W9-BJE-660

Critical acclaim for
ORSON WELLES:
A Biography

"It is as wonderful to hear him speak in print as to hear that marvelous butterscotch voice in movies. Here is a man of appetites, of supreme self-confidence and deep insecurity. But above all here is the *man*."
—*The New York Times Book Review*

"Barbara Leaming has successfully captured that overwhelming personality in a fascinating, skillfully assembled biography which . . . will almost certainly remain the definitive book on the phenomenon which he undoubtedly was."
—*Spectator*

"To know Welles through the book is to meet a spectacular, one-man entertainment factory in all his outlandish facets."
—*People*

"Excellent biography—the first real life of Welles"
—*Boston Globe*

"Orson Welles entertains, outrages, and seduces his biographer and us."
—*Vogue*

"An essential sourcebook for anyone interested in Welles, the cinema, or the life of the artist in America . . . a delightful read."
—*Boston Herald*

PENGUIN BOOKS

ORSON WELLES

Barbara Leaming is a professor of theater and film at Hunter College, New York, and is the author of numerous books and articles on film. She has built *Orson Welles* on two years of in-depth, uninhibited interviews with Welles and hours of painstaking research in archives and among Welles's contemporaries. Leaming lives in New York City.

ORSON WELLES

A Biography by
Barbara Leaming

PENGUIN BOOKS

PENGUIN BOOKS

Viking Penguin Inc., 40 West 23rd Street,
New York, New York 10010, U.S.A.
Penguin Books Ltd, Harmondsworth,
Middlesex, England
Penguin Books Australia Ltd, Ringwood,
Victoria, Australia
Penguin Books Canada Limited, 2801 John Street,
Markham, Ontario, Canada L3R 1B4
Penguin Books (N.Z.) Ltd, 182-190 Wairau Road,
Auckland 10, New Zealand

First published in the United States of America by
Viking Penguin Inc. 1985
Published in Penguin Books 1986

A portion of this book appeared originally in *Playboy* magazine,
under the title "The Genius Takes on Tinseltown."

LIBRARY OF CONGRESS CATALOGING IN PUBLICATION DATA
Leaming, Barbara.
Orson Welles: a biography.
Bibliography: p.
Includes index.
1. Welles, Orson, 1915–   2. Moving-picture
producers and directors—United States—Biography.
I. Title.
[PN1998.A3W447   1986]   791.43'0233'0924   [B]   86-9343
ISBN 0 14 00.9620 5 (pbk.)

Printed in the United States of America by
Offset Paperback Mfrs., Inc., Dallas, Pennsylvania
Set in Times Roman

Author's Note

In life. It is the expression he uses to describe the stars offscreen and out of the public eye. I took a while to catch on to what he meant when without explanation he would say "Rita *in life*" or "Marlene *in life*," but once I did, I realized that even more than the artist, the genius, the wonder boy, this was the true subject of my biography of Orson Welles, what I had wanted to discover and write about all along: Orson Welles *in life*.

Orson Welles generously gave me his complete cooperation for this book. Although he knew that to find out everything I could about him I talked to numerous other people (some of whom he regards as enemies), and examined masses of documents (letters, memos, daily production reports, contracts), he did not ask to control what I wrote.

Our many, many hours of interviews over some twenty months, sometimes several times a week, even several times a day, allowed him to speak freely and openly as I dare say he has never done before. The man I slowly came to know is very different from the legendary *monstre sacré*. While *in life* he is as dazzlingly brilliant, as witty, caustic, and charming as his reputation suggests, he is also shy, introspective, and vulnerable.

Orson Welles has made history, he has created masterpieces in three art forms: film, theater, and radio—but his most fascinating and enigmatic creation may be himself. I was amazed to discover that, *in life*, he was as curious about his own legend as I was. As his biographer, I have tried to depict the duality intrinsic to his experience: both the legend, the public persona, as it emerged over more than half a century, and how Orson himself felt about it all *in life*. While I might have been able to record the former on my own, without Orson's intimate recollections I could only have speculated about the latter.

B.L.
New York, October 1984

Acknowledgments

I would like to thank the many people who helped me with this project. Some of those who shared their memories and perceptions of Orson Welles are listed in the source notes. I also depended on the librarians, archivists, and historians who have preserved important documents regarding the life of Orson Welles. Special thanks are due to Saundra Taylor and her staff at the Lilly Library of Indiana University, who enabled me to examine the nearly 20,000 items of Welles's papers. I also wish to acknowledge the kindness of Lorraine Brown at George Mason University, John Hall at RKO, Dean Fallon and Karen Nixon at the Florida State University, and Robert Knutson and Ned Comstock at USC Special Collections.

Amanda Vaill, my editor at Viking, worked closely with the project from the first, and was a consistent source of enthusiasm, support, and sage advice. Her contribution to the book was enormous. At Weidenfeld and Nicolson, my editor, John Curtis, provided the warmth, encouragement, and counsel I needed. I will always be immensely grateful to both of them, as well as to Stacy Schiff at Viking, Alex MacCormick at Weidenfeld and Nicolson, and my agents Lois Wallace in New York and Anthony Sheil in London.

There are five people within whom this book could never have been written. The first of course is Orson Welles, who, day after day, month after month, patiently subjected himself to my barrage of questions, and also arranged for me to meet and interview some of the important people in his life. No one could have spent as much time talking to Orson as I have without coming to feel the deepest affection and respect for him. I can only hope that this book does some small justice to a very great man, whose laughter and friendship I cherish, and whose joy in living has been a lesson to me. How can I ever thank Henry Jaglom for arranging my first meeting with Orson? Because Henry has been such a close friend of Orson's, he knows what a special gift he gave me in introducing me to him. Another of Orson's dearest friends to whom I am grateful is his mentor Roger "Skipper" Hill, who, besides talking to me at length, gave me access to Orson's boyhood letters and diaries, as well as other precious documents from Orson's later life. I have dedicated this book to Skipper by way of acknowledging his formative impact on Orson. Long before I met Orson himself, it was Shifra Haran who first made me truly feel what she likes to call his "wonderfulness." I am grateful to her for this, for the innumerable details about Orson and Rita Hayworth with which she provided me, but above all for the "wonderfulness" of her friendship. Finally, I want to thank my husband, David. I think he knows how much I depend on him and how much I love him.

Contents

Illustrations follow page 288.

ORSON
WELLES

"I've just walked across Lake Michigan, I suppose," Orson Welles says to me when I report that I've just finished writing about him at the age of three. Early on in our conversations he tells me to stop calling him Mr. Welles. "Everybody calls me Orson," he says. "On the phone people who've never met me say, 'Hello, Orson!,' and I don't even know what they look like." To talk about his life there are lunches and dinners at Orson's Los Angeles hangout, Ma Maison: "Meet me at nine at the saloon," Orson says when he calls me— by which, I learn, he means his regular table for four behind a latticework screen at the only restaurant in town with an unlisted telephone number. At dinner we are joined by his regular evening companion, a two-year-old black toy poodle named Kiki, who, seated on a chair to his left, growls and snaps her tiny teeth at anyone who gets too close to her gargantuan master. "Kiki's terrible," Orson laughs. "She finally gets to know somebody who comes to see me on business all the time and gives him little kisses and all that, but when he gets up to walk out, she runs and bites him on the ankle."

In New York, where he is stopping over on his way back from the Cannes Film Festival, when Orson receives me in his suite at the Hotel Carlyle, there is Kiki cradled in his massive arms, which issue from a voluminous red, orange, and yellow striped burnoose that grazes the thick rug as he walks on stockinged feet. "Don't bite the biographer," I say, drawing back slightly. "No, " says Orson, chuckling and shaking his head. "That would not be a good idea!"

When we haven't talked for a while, Orson calls me and says, "Ask me a question!"—at which we both laugh; about a career so illustrious just where does one begin? Says Orson: "I only remember the pieces I tell you about. I don't remember the things I don't tell you. I know people who have a much better recollection of their childhood than I do. They remember very well when they were a year and a half and two years old. I've only one or two dim daguerreotypes that come to mind." He is wistfully aware that, even to him, his long life is available only in partial views. When he sends me to Illinois to meet the man he calls his oldest and best friend, his childhood mentor and former headmaster of the fabled Todd School for Boys, eighty-eight-year-old Roger "Skipper" Hill, Orson says, "His memory is very good. As far as I know it's very accurate, except I've found talking to him, as one does, I remember one thing, which he's forgotten, and he remembers another, which I've forgotten. So it sort of patches things up."

Although Orson likes to tell me that mine is a "vile profession"— bee-ography, as he pronounces it—he is often eager to try to retrieve those fragments of the past he can. While his biography is being written, as he grows from three to thirty to sixty, sometimes there are inscrutable disparities between what Orson remembers and the data I unearth.

Once, when Orson mentions that his father died at a "great age," no sooner do I blurt out that, no, he was fifty-eight, than I realize that I certainly ought to have refrained from correcting Orson on so delicate a subject. Orson is perplexed. He has always thought of his father as being very old when he died—but here is someone who has just been looking at Dick Welles's death certificate, so Orson must somehow readjust his memory.

"I think there is a movie in the story of somebody who's getting a biography written about him," Orson tells me. "I think finally the biographer comes with a pistol and shoots the subject. . . . There is a wonderful movie in it: you know, a public figure of some kind who makes the mistake of getting to know the unauthorized biographer. I see a professional charmer—like a John Huston or an Alex Korda—who never fails, with the bankers, with the women, with the actors, who cannot be resisted, and who cannot figure out or conquer this biographer-woman. He tries everything, and it stops his career. He begins to examine his own past. For example, you said one thing to me that started me off on this plot, oh, some time ago. You said, 'You know, your father wasn't old at all when he died'—and then I said, 'But I've always been told he was old!' Then I began to think, how could that possibly have happened? If it were true, why did it happen? If it were not true, why was I lied to?"

Later: "One has organized one's life," says Orson, "and forgotten—perhaps deliberately and certainly unconsciously—what one wants to forget, and here is somebody coming up with the proof of things you're forced to remember or believe happened. I see the situation as a fascinating way to get into what a man's life is really like. And of course, at the end of it, neither one of them knows. I think that's the end of the story."

Although Orson is never keen to hear what others have said about him, he is evidently fascinated that they are all out there, remembering him, giving interviews about him, even writing memoirs about him. "Has it occurred to you," he asks me, '—I don't know how you're writing this, this is an incredible impertinence on my part even to suggest something—has it occurred to you that maybe your final form of this ought to be a narrative of your writing it, rather

than the novel-like story of me, the people you talked to?"
At which curious proposal I protest that it would be hubris
to include myself in his story. "I think you're dead wrong,"
says the man who made Citizen Kane, *the prismatic story*
of a reporter's interviewing sundry people who knew an
enigmatic media figure named Charles Foster Kane. "I
think it's still going to be about me—and overwhelmingly
about me. It's just another way of doing it. I think there's
no biography so interesting as the one in which the biog-
rapher is present. I think it's a wonderful story, the whole
thing: trying to get me, the people who won't speak, the
people who do speak, the different versions, the meetings,
the sources—and out of this comes the story. I think you'll
understand me better that way than the other way. I don't
want you to understand that I think you should do every
chapter that way. Eventually you would interrupt the book
anything from six to twelve times by descriptions of what
you had to go through to get what you are now going to
tell. I don't think there's hubris at all about it—not a bit.
Don't listen to the publishers, because the biography is twice
as interesting if I am friends with the biographer. It becomes
a dialogue of a certain kind, a drama between two people.
You're not inserting yourself, you are admitting—which is
always a tremendously good formula in any art form, I
think—the limitation of the form. In other words, you are
not God. You are not looking down on this from above. You
had a tremendous amount of sources—some of them comic,
some of them casting a clearer light on the story you're
going to tell than the story itself will. It fascinates me. I
think it's a wonderful way to do a biography, particularly
because you are telling, excuse the expression, a rather
dense story. I can be frank with you without sounding
fake modest, but you're talking about—alas—some kind of
legend."

CHAPTER 1
The Genius

"My mother and father were both much more remarkable than any story of mine can make them," says Orson Welles. "They seem to me just mythically wonderful." Born in Missouri in 1872, Richard Head Welles made his money as a manufacturer of bicycle and automobile lamps in Kenosha, Wisconsin, but sold his business to avoid shifting from the popular carbide lamp he had invented to what he viewed as the newfangled electrical model, because he thought the latter likely to explode on bumpy roads. Among his many odd inventions, from which no profit was earned, was a glider attached to a steam-driven engine because, by some twisted logic, he thought the best place for an airplane's engine was on the ground. With Dick Welles at the wheel below, a servant rode the glider high above until, blinded by gusts of steam, the poor fellow crash-landed, thereby causing a disappointed Welles to abandon the entire project.

More than any of his failed inventions, however, Dick Welles's greatest disappointment in life was that he had not managed to accumulate a great personal fortune. "He was lost because he wasn't a multimillionaire," says his son. "You see, he was born with more money than he had when he died, and to him, I believe, that was a great *shame*." It

wasn't that Dick Welles ever lacked the funds to live in a
reasonably grand style—but he never quite became the great
American nabob he fancied himself. "A *very* rich banker—
that's what he would have liked to be," recalls Orson Welles,
which probably explains the reserve with which Dick dressed
and generally deported himself, as well as his wistful sense
of having failed in life. Always a dreamer, he acted the part
of the man of immense wealth he knew he really wasn't.
Among his friends in the staid men's clubs he liked to
frequent were those "aristocratic philistines," as his son calls
them, who actively cultivated a dislike of the arts. Not for
them the reputedly uplifting virtues of culture advocated by
some Americans—who were principally feather-brained
women as far as Dick and his men's club cronies could see.
By contrast with the relentless pursuit of money, the arts
seemed frivolous, morally objectionable. Although they distracted a fellow from the serious business of making money,
they couldn't possibly afford him the pleasure or relaxation
to be had in a good cigar, a racehorse, or a show girl.

Dick Welles had spent his twenties in the tireless pursuit
of show girls and other beauties with whom he sought no
lasting bond, but he changed his mind about settling down
when, in the first decade of this century, he met and fell in
love with a tall, statuesque, dark-haired young woman from
a fine family in Springfield, Ohio. An accomplished pianist,
an advocate of women's rights, and a literary intellectual
with an interest in Sanskrit, the awesome Beatrice Ives was
an unlikely match for a sport like Dick Welles, for whom
music was mainly what show girls sang and danced to.
Beatrice was abundantly different from the women he had
collected, and cast off, in the past. Her graceful height, her
resonant voice, and—above all—her refined beauty afforded Miss Ives the sort of commanding presence that
Dick's silly show girls had so entirely lacked. He loved the
fact that people seemed rather frightened of her. It was
difficult to argue against women's rights with someone who

spoke in a voice as rich and overpowering as hers. A simple
look from her was enough to silence a man. But what really
intrigued Dick was that, for all her stately seriousness, she
possessed a wicked sense of humor. As much as any man,
she took delight in playing outrageous practical jokes that,
on account of her genteel demeanor, were all the more
unexpected by her victims. In recent years financial ruin
had befallen the Iveses of Springfield when Beatrice's father,
Benjamin, lost his coal mines to creditors. In youth, however, Beatrice, an only child, had had all the comforts that
wealth provided. Says her son Orson: "She had a life somewhat like mine in that she was raised in conditions which
I call *great wealth*, but which in those patrician circles in
the old days was called *being comfortable*. Wealth was
something that was measured in terms of J. P. Morgan's
yacht—and everything under that was just *being comfortable*. Nobody else would ever dream of thinking they were
rich." Since she had been a little girl, Beatrice had been
much closer to her father, whom she adored, but her relationship with her difficult mother, Lucy, was fraught with
tension. Nor was Lucy the only older woman with whom
Beatrice came into irreconcilable conflict. Her romance with
and ensuing marriage to Dick Welles met with her mother-
in-law Mary's vehement opposition. The single time the
homely and mean-spirited Mary addressed her was at their
first and last meeting when, having married Beatrice over
his mother's objections, Dick proudly brought her home to
Kenosha in hopes of Mary's relenting, and accepting Beatrice into the family. But this was not to be. Even before
she ever laid eyes on her, Dick's mother had pronounced
the Ives girl a *radical* who was probably only after him for
his money. When Beatrice married Dick Welles against his
mother's wishes it confirmed Mary's worst suspicions. Their
encounter was strained, unpleasant, and not to be repeated.
But Beatrice had more than held her own.

She also held her own in the marriage. For however much

Dick and Beatrice were in love with each other, there were
from the first vast temperamental differences between them.
Dick's ingrained contempt for the arts may have caused him
to attribute less importance than he should have to his bride-
to-be's devotion to her study of classical music. After the
economic ruin of the Iveses she had resolved to become a
stenographer so that she could go on with her studies. Now
that would no longer be necessary. But never had Dick
anticipated that after marriage she would so vigorously persist in her artistic aspirations. When she became Mrs. Richard Welles, however, Beatrice not only threw herself into
her musical studies with fully as much passion as before,
but, more and more, she sought to establish herself in Chicago-area artistic and bohemian circles. Not for her the
"aristocratic philistines" whom Dick seemed so much to
enjoy. To make matters worse, it wasn't long after they were
married and had settled in Kenosha that Dick began returning periodically to the music halls, taverns, and other low
spots he had frequented in his bachelor days, so that although he numbered among his *sporting* cronies authors like
Booth Tarkington and George Ade, he also kept somewhat
less suitable company of whose influence Beatrice openly
disapproved—but no less than Dick turned up his nose at
the sensitive artistic souls she preferred.

Dick and Beatrice Welles would have two sons, Richard
Ives and, a decade later, George Orson, whose birth initiated
the final phase of their marriage. Conceived in Rio de Ja-
neiro, where his parents were on holiday, Orson was named
for two of Dick's cronies who were in transit with them:
George Ade and a businessman called, by coincidence, Orson Wells. At length, the first name, George, would be
dropped when Dick Welles decided it was more appropriate
for a railroad porter than for any son of his. But it was as
George Orson Welles that the baby was born on May 6,
1915, at seven a.m. in his parents' fashionable home at 463

Park Avenue in Kenosha, Wisconsin. The newcomer was sickly—born with anomalies of the spine that would cause him pain for all his long life.

When Orson Welles was eighteen months old, he was, as they say, "discovered"—not by a theatrical agent, a movie producer, or a talent scout, as might be expected, but by a Russian-Jewish orthopedist, who, as a family friend, had been summoned to inspect a head wound sustained by young Richard. Legend has it that in the course of his visit to 463 Park Avenue, Dr. Maurice Bernstein happened to look in on the younger Welles boy, who, peering up out of his crib at the distinguished-looking doctor, said, "The desire to take medicine is one of the greatest features which distinguishes men from animals." At least that is what Bernstein reported to Dick and Beatrice when, in a great flurry of excitement, he issued from the nursery. He had been alone there with the baby, who, he explained somewhat breathlessly, *must* be a prodigy, a genius. Never had Bernstein encountered a remarkable specimen like this! Could he see the boy again, and how soon? As soon as he liked, Dick and Beatrice agreed. Richard had been a fractious, difficult child with a local reputation for mischief-making, so the Welleses couldn't have been more delighted at Dr. Bernstein's so effusively praising their other youngster, even if that praise were based on an utterance that nobody else had heard.

There began a series of educational gifts from the doctor, who came by every day now: a violin (although Orson was much too tiny to grasp it properly); a conductor's baton; painting and sculpting equipment; a puppet theater; a theatrical makeup case; a magic kit. Bernstein coined an affectionate nickname for his protégé—*Pookles*; and Pookles in turn called him *Dadda*—a nickname that gave Dick Welles second thoughts about just what Dadda Bernstein was up to.

But it was too late. Dadda had successfully wheedled his

way into Dick's home, and now he had become a fixture
there. In collusion with Beatrice, Dadda seemed intent on
turning the boy into some sort of artist. But that wasn't the
only trouble. Although the ostensible purpose of Dadda's
visits was to study and to nurture young Orson, he seemed
every bit as attentive to the beautiful Beatrice. Matters were
further complicated by Beatrice's recent poor health: attending to her medical needs gradually became another reason for Dadda's spending so much time with a married
woman. Nor did Beatrice seem to discourage Dadda's attentions. A trim, compact man, always impeccably tailored,
Maurice Bernstein was something of a dandy. He wore his
dark hair swept back to one side of his high forehead, which
had the effect of drawing attention to the strong features of
his handsome face. His soft dark eyes radiated humor, intelligence, and compassion. The strong aquiline nose and
broad sensuous mouth gave him the air of a much larger
man. He was, as Orson recalls, "irresistible to women,"
whom he typically charmed with his mighty fund of Jewish
jokes. He further appealed to Beatrice on account of the
wide-ranging musical erudition that had allowed him to
move with ease in Chicago musical society, with many of
whose leading performers he was on intimate terms.

Just *how* intimately Dadda Bernstein knew several of the
local opera's prima donnas Beatrice may not as yet have
suspected. But she was by no means the first musically
inclined beauty of whom Dadda found himself enamored.
Nor was this the first marriage into which he had deftly
insinuated himself. "He had this way of getting himself into
triangles as the third party," says Orson of his mentor, one
of whose most enduring relationships was with the wife of
a prominent Chicago music critic who not only knew of,
and countenanced, Bernstein's infatuation with his wife, but
went into jealous sulks when, as with Beatrice, Dadda lavished his courtly attentions on other women. With some of

these women—but not with all—his love affairs were chaste, platonic. A "crazy romantic Russian," as Orson describes him, he loved being in love. Although he was no stranger in the bedroom, he was, says Orson, "satisfied with the balcony"—and so it was with Beatrice, in whom he found a worthy object of adoration, for the years had only enhanced the vivid presence and air of authority that she had already commanded in her early twenties. In past months, an affliction of the liver had weakened her considerably, but she was not the sort of woman to settle comfortably into illness, and this staunch refusal to do so made her all the more exciting to Dadda.

But if Dick Welles couldn't figure out exactly what was going on between his wife and the handsome doctor, it was partly because Dadda was also quite genuinely obsessed with Pookles. A platonic affair with a married woman that included a no less powerful infatuation with her look-alike son were human possibilities that simply would not have occurred to Dick Welles—or perhaps to most other men. But curious combinations were Dadda's style. As for his claims that Orson was a born genius: while Dadda almost certainly exaggerated his words of wisdom from the crib, Orson was indeed a gifted child whose decisive early development profited immeasurably from the doctor's constant encouragement. "The word *genius* was whispered into my ear the first thing I ever heard while I was still mewling in my crib," laughs Orson, "so it never occurred to me that I wasn't until middle age!" Told that he was a prodigy for as long as he could remember, young Orson developed an air of confidence, of knowing just what he was about. He appeared to have inherited his mother's boldness. But for all his outward assurance, the child lived in constant fear of not coming up to his parents' expectations. "I always felt I was letting them down," he says now. "That's why I worked so hard. That's the stuff that turned the motor." Not

that he ever questioned his being a genius—with Dadda
there to praise and to advise him, how could he doubt it?
But precisely because he was supposed to be superior to
other children, his parents seemed to expect so much more
of him. "The opposite to Dadda Bernstein the mindless
worrier and worshiper, my mother and father were much
cooler and more distant," says Orson. "I trusted and feared
their judgment." He would do anything for their approval.
By the time Orson was three, Dick and Beatrice were sending him on errands to the other side of town. Terrifed to go
off alone, but longing to please them, the three-year-old
repeatedly forced himself to do as they asked without flinch-
ing. "I was *taught* to feel secure, it was not in my character,"
he says of their rationale for treating him as a considerably
older child. In time, too, Orson grew accustomed to Dadda's
shamelessly pushing him in front of the touring musical
celebrities with whom they regularly visited backstage. But
although he learned to seem supremely confident, Orson
never really overcame his innate shyness. These painful
experiences were his first acting lessons.

After Dick Welles moved his family to Chicago, little
Orson's painfully acquired social skills came in handy.
Through Dadda's intervention, Beatrice and the prodigy
were admitted to the select and cultivated set that gathered
at music critic Ned Moore's home in Ravinia, where Dr.
Bernstein was always an honored guest on account of his
off-again, on-again liaison with Moore's wife, Hazel. In
those days Chicago was a center of artistic and intellectual
ferment nearly equal to New York's, and many of its leaders
visited the Moores' salon, where Orson took to listening,
even contributing, to the high-toned conversation. It was
the start of his youthful alienation from his peers, for enamored of the attention he received from the Moores' guests,
he recoiled from mingling with other boys his age, who
might not offer him the adulation to which he was growing
accustomed.

Besides, he had far more interesting things to do than playing children's games. The playing *he* liked was onstage. Recruited for a walk-on stint in *Samson and Delilah* at the Chicago Opera, Orson then became a big hit as "Trouble" in *Madame Butterfly*, whose title role was sung by another of Dadda Bernstein's conquests (of which, by now, Beatrice had been amused to discover, there was a long and illustrious list). Beneath the dark hair that Beatrice combed down over Orson's forehead, the slight tilt of his almond-shaped brown eyes gave his face a distinctly Eurasian cast, so that he seemed a natural for the part of Madame Butterfly's love child. Encouraged to perform, and thrilled by the attention it brought him, five-year-old Orson also portrayed a somewhat less artistic role at the entrance to Marshall Field's department store, where, costumed as a rabbit, he periodically exclaimed to curious passersby: "I must hurry—or else it will be too late to see the woolen underwear on the eighth floor!" If Orson simply had to act, his father preferred that he do it in a department store, with its healthy atmosphere of buying and selling, rather than in *Madame Butterfly*.

Not long after the Welleses left Kenosha for Chicago, Dadda Bernstein followed them to take up residence in the great city. However many other women there were in his tangled personal life, Beatrice had become his principal obsession. "He left Kenosha to be near my mother," says Orson, who remembers the despair that having to abandon small-town life occasioned in Dr. Bernstein. He had come from Russia in poverty, and had labored for years to establish a medical practice in what struck him as the ideal American small town. Now that he had to abandon it in pursuit of Beatrice Welles, he often spoke wistfully of Kenosha as "a paradise that he'd lost." But he found little sympathy for this nostalgia in Beatrice. "My mother used to make *heartless* fun of that," says Orson of Beatrice's inevitably sarcastic response to Dadda's dream of small-town life.

Provincialism was exactly what she had hoped to put behind her by moving to Chicago, and—ironically—at first it was in large part through Dadda's contacts there that she so brilliantly succeeded. Given access to Chicago's artistic elite, her magnetic presence and personality quickly established her among them. Increasingly independent of her husband, Beatrice's musical career also began to come into its own. She was hailed as "a pianist of exquisite feeling and polished technique" when, at the Milwaukee Art Institute, she performed original compositions, to which she sang in the "deep lovely voice" that was to be a decisive legacy to Orson. But her illness had not abated, so that the strain of a more prolonged concert tour was out of the question.

By now Bernstein's attachment to Beatrice and her son was having an effect on Dick Welles. Embittered by what he perceived as the loss of Beatrice and Orson, and disappointed by his own failures in business, Dick had taken to drink. "To him, Dadda Bernstein represented everything that had made his marriage with my mother impossible," says Orson. Finally, Dick used Beatrice's illness as an excuse to travel alone. But time apart did not help them. No sooner had he returned than they began fighting bitterly again. Unlike Bernstein, however, Dick Welles did not enjoy being deftly cut apart by the exquisitely articulate Beatrice. So constantly tense was the atmosphere at home that young Orson took the discord between his parents as a given; at the age of six he listened quietly the night of their last quarrel, after which, by mutual agreement, Dick and Beatrice separated forever. Orson was neither surprised nor terribly shaken. He would reside primarily with his mother in Chicago, while frequently visiting and traveling with his father, whose subsequent liberty permitted him to indulge a taste for globe-trotting that domestic life had hitherto curtailed. "When they separated I felt no partisanship," says Orson, who blamed neither parent for the rift. In a curious

way, young Orson thought of himself as having actually
benefited from the separation, because always seeing his
parents individually afforded him "twice the love."

As for Orson's older brother, Richard, perhaps since the
day his head wound caused Dr. Bernstein to pay a fateful
call, he was clearly the less favored of the Welles boys.
"My father hated him," says Orson—so that, finally, as a
result of the boy's repeated misdeeds, including his expul-
sion from the Todd School, where he had been sent in hopes
of straightening him out, Dick Welles had banished Richard
from the family. Nor was Dick remorseful for having scorned
his eldest son when, subsequently, a corpse reported to be
Richard's washed up on the banks of the Mississippi. "That's
good," Orson remembers his father's having said, "at least
the family is rid of him!" Some years later, much to everybody's surprise, Richard suddenly reappeared, no less surprised that he had been thought dead.

After the separation, while Dick Welles wandered aimlessly around the world, Beatrice seemed to flourish in Chicago, where, much as she had always dreamed of doing,
she established a salon, one of whose principal attractions
was her talkative son Orson. Life with mother was especially
challenging because of her strict policy that, as he puts it,
"children could be treated as adults as long as they were
amusing. The moment you became boring, it was off to the
nursery." One suspects that this early compulsion to amuse,
to charm, to seduce, was a vital factor in shaping what
would become the classic Welles persona. Nor did he fail
to charm the classical musicians who, among other artists
and intellectuals, frequented his mother's apartment. When
they gave chamber concerts there, he pretended to conduct
with his baton, grandly turning the pages of music before
him at all the right moments. To be polite to his mother,
who was after all their hostess, the musicians inevitably
praised the child as a *genius*, which powerfully reinforced

what Dadda had been telling him all along. By now it had
been quietly settled that Orson would succeed his ailing
mother in a musical career. "Everybody thought I was going
to be *a great musician*, you see," says Orson (who abandoned playing publicly after his mother's death). As for his
fabled status as a prodigy, Orson is decidedly modest: "Look
at the real prodigies and I look like nothing compared to
them." Despite this disclaimer, however, Orson evidently
was a truly gifted boy musician. "If you tell a small child
he's going to be *a great musician*," Orson explains, "and
you keep after it, and if he's pretty good—you know, you
have to be fairly good to sustain it—it gives you a certain
authority."

Although it nurtured his self-confdence, mingling exclusively with grown-ups was not without disturbing incident,
as when some of the male Italian opera singers among Dadda's friends made indecent advances to the confused child.
"You see," says Orson, "the Italians believe any young boy
is meat for a quick seduction, and it will have no effect on
him or the masculinity of the grown man." Since they left
him with "a strange sense of shame," Orson kept the men's
advances a secret from his mother and Dadda.

Because in early childhood Orson had suffered from a
myriad of diseases, diphtheria, scarlet fever, malaria, and
rheumatism among them, there had been no rush for him
to begin school. On the basis of Orson's severe asthma
alone, Dr. Bernstein was more than willing to submit the
necessary documentation to keep the boy with his mother.
Finally, in Chicago, an abortive attempt was made to place
Orson in public school; but he was so frequently bullied for
his clearly not fitting in that he had to be removed almost
at once lest he sustain serious injury from the terrible pum-
melings. It followed that, aside from violin and piano lessons, Orson's education was largely informal: drawing and
painting; reading Shakespeare aloud with Beatrice (who used

A Midsummer Night's Dream as his first primer); picking up a bit of spoken German from his nanny; performing elaborate puppet shows for Dadda; regularly attending the theater and the opera; painstakingly making himself up as, and learning the lines of, King Lear, and playing other favorite dramatic characters who imaginatively satisfied what he calls his "determination to escape the conditions of childhood."

But imagination would not allow him to escape the fact of his mother's illness, which appeared suddenly to worsen with the passing months. Beatrice's continuing role of popular hostess brought the world to her living room, so eight-year-old Orson's public life went on as before. But secretly he worried constantly about her—she had grown much weaker of late despite the great outward show of vitality that concealed her poor health from others. An incident in the park one morning deepened his anxieties: as was his custom, he had been riding a horse quite alone when he came upon a woman whose horse appeared to have thrown her. Orson had no way of knowing that her gurgling and mad thrashing about was an epileptic fit. It seemed to him that she was dying, and that he could do nothing for her. Even when the woman mysteriously came to, and explained what he had seen, his thoughts held on to that terrible image of death, and the feeling of utter helplessness that went with it. Fearful that his mother was about to die, he began to resist losing sight of her, and often sobbed when he did. Orson's worst fears were confirmed when, two days after his ninth birthday, his mother was taken to Chicago Memorial Hospital, where, two days after that, she died of "acute yellow atrophy of the liver" at the age of forty-three. The news left him with a sense of "anguished loss."

After his mother's death, Orson spent four weeks with her relatives in upstate Woodstock, New York, where his girl cousins initiated him into sex. Until then Orson's en-

counters with sex had been limited to fending off the advances of men. But for the first time now, the girl cousins,
particularly one a bit older than he, suggested other possibilities. "The children, who had a witches' coven of sex,
had their way with me to whatever extent that may be,"
laughs Welles now. But these first fumbling heterosexual
experiences, however limited, left him with a keen appetite
for more. He had lost his mother and discovered sex, all in
the space of little more than a month, so that nine-year-old
Orson had grown up considerably when Dick Welles sent
for him.

Expressly to steal him away from Dr. Bernstein, who,
more than ever now, laid claim to the boy's mind and affections, Dick took Orson on far-flung travels in Europe,
Africa, and Asia—but not without Dadda's carefully monitoring their every move from afar. "I *was* my mother, and
I kept the flame," says Orson of Dadda's passionate preoccupation with him after Beatrice died. Orson had noticed
that, since his parents' separation, his mother had seemed
at intervals to weary of Dadda's nagging. One day in a fit
of exasperation she had even thrown him out of her car in
the middle of Michigan Avenue. Not that she meant to
eliminate him from her life—but she *had* begun to find his
single-mindedness about her rather cloying. Now that Beatrice was dead, however, Dadda could be every bit as
maddeningly obsessive as he liked. But by expecting Pookles to join him in forever lamenting the death of the beautiful Beatrice, Dadda badly confused the child about just
what he was supposed to be feeling now. "It wasn't that I
didn't love my mother," says Orson, who had to sort it out
for himself, "I didn't love her *the way* he did."

Suddenly the boy perceived himself as the center of a
fierce dispute between Dadda Bernstein and Dick Welles,
each of them anxious to determine his future course in life.
It was the old debate between art and commerce that the

Welleses had never resolved. Besides resenting Dadda's powerful influence on Orson, Dick was furious about his swift annexation of virtually the entire contents of Beatrice's apartment, including her piano, as well as various items that Dick considered rightfully his, among them an old prayer rug. Dick knew that he was in no shape for a prolonged fight with Dadda, to whom he had lost once before. After the breakup of his marriage, heavy drinking, coupled with gambling, opium smoking, and whoring, had considerably impaired his physical and mental health. At the moment it was enough for him to have successfully made off with Orson.

But now Dr. Bernstein tried to win a round. Fearing that Dick was a bad influence on the child, and acting in his handy capacity as a physician, Dr. Bernstein arranged for Pookles to spend a year in Wisconsin in the charge of an eminent German psychologist who specialized in unusual children. Who better than such a man would know how to measure the young genius's capacities and care for his special needs? Even Dick had to agree that it was too good an opportunity to miss. Wary of giving in to any suggestion of Dadda's, he grudgingly consented to Orson's year with Herr Professor. In Wisconsin, Orson boarded with the sturdy doctor and his wife, and was enrolled in the local public school; there he caused an uproar by delivering an art lecture to the student body in which he lambasted his teachers for lacking creativity. "You mustn't criticize the public school system, Orson," one teacher called out, to which the fourth-grader responded, "If the public school system needs criticizing, I will criticize it!" Acutely conscious of his role as *wunderkind*, when Orson discovered that he was to be photographed for a local newspaper article on the incident, he instructed Dadda to secure an eccentric Oscar Wilde tie that would afford a proper image for his public. Nor, as the inky news photo would attest, did Bernstein fail him—for it was

Dadda who had spent years nurturing that very self-consciousness in the first place, and it therefore seemed perfectly natural to him that Pookles would think of himself as having a public.

But the art lecture was far from his only public appearance in Wisconsin, where Herr Professor liked to exhibit Orson before psychology students who questioned him about his dreams. Taught by his mother that a child must always be entertaining, Orson shrewdly calculated what Herr Professor's group would be interested to hear. Since he'd been brought to town as a prodigy, he'd better have a prodigy's dreams. Afraid that his own would be much too dull, he routinely memorized dreams from the case studies in Herr Professor's library at home for impassioned recital the next day. Before long, however, Orson feared that the lurid dreams he had chosen to keep his audience entertained were attracting the wrong kind of interest from Herr Professor. Although one of the principal purposes of Orson's stay in Wisconsin was so that his host might examine him, Orson noticed that the large powerful German had been staring at and circling him a bit too keenly. Herr Professor's sudden interest seemed to hark back to "earlier passions." Finding himself the object of homosexual advances was nothing new to Orson, who, having been frightened and ashamed the first few times it happened, soon knew just what to say when the bohemians who frequented his mother's salon made their move. "I had all this experience, you see," says Orson. "From my earliest childhood I was the Lillie Langtry of the older homosexual set. Everybody wanted me. I had a very bad way of turning these guys off. I thought it would embarrass them if I said I wasn't homosexual, that that would be a rebuke, so I always had a headache. You know, I was like an eternal virgin." But Orson doubted whether a simple headache would do now when, with evident difficulty, Herr Professor finally made his move. Because they were quite alone in the house, since the German's wife was out for the evening, Orson decided it was best to slip out a back window, find the local train station, and flee to Dadda Bernstein in Chicago.

CHAPTER 2

Island
of Lost Boys

After Orson's escape from the lascivious child psychologist, the battle between Dick Welles and Dadda Bernstein resumed. Dick was back in the States, living in a defunct hotel he had bought in rural Grand Detour, Illinois. Dadda was appalled at the very thought of Orson's taking up residence there. Dick had lately cultivated the friendship of an assortment of dubious vaudevillians whom he'd liberally invited to stay with him at the Sheffield should they ever find themselves in or around Grand Detour. The place was often packed. One guest, a magician, taught Orson magic tricks. A pair of sisters, both with prominent gold teeth, demonstrated how to play "The Stars and Stripes Forever" on bottles filled with various amounts of water. Another visitor swallowed several goldfish only to reveal to the boy that they were really just carrots and that Orson could create the same illusion with an adroit mixture of double-talk and manual dexterity. These people obviously weren't the opera singers and classical musicians with whom Dadda wanted his protégé to mingle, but Orson was fascinated. It seemed to Dadda that the only way of getting him out of Grand Detour was to persuade Dick to enroll him in school, a prospect that didn't appeal to Orson; following the example of his vaudeville friends, he dreamed of becoming a boy showman. The visit to Grand Detour of the younger of the memorable girl cousins from "the witches' coven of sex" in upstate New York emboldened him suddenly to run away with her; the pair of them planned to sleep in the woods and support themselves by magic and minstrel shows. Two days later, identified and apprehended while performing in blackface on an Illinois street corner, the hungry runaways were returned by police. When the girl cousin had been shipped back to New York, Dick Welles warned Orson that if he didn't "straighten up and behave," he'd be sent to that "Bible-pounding, reading, writing, and arithmetic place" called the Todd School in Woodstock, Illinois, from which his older brother Richard had been expelled. In those days, Todd was, as one alumnus recalls it, an "island of lost boys." From Richard, says Orson, he "knew about Todd as criminals know about San Quentin." Inspecting Richard's old Todd catalogue, Orson had seen a grim photo "with a lot of little boys in Eton collars," which struck him as "the ultimate in humiliation," for he imagined himself wearing one too. One more untoward incident like his running away with his cousin, and it would be off to Todd.

Dick was particularly concerned that Orson behave himself during the time he would be staying with Dadda while Dick was briefly in Trinidad. But no sooner had Orson moved in with Dadda in Chicago than he began playing doctor with a neighbor girl and her friends. "She had a group that met in the cellar of an apartment house," recalls Orson. Although there were several children in the group, Orson was particularly impressed by the girl leader, who struck him as unusually experienced for her age. But when the girl's mother suddenly found out what her daughter had been up to, it was Orson whom she blamed. The indignant woman visited Dadda to complain about the boy genius who had corrupted her innocent child. Because Orson had been studied in Wisconsin as a child prodigy, the woman assumed

there must be something wrong with him. "You know about
this Leopold and Loeb case," she said to Dadda, referring
to the pair of Chicago boy geniuses who had wantonly
murdered a young boy. "This is something just like it. That's
what this child of yours has been doing with my daughter!"
Since the girl had evidently been conducting her basement
sessions long before he arrived on the block, Orson was
dumbfounded by her mother's accusations. Nor could he
figure out what playing doctor had to do with the famous
murder case. "I was convinced that there was some connection that I didn't understand," says Orson. But the incident had sealed his fate. Although his going to Todd was
ostensibly a punishment, both Dick and Dadda saw it as a
way of freeing the boy from the bad influence of the other.
"I was sent to Todd in order to settle their hopeless battle,"
says Orson. Dadda privately told the boy that going to Todd
would allow him to resume his artistic pursuits, whereas
Dick said it was for the kind of strictly practical education
Dadda had always kept him from getting. Of his forlorn
departure for Todd, Orson recalls that he "left in the spirit
of one sent to the slammer."

   "I hear we've got another *Welles* boy," groaned the elderly
headmaster, Noble Hill, the day Orson checked into Clover
Hall. "I hope he's nothing like his brother!" Founded in
1848 by Reverend Richard Kimble Todd—whom Orson
imagined as having "a beard down to his knees"—in 1892
the Todd Seminary was purchased by one of its teachers,
this very same Noble Hill, recalled by Orson as "a Nova
Scotia Puritan ministerial type who was several years before
the mast and all that sort of thing." Under Noble Hill (even
his son called him by both names), Todd stressed public
speaking, sports, and—above all—leadership. Although
Todd Seminary had offered a full preparatory program, Noble Hill made the eccentric decision to eliminate the final
two years, so that, after the tenth grade, boys had to finish
high school elsewhere. His rationale was to focus all pe-

dagogical effort on *early* leadership training, since he felt
that the sooner his boys knew how to lead others, the better
they would do for themselves. Known to terrified students
and faculty alike as "the King," Noble Hill dearly loved the
sound of his own voice, and delivered countless rousing
speeches to the boys about keeping "the snow untrodden"—
a reference to what he envisioned as Todd's mission of
keeping them all from sexual temptation. Typically, his
speeches were peppered with the expression, "I feel constrained to—" presumably to show that he too knew how
to keep himself in check.

The King held a much-anticipated yearly oratory contest
for which the boys practiced every afternoon. Athletics were
left to Noble Hill's son, the charismatic Roger, whom Orson
Welles's eldest daughter aptly describes as "puckish," and
whom Orson himself compares to Ronald Colman—"but
with much more energy of course than Ronald Colman."
For it was characteristic of Roger's wiry, compact frame to
exude phenomenal amounts of energy even when ostensibly
at rest, his left hand typically posed on his hip or in his
pants pocket. His gait Orson fondly describes as a "sailor's
swagger"—hence the affectionate nickname by which all
Todd called him: Skipper. Notwithstanding a long history
of childhood illness that led to his boyhood nickname "Puny,"
after a brief stint in advertising, Skipper had spent a semester
at the Bernarr MacFadden American College of Physical
Education in hopes of becoming Todd's gym teacher and
basketball coach. With the surefire MacFadden method,
Skipper, then in his early thirties, had all Todd flexing its
muscles. Whether on balance bars or the basketball court,
Skipper's agile young jocks were champions of the Midwest
schoolboy circuit. So successful a coach was he that his
basketball manual, written in his spare time and privately
published by the Todd Press, became an unexpected best-
seller.

On two counts Skipper was a man of great mystery at

Todd. For one thing, to the stupefaction of all, he never appeared to eat a normal meal, preferring to subsist—almost entirely it seemed—on Hershey Bars, an unexpected habit in an official purveyor of health education whose abundant energy would certainly have seemed to recommend this singularly unhealthy diet. Stranger still was his tendency to disappear at intervals into the boiler room to indulge in what was widely said to be his single vice. Its exact identity was the object of much speculation among the Todd boys, none of whom had ever managed to follow him there. Only some of them guessed correctly from certain telltale signs that, even as they debated, Skipper was enjoying what Orson calls "secretive puffs at a Camel cigarette." Skipper's secret life in the lower depths was necessitated by the King's having strictly prohibited the foul and ungodly practice of smoking on campus.

When Orson Welles got to Todd, he "fell in love with Roger Hill." Almost certainly it was Skipper's matchless zest to which he was attracted. "He's always been galloping on some sort of hobbyhorse all of his life with tremendous enthusiasm and a kind of youth that I never had," says Orson. "He was always younger than I was." Of course, in a fusty institution like Todd, over all of whose most picayune affairs old Noble Hill still exerted his imperious domination, Skipper was immensely attractive to all the boys, for whom he epitomized an almost subversive sort of excitement. But Orson's needs were special. Initially perplexed by the abrupt transition between his erratic life of recent years and the monotonously regular rhythms of morning prayer and classes in which he now found himself, Orson saw in Skipper a chance to reproduce at least one familiar relationship from his exceedingly peculiar past—the bond he had maintained with his mentor, Dadda Bernstein, who was always willing to intercede on the boy's behalf. The ferocious bullying to which Orson had been subjected in the Chicago public school, as well as the dreadful tales he had heard about Todd from

Richard, made him think he needed a protector. Extensive experience with adults, with whom he had hitherto spent far more time than with children, had shown him how—with a bit of calculation on his part—some of them were rather easily manipulated by a child as bright and unusual as he. Sizing up the Todd hierarchy, Orson astutely perceived that Skipper might be such an adult. All that was needed was for Orson to court, to *woo* him: for the boy's designs on the older man were admittedly nothing less than romantic. "I'm the boy you could have had," Orson would tell Skipper many decades later, thereby suggesting what *might* have occurred had Skipper not been quite so happily married and single-mindedly heterosexual. Making Skipper his friend wasn't going to be easy, since everyone else at Todd was competing for his interest and approval through feats of athletic prowess. Conscious of his insurmountable physical awkwardness, his flat feet, his weak ankles, his asthma, Orson knew sports weren't going to be his way to Skipper, so he devised another stratagem.

Every year, the students put together a Halloween Eve show in Todd's gymnasium, which was usually the province of the older boys. So the appearance of an eleven-year-old sixth-grader in an elaborate Sherlock Holmes suit and deer-stalker cap, which he promptly shed in favor of a massive billowing cape, created a kind of bemused sensation. This was Orson's plan for capturing Skipper's attention: a magic show in which the most magical element of all was his own sudden physical metamorphosis. No sooner was he onstage than the awkward, somewhat unhealthy boy was instantly replaced by the epitome of theatrical presence: a mesmerizing (some said *spiritual*) power that issued, it seemed, from everywhere—the hands, the rich, unexpectedly mature voice, the dark, vaguely Oriental eyes—all orchestrated so majestically that one hardly knew his main trick didn't work. For the miniature building that he caused to materialize from beneath a handkerchief wasn't aflame as

Orson intended. Among those few spectators conscious of
this small failure was Skipper, who also saw how Orson's
rapid-fire inventive banter, delivered in stentorian tones and
with much accompanying choreography, almost entirely obscured what had really happened—a sort of stage magic far
more impressive than if the little house had merely blazed
as it was supposed to.

While his students had always perceived Skipper as an
iconoclastic figure at Todd, until Orson's appearance he had
been an iconoclast without an agenda. But he was instantly
attracted to Orson's abundant creativity, and perceived in
him the outlines of a bold new direction for his own teaching
career—not just as the boy's mentor, although he would be
that too, but as one who would seek to nurture the creative
potential in all his charges. Although it has been mistakenly
reported that Skipper actively recruited the prodigy for Todd,
he actually knew no more about Orson's background than
anybody else, so he could not yet have understood precisely
what, if anything, in that mysterious childhood might have
contributed to the boy showman's curious self-confidence.

After the Halloween show, Orson became a regular visitor
to the campus apartment Skipper shared with his wife Hortense and their three children—and at first, Orson felt acutely
threatened by Hortense. She, in turn, resented his incessant
intrusion into their family life, and she complained angrily
to Skipper; for unlike other Todd boys, Orson came and
went freely at the Hill residence. Nor was Hortense amused
by Orson's constant lounging in her bed, a state of affairs
that suggests that she was initially as threatened by Orson
as he admits to having been by her. Hortense probably saw
what Skipper in his refreshing innocence did not: that this
was the boy he could have had. Skipper appears to have
been much too busy discussing Shakespeare and magic and
opera with his peculiar little companion for the possibility
of such indiscretion to occur to him. Before long, however,
Orson and Hortense became curious about each other, and

he began to court her as earnestly as he had her husband. From then on, although Orson's relations were always primarily—and publicly—with Skipper, he was no less devoted to Hortense. "It's that Christian marriage that we were supposed to believe in," says this thrice-married child of a broken home about his mentor's model home life. Orson's eldest daughter speculates that Skipper and Hortense were the closest he ever came to having a true family—a fact that did not go unnoticed by the Hills' own children, whom Orson perceives as having always "despised" him as "this gosling in the midst of the chicken run."

Orson's everyday life at Todd was as dramatic and flamboyant as his magical debut. His snide marginalia on his IQ exam showed Skipper that, at intervals, the child's experience and knowledge of the world outstripped the anonymous pedagogue who'd composed the questions, and—most terrible—that Orson knew it. "Underline the animal that crosses the desert," went one question, to which alternative answers were *horse, elephant, camel*, or *donkey*—of which the boy was expected to choose the third. Having actually explored a desert in his travels with Dick, and knowing not only that each of these animals could be observed in transit there but also that the conventional, if hopelessly incomplete, answer was *camel*, Orson defiantly—and correctly—underlined all four, beside which he scrawled: "but obviously not by the dumbhead that wrote this test."

This kind of behavior won him the admiration of his peers, but not friendship. Says one of his fellow students, Hascy Tarbox—a rival for Skipper's affections—known as Todd's *other* genius: "Orson had no friends. Not as you and I know of friends. With the possible exception of Roger E. Hill, he was totally void of any human relationship of needing and being needed." Nonetheless—mainly because of his advantageous connection with Skipper—Todd wasn't at all the loathsome place Orson had fearfully anticipated. He

had an audience of his fellow students, and with them made
judicious use of the spate of rumors concerning his curious
past. Says Hascy Tarbox: "During his stay at Todd, Orson
gave off the impression that he was in direct contact with
all the great creators, philosophers, thinkers, religious leaders, wits, and whores of all time." How odd it must have
seemed to those ordinary boys at Todd for one so young to
possess anything so distinctly adult as a *past*! Says Skipper:
"In some ways, he was never really a young boy, you know."
And Hascy Tarbox: "He was never a boy. Or if he had been,
he tried to pass that phase in development so fast that he
gave the illusion to we mere mortals that he was indeed
ageless." His early play with stage makeup, phony noses,
and snow-white hair (such as that he had used to disguise
himself as King Lear) had been an effort to appear vastly
older; by the time he came to Todd, Orson was straining
frantically beyond his meager years, all the while glancing
fondly, sentimentally backward, at a fabled childhood from
which, paradoxically, he had ever been in flight.

In addition to coaching basketball, another of Skipper's
activities at Todd was staging drag chorus lines—little boys
dressed as showgirls—for whose production numbers he
wrote sparkling lyrics. At the Christmas Nativity play the
year Orson arrived, the newcomer portrayed the Virgin Mary,
so when it came time for the annual Spring travesty, a revue
entitled *Finesse the Queen*, Skipper initially presumed that
this "chubby eleven-year-old was just the size and shape
for the chorus." But Orson's curiously adult manner, and,
in particular, his already resonant baritone, destined him to
be cast instead as a male lead. Dapper in a suit and tie, with
hair smartly slicked back, he had to glance upward at his
gangling "female" counterpart, an older boy much too tall
for the part.

The King was a fervent enthusiast of drama, so when
Orson got to Todd, playacting was already an important part
of the curriculum—but not the intensely serious sort of

playacting Orson favored. Preferring Shakespeare and the classic canon to the lighter, more trivial dramatic fare to which Todd audiences had hitherto been accustomed, Orson persuaded Skipper to revise the school repertoire. Says Orson: "Because I wanted to attract his attention, and couldn't do so on the trampoline, I encouraged dramatics where I thought I would be able to get the attention of this marvelous man with whom I was in love." There followed a startling succession of plays—variously adapted, designed, directed, and acted by Orson. There was Orson as Cassius; Orson as Marc Antony; Orson as Richard III; Orson as Dr. Jekyll and Mr. Hyde; Orson as both Androcles and the Lion; even Orson as Jesus Christ ("the late J.C.," as Hascy Tarbox says), for which he posed for photographs looking strangely ethereal. Normally he adopted a directorial persona, which Hascy Tarbox recalls as being somewhat closer to Genghis Khan's: for effect, he directed with a big stick with which he periodically slammed the footlights to betoken his displeasure. If the other boys condoned his dictatorial guise it was because, encouraged by Skipper, they all self-consciously perceived themselves as somehow sharing with the prodigy a moment in theatrical history.

On the advice of an office assistant who had said, "You'd better keep a file on this kid," Skipper Hill began what would grow to be a vast collection of youthful Wellesiana, of which perhaps the most curious, and revealing, item was a shot of a wide-eyed Orson peeking through the curtain at the audience for a production entitled *Wings over Europe*, meanwhile sucking in his cheeks to make his face appear thinner—and, he must have thought, more handsome—for the camera, and for posterity. But there was another observer of this scene, one whom Orson had not expected. Dick Welles was terribly disappointed by Orson's having obviously devoted himself to acting and directing. "He loved me like an Arab," says Orson of his father, whom Skipper Hill less fondly recalls as by then "a sad drunk." Says

Skipper: "He was rather frightening, and usually pretty heavily cocked with alcohol." Mainly he steered clear of Todd, but the night Orson appeared in *Wings over Europe*, Dick couldn't resist coming secretly to see what it was all about. Without having told Orson that he was coming he stood in the back of the auditorium, and left before the play was over, because, says Orson, "He didn't want to admit he was interested in my acting career or some damn thing." Nor did he mention it later. But when Orson peeked through the curtains and sucked in his cheeks for posterity, there beyond the camera, looming in the back, was his father, who knew by now that once again, and probably forever, he was losing the battle for his son.

CHAPTER 3
Untrodden Snow

Dadda Bernstein liked to reminisce about Baby Orson's puppet theater, for which Orson had devised a show featuring an elderly gentleman who struggled comically to untangle his beard, which was glued to a book by candle wax. A decade or so later at Todd, Hascy Tarbox recalls, having introduced puppeteering as "almost the greatest art form there ever was," Orson supervised the construction of a new, much larger and more ornate marionette theater, where he directed a two-part puppet revue consisting of a brief melodrama, followed by a song and dance number. The principal setting for the melodrama was the J. P. Bloodshed Bank, run by a despised villain named Julius Peabody. Showman that he was, Orson knew that his second act simply had to top the first. So imagine the collective astonishment when, as the finale began, each of the singing and dancing blockheads was seen to resemble, vividly and parodistically, one of the so-called Olympians of the Todd faculty. Only those few students who had attended rehearsals knew that these had been even more outrageous, since in private the puppet-teachers were made to copulate vertically, horizontally, onstage, in the air, and every which probable and improbable way. Nor had the generally imperious Orson balked at this sudden violation of his script but, from the bedazzled look on his face, seemed rather to enjoy the view, for as Hascy Tarbox says, "He was as lascivious as the rest of us."

When Orson arrived at Todd, although he was much taller than the other sixth-graders, his perfectly round, chubby-cheeked baby face betrayed the fact that he was still very much a child. As he entered his teens, however, Orson metamorphosed. He suddenly seemed all gangly arms and legs. To his immense delight, Orson was thin! Most striking of all was the effect his sudden slenderness had on his face. It remained soft, but it had acquired an almost decadent aura, so that he looked like what he calls "a dissipated choirboy." His cheeks had hollowed out, and his full, sensuous lower lip took on new prominence. For the first time now there was something that Orson terms "ambiguous" about his looks, and the overall effect was enormously attractive. With his strange Asian eyes and striking high forehead—to which he had an unconscious habit of calling attention by running his slim fingers through his long unruly hair—Orson appeared quite unlike any of the other boys his age. There was something soft, almost feminine about him, and yet, his deep, resonant voice, great height, and huge-boned form left no doubt in an observer that he was unmistakably male.

During summer vacation, the year he was fourteen, while crossing the Atlantic from Italy, Orson had had his first "grown-up" sexual experience with a girl two or three years his senior. "I had no idea how to go about it!" laughs Orson, who depended on the older girl's experience (*his* having been limited to playing doctor). By tipping a steward Orson and his girlfriend had the use of a large first-class cabin all day long. Of having lost his virginity Orson chuckles: "I was, however, not a *wunderkind* in that department, merely precocious."

Back at Todd, Orson was anxious to practice what he had

learned at sea, but since the boys were without town priv-
ileges there were few opportunities for meeting girls. Despite the naughty puppet show, sex on campus was mostly
limited to the dismal likes of watching the penmanship teacher
summon boys to his desk so that he might slide his hand
into their pockets and fondle them while making a great
show of reviewing their lessons. The demented teacher
seemed to have convinced himself that no one noticed what
he was up to. Among themselves however the boys whispered about who would be next since he didn't do it to
everyone or every time. While he pretended to devote himself to his lessons, Orson watched intently as each boy in
turn was summoned to the front of the room. Much to
Orson's repeated relief, the feeler never did it to him, but
he did it one time too many to other boys, and, at length,
was discreetly dismissed (although the giggling double-
entendres about the Palmer method of handwriting persisted
on campus). "How they *hired* him I don't know," moans
Orson, "because he walked like a willow in a blizzard!"
While for once Orson had had nothing to fear from the
penmanship teacher, he had a more difficult time with a
much-respected Todd father whose son, a classmate of Orson's, invited him home for the weekend. "We don't have
another bed, and you and I will sleep here," the boy's pipe-
smoking parent told Orson, who cheerfully complied—until
his bedmate pounced, at which Orson awkwardly climbed
over him, and dashed out of the room. He was probably
much more embarrassed than his would-be seducer. Although he frequently saw the man again at Todd, neither
mentioned the untoward incident.

With his classmates Orson dutifully went to chapel twice
daily, and on Sundays walked "in crocodiles" to the Presbyterian church, where, as if they hadn't heard enough of
the King's ranting about "untrodden snow," the local minister sternly harangued them some more. There Orson spotted a pretty girl in the church choir with whom he promptly

arranged a date. But since, by order of the King, Todd boys
were not allowed to go into town unescorted, Orson climbed
out the dormitory window and slid down a rain gutter. Thus
began Orson's regular forays into Woodstock, Illinois, where,
the minister's harangues notwithstanding, he conducted affairs with several girls in the Presbyterian choir. If he felt
guilt about any of his sexual activities, it wasn't about actually having sex, but about looking at pornographic pictures. "What I *did* was never connected with what I *saw* in
pornography," says Orson, "and what I saw seemed to me
an indication of the depravity of man. I thought what I was
doing was all right, but the pictures of it, of grown-up people
doing it, seemed to me a terrible revelation of humanity."
Still, these nasty images were much in his thoughts. "I was
obsessed, terribly worried, by pornography, deeply depressed by it, like the snake house—I kept going back and
looking at it. The pornography of my childhood was so
much worse than now because it was unwashed, you know.
I'll never forget seeing a picture of something like eleven
Swedes, all men, all sodomizing each other, and all with
their socks on." To Orson, pornography was "a view into
hell."

Orson's mature appearance—he looked and sounded considerably older than his classmates—presented problems
when Skipper's Todd Troupers entered its production of
Julius Caesar in the Chicago Drama League contest. Orson
took two parts. With an eye toward displaying the flexibility
of his voice and mood and manner, he played Cassius and
he also stepped in for the boy who played Antony to do
Antony's important oration. If more than ever now Orson
felt the need to distinguish himself, it was because he had
come to regard Skipper as the more judgmental and demanding of his two mentors. To others it may have appeared
as if Skipper badly spoiled the boy. "Orson would have been
better off if he hadn't had so much adulation, and he'd had
to play ball with the rest of the world," says Hascy Tarbox,

echoing a common sentiment. But from Orson's point of view, it was precisely *because* of Skipper's adulation that he drove himself so relentlessly to earn it. On stage in *Caesar* at Chicago's Goodman Theatre, Orson was by all accounts so outstanding, so professional, that the judges instantly disqualified Todd for having hired two "ringers": adults masquerading as children for purposes of competition. What ringers? Todd angrily demanded, to which the jury replied that the *men* playing Cassius and Antony were obviously not students but professional actors. So before the truth could be told, the Silver Cup was awarded to Senn High School. It was only afterwards that Orson's age (*but he was so large and mature, and his voice so resonant!*) and dual role (*but Cassius and Antony looked and sounded nothing alike!*) were verified. But in the meantime at least two members of the audience were utterly appalled that Senn, not Todd, had been victorious. The much younger of the pair, Hiram "Chubby" Sherman, whispered something into the ear of his mentor, the Goodman Theatre's director, Whitford Kane, who publicly awarded a belated unofficial prize as tribute to Orson's ability. No Silver Cup was involved, just the immense admiration of Kane and his discerning protégé, for both of whom this was not to be the last encounter with Orson Welles.

The summer after the mixup of *Julius Caesar*, Orson accompanied his ailing father on a voyage to the Far East. Despite the great love between them, there was also considerable tension. Dick made no bones about being terribly disappointed with Orson, who, he kept sadly repeating, had passed from him. "I think he felt he'd lost me in the great struggle for my psyche," says Orson, "not in my love for him, but in what I was going to be." Although by now Dick's alcoholism had irreversibly dissipated his health, both of them avoided references to his drinking. "I knew he'd come to the end of the road," says Orson, who boyishly dreamed of finding a drink for his father that wouldn't make

him sick. Orson didn't resent Dick's perpetual inebriation
because he understood how "lonely and unhappy" his father
had been since the separation from Beatrice, whose life had
seemed to flourish at the very moment she was rid of him.
Dick's health was so poor in general that he was afraid of
dying in the Orient, and he had Orson sign a paper promising
that "he wouldn't be buried in the ground." Orson was to
have him either buried at sea or cremated.

Although Dick survived, the Oriental journey was not
without unfortunate incident. Explains Orson: "On the ferry
going over to the mainland from Hong Kong with an awful
lot of typical colonial British who'd just finished a party as
our fellow passengers, my father was drunk enough to lose
his trousers, and I had to get them on." Of his father's
embarrassment on the boat from Hong Kong, Orson says,
"I can imagine a child hating his father for that. I didn't at
all. I still looked up to him." Over the years Orson's public
accounts of the China trip would be shot through with humor—notably the charming and oft-repeated tale of his
having run up a huge tab in the men's bar, where he caroused
with fellow travelers while Dick (who, much to his consternation, would have to pay for it all later) snoozed oblivi-
ously in his cabin. But the humor seems hollow: the *whole*
story is actually terribly sad. Drunk in his cabin, Dick was
jolted out of his stupor when he saw Orson stumble in after
a merry session of drinking in the ship's bar. "Your father
was a drunk, your aunts were drunks, and here you are!"
Dick blurted out from where he lay, at which wounding
reprimand Orson spun around on his heels to return straight-
away to the bar, where—with much ado—he ordered a
round of drinks for all. Neither a clever prank nor an act
of spite, it betokened Orson's pain at finding himself unable
to help his father, or to patch things up with him. Respecting
and fearing Dick's judgment as he did, he knew his father
was right: he *had* passed from him.

Never was this clearer than when, back in the States,

Orson allowed the Hills to talk him into not seeing his father
again unless he stopped drinking. This wasn't like Dadda's
complaining that Dick was a bad influence on Orson because
he was a philistine. Hortense Hill was genuinely concerned
about Orson's safety with Dick, who, in a drunken stupor,
narrowly escaped death when the Hotel Sheffield burned
down. Perhaps if his son refused to see him, Dick would
feel compelled to sober up. So Orson bluntly told Dick that
he had decided to follow the Hills' suggestion, and "that
was the last I ever saw of him." On December 28, 1930,
having escaped the Hotel Sheffield fire, Dick Welles died
in another hotel at 171 North Randolph Street in Chicago,
where the man he thought of as his greatest enemy in the
world, Dadda Bernstein, was called in as a family friend to
issue the death certificate. Dick was fifty-eight. The cause
of death was heart and kidney failure. But in the ensuing
years Orson has variously implied that his father killed himself, or—more mysterious yet—that he thinks of himself
as having killed his father. As to the question of Dick Welles's
fabled suicide, it was, and remains, Orson's feeling that his
father "drank himself to death." For Orson, the heart and
kidney failure were only the apparent causes of death—
they seemed to him the culmination of Dick's long course
of self-destruction that had begun with the loss of Beatrice.
And the son believed that the father's unequivocal loss of
the "tug of war" for Orson, coupled with the boy's sudden
refusal to see him, had been too much for him to bear. So
the young Orson told people that he was present at his
father's suicide, although he was undoubtedly alluding to
the last summer they had spent together, when the boy
watched helplessly as Dick seemed hell-bent on doing himself in with alcohol. And when Orson claimed that he thought
of himself as having killed his father, he only reflected his
own intense guilt: "I've always *thought* I killed him," says
Orson about a lifetime of despair at having betrayed Dick
when he needed him.

Although family members of alcoholics are frequently advised by professionals to eject the offenders until they stop drinking, Orson feels he made the wrong decision, if only in *human* terms: "I didn't think I was doing the right thing, that's why it's so inexcusable. I didn't think my father's drinking was a terrible thing, or that it was endangering me at all. I simply wanted to please the Hills. So it's really inexcusable. I didn't have a moral position about it at all." Orson also says that while he had been somewhat prepared for his mother's death, the news about Dick stunned him: "I wasn't prepared for my father's death, in spite of the fact that he thought he was dying the summer before." Worst of all perhaps were Orson's incessant thoughts of Dick's "lonely death," which filled him with what he describes as "anguish and pity." Summoned to Chicago by a telegram that reached him at Todd, Orson found himself unable to confide his guilt to Dadda. "I didn't discuss it with him," says Orson, "there was so much *hatred* between the two of them." Nor is the fact that he was so young when he acceded to the Hills' wishes any solace to him now: "I was supposed to be a big grown-up prodigy, so there's no excuse for it on any level—particularly feeling as I did about my father. If I had worked myself up to thinking that my life was being ruined by him—but I didn't believe that at all. I just understood that that's what they thought, and that's what's so awful about it." He could not broach the subject with the Hills, to whom he ordinarily would have turned concerning most personal quandaries: "I felt that they had been, momentarily, false gods; that I had followed the wrong adults, you know, and for the wrong reasons. I've never, never . . . I don't want to forgive myself. That's why I hate psychoanalysis. I think if you're guilty of something you should live with it. Get rid of it—how can you get rid of a *real* guilt? I think people should live with it, face up to it."

Remembering his father's request for burial at sea or

cremation should he die during the voyage to the Orient, Orson was appalled at the standard below-ground burial arranged by Dick's mother and half-brother in Kenosha, Wisconsin. "I couldn't stop it!" says Orson, still obviously upset, fifty-three years later, by his father's having been embalmed and placed in a coffin for viewing. It seemed to the boy just one more betrayal of Dick Welles. It was as an outsider that Orson attended his father's funeral—he had left Kenosha as a small child and barely knew his paternal grandmother—and this experience of perplexed alienation, mingled with intense guilt about his father, made the entire affair unbearable to one so young, who was simply not yet equipped to cope with all he was now feeling. Nor did the antipathy he felt toward his grandmother help matters. Decades later, Mary's public denials notwithstanding, Orson sticks to his original story about her, first circulated in the 1930s, that she was a witch who performed Satanic rites at Dick's funeral. Her response—that she was a devout Christian Scientist and that it was Orson who had made a tasteless scene at the funeral—he dismisses. "She was a witch," he insists, "a genuine witch—short, fat, and foul-smelling." In the end, one suspects that Orson's disdain for his grandmother is mainly owing to what he characterizes as her having put a curse on his parents' marriage—which, in somewhat less Satanic (and metaphoric) terms, was simply her sustained refusal to come to terms with Beatrice. If for Orson his grandmother seems utterly profane, perhaps it is because, in opposing the union of his parents, she became somehow antithetical to the halcyon days of earliest childhood that remain so sacred to him.

After the funeral, when Dick's will was read, it was discovered that fifteen-year-old Orson was to choose his guardian, a delicate matter since the contest would obviously be between his two mentors, Skipper and Dadda, both of whom had been greatly devoted to him. It didn't take long for Orson to make his decision. He called Skipper at Todd to request a meeting on his arrival at Chicago's Union Station; and there, they talked on a bench for a very long time about all that had happened. But when Orson asked Skipper to become his legal guardian, Skipper declined on the grounds that this was sure to break Dadda's heart. Orson must never tell Dadda about their conversation; he must pretend that Dadda, not Skipper, had been his first choice. As close as Orson had always been to Dadda, he had chosen Skipper in hopes of becoming part of the Hill family with Hortense as his mother. Dadda's domestic arrangements were considerably less attractive to him. The year before, Dadda had entered into a short-lived marriage with an opera singer whose daughter and ex-husband, an Italian conductor, lived with them—which appealed to Dadda's taste for threesomes. When Orson, on holiday from Todd, came to stay, he found himself sternly forbidden by the ex-husband to come into any sort of physical contact with either of the women of the house—"I wasn't allowed to touch anybody because of possible infection or dirt. I'd been playing outside, and I'd bring in microbes and all that." Since he would be back at Todd soon enough, Orson scrupulously kept to himself, but even that didn't keep him out of trouble. Before long, what seemed like his perennial problem cropped up again. Having forbidden the boy to touch anybody didn't stop the ex-husband from suddenly trying to touch *him* when they were alone. "I have a headache, Maestro!" Orson recalls having cried as he rushed from the room.

By the time Dick Welles died, this brief marriage of Dadda's was over. Unfortunately, however, Dadda's latest circumstances, cohabiting with the Moores, were no more appealing to Orson, who vehemently disliked the autocratic Hazel Moore, a former gym teacher whose shrill commands he still likes to mimic: "Orson, you haven't washed the bowl in your bathroom!" Dadda had resumed his affair with Hazel, who fiercely resented his devotion to Orson and treated the boy accordingly.

Skipper had second thoughts about his having foisted Orson on Dadda when, in his capacity as legal guardian, Dadda used part of Orson's legacy to buy a house in Ravinia where he was joined by the Moores. But there was no question of Dadda's thinking he was misusing Orson's money. He quite sincerely believed he was establishing a home where Pookles would feel comfortable, especially because it was decorated with furniture that Orson recognized from his mother's apartment—above all, her piano. But Orson's acute antipathy toward Hazel mostly kept him away. He preferred the solitude of his digs at Todd, where one of the latest mysteries about him was precisely how he had secured a private room when everybody—absolutely everybody—else shared accommodations. Was it a mark of wealth, superiority, or just downright peculiarity? Rumor among the boys was that no one else on campus would live at close quarters with the guy. But whatever the real reason, it was an unquestionable fact of life at Todd that Orson resided alone, apart, and entirely unto himself. His secluded bedroom was actually no larger than a broom closet from which vast clouds of incense periodically wafted through the dormitory halls, thereby suggesting to covetous classmates yet another Wellesian enigma: why was Orson allowed to have matches when nobody else was?

The fifteen-year-old Orson was now in his last year at Todd, and he launched into what would be his student finale: an ambitious adaptation of Shakespeare's history plays that, in retrospect, clearly foreshadowed what would be his legendary Mercury Theatre production, entitled *Five Kings*. The Todd version was slated for Orson's graduation ceremony. Orson's technique of adaptation consisted of using a crayon to excise and rearrange passages in a huge one-volume Shakespeare that he seemed to carry about with him at all times. Although his senior show was initially to have been of *Richard III*, Orson kept grafting on fragments of other plays so that the result was decidedly a most per-

sonal—and unprecedented—concoction. In rehearsal it was
a sprawling and unwieldly affair into which Orson tried to
cram what seemed to the boys like "casts of thousands."
Because there were not enough older boys to fill the ranks
of Orson's armies, he dug down into the fifth grade for fresh
recruits. Even then, a few willing daughters of faculty members had to be inducted and disguised as boys. In rehearsal
the play ran to three and a half hours, and felt like forever—
which, says Hascy Tarbox, led to the faculty's stepping in:
"It was one of the few times the staff suggested to Skipper
that maybe somebody should pull Welles's cork, and do a
little cutting on this thing." So the commencement performance was a truncated extravaganza—but an extravaganza
nonetheless; and if some of the action didn't entirely make
sense, no one in the delighted audience seemed to care.
Through last-minute cutting, insignificant characters and
ambiguous snippets of dialogue somehow assumed featured
status so that, for instance, Hascy Tarbox's minor role as a
messenger became almost a lead since he was onstage nearly
as much as Orson, who played the hunchbacked Richard
III. All in all, Orson's senior show was the grandest exit
Woodstock was likely to see in a while—not counting the
Presbyterian minister's suicide, that is, when, in a nearby
cornfield, he doused himself in kerosene and went up in
flames. As to why he did himself in, the Todd boys never
found out. "I think maybe he was caught with his hand in
the till," Orson muses, "or up somebody's skirt!"

CHAPTER 4

Sodom
and Begorrah

When Orson graduated from Todd his mentors parted ways about what he should do next. Skipper had fixed his sights on Harvard and arranged for an assortment of Chicago-area intelligentsia to write glowing letters of recommendation on Orson's behalf. An exception would have to be made, since Orson would be skipping the last two years of high school that most Todd graduates went on to complete at other prep schools. Harvard especially appealed to Skipper because of what he had heard about George Pierce Baker's celebrated 47 Workshop in playwriting there (although, as it turned out, Baker was no longer holding forth in Cambridge). By contrast with Skipper, who, on the basis of the Todd productions, envisioned a theatrical career for the boy, Dadda pronounced that Orson had been devoting far too much of himself solely to theatrical pursuits (which Dadda somewhat jealously associated with Skipper's influence), and that a more catholic education was in order. This in mind, Dadda's first choice was Cornell. But if his mentors had each of them already planned his next four years for him, sixteen-year-old Orson had other ideas. When Orson was in his last year at Todd, a curious item about him had appeared in Ashton Stevens's important column in the Hearst *Chicago*

American: "Given as good an education as will adhere to him at a good college, young and not ill-looking Orson Welles is as likely as not to become my favorite actor. True, it will be four or five years before he has attained his majority and a degree, and I have yet to see him act. But I like the way he handles a situation and to lay my plays long ahead I am going to put a clipping of this paragraph in my betting book. If Orson is not at least a leading man by the time it has yellowed, I'll never make another prophecy." A good friend of Dadda's, the courtly Stevens hadn't exactly written about Orson out of the blue. Nor was it the first time he had shown a friendly interest in the boy whose articles on music for the local *Highland Park News* the eminent Chicago columnist had vetted. Still, a prophecy in print was a great thrill for Orson, who didn't really see in the slightest what college had to do with his promptly fulfilling it. In May of 1931, in hopes of forestalling his mentors' shipping him off to either Harvard or Cornell, Orson took the bold measure of placing an ad in the "At Liberty" column of the show-business periodical *Billboard* that read: "ORSON WELLES—Stock Characters, Heavies, Juveniles or as cast. Also specialties, chalk talk or can handle stage. Young, excellent appearance, quick sure study. Lots of pep, experience and ability. Close in Chicago early in June and want place in good stock company for remainder of season. Salary according to late date of opening and business conditions. Photos on request." Orson figured that he'd be more likely to lure prospective theatrical employers by implying that he was already working on stage—although his ostensible *closing* in Chicago was really just his high school graduation play. In the meantime, he halfheartedly enrolled at the Chicago Art Institute, mainly to convince his mentors that he was indeed pursuing an education, while in truth he eagerly anticipated stealing off to some distant theater the moment an offer, any offer, turned up.

When by June there had been not a single response to

the ad, Orson decided to escalate the stakes. His new, more hard-hitting copy in *Billboard* read: "I will invest moderate amount of cash and my own services as Heavy, Character and Juvenile in good summer stock or repertory proposition." At Dadda's in Ravinia there followed a terrible battle of wills between Orson and his guardian, each of them stubbornly holding his ground. Dadda had considerable leverage, however, as he legally controlled the money Dick had left Orson. Intent on the boy's going to a good college, Dadda was unlikely to approve Orson's squandering his money on the theater. Finally, three days of frantic quarreling was interrupted when Orson suffered a timely hayfever attack. Whereupon a genuinely sympathetic Dadda proposed sending him somewhere far away, at least until the hay-fever season was over. It seemed to Dadda like the best way of ending the argument. Much to Orson's amazement, Dadda spontaneously came up with the marvelously improbable idea of a walking and painting tour of Ireland and Scotland, during which Orson would keep a copious diary that might even afford material for a travel book. Orson could barely believe what he was hearing. But within four days of this entirely unexpected turn in the conversation, having sworn to keep painting and writing about all he saw wherever he saw it, a still very surprised Orson found himself in New York, excitedly preparing to board the SS *Baltic*—destination (or so he imagined it) the great theaters of Europe.

When he disembarked in Galway that August of 1931, Orson checked his baggage, after which, with only an army knapsack hastily stuffed with painting equipment, he began his hike through the Irish countryside. Two miles beyond Galway, however, the knapsack split asunder. Dripping with paint, he began to haul his belongings to a nearby pub, until the sight of a passing donkey cart inspired him to acquire one for himself. From then on, touring about by day with his new blue and orange cart drawn by a three-year-old

donkey named Sheeog, Orson would camp at the edge of
the road, where he built a turf fire and slept under the stars.
Back in the States, Orson's adventures were meticulously
monitored through letters addressed to "My Dearest
Dadda"—which in turn were dispatched from Ravinia to
Todd, where, after studying them intently, Skipper had his
secretaries type multiple copies, all but one of which were
returned to Dadda, who promptly sent them to Ashton Stevens and other eminent Chicagoans lest they be wondering
(as Dadda matter-of-factly assumed they would) about Orson. Painfully sensitive to the expectations of his audience,
Orson knew that Dadda above all would want some word
of the serious writing and painting that was to have been
the principal justification for traveling abroad. But the news
was disappointing. From Inisheer, in the Aran Islands, he
complained of having written nothing and painted six "hideous" abortions that he used to pay for lodgings. His night
life on the tiny island was considerably more successful,
however. He had become a regular at the raucous Irish home
dances, where, known to the admiring locals as Paddy, it
was his custom to jig well into the morning.

By October, Orson found his way to Dublin—for if it
was *theater* he wanted, the home of the Abbey and the Gate
was clearly the place to find it. He spent his first hours in
Dublin in a downcast mood, lonely and homesick, since at
the American Express office no mail—or money—from
the States awaited him. Low on cash, and having already
written desperately to Dadda for more, he worried about
what he was possibly going to do when he'd spent his scant
remaining funds. That night, returning to the little room he
had rented, he found the electricity shut off—all in all, not
an auspicious start. Next morning Orson wasted no time
finding a theater, the Gate as it happened, so that on his
second night in Dublin he saw a performance of the Earl
of Longford's *The Melians*, in which he was relieved to
spot a familiar face onstage—a fellow he had met tramping

about the countryside. His young acquaintance played only an obscure role in the play, but it was enough of an excuse for Orson to present himself backstage, where he caught the eye of Hilton Edwards, the plump, homely co-director of the Gate. (His producing career had begun, he liked to say, when, glancing at himself in the mirror, he decided that "it doesn't matter what a producer looks like.") Edwards and the boy quickly fell into animated conversation, during which, hoping to be hired in some small capacity, Orson announced that he was a visiting actor from New York, where he had just wrapped up a season with the Theatre Guild. But Orson need not have lied to interest Edwards in hiring him. With his partner at the Gate, Micheal Mac-Liammoir, Edwards had been looking for someone to play Karl Alexander, the Duke in the impending production of Ashley Dukes's adaptation of Lion Feuchtwanger's *Jew Süss* (unlike the national repertory of the more-established Abbey Theatre, the Gate's was broadly international). He had nearly despaired of finding the right actor in Dublin, and was about to substitute another play altogether when by chance Orson wandered backstage. At a glance he looked and sounded right for the part, but could he act? When an impromptu audition showed that indeed he could (although his reading of the part suffered at first because he was nervous), Orson was offered, and promptly accepted, a place in the company. He left the theater heady with the excitement of having become a *professional* overnight, and being able to write home about it in triumph. Back in his room he scribbled an ecstatic letter to Skipper to declare that John Barrymore and Gordon Craig should "step back" because he, *Orson Welles*, had arrived.

It had all happened so quickly. Yesterday he had been depressed about his failure to have written or painted anything that met the high standards to which he had been taught to hold himself—and now suddenly he was about to go into rehearsal for a lead role in a major play due to

premiere in three weeks. He couldn't get it out of his head
that Ashton Stevens's prediction had been confirmed in a
matter of months, not years. In the weeks that followed,
Orson was much too charged up to sleep. After long days
of rehearsal, it was his custom to buzz about nighttime
Dublin, afterward returning to the Gate to work till morning
painting scenery. Having told everyone that he was eighteen
years old (two years seemed to make all the difference to
him), he acted as if it were the most natural thing in the
world for him to be starring in one of the best theaters in
Dublin. The supreme self-confidence that Dadda and Skipper had nurtured with their lavish attentions stood him in
good stead now that he was about to appear before an audience that would not consist of the predictably admiring
teachers, peers, and parents to whom he'd grown accustomed at Todd: "I knew that it was a more important audience, but I had a *very* high opinion of myself as an actor,
which I've never lost, one which is seldom shared by anybody else," he laughs mischievously, "so it didn't seem to
me that I was at hazard in any way. I'd seen all the other
actors and what they were doing, and it was clear to me
that I would walk away with the play—and I *did*, you see."

Orson's aplomb was among the first things that struck
Micheal MacLiammoir about him. "He knew that he was
precisely what he himself would have been had God consulted him on the subject at his birth," says MacLiammoir.
"He fully appreciated and approved of what had been bestowed, and realized that he couldn't have done the job
better himself, in fact he would not have changed a single
item." But MacLiammoir was not entirely amused by Orson's posing. From the first he was insanely jealous of the
handsome young newcomer in whom his lover Hilton Edwards seemed to have taken a special interest. Even Hilton's
telling him truthfully that nothing untoward had gone on
with the boy did not soothe him. "He was so jealous of
Hilton," says Orson, "the possibility of Hilton's being in-

terested in anybody else, and when he discovered I was not inclined in their direction, he remained jealous of me and Hilton, because Hilton and I enjoyed each other's company very much."

Only gradually, however, did Orson begin to comprehend the dynamics of Hilton and Micheal's passionate relationship. The doyens of the theater, known fondly about Dublin as Sodom and Begorrah, had first met as actors in Anew McMaster's legendary Intimate Shakespeare Company. "His story is absolutely extraordinary!" says Orson of the outrageous Irish actor-manager Anew McMaster, better known as "Mac." "He played only in small Irish towns, and was the *best* living Shakespearean actor. He was the most *beautiful* man you ever saw in your life—and with a marvelous voice. He had everything! He had come to London and got bad notices in his first play, and he refused to go back ever again. He spent the rest of his life touring in the Irish smalls, you know, they'd build a stage, put up scenery, and so on. McMaster had an absolutely fabulous personality. When he played Shylock, he took off his Shylock makeup and put on juvenile makeup to take his bow—and he always made the same curtain speech no matter where he was: 'I want to come back next year to your dear little city by the sea.' He'd be inland, you know, two hundred miles from the sea—these poor peasants would stare at him!" About McMaster's notorious reputation in England and Ireland, Orson laughs: "Smaller and smaller amount of places he could play because he was a raging queen and went through the choirboys of each town like a withering flame!" His homosexuality notwithstanding, Mac was married to Micheal MacLiammoir's sister, with whom he shared a devotion to the occult teachings of Aleister Crowley. Mac was especially delighted when Mrs. McMaster's aquiline beauty of a brother, Micheal, joined the company, because like McMaster, MacLiammoir liked to wear heavy makeup offstage as well as on. "They had their little compacts with

powder puffs," says Orson of Mac and his brother-in-law.
"They would sit at tea after they'd been to the *fil-ums* in
Dublin, and amaze the locals by bringing out their powder
puffs—this is the day when the powder puff was a real
puff, you know—and fix themselves up and bead their
eyelashes, and so on. They were wild—*so* wild that everybody just stared in wonderment at them." For all Micheal's
beauty and eccentricity, however, beside McMaster he was
clearly the lesser light. "Micheal was kind of the less glamorous and extraordinary *sister* of his brother-in-law," Orson
explains. "He was remarkable, he was a really great Hamlet,
he was a tremendously amusing writer and a formidable
personality, but compared to Mac he was *nothing*! Mac had
his eye wiped, as they say in Dublin."

Micheal was twenty-eight, but still exceedingly boyish
in appearance, when he joined the Intimate Shakespeare
Company. His only physical flaw was a toupée that, says
Orson, "lived a life of its own." In boyhood he had been a
celebrated child actor in London whose roles included Macduff's son in Sir Herbert Beerbohm Tree's *Macbeth*, *Oliver
Twist*, and several seasons in *Peter Pan*. "In those days
there were all kinds of very high-society elderly gentlemen
who would be waiting for him with bouquets of flowers
when he came out," says Orson. "He'd been *enormously*
spoiled because he was the toast of the town, and apparently
in the West End it was perfectly all right for a child actor
to be a sexual object and carry on like a leading lady." When
he joined the Intimate Shakespeare Company, Micheal found
himself instantly attracted to Hilton Edwards, four years his
junior, a beefy English opera singer and actor whose stage
experience included four years with the Shakespearean company of the Old Vic Theatre. "What Micheal liked was
vigorous nonhomosexual types," says Orson, "good family
men, preferably with large black mustaches, and ideally,
members of the police force." Although he wasn't a po-
liceman, and didn't have a large black mustache, Hilton

Edwards thought of, and conducted himself as, a heterosexual—at least he had until he met up with Micheal. "Hilton Edwards was a perfectly normal man," says Orson, "that
is, as normal as *any* English actor is, and was *seduced* by
Micheal." So that four years later, after they had settled in
together and founded the Dublin Gate, Micheal constantly
feared that Hilton might drift back to heterosexuality. "Hilton was a born hetero," Orson explains, "and our friendship
was the friendship of two men, with no sexual overtones.
I think that bothered Micheal, that put him out of it, you
see—the *worst* threat you can imagine."

In Hilton Edwards, Orson felt the familiar lure of the
mentor type—the powerful older man who could assist him
in the great world. His friendship with Edwards gave him
more than just the coveted opportunity to appear onstage in
Dublin. It helped shape his aesthetic point of view by exposing him to the theory of modern theater at the heart of
the Gate's international repertory and often eccentric staging. When Orson wrote home to say that he was getting a
better education in Dublin than he possibly could at any
college, he wasn't merely rationalizing a decision to postpone returning to the States. For many years hence, both
in theater and film, his own work would bear the decisive
influence of his brief tenure at the Gate, where he picked
up a quick course in antinaturalist stage theory, which Edwards had synthesized and dubbed the *Theatre Theatrical*.
Much as Orson admired his brilliant directing, it was less
Edwards's theatrical practice—that is, the way he actually
directed at the Gate—than his artistic theory—the way he
thought about the theater and what it should be—that had
such a profound and lasting effect on the boy's ideas about
the stage. In short, and by contrast with the modern naturalistic theater's attempts to create an illusion of reality onstage, Edwards's Theatre Theatrical would make no effort
to conceal its intricate artifice—its audience was never to
forget for one moment that they were in a *theater* where

actors were *performing*. According to Edwards, "an attempt to create an illusion of reality is essential to many plays, but limiting, misleading, and even degrading when applied to works that have no intrinsic relation to reality." What especially disturbed Edwards was that naturalism was widely regarded as the *only* serious means of presenting drama—so that the ultimate accolade for an actor might be, "Isn't he natural?" or for a stage set, "Isn't it realistic?" From Edwards, however, Orson learned the seminal lesson that naturalism was but one of various possible styles to be considered in staging a play; it was an artistic convention like any other. Edwards argued that theater should not be confused with film, which, owing to its photographic nature, was intrinsically prone to create an illusion of reality. Because of this unfortunate confusion, however, cinema had had a detrimental effect on modern theater, which, against the grain of its basic nature, strove to compete with film's stark realism. Wrote Edwards: "An attempt to obey the trite command to let art conceal art has become so successful that the art of the theatre has become indistinguishable from the art of the camera." The Theatre Theatrical's antidote was in intense stylization: "When the theatre once again makes its audiences conscious of the presence of its art," said Edwards, "people will go to the theatre to see and hear a theatrical performance, and to the cinema to see and hear a cinematic one. The theatre will be the theatre precisely because it is theatrical, and the preservation of its individuality will result in the preservation of the two art forms that are, however similar, separate and distinct." While Orson did not consciously imitate, or borrow from, Edwards's program for the Theatre Theatrical, who can say how different his early work as a director in New York and Hollywood might have been had his first formative professional experience been with a company of an entirely different theatrical bent? Like his mentor Edwards, Orson would take an antinaturalistic stance in his early stage productions in

New York whose unabashed theatricality was antithetical to the tendencies of, say, the Group Theatre. Later, in Hollywood, Orson would give Edwards's ideas an ironic twist by imbuing the photographic medium of film with an unmistakably theatrical element of extreme stylization. Observers of Orson's career have frequently been puzzled by his having sprung seemingly full-blown as a vanguard director in New York—when his only prior directing experience was a handful of school productions at Todd. The theatrical theory of Hilton Edwards, which Orson rapidly assimilated at the Gate, is the missing link between his juvenile productions and what came later.

As the Dublin premiere of *Jew Süss* approached, Orson maintained his air of perfect assurance. Nor was it just an act. It never really occurred to the boy that the first-night audience would be mercilessly judging his performance—or if it did, he wasn't conscious of it. His thoughts were filled with the exciting new ideas about theater he was soaking up at the Gate—and also, as it happened, with his co-star, the beautiful Betty Chancellor, with whom he was wildly infatuated. If he was nervous about *anything* when he stepped out on stage on opening night, October 13, 1931, it was about Betty, with whom his lurid scenes had fired up the sixteen-year-old's imagination so much that at first he was barely aware of the audience. He was much more interested in what *she* thought of him. "She was the *sexiest* thing that ever lived," says Orson, still obviously smitten. "She was one of those absolutely black-haired girls, with skin as white as Carrara marble, you know, and eyelashes that you could trip on, and all that! She played Jew Süss's daughter, and I had to rape her—that was offscene—and I came on disheveled, practically unbuttoned, having had my way with her." The rather abstract presence of numerous spectators merely heightened his excitement. Finally, however, they made themselves felt even by Orson when at the end they wildly applauded him and called his name. "It was

thunderous and *totally* unexpected," recalls Orson, who had
been so entirely focused on Betty all evening that the ovation
came as a sudden shock. Only then was he hit with the full
impact of the momentous evening. He forgot about Betty
for the moment, and took his bows in a daze. What if they
hadn't liked him? What if he'd flopped? What would he
have written home? Thank God they loved him! "That was
the night I had *all* the applause I needed for my life," says
Orson, to whom the delicious ovation seemed never to stop.
"I got more acclaim for that than for *anything* I've done
since!" Orson muses. Of all the accolades that he was to
receive, and there were many, probably the most gratifying
to Orson came from America, when, on November 8, 1931,
The New York Times ran a review of the Gate's *Jew Süss*
that focused in large part on him. Said the *Times*, "This
somewhat unpleasant play has been magnificently produced
by Hilton Edwards, who also plays the title role. His is a
most difficult part because for more than half of the play it
is second to that of the Duke Karl Alexander, and when
Jew Süss's great moment comes it is too late as the play
belongs to the Duke. This is particularly true in the case of
the Gate production in which the Duke is played by a young
American actor, eighteen years old, whose performance is
amazingly fine. This young man is Orson Welles, who came
to Ireland during the summer on a painting expedition. . . .
Welles, who had appeared occasionally at the Goodman
Memorial Theatre in Chicago, and in small parts with the
Theatre Guild in New York, journeyed to Dublin and offered
his services to the Gate. His fine voice, unusual in a youth
of his age, recommended him and he was given the part of
the Duke in 'Jew Süss' to read. There are a naturalness and
ease about his acting, which at once caught the packed house
on his first appearance. When the last curtain fell he had
acquitted himself so well that he was given an ovation.
Dublin is eager to see him in other roles, and he has an-

nounced his intention of remaining with the Gate for the entire season." Orson was particularly delighted that, having pretended to have recently completed a successful theatrical run in New York, he was now being acclaimed in the major paper of that very city, and with an explicit reference to his bogus work in the Theatre Guild there!

But while Dublin may have been eager to see him in other roles, Micheal, more jealous than ever, certainly wasn't. "From then on," says Orson, "whenever I was anywhere near the Gate it was one long plot to cut me down." Although Orson didn't quite perceive it at the time, he realizes now that Micheal worked on stirring up Hilton's jealousy about the young American's having stolen the show. Although there was considerable praise for Hilton's portrayal of the Jew, Orson was clearly the greater sensation, and Hilton bristled to find himself sharing the limelight with a child. For his part, Orson was much too preoccupied with his sudden success and too little experienced with the mechanisms of professional jealousy to worry much about Hilton's still-subtle antipathy. "At that point," says Orson, "I chose to think they were my friends and that they adored me." Onstage during curtain calls for *Jew Süss*, Orson could frequently be seen affectionately putting his arm around Hilton. He even worked on winning over Micheal by camping it up with him. "It was right back to my childhood, playing parts to keep various people interested," says Orson. "I had an entire persona for Micheal, which has no relation to anything I was ever like before or since, or with anybody else—but it was what he *wanted*, and what amused him— it was a kind of *camp*." Now and then, particularly when he had been drinking, Micheal would forget about his jealousy and relax with Orson, who genuinely admired his fine acting and mordant wit. Very late one besotted night when the two of them were alone, Micheal abruptly and mysteriously turned to Orson and said, "Never trust us!" "What

do you mean?" asked Orson. "You and Hilton?" "Ah, no,"
replied Micheal. "It's the *queens* you must never trust! We're
like weathervanes. We go where the wind blows." Another
evening when he had Micheal in a good mood, in the faintly
English accent Orson had affected since arriving in Dublin,
he asked him to define the Irish character in one word.
"Malice!" Micheal shot back without hesitation.

After *Jew Süss*, Orson's roles at the Gate in David Sears's
The Dead Ride Fast, Percy Robinson's *The Archdupe*, Pad-
raic Colum's *Mogu of the Desert*, Walter Ferris's *Death
Takes a Holiday*, and Shakespeare's *Hamlet* were not as
substantial as he—or the theatergoing public—had hoped
for on the basis of his unequivocally spectacular debut.
Within weeks of arriving in Dublin, he had become a minor
star there, recognized almost wherever he went. But he
couldn't possibly sustain that stardom afterward without the
exposure Micheal and Hilton made certain he didn't get.
He needed the leads in *The Apple Cart*, in *Coriolanus*, with
which they tempted him, then mysteriously withheld. It was
three or four months before he came to understand that, this
time, his liking and admiring people did not guarantee their
being nice to him in return—even though their having
spurned him for the moment was in its curious way a great
compliment to his acting ability.

On the basis of *Jew Süss*, the British impresario Charles
Blake Cochran approached him about appearing on stage
in London. But before he left Ireland, Orson finally got
to meet Micheal and Hilton's mentor, the great Anew
McMaster, who asked him to paint a series of angels on
some drapes for one of his traveling productions. When the
curtains Orson had designed didn't fit the makeshift stage
in one of the bogs where the Intimate Shakespeare Company
had landed, Mac ordered the angels' heads temporarily cut
off. Not having heard anything about this, Orson excitedly
went to see the show in the next country town where Mac

played, but much to his horror the heads had been sewn back on—under the angel's feet! "Mac," said Orson respectfully, "there are no angels like that." Mac looked intently at the misshapen angels for a long moment, then back at Orson. "*Dear*, who'll notice?" he said, as if declaring the obvious. "Nobody notices! They're all looking *at me*, love! You're such a pedant!"

On his departure from Ireland Orson was careful to remain on the best of terms with the Gate's co-directors. Even if they had done their best to diminish him afterward, they had, after all, provided the circumstances for Orson's auspicious debut. Although by now even Micheal had grown genuinely fond of Orson, they were not sad to see him go.

To Orson's grave disappointment, he learned when he got to London that the regulations governing the employment of foreigners prohibited Cochran from hiring him as planned. This being so, Orson resolved that he had had enough of Europe for the moment; he figured his publicity in the *Times* would undoubtedly help him to secure suitable theatrical employment in New York. If Orson was dismayed by the unanticipated withdrawal of the offer to act for a season in London, he was nonetheless in exceptionally good spirits as he sailed back to the States. On balance, his months in Europe had confirmed the vague air of artistic success that always hung about him at school—confirmed it for those back at Todd who, despite all their lavish praise of the prodigy, must have sometimes secretly wondered just how he would fare in the real world; and confirmed it for Orson as well, who, despite that very praise, must have sometimes secretly wondered himself. Orson left Europe now with a sense of how instantly success could be his. For, in perspective, the fruitless weeks of tramping about Ireland seemed insignificant beside his overnight triumph at the Gate. Stuffed in his pockets were newspaper clippings that proved it wasn't all just another of Orson's charming little fictions. When he studied the faces of those to whom he now recounted his theatrical career, if he detected even the slightest doubt, a raised eyebrow, a repressed smirk, here, sir, was the *Irish Independent*, and here the *Irish Press*, and here—in particular—*The New York Times*, all of them hailing Mr. Orson Welles. If he was headed for New York, you see, it was because he was *already* well known there.

CHAPTER 5
Marching Song

No sooner did Orson get to New York than something dreadful happened. Another young actor might have overlooked the routine offense to which Orson was subjected in the rather forbidding office of the Shuberts, where he presented himself in response to their casting call, but he was utterly appalled. Had he been given the opportunity, he would have told them about his work at the Dublin Gate, and especially about *Jew Süss*. He would have shown them his notices— mostly to refresh their memories, of course, for surely they had read the *Jew Süss* review in the *Times*. All this he would have done, and more—since young Orson was never one to contain himself about himself. Having been hired so swiftly at the Gate, Orson assumed that he would do equally well with the Shuberts. It was not exactly the Shuberts, however, to whom Orson presented himself now, but to an office boy who sternly refused to let him pass. No, he had not heard about *Jew Süss*. No, he had not read the reviews. No, Orson could not go inside. Far more devastating than any of this was what, at length, the office boy called him. Not having got this pest's name, the office boy imperiously addressed Orson as *kiddie*. Kiddie! How Orson growled within. Kiddie! How could the office boy have known that to Orson this would surely be the most revolting, the most insulting of epithets? All through Todd he had felt somehow older than the other boys, and more experienced. Now especially Orson perceived himself as having mysteriously grown up in Dublin, of having had experiences that made him a man—more of a man certainly than this insipid office boy who had the audacity now so to abuse him.

Some years hence it would be to this black incident that Orson would return when trying to explain why, contrary to plan, he left New York almost as soon as he arrived there. The instant gratification of having been hired so quickly in Dublin made it difficult for Orson to fathom the chilly indifference he was encountering now. Another factor in Orson's return to Illinois was that he was homesick for the comforting environment that he could almost always count on with the Hills. For all his nagging, even Dadda was a sunny alternative to rejection and isolation in New York. Unlike Edwards and MacLiammoir, whose complicated attitudes toward him and toward each other Orson couldn't always entirely decipher, Skipper and Dadda were utterly transparent in their boundless affection for him—which was exactly the sort of unqualified support Orson needed after the curious mixture of success and disappointment of recent months. In Illinois he could expound on every precious detail of his newfound fame, while quietly sorting out for himself just why and how it had all so suddenly escaped him.

By now, Skipper had taken charge of Todd, and was occupied by converting it into the progressive "paradise for boys" that, for years thereafter, he liked to tell people Orson attended. When it was evident that Orson had no intention of returning immediately to New York or Europe—for reasons he never really disclosed—Skipper offered him the chance to stay on at Todd, during which peaceful hiatus Orson figured he could plot out his next moves. Nearly seventeen now, Orson was hired as Todd's drama coach. It was about as close to returning to one's blissful childhood as could be imagined. Skipper assigned him to prepare the boys for that year's Chicago Drama League competition—the very competition that had once meant so much to Orson for the manner in which Chicago stood for *the great world* outside Todd. In the meantime, however, Orson had been to *the great world* and back. Planning a child's assault on Chicago felt insignificant after the exhilaration of his recent conquest at the Gate—a disparity that Skipper could not entirely have understood, since he was now substantially less experienced in *the great world* than Orson. Many decades later Skipper would persist in attributing Orson's lack of enthusiasm about the competition—a production of *Twelfth Night* with Hascy Tarbox as Sir Andrew Aguecheek—to its having been merely an adaptation of a production Skipper had seen by Kenneth MacGowan. Orson, Skipper would argue, vastly preferred doing original productions. More likely, while this regression to past pursuits must have been soothing for Orson, by contrast with Dublin it was also somewhat depressing. Still Orson persisted. Unlike Orson's previous foray into Chicago, this time Todd easily took the Silver Cup. But Orson could not work up much enthusiasm about the victory. The once-coveted trophy hardly compared with a rave in the *Times*—but it would have to do for now.

Another of the main activities at Todd that spring term of 1932 was a bus tour to Niagara Falls and the newly built Empire State Building. The refurbished Todd bus was christened Big Bertha, and it doubled as a rolling classroom and dormitory. Skipper did the driving, with Orson at his side to keep him awake with conversation, which more often than not had to do with Orson and what he was going to do next in life. Finally, Skipper suggested that instead of acting Orson might want to try playwriting. He even sug-

gested a topic about which Orson already knew a great deal.
When Orson was still a Todd boy he had declaimed John
Brown's gallows speech in one of Noble Hill's annual oratory contests. To get his character exactly right, Orson had
done abundant historical research on the legendary abolitionist—why not write a play about him now? To encourage
Orson to try—"I wanted to get him out of my hair!" laughs
Skipper—Skipper offered to collaborate on the play. Since
he was about to embark on the yearly Todd recruiting campaign his participation would have to be limited to writing
a draft of the first act, whereas the rest would be in Orson's
hands. Thus, by the time Big Bertha rolled back into
Woodstock, although he had not yet put a word on paper,
Orson was excitedly thinking of himself as a playwright who
needed seclusion to work. With summer growing near, to
avoid the hay fever he would be certain to suffer in Ravinia,
and also to avoid Dadda, whose beloved but overbearing
presence was not exactly conducive to Orson's working with
total concentration, the aspiring playwright boarded a train
headed for Lake Mercer, Wisconsin.

On the train, however, he met a Todd father (happily not
the fellow who had made sexual advances to him) who
seemed horrifed at the thought of Orson's going to Lake
Mercer, although he didn't explain why. One of his sons
had been in Orson's class. Why didn't Orson remain on
board a few stops beyond his destination? In Lake Falambeau Orson could stay with his classmate's family until he
secured accommodations of his own. At 6:30 in the morning
Orson was scheduled to get off the train at Woodruff, where
he had arranged in advance to have someone drive him to
Lake Mercer. He was very glad he had changed his plans
when at Woodruff he found a drunk "cross-eyed half-breed"
waiting for him in a Model-T. His new destination, Lake
Falambeau, was in the midst of the Ojibway Indian Reservation, where Orson promptly hired several "squaws and a

few antiques in the neuter gender," as he wrote to Skipper, to build a birchbark and deerskin wigwam on a parcel of land in a pine grove that his hosts had offered for this purpose. The pine grove was separated from their summer house by a stretch of water across which Orson—never one to miss a meal—paddled three times daily. Before long Orson was short of cash, for which he appealed to Dadda, who adamantly refused. Money had become a constant point of contention between Orson and Dadda, who as his guardian was responsible for doling out small amounts of Orson's trust, until at the age of twenty-five Orson could do as he wished with his dwindling inheritance. In this case, Dadda disapproved of Orson's wasting time on a play when he should be in college. There was also a covert element of jealousy involved—playwriting had been Skipper's idea. Refused by Dadda, Orson played on the rivalry between his mentors by writing to Skipper about the dreadful effect Dadda's intransigence was having on his writing. Thus, Orson seemed to imply, Skipper's lending him twenty-five dollars was doubtless because of his greater sensitivity to Orson's creative life. Unmentioned was that Orson's principal expenses just now were the malted milkshakes for which he made regular treks into town. Within days of receiving the loan, however, Orson's guilt at having wheedled funds out of Skipper led to a nightmare in which his mentor had gone bankrupt. There was even a public auction of all Skipper's worldly goods at which Orson bought the model ship that was one of his mentor's prized possessions, and for which noble purchase he used his last five dollars, which, he realized with horror, had come from Skipper in the first place. Orson's guilt notwithstanding, Skipper's twenty-five dollars came in handy when a powerful East wind and the impending rainy season forced him to abandon his wigwam for the pine-log hunting lodge of a taciturn archer named Larry, where he completed a draft of the second act of the John Brown play and suggested extensive revisions in the language and structure of the first act Skipper had sent him.

That fall Orson returned to Illinois. Having grown accustomed to the spooky silence of his hulking archer roommate, Orson was thrown into a fit of agitation by the noise and general commotion he discovered in Ravinia, where Dadda and Ned Moore seemed constantly to be bickering about Dadda's paying attention to women other than Ned's wife, Hazel. Nothing had changed. When Dadda wasn't carrying on with the Moores, he liked to bemoan wearily Orson's ill-spent summer, so that Orson had little peace to work on the drama, which by now he had titled *Marching Song*. To make matters worse, no sooner had Orson arrived than word came from his brother Richard, who had been confined to a mental institution, that he hoped to pay everyone a visit for his birthday. Orson had not talked to Richard in three years, and he certainly didn't want to see his vexing older brother now that he was trying to work diligently on revisions. Everyone else in the household seemed overjoyed at the impending arrival, however, which made Orson feel terribly callous about being in no mood for Richard's unpredictable antics. The responsibility would fall on Orson to see that Richard didn't steal the silverware—as he had been known to do—or otherwise disgrace himself. To Orson, Richard was a nuisance, but also something more: a loathsome and distorted image of his own strangeness. Orson had finally come to terms with temporarily putting the play aside to make Richard's time off from the institution as pleasant as possible when, at the last minute, Dadda abruptly canceled the visit because he was too busy with his medical practice.

Despite these rampant distractions, Orson managed somehow to finish *Marching Song* and to dispatch the play to Skipper, whose letters—and small loans—had proved decisive in sustaining the boy's intense focus on writing and revising. The title page of *Marching Song* describes it as "a play of the stirring days just before the Civil War, concerning chiefly John Brown, prophet—warrior—zealot—the most dramatic and incredible figure in American history." But on examination the play is less about John Brown himself than his public persona and the legend that circulated about it. The device Orson uses dramatically to examine that legend is to send a newspaperman in quest of the mysterious abolitionist about whom so little is known, and so much said. Long before John Brown actually appears on stage we have examined a variety of conflicting points of view about him by listening to the people whom the correspondent encounters. It is not surprising that Orson would be interested in how the public perceives a figure such as Brown about whom they know mostly from the press or from what they had heard indirectly. Having aspired to—and achieved—a degree of fabled status himself (the press had been covering him at intervals since age ten), Orson was drawn to the story of John Brown as one in which he could explore a public self's gossamer existence. Some readers of *Marching Song* may complain that its John Brown lacks psychological depth—but this ostensible defect is intrinsic to the play's central theme of the public persona who is not really a three-dimensional personality, but a mask, a name, a voice, a cobweb of legends. In a far more developed—and aesthetically satisfying—form than in *Marching Song*, the negotiations between the public and private self would be a decisive theme of his first feature film, *Citizen Kane*, whose protagonist is in a way rather like John Brown: a public figure of immense mystery about whom there are various and conflicting points of view. Besides the motif of the correspondent's search for the enigmatic public self, both *Marching Song* and *Citizen Kane* share a delight in the way newspaper headlines punctuate—and per-

meate—daily life: the headlines that, both thematically and
formally, play so vital a role in *Citizen Kane* are predated
in *Marching Song* by stereopticon slides of headlines about
John Brown that were to be projected before each act, all
of them "blending into each other with kaleidoscopic effect." This obscure instance of Wellesian juvenilia is an
important piece of evidence that clearly belies the spurious
charge that Orson Welles was in no way responsible for the
screenplay of *Citizen Kane*. Written in 1932, long before
he met screenwriter Herman Mankiewicz, *Marching Song*
unquestionably adumbrates some of the principal concerns
of Welles's first feature film. Anyone who doubts Welles's
major role in writing the film will discover in *Marching
Song* significant textual evidence that *Citizen Kane* is in
important ways a vastly more mature and resonant artistic
reworking of aspects of Orson's boyhood play—and the
lifelong obsessions it reflects.

Thrilled by what he read, Skipper packed Orson and
Hortense into Big Bertha for the long trip to Manhattan,
where he had appropriately reserved a suite at the Algonquin. Although Skipper envisioned that at the Algonquin he
and Orson would entertain a host of Broadway producers,
and that he would carefully compare the merits of their offers
before selecting the right man for the job, he was already
especially keen on the renowned Dwight Deere Wiman, who
had been his childhood schoolmate many years back at the
old Todd Seminary. In New York, however, their reception
was hardly what the co-authors had hoped for. Wiman was
polite of course—after all he had been a Todd boy himself—
but expressed no genuine interest in *Marching Song*. Nor
was there the anticipated rush of producers into the Hills'
hotel suite, for which Skipper had paid far too much to
remain there for long. Within days Orson found himself left
behind in New York, with instructions to make the rounds
systematically of the very same producers who had declined

to call on the now-vacated Algonquin suite in which the co-authors and Hortense had very temporarily held court.

Orson moved to a dismal walk-up room without a bath on West 77th Street off Riverside Drive. Greatly depressed by Skipper's having abandoned him in New York, where, however much he padded from office to office, he couldn't seem to get anyone even to read the play, let alone to buy it, Orson wanted to move to a bigger, more comfortable room with a private bath and a kitchenette to prepare snacks. Skipper maintained that Orson's changing addresses again might only confuse any eager producers who were trying to track him down, so Orson resolved to stay put. He need not have done so, since the only person trying to track him down was Dadda, from whom Orson received long hysterical letters imploring him to return to Ravinia at once and stop trifling in Manhattan. "I do hope you won't continue to waste your youth aimlessly," wrote Dadda, who followed this with an urgent telegram, "Leave play with agent and come home." At times Orson began to suspect that Dadda might be right after all. Maybe Orson was wasting his time in New York. Having left a copy of his manuscript with the receptionist in one producer's office, Orson returned some days later to be told that nobody there remembered anything about him or his play, but that they would be glad to check the files. When they did, however, *Marching Song* was nowhere to be found. At a loss for what to say, the embarrassed receptionist summoned the playreader—an actual specimen of that inscrutable class of New Yorkers that Orson had never before managed to glimpse. Expecting the worst, he was infinitely relieved when a rather sweet, matronly woman appeared. For the first time in any of these brusque, impersonal offices, Orson found himself treated with a measure of human kindness. Although the nice lady had not yet read the play, she planned to do so that very Saturday, that is, if Mr. Welles did not need it back before then. It was

Friday. Back on West 77th Street, with renewed enthusiasm Orson wrote to Skipper of his new friend's sincere intention "to do the play full justice." He barely survived the weekend till Monday, when, returning to see her, he found only his manuscript and a written rejection waiting at the front desk. *Marching Song*, she noted, was unsuitable for the market— for which crisp critique Orson was expected to pay five dollars. Perhaps, he feared, she really had done his play the "full justice" she had promised.

To lure Orson back to Ravinia, Dadda told him that a friend of his was putting together a radio show to be broadcast from Chicago for some twenty-six weeks. Would Orson be interested in a dramatic role? Orson said yes, that is if they paid him three hundred dollars a week and billed him as "the internationally famous actor, Mr. Orson Welles." How utterly jubilant was Dadda when *Mr. Orson Welles* suddenly appeared at his and Hazel and Ned's doorstep in Ravinia, and how depressed was that *internationally famous actor* when the plans for the radio show just as suddenly collapsed. Not long after Orson had left New York, however, a producer named George Tyler optioned *Marching Song* from the happy co-authors (although as it turned out, he never managed to stage it). Lest Orson decide to start another play, Dadda announced that he should honor his mother's memory instead by touring the country with a program of elegant musical readings. Beatrice had liked to recite Tagore to piano accompaniment. For Orson, Dadda suggested Oscar Wilde with a background of Debussy. Predictably, Ned and Hazel thought it a splendid idea, but Orson was ambivalent from the first. He briefly considered pulling out his Irish diaries and letters to make a book of the stories they contained. But if it was a book Orson wanted to write now, Skipper as usual had a better idea. He proposed their collaborating on editions of Shakespeare's plays, specifically intended for classroom use. These were all plays to be *performed*—Skipper and Orson agreed—something that was often woefully forgotten by teachers and pupils alike who read Shakespeare silently as they would a novel, thereby missing a good deal of what the dramatic poetry was all about. Skipper would pen a general introduction to be used throughout their *Everybody's Shakespeare* series, while Orson would contribute an essay on stagecraft, as well as complete stage directions and illustrations for each play chosen.

Orson shrewdly decided to use his work on *Everybody's Shakespeare* as an excuse for repairing abroad again—this time to Morocco, where, he finally managed to convince a very skeptical Dadda, he would be able to write with greater facility. Before Dadda had time to change his mind Orson had gleefully boarded the American Export Line freighter, the *Exermont*, headed for Tangier. While he traveled about Morocco on stinking buses filled with chickens, Orson made the acquaintance of a very elderly and aristocratic curator at the Rijksmuseum in Amsterdam, who was on a painting tour of North Africa. As he watched him work, Orson was fascinated by his tiny paint box, which also served as his palette. Grasping the box with the thumb of one hand, the old man painted exquisite miniature landscapes about four times the size of a postage stamp with little brushes in the other hand. After they had chatted for a while, the artist, who was in his mid-eighties, invited Orson to travel with him.

Only when they had been happily tramping about together for several weeks did the old man happen to mention that he was expected presently by the famous Thami el Glaoui, Pasha of Marrakesh, and leader of the Glawa tribe of the Western Atlas. A loyal friend of the French protectorate (who paid him well), Thami el Glaoui was despised by Moroccan nationalists, who resented his having maintained peace between the Berbers and the French. But the Glaoui was not about to lead the Berber warriors against the French, whose culture he cherished, especially its writers, among whom he counted Colette as one of his dearest friends. His modern European education had not, however, extinguished the eleventh-century warrior in him. "He had killed one of his sons with a bow string," says Orson of the Glaoui's mass of contradictions, "but he also knew how to sit in the Ritz Hotel and chat it up with Claudel." As a warrior, one of the Glaoui's most celebrated feats had been to subdue an infamous North African bandit, whom he imprisoned in an iron cage that, placed atop a donkey, was paraded about Morocco as a warning to anyone who might defy him. (Many years later Orson would consciously draw on this image by displaying Iago in a similar cage in his film version of *Othello*.) The Glaoui was known as an insatiable ladies' man, and one of his many conquests was a well-known French actress to whom, after his death, he left a parcel of land in Morocco. At home at the Dar el Glaoui in Marrakesh, where he was said to have some one hundred and fifty girls in his harem, he liked to entertain visiting European dignitaries such as Winston Churchill with sumptuous Moroccan feasts, champagne, and the favors of concubines.

"He lived on a level of grandeur that was beyond description!" says Orson, who found himself now accompanying the old Dutchman to see the Glaoui. For all he had heard about the Glaoui, Orson was startled at first to see buses filled with concubines and Berber boy dancers. It seemed that the Glaoui was just then planning to take his many guests on a two-week picnic. "An unforgettable moment for me," Orson recalls, "was when we first started off. I saw this bus with a little tiny window in the back. The little curtain opened, and a head, all done up in veils, looked right at me and winked—it was one of the most erotic moments I ever experienced in my life—and away went the bus!" Nor was this the last Orson saw of the

Glaoui's concubines. That night, as on every other night for the next two weeks, after an exotic feast, which was accompanied by a serenade of Moroccan music and the dancing of the Berber boys, the Europeans retired, six to a tent, where they shared amongst them one of the concubines. "Into our tent would creep, nobody of our choice, but somebody sent over by the Glaoui," says Orson, who had no way of really knowing whether this was the veiled creature who had winked at him, but he *imagined* she was. For a seventeen-year-old boy it was, Orson sighs, an "entrancing experience." But the dignified old Dutchman who had taken him there in the first place seemed absolutely unfazed by any of it. "He reacted exactly the same to being in a bus full of chickens," laughs Orson. After they had spent several weeks in each other's company, the friends were about to part ways. As they walked together to the bus that was to take the Dutchman to Casablanca, Orson worried about how properly to say goodbye to the old aristocrat, whom he would probably never see again. How could he possibly thank him for the two ineffable weeks with the Glaoui? Filled with a teenager's anxiety about precisely what words would express how glad he was to have met him, Orson was startled when the old man simply said "Goodbye" and got on the stinking bus, where, without another glance at Orson, he calmly positioned himself among the chickens. "I've always admired him enormously for that!" says Orson.

Some weeks before he left Morocco for Spain, Orson quickly wrote a series of five short stories about a young detective who lived in Baltimore with his aunt. A dilettante and a playboy of sorts, the colorful character was expressly based on what Orson imagined his father's youth to have been like. These he sent to a friend of Dadda's in Chicago whose wife had once offered to intercede for Orson with the publishers of pulp magazines should he have anything to offer them. When at length he reached Seville, Orson was thrilled to discover a check waiting for him there, which enabled him to rent a flat above a busy bordello. In Seville, when he wasn't working on *Everybody's Shakespeare*, Orson studied bullfighting with a matador, and then turned over a considerable portion of his earnings from the pulp magazines to an impresario who booked him in a succession of pitiful bullfights in which he had himself billed as "The American." But the hot-blooded spectators were typically unamused by the incompetent's having bought his way into the arena, and showered him with beer bottles (from which he still bears a slight scar on his upper lip). It was the custom of triumphant matadors to offer friends and fans cups of sherry to betoken their jubilance. Orson saw no reason why he couldn't do the same. While he mainly spent his time in the arena ducking bottles, he always at least *acted* like a winner, graciously distributing the symbolic cups of sherry—although in place of the usual friends and fans, the beneficiaries of Orson's generosity were the whores and their customers from the bordello downstairs.

When he returned to America during the summer of 1933, Orson was so thoroughly immersed in *Everybody's Shakespeare*, the text for which was nearly completed, that Skipper had the good sense to keep the boy away from the usual commotion in Ravinia by installing him in a tiny room in Chicago's Old Town district while he worked on the illustrations. One night not long after he returned, he took off a few hours from his art work to attend a party of local literati, many of them connected with the University of Chicago. There he noticed that a man he didn't know was watching him with evident interest and following him all about the room. When at last the stranger spoke to him, he inquired if by chance Orson was an actor. "Here's another queen!" Orson told himself. "No, I'm a writer," Orson answered curtly before edging away from the stranger, who called after him, "Aren't you from Dublin?" "Well," said

Orson, suddenly curious, "I was there, yes." "Aren't you *Orson Welles?*" Orson had not been recognized like this since the days of his triumph in Dublin, which seemed but a frail memory now. Just as all else had come very early to Orson, so too, it appeared, had the end of his acting career. Nobody seemed to remember, or even to have heard of, *Jew Süss* at the Gate, nobody except the stranger, that is. He turned out to be playwright-novelist Thornton Wilder, who, in the ensuing weeks, listening to all that had happened to Orson since Dublin, suggested that the boy return to New York with suitable letters of recommendation from him, among them an introduction to writer-raconteur Alexander Woollcott.

In New York that August, strictly on Wilder's say-so, Woollcott put Orson in touch with producer-director Guthrie McClintic and his wife, Katharine "Kit" Cornell, who were about to embark on a seventeen-thousand-mile theatrical tour for which they were assembling a company of forty actors to appear in a repertory consisting of *Romeo and Juliet, The Barretts of Wimpole Street*, and *Candida*. When Orson nervously called on McClintic in his Beekman Place apartment, the speed with which he was hired reminded him of his fateful first visit to the Dublin Gate, except that this time he didn't even have to audition to find himself cast as Mercutio in *Romeo and Juliet*, Octavius in *The Barretts of Wimpole Street*, and Marchbanks in *Candida*. Woollcott's recommendation was really all it took. McClintic briskly explained that there would be five weeks of intensive rehearsal before they opened at the Erlanger Theatre in Kit Cornell's hometown of Buffalo, New York, during which Orson would be coached by the formidable Mrs. Robert Edmond Jones, who had the special distinction of having worked with John Barrymore. When he left Beekman Place, Orson's head was spinning. Weeks before, in Chicago, when Thornton Wilder had asked him whether he was an actor,

Orson had quite honestly—if resignedly—declared that, no, he was a writer. Now suddenly he was an actor again! That evening, back at the Algonquin, thinking of himself as on the road to Broadway at long last, a very elated Orson wrote to Skipper, "Looks rather like the saga has begun."

Trying to get me—Orson suggests I begin there. How does one get Orson Welles? Orson jokes about my having done so because he knows how exceedingly difficult he was about it. Suggesting I tell this particular story, he is a bit like a naughty boy who wants someone to recount just how naughty he was. Of course, his avoiding me wasn't really being naughty at all. He was under no obligation to make himself available to me, someone he had never met, a writer he had never heard of. I certainly wasn't the first person in recent years to approach him about writing his biography, to ask that he dig into his most private memories. Why would he possibly say yes to me?

But you don't feel that way when you're a writer embarking on a project that you know will consume your own life for the next few years. To write about somebody else's life is to give up your own, to spend your time with his friends and associates, to pore over his mail and bills and laundry lists. "You had trouble getting me before, now you have trouble getting rid of me," Orson would laugh once we'd come to know each other. Whenever he would call me up for our marathon conversations he would know that, at the very moment the phone rang, I would probably be writ-

ing, reading, thinking about him. Although he never visited
my apartment in New York, he knew that it was piled with
documents, photos, clippings, tape-recorded interviews—
all about Orson Welles, a character we sometimes discussed
as if it were an attractive mutual friend about whom we
liked to gossip incessantly. It both amused and appalled
Orson that from morning till night I spent as much time
thinking about him as he did—and probably even more.
Sometimes in the course of my writing his biography he
would try to divert, to amuse me—when he suggested that
I read a travel book or two to take my mind off my work,
I gasped that, yes, I was desperate for the new information
such books afford. "Yes," he laughed ruefully, "information
on any subject except the pie-faced actor!"

   But how did I get him? That's what I started out to tell
here. The first step was to make contact with him, which,
in his case, wasn't easy since he doesn't have an agent.
The contact number I turned up belonged to a lawyer—a
lawyer who unfortunately was dead. But still, important
people assured me, this dead lawyer's office was where one
writes to contact his erstwhile client Orson Welles. I felt not
a little foolish writing in care of a dead man, to someone
who had always seemed, well, larger than life to me. An
inauspicious start. Since there were no answers to any of
the several notes I wrote care of the dead-letter office, I
had no way of knowing if Welles (the picture above my desk,
the name I kept typing over and over) had received them.
"Any word from Welles?" my sadistic husband would ask
almost daily. "Not yet," I would reply, having long since
plunged into the first stages of research about the man to
whom I had almost run out of winning things to say about
why he should agree to see me.

   There were endless interviews with people who had known
him intimately for six weeks in 1938, or a month in 1944,
or a day in 1952. Charming people. Theatrical people.
Sometimes they had even run into him many years afterward

late one night on Park Avenue in New York, a sunny after-
noon on Santa Monica Boulevard in Los Angeles. Was he
deliberately ignoring them, they wondered, or (even worse)
did he just not remember who they were? If gradually I
stopped being anxious about Welles's not having answered
my letters, it was because no one I spoke to had the slightest
expectation that he ever would. That's not how it usually
works when you're writing a biography of a living man.
Inevitably the first question the people you've come to in-
terview ask is, "Have you talked to him yet?" No one asked
that about Orson Welles.

"I do tend to hide from people," Orson would tell me
later. "I get it in my mind that I'd rather die than see them.
I get a mild persecution complex if somebody keeps after
me. The dearest thing in life becomes not seeing them,
you know. Have I told you the story about Carl Laemmle,
Sr.? This is a little Anglo-Saxonish, but it's worth it. This
fellow had been sitting out there for a couple of days re-
fusing to move. The third day Laemmle wanted to go to
lunch and he said, 'Is that fellow still sitting out there?'
The secretary said, 'Yes, what am I going to tell him?'
Laemmle said, 'Give him an evasive answer. Tell him to
go fuck himself.' "

For a long time, however, I didn't know if Welles was
hiding from me, or just hadn't received my letters. In my
thoughts the man I kept writing to had become rather like
one of Gogol's dead souls. I stopped expecting a response,
merely went through the motions of writing to whatever new
address various important people gave me. Far more pal-
pable to me than the shadow-Welles I was supposedly trying
to find were the mountains of documents, no, the mountains
of Xeroxes of documents, accumulating in my apartment.
Cryptic telegrams to and from Orson Welles, doodles on
the backs of menus, telephone numbers he'd scribbled on
torn bits of paper. They reminded me of the relics of saints,
teeth and fingers, drops of sweat, preserved in medieval

*churches and monasteries. Out of them I began to construct
Orson Welles, to decipher the story of his life, of where he
had been, whom he had known, what he had done. Who
needs Orson Welles, I kept telling myself, when his relics
are preserved in scholarly archives across the country? If
I gathered, and Xeroxed, enough of them, eventually I'd
have a whole man.*

*But if I had almost managed to convince myself of this
in New York—a continent away from where I knew he was—
my rationalizations crumbled the moment I got to Los Angeles to interview people and work in the archives there.
This was the most frustrating period because I knew he was
in town, I even knew where I could find him. It was no
secret that he ate lunch regularly at Ma Maison. In a B
movie of all this, I would simply drive over there and wait
till he came out the door. Just one glance at me with my
briefcase of Xeroxes and my tape recorder and he'd know
he should tell me everything, answer every question, disclose every secret. But in life I steered clear of Ma Maison.
Even in my B-movie fantasies of just turning up there and
presenting myself I was so frightened I could barely bring
it off. How would I possibly be capable of doing it in life?*

*Maybe I should call him! I told myself as an excuse for
not being brave enough—rude enough—to accost him on
the street. Then Charlton Heston, who has known Orson
for many years, gave me a good excuse for not doing that
either. "If you're in town, it's almost impossible to get him
on the phone," Heston told me when I interviewed him. "If
he's in Borneo you can get him on the phone—or if you're
in Borneo, he will get you on the phone. He's very mysterious." Maybe I should go to Borneo, I thought.*

*Instead, I went to see Richard Wilson, a former associate
and business partner of Orson's, who a number of people
hinted to me might be the entrée to Orson Welles I was
looking for. "You thought he was my Rosebud!" Orson
sneered, when I told him about this later. No stranger to*

*giving interviews about Orson Welles, Wilson mysteriously
hesitated at first, then limited me to ten questions. This, he
said, would be his last interview on the subject—although
when I got there another interview was scheduled after mine.
At the end of a basically superficial interview (my own fault
mostly, because I had so much difficulty picking* ten *questions), I came to the one question I had been waiting to ask
all along.*

*"My biggest and most important question," I said, "is
how am I going to get to Welles."*

"I won't, I can't help you," Wilson replied.

*A moment later I tried another tack: "What do you rec-
ommend just in general? I'm not asking you to do it. Should
I just keep writing, or should I find someone who will take
me to him?"*

*"I don't think you'll find such a person, because your
cause is not just."*

*Wilson went on to tell me about two previous would-be
biographers whom Welles had agreed to see, then eluded.*

*"Do you think he would talk just for an interview?" I
asked, embarrassed by now. "I don't want to do an autho-
rized book . . . but I would like to talk to him."*

*"Well, I've no recommendation," said Wilson. "If you
see him, it'll be a fluke, and if you get to talk to him, it'll
be happenstance."*

Depressed at being told that my cause is not just—*what
did he mean? was I doing something dreadful?—I drove
about aimlessly for a while, stopping finally on impulse to
buy a "star map" from a scrawny little boy. Here and there
throughout Los Angeles one sees such little boys at roadsides
selling star maps for a dollar or so. Basically they are street
maps of Los Angeles with the addresses of movie stars
marked off for the tourists. But it had never occurred to me
before to look at one. Maybe it would tell me how to get
to Orson Welles—or at least how to get to where he lives.
(Going to his house when I didn't dare approach him outside*

the restaurant was irrational, I know, but I was depressed and not thinking clearly just then.) Not wanting the kid to see how anxious I was to open the map, I drove for another five minutes before turning off the road and stopping the motor. There it was—Orson Wells (misspelled), and an address in the Hollywood Hills. So that's where he's been hiding! I told myself I'd write to him there. But first I wanted to see for myself, so I circled farther and farther up into the hills, until at last finding where the house on the map should be, I saw that it was no longer there, having been washed away years ago in a mud slide.

Having hauled several suitcases of Xeroxes and taped interviews back to New York, at long last I found the letter I had been waiting for. I didn't even have to open it. There on the back flap of the envelope was typed O. Welles (probably so the fellows in the post office wouldn't know who it was) and an address in Las Vegas. My excitement died quickly, however, when I read my subject's very gentlemanly refusal to see me. It was written in a literary style I recognized from the countless letters of his I had read, but I matched the signature against one of my Xeroxes just to make sure. It was Orson Welles, all right—and he had refused to cooperate.

But how after that did I get to him? Now that I had been politely refused like that—he didn't tell me that my cause wasn't just, just that he wasn't about to further it—I decided to be bold in a way I hadn't in Los Angeles. I'd show up in Las Vegas, call him from there, and count on his agreeing to give me an interview, one interview, since I'd come so far for that purpose. I made a reservation at Caesar's Palace, dashed off a telegram to tell him I was arriving, and flew to Nevada without further ado. There, as the bellboy hauled my tired suitcases into my turquoise-tinted room, Orson Welles was waiting for me. "Hello," said a familiar voice when the bellboy switched on my closed-circuit TV. "I'm Orson Welles." (This was no accident, I learned. At

Caesar's Palace bellboys are supposed to turn on the closed-circuit TV the minute you get there.) "I've been asked by Caesar's Palace to tell you a little about gaming," Welles continued. "I guess they've asked me because I know a little about cards, a little about history, and, well, because I've been known to take a long shot or two." I couldn't believe what I was hearing. Nor could I believe it when moments later I dialed Welles's number and got Mrs. Welles, the Italian Countess di Girfalco, who told me that her husband wasn't there and that she didn't expect him. He was, she said ambiguously, on location.

Having come this far, to watch my subject on TV, and talk to Mrs. Welles on the telephone, I figured I might as well drive out to see where he lived. But when I found the address he had given me, and—like a good reporter—asked some children playing nearby what they knew about the Welles house, *they looked terribly puzzled. The Welles house? Orson Welles! I said. Don't you know who Orson Welles is? Sure, they said, but* he *doesn't live here. Wayne Newton lives here. Robert Goulet lives here. Totie Fields used to live here. But not Orson Welles! Finally, I found a gardener who knew what I meant by the* Welles *house. "Yeah," he said, "Orson Welles's mother and sister live there." What mother and sister? I muttered to myself. His mother died more than sixty years ago—and he never had a sister. About to head back to Caesar's Palace, where at least I knew that I'd be able to get Orson Welles, to make him materialize whenever I liked by turning on the TV, I stopped one last gardener to ask if he knew anything about* . . . "Oh yeah, Orson Welles," *he replied, "he comes and goes by night."* Like Charlton Heston said, very mysterious.

Back in New York again, *I seemed to have begun a new phase of research. Suddenly everyone I called seemed to be writing, or about to write, or already to have written, a memoir that included, was largely based on, or entirely devoted to, his or her association with Orson Welles.* Living

*relics, they had touched the saint—and wanted a publisher's
advance to write about the experience. Much to my horror,
I saw in them my parodic doubles—except that they had
indeed got to Welles, if only for six months in 1942, eight
months in 1947. . . . In the midst of all this madness, happy
for any chance to get out of my apartment, which looked
and smelled like a photocopy center, I met with filmmaker
Henry Jaglom in a bar on the Upper West Side to talk about
his experience directing Welles in* A Safe Place *in 1970. In
the course of the conversation, I kept waiting for Jaglom
to say that he was writing a memoir about Welles or that
he had run into Welles late one night on Park Avenue, or
maybe even that my cause was not just. But no, Jaglom
matter-of-factly offered to introduce me to Welles. He was
going to Los Angeles in a couple of days, and he'd set up
a meeting if I liked. Nodding yes (I was speechless) and
smiling sweetly, I was absolutely sure he was still going to
tell me about his memoir.*

*Quick cut to Los Angeles. Super Bowl weekend. The B
movie again, except this time it's* in life: *we're driving to
Ma Maison in Henry's rickety old car. I feel like a mail-
order bride. First I keep thinking with horror about Na-
bokov's having once complained that he was forever doomed
to exist on the library shelf with a critic who had written a
particularly detestable book about him. Is this how my subject feels about me?*

*"I thought it was best to know my enemy," Orson told
me many months after that first day in Ma Maison about
why he had finally agreed to see me.*

*As the car neared the restaurant, I suddenly found myself
wondering like a schoolgirl before a blind date: Will I like
him? What if I don't? I don't want to write a book about
someone I don't like. Maybe I should get back to my Xeroxes. Maybe I shouldn't go in. Then I imagine he's not
going to be there. As Henry leads me into the crowded
restaurant I remember* Dead Souls, *the star map, the mud*

*slide, the closed-circuit TV in Caesar's Palace in which my
subject keeps saying Hello, I'm Orson Welles Hello, I'm
Orson Welles, twenty-four hours a day, even now. Quickly
I run through all the things I've heard and read about him,
the Christmas gift lists, the telephone numbers, the mash
notes from girls he apparently loved and left in Rio. All the*
Orson Welleses *people have told me about are superimposed
in my thoughts—lunatic, sybarite, bastard, genius—and
suddenly there* he *is—Orson Welles in life—his great head
bobbing out to see us from behind a latticework screen.*

*Small talk. Hello. How are you? Fine. Pleased to meet
you. I sense this is every bit as unnerving for him as it is
for me—and that's when I know that the golem, the Xerox-
paper-doll, I've been fashioning at home is necessarily missing* his *personal voice,* his *sensitivity—his spirit. We start
joking, laughing, swapping stories of his past about which,
much to our mingled horror and mirth, I seem to know
things he doesn't. He doesn't know the line that Shorty the
dwarf chauffeur used to say when the Boss (as Shorty called
him) made love to young ladies in the back seat. "Yes, yes,*
that's *Shorty! that's Shorty!" Orson exclaims when I tell
him. He doesn't know that his mad brother Richard met his
wife in a midnight mission. "I'm* sure *it's so," he muses.
"That's* just *like Richard!" But there is so much about him
that I don't, can't possibly, know, that* only *he knows, and
only he can tell me. It's the real reason for writing a biography of a living person, I discover: the memories, dreams,
and images that will die with him unless someone records
them for posterity. But first, you have to* get *to him.*

CHAPTER 6

Roaring Pansies and Nubile Virgins

"I found myself wondering skeptically if Mr. Wilder and I had done well by Miss Cornell," wrote Alexander Woollcott of his having recommended Orson to Guthrie McClintic. No sooner had the Cornell tour begun than the McClintics found themselves wondering the same thing. As they criss-crossed the nation in a breathless itinerary that crammed seventy-four stops and two hundred and twenty-five performances into seven months, other members of the troupe, not the least of them Miss Cornell herself, were often irritated by Orson's sophomoric behavior, such as his dressing up in a billowing cape and fake mustache, and throwing a sedate hotel restaurant into chaos by barking commands at the staff in a mock-foreign accent. Miss Cornell, who happened to be dining there at the time, was most definitely not amused. (What confused eighteen-year-old Orson was that the zany MacLiammoir and Edwards probably *would* have been.) Another of Orson's antics was to take up temporary residence in an abandoned store in whose display window he announced himself to the baffled locals as Mr. Swami—"the corniest name I could think of!" laughs Orson. In boyhood a professional mind reader of his father's acquaintance had once told Orson that the moment one begins

to believe seriously in one's occult powers, it's time to quit.
Orson had occasion to recall this stern warning when he
saw a lady enter the inscrutable Mr. Swami's parlor, and
heard himself saying to her, "You are suddenly a widow!"
How did he know this? the excited woman begged to know.
Wishing he knew himself how he had done it, Mr. Swami
promptly turned in his turban and was heard from no more
during the Cornell tour.

But antics like these weren't the only trouble as far as
Miss Cornell was concerned. Sometimes he was late for
rehearsals, and once even missed the train that was to take
the company to its next booking, so that not until show time
was it known whether Mercutio was going to show up.
"They'd have the matinee either on Wednesday *or* Thursday," Orson groans many years later, "so I was in a constant
sweat all week long, sure that I had missed the matinee!"
Never did Orson actually miss a single performance, but
still nerves were frazzled all round by what was widely
deemed his rampant unpredictability. Fortunately for Orson,
however, his performance in the all-important *Romeo and
Juliet* gave little cause for complaint. The *Chicago Tribune*'s
Charles Collins wrote, "Passing over Basil Rathbone's Romeo, already described as handsome but cold, attention
focuses at first on Orson Welles's Mercutio—a new treatment of the character. . . . Welles swaggered out to prove
that the critics of Dublin, who hailed him as a wonder boy,
were not crazy. Welles is flamboyant, some will say—but
so is Mercutio. Welles violates tradition by wearing a half-
fledged beard—but it gives his boyish face a definite Tudor
look. He reads the Queen Mab speech with merry flourishes,
and he plunges into the duel scene with a fine fury of
swordsmanship." Excellent notices like this should have
more than compensated for any of young Orson's "merry
flourishes" offstage.

After he had dueled his way through thirty-four states,
Orson was crestfallen to learn that the Cornell tour would

not be taking him to Broadway as he had keenly anticipated, but several very significant miles away, to the Brooklyn Academy of Music. It was spring and, with nothing to do until the fall, when McClintic held out hope for a Broadway opening, Orson planned a stay at Todd, where he would launch a summer theater festival with Whitford Kane, his erstwhile champion at the Goodman Theatre in Chicago, as its head, and Micheal MacLiammoir and Hilton Edwards as its leading lights. Although in the end he never actually showed up for the job, Kane promptly accepted the post of summer festival director. In Dublin, Edwards and Mac-Liammoir were more hesitant about Orson's invitation (the last they had heard from him was when he tried unsuccessfully to interest them in staging *Marching Song* at the Gate), principally because of what Edwards took as Orson's effrontery in presuming that he could work on equal footing with them. Orson had written to say that the summer festival would feature three plays, two of them directed by the Dubliners, and one by Orson, which struck Edwards as utterly preposterous. Orson Welles *direct* a play? But Micheal finally prevailed on Hilton to accept the invitation— especially since Skipper Hill was picking up the tab.

When they stepped off their steamship, the *President Harding*, in New York, a beaming Orson was there to meet them, and so were several newspaper photographers he had conned into snapping their arrival by disclosing that these were the two grand old men of the European theater even if the boys in the city room had never heard of them. Orson had obvious personal reasons for wanting to impress Micheal and Hilton, whom he installed in elaborate quarters at the Algonquin and treated to a grand tour of the city. He charged everything to Todd, which faced imminent economic ruin if Orson's festival didn't at least break even.

Orson's importing two such thoroughly uncloseted homosexuals as MacLiammoir and Edwards came as an immense shock to provincial Woodstock, which still hadn't gotten over the infamous penmanship teacher they'd had to run out of town. "Oh, it was wild because these two fellows were at the absolute high pitch of their sexuality!" Orson recalls the splash the Dubliners made at Todd. "They were away from home, and they went through Woodstock like a withering flame. *Nobody* was safe, you know. It was a rich harvest there for both of them, and they knew no shame. Hortense was faced with something she'd never known about in her life. You know, in front of her eyes people were tumbling over. It was a very strange summer, because Micheal wore what were then shorts of a briefness unseen on the Riviera—and up and down the main street of Woodstock went Micheal, you know, with beaded eyelashes with the black running slightly down the side of his face because he never could get it right, and his toupée slipping, but still full of beauty. Hilton couldn't keep his hands off his genitals—he went dancing around caressing himself and sputtering. Everywhere were these four eyes darting about for the next victim. I felt rather guilty about it all because I hadn't stopped to think that I was bringing Sodom and Begorrah to the Reverend Todd's old establishment. Luckily, Noble Hill was happily in California."

Orson adds that through it all Skipper "was shocked, pretending not to be." Behind their backs the headmaster snidely referred to his esteemed visitors as the "roaring pansies." Much to his and Hortense's stupefaction, so widespread was homosexuality that summer at Todd that Leslie Howard's mistress, the steamily beautiful Louise Prussing, whom Orson had hired as the festival's leading lady, was, quips Hascy Tarbox, "probably the only one in the place that got enough sleep." By now, Hascy Tarbox was what Skipper describes as a "beautiful sixteen-year-old." Skipper recalls Hascy's "being chased all over campus that summer." Says Hascy himself of Orson's Irish imports: "Both of these characters introduced me into homosexuality with a vengeance." Not that Hascy accepted, however. Now that he

had graduated from Todd, Hascy was what he calls a "hanger-
on at the campus," of whom there were quite a few, who
participated in the summer productions without paying or
being paid. "Hilton and Micheal were something else to a
young man just emerging into the world," Hascy recalls.
"Instead of poking my head into reality I bumped into these
two, who managed to exist in never-never land and gave
me a pretty screwed-up version of what it all meant." At
that time Hascy suffered from migraine headaches, one of
which overtook him in the Dubliners' presence. "It all started
innocently enough with a migraine headache," says Hascy.
"Migraines were the only indication to me that I was really
very bright. For it was tacitly understood that only the real
brains had migraine headaches. Understood by whom is still
a mystery. Anyway, I get this goddamned head that has the
eyes spinning, out of focus, tunnel vision, the stomach
turning, and the will to live ebbing. Both of these characters
run for the Yardley's English Lavender after-shave lotion,
start slopping it all over me. Particularly where I don't ache.
I'm yelling, 'Cease and desist!' They get the picture. They
let up. Take back their bottles of Old English Lavender.
And don't bother me for the rest of the summer." Hascy
was by no means alone in being chased by the Dubliners.
Another of their special targets that summer at Todd was
the actor Charles "Blackie" O'Neal, who is remembered
today less as a tragedian perhaps than as the father of Ryan
and grandfather of Tatum and Griffin O'Neal. Blackie came
to Todd with actress Constance Heron, whom Skipper had
hired to play Ophelia in *Hamlet* on the basis of her performance in *The Drunkard* in Chicago. Since they had "inherited" Blackie—as Orson puts it—when the handsome,
rough-hewn actor turned up with Miss Heron, the summer
festival assigned him to play Horatio to Micheal Mac-
Liammoir's Hamlet. "I'll get that one!" Micheal excitedly
told Orson when he laid eyes on Blackie. "Just watch me!"
Suddenly it occurred to Orson that O'Neal was precisely

the sort of "vigorous nonhomosexual" type Micheal preferred.

For all Skipper's troubled homophobic visions of "pansies" everywhere (Skipper was not especially disturbed when,
because he had gone to Hollywood to look for film work,
Whitford Kane failed to show up, since he too, it seemed,
was a "pansy"), there were also abundant heterosexual
goings-on that summer, what with the handful of innocent
young girls—"nubile virgins," Skipper called them—who
had joined the theater program. *Girls* were a new invention
at Todd, and Hortense, madly drinking coffee to stay awake,
prowled the dormitory nightly to be certain the boys were
not *too* curious about them. The idea was to return the
"nubile virgins" to their parents absolutely intact. One of
the female students was actually an English teacher from
rural Iowa, whose exceedingly large bosom was a topic of
much animated speculation among the Todd boys. Eager to
abandon the constraints to which she was accustomed as a
small-town schoolmarm, she spent much of her time in
feverish pursuit of a Todd faculty member—although in this
case her erotic passion was unrequited.

But of all the boy-girl romances, certainly the most talked
about was Orson's. The girl was a petite, porcelain-skinned
beauty of eighteen. From a prominent Chicago family, Virginia Nicolson was a pupil at Miss Hare's University School
for girls, where Skipper's daughters, Joanne and Bette, were
weekly boarders. Virginia had heard from them about Orson's impending summer theater festival. Because she was
keenly interested in dramatics, her father, Leo Nicolson,
permitted her to enroll as a student in lieu of throwing a
debutante party. To make what was in those hard times the
very substantial tuition of two hundred and fifty dollars for
two months appear somehow more palatable to parents,
Orson had come up with the idea of pretending that not
everyone who applied would be accepted. Prospective summer students would have to submit to an audition, even

though the real test of an applicant's suitability was whether
his or her parents could afford to pay. Even Skipper admits
that "the school was a phony"—since formal instruction
wasn't really offered, just a chance for professional experience. As Hascy Tarbox puts it, Virginia and the others
were only "laughably referred to as students." Slave labor
would have been more like it, in that the kids were really
there just to help Orson and company on the productions.
When Virginia read Shakespeare at her audition, the results
were positive, as Orson made certain they always were, and
she was promptly signed up for the Todd Summer Theatre
School. But this particular audition had been distinctly different from all the others on account of the special attention
Orson paid to it. From the first he felt himself powerfully
attracted to the fragile, almost childlike blond, whose waist
was so narrow he could nearly circle it with one of his great
hands. Beyond the perfect breeding betokened by her graceful string of pearls and beautifully tailored clothes, he soon
detected something else, a bold streak of fantasy that disclosed itself in the wonderfully outrageous stories she would
tell him when they were alone. He liked to think he knew
a wonderful secret about her, that despite her perfect de-
portment, her flawless boarding-school breeding, she was
every bit as drawn to wildly eccentric, theatrical people and
situations as he. He thrilled to the way they looked together
in public, he the towering lanky-limbed boy, all huge raw
bones and hands, and she the delicately exquisite china doll.
Orson and Virginia co-starred in a short, rather silly home
movie one Sunday afternoon, a send-up of Buñuel and Dali's
An Andalusian Dog and Cocteau's *The Blood of a Poet*,
which Orson had seen and detested in New York. Watching these two children at play on screen in their floppy
grown-ups' clothes is a bracing reminder of just how startlingly young nineteen-year-old Orson still was.

When they saw that Orson was absolutely enchanted by
Virginia, the Dubliners made it clear to him that they didn't

like her. They made a great show of turning up their noses
at her supposedly being an aristocrat when in fact she was
only an American. How could an American *possibly* be an
aristocrat? Partly as a reaction against Hilton and Micheal,
whose decadent influence on Orson he feared, Skipper encouraged Orson's romance with Virginia. But whatever
Skipper's anxieties, at this point the Dubliners weren't so
much interested in seducing Orson as in humiliating him,
making him feel foolish. "I was in very small danger from
Micheal and Hilton in Woodstock," laughs Orson. "No, they
were too busy hating me, you know, which they were that
summer. It was a real vendetta against me, and it would
have been unthinkable that I would have been *chosen* by
them." Orson was mortifed in front of Skipper when Micheal
and Hilton openly needled him. "They were really, I think,
rather mean to Orson," says Skipper, who was baffled by
their resentment. Even nineteen-year-old Orson didn't entirely comprehend how much Micheal and Hilton despised
having to function as his equals. He had invited them in
hopes of patching things up, but he discovered to his be-
wilderment that the old conflicts had only grown deeper.
He revered them far too much to fight back. As in Dublin,
he outwardly pretended that all was as it should be, but
secretly he was miserable.

Orson's festival consisted of three productions: George
du Maurier's *Trilby*; Merejkowski's *Czar Paul*; and Shakespeare's *Hamlet*. The agreement at the outset was for Orson
to direct *Trilby*, and for the Dubliners to handle the other
two. Explains Hascy Tarbox: "No matter how it hurt, each
would shut up and let the other have his way. How else
could such temperamentals get on with it?" But if Micheal
and Hilton were going to refrain from making suggestions
when Orson directed his first professional play, they would
not help him even when he asked—an attitude that enraged
Skipper one day shortly before the opening of *Trilby* when
he overheard Orson desperately requesting Hilton's advice

about lighting, and Hilton's blunt refusal. As far as Edwards
was concerned the boy had already learned enough from
him—too much, in fact. While he tried to conceal his embarrassment, a very flustered Orson turned to his assistant,
one of the "nubile virgins," who dutifully carried about with
her at all times a textbook on stagecraft in which he ordered
her to look up the information. At length the completed
production itself, which like the others ran for a fortnight,
MacLiammoir pronounced "disappointingly vague and in-
definite"—although one wonders whether it was truly disappointment the Dubliners felt in declaring Orson's *Trilby*
a failure.

There is little question that the big hit of the festival was
Micheal MacLiammoir's *Hamlet*. In addition to his role as
Claudius, Orson also played the ghost; a costume change
was therefore necessary, for which enervating task Hascy
Tarbox was assigned as Orson's dresser in a 3-by-3 nook
backstage, where the two of them struggled frantically to
get Orson into what Hascy describes as "his fake chain-mail
underwear and his pasteboard helmet." Hascy's part in the
play was the Player Queen: "Pretty dangerous around that
place at that time playing any kind of a queen!" he recalls.
Backstage with Orson his drag costume posed other problems: "My off-the-shoulder dress was really off the ass most
of the time, falling down," he says. "Orson was beginning
to get a little fleshy, to put it kindly, and there was just no
room for it. All this done in the dark by Braille, Welles was
sure that I was trying to attack him." The pasteboard helmet
was too small for Orson's head, so Hascy had to jam it on
crookedly, which gave it the appearance of being dented.
Orson looked, says Hascy, "like he had been done in in a
battle or had had one hell of a night and was coming home
late to the castle."

By some miracle the Todd Summer Theatre Festival broke
even, with an audience consisting mainly of Chicago-area
socialites whom Skipper had invited to a preopening gala

at the swank Tavern Club with drinks and dinner at Todd's expense. The guest list was culled from the *Social Register*. Skipper's anxious investment paid off handsomely when, in turn, the blue bloods paid top dollar to sit in the first few rows of the rickety old Woodstock Opera House, which the Todd boys roped off and called the "dress circle," even though, as anybody who had ever been there knew, the best seats in the house were really in the gallery. In the end, Todd didn't make any money on Orson's festival, but it didn't lose any either. Still, Skipper and Hortense seemed most unlikely to throw open the school's doors to a sequel next year. Trying to protect the Todd boys from the Dubliners and the "nubile virgins" from the Todd boys had been too much for them to bear.

Having heard that Kit Cornell's *Romeo and Juliet* would indeed be opening on Broadway in December, Orson went to New York to look for acting work after he had finished at Todd that August. But the search was fruitless. To make matters worse, his acute asthma kept him from sleeping at night. The one consolation should have been that, on his own again, he could freely resume his activities with the young ladies. But Hortense's watchful eye was replaced by that of the manager of the Algonquin, who, without specifically mentioning Orson's lady friends, complained about his so frequently ordering two breakfasts in the morning. "Couldn't you order larger breakfasts?" asked the manager. "What do you mean, Frank?" asked a genuinely puzzled Orson. "Well, order double breakfasts—don't order two breakfasts." Delivering two breakfasts to young Orson's room would mean that the hotel countenanced his sleeping with women to whom he was not married. This was no special quirk of the manager's. While it is difficult to imagine today, it was then not uncommon for the better hotels to ask to see a couple's marriage certificate. Nor, as Orson recalls, was it unheard of in some hotels for the house detective to unlock a door with a passkey in the middle of the night to be certain that the people in bed together were indeed legally married. At the Algonquin, faced only with the manager's euphemistic dismay, Orson refrained from ordering the telltale two breakfasts: "I had to order *big* breakfasts," he laughs, "and whoever my companion of the night was, poor little thing, had to go and hide in the bathroom."

Out of work but sustained by the expectation of playing Mercutio on Broadway in December, Orson busied himself with two literary projects: his essay on Shakespeare that, much to Skipper's consternation, Orson had not yet fnished, as well as a fresh idea for a new play that he promised himself not to begin until the earlier project was completed. Todd Press (whose editorial board consisted solely of Skipper) wanted to follow up the best-selling basketball manual of several seasons back with the long-overdue *Everybody's Shakspeare*. "Fix up a platform in a classroom, a gymnasium, a dancehall or a backyard and give Shakespeare a chance," wrote Orson, a schoolboy addressing other schoolboys. "I do think that in studying these plays you ought to act them out, if only in the theater of your own mind. Mr. Hill, who is a scholar and a teacher and ought to know, agrees with me." Mr. Hill also agreed with him that it was a good idea to have a steady girl in his life just now, so that when Leo Nicolson asked him to intercede with Orson, who had invited Virginia to join him in New York, Skipper shocked everyone by declaring himself a staunch supporter of whatever plans the teenage couple might have. At the time, however, marriage was not part of those plans. "She really did run away to see the bright lights, and because she was kind of stuck on me—and no more," says Orson, who figured that he had to come up with a good excuse for her to give her parents about why she was leaving Chicago. "She couldn't say, *I'm going to live with Orson*," he recalls. "She had to say she had a job." But Virginia's father saw through the subterfuge of her supposedly coming to New

York to assist Orson's friend Francis Carpenter in staging yet another production of *Romeo and Juliet*. Hence his appeal to Skipper, as well as his hushed offer of a seat on the stock exchange for young Orson, on the condition that he leave Virginia alone.

Meanwhile, Orson suffered what he perceived as a devastating setback in New York when, having begun to suspect that Guthrie McClintic was trying to avoid him, he learned that the producer-director wasn't returning any of his calls because he dreaded telling the boy that, for the Broadway run, he'd lost the role of Mercutio to another actor. In the interval since the Cornell tour, McClintic had hired Brian Aherne to play Robert Browning in *The Barretts of Wimpole Street*—a role for which he seemed especially well suited. In *Romeo and Juliet*, however, McClintic determined that no less important a role than Mercutio could be assigned an actor of Aherne's caliber, so that it was in the company's best interest to relegate Orson to the less-rewarding role of Tybalt—a cruel logic McClintic knew Orson was most unlikely to follow. However terribly unjust his fate may have seemed, Orson had little choice but to accept since the Broadway debut he longed for was still at stake. After this, Virginia's arrival in New York that fall greatly picked up his spirits. "She was the essence of innocent youth when she came to New York," Orson fondly recalls, "and it brought out a wonderful spirit of *let's go with whatever's going* in her." Her excitement about being in New York, and with him, made him abandon the cynicism he had just been beginning to feel. No sooner had she gotten there, however, than Orson was confronted with a major new problem. Obviously, he couldn't order a big breakfast and Virginia couldn't hide in the bathroom *every* morning. Prying managers and house detectives made living together at a decent hotel out of the question. So although they certainly hadn't intended to do so when they first dreamed of being in New York together, suddenly that November of 1934 they de-

cided to marry secretly. "We really only got married in order
to live together," says Orson. "It wasn't taken very seriously
by either of us." Their impulsive nuptials weren't so secret
that Orson could resist calling Skipper and Hortense to invite
them to bear witness the very next day, November 14.
Thinking that Orson sounded "frightened," Skipper told the
nineteen-year-old prospective bridegroom that he thought
marriage an excellent idea, and that, yes, he and Hortense
would most certainly be there tomorrow.

When they learned of their daughter's secret marriage,
the Nicolsons were shocked. If Virginia was to be married,
at least there should be a *proper* wedding—all of it duly
recorded in the Chicago society columns signed "Bunny"
and "The Dowager." This being so, further secrecy was
urged. Orson and Virginia were to say nothing of the step
they had taken. They were to claim merely to be engaged.
Announcements would be dispatched, these followed by
wedding invitations. After they were married they would
move to a proper apartment in suburban Rye, New York.
Although initial plans were for the second wedding to occur
at the Little Church Around the Corner in Manhattan, at
length the site was shifted to the more intimate setting afforded by the West Orange, New Jersey, home of Virginia's
godmother, Mrs. Herbert Gay. Virginia's attendant would
be her younger sister, Caryl, and Orson's best man the much-
neglected Dadda Bernstein, who, profoundly dismayed that
he had not been invited to the secret wedding along with
Skipper, was thrilled by the Nicolsons' shrewd decision to
get things right *this time*.

But while Dadda and the Nicolsons threw themselves into
preparing frantically for the big day, Orson's thoughts were
mostly elsewhere, on rehearsals for his imminent Broadway
opening on December 20 at the Martin Beck Theatre. In
Romeo and Juliet, besides playing Tybalt, a masked Orson
spoke the choral prologue, so that on opening night he was
the first of the company to be seen or heard, even before

the parting of the curtains, each of them decorated with the crest of either the Montagues or the Capulets. Thereafter Orson was by all accounts an eloquent Tybalt—played with such brio that, on the second night of the successful run, he was noticed with unusual interest by a fledgling New York producer, whose own august manner and Ciceronian diction seemed to make him well qualifed to judge the nineteen-year-old's potential. After Tybalt's death, Orson was required to hover offstage until the curtain call. During this interval he repaired to the Martin Beck's third floor to work on the new drama he had mentioned to Skipper, which by now had a title, *Bright Lucifer*, and was well under way. Night after night, he slipped away to this secret workplace— and there it was, some weeks after the fledgling producer had first spotted him, that a massive shirtless Orson glanced up to see the fine features and noble bearing of a nonetheless excited man who introduced himself as John Houseman.

CHAPTER 7
Bright Lucifer

Houseman started out being in love with me, and then turned to hate," says Orson. "There must be something else to think about. It's a real Russian novel, you know." If there exists no such Russian novel, there *is Run-Through*, the maiden volume of Houseman's well-turned autobiographical trilogy. In *Run-Through*, from the moment Houseman first glimpses a scarlet-and-black Orson on stage in *Romeo and Juliet*, already his language betokens a morbid obsession with this "monstrous boy," as he calls him, in whom he excitedly senses something "obscene and terrible," an "irresistible interior violence," which suggests how much, at the outset, Houseman was drawn to what he perceived as simultaneously frightening and fascinating in Orson.

No less curious is Houseman's metaphor of himself as lover, and Orson as his beloved: "I left without seeing him," he writes, "yet in the days that followed, he was seldom out of my mind. My agitation grew and I did nothing about it—in much the same way as a man nurtures his sense of excited anticipation over a woman the sight of whom has deeply disturbed him and of whom he feels quite certain that there will one day be something between them. He postpones their meeting until the feared and eagerly awaited moment when their confrontation, with its predictable consequences, can no longer be delayed." When at last, some weeks later, Houseman pays what he calls a "secret visit" to Orson's dressing room—why *secret*? from whom?—there is a faint lubricity in his description of Orson "naked to the waist, before his mirror under the glaring bulbs. . . . His black-and-scarlet Tybalt costume, stiff and heavy with sweat, lay over the back of a chair." For full effect, there is no reported dialogue, just Orson's paraphrased remark, accompanied by the handsome young actor's smile, that he was working on a play about the Devil. Later that evening, having agreed to meet Houseman in a bar across the street, Orson approaches his table in a manner that Houseman describes as "frightening."

These details would be relatively inconsequential if they did not so vividly establish Houseman's view of Orson Welles. In his account one senses that Houseman was initially enthralled by the young actor's apparent impassivity, what seemed like an inscrutable, and invincible, autonomy—all the more mysterious in one so young. If subsequently Houseman suffered in his relations with Welles, how, one wonders, could it have been otherwise—when it was precisely this indifference that appears to have excited him from the start?

Consummately intelligent, acutely cultivated, the thirty-two-year-old Rumanian-born Houseman was just then in quest of an artistic career. Having toiled as a grain merchant in his twenties, Houseman turned to the arts as a profession relatively late when, in 1934, he found himself invited by his friend Virgil Thomson to become general director-manager of his and Gertrude Stein's opera *Four Saints in Three Acts* (one of whose innovations was to use black actors and actresses in nonblack roles). It was a remarkable opportunity for one so inexperienced as Houseman, but he brought it off with an impeccable sense of style that was not unnoticed in the vanguard artistic circles to which he was to introduce

Orson. There followed his direction of Maxwell Anderson's play *Valley Forge*, from which project he was fired before the opening and replaced by another director. Almost certainly when he spotted the "monstrous boy" in *Romeo and Juliet*, Houseman could not have remotely suspected what Orson would mean to him—and he to Orson—in the years to come. When he returned, weeks later, for his "secret visit," it was to offer Orson a role in a new play by the Pulitzer prize–winning poet Archibald MacLeish entitled *Panic*, which, in the interim, Houseman had signed on to produce. Nonetheless, the thrill, the fear, the fatal attraction—all appear to have been there from the first.

Orson discovered in Houseman a fresh incarnation of the mentor type—the older male to whom young Orson persisted in turning for sage counsel. Orson was intrigued by the proffered role of the failed industrialist McGafferty—but no less so by Houseman's connections in New York artistic circles. Before long Houseman shrewdly perceived in Orson much more than just an actor for the MacLeish play. Houseman's abandoned mercantile career had prepared him to be a boldly adventuresome theatrical entrepreneur—and what better product to market than the wonder boy from Wisconsin? For all the adulation with which Orson had been garlanded in the past, perhaps it was Houseman who was the first to have any real idea of just what Orson was capable of achieving—particularly with Houseman there to help him achieve it.

The trouble with Houseman's literary portrait of Orson in this period is also the source of its immense interest: the obsessive (and obfuscating) tone with which it is shot through. Here, for instance, is Houseman on Orson, a passage that probably discloses far more about the former than the latter: "No sooner were his eyes closed than, out of the darkness, troupes of demons—the symbols of his sins—surrounded and claimed him, body and soul, in retribution for crimes of which he could not remember the nature, but of which he never for a moment doubted that he was guilty. Neither running nor hiding could save him from their clutches. And when they had seized him with their bleeding claws, they would drag him off into some infernal darkness, there to inflict upon him, through all eternity, those unspeakable torments which he felt he so richly deserved." It is a most peculiar picture of a young man about whom the only thing remotely *infernal* was the hell he'd raised on the Katharine Cornell tour. The trouble with Houseman's "Orson" is that he never develops beyond the initial fantasy image. But to get into Orson's head, as they say, to comprehend anything of why he acted as he did would be to destroy that fantasy— something Houseman seems unwilling to do. Significantly, it is his self-appointed role to protect the "monstrous boy" from destroying himself. So fixated on saving Orson is Houseman that when Orson shows interest in another potential partner like Marc Blitzstein Houseman feels, by his own account, jealous and rejected. Not that Houseman is so morbid in his affections that he fails to involve himself with others—he even reports an occasional romance from this period, such as the liaison with a Viennese woman born the same year, the same day, and even the same hour as Orson!

Still it must be said that on his part young Orson did nothing whatsoever to discourage Houseman's demoniacal fantasy of him. At the Gate, Orson had actively sought out MacLiammoir and Edwards, as earlier at Todd he had sought out Skipper, but this time it was the mentor who would seek out the protégé, and Orson thought it best to keep their relationship that way. With MacLiammoir and Edwards, one of the fatal mistakes he made was to evince too much keen interest, to be too receptive, to show himself too anxious— whereas it had been his air of absolute autonomy that, at first, seemed to have fascinated them. By the time he met

Houseman, Orson understood the dynamics of the impassive role he was expected to play if he were to avoid shattering other people's useful fantasies of him. One's suspicions that Orson was calculating his every move are confirmed in the odd episode in *Run-Through* in which Houseman visits the Welleses' Riverside Drive studio apartment to be greeted by a quite unabashedly nude Orson posed in his bathtub. The scene's erotic implication is signaled by the detail that, by night, with a board and mattress atop it, the tub was Orson and Virginia's "marriage bed"—not just a bed, but a *marriage* bed, where Houseman now discovers his friend in the raw. Writes Houseman: "Orson was lying there, inert and covered with water, through which his huge, dead-white body appeared swollen to gigantic proportions. When he got up, full of apologies, with a great splashing and cascading of waters, I discovered that his bulk owed nothing to refraction—that he was, in reality, just as enormous outside as inside the tub...." Intrigued by Orson's enormity—specifics Houseman leaves to the reader's imagination—he says nothing of what were obviously Orson's calculated efforts to shock and disconcert him. Mentioning them would undermine the guise of impassivity upon which the visitor's rapt fascination—and fantasy—apparently depends. Also Houseman's subsequent sense of himself as mentor and manager was based in large part on Orson's being always the "monstrous boy" whose very monstrousness needed taming.

To adduce that from the first Orson was playing a role for Houseman might be mere speculation were it not for a remarkable unpublished literary document that lets us get inside Orson's head at the time of the two men's initial encounter. For on the night of Houseman's first and fateful "secret visit" to Orson's dressing room at the Martin Beck Theatre, had Houseman averted his gaze from the "monstrous boy" to steal a look at what he was then writing, the visitor would have had a very good notion indeed (as evidently he still did not, so many decades later, when he composed his memoir) of just how shrewdly self-conscious young Orson was. In *Bright Lucifer* Orson was fleshing out an acutely ironic self-image in the dramatic character of Eldred Brand—the very sort of "monstrous boy" whom Houseman discovered in Orson. For anyone with a knowledge of Welles's early life it will be clear that Eldred (a stage role Orson planned to play himself) must be counted as young Orson's literary avatar. Like Orson, Eldred suffers from hay fever—and like Dick Welles, Eldred's father is said to have been similarly afflicted. As an orphan, Eldred is the ward of a man, Bill Flynn, whom he accuses of having been in love with his mother, much as Dadda was indiscreetly attached to Beatrice Welles. "You've tried to be just like a father to me, haven't you?" asks Eldred, which calls to mind how Bernstein frequently interposed himself between Orson and his real father so that the boy even called him Dadda. And Eldred's "I have my mother's eyes, haven't I?" suggests Orson's own distinct resemblance to his mother, as well as Dadda's having transferred his attachment entirely to Orson after Beatrice's death. Although Bill proclaims his devotion to Eldred, the orphan is jealous of his affections. "She hates me!" Eldred complains of Bill's wife, Martha, much as Hazel Moore fiercely resented him (and much as Hortense Hill felt about him at first). "She hates me, Bill! It's true! She's jealous! . . . She's jealous of our love for each other." Recalling what both Skipper and Hascy Tarbox said about Orson's never having really been a boy, one is struck by the line: "There's nothing young about Eldred. He's as old as Egypt." And if, in youth, Orson seemed rather more than routinely attached to Skipper— much to Hortense's alarm—one notes with special interest Bill's assessment that "Eldred doesn't go much yet for the girls." Finally, the drama's setting, an island in a North

Woods lake near an Indian reservation, whose natives play an important part in the action, surely draws on Orson's Lake Falambeau holiday.

The slender plot of *Bright Lucifer* is perhaps less interesting artistically than as an indication of the acute irony with which young Orson viewed the demoniacal image that Houseman depicts quite unironically in *Run-Through*. To recuperate from the humiliation of having been publicly jilted by the woman he loved, a Hollywood actor named Jack is visiting his older brother Bill, whom he finds excessively devoted to his petulant and peculiar ward Eldred Brand. Jack insists that Eldred is a "troublemaker," a "goddam little brat," and a "busy little bitch boy"—but against these charges Bill adamantly defends him by calling Brand "a sweet kid" or by fondly proclaiming "Eldred's my boy." *"Your boy!"* Jack exclaims, evidently alarmed by something morbid in Bill and Eldred's relationship. "I've half a mind to tell you—" but thinking better of it, he discreetly breaks off: Bill is his respected older brother, after all, and Jack cannot quite substantiate, let alone articulate, his worst suspicions. The demoniacal theme is introduced when Jack hears the thumping of Indian drums—"devil drums," Bill informs him—to ward off the devil, for "someone must be dead or dying." When Jack scoffs at the very idea of real devils, Bill insists, "I believe in devils," and at precisely this point Eldred appears. "Hi, Eldred," Bill says, almost in the same breath, so that the link between Eldred and those devils is implicit, ironic—just as Bill believes in devils, he believes in Eldred.

The ironic distance with which young Orson viewed his manipulations of his elders is suggested in Eldred's shrewdly—and comically—playing Bill and Jack against each other. "I think you love that man more than you love me," Eldred accuses Bill. With Jack, Eldred is a "persuasive little bitch" who eggs on the actor to costume himself as a hideous ghoul who will terrify the Indians—and Bill. When initially Jack resists, Eldred is slyly seductive, in turn flattering and calling into question the actor's ability to convincingly make himself up as the fiend. Predictably the outcome of the masquerade is disastrous: the Indians panic and Bill dies of fright. Less predictable is that young Orson could so heartily laugh at himself and—especially—at his image, something of which one doubts the irredeemably possessed, tormented soul Houseman describes would be even remotely capable.

With its private allusions to Dadda and Skipper, *Bright Lucifer* may be read as Orson's caricature of his frequently manipulative boyhood relations with them. One wonders, though, whether Houseman himself doesn't put in a swift appearance in *Bright Lucifer*—after all, Orson was writing the play when they met and only completed it several months later, after the dynamics of their relationship had crystallized. As the play draws to a close, after Jack's ludicrous ghoul has wrought immense havoc, Eldred proclaims that he has decided to become Jack's "manager": "I'll let you out to house-parties!—to Kings and Countries. . . . You'll have offices in—London, Moscow. Hundreds of secretaries . . . I offer you the earth! . . . And I'll throw in some immortality." Curiously enough, it was Jack Houseman who was about to become Orson's "manager," to offer him all these things, and more—although, as *Bright Lucifer* suggests, in his own way perhaps Orson thought of himself as *Jack's* "manager"—secretly, of course, so as not to spoil things.

After Paul Muni and Alfred Lunt had shown no interest in playing McGafferty, the ruined banker in Archibald MacLeish's Depression drama *Panic*, which was to be directed by James Light, Houseman paid his "secret visit" to Orson to talk about the part. Because *Panic* was slated to run for only three nights, the most seasoned and celebrated

actors in town were not inclined to invest the time and effort
rehearsing it—something only a relative newcomer like
Orson could afford to do. So when Houseman proposed
McGafferty, Orson merely went through the motions of
taking his time to decide lest Houseman find him excessively—and unappealingly—anxious. As Orson excitedly
wrote to Skipper (with whom he didn't have to pretend to
be blasé), Houseman could introduce him to plenty of the
right people in New York—like Virgil Thomson and Martha
Graham—besides getting him into the play.

In private, Orson noticed that Virginia was not as enthusiastic about Houseman as he, and at first, without saying
so, Orson ascribed her reservations to jealousy about all the
many hours he was suddenly spending with his new companion. But even when she was enlisted as a member of
the play's chorus she did not change her attitude. When
Virginia warned him that one day Houseman would be his
Iago, that is, a jealous betrayer, Orson chose to regard this
as nonsense. He saw his rapidly evolving relationship with
Houseman as a shrewd strategy for advancing himself in
New York's theatrical world. Orson recalls that once, amid
a typically intense and impassioned conversation about theatrical affairs, Houseman told him that he had dreamt of
Orson's riding bareback on a horse—a dream image that
probably should have warned both of them that their professional relations would often grow dangerously, destructively
personal. If Orson chose to ignore this warning signal, it
was because he was delighted to have hit upon so appre-
ciative an audience as Houseman, to whom, in turn, he
related his dreams of success on stage.

Orson's run as Tybalt in the Katharine Cornell *Romeo
and Juliet* drew to a close in time for him to work on *Panic*
without conflict. While his performance in *Panic* did indeed
meet with critical acclaim—and resulted in one more *New
York Times* review for Orson—it had another effect on him

as well. When MacLeish's play about the banking crisis of
1933 opened on March 15, 1935, at the Imperial Theatre,
it introduced Orson to an explicitly political theater. At a
time when about fifteen million Americans were unemployed, among them destitute actors who lined up for handouts at the Actors' Dinner Club or the Stage Relief Fund
in New York, Orson's idea of depression was what he had
felt when Brian Aherne took the role of Mercutio from him.
"Politics" in the theater had meant his internecine feuds with
MacLiammoir and Edwards at the Todd Summer Theatre
Festival. Single-mindedly interested in his own career, Orson found the rampant political talk among Houseman and
his left-wing cronies to be hopelessly phony at first. He had
trouble tuning in to the sense of social responsibility many
artists felt in Depression America. Although he tried to
refrain from saying so, their political rhetoric struck him as
merely an attempt to be chic. Finally, however, he couldn't
resist making himself heard on the third and last night of
the play, a benefit for the journals *New Masses* and *New
Theatre*, which was followed by a symposium featuring left-
wing intellectual John Howard Lawson and Communist Party
cultural commissar V. J. Jerome. It wasn't long before Orson
wearied of what seemed to him like their droning on and
on. "I thought they were talking such nonsense that I began
to hoot and holler," Orson recalls. Unamused by the embarrassing spectacle the young star was making in back of
the auditorium, the leftists ordered him ejected from the
theater.

After *Panic*, Orson had several offers for relatively in-
substantial stage roles, but having starred in one play, he
thought it best not to seek, or accept, anything less than a
Broadway lead. In the spring of 1935 the Welleses were
living in the murky efficiency apartment on Riverside Drive.
There was serious talk of Orson and Houseman's staging
John Ford's *'Tis Pity She's a Whore*, but despite their am-

bitious plans, funds were not forthcoming, and they abandoned the project with regret. In the meantime, Orson and
Virginia got by on loans from Skipper and on the radio work
for which Orson's magnificent voice made him particularly
well-suited. Waiting around for an appropriate Broadway
part, or for Houseman to come up with the money for him
to do a play of his own, Orson devoted himself to working
on *Bright Lucifer*.

CHAPTER 8

The Bitch Boy

During the winter and spring of 1935 Orson wired Skipper so frequently for cash that the disapproving telegraph operator in Woodstock—a hardworking fellow named Joe whose office was a nook in the local railroad station—began to needle Todd's headmaster about him. "Roger, I thought you wasn't gonna send him no more money," Joe would say. "What do you mean?" Skipper would reply. "Well, what's he thankin' ya for?" said Joe. "I didn't send him any money!" Skipper insisted. "Well, what's he thankin' ya for?" Joe repeated. Only after this little ritual would Joe give him the latest frantic plea from New York.

What seemed like the perfect opportunity for Orson to finish *Bright Lucifer* without the bothersome distractions of having to pay for food or lodgings presented itself when his eccentric theatrical friend Francis Carpenter invited the Welleses to join him for a month at what he described as a palatial Long Island estate. Having frivolously spent their scant remaining funds on preparations for the month's holiday, the Welleses took off for Long Island, where, at the appointed address, they discovered a forlorn and tumbledown mansion, whose owners appeared long since to have died or otherwise departed, and whose larder, contrary to

Orson's fond expectations, was empty but for a single
wretched cauliflower. Especially in Orson's case, hunger
was decidedly not conducive to creativity, so within three
days' time the decision was made to return to New York
on the few coins Orson and Virginia were able to amass
from their pockets and luggage.

In New York, the Welleses checked into the Algonquin
and proceeded to run up a large tab. After three days of
hardship and near-starvation on Long Island, Orson needed
his comfort. Without cash, however, he had little choice
but to start signing for things. The monthly fifty dollars
Skipper had begun to give him as advance royalty for *Everybody's Shakespeare* was hardly enough to pay the bills at
the Algonquin. In fact this stipend was really just another
of Skipper's handouts, since thus far *Everybody's Shakespeare* had not made a cent, and it seemed unlikely to do
so in the near future. Skipper's handling of its publication
proved an immense disappointment to Orson, whose New
York friends had not been able to find it in bookstores. As
far as he could tell it was on sale only in a local shop in
Chicago. For Orson the book was worthless if it wasn't
distributed and reviewed in Manhattan, so that on the advice
of Katharine Cornell's press agent, he had Skipper send
complimentary copies to a list of drama editors, as well as
to Alexander Woollcott and other New York literary figures.

By the time he had finished *Bright Lucifer*, Orson feared
that the hotel desk clerk, whom he described to Skipper as
"a greedy little rodent," had begun to suspect his spendthrift
guests. Skipper sent more money when Orson joked that he
was going to wind up in jail if he couldn't pay his bill, and
more money still when Orson lamented that, having paid
off part of his previous bill, he had since run up further
charges. Orson seemed almost to have forgotten that Skipper
was only a modest Depression-time schoolmaster with a
wife and three children for all of whom the repeated handouts must have caused a considerable strain. This was in

no way lessened by Orson's giving Skipper a share in the potential profits from *Bright Lucifer* or anything else he might write. Orson was genuinely surprised when Skipper passed up his offer to stage *Bright Lucifer* at the Woodstock Opera House that summer as a follow-up to last year's festival. Nor was Skipper interested in backing the all-boy production of *Tom Sawyer* that Orson proposed next. The ultimate goal would be Broadway at Christmastime, starring Orson as the biggest of the boys, but in the meantime Orson envisioned a core of Todd Troupers, past and present, tooling about the nation in Big Bertha to play mainly one-night stands under the supervision of Whitford Kane—that is if Skipper would overlook Kane's having failed to show up last summer. Skipper demurred by saying that there simply were not enough funds in the Todd budget. Fearful of discouraging Orson too much, however, Skipper generously proposed increasing his stipend so that, on a strict budget, the Welleses could summer someplace where the living was cheap and where Orson could get some more writing done.

Skipper's suggestion notwithstanding, the Welleses repaired to Todd, where Orson put on an impromptu *Uncle Tom's Cabin* with the Todd Troupers. Still anxious for Orson to seclude himself elsewhere to write, Skipper rented a rustic cabin for the Welleses in Lake Geneva, Wisconsin, where Orson happily scribbled away at his never-completed Irish travelogue, as well as an essay portentously titled "Now I Am 21" (although he was only twenty). Toward the end of the summer, anxious that Orson return to New York, where he clearly belonged, Skipper gave the Welleses a beat-up thirty-five-dollar Essex automobile for the long trip home. Virginia drove (Orson couldn't) while her husband entertained her by reciting poetry. Rolling into New York at last, they maneuvered their hopeless wreck of a car into the garage at the Waldorf, never to return for it.

Shortly thereafter the Welleses installed themselves in what Orson described to Skipper as "the loveliest English basement apartment," on the outskirts of Greenwich Village at 319 West 14th Street, next to a Chinese laundry and a flophouse and only a few doors away from the flat shared by Whitford Kane and Chubby Sherman. The rent was fifty-five dollars a month, paid for mainly by Orson's frequent radio work. It had taken time, but more and more radio producers were becoming aware of Orson's extraordinary voice, as well as his amazing talent as a mimic, and the unusual ease with which he could assume and cast off accents, dialects, and ages. These talents had been definitively demonstrated the year before in at least two of Orson's appearances on *The March of Time*, a brisk, newsreel-style account of current events enacted with melodramatic flair by prodigiously flexible actors capable of playing several roles in a single show. In one of Orson's *March of Time* roles, he played the late German president von Hindenburg. Since the script took Hindenburg from youth to decrepit old age, Orson concocted subtly different voices for different stages of the character's long life. As at-home listeners *heard* Hindenburg's aging process reflected in Orson's ingenious vocal permutations, those in the studio watched in wonder as Orson's face and body seemed to age as well, metamorphosing entirely as the president reached his eighties. On another show, Orson demonstrated the unusual elasticity of his voice when he attempted to portray the gooing and cooing and crying of each of the newborn Dionne quintuplets so that listeners could seem to tell one baby from the other. But his virtuosity had not really begun to pay off until he returned to New York in the fall of 1935.

"*Suddenly*," recalls Orson, and today he seems as truly amazed by the abruptness of his success as he was then, "I was one of the most successful radio actors ever." For the time being, Orson's mammoth appetite for work and his newfound ability to secure plenty of it eliminated the financial troubles that had preoccupied him in the past. Before very long, he found himself earning "never less than $1,000

a week," he says, "as an unnamed, anonymous radio actor."
For someone with so well developed an ego as Orson, an-
onymity posed a special challenge. Accustomed to asserting
himself in whatever stage role he portrayed, Orson Welles
now would have to disappear entirely.

Although at the outset of their marriage Orson and Virginia had had to live frugally, there was now money for
luxuries, like the mink stole Orson bought for Virginia on
Christmas Eve in Saks Fifth Avenue. To maneuver himself
through the crush of last-minute shoppers Orson arrived in
a wheelchair, so that people would step aside to make way
for him. "Just as the lights were being turned off in Saks,"
Orson recalls, "I picked this one little mink." After a forlorn
glance at the price tag, he looked up at the hovering salesman, to whom he pointed out that since the stole was doubtless going to be discounted right after Christmas, he should
be able to buy it *now* at the sale price. "Otherwise I have
nothing for my wife," lamented the big man in the wheelchair. The various salesmen briefly huddled off to the side,
and finally agreed to Orson's proposal. "I never did anything
remotely that intelligent again," quips Orson. "It was a flash
of Christmas sentiment on their part. But I always regard
it as great shrewdness on mine."

A half century after the Todd Press put out the first edition of Everybody's Shakespeare, *eighty-eight-year-old Roger "Skipper" Hill asks me to help secure a new publisher in New York for it. The Todd School for Boys was shut down long ago, and Skipper and Hortense retired to Florida, where he ran a charter yacht business. In 1983, Skipper, now a widower, lives alone in an expensive, ultra-modern apartment—with a waterbed—in Rockford, Illinois. Prominently displayed on a shelf, encased in glass, is the prized model ship that had burned up in Orson's nightmare. Here it is, perfectly intact.*

The four-room flat is cluttered with what Skipper calls his archives—a sprawling collection of Todd memorabilia that includes films, video and audio tapes, and great mounds of yellowing paper documenting whole decades of minutiae, much of it pertaining to Todd's pair of geniuses: Orson Welles and Hascy Tarbox. All of the most inconsequential telephone calls have been recorded and precisely filed away—calls from Orson, calls from Orson's eldest daughter, Christopher, and now—I shudder to think—calls from me, Orson's biographer.

Buried in Skipper's morass of paper and plastic is a big

chunk of Orson Welles's personal mythology: the intimate frame of reference he shares with Skipper, and without which it is impossible to understand what has driven him all these years. Although he has never been to this place, Orson is strangely in touch with the most trivial, seemingly inconsequential, details recorded here. Sometimes, Skipper and Todd and Hortense and Hascy Tarbox seem more real to him, more vivid, than many—no, most—of the events, the people, the places, he has known in the intervening years. But it isn't nostalgia that so frequently lures Orson's thoughts back to Todd; it isn't simply that he longs for the abundant praise and success that he knew there. The image he had of himself at Todd is what he has struggled to live up to all his life. ("Considering what I thought of myself at fourteen, I'm a mess!" a sixty-nine-year-old Orson tells me one afternoon.) Skipper's—and his own—expectations of himself back then are what, many, many years later, he continues to measure himself, and his life's achievement, against. For his part, Skipper is as wrapped up in the hopes and dreams of their shared past as Orson, whom he continues to regard as the beloved protégé who needs all the help the older, wiser mentor can give him. I witness this when, from his immense hoard of Wellesiana, intact since Todd (crumbly photos and cryptic copies of Orson's letters and diaries), Skipper gingerly extracts a rare old edition of Everybody's Shakespeare, *which he presses upon me in hopes that I know an agent or publisher who might be interested in reissuing it. No need to mention any of this to Orson, he informs me—but if we succeed perhaps it will bring Orson a little extra cash, which, his mentor says ruefully, he could use just now. Hearing all this, I feel as if I have entered a time warp.*

When Orson sent me to see Skipper, he announced that he had asked his mentor not to introduce me to the rest of the Hills, who live in Rockford now. "They all hate me, of course," said Orson, "the grandchildren, great-grandchil-

dren, and great-great-grandchildren, because not only was I a sort of adopted child, but my eldest daughter, Christopher, went to the boys' school as the only female pupil. Christopher still considers Roger and Hortense—who's just gone—as kind of her parents. Of course, the real children despise us both, and I have told him, not giving him that reason, that it would save your time if he didn't subject you to the children."

No sooner do I arrive in Rockford, however, than Skipper packs me into his talking convertible to go see the children, all of whom eye me with curiosity, unsure of whether I am Orson's emissary—Orson not having been seen or heard from by any of them for many years—or a reporter in search of what one of them snidely calls "some apocryphal crap." In the living room of one of Skipper's granddaughters stands an immense silver cup that seems somehow to dominate the room. It is, I recognize at once, the famous Chicago Drama League contest trophy, carted off for Orson's Twelfth Night—evidently now among Skipper's heirlooms.

But of all Skipper's family, the one Orson is most anxious that his biographer not meet is Hascy Tarbox, who married one of the Hill girls, and who collaborated with Skipper on the short film Rip Van Winkle Renascent that I spend part of the afternoon watching, and that Skipper says he is considering asking Orson to help re-edit. "It's best not to tell Orson that you saw Hascy," Skipper warns me before we go to see him. "Don't let that bastard near her!" Orson told Skipper before I got to Rockford—or so Skipper informs me now with a mischievous wink.

"There's this boy, Hascy Tarbox," Orson tells me afterward, unaware that I have already met him—although to my eyes Hascy Tarbox is hardly a boy, but a distinguished, silver-haired grandfather in his sixties. (But to Orson's eyes—and this is key to comprehending him—Hascy is still a boy, still Todd's other genius, with whom he is in competition for Skipper's love and respect.) "There's this boy, Hascy

Tarbox, who was younger than I, was in a class younger than mine, and became a commercial artist and a cartoonist—with a lot of talent, but at the beginning, totally derived from imitating me. He could have gone out into the great world and made a big success, but he stayed and married one of Roger's daughters and adores Roger. So there can be nobody who hates me like Hascy, you see, because he's the one who gave up the world career to be near Roger."

On the matter of his having imitated Orson, Hascy tells me that, following the publication of Everybody's Shakespeare, Skipper commissioned him to forge Orson's name on many volumes so that they could be sold at a higher price as autographed editions. *"I got terribly good,"* says Hascy. *"As a matter of fact, it's my one talent. If I had ever known anybody whose signature was worth forging I certainly would have taken a different course in life."*

After he had achieved great fame on the New York stage, Orson returned to Chicago, where he and Virginia dined at the Sherman House with the Hills, Hascy, and his wife, Joanne. Recalls Hascy: *"Some babe runs up with the usual crap, 'Oh, are you Orson Welles? Oooh, would you autograph this menu?' Orson just looks at her, and the old man says, 'Here, let* him *autograph it'—which I did!"* As I listen to this story, I find myself trying to recall whether the withered copy of Everybody's Shakespeare Skipper showed me was itself one of these precious signed editions—signed by this boy, Hascy Tarbox, that is.

CHAPTER 9
A Free Soul

If in radio Orson had cheerfully accepted the need for momentarily extinguishing his ego for high pay, there was soon to be plenty of opportunity to assert himself in the theater. While he and Virginia had summered at Lake Geneva, Wisconsin, in 1935, a chain of events had begun in Washington, D.C., that, unbeknownst to twenty-year-old Orson, would make it possible for him to have his New York directorial debut. Harry Hopkins, the head of Franklin Delano Roosevelt's Works Progress Administration, the WPA, had announced the appointment of Hallie Flanagan, the head of Vassar College's Experimental Theatre Workshop, as national director of the newly formed Federal Theatre project, whose aim was to provide work for the nation's unemployed theatrical professionals. Faced with an overall fifteen million unemployed Americans, Congress had appropriated five billion dollars for the WPA. Roosevelt had argued that federal relief merely sapped the vitality of the American people. Instead of idly waiting on the breadlines, which had been so ubiquitous in these hard times, a man deserved the basic dignity of earning a living for himself. Although the pay they would receive was minimal—$23.86 a week, slightly more than half the rock-bottom forty-dollar Equity minimum—in Depression America unemployed actors, musicians, playwrights, and technicians were eager to get off the dole by doing what they knew best. Hopkins's choice of Mrs. Flanagan to organize and implement the Federal Theatre Project was significant since she was not a member of the Broadway commercial establishment, but an academic with a taste for experimental and regional theater. Flanagan's determination to vitalize American regional theater notwithstanding, it was only natural that the largest of the Federal Theatre Project's operations would be in New York, where most theater professionals lived and—in better times—worked. When word got around town that the government was about to hire approximately 5,000 New Yorkers for the production companies that were forming in the area, professionals and nonprofessionals alike swarmed into the local Federal Theatre Project offices to apply. By rule, ten percent of each unit could consist of theater people who had not been receiving relief, thereby ensuring the presence of expert professional talent to counterbalance the inevitable amateurs who found working in the theater more appealing than a government construction project. This elite ten percent was where Orson came in.

The events that began with Flanagan's appointment led next to the distinguished black actress Rose MacClendon, who was named co-director of Harlem's Negro Theatre unit. For the other top position she in turn recommended John Houseman, whose credentials for the job were his having served as general director-manager of the all-black *Four Saints in Three Acts*. At Virgil Thomson's suggestion, Houseman divided the Negro unit into two sections, one devoted to plays on black themes, the other to European classics—for the latter of which he wasted no time in calling on Orson Welles. Having been without the cash to stage a play only the season before, here they were, thanks to the Depression, not only with the means to mount a classic production of their choice, but with far more money for that production than they would ever have been able to raise on their own given Orson's age and relative inexperience as a director.

Orson was not unaware of the near-miracle of a callow twenty-year-old's directing a major New York production when far more seasoned directors were out of work. He expected people to resent him. He knew that he would have to transcend somehow his extreme youth if he were to command the authority of an entire cast and crew, most of them far older than he. The actor in Orson sensed that he had to invent himself in a new role: as a director. What he lacked in actual directorial experience he would compensate for with innate acting ability. The year before, when Orson had directed *Trilby* at the Todd Summer Theatre Festival, his persona was not entirely adequate to the task, having been undermined by the resentful and rebellious presences of MacLiammoir and Edwards, who, far from helping the novice director, cruelly sought to make Orson more flustered than he already was. Given Orson's disagreeable experience with *Trilby*, it is not surprising that he would now formulate a definition of the *director* as absolute "master." An explicit statement of that definition can be found in a speech entitled "The Director in the Theatre Today" that Orson delivered to the Theatre Education League in 1939. Orson's ideal director was in complete control of every aspect of the production—something young Orson naturally feared he might not be. "Someone eventually has to shut up," said Orson, who surely didn't have himself in mind. "The composer, the light man, the scene designer, the choreographer and the actors ... cannot all decide upon individual conceptions of the play. That would result in chaos. The director must know what he wants of each of these; he must know what is right for that conception he has of the play." That is, whatever the myriad—and undeniable—contributions of the individual members of the company, finally a production must express the director's vision. "At about the same time in the history of the theater that the director came in the old-time star went out," said Orson. "The horrible truth is that nobody has read the last chapter of the detective story and discovered that the old-time star did not go out. He merely sits in the fifth row now and is the director."

Orson's strategy for asserting his directorial presence at his WPA debut started out as an idea of Virginia's: staging an all-black *Macbeth* by transposing its action from Scotland to Haiti, a startlingly new setting with important artistic advantages, not the least of them the rich possibilities for music and decor. Orson worked quickly. Preferring not to anchor the action too firmly in Haiti he had in mind a mythic island more like the fantasy setting of *The Tempest* than any actual place. But as Orson saw it, there was a significant gain in realism as well: by alluding to Haitian voodooism the production could make credible the role of the witches that modern audiences of *Macbeth* often have trouble accepting.

When he got the go-ahead to stage *Macbeth* at Harlem's Lafayette Theatre, Orson knew that among his most crucial early decisions would be casting the two leads. For Macbeth he chose the slender, muscular, light-skinned Jack Carter, who had played Crown in the original *Porgy*. "He was beautiful!" says Orson. "He had pale gray eyes and a wonderful face. He was absolutely superb onstage." His one physical flaw—of which he was painfully self-conscious—was a head slightly too small for the rest of his body. If he chose, Carter could have passed for white. So fair was his complexion that to appear in the all-black *Macbeth* he darkened himself with makeup. The fascination he held for Orson was not limited to his physical presence or acting ability: "He served time for murder and had close connections with the mob," reports Orson, who was intrigued by the air of violence and danger that hung about him. Carter talked about

his past far less than everyone else did. Depending upon
whom one asked in Harlem, he was the son either of a black
American show girl and a white European nobleman, or of
a famous white actress and her black servant. Before he
came to New York he was said to have run a brothel in
Washington, D.C. In Depression Harlem he held court in a
luxurious apartment and dressed impeccably. A chronic alcoholic—Orson calls him a "black Barrymore"—he would
slip off on drunken binges for weeks, even months at a time,
only to return as handsome and, inexplicably, as fit as ever.
As intensely curious as he was about Carter's past and private life, Orson asked no questions: "Our conversation was
never about anything that would intrude on his personal or
private life, because he was a murderer and ex-gangster,"
says Orson. "You know, Harlem was full of white amateur psychoanalysts and members of the Communist Party,
and I didn't want to join that chorus with him. If he ever
wanted to tell me something, he would. That was the way
we left it."

Carter's unpredictability had scared off other directors,
but not Orson, who, as much as he seeks to assert complete
directorial control, has always been thrilled by the possibility of anything being able to happen at any moment in
a theatrical performance of live actors. This sense of peril
he defined as the essence of theatricality. As director,
Orson knew that probably the gravest danger from Carter
was his going on a drinking binge, which the production
could ill afford. Orson's problem was how to avoid this.
"I seduce actors, make them fall in love with me," says
Orson—and so it was with Jack Carter. Befriending Carter
inevitably meant boozing it up with him—and this Orson
did, partly out of innate fascination with him, of course,
partly to monitor and to keep safely in check the actor's
self-destructive impulses. For his part, Carter was no less
vividly attracted to Orson. As John Houseman says: "Jack

Carter was no fool, and he knew that through his association with Orson he would achieve a quality and a fame as an actor, which he had no chance whatever of doing without Orson."

Although Rose MacClendon had initially been slated to play Lady Macbeth, her fatal illness led to Orson's selection of Edna Thomas, whose genteel manner was in stark contrast to Carter's volatility. In directing Edna Thomas and Jack Carter, Orson used the real-life contrast between them. Says Orson: "Lady Macbeth *ought* to be the mother in the family to a weak-willed husband, and Edna Thomas was the mother. She had that kind of strength and that kind of authority, and Carter had that sort of slightly derailed energy which was fascinating. They were great together." A beautiful lesbian with a passionate attachment to a European lady of considerable means, Thomas—like Carter—was particularly light-skinned and used makeup to appear darker on stage. From the outset it was evident that winning over Edna Thomas would be a major test for Orson. A veteran of many stage productions, she would carefully observe his every move to be certain the novice director knew what he was doing. As *Macbeth*'s choral director Leonard De Paur recalls: "He would never have gotten Edna to work as well as she did if she hadn't believed in what he was trying to do." Much to Orson's relief, before long she generally accepted his authority, although she persisted in publicly offering the youngster advice when she judged he needed it.

For the rest of his cast Orson had decided to try out anyone in Harlem who wanted to audition. For countless hours Orson looked and listened intently as applicants paraded before him, quite a few of them unable to read. Of the cast he painstakingly assembled Orson says: "They really threw themselves into it. None of them had played Shakespeare or even seen a Shakespearean play. It was marvelous to hear what they did with it. They preserved the poetry in a funny way because they found innately the rhythm of the iambic pentameter and observed it without any instruction." Orson contrasts his cast with young actors today who misguidedly—he thinks—"turn the poetry into conversation, which is just an easy way out. The black cast didn't do that. They made it sound real, but they kept it on the level of what it's supposed to be." At rehearsals, behind the balcony in the lounge of the Lafayette Theatre were tables crammed with food and drink Orson bought with his abundant radio money. "They thought he was wonderful," says *Macbeth*'s lighting director, Abe Feder, of how the company felt about Orson's generosity. "They just loved him. They ate, and the liquor flowed—and they were being paid. It was a kind of Valhalla. Everybody was amenable. It was suddenly a state within a state." Orson's munificence had created a community around him.

The uniqueness of this community was intensifed by rehearsals' beginning after midnight, when Orson was through with his radio commitments. Orson's colossal—evidently contagious—energy allowed him to work around the clock. (Exhausted, he sometimes napped secretly in the projection booth.) "In those days I seemed to be able to go without any sleep at all," recalls Orson. "The most sleepless period of my life was during the Harlem days. Because then I was doing radio all day long—nine o'clock till five or six, with the *March of Time* at the end of the day. We rehearsed from midnight till dawn. And then after dawn would rise, I would walk through Central Park. Imagine what New York was like in those days: I'd walk through Harlem, through Central Park, and with that exercise under my belt, take a shower and go to whatever studio I had to be at. It was an incredible regime. Of course I only did that during the rehearsals of *Macbeth*, but they were spread over a couple of months. It was a couple of months with really no sleep at all."

In rehearsal Orson could be as explosive as he was tireless, but this too was part of his persona. "When I shouted it was theater," says Orson. If something went wrong he liked to roll his enormous dark brown eyes to intimidate cast or crew members into getting it right. Explains Leonard De Paur: "When you're young, you've got to resort to all sorts of crazy devices." While Orson's orneriness was mainly a young man's tactic for securing and sustaining control, he appears quite genuinely to have lost control of himself on occasion. "Like everybody else at that age he was capable of temper tantrums," says De Paur, who maintains nonetheless that ninety percent of these tantrums were merely "a posture" calculated to afford Orson the authority twenty-year-olds don't generally have. One apparently authentic tantrum erupted at the dress rehearsal. It was about four in the morning. After they had labored almost continuously for nearly seventy-two hours (with time out only for catnaps) cast and crew were exhausted and exhilarated. Looming on the balcony was Orson, inevitably anxious about the opening. Sullen, brooding, he appeared to have had too much to drink—but this was perfectly understandable. The cast wanted to celebrate. "You're coming with us!" someone called up to Orson. "You're coming with us!" repeated another. Silence. More silence. Could it be that he just had not heard them? Then: "I come with no man!" he bellowed drunkenly. "I am a free soul!" Abe Feder's assistant tore up the aisle. "Get him the hell out of here before they hit him!" he urged Feder. Although Feder nervously ushered him out of the theater and into a cab, there was really no genuine threat of violence. Instead, the insulted company members just stood there, all of them immensely disappointed at having glimpsed something they knew they shouldn't and wished they hadn't: the director's reverse metamorphosis into an arrogant schoolboy. For one terrible moment, seeking to exert, to exude, complete control, the young Orson had entirely lost it.

Orson's preopening anxieties were compounded by the racial tension the Harlem Communists had whipped up between his production and the local black community. "The atmosphere during rehearsals was one of wild hatred," says Orson, who could have been badly hurt or killed when, convinced that the Federal Theatre Project's *Macbeth* was an insult to black people, a man slashed at him in the lobby of the Lafayette Theatre. "The fellow had a razor blade strapped with adhesive to his wrist," Orson recalls. "He was going to cut me up by running his hand up and down my face. Canada Lee saved me." No sooner had the waiting attacker pounced than Lee, a powerful former boxer hired to play Banquo, quickly subdued him. He was not alone in his anger; the Harlem Communists assumed that Orson had come uptown to do a black travesty of *Macbeth*. "We were picketed all the time for white chauvinism," says Orson of the debilitating rehearsal period. "They were disturbed at the idea that I was doing Shakespeare because they were sure it was going to be *funny* Shakespeare—and they wouldn't listen when I said we weren't. So the black Communist Party, which was very strongly organized, gave us hell all the time."

Convinced that once it opened the production would vindicate him in the community's eyes, Orson resolved not to let the violent incident or the picketing keep him from continuing to explore nighttime Harlem as he liked to do, often in the congenial company of Jack Carter. One night: "I was caught in a raid at a rent party at about six in the morning," says Orson. "A narcotics raid! Out on the street we were all on our way into a paddywagon, and a cop grabbed me and said, 'Move along there! Don't obstruct the traffic!' and got me out of it. Just a nice cop. I told Houseman this story, and he said, 'Well, why were you raided?' and I said, 'Because we were all shooting up.' He believed me!" Orson was again toying with his appalled producer—as he appears, somewhat perversely, to have generally enjoyed doing. "I intended to torture him," Orson recalls, "but when I realized it was giving him a little pleasure, I dropped it."

While he had clearly profited from Houseman's intense interest in him, Orson also found it rather cloying. In addition, Orson was put off by what he perceived as Houseman's newly acquired bureaucratic air since his appointment to the Federal Theatre. "What was so astonishing was the change in Houseman," Orson remarks. "He didn't sound like a bureaucrat when I first talked to him and we discussed the theater. The minute he joined the WPA he began talking as though he was the robot who'd got the brochure programmed into him!" Because Houseman's presence at rehearsals made him uncomfortable, Orson forbade him to attend. But since Orson could hardly say that he didn't want Houseman there because he found him personally irritating, he came up with another excuse. "Houseman never came to rehearsals unless he had a group of people he wanted to impress," says Orson. "On more than one occasion I asked them all to leave. I said, 'Jack, if it is possible for you to be at the rehearsals from the day we start, all the way through every day, you are very welcome. But as an occasional visitor you represent an invasion of privacy, and you disturb everybody—particularly me. It is only because you are only occasionally here that I have to say, don't come at all.' I thought it a very skillful way of putting him out." If, as he says, it amused Orson to "torture" his boss at the Negro Theatre unit, Houseman in turn was not unskilled at rattling Orson, such as when he and Virgil Thomson carried on long conversations in French so that Orson couldn't understand what they were saying. Nor, it appeared to Orson, was he supposed to. These incidents suggest the sustained, mostly unspoken, psychological tensions between Houseman and Welles even at this stage of their professional relations. Although he depended on Houseman's administrative skills for the day-to-day running of the theater, Orson was both aware of and irritated by Houseman's sense of himself as somehow taming his incorrigible young partner. Probably Orson had hoped that Houseman's image of him would change when he had proved with what authority he could work. Perhaps then Orson and Houseman would have come closer to the sort of genuine friendship others assumed they had.

CHAPTER 10
King of Harlem

Orson could not explain how or why it happened—but he was grateful it had. The "wild hatred" he had confronted in Harlem during rehearsals magically disappeared on opening night. "Suddenly, for no reason at all, on opening night it seemed that all Harlem had decided it was the triumph of their lives," says Orson. "Everybody who's ever been to that opening describes it as the greatest opening in Harlem's history, if not the world's!" Initially scheduled to rise at 8:45, the curtain didn't budge until 9:25, for there was an extravaganza outside the dramatically floodlit Lafayette Theatre as well as inside. Along 7th Avenue, ten whole blocks were closed to traffic and the streets crammed with many more would-be first-nighters than the 1,223 seats could hold. "Nothing like it has been seen in Harlem since," says Orson. There were "all the Harlem gangs," Orson recalls, "and all the respectable black bourgeoisie, and then the terribly chic crowd from downtown headed by people like Cecil Beaton." As the crowds swarmed in past the Elk Lodge of Harlem, who were giving a full-dress concert of their brass band, and past Hallie Flanagan, who was earnestly lecturing newsreel makers about the Federal Theatre, others tried to push back out again, having seen that the one hundred legal standing-room spots were already taken. After the heavy drinking of the night before, Orson suddenly realized that he had not changed into a clean shirt, "Who wears a size-sixteen shirt around here?" he could be heard backstage. He ultimately found a company member with a shirt to spare, but although the neck fit properly, the sleeves came only to midarm on him. Moments later, wild applause and gasps of pleasure could be heard from the auditorium when at last the curtain rose on the intricate jungle settings, piquant costumes, and sensuous lighting of Orson Welles's black *Macbeth*. "As an experiment in Afro-American showmanship the *Macbeth* fairly rocked the Lafayette Theatre," judged Brooks Atkinson of *The New York Times*. "If it is witches you want, Harlem knows how to overwhelm you with their fury and phantom splendor." In the *New York Daily News*, Burns Mantle hailed Orson's show as "a spectacular theatre experience. This West Indian *Macbeth* is the most colorful, certainly the most startling, of any performance that gory tragedy has ever been given on this continent." On opening night, even Orson appeared onstage—"virtually dragged out of the wings by members of the company and forced to take a bow," reported the *Times*—although one wonders how much dragging and forcing were really necessary. ("The fact that we don't take bows at the end doesn't really matter," Orson would say of the star-director in "The Director in the Theatre Today." "A few of us even manage to overcome the handicap. We come out and take them anyway.")

Orson figured that Percy Hammond's vicious mockery in the *Herald Tribune* would only stir up interest that would pay off at the box office. "What surprised me last night was the inability of so melodious a race to sing the music of Shakespeare," wrote Hammond. "The actors sounded the notes with a muffled timidity that was often unintelligible.

They seemed to be afraid of the Bard, though they were playing him on their home grounds." Incensed by Hammond's mockery, one of the African drummers, whom Orson had hired to accompany the ranting of the three witches, assembled a voodoo doll to stand for the critic. After piercing the effigy with pins, he hung it symbolically. Asked what he was doing by Feder the lighting man, the African replied, "He's bad man." "How do you know?" said Feder. "He had a right to his opinion." "No," replied the African. "Bad man. Bad man. Voodoo." Earlier, over beer and pretzels in nearby Watson's Bar and Grill, the African drummer had discussed Percy Hammond with Orson, who, mostly to humor his earnest drinking companion whose gold teeth had diamonds in them, had agreed to his putting a curse on the critic. The African made one stipulation: the responsibility for Hammond's death would be Orson's alone. As a pretzel disappeared into his mouth, Orson nodded agreement. The rest of the company, Orson among them, watched with amusement as the voodoo practitioners blessed their drums before pounding on them backstage for several days. He barely gave it another thought until, shortly thereafter, he gasped to learn that Percy Hammond had just died.

As the African drums pounded Percy Hammond's life away, Orson's *Macbeth* had become among the most popular tickets in town and ran for nine packed weeks at the Lafayette. Suddenly everyone in New York seemed to have heard about Orson Welles, and wanted to see his spectacular new show. The Negro Theatre unit announced that on Monday nights home-reliefers would be admitted free until two-thirds of the house was filled, but on the first such evening there were 3,000 too many charity-playgoers waiting intently at the door, and the cops had to be called to turn them away. After Harlem, there followed a brief run at the Adelphi Theatre on West 54th Street, where a besotted Jack Carter had to be quickly replaced after he stormed out during

the intermission. His understudy was shorter and darker than
he, but expecting the unexpected many spectators interpreted this sudden shift as yet another of Orson Welles's
audacious devices about which they had read so much in
the press. If only they could figure out what it meant! Carter's breakdown appeared to have been precipitated by several scornful references to his acting in the reviews, such
as when *Variety* complained that he "seemed a bit too conscious of his handsome physique and a bit closer to the
Emperor Jones than Macbeth." Along these lines Brooks
Atkinson wrote in the *Times*: "As Macbeth, Jack Carter is
a fine figure of a Negro in tight-fitting trousers that do justice
to his anatomy. He has no command of poetry or character."
Having disappeared on a binge, Carter had to be permanently replaced when *Macbeth* embarked on a triumphant
4,000-mile tour that took the company as far as the Texas
Centennial Exposition in Dallas.

In Indianapolis, Carter's replacement fell ill only to be
replaced by Orson himself—"the only time anybody's ever
blacked up to play Macbeth!" Orson laughs. "I was a much
darker Macbeth than Jack was. I had to prove that I belonged." If no one in the audience recognized him, it was
because "they didn't know who I was. I was an anonymous
radio actor. This was a Negro *Macbeth*, so why was anybody
going to think I was passing? The cast thought it was very
funny. I think this has disappeared, but they had an expression in black show business, which is: instead of 'making
up,' you 'make down'—make yourself darker. So they said,
'There's Orson making down again!' " Back in New York
Orson declined an invitation from the British impresario
Charles Blake Cochran to bring his black *Macbeth* to London. He thought he had better capitalize on his great success
in New York right now, lest it disappear as abruptly as it
had been attained. Besides he was having too much fun in
Harlem, where, instead of being the pariah he once was,

he found himself welcomed and cheered wherever he went. "I had conquered Harlem!" says Orson. "I would go up two or three nights a week to Harlem, where I was the King. I really was the King!"

CHAPTER 11
The Magic Box

On May 15, 1936, Orson Welles was twenty-one. The summer before, when he began writing an essay titled "Now I Am 21," he could not have anticipated the wild success that would be his at that early age. While he summered in Wisconsin he had wondered how he was possibly going to support his wife and himself when they returned to New York, and whether he would ever really get the leading roles he longed for, let alone the chance to direct. Now at age twenty-one Orson was a highly paid radio actor, who frequently had to turn down lucrative on-the-air work because he could not fit it into his crowded schedule, as well as a critically acclaimed stage director whose likely next step was an independent production on Broadway. Hallie Flanagan knew that the producers were about to snap up young Welles if she did not quickly do something dramatic to keep him with the Federal Theatre. In a few months he had had far too much praise and publicity, he had become too *hot*, to be content with anything less than the big offer she braced herself to make. The federal government could afford to do what independent producers probably could not, and certainly would not. So instead of merely giving Orson another major production to direct, which was all he could really hope for from the independents, she gave him his own theater in New York, one of the great stage capitals of the world. Ironically, the Depression, and Roosevelt's efforts to allay the misery it caused, had made Orson's great good fortune possible. Less than a month after he had turned twenty-one, Orson was in possession of the personal showcase he privately liked to call his "magic box": the old Maxine Elliott's Theatre at 109 West 39th Street, where, with Houseman as his partner in charge of administration, he was to inaugurate the Federal Theatre's classical unit. It was the most glorious birthday present a young man could imagine.

The one thing Flanagan could not give Orson was a conventional company of actors, since prior Federal Theatre units had already engaged most of the reasonably desirable actors on the dole. No one else had wanted most of the people who flocked to Orson now when they heard he was hiring. They were, says Orson, "beaten by life." At times it seemed that only the dregs were left: surprisingly foul-mouthed old folks, has-beens, and never-was's, whose acting experience, when they had any, was often limited to circuses, burlesques, and honky-tonks. Instead of appalling Orson, they brought back happy memories of the show-business flotsam who used to drift in and out of Dick Welles's Hotel Sheffield when Orson was a boy. He felt right at home with them. Their age and general ill-fortune made his extreme youth and success even more obvious. He was a winner among losers, considerably younger than the youngest of them. But they didn't resent him. While there was great potential for discord between the impoverished old-timers and their kid director, from the first he won them over with the same innate respect he had felt for Dick's vaudeville drinking cronies. It would never have occurred to him to think or act otherwise. Through no fault of her own, Virginia Welles was not so easily accepted by certain of the impoverished actors, who regarded her with suspicion. "I think she got herself disliked by the less fortunate members of the relief group," Orson recalls. "That would have been inevitable because she exuded that thing that you do if you've gone to those schools, even if you don't have on a sweater and that chain of pearls they all had. You know, everybody was out there freezing, and here was this privileged creature." Not that Virginia hadn't sincerely tried to fit in with the group: "She threw herself into the life of the bohemian theater world," says Orson of her earnest attempt. "She wasn't being at all finishing school about it. She just couldn't help it. It was like bringing in Katharine Hepburn to *The Front Page*."

If Orson was not terribly worried about doing classic plays with his motley new company, it was because he knew he had a secret weapon: the ten percent nonrelief quota that allowed him to hire a handful of working actors, among them colleagues from the radio. "The backbone of the WPA was actors who really had money from other sources," says Orson. Some of the down-and-outers liked to buzz among themselves about the elegant attire Arlene Francis or Joseph Cotten wore to rehearsals. "Ah, relief-orchids I see you're wearing!" one of them teased Miss Francis about the expensive flowers pinned to her dress. Nor did Joseph Cotten's beautiful chamois gloves go unnoticed. But Orson hadn't hired these actors for their pretty clothes. "By bringing in Arlene Francis, Joe Cotten, and Chubby Sherman," he explains, "we had what looked like a company of actors." He had gone without much sleep during *Macbeth*, but he seemed even busier now, what with a whole new theater to organize, abundant radio work that sometimes took him as far afield as Chicago, and even a leading role in Sidney Kingsley's new play, *Ten Million Ghosts*, set to open in October at the St. James Theatre. Why he had accepted a Broadway lead in the middle of his myriad other responsibilities, and how he was possibly going to handle it all, kept everyone guessing. What New York didn't know was that since earliest

childhood Orson had felt compelled to live up to whatever
marvelous things people said about him. Called a genius,
he struggled to prove that indeed he was one. Now, in New
York, they called him "Wonder Boy Welles," and he would
go to any lengths, even drive himself to the brink of exhaustion, not to disappoint them. Fueled by his sudden
success, high on power and publicity, he discovered that
the more he did the more energy he seemed to have.

Although his new theater was to be the Federal Theatre's
classical unit, Orson decided that calling it by that name
might attract too stodgy an audience, entirely inappropriate
for his audacious directorial image. A proponent of theater
as a "popular art," Orson wanted to appeal to what he called
"a democracy of an audience" that encompassed the city's
rich and poor (the *everybody* of *Everybody's Shakespeare*).
Any name with *classical* in it seemed to him to have elitist
connotations, so that at length he and Houseman settled on
a name without any connotations at all: Project 891—the
new unit's government project number. Of their decision
Orson told the *World Telegram*: "No sooner would you open
a Classical Theater than what public you might have would
be sure that they were going to have a feast of Ibsen and
Shakespeare. That would provide you with a self-conscious
theater full of self-conscious actors, impressed with revering
the immortal bard. Damn—he's immortal only as long as
people want to see him! That's why we call it '891 Presents'
and are opening the season with a farce."

The farce was *Horse Eats Hat*, which he and poet Edwin
Denby had very freely adapted from Eugène Labiche's *The
Italian Straw Hat*. Orson thought it wise to make the second
play he directed in New York even more unusual and outrageous than the black *Macbeth* had been. This time, the
springboard of the action was a silly little story. Freddy
(Joseph Cotten) is on his way to his wedding when his horse
munches Agatha's (Paula Laurence) straw hat. Evidently
Agatha has been cheating on her husband and fears he will

find out if she comes home without her hat. So the prospective bridegroom sets out in search of a replacement, thereby keeping his bride (Virginia Welles) waiting. Sounds simple—but the ensuing action was every bit as intricate as Orson's schedule. Orson's staging of *Horse Eats Hat* had the action constantly spilling off the stage—beyond the frame of the play—into the audience. Nor did the action let up during intermissions, when by convention, a play stops. During these interludes, an actress dressed in white jodhpurs and a military coat played a trumpet from one of the balcony boxes, while in another, actor Bil Baird seemed to pound out a tune on a player piano. Certainly the audience knew that all this was no more real than the play. What followed was more ambiguous: Baird recalls that he would climb onto the piano, ostensibly to fix it, then would pretend to fall off, grasping the balcony rail as if to save himself from plunging into the audience, some of whom were greatly alarmed. Another mock-accident had the set collapsing to disclose a presumably startled actor in his underwear. "Orson would have had him naked if he could," says Baird. All of which—the flamboyant intermissions, the active audiences, the mock-accidents—had the effect of wearing away the borders of the artistic space in a way that, more and more, Orson would like to do. Having been required in boyhood always to be entertaining, to be *on*, as an adult Orson was instinctively drawn to those theatrical moments when people were unsure whether he or his actors were on or off. Every now and again even Orson appeared uncertain whether the action was staged or real. In the play Bil Baird in a sailor suit and yellow wig did a routine as an obnoxious schoolboy who kept bumping into everyone, until Orson, as Mugglethorpe, the father of the bride, socked him, at which Baird would go into a backward flip. One night, however, Orson got carried away with his role and really socked him as hard as he could—or so it seemed to Baird. "He loses his mind in a case like that," laughs Baird. "That's *very Orson*!" Had Welles really forgotten himself, or did he just want the other actor to think he had? Afterward, backstage, a furious Baird inquired why Orson had pounded him like that. "He didn't remember," Baird says. "At least he pretended he didn't."

Since Orson's earliest formative directorial experience was with the WPA, he quickly became accustomed to the abundant manpower these work-relief productions encouraged him to use to get as many individuals as possible off the dole. But this was an expensive habit that would prove troublesome later on, when the government wasn't footing the bills. Not that, even in the early days, Orson wasn't pouring plenty of his own money into the production: something he would also find himself doing in the movies. Much too impatient, and too busy, to fill out requisitions when he needed props, he would take the cash out of his pocket and send someone to buy what he needed. Nor would he get his money back later. "The whole time I was at the WPA I never collected a dime because you had to go stand in line," Orson explains. "I'm the only man who ever dishonestly put money into a government project!"

When at last it opened on September 26, 1936, *Horse Eats Hat*—and the new theater it inaugurated—was the startling, controversial event Orson had hoped for. People either loved it or hated it, but either way they were talking about Wonder Boy Welles, who had unquestionably established himself as a provocative force in the New York theatrical world. "It was as though Gertrude Stein had dreamed a dream after a late supper of pickles and ice cream, the ensuing revelations being crisply acted by giants and midgets, caricatures, lunatics and a prop nag," said *The New York Times*. Wrote the *World Telegram*: "Adaptors Edwin Denby and Orson Welles must have had a riotous time rejuvenating the whirligig and it is of a certainty that spectators will have an equally mirthful time digesting it." Even those who despised what they saw had to admit that they had never seen anything quite like it before: "The WPA must have the satisfaction of knowing that, whatever *Horse Eats Hat* may be, it is the only one there is of it," sighed the bewildered *Daily News*. By emphasizing the unprecedented strangeness of the event, even the bad reviews sold tickets. Quite a few first-nighters adored the show so much that they came back to see it night after night; from the audience, they recited the nutty lines with the actors.

Having made a commitment to appear in Sidney Kingsley's *Ten Million Ghosts*, for which Kingsley's assistant Martin Gabel had recommended him, Orson briefly took off from *Horse Eats Hat*. By now, however, like everyone else in town he was wondering why he had agreed to do the show in the first place. Having been the sovereign boss of his own theater, he was suddenly again a young actor in another man's show. It was a most unfortunate interlude. "He didn't like anybody directing him," says Gabel of Orson's overt antipathy toward Kingsley. "He couldn't stand the idea of Kingsley's telling him what to do." So unenthusiastic was he about *Ten Million Ghosts*, and so exhausted from his many commitments, that on opening night, October 23, 1936, at the St. James Theatre, when he made his entrance as a wounded soldier on a stretcher, Orson actually dozed off onstage for a few moments. The audience may have been sleeping too, for no sooner had the play opened than it shut down, and Orson was back in *Horse Eats Hat*, having been replaced in the interim by an ex–Todd Trouper.

When he had been off working on Kingsley's play a small scandal erupted at Project 891, when Washington moved to censor salacious portions of *Horse Eats Hat*. Some of the reviews had voiced their outrage at the evening's pronounced bawdiness. Charged Hearst's *New York American*: "An outmoded farce has been garnished with sewage in apparent attempt to appeal to devotees of filthy drama sufficiently to overcome the stupidity of plot and ineptness of production." But the real trouble began when the very offended wife of a high-ranking government official put her husband up to trying to close the play on moral grounds. Instead, the WPA sent a representative to report on possible improprieties of language or action. These included the lines "It's nice to see a pretty little pussy" (spoken to a maid who has just "tossed her skirts behind her"); "girls don't belong in the bushes with horse-marines" (which remark of Joseph Cotten's the WPA found "definitely suggestive"); "My woolens are so wet" (uttered by a sentry who—the government noted with alarm—places "his hands on that portion of his anatomy which might be responsible for such a condition"); "He told me our love was like a gorgeous volcano. . . . Then he left me in the ladies' room," exclaimed by Arlene Francis, to which Joseph Cotten responded, "What's the matter? Weren't you comfortable?" ("These are unmistakably suggestive lines," pronounced the report); and Virginia Welles's "I can't stand it; I've got to sit down," to which Orson replied, "Not in the street" ("Obviously she refers to her state of fatigue," judged Uncle Sam, "but— the audience chooses to make something else of it"). That certain "vulgar members of the audience" might be placing "a soiled construction" on actually quite innocent lines the government did not deny. But since "it only requires the laughter of a very few to infect the audience," all double entendres were to be eliminated immediately.

As censorship goes, Washington's annoying demands were relatively insignificant, and easily accommodated. But they presaged the far more serious governmental intervention that Orson and his company were to experience in the very near future.

CHAPTER 12
Wild Camp

He was daring, bold, provocative—after the black *Macbeth* and *Horse Eats Hat* there was no question of it. But one question remained. Was he merely naughty? A young rebel whose audacities would soon grow mannered and tiresome? Even before *Horse Eats Hat* was finished, Orson calculated that his next production had to do more than shock. He needed to show himself a master craftsman, a virtuoso, a wizard. From the first, having thought of Project 891 as his "magic box," Orson decided that now was the time to pull out all his tricks, to demonstrate a bit of the conjurer's exquisite art—hence his idea of following *Horse Eats Hat* with Christopher Marlowe's classic drama of black magic, *Doctor Faustus*, in which Orson would play the title role. Orson enlisted the prodigious Abe Feder to design an intricate—and unprecedented—lighting scheme whereby shafts of sheer light made actors seem inexplicably to appear, then disappear amid the prevailing gloom of a bare stage draped all in black velvet. Besides this, there were to be assorted trapdoors into which actors might suddenly slip away, as well as two black cones, each six feet in diameter, suspended from ropes above the stage, which could be lowered or raised, rapidly and invisibly, to conceal or reveal actors.

Next Orson ordered a platform stage that extended out into the auditorium. Although this design concept harked back to the Elizabethans, Orson chose it not for its historical connotations, however appropriate they might have been, but for the fact that the actors were surrounded on three sides by spectators, which allowed the cast blatantly to acknowledge the spectators, and, even more, to confront them. To add nervous energy to the dramatic encounter between actor and audience, Orson took the chance of casting the fiery Jack Carter as Mephistophilis: tempter and seducer. Given his prior experience with the alcoholic actor, people thought Orson mad even to consider hiring Carter again. But despite the basically negative reviews Carter had had in *Macbeth*, Orson always thought he had been quite marvelous in it. As far as Carter's drinking was concerned, Orson thought the electric excitement he would inevitably bring to the show well worth the risk. "We kept him in our little apartment on 14th Street for ten days before the opening to keep him from going on a binge or doing something Barrymoresque," says Orson, who could not have avoided thinking that if he had treated his alcoholic father as sensitively as he did Carter, Dick Welles's life might not have ended as badly as it did.

When Carter got there, the atmosphere on 14th Street was anything but restful. Orson and Virginia were so frantically busy keeping his career going that, although they could easily have afforded to move, they just hadn't had the time. Every now and again, Leo Nicolson came to town, where, confused by the modesty of their basement apartment, he frequently slipped Virginia "household money," which, in turn, she hid in a crack in the wall behind his picture. Still dismayed by his theatrical son-in-law, Nicolson would take Virginia out for a steak since he feared his slender daughter wasn't eating properly. Although the apartment was rather cramped even for just Orson and Virginia, there were frequent houseguests staying for extended periods. The actress Paula Laurence (set to play Helen in *Faustus*) had been in residence for a while, and now there was the flamboyant would-be impresario Francis Carpenter, who, when his hosts were at the theater, would grandly answer the telephone, "Orson Welles's residence—this is Francis Carpenter the maid speaking!" Once the Welleses returned from a rehearsal to find Francis lamenting over a tiny pile of ashes on the floor. Gazing up at them with a great show of anguish—Francis was a man of the theater, after all—he disclosed that there had just been a terrible fire in which Virginia's mink stole (the one Orson had gotten her at Saks for Christmas) had burned. The ashes before him were all that remained of it. Checking the closet, from which the fur was indeed missing, Orson carefully inspected the purported remains while Francis attempted to console Virginia. Close up, Orson could easily see that the ashes were really a pile of burnt paper. "Okay, Francis, give me the pawn ticket," said Orson matter-of-factly, after which the three of them went to retrieve the stole.

Despite all this madness at the Welleses', Carter managed to stay remarkably tranquil. When *Doctor Faustus* opened at Maxine Elliott's Theatre on January 8, 1937, he was in fine form, and he lasted that way throughout its immensely successful run. Opening night was every bit the unqualified artistic triumph Orson had wanted. Next morning in the papers there was one rave review after another. In the *Times*, Brooks Atkinson hailed *Faustus* as "a brilliantly original production." "The play is produced with arresting originality," wrote Richard Lockridge in the *Sun*. Returning to the topic some days later when *Faustus* was regularly playing to standing-room-only audiences, Brooks Atkinson called it the Federal Theatre's "principal artistic achievement." As for Orson, the recipient of all this incredible praise was *still* only twenty-one! Since returning to New York in the broken-down thirty-five-dollar Essex that he and Virginia had abandoned in the garage at the Waldorf, Orson Welles had directed three major New York stage productions, each one more successful than the last. But this latest triumph was clearly the most gratifying of all because of the utmost seriousness with which *Faustus* was uniformly regarded. "The world was treating me so well that I was like somebody at his own birthday party!" says Orson.

Faustus had an unusually late curtain—at nine p.m.—because Orson had a twice-weekly radio commitment at eight p.m. In full *Faustus* makeup Orson arrived at the radio station to do the program live before a studio audience—for whom he was required to wear a dinner jacket. Finishing moments before nine, he scurried downstairs to a waiting cab that sped him to the Maxine Elliott, where the curtain was just rising on the chorus, who would occupy the stage till Orson appeared, having traded his dinner jacket for the proper sixteenth-century getup. At eleven o'clock when the curtain fell, and everybody else went home, Orson sped back to the radio studio to do a rebroadcast for the Pacific Coast. In addition to his evening radio spots, he had so many on-the-air commitments during the day that he often did not know in advance what part he was going to be called upon to play. "They'd open the door just as the music was starting," recalls Orson. "They'd say 'eighty-year-old Chinaman'; they'd hand me a script, and I'd do it." Baffled by Orson's uncanny ability to perform a role he hadn't rehearsed, the radio personnel didn't know that getting there late and without preparation immensely appealed to Orson's innermost sense of theatricality. It was precisely the risk, the vertigo of it all that got his juices going—and the risk was made more exciting when he took to riding screeching ambulances between radio engagements. "There's no law against using an ambulance if you're not sick," insists Orson today, "in those days anyway."

His great triumph in *Faustus* was followed by an enviable series of offers—or birthday presents, as Orson thought of them: his first radio directing assignment; the leading role in a radio drama, *The Shadow*; a movie contract with Warner Brothers. He accepted the first two offers. That February he directed a condensed version of *Macbeth* on the air, and in March he put in his first radio appearance as Lamont Cranston, alias The Shadow. Thus Orson was introduced weekly on the exceedingly popular radio drama: "The Shadow, Lamont Cranston, a man of wealth, a student of science, and a master of other people's minds, devotes his life to righting wrongs, protecting the innocent, and punishing the guilty. Using advanced methods that may ultimately become available to all law-enforcement agencies, Cranston is known to the underworld as the Shadow—never seen, only heard, as haunting to superstitious minds as a ghost, as inevitable as a guilty conscience." In May, Orson would negotiate with Warner Brothers, who wanted him to come to Hollywood to act in the movies. But although the studio was willing to let Orson return regularly to work on the Broadway stage, it would not agree to the $2,500 weekly salary he demanded if he were to give up the wonderful life he had in New York.

Orson and Virginia had finally moved to a country house with a swimming pool in Snedens Landing on the Hudson. To get into town he would take a motorboat across the river to a waiting chauffeur-driven Rolls Royce limousine. Consciously modeling himself on his playboy father, who, Orson says "never shaved himself in his life," Orson went for a daily shave and manicure before lunch at the swank Manhattan restaurant "21": "I found this wonderful barber at the top of '21'—used to be a very gay sporting crowd there in the morning—and he would put the hot towel on and shave me, and the girl would do my nails. I tell you, I was a dude!" When he lunched at "21" Orson rarely ate very much because he was taking what he describes as "great pains" to starve himself down to an unnatural slenderness—and before long he had indeed lost weight so that his clothes hung very loose. "I hadn't time to get new suits!" laughs Orson about his clothes, which had actually been fashionably baggy in the first place. "That was the day when the style of trousers was very nice for people with fat thighs, you know!"

By deliberately copying the style of Alfred Lunt, Orson affected a manner of behavior he describes as "wild camp." "Well," says Orson, "I see myself in those old stills, and I see somebody that could very easily be thought of as a faggot." Orson points out that this very same camp style was adopted by, among others, Jack Benny and Bob Hope. "I looked just exactly like Bob Hope," he recalls of the image he cultivated. "You just put Hope's nose on. We were so similar you can't believe it. We walked the same way and everything. It's all camp—like Alfred Lunt, who was as normal as anybody." Of Lunt's camp mannerisms Orson says: "You'd swear he was a homosexual—and it was all that great camp style. Those great long takes, those thoughtful moments, give it the flavor of camp, you know, which was hysterical. Lunt was the master of that! He was one of the best actors we ever had! He moved on the stage more beautifully than any actor I've ever seen—and also with a Benny-ish languor. He had that same quality of walking under water."

But if on account of his newly, and quite self-consciously, acquired camp style, people were whispering that Orson Welles had become a homosexual, the truth was that he had embarked on his first extramarital affair. The woman in question was a beautiful ballerina older than he. Orson's predecessor for her affections had been George Balanchine.

As it turned out, she was only the first of several dancers with whom Orson was to conduct affairs. "This was my period of ballerinas," he laughs, "and none of them were a disappointment. I may have gravely disappointed them, but they certainly didn't disappoint me. I got terribly interested in ballerinas. I didn't consciously go out to collect them, but life just worked out that way." When he made love to the first of his ballerinas, he discovered the unmatched beauty of the dancer's body, "which I found terribly erotic suddenly," says Orson. "I had never noticed those calves before!" Although he was still very much married to Virginia, the move to Snedens Landing, where she spent a great deal of time, made him considerably more independent of her. Orson points out that as teenagers he and Virginia had married in haste without necessarily viewing their marriage as a life-long commitment. Now his great celebrity after *Faustus* had presented him with far too many irresistible temptations, among them the beautiful ballerina with whom he began openly meeting for lunch at the Colony. Throughout the affair he continued to go home at night, where he fondly recalls lying naked on the floor so that Virginia could walk on his tired back.

Orson reports getting away for his "first adulterous weekend" by telling his wife "a big lie about going to Washington." As smoothly as it all seemed to be going, however, he approached his rendezvous with what he describes as "enormous guilt." It was Orson's supreme misfortune that in the hotel room just as he and the danseuse were about to have a go at it, he suddenly heard all too familiar words issuing from the radio: "Who knows what evil lurks in the hearts of men? The Shadow knows!" Today Orson can laugh heartily about what was then a debilitating experience. "Imagine what it did!" he says of suddenly hearing another voice delivering his famous line, especially when he was feeling so unspeakably guilty in the first place.

He adds ruefully that "the impotence lasted for one night."

Having strayed from his marriage, Orson was also seriously considering abandoning Houseman and the Federal Theatre. In May it was reported in the press that the eminent producer Arthur Hopkins, who had been a driving force behind John Barrymore, had offered to back Orson's production of *King Lear*. Orson's weariness with the red tape and bureaucracy he constantly encountered in the Federal Theatre made the idea of independent financing seem very attractive. The Federal Theatre already resented Orson's making his own artistic decisions without consulting them, and his pouring $1,000 a week or more of his own radio money into the shows only made him more independent. As long as he was being hailed as the star of the Federal Theatre they wanted to be certain they knew his every move. A man who didn't fill out forms or stand in line might be dangerous. They regarded him as a runaway horse. But Orson could not see what all the fuss was about. He was far too busy, and enjoying himself far too much, working and playing, to waste time at meetings of government bureaucrats. These he left to Houseman, who seemed intent on keeping the peace with Hallie Flanagan. "He was always busy patching things up," Orson recalls of Houseman, "and I could never understand what the hell had to be patched up!" Orson figured that the Federal Theatre should, and would, be happy that he was putting on one hit play after another—and still didn't entirely understand that his extreme success was precisely why Hallie Flanagan and the other bureaucrats wanted to watch him so carefully. Another reason Orson was resistant to dealing with them was that, of late, he had been operating on a much higher level of government. WPA head Harry Hopkins had befriended him backstage after a performance of *Horse Eats Hat*. Since then, Orson had quietly visited Hopkins in Washington, where he had met and been a guest of President Roosevelt.

With an eye toward his future, Orson kept his meetings with Hopkins and Roosevelt a secret from Houseman and the others at the WPA. Better to keep his connections in Washington for himself should he ever think about a political career. At this point after so much swift success, anything, any dream, seemed possible.

"The one thing I find, digging into my memory, is how lighthearted I was in that period, and how blithe," says Orson. He and Virginia liked to entertain at Snedens Landing, where the new friends celebrity had brought him gathered for "weenie roasts" and swimming. One weekend he and his chum, screenwriter Charles MacArthur, the husband of Helen Hayes, had been joking about which of Orson's elegant and sophisticated guests secretly urinated in his swimming pool. They soon devised a wicked plan to embarrass any who did. "Charles MacArthur and I found a chemist who had developed a liquid, a clear, colorless liquid, which if put in the pool immediately detected urine when anybody would pee. We put this stuff in and we invited our friends out, naturally, at the weekend, and they were swimming around in raspberry-colored clouds. They were *all* doing it, you see!" Instead of being absolutely mortifed, however, the people who had been caught in the act let loose with "howls of laughter" when the water turned color. "We discovered during our scientific investigation that it was overwhelmingly the men who did it," Orson points out, "and women of advanced years—but we put that down to weak kidneys." But if his friends thought the whole thing very funny, Orson was appalled by the "awful revelation" that so many people he knew and respected habitually peed in his pool. "I spread a rumor that I had two rattlesnakes and a water moccasin in the vicinity, and that until we got them killed, nobody was to go in. In fact, I had two rattlesnakes under the house and a water moccasin that used to get into the pool at night. I'd find myself swimming in the moonlight next to a water moccasin. But that was better than the pee." As for their revealing little experiment, Orson and MacArthur soon desisted. "My wife made me stop it," Orson recalls, "and Helen Hayes made Charles MacArthur stop."

"It was lovely talking to you," Orson laughs, "I'm glad to have passed on some health advice." His telling me the story of his and Charlie MacArthur's prank on their less than fastidious friends has launched Orson on a mock-serious speech in which he sternly warns me of the ever-lurking hazard of finding myself in a pool tainted by a stranger's urine. I must be ever-vigilant, he says—for he knows that we share a fondness for swimming. "I will not swim in public swimming pools because I have a mania about people peeing in the pool," he tells me—which, after the Sneden's Landing story, seems less paranoid than it would have otherwise. "Now I know that everybody pees in a pool," he continues. "I won't go into a pool unless it's my own."

"People you knew?" I ask him incredulously.

"Oh," Orson assures me, "but the nicest, cleanest, most respectable people—and there it'd be suddenly surrounded with clouds of raspberry-colored juice. That shows you must never swim in a public pool, much less a private pool. I don't let anybody swim in my pool. I just cannot bear to swim around in somebody's pee."

"*That I can understand,*" *I say,* "*I just never thought about it very much.*"

Not thought about it? Orson is appalled. "*They do it in the pool because it's so comforting,*" *he patiently explains, as if lecturing a hygiene class.* "*And the damnedest people do it. Your trusted clean friends.*"

"*I'm thinking that I must have been swimming in pools of pee for my entire life,*" *I giggle.*

"*You have,*" *Orson says triumphantly.* "*The change of temperature tends to bring on a need to go to the little room. And instead of getting out and doing it, the people just say, 'Well, just this once.'*"

But how can I know when someone nearby is peeing in the pool?

"*I know that faraway look which men get when they're peeing,*" *Orson explains with absolute authority.* "*If you ever watched them in the old days, when the* pissoirs *gave you an opportunity to watch the play of expression as you walked down the street: it's a sort of terrible dreamy expression that comes over men's faces when they're peeing.*" *He pauses, apparently to give me time to search my memory for a familiar male face covered with the tell-tale dreamy expression.* "*And when you see that in a pool, you know, it's most unnerving,*" *Orson continues.*

"*Now,*" *I sigh,* "*forever in a pool I'll be watching everyone's face. I won't get any swimming done.*"

"*I have now cut you off forever from the swimming pool in the hotel,*" *says Orson, who knows how much I like to swim in hotel pools when I'm traveling.* "*I'm sorry I did it. But I think it's for your own good, dear.*"

By now I'm used to Orson's advice. He is a wealth of it—though not always in the areas one expects. For instance, he has also advised me on traveling with a bad back, since in addition to our common pleasure in swimming, we have similar chronic back problems. "*When I*

don't have my bed," Orson says, referring to the adjustable
hospital bed he adores, *"I travel with two suitcases of pillows. I can't sleep without them."* Orson isn't kidding. A
friend of mine who once saw Orson checking out of a hotel
assumed that the suitcases—to accommodate which an additional taxi had to be hired to go to the airport—must
certainly contain an extensive wardrobe. I didn't have the
energy to explain that, no, there were pillows inside.

Another Orson must: extra-spacious tables in restaurants, even if he is dining alone. *"You know I always ask
for a table for at least one more than will be in the party"*
says Orson. *"In other words, if there are three people, ask
for a table for five, you know."* But why? I am obviously
wondering. *"So you have a better table,"* he says, appalled
at my lack of Orsonian savoir-faire. *"If it's for two,"* he
says, patiently instructing me now, *"never admit that. It's*
always three or four. You get one of those little tiny tables
for two otherwise. Then you do the whole thing about 'Do
you think she's coming? Well, never mind, let's go ahead.'
It works wonderfully!"*

All of this advice is lavished upon me on an evening when
both Roger "Skipper" Hill and I are in Los Angeles to see
Orson, who isn't feeling his best and decides to send us off
for dinner together at Chasen's. Even if Orson won't be
joining us, he wants to be absolutely certain that we don't
have to suffer the humiliation of a mere table for two. To
protect us, he knows that he'd better call Chasen's himself
lest our nerve fail us and we admit that there will be only
two of us. *"I'll make the reservation,"* Orson announces,
*"and pretend that I'll be there so you'll have a good table.
Then you say, 'Mr. Welles should be here pretty soon.' And
then after you've had your opening drink, you say, 'Well,
we won't wait for him,' and you order, you see."*

More appealing than the idea of a good table, I love the
idea of Orson's giving Skipper Hill and me our lines.

"Say, 'Mr. Welles's table,' " Orson runs through it once

more with me before retiring, "and then if I'm awake I'll even call up. Otherwise you wait ten minutes and say, 'He told us that if he couldn't get in from the airport, we should go ahead and eat.' "

"Okay," I say.

"It works wonderfully," Orson assures me, in case I'm nervous.

"We'll do the Orson Welles lines," I say confidently.

"Roger, of course," says Orson of his boyhood mentor, "will give it all away with some loud *remark that will ruin—"*

"No," I cut in, "Roger will not say anything. I'll do the line. Tell Roger he can't do the line."

"You see," Orson laughs, "he's got this terrible streak of honesty. It's not very broad, but it's there."

After dinner at Chasen's—where indeed Skipper and I had a large, well-positioned table—I drive back to my hotel, laughing about the moment when Roger began exuberantly reciting the Orson Welles *lines to the waiter, and I seriously feared he might be overcome by an honesty attack and reveal that Mr. Welles wasn't* really *on his way. But no, we brought it off perfectly, just as Orson advised us. It has been a long, full day. As I pull the car into the driveway, I ponder taking a refreshing swim in the hotel pool, but remembering Orson's other sage advice, decide it is best to go straight to bed.*

CHAPTER 13

Saint
of the Barricades

During the run of *Horse Eats Hat*, a handsome, dark-haired, brilliant young man in his early thirties, named Marc Blitzstein, had visited Orson backstage to show him the score of what he described as his "labor opera." Would Orson be interested in directing *The Cradle Will Rock* for the radical Actors' Repertory Company? From the time of their first meeting, Orson found Blitzstein irresistible. "He was almost a saint," Orson recalls. "He was so totally and serenely convinced of the Eden which was waiting for us all on the other side of the Revolution that there was no way of talking politics to him. He didn't care who was in the Senate, or what Mr. Roosevelt said—*he* was just the spokesman for the bourgeoisie!" Until now Orson had been disgusted by what struck him as the phony political rhetoric of most of the left-wing intellectuals he had encountered in New York. But Blitzstein wasn't like that. "He wasn't a finger-wagger," says Orson. "When he came into the room the lights got brighter." Even if by instinct Orson didn't share his radical politics, he was absolutely charmed by Blitzstein's sincerity and single-mindedness. "He was an engine," Orson recalls, "a rocket, directed in one direction, which was his opera— which he almost believed had only to be performed to start the Revolution. You can't imagine how simple he was about it. They were going to hear it, and that would be it!" As far as Orson could determine at the time, Blitzstein's belief in the coming revolution, and his role in it, was unshakable. "He had been 'converted,' " says Orson, "and he was like one of those little gray friars hopping around after St. Francis had spoken." Although he was preoccupied with his own "magic box," the newly formed Project 891, Orson found himself so personally taken with Blitzstein, and so delighted by *Cradle*'s marvelous score, that at length he agreed to direct the opera for the other company.

As it happened, however, the Actors' Repertory Company did not have the money to do the show, and Blitzstein had to wait until after the triumph of *Faustus*, when Project 891 announced *Cradle* as its next production. In the meantime, Orson briefly staged Aaron Copland's children's opera *Second Hurricane* at the Henry Street Settlement House; that production only whetted his appetite for doing an opera on the grand scale he envisioned for *Cradle*. While he knew that Blitzstein wanted to do his labor opera in a spare agit-prop style that would put across his political message as directly and emphatically as possible, Orson wanted to stage it as a flashy Broadway show. Since he anticipated that Blitzstein would almost certainly balk at the idea of Orson's transforming *Cradle* into a Broadway extravaganza, Orson was prepared to argue that only by doing so could they get people to take the show seriously rather than write it off as merely a left-wing exercise. When they met to discuss the production Orson told Blitzstein that he could mount it in one of two ways. The first was to commission a primitive painter he knew in Havana to design modest backdrops on canvas. While that sort of staging might satisfy a few leftists and intellectuals who already sympathized with Blitzstein's politics anyway, it would certainly not attract the kind of broad and diversified audience that "a big Broadway smash hit" would. However decadent and distasteful it might at first seem to him, a lavish and spectacular production would best serve his purposes by enabling him to communicate with large numbers of people.

When he had finally sold Blitzstein on the concept of a flashy Broadway show, Orson secretly wondered about his own motives. Was he really trying to serve Blitzstein's labor opera as he said, and hoped, he was, or was he merely manipulating his friend to serve his own career? In his heart Orson wasn't sure. As a political progressive he very strongly concurred with *Cradle*'s pro-union sentiments, but he was not eagerly awaiting the revolution Blitzstein envisioned. It had been Blitzstein's brilliance and refreshing sincerity that had attracted Orson to him in the first place. Now, pretending to have been politicized by Blitzstein, Orson sometimes found himself being insincere, professing revolutionary principals he didn't believe in. "I was only radical because I was showing off," Orson reflects. "I've never been anything more than a progressive. I allowed myself to be thought of as farther to the left than I was because I didn't want to lose his friendship."

Their relationship took a curious new twist when, at Orson's invitation, Blitzstein regularly began accompanying him to "21" and other fashionable spots where the Revolution, if it ever came, was unlikely to be greeted with much enthusiasm. Orson wondered whether he was somehow trying to "tempt" his friend with celebrity and glamour. Was his purpose, as he mostly told himself it was, to keep Blitzstein in tune with his plans for a lavish production, or, as he sometimes feared, did he merely wish to see if the "saint of the barricades" could be led astray? One evening the two were waiting for the limousine to take them to the motorboat to Snedens Landing, where Virginia had invited Blitzstein to stay during the show's incubation. Orson said to Blitzstein, "You think you'll have all this after your revolution?" "Everybody will have it," Blitzstein replied serenely.

Orson's friendship with Blitzstein caused further tension

with Houseman, who, in *Run-Through*, speaks of his "ill-concealed sense of rejection" at Orson's excitement about *Cradle*. "He and Virgil were in a huff because of this marriage between Marc and myself," says Orson of Houseman and his oft-quoted roommate Virgil Thomson. Virginia's having invited Blitzstein to stay with them only made matters worse because the Welleses had never really included Houseman in their new social set in Sneden's Landing. Orson's money and celebrity had already put an immense distance between him and Houseman that caused discomfort on both sides. Now, Blitzstein's creative and personal involvement with Orson made it all too painfully obvious that Houseman was limited to a useful, but strictly bureaucratic, role in Orson's productions.

Orson planned temporarily to shut down *Doctor Faustus* on May 29, while he staged what he had promised Blitzstein would be a "magical production" of *Cradle* that was, as he described it, "full of metal and glass and the horror of Steeltown." When *Cradle* opened, if indeed it was the "hot ticket" he assured Blitzstein it would be, he would run it in repertory with *Doctor Faustus*—each for a week at a time. That May Orson turned twenty-two. Although he was exhilarated by the idea of there being two Orson Welles productions running in New York, he quickly came to think of *Cradle* as not his so much as Blitzstein's show. "It really belonged to Marc," says Orson. If at first perhaps there had been a bit of cynicism involved in his having sold Blitzstein on a big flashy show, now he saw himself as seriously working toward making Blitzstein's personal triumph as great as it could possibly be. "I really did love him very much," says Orson.

Not long after Orson had begun work on *Cradle*—for which late-night rehearsals would sometimes go on till four a.m.—his plans became a subject of great controversy in Washington. This time the government was worried about something far more serious than naughty words or sexual innuendos. *Cradle*'s theme, the unionization of the steel industry, was a particularly sensitive issue then. At Tom Girdler's Republic Steel plant in Chicago, police had opened fire on strikers, killing ten of them, seven of whom had been shot in the back. The Wagner Act, initiated by New York's Senator Robert Wagner, had prohibited blatant union-busting, and gave workers new hope in their struggle to organize for decent wages and conditions. But while giants like U.S. Steel bowed to unionization, holdouts like Girdler at Republic stubbornly resisted with lockouts, strikebreakers, and violence against unarmed strikers. That the government was paying for a bunch of radical New Yorkers to stage a pro-union extravaganza was intolerable to the conservative steel industry's management, who had never thought much of the WPA anyway, and who were determined to put a stop to the offensive show at any cost. Their resentment reflected the more general suspicion among conservative elements in Washington that the Federal Theatre had been designed expressly as a medium of propaganda for the radical social and economic ideas of the Roosevelt administration. In the Congress, Southern Democrats had teamed up with Republicans to cut back government cash for the WPA, thereby panicking work-reliefers in the Federal Theatre who feared that they would be among the twenty-five percent slated to get the boot. They reacted with sitdowns, pickets, and other forms of protest, but none of these tactics were terribly effective against the conservative congressmen, who were determined at once to weaken the work-relief programs and to constrain what they perceived as the militant elements in the Federal Theatre.

Congress may have been sensitive to the concerns of the steel barons, but the government was hesitant to censor *Cradle* overtly. That would cause far too much public furor, something Washington wished to avoid in the face of the mounting public protests with regard to the general WPA cuts. When on June 11, 1937, Hallie Flanagan was curtly notified that because of impending budget cuts and the attendant reshuffling of the WPA, no new shows were to be opened until the start of the government's next fiscal year in July, it was actually Washington's way of forestalling the opening of *Cradle* without seeming to have censored it.

Orson was in a quandary about what, if anything, to do in response. Although his marriage to Virginia had been rather precarious lately, he knew that she had his best interests at heart when she counseled him against going ahead with the production. Suddenly it seemed to Orson that she had grown up far more than he, and that her judgment was wiser, steadier. Although she was personally devoted to Blitzstein, she recognized that his dreams of revolution had nothing whatsoever to do with what Orson wanted in life. She didn't want to see Orson lose his beloved theater, or his chances for future success, over revolutionary ideals he didn't really believe in. Orson recognized that part of her antipathy toward the political radicalism he had been halfheartedly professing was based on her viewing it as an attack on the privileged social class from which she came, and with which she continued to identify. Slightly embarrassed about not having been so honest himself, he greatly respected her for her forthrightness. "She didn't become a bohemian," he recalls. "She kept her persona with her pearls around the nice sweater and all that. That was part of her great charm to me. If she'd turned into a little bit of Greenwich Village, I would have been horrified. She stayed true to herself." In the midst of this crisis, he felt renewed affection for her.

Not wanting unnecessarily to jeopardize his theater, or, even more, to hurt the work-reliefers who depended on its existence (Orson could always work elsewhere—they probably could not), he was basically inclined to obey the orders from Washington if he couldn't somehow persuade the government to change its mind. To fine-tune his show, Orson had previously put off the opening from June 15 to June

21, but previews were scheduled to start June 16. Approximately 18,000 tickets had been sold already, mainly to theater parties of assorted leftist groups who used the outings to raise funds. Hoping that word of the show's splendor might save the production, Orson announced that on June 14, Project 891 would mount a special invitational preview for assorted New York notables. In the innocence of his good intentions, it did not seem to occur to Orson that the steel barons and their sympathizers who had worked so hard to shut down his show were most unlikely to be moved to change their minds now by, say, the plaudits of the critic of the Communist *Daily Worker*.

The day after the invitational preview, guards officially sealed Maxine Elliott's Theatre to eliminate the possibility of Orson's violating the government ban. What Washington did not know was that until now Orson had been inclined to obey its order not to open, but the sealing off of the theater changed his mind. Allowed inside by the guards, 891 struggled to plot a coherent strategy. Orson regretfully argued for moving *Cradle* elsewhere to start previews as scheduled. "I was very ambiguous in my feeling," Orson admits, "and I wasn't sure that we weren't wrecking the Federal Theatre by what we were doing. But I thought if you padlock a theater, then the argument is closed. If they hadn't padlocked the theater, I would never have taken that strong a stand. The padlock was an insult. That's what unified everybody, you know. The padlock was the thing that made us move." Consulted about the legality of moving the show, the attorney Arnold Weissberger (the brother of Orson and Houseman's secretary, Augusta) advised them that technically they could stage Cradle anywhere except on federal property. A major complication, however, was a ruling from the Actors' Equity Association that its members were to refrain from appearing onstage in *Cradle* as long as Washington chose not to open it, since, like any other moneyman, the government could legitimately choose to postpone a production it had bankrolled. Another complication for the cast was that, although 891 had not been slated for the personnel cuts that had hit other Federal Theatre companies, the work-reliefers involved with *Cradle* had reason to fear getting kicked out of the WPA if they violated the government ban. Finally, the guards were not going to allow 891 to haul out the elaborate sets and costumes, the myriad trappings of the big Broadway show, of whose absolute importance Orson had so completely convinced Blitzstein, that the composer hated the thought of their having to be left behind as government property. Both men were strangely ambivalent about the dramatic course of action the government had forced them to take, Blitzstein on account of losing the lavish production, Orson on account of his continued discomfort with making himself seem more politically radical than he really was: "My feeling, I realize now, was not only wondering about the political wisdom of doing it—at the time I was supposed to have been politicized by Marc; I was really wondering in a regrettably liberal way whether we should do it at all."

Even before 891 had figured out the logistics of moving *Cradle*, the news that they intended to flout the government ruling whipped up anxious ticket holders, many of them members of various leftist groups who looked forward now to witnessing, and participating in, an act of public defiance, as much as, if not more than, they did the play itself. Very quickly the public drama of government repression and artistic rebellion transfigured the play that had started it all. Orson realized that as marvelous as *Cradle* would have been as an extravaganza, now it would be something more: an *event*. Since Equity had ruled against actors appearing onstage, he would let the cast of *Cradle* fan out among the audience. Alone on the stage, Blitzstein would perform on a piano with the voices of cast members joining him from the depths of the auditorium. As he thought about it all in advance, Orson had to admit that, under the circumstances, this rigidly spartan production would be infinitely more theatrical than his initial ornate conception. Now all he had to do was convince a very disappointed Blitzstein that they were far better off this way.

Only at the last moment, the very day of the scheduled first preview, was a new auditorium secured: just before show time, ticket holders milling outside the Maxine Elliott were directed uptown to the old Venice Theatre. Before a packed house that included one hundred or so standees, in what Virgil Thomson calls "the most beautiful voice in the world," an exhilarated Orson told the audience what they might have seen onstage had the government not stepped in. Instead Marc Blitzstein, seated at a beat-up piano, began to tell the story of *Cradle*. Feder, the lighting man, had only a single spotlight, so that when actors suddenly spoke out from the auditorium, he had to scan the theater with his spot in hopes of quickly finding them. All of which added immeasurable tension to the play: Would the show go on? Who would sing the parts of actors who didn't show up? Would the spotlight find the actors before they had stopped singing? Would the government suddenly barge in to stop the proceedings? What would be the evening's repercussions? Afterward, Orson told the audience: "This performance was not a political protest but an artistic one." And in a way he was right. *His* motives, anyway, were artistic—but, as he should have anticipated, next day the government did not see it like that. "WPA Opera Cast Fears Spanking" read the *New York Post* headline.

Accompanied by Archibald MacLeish, Orson flew to Washington to request permission from the WPA to return *Cradle* to the Maxine Elliott that evening. By eight p.m., however, when Houseman, still in New York, had not heard from them, he announced that there would be no show that night. After he had failed in his mission to Washington on the 17th, Orson flew back to New York immediately, where he and Houseman decided to run the show in its present spartan form for two weeks at the Venice, starting that Friday, June 18. Although in the meantime Equity had reversed its decision, so that now its actors could go onstage in *Cradle*, Orson astutely chose to keep them out there in the auditorium because it was—as 891 told the press— "good showmanship" to do so.

CHAPTER 14

Declaration of Principles

"What do you think you could do in the Federal Theatre now?" Harry Hopkins, the head of the WPA, asked Orson, who had come to him for advice about his next move. Harry Hopkins merely confirmed Orson's opinion that there was no turning back. When he opened *Cradle* despite the government ban, Orson had forfeited Project 891, his "magic box." But he had also propelled himself into the headlines: "WPA Actors Take Over Play, Act from Seats," "Strike Play Opens Despite WPA Ban," "WPA Opera Put on as Private Show." Suddenly he was more than just a stage star, he was a name in the news. Even people who didn't follow the theater were reading and talking about Orson Welles. With the Federal Theatre behind him, he decided that now was the time to catapult himself to even greater personal fame by accepting producer Arthur Hopkins's offer to make him the new Barrymore by mounting *Lear* on Broadway that fall. Orson was relieved that, by contrast with Houseman, Arthur Hopkins did not have "the least emotional interest in me."

While Orson had decided to break with Houseman in the aftermath of *Cradle*, he felt closer than ever to Virginia, whose solicitude and support had meant a great deal to him during the crisis with Washington. When the ballerina with whom Orson had been conducting his affair went to Europe for the summer, they made no mention of seeing each other again in the fall. By summer Virginia was pregnant. Orson looked forward to spending the summer planning *Lear* with Arthur Hopkins, who was going to promote him as "a great star." Having commissioned Pavel Tchelitchew to design costumes and scenery for the production, Orson grew increasingly alarmed at Hopkins's perpetual silence. "I am totally defeated by silence," he explains. Although mutual friends assured him that Hopkins was taciturn by nature and that he need not worry, Orson's intuition told him that something was indeed very wrong, and eventually he figured out what it was. "He didn't have the money," Orson recalls, "and that was why he couldn't bring himself to say anything. I finally said to him, 'Arthur, what do you say we don't do it?' and he didn't answer that, so after a little while I left the office and that was the end of *King Lear*."

It was now well into August. To his great dismay, Orson found himself with only a new baby to look forward to in the impending dramatic season. Although it had been he who so recently had sundered the partnership with Houseman, he wasted no time in patching things up between them now by proposing that they start a new theater together that fall. Having just received his pink slip from the Federal Theatre, Houseman promptly accepted. Whatever resentments may have lingered on both sides, neither man was in the position to be proud. They knew they had to work quickly if there were to be even the slimmest chance of their establishing themselves in time for the new season.

This was the kind of unreasonable pressure Orson throve on. By August 29, they had pulled off what seemed like a miracle: the publication of the Mercury Theatre's *declaration of principles* on the front page of *The New York Times*

Sunday drama section (much as Charles Foster Kane would later publish his new newspaper's principles on its front page). There was no actual theater yet, of course, but this front-page coverage (courtesy of Orson's steadfast admirer, Brooks Atkinson) conferred public existence upon the idea. Beginning with *Julius Caesar* that November, the Mercury would mount in the course of the season four or five classical plays that were relevant to contemporary affairs. But although politics was important, aesthetics came first. The Mercury would never choose a particular drama just because it expressed, or could be made to express, the proper political views. In an attempt to recapture the wonderfully heterogeneous audience that had flocked to Project 891 the year before, Mercury would continue the popular low-price policy, and the top ticket price was set at two dollars.

After the coverage in the *Times* had attracted the first minimal funds the Mercury needed to get started at the Comedy Theatre on West 41st Street, Orson repaired to New Hampshire for ten days of furiously X-ing out, cutting, pasting, and generally overhauling *Julius Caesar*. In spare moments he also worked on the second production Mercury planned: Thomas Dekker's *The Shoemaker's Holiday*. By the time he got back to New York he had mapped out a modern-dress *Caesar* that was a parable of the threat of fascism in Europe and demagoguery at home. Lest anyone miss the point, a press release spelled out Orson's intentions: "Our *Julius Caesar* gives a picture of the same kind of hysteria that exists in certain dictator-ruled countries of today. We see the bitter resentment of free-born men against the imposition of a dictatorship. We see a political assassination, such as that of Huey Long. We see the hope on the part of Brutus for a more democratic government vanish with the rise of a demagogue (Antony) who succeeds the dictator. Our moral, if you will, is that not assassination, but education of the masses, permanently removes dictatorships."

As in *Faustus*, Orson called for a spare setting, in this case a network of platforms in front of the theater's bare brick wall, which was painted a vivid red. "His great thing was an invention of the mise-en-scène in a way that no one had done before," says Martin Gabel, who played Cassius. "For example, at the time we used to see newsreels of the Nuremberg rallies, with the great stream of light going from the ground into the heavens—very effective theatrically. And Orson thought *Julius Caesar* might be adapted as a parallel to that, to Hitler. He had no money, or very little, but he was immensely inventive: he put these beams in the floor, and at the appropriate moment they lit the stage. It was just dazzling! That's his genius!" From the moment they shot on, the production's famous Nuremberg lights crystallized Orson's interpretation of the play in a single startling image. Stage manager Walter Ash quickly saw that Orson typically regarded the stage as a vast picture to be composed. "He started out as an artist," says Ash, alluding to Orson's early paintings and drawings, "and when he directed it was visual—he saw how it would *look*. Then he would put people there. An actor would say, 'Why am I over here?'—the old cliché of *what's my motivation*? He gave cliché answers: 'It's your salary on Friday!' "

An important part of the production's visual impact was the contemporary costumes, especially Orson's: the impeccably custom-tailored, pin-striped James Bell suit that, as Brutus, he wore vividly to distinguish him from everyone else's drab military uniforms and dark rumpled street clothes. The press release detailed Orson's concept of the character: "Brutus is the classical picture of the eternal, impotent, ineffectual liberal; the reformer who wants to do something about things but doesn't know how and gets it in the neck in the end. He's dead right all the time, and dead at the final curtain. He's Shakespeare's favorite hero—the fellow who thinks the times are out of joint, but who is really out of joint with his time. He's the bourgeois intellectual, who, under a modern dictatorship, would be the first to be put up against a wall and shot." Determined to make Brutus *his* role, Orson very consciously regarded it as a way to launch his career as a great leading man. What Arthur Hopkins had been unable to do for him, Orson would do for himself. Hence the elegant suit and the absence of his usual heavily layered makeup: unlike the two previous roles with which he was widely associated, old Mugglethorpe and Faustus, Brutus allowed him to show the audience a star's handsome face and form.

Counting on *Caesar* to usher in both his new theater and his new leading-man image, Orson grew terribly alarmed when, after several postponements, the play seemed to drag on far too long at its previews. It was clear that something was wrong when at the third preview the final curtain dropped, and much to the vexation of the actors onstage, there was not a single curtain call. "We didn't get a call! We didn't get a call!" exclaimed the diminutive p.r. man as he rushed backstage. There he ran into Orson, who, glaring down at him, angrily spit in his eye. The little fellow tried to sock the giant, who reached over to restrain him easily. "Spit in *my* eye!" Orson rumbled. There followed a postponement of five days, during which Orson mercilessly trimmed what he judged to be slack time in the play, so that by opening night, November 11, 1937, the audience response could not have been more different—or more effusive. Now at last, the play's timing was absolutely perfect. The next morning, *Caesar* was critically acclaimed with even greater fervor than *Doctor Faustus* had been. "Move over and make room for the Mercury Theatre," wrote Brooks Atkinson in the *Times*. "After a glimpse of the modern version of *Julius Caesar*, which opened at the old playhouse in 41st Street last evening, it is plain that a place must be found for so much original acting talent. This is the theater Orson Welles and John Houseman have modestly founded on the reputations they acquired in producing *Macbeth* and

Dr. Faustus for the Federal Theatre. To judge by their first production, the Mercury will be a theater where enthusiasm for acting and boldness in production are to be generously indulged by young actors with minds of their own. Mr. Welles's mind is not only his own but it is theatrically brilliant and he is an actor of remarkable cogency." In the *Daily Mirror*, Robert Coleman, who urged his readers to place *Julius Caesar* at the head of their "must see list," wrote that "directed by young Mr. Welles, the production proves that intelligence can amply atone for the lack of a fat bankroll."

Given precisely this "lack of a fat bankroll" the Mercury probably should have made a quick business decision, and at least temporarily abandoned its announced status as a repertory company. From a strictly practical point of view, instead of preparing yet another production to alternate with *Caesar*, they should have stuck with this, the Mercury's first solid hit, thereby eliminating the considerable extra costs a new show would entail. What Houseman and Welles seemed to have forgotten was that, for all its resemblances to Project 891, there was a decisive difference now: the Mercury was an independent enterprise, a business, without the cushion of government backing that kept the Federal Theatre afloat. What they overlooked in the excitement of the moment was that cheap tickets were likely to fill the house night after night, but unlikely to turn a profit. No matter how cheaply Orson staged his productions, they still had to be paid for by the Mercury, not by the government. If at length the Mercury did not make enough money, other people certainly made money on the Mercury: as Joseph Cotten has pointed out, scalpers outside the theater typically sold choice two-dollar seats for fifteen or twenty dollars, which brought no extra income to Orson and company. The paradox of the Mercury was this: they would consistently play to jam-packed houses and go broke doing so.

CHAPTER 15

Bewigged
and Bewhiskered

Rehearsals for *Shoemaker's Holiday* began November 12 —
the day after *Caesar* opened — and lasted through December. Because of its vivid contrast with *Caesar*, Thomas
Dekker's bawdy Elizabethan comedy was chosen to demonstrate the Mercury's immense range, especially since some
of the actors (although not Orson) appeared in both shows.
Orson persisted in his fondness for nocturnal business hours,
largely because like him, a number of the Mercury players
worked in radio by day, making late-night rehearsals more
convenient. The morning after, a thoroughly exhausted Orson would sometimes be seen at ten a.m. deeply asleep in
the second row of the theater. At noon, Mrs. Anna Weissberger, the mother of Orson's secretary, Augusta, would
appear with a pot of chicken soup to fortify him. Typically
Orson did a great deal of eating in the theater. While he
prepared *Caesar*, he had initiated the practice of sitting on
a high stool in the orchestra pit to dine heartily on steak
and mushrooms from Longchamps while directing, and he
continued this practice with *Shoemaker*. A big-boned young
man with surprisingly flaccid musculature, Orson was still
disinclined to exercise, and worried about going all to fat

again now that he had managed to slim himself down; after a jumbo steak it was his custom to order a dietetic dessert, most often half a grapefruit.

Prudence was also called for in the production, since there wasn't the cash to pay for an entirely new set. Instead, the platform used for *Caesar* was reversed on rollers. On it designer Samuel Leve built houses for a London street from the slats of orange crates. "I want to give the audience a hint of a scene," Orson told the press. "No more than that. Give them too much and they won't contribute anything themselves. Give them just a suggestion and you get them working with you." The theory was sound, but the minimalist set had *really* been the result of Mercury's not having had the money to do anything else. Fully as ingenious as the set were Millia Davenport's costumes, which included the much talked-about gargantuan codpieces Orson had ordered. So vast were they that no sooner had he come out onstage than Francis Carpenter as Dodger would obscenely straddle the codpiece of another actor. Despite their ridiculous size, the codpieces were specially fitted to each actor's proportions by Miss Davenport—who before taking their measurements gleefully announced, "Now look, dears, grandma has seen everything. Will you please take off every living stitch so I can put it together with safety pins, and I will not stick or tickle you."

Evidently, preparing for one play and putting on another were not enough to satisfy Orson's hunger for theatrical activity. Accordingly the Mercury announced that Sunday nights, beginning November 28, when *Caesar* was dark, there would be special performances of *The Cradle Will Rock*, this as part of a projected program of experimental drama they called the Worklight Theatre. (As it turned out, *Cradle* was the first and last of the Worklight productions— so critically successful was it that Mercury figured they had better keep it running.) In the midst of all this, in response to a new movie offer from Metro, Orson abruptly flew to Hollywood for screen tests. Before long, Metro had offered him a lucrative acting contract that, as Warner Brothers had done, expressly gave him several free months a year to work onstage in New York. Despite Metro's generosity and the enthusiasm with which they made their offer, Orson decided he was far too busy with Mercury to accept. Once again, the future looked much too promising in New York. At this point Orson's thinking about cinema was still mainly limited to canned theater: he harbored a vague notion of someday founding an independent production group in New York to film Mercury's repertory for posterity. Only later would he hit on the idea of making original movies that shrewdly adapted the theatrical pyrotechnics for which he was celebrated.

Slated to open New Year's Day, 1938, *Shoemaker* seemed ready to show to an audience by Christmas Eve, so after the final curtain fell on *Caesar*, at about eleven p.m., Orson invited the audience to stay into the wee hours for the scheduled dress rehearsal. When *Shoemaker* broke that morning, about two-thirty a.m., Orson returned to Snedens Landing confident that he had another big hit. He looked forward to spending Christmas Day totally secluded in the country with Virginia and their cocker spaniel, Budget. The couple had not seen a great deal of each other during the early months of Virginia's pregnancy. While Orson was preoccupied with planning the new theater, Hortense Hill had kept Virginia company. Later, accompanied by the wife of a journalist who had written about and been befriended by Orson, Virginia had taken a pleasure cruise on a Dutch ship, during which she cabled and wrote Orson about how homesick she was. This was to be their single idyllic day together, with nothing to do, and no one to see. Whatever grave problems there may have been in their marriage, and however often he may have strayed from it, Orson still cherished Virginia for understanding, and sharing, his occasional need for complete quiet and solitude. She seemed to know, as few people did, how basically shy and retiring he really was. That morning, they were both filled with horror when they looked out the window: from across the snowy fields "we saw, from all directions, our neighbors moving toward us to wish us a Merry Christmas," recalls Orson. Without a word, Orson and Virginia quickly closed all the shutters to signal the well-wishers to leave them alone and go away.

Orson Welles's *The Shoemaker's Holiday* opened on New Year's Day, 1938, the three hundred and thirty-eighth anniversary of its first performance. "If there was any doubt after *Julius Caesar* that the Mercury Theatre is the liveliest drama household in this town, *The Shoemaker's Holiday* should dispel it," wrote Brooks Atkinson in the *Times*, "for the Dekker comedy is the funniest of the season and the new year has begun with a burst of theatrical hilarity." In the *New York Post*, John Mason Brown effused: "It is but further proof of Mr. Welles's astonishing genius as a director to see the ease with which he is able to turn from the brilliant innuendoes and ominous excitement of his Fascist *Caesar* to the gleeful exuberance and frank horseplay of his *Shoemaker's Holiday*." For all the loud praise he was accorded, Orson was especially delighted to have repaid what he considered a longstanding debt to Chubby Sherman, who, as Firk the journeyman, was widely hailed for his brilliant comic acting. Orson had never forgotten that it was Chubby who had urged his mentor Whitford Kane to award Orson a special prize for the Todd Troupers' *Caesar* at Chicago's Goodman Theatre in 1930. Now, eight years later, *The Shoemaker's Holiday* brought Chubby Sherman the Broadway stardom he deserved.

With *Shoemaker* successfully open, Mercury dispatched a road tour of *Julius Caesar* and temporarily moved *Cradle*

to the Windsor Theatre, where it would run daily instead
of on Sunday evenings only. Very soon thereafter, it became
clear that business for *Shoemaker* and *Caesar* was brisk
enough to move to a larger theater, the nearby National
(later the Billy Rose), so *Cradle* could shift back to the
Mercury Theatre for its regular run. By January, Mercury
had been operating for only three months on Broadway, and
was running three productions, all of them hits, when Orson
embarked on yet another show, this entitled *Five Kings*. For
Orson, *Five Kings* had intensely personal connotations, as
it recalled his notorious Todd graduation project in which,
at age fifteen, he had stitched together a crazy quilt of
Shakespeare's history plays. In the years since, Orson had
never quite gotten over the fact that at Todd required cuts
had made his Shakespearean extravaganza difficult, perhaps
impossible, to follow. This was the first time that the faculty
had implored Skipper to "pull Orson's cork." Now, at twenty-
two, having unquestionably established himself on the New
York stage, Orson returned to his lamented boyhood project,
intending to get it absolutely right this time. The triumphs
of the past three months would only be a prelude to this,
Orson's ultimate theatrical act. Perhaps the entire enterprise
was too personally charged, for there was trouble from the
start. As early as March 4, the press was talking about
Orson's having delayed rehearsals, ostensibly because he
was anxious about his "momentarily expected heir"—although in light of Orson's general obliviousness to domestic
matters, this was probably just a convenient excuse. What
he was truly most anxious about was the unusually massive
production he was planning, a sprawling hodgepodge of
Henry IV, Henry V, Henry VI, Richard II, and *Richard III*.
Pleasantly overwhelmed by the thought of it all, he didn't
want to start until every detail in the gargantuan script was
right. As it stood, *Five Kings* was so long that playgoers
would have to show up twice—two nights in a row, or for

a matinee and an evening performance—to see the whole thing.

That it wasn't the new baby that was keeping Orson from getting started was clear by March 7, when he announced that instead of *Five Kings*, which he somewhat anxiously put on hold, he would direct Webster's *The Duchess of Malfi* next. A cast was announced, a design by Pavel Tchelitchew commissioned, and a first reading scheduled for that very evening. Next day, however, Orson decided against the show. "We didn't have a strong enough company," recalls Orson. "No matter what people say, *that's* why we didn't do *The Duchess of Malfi*. I saw they weren't up to it, and I didn't have people for three of the leading parts. They just weren't disciplined classic actors."

Since he conceived of the Mercury as in essence a director's theater, Orson figured the most judicious tactic would be to seek other directors to expand the company's range. Says Orson: "I had a company pretending to be an Abbey or a Moscow Art, and I knew perfectly well it was a group of people cast for *Julius Caesar*. It was no repertory company at all. It was a great fake. That's why I wanted, not only better actors, of whom I must say I despaired, but another director—a director for the kind of plays that were closer to what the Group was doing and that I wasn't so interested in. That would enlarge our audience and all of that. I thought of that director as another young and vigorous, untried fellow, rather than a reformed grain merchant, you know." By which he means, of course, Houseman. Nonetheless, after his decision to abandon *Duchess of Malfi*, when Orson decided to take on another director to do *Measure for Measure*, he felt obliged to ask Houseman. Much to Orson's relief, Houseman declined, and Orson suggested that they try Chubby Sherman, who enthusiastically accepted. There followed three weeks of rehearsal under Chubby's direction, which ended when, to Orson's great

dismay, Houseman canceled the production. Orson was terribly puzzled by the cancellation. "What I heard before it
was canceled," reports Orson, "was that it was really very
good." In *Run-Through*, Houseman suggests that the ultimate downfall of the Mercury was due to the fact that its
success "had little to do with the quality of our work but
seemed to proliferate around the person of Orson Welles
with a wild, monstrous growth of its own." But in fact, the
whole idea of developing alternate directors—which might
have lessened the Mercury's dependency on Orson's personality—was extinguished by the cancellation of Chubby's
Measure for Measure.

Meanwhile, in England, George Bernard Shaw had received a telegram from New York requesting rights to stage
Heartbreak House. "Who are you?" Shaw wired back, evidently never having heard of Orson Welles. If Shaw eventually sold the Mercury the rights to put on his play, there
was one thing he stubbornly would not agree to: he prohibited Orson from reworking the text. Not a word was to
be changed, cut, or added. Nothing was more likely to
cramp Orson's style. Peeved by Shaw's obstinacy, Orson
was heard to remark: "The play's not good enough to cut."
Since he could not touch the text, the whole project now
held considerably less interest for him, but still he pressed
on furiously with rehearsals for *Heartbreak House*. Intent
on assembling an incomparably rich repertory, Orson was
not about to stop after only three plays. And to prove that
the Mercury was capable of any kind of production, he
decided to stage *Heartbreak House* without the pyrotechnics
that people associated with his last two shows. He wanted
to prove that Orson Welles could do anything: even play it
straight.

On March 27, 1938, Orson's close friends received a
most peculiar telegram: "Christopher, she is born." It was
no joke. Virginia had given birth to a girl at Harkness

Pavilion at the Presbyterian Hospital. (Years later, Christopher would speculate that one of her father's reasons for giving her a boy's name was the turn of phrase for the telegram.) The joyous telegram masked the guilt Orson had experienced in the hospital waiting room just before the baby was born. Virginia had become pregnant at a moment when they were trying to salvage their marriage after Orson's affair with his ballerina. Since then, however, Orson had persisted in being unfaithful to Virginia with other ballerinas, for whose highly cultivated bodies he found he had developed a very special taste. "I learned it when my first child was born, and I was unfortunately steaming up various hired cars around New York with one of the ballerinas," says Orson. When Virginia was about to give birth, he rushed to the hospital to await the big event, but even there his thoughts were on ballerinas. "The nurse kept coming in to report to me about when the child would arrive," Orson recalls. "After her second walk forward, I said, 'You're a ballerina,' and she said, 'How do you know?' I said, 'Because of the way you walk.' " Suddenly it occurred to him that an expectant father certainly should not be flirting with his wife's nurse. His thoughts should be on the baby. Nor was he any more comfortable with his role once the baby was born. His secretary noticed that Orson did not seem to know what to do with his new daughter. It even appeared to her that, in his own curious way, he expected the baby somehow to initiate their relationship. When of course this did not happen, he seemed almost to lose whatever interest he had had in the first place.

In April, Orson capped the Mercury's first season with the much anticipated premiere of *Heartbreak House*, in which he appeared in the role of Captain Shotover. Since this was the Mercury Theatre, the prospect of period sets and costumes in *Heartbreak House* caused as much stir as the lack of them had in *Caesar*. It was rather as if a famous abstract painter had announced that his next gallery show would consist entirely of realistic pictures. A great many people doubted Orson could do it—but the premiere, and the laudatory reviews that followed, proved them wrong. In the *News*, Burns Mantle wrote: "The Mercury Theatre, and Orson Welles, who did the staging, achieve a new triumph with the production. There are none of the tricks of novelty about this one." The *New York Sun*'s Richard Lockridge saw the irony of the least unusual of the Mercury's productions being explicitly intended, and received, as a dramatic departure: "This time their experiment is merely the simple, and fine, one of putting on a provocative, stimulating play as straightforwardly and effectively as they know how. And, under Orson Welles's perceptive direction, they prove that they can do this too. . . ." In the *Times*, Brooks Atkinson said: "Although the prospect of a conventional production worried some of the Mercury's friends . . . they can be reassured this morning. The Mercury can step as lightly as Bernard Shaw."

With Mercury set to close for the summer on June 11, Orson put *Shoemaker* on hold, so that he could alternate *Caesar* and *Heartbreak House*. Having staged an incredible four hit plays in a span of six months, he could now be seen nightly on Broadway as either the handsome Brutus or the bewigged and bewhiskered Captain Shotover. It was in his grotesque octogenarian disguise for *Heartbreak House* that on May 9, 1938, three days after his twenty-third birthday, Orson Welles glared out at the world from the cover of *Time* magazine. Before the introduction of contact lenses, actors could not make their eyes age, which accounts for the creepy effect of Orson's unmistakably young eyes peering out from all this encrusted putty and fake hair. The *Time* cover was not without irony; it seemed more likely that the old-timer on the cover was responsible for all of Orson's accomplishments than the wide-eyed kid in the interior photo spread. The gist of the article was that what Orson had done to date on the New York stage might have served as an entire career for other men—and a distinguished one at that. But for Orson Welles all this was only a start.

CHAPTER 16

First Person
Singular

Orson had spent a good part of the spring of 1938 competing
with George Balanchine for yet another of his dancers. "He
was used to it," laughs Orson of their sexual rivalry. But
still Orson did not want Balanchine to know that he was
pursuing this particular twenty-one-year-old, so when he
met her in her hotel in New Haven, where he knew Balanchine would be staying, Orson wore a disguise. "I went
to New Haven in a raincoat and with a mustache and glasses,
so as not to be recognized," Orson recalls. "As I came into
the hotel, I got into the elevator with George Balanchine,
who said, 'Hello, Orson, I didn't know you were here!'"
From their mutual sweetheart Orson learned that Balanchine
was just then doing something to make himself an even
more formidable rival: "At that time, according to her, George
was having treatments to enlarge his penis," reports Orson,
who discreetly refrained from ever asking her whether the
treatments had worked. Orson soon discovered that, in addition to Balanchine, he had another serious rival: a very
famous European film actress who liked to fill the ballerina's
room with flowers. "It's her trying to get in," his girlfriend
would say, when she saw Orson looking nervously at all
the flowers.

Although his liaison with this latest ballerina was what Orson describes as a "passionate courtship on both sides," it all had to be "carefully hidden" because of the very protective mother with whom she lived. There were no long lunches at the Colony, like those Orson had enjoyed during his first extramarital affair. "Mama wouldn't have allowed it," he explains. "It was all very difficult, which was the ideal situation for me because I—thank God—matured before the sexual revolution. I like it to be hard to get at!" Thus, he characterizes the obstacles the mother threw in their path as actually "a big help." Longing to get away alone together, Orson and his girlfriend borrowed Walter Slezak's country house. Soon after they got there, an alarm clock went off somewhere in the house, and Orson had to search all over to find it to turn it off. Orson settled in again with his beautiful dancer, when, much to their astonishment, they heard the ringing of another clock, for which, in turn, Orson had to search high and low. Having finally silenced it, he returned to his companion, when fifteen minutes later they heard the shrill voice of a third clock. By now Orson realized that all this was Slezak's little practical joke, a bit of what Orson fondly recalls as his "Viennese malice." Having lent his house to Orson for a weekend of pleasure, Slezak could not resist hiding alarm clocks everywhere, each set for a different time.

After this, Orson decided to rent a room where he could conduct affairs easily and discreetly. He had wearied of hired cars and borrowed country houses. Much of that summer he lived at the Hotel St. Regis on the pretext that Snedens Landing was hard on his hay fever. (He would not have his freedom for long; by the time rehearsals for the Mercury's fall season had begun, Virginia had found a duplex apartment for them on East 57th Street, which left Orson without a good excuse for sleeping in an East 55th Street hotel room.)

Before the Mercury had shut down for the summer, there

had been talk of touring the country with *Five Kings*, but nothing ever came of the idea, in part, some thought, because Orson could not bear to abandon his dancer-mistress. Orson put the production off for late the following season. Next, plans to try out Oscar Wilde's *The Importance of Being Earnest* on Cape Cod in preparation for a Broadway run in early fall were abruptly canceled when its star, Chubby Sherman, quit the Mercury. With his theatrical plans for the fall still unclear, Orson was approached to write, produce, and direct a weekly series of hour-long radio dramas to be cast mainly from among his Mercury players. Immensely excited about the series—to be titled *First Person Singular*—Orson told the press: "I think it is time that radio came to realize the fact that, no matter how wonderful a play may be for the stage, it cannot be as wonderful for the air. The Mercury Theatre has no intention of producing its stage repertoire in these broadcasts. Instead, we plan to bring to radio the experimental techniques which have proved so successful in another medium, and to treat radio itself with the intelligence and respect such a beautiful and powerful medium deserves." This new series heralded a major shift in his attitude toward the medium—because, at long last, he would have complete control of the shows to which he would lend his mighty voice. Later, Orson would apply the strategy he was now adopting for radio to film: he would make full use of what he had learned in the theater, all the while respecting the unique properties of whatever artistic medium he found himself working in. When one considers that initially Orson had envisioned working in cinema as a question of merely recording stage productions, it is evident that his statement about *First Person Singular* represents a major conceptual advance.

Slotted on Monday nights at nine p.m. on CBS, *First Person Singular* was a sustaining series—that is, presented by the network without commercial sponsorship. Before the new show got under way on July 11, a contract had to be drawn up, and for the first time he called on a lawyer for the job. His secretary, Augusta, had suggested that he visit her brother Arnold Weissberger, then employed at the Wall Street firm Liederman, Hess, Strauser and Schwartz. Orson decided he would take her advice, since she had recently recommended a marvelous psychiatrist who treated allergies as psychosomatic illnesses, and had been remarkably successful with Orson's hay fever and asthma. So Orson strolled into the Liederman, Hess offices asking where Mr. Weissberger might be found. By then Orson's voice was known across the country as Lamont Cranston's. "The Shadow is here! The Shadow is here!" cried an excited office boy as he rushed into Weissberger's office, followed by Orson. Neither Orson nor Weissberger (who had advised him about opening *Cradle*) could possibly have suspected how momentous this little visit was to prove. When he perused the CBS contract Orson was about to sign, the lawyer was alarmed that, although Columbia had final review of a script, Orson himself was legally responsible if any trouble ensued from its broadcast. This blanket indemnity struck the meticulous Weissberger as illogical. It was acceptable for Orson to be held responsible for libel or plagiarism—but certainly not for unforeseen and unknown results of his broadcasts. He wisely told Orson that if Columbia was to have the final say on scripts, then they—not he—should be responsible for any such problems. When he conferred with one of the partners in his own firm, Weissberger was told that Columbia's powerful legal staff would probably kill his bid for such a rider. Undaunted, Weissberger pitched his argument to CBS, who wanted Orson badly enough to let his lawyer have what he wanted. They figured that Weissberger had won a minuscule and inconsequential point. If in fact there was anything potentially problematic in a script, they would certainly be sure to spot it.

The title *First Person Singular* designated Orson's trademark approach to radio drama. Orson would tell stories like

Dracula or *Treasure Island* in the first person. As narrator, he interacted with other characters, some of them played by Orson himself, others by Mercury actors. Although he was introduced as Orson Welles, he would sometimes take on the voice of one of the characters in a drama, then another, thereby subtly blurring the line between fact and fiction. To help him with the complicated job of putting the new show together, Orson called upon Houseman, with whom he had worked in relative harmony throughout the Mercury's spectacular first season. Orson figured Houseman could use the extra money. Ultimately Orson would come to realize that Houseman's joining him for *First Person Singular* only revived, and intensifed, the old hostilities. In Harlem, although Orson had been responsible for the artistic success of *Macbeth*, he had been working for Houseman. In Project 891 and the Mercury Theatre, while Orson continued to be the creative force behind their success, he and Houseman were partners. By hiring Houseman for *First Person Singular*, Orson had changed all that. "He was working for me," says Orson to explain the new tensions and resentments that, from that moment on, began to creep into their already troubled relationship. But none of this was obvious as they began to work on the new radio show and make great plans for the Mercury's fall season.

Orson had not forgotten *Five Kings*, but he picked a farce by William Gillette, *Too Much Johnson*, to open the second season, this to be followed, at the suggestion of Martin Gabel, by Georg Buechner's somewhat peculiar play *Danton's Death*. After which, if all went well, Orson would finally put on *Five Kings*, presumably sparing no expense since he would have staged the first two productions on a shoestring. With *Too Much Johnson*, which Orson planned to preview in August at the Stony Creek Theatre in Connecticut, the shoestring was almost instantly abandoned when Orson decided to shoot a bit of film as part of the play. Set designer James Morcom says that *Too Much John-*

son "was a real turning point in Orson's life because that's the first time he was exposed to movies. It was like a fly being stuck on flypaper. The flypaper was the movies and Orson came along and got stuck on it. That was the end of everything. He knew that this was *it*." Orson had, in fact, briefly worked on a film before, *The Hearts of Age*, made at the Todd Summer Theatre Festival, but it had been little more than "a home movie," as he calls it. Back then, moviemaking had not yet captured his imagination. This time, however, with a great deal of theatrical experience behind him, no sooner had he begun tinkering with a camera than, as Morcom points out, "he got the bug. He saw what he could do. He's so clever and imaginative—he saw means that you could do things, all kinds of things you can't do on the living stage." Increasingly conscious that each artistic medium has capacities and potentialities specific to it, Orson now abandoned the idea of the camera as simply a recording instrument. When he made a movie, he could achieve on the editing table the kinds of abrupt leaps in time and space that lighting and stage design had made possible in *Doctor Faustus*. Orson enthusiastically set to work on, and kept at, the film footage he wanted to incorporate into the play. He ordered an editing table installed in his room at the St. Regis, where he sat mesmerized for hours studying the new footage he and his cohorts had shot and painstakingly teaching himself to shape it. But Orson had not finished these filmed sequences by the time of the August 16 preview in Connecticut, so the play went on without them, much to the consternation of the members of the company, who, as Joseph Cotten points out, had not really rehearsed beyond Act One. (It was a big break, nonetheless, for Cotten, whom Katharine Hepburn spotted one night of the run, admiring him so much that she later cast him for *The Philadelphia Story*.)

It is tempting to imagine that suddenly Orson found himself rather more interested in the film footage than in the

play of which it was to have been an important part. At the
time of *Caesar* he had privately regarded film acting as a
convenient escape should the Mercury encounter serious
financial problems: "I was going to have to go to Hollywood
the minute we lost money," says Orson. Several months
later, however, he had discovered the vague and tantalizing
possibility of directing movies as well as acting in them.
The disastrous second theater season that followed sometimes seemed almost like an afterthought.

CHAPTER 17
Day of Doom

After the calamitous previews for *Too Much Johnson* in Connecticut, Orson decided to open the new season with *Danton's Death* instead. But here too there was trouble from the first. Unfortunately, as even Martin Gabel, who had initially recommended it and played the title role, admits, *Danton's Death* is not a particularly compelling drama. "*Danton's Death* is by a young boy named Buechner," says Gabel, "and it's not much of a play, though every time it's done they say, 'This great play! It didn't have a good production this time!' Actually it's not a great play, a piece of shit, really. But it has some wonderful things in it." Undaunted, Orson believed that he could compensate for the play's inherent dramatic weakness with spectacular staging. If at the Mercury, and later in the cinema, Orson sometimes seemed preoccupied with staging, with mise-en-scène, at the expense of psychological, or otherwise purely human, concerns, it was in part because in the Federal Theatre from *Macbeth* on, he had often had to work with somewhat marginal actors whom—as if they were the blockheads, the marionettes, he had exhibited back at Todd—he took to choreographing, to manipulating, for purely pictorial effect. At the Federal Theatre too, postponing a show had never been a serious problem; with the government footing the bill, Orson thought nothing of stalling the premieres of his elaborate shows until every visual element was perfectly in place. He could hardly now afford this directorial luxury, however.

Of all the plays he had done, *Danton's Death* seemed most in need of the abundant money and manpower he had had at his disposal at the Federal Theatre—and that was simply not available now. "When Reinhardt did it—and he had a great success with it," says Martin Gabel of *Danton's Death*, "he must have realized it wasn't much because Reinhardt combined it with a play on Danton by Romain Rolland, and then, still not satisfied, I presume, he made it a gigantic spectacle. He had the whole great Reinhardt company in it—all famous actors and actresses. It was a gigantic spectacle when he did it. When Orson did it, he had no money, so he had to invent." Orson's practical problem was how to invent a cheap substitute for the massive Parisian revolutionary mob: "He did something," recalls Gabel, "that, I submit, nobody else in the history of the theater would have thought of: he went out and bought all the Halloween masks extant. Since we couldn't afford a crowd, he made a cyclorama. He had these all tied together, these grinning devilish masks all across the stage, and they represented the people of France. That's an example of what his great gift is." Such ingenuity notwithstanding, Orson still could not breathe dramatic life into the troubled play. Sensing that the first production of his new season was going to flop, Orson panicked. He installed a bed in the aisle of the theater to signify that he did not intend to leave until the production was absolutely right and that he did not expect anyone else to leave either. Says stage manager Walter Ash: "When it became obvious that there were problems with *Danton*, Welles did what all directors do when it doesn't work: he started to embellish with lighting and technical effects." Of all these effects perhaps the most controversial was an elevator stage that, when raised, was supposed to suggest the threat of the guillotine. Since there wasn't any cash to secure a proper elevator, the one they used was defective and creaked as it ascended or descended. Once it collapsed altogether, sending several injured actors to the hospital.

Late in October, as the November opening of *Danton's Death*, and the Mercury's second season, approached, it seemed to Orson as if everything was going wrong. He feared that in *Danton's Death* he might have a disaster on his hands: a disaster that the thinly financed Mercury could ill afford. The only thing that seemed to have gone right for him lately was his radio show, which was renewed for another twenty-six weeks after its initial nine-week tryout. But even this had its negative side. CBS slotted Orson's program opposite America's most popular radio show, ventriloquist Edgar Bergen's *Chase and Sanborn Hour* on Sunday nights. Bergen and his famous dummy Charlie McCarthy were well-nigh impossible to beat. Orson's new show had begun in mid-September with Howard Koch writing and Paul Stewart producing. For more than a month, it had existed in relative obscurity. Each week their one big chance to attract listeners came when Edgar Bergen introduced a guest performer. At that moment, if the performer was not especially good, people across America would quickly turn the dial to hear what else was on before switching back to Charlie McCarthy. Until now, Orson had not had much success at keeping the listeners who briefly alighted on CBS. Nor was anyone particularly optimistic the last week of October, 1938, when, on his Halloween show, Orson planned to do a corny update of H. G. Wells's *The War of the Worlds*, in which men from Mars invaded New Jersey.

The script's conceit was that the listener had just tuned in to a program of live dance music which, at intervals, was interrupted by news flashes about "a huge flaming object, believed to be a meteorite," that had landed on a New Jersey farm, and that turned out to be the first assault of a

full-scale Martian invasion of earth. Routinely submitted to
the CBS censors, the script suffered twenty-seven minor
changes, such as the substitution of the made-up Hotel Park
Plaza for the all-too-real Hotel Biltmore, and Jersey State
Militia for Jersey State Guard—all in the interest of diminishing verisimilitude. Just before he went on the air,
Halloween Eve, Orson made last-minute changes in the
script, which appeared to make it even duller than it already
was. While it seemed far more logical to stress the mock-
newscasts rather than the silly music, Orson wanted to keep
the music playing for unbearable stretches of time. No sooner
would listeners have begun to listen to a newsflash than
they would find themselves bored by the music again. The
crises of *Too Much Johnson* and *Danton's Death* had led
some close observers to speculate that at twenty-three the
wonder boy might be losing his touch. Now, as he prepared
to go on the air, his determination to drag out the insipid
musical interludes seemed only to confirm that rumor.

It was eight o'clock, time to begin. After the announcer
had clearly introduced this as "Orson Welles and the Mercury Theatre on the Air in 'The War of the Worlds' by
H. G. Wells," the fictive action began in the Meridien Room
in the Hotel Park Plaza, where Ramon Raquello and His
Orchestra were performing. Then: "Ladies and gentlemen,"
an announcer broke in, "we interrupt our program of dance
music to bring you a special bulletin from the Interconti-
nental Radio News." It was the first of several such interruptions to report a series of mysterious explosions on Mars,
then that a "huge flaming object" had dropped on a farm
near Grovers Mill, New Jersey. When eventually a make-
believe newsman, "Carl Phillips," made his way to Grovers
Mill, he broke in to report that this was not a meteorite,
but an unidentified flying object around which mobs of the
curious had gathered. As Phillips watched in horror, a hideous alien began to issue from the spaceship. "Ladies and
gentlemen," gasped the newsman, "this is the most terri-

fying thing I have ever witnessed. . . . Wait a minute, some-one's crawling. Someone or . . . something. I can see peering out of that black hole two luminous disks . . . are they eyes? It might be a face. It might be . . . good heavens, something's wriggling out of the shadow like a gray snake. Now it's another one, and another one, and another one. They look like tentacles to me. There, I can see the thing's body. It's large as a bear and it glistens like wet leather. But that face. It . . . ladies and gentlemen, it's indescribable. I can hardly force myself to keep looking at it, it's so awful. The eyes are black and gleam like a serpent. The mouth is kind of V-shaped with saliva dripping from its rimless lips that seem to quiver and pulsate."

So it went on and on, the increasingly agitated bulletins alternating with the insipid music. Orson played the eminent astronomer Professor Pierson, who was called upon to ex-plain how the aliens had just burned to death a number of human onlookers, including newsman Carl Phillips. "Of their destructive instrument," declared Orson, "I might ven-ture some conjectural explanation. For want of a better term, I shall refer to the mysterious weapon as a heat-ray. It's all too evident that these creatures have scientific knowledge far in advance of our own." Then an announcer warned listeners of the larger implications of the bizarre incident in New Jersey: "Ladies and gentlemen, I have a grave an-nouncement to make. Incredible as it may seem, both the observations of science and the evidence of our eyes lead to the inescapable assumption that those strange beings who landed in the Jersey farmlands tonight are the vanguard of an invading army from the planet Mars."

Did Orson Welles know exactly what he was doing? Had he been counting on the fact that the millions of listeners tuned to Edgar Bergen wouldn't begin idly switching sta-tions until long after the Mercury announcer had said that this was really just an adaptation of *The War of the Worlds*? Could Orson have suspected that moments after Edgar Ber-

gen had introduced a singer, people across America would
gasp at the "news" on CBS? For once Orson succeeded
magnificently in keeping listeners from tuning back to Charlie McCarthy. He had dragged out the boring music to in-
tensify suspense, to make it seem that considerably more
time had passed in the interval since the last news bulletin
than really had. It was all a question of framing. Not having
heard the usual introduction that framed the scenario as
fiction, countless people took it for fact. Orson's prior work
in theater and radio certainly suggests that he was amused
by the idea of breaking down the frame, of deliberately
blurring the reassuring distinctions between fiction and fact
that serve as signposts, orienting us whenever we are exposed to made-up stories, whether in novels, the theater,
radio, or the movies.

Today Americans are pleasantly disoriented when on television's popular *Saturday Night Live* there is a break to a
commercial that is not really a commercial. It comes when
a commercial is supposed to come, it looks and sounds like
a commercial, but it's only a travesty, a mock-commercial
that is meant to amuse. Similarly on Mercury's "War of the
Worlds," when newsflashes periodically interrupted a live
performance of dance music by the fictive Ramon Raquello
and His Orchestra or Bobby Milette to say that the Martians
had come, the broadcast conceit afforded the fiction maximum verisimilitude. Without the broadcast conceit, Orson's
Martian show wouldn't have scared anyone. It sounded real
precisely because it sounded like a radio show (much as,
later, the news footage in *Citizen Kane* seemed real because
it looked like news footage). Today Americans are sophisticated and immensely amused about this sort of violation
of the frame, this pretending that what follows is real when
it isn't, but in 1938 no such sophistication existed. (Perhaps
it was one of the ultimate effects of Orson's Martian scare
to begin making our contemporary style of sophistication
possible.) The recent news of Hitler's annexation of Austria

probably made Americans ready to believe Orson. Most of them knew about the Nazi invasion only indirectly, from the media. They trusted the media and believed what they learned from radio or the papers, so why not believe what they heard now? Much as the broadcast described swarms of hysterical people rushing aimlessly through the streets of New York, so in fact on some streets it happened, although unlike the broadcast, in reality there were surely no Martians in sight—which did not stop some people from reporting to the police and the press that they had seen them anyway.

Although the shrewd manner in which Orson timed his broadcast suggests he intended to mislead his listeners, afterward he firmly denied having meant to do so. Still, if one turns to *Bright Lucifer*, Orson's revealing play of 1935, one discovers an account of a hoax that, in a curious way, foreshadows the Martian scare. Dressed as a ghoul at Eldred's (Orson's) instigation, Jack the Actor stirs up havoc on an Indian reservation when people actually believe he is a supernatural being. So convincing is he that he is said to have developed "quite a following" among panicked believers, some of whom interpret the ghoul as signaling the Day of Doom. Afterward, the reaction of the populace is described thus: "God! the whole country's up in arms against me!"— much as all America was the day after Orson's Martian scare.

The next morning Orson found himself on the front page of the *Times* as the perpetrator of a hoax that had panicked the nation. Seeing him there with no little horror, his lawyer, Arnold Weissberger, phoned him instantly to instruct the typically expansive Orson neither to talk to reporters nor to apologize for all that had happened lest he appear to admit any indiscretion. A spate of lawsuits—$200,000 worth, all told—was about to begin. While no one had died (although one hysterical lady was about to swallow poison when her husband found her), plenty of broken legs and miscarriages had resulted from the broadcast. In addition, there were

numerous crank suits, like that of the lifelong stutterer who
had just been cured by psychoanalysis only to begin stut-
tering again after the hoax, and who sued Orson for $2,000
in order to return to therapy. Fearing that he would be
ruined—both financially and professionally—Orson was
immensely relieved to learn that the rider Weissberger had
sagely tacked on to his CBS contract freed him from any
responsibility whatsoever for unforeseen and unknown results of his broadcasts. CBS would have to settle the suits,
not Orson. Despite the initial uproar against him, which
included a threatened FCC investigation, it soon became
obvious that the scare had worked largely in Orson's favor,
affording him a vast celebrity that even his recent *Time*
cover had not. Overnight, he had made himself known around
the world. As a result of the brouhaha, his radio show gained
in popularity; Campbell's Soup in fact offered to sponsor it
for an additional thirteen weeks of one-hour slots.

From Orson's point of view, the most curious result of
the Martian scare was a letter he received from a lady in
Marin County, California, to say that a local amateur theater
group was planning to put on a reenactment of the Halloween broadcast. Enclosed was a clipping from a local paper
detailing how the cream of Marin County had gathered at
the home of Mr. and Mrs. Eldred Ireland to discuss the
project. None of this would have merited Orson's attention
were it not for the fact that the production was to be headed
by Richard I. Welles, of whom the letter said: "He is planning to put on a presentation of 'The War of the Worlds,'
which he wrote for you." It was the first Orson had heard
of his daffy brother for some time. After having been confined on and off at various mental institutions, Richard had
spent a brief stint in a monastery, then gone on to become
a social worker in Chicago's Hull House until a scandal
ended his tenure there. "He got fired from Hull House,"
explains Orson, "because he took a hooker upstairs and
locked himself in with her, and they couldn't get him down

for days." In the meantime, Richard had sent word to Orson that the latter's theatrical shenanigans had brought disgrace to the Welles name. "Richard's reaction to the early stages of my fame," says Orson, "was that I had disgraced the family by becoming a *player*." After the *Time* cover and now the Martian scare, however, Richard's view had changed considerably, so that he hoped to cash in on his celebrated sibling by passing himself off as Orson's creative collaborator.

Although it was snidely hinted in some quarters that Orson had staged the Martian hoax expressly to draw attention to the upcoming opening of *Danton's Death*, even the abundant publicity the Mercury did get could not save the ill-fated theatrical production. When it opened that November, Brooks Atkinson called the production "a worthy successor to the *Caesar* and *Shoemaker's Holiday* of last season," but his was distinctly a minority view. "It is all stunt and no play," complained John Mason Brown in the *News*. Worst of all was Richard Watts Jr.'s grim verdict in the *Herald Tribune*: "For the Mercury Theatre, the honeymoon is over." Duly warned, the audiences stayed away, and after twenty-one performances, an impoverished Mercury shut its doors.

Without funds, Mercury could hardly proceed with *Five Kings*. Exhausted and depressed, his professional and personal life in shambles, Orson repaired to Todd with Virginia. Once a week for several weeks, he flew to New York for two days of radio work, then back to Chicago, where with Skipper's encouragement he hoped to hatch a new plan for *Five Kings*, and with Hortense's encouragement, to try one last time to salvage a marriage that no longer made him entirely happy. The trip was only partially successful. At the end of his hiatus in Woodstock, Orson told himself that, although he did not plan to do anything about it just yet, his marriage was over. He did manage to salvage his great plans to stage *Five Kings*, however, for which he had outlined a condensed one-night version in which he planned to play Falstaff. In New York a deal was struck with the Theatre Guild to put up the cash to revive the Mercury for the new production. Orson intended to rehearse in New York before going on tour in February to Boston, Washington, and Philadelphia on the way back to Broadway in the spring. Key to his visual concept was an elaborate revolving stage that enabled actors to seem to move from one locale to another when actually it was the stage that had turned to disclose a new setting. "It was done like a film," says stage manager Walter Ash. This was not surprising considering Orson's recently acquired fascination with film's plastic possibilities. Having spent countless hours at an editing table working with the raw footage for *Too Much Johnson*, Orson had thrilled to the ability to move the film strip forward and backward to advance or reverse the action.

For all Orson's insistence on maintaining complete control, however, when the sprawling production landed at the Colonial Theatre in Boston that February, it seemed not to have been properly, even entirely, rehearsed. Too often actors did not really know their lines or how precisely to maneuver themselves in relation to the revolving stage; on opening night the stage motor proved defective and scenery fell off in every which way, much to the alarm of the audience. In the midst of this chaos, Virginia unexpectedly arrived in Boston, which only further agitated Orson, who had resolved to break off with her.

By the time the production reached the Chestnut Street Theatre in Philadelphia, *Five Kings* seemed more chaotic than ever. Orson soon discovered with horror that the motor was incompatible with the current in the theater, something he presumed Houseman would have checked on in advance. In the absence of an adaptor, the revolve had to be hand-operated on opening night. This meant that the scenery did not always change rapidly enough to keep pace with the action. And Orson kept cutting parts out to trim the production to a manageable length, which made the play difficult for audiences, who could not follow the historical sweep of events. This nightly cutting and restoring made for even more confusion among the actors, who were never any of them quite sure of what they were supposed to be saying or doing. When in Philadelphia the Theatre Guild withdrew its support for the obviously troubled production, Orson madly scrounged around for the cash he needed to bring *Five Kings* to New York, unsuccessfully soliciting from prospects as farflung as Tallulah Bankhead (whose husband, John Emery, was in the show) and Dadda Bernstein. Finally the Broadway character Toots Shor turned up in Philadelphia with several thousand dollars he had been saving to open a restaurant in New York, and he offered this sum to Orson to save his show. As desperate as he was, Orson turned down his friend; Shor would not have been able to open his famous New York restaurant had Orson accepted. Undaunted by his inability to raise funds, Orson had the sets shipped back to New York to be put in storage for a time when he might have the money to resuscitate the show.

CHAPTER 18
Bananas and Milk

The year before *Five Kings*, when the Mercury was at its most vital, Orson had spent an occasional afternoon in a 42nd Street burlesque house, whose management let him appear as a straight man to the baggy-pants comedians. For all his devotion to the theatrical classics, he was no less devoted to low forms of theater, burlesque and vaudeville principal among them. Thus, after the failure of *Five Kings*, it occurred to Orson that on the vaudeville circuit he might be able to raise the funds to get the costumes and scenery out of storage and revive his show on Broadway in the fall. It was April. The summer hiatus of his weekly radio broadcast for Campbell's Soup was coming up in June, so Orson threw himself into concocting a vaudeville act.

In the meantime, at Chicago's Selwyn Theatre in May, John Barrymore was set to open in *My Dear Children*, and Orson liked to fly in to see the show, and to dine with the ailing fifty-seven-year-old star. "He was so generous to a young theater man like myself, and so kindly and so gentlemanly and so warm," says Orson. "He was such a *good* man!" Once, having heard in New York that the great actor was dying, Orson rushed to Chicago, where, at the Ambassador Hotel, he found the elder Barrymores, Lionel and Ethel. "They were there to be at his deathbed, and he wasn't there!" recalls Orson. "So Lionel and Ethel and I had dinner, and then we went out looking for him and finally located him in a cathouse on the South Side and got him back. He wasn't dying at all—of course he *was* dying, but he wasn't dying any *more* than he was any other day." It is Orson's curious theory that, like Rita Hayworth, John Barrymore suffered from Alzheimer's disease. His excessive drinking, Orson argues, was merely an attempt to cover up his imperiled state of mind. According to Orson, Barrymore was terrifed by his own mental deterioration, as well as by the prospect of finding himself institutionalized. "He preferred to be thought of as a drunk," says Orson. Barrymore's appearance in *My Dear Children*—a play about a Shakespearean actor whose career has reached its nadir—seemed appropriate to many. But audiences came less for the play than for Barrymore, who, forgetting or ignoring his lines, liked to launch into self-mocking improvisations. Fascinated though he was by the breakdown of the frame, whereby Barrymore suddenly slipped out of the play into playing himself, Orson was also terribly upset to see his friend in this condition. "He was so sick he could hardly get through it, and pretended to be drunk," says Orson. "He knew he was prostituting himself, and that everybody he cared about was ashamed of him, but he managed to play it as though it were a great lark, and to bring the audience into it as though they were at a party. A great performance, really."

Back in New York, Orson had begun to receive a spate of inquiries from RKO's new president, George J. Schaefer, who, impressed by all he had read and heard about Orson, was determined to hire the genius who had staged the Martian hoax. But Orson was equally determined to remain on the East Coast to stage *Five Kings*, so that on May 16, his agent, Albert Schneider of Columbia Management, wired

Schaefer that "new developments regarding Welles make it impossible to consider films at this time." Orson's obstinacy seemed only to titillate Schaefer, who, thus rebuffed, wanted him all the more. But Hollywood would once again have to wait. For on June 8, Orson's twenty-minute vaudeville act, *The Green Goddess*, opened for a week's engagement at the Palace in Chicago. Six times a day he played the Rajah in his shortened version of the old William Archer melodrama, in which he impersonated the likes of John Barrymore, Charles Laughton, Alfred Lunt, or Herbert Marshall. *Here* was the Rajah as Barrymore would have played him, and *here* as Laughton would have done. It all sounds promising, but audiences didn't seem to think so. "Nobody had ever done worse business than I did," says Orson. "You could shoot deer on the main floors of all the great vaudeville houses of America. But I had a lot of fun. It was great to be a vaudeville headliner even if there was nobody out front because it's *real* stardom in vaudeville. They had dressing rooms like you saw in the musicals about backstage—which don't exist on Broadway—you know, with three rooms and bathrooms and a grand piano. All the other acts always stand in the wings and watch you because *you're* the head-liner, no matter how bad you are—I certainly was!" Onstage everything that could possibly go wrong seemed to do so. A p.a. system broke down, actors missed cues or appeared in the wrong costumes, and Orson tripped on a wire.

In Pittsburgh, Orson gave up *The Green Goddess* altogether. Empty houses wouldn't pay for *Five Kings*. Every day cost Orson additional money for storing the show's costumes and scenery, and Schaefer's offer at RKO began to look better and better. Orson figured that if he went to Hollywood it would take him three to six months to shoot a movie there, and the profits would pay for a Broadway season, one he planned would begin sometime after January and culminate with *Five Kings*. Doing several other productions, *The Playboy of the Western World*, *Peer Gynt*, and something by John Ford, would give him the time he needed to perfect the troubled show, which had vexed him in one form or another since Todd. Since he'd never made a feature film before—besides *The Hearts of Age* and the footage for *Too Much Johnson*, he had done some film work to accompany *The Green Goddess*—Orson's scheduling was somewhat unrealistic. Nonetheless, he planned a temporary foray; he fully intended to return to New York, as his having left the business end of Mercury there suggests. Houseman would go with him to Hollywood, but Augusta, their secretary, would stay behind to keep Mercury's books balanced.

When Orson arrived in Los Angeles on July 20, 1939, he checked into the Chateau Marmont Hotel at the foot of the Hollywood Hills. Shortly thereafter, he moved to a palatial rented house at 426 Rockingham Drive in Brentwood, in which Mary Pickford and Buddy Rogers had spent their honeymoon. There were maids, a butler, a pool, and cabanas. Orson's neighbors were Shirley Temple and Greta Garbo. In no time, Orson was spending eight hundred dollars a week on personal living expenses, exclusive of rent. All of this may have seemed a bit opulent for a recently failed vaudevillian who had come to Hollywood to raise money, not to spend it, but Orson didn't think so. Two days after Orson's arrival, the first version of the summary agreement between RKO and Welles was ready, although it would not be until August 21 that Orson would sign the full-length sixty-three-page contract that Arnold Weissberger had shrewdly drawn up. The deal was for Orson to act, direct, produce, and write two films, for which he and Mercury Productions would receive a fixed $100,000 for the first picture (due before January 1, 1940) plus twenty percent of the profits after RKO had recouped $500,000; and a fixed $125,000 for the second picture (due before January 1, 1941) plus twenty-five percent of the profits after RKO's

$500,000. RKO knew quite well that Orson had never made a feature film in his life; nonetheless, in an unprecedented arrangement, they gave him creative carte blanche. As long as RKO initially approved a project, they had no right to see a single millimeter of film until Orson chose to show it to them. Nor could they cut a single frame, or make any alteration whatsoever, without Orson's approval. All Hollywood was abuzz with talk of Orson and his amazing contract. No one could quite believe that the studio was willing to bet so much on a novice. His outsider status did not endear him to those who felt they'd paid their dues. Why had RKO given a know-nothing kid from New York the most advantageous contract ever? "I would have hated myself too," laughs Orson. One of today's leading filmmakers, Martin Scorsese, suggests that people in Hollywood were just plain "frightened" by Orson. Says Scorsese: "I think that people may have resented him for the power of his ambition." What seemed to upset them most was the announcement that Orson's movies would be written, directed, produced, and acted all by one person. "There's a tendency for the audience to hate that person," explains Scorsese, "to say 'Who the hell is that? How dare he take credit for *everything*?' "

Although the current in Hollywood ran against him, Orson found that some of America's biggest directors, men like John Ford and King Vidor, were generous enough to welcome the newcomer. "I had all these wonderful directors who gave me advice," says Orson. "They were the *only* people who were nice to me, and you'd think it would have been the opposite. Logically they should have been envious and bitchy. They were wonderful, the ones I became friendly with, Ford and Vidor. And Woody Van Dyke gave me wonderful advice. He said, 'Keep the camera close and keep it moving.' That's as good advice as you can give anybody. And King Vidor said to me a thing I never forgot. He said,

'A good director is a fellow who doesn't go on trying to get everything right, who knows when to walk away from something, and when to stay with something.' I think that's a wonderful definition, and I never forgot it. I leave some things rough, and I stay on other things, because I think he's absolutely right. If you paint a picture, you're not going to spend the rest of your life on the lower left-hand corner. And there are so many directors of the Wyler and Zinnemann school, who paint the lower left-hand corner with so much intensity and good taste that they're left with schlock." Only the ruined D. W. Griffith, Orson recalls, was distinctly unpleasant when they met, but Orson could well understand his resentment. Here was one of the mightiest directors, tragically unable to work in Hollywood, and here was a youngster who had never even made a feature film before walking around with the best contract the studios had ever offered.

For all his bravado in public, Orson wasn't entirely certain himself how he had managed to get this prize contract. The answer was to be found with George Schaefer. Before he became president of RKO the previous October, about the time of the Martian scare, Schaefer had had experience mainly in film sales and distribution. A shrewd businessman, unlikely to be taken in by a glib twenty-four-year-old, he had no illusions about Orson's experience with film. It was Orson's image, and his uncanny ability to attract attention to it, that impressed Schaefer. And, as he saw it, the generous contract was actually a publicity gimmick— a shrewd investment that began paying off the moment it became public.

Suddenly Orson was very rich—or so he seemed to believe. To read the press accounts anyone would have thought so, although Orson was really still living on his own money, mainly from radio, until he got his first picture under way— which, with his usual abundant self-confidence, he figured he would be able to do almost instantly. Says Martin Gabel: "Hollywood means big houses on the hill, it really does. And limousines and chauffeurs. It's an extremely seductive thing if you're attracted—and most of the people are—to that sort of life. And Orson seems to have gone for it— like a *royal* personage would." Appalled by the gaudy establishment Orson had acquired for himself so soon after arriving from New York, Arnold Weissberger issued stern warnings to economize at once, to which end the lawyer opened a special account to be managed by Orson's assistant, Richard Baer, whom he and Houseman had brought with them from the East Coast. It was Baer's responsibility to dole out cash as Orson needed it; if Orson's requests seemed especially unreasonable, Baer was to notify Weissberger immediately. "Orson's psychology in spending"—as Weissberger called it—was to spend as much as he wanted to, and to worry about his bills later—a psychology that his income did not necessarily justify.

The day after Orson installed himself in Brentwood, he invited the press to accompany him for a neighborly call on the nearby Shirley Temple estate. From his rented garden, he assembled a bouquet of eglantines and forget-me-nots, which, to the abundant clicking of cameras, he presented to his eleven-year-old hostess. With all the youthful spontaneity the two seasoned actors could muster, they posed in Shirley's playground, first on the merry-go-round, then on a slide, after which they seemed to lose themselves in a game of croquet. Invited to sign Shirley's guest book, Orson drew himself presenting her with the croquet mallet, beneath which he scrawled: "From one chap to another." Wrote one reporter: "Then they chased the photographers away, and over the privacy of their tea cups talked about, well, Heaven knows what." Since their meeting had been staged for these photographers in the first place, one imagines that they weren't chased *too* seriously, and that it was precisely about the photographers and the wonderful pictures they had just taken that Orson and Shirley were talking now in their tête-à-tête. After this short intimate tea party Orson invited the still-present press for a tour of his photogenic new home. His hospitality paid off in a statement in the next day's paper: "The gentlemen of the press passed a pleasant afternoon, and left with the conviction that Mr. Welles, who is only thirteen years older than Shirley Temple, is as agreeable as he is talented."

More authentically private than his staged tea party with Shirley Temple were his encounters with Greta Garbo. Shortly after Orson moved to Brentwood, he received word that his new neighbor was without a pool and would like to use his. But Garbo required total privacy. At first, he could catch a glimpse of her only if he watched from a window. One day, however, Orson could not resist appearing at poolside, where Garbo was doing laps. Anticipating a chilly reception, Orson was relieved that Garbo actually seemed happy for someone to talk to, and from then on Orson felt free to join her whenever she arrived for a swim.

For all the publicity he—and his contract—were getting in Hollywood, there was still a side of his life that Orson was anxious to conceal from the public. When Orson went to California, there had been no question of Virginia's coming also. Instead, she went to Ireland as the guest of Mercury actress Geraldine Fitzgerald. Baby Christopher was left behind in New York with her devoted Irish nanny. Orson told people that if Mrs. Welles hadn't joined him in Hollywood, it was simply because she preferred the East. Later, although RKO admitted that Orson's wife was in Ireland, the studio told the press that she had "left their son with him." Evidently RKO had been apprised neither that Christopher was a girl, nor that she was in the care of a domestic in New York. At pains to quell any rumors of trouble between the Welleses, RKO announced: "The truth is, the Welles family are cosmopolitans who care little for the traditional picture of a happy domestic group."

In the absence of his real family that summer, Orson wired Dadda and his wife Hazel (Edward Moore had died) to invite them to stay with him for a few weeks in Brentwood. Considering that Orson had spent years *avoiding* Dadda—sometimes, in Chicago, Orson even asked Skipper not to tell Dadda he was in town—Dadda was thrilled by Pookles's unanticipated invitation. No sooner had he received it in his Bellevue Place home in Chicago than he wired back his acceptance: "Oh somewhere in this favorite land the sun is shining bright. The band is playing somewhere, and somewhere hearts are light and somewhere men are laughing and somewhere children shout but there is no joy in all the world like that on Bellevue Place. Thanks. We're coming." That same day, Hazel Bernstein, whom Orson had always found to be somewhat irritating, sent him a fond note explaining what a big difference hearing from Pookles had made to Dadda's spirits. She assured him that Dadda and she understood that Pookles would be "busy to distraction," and that both of them would simply "be glad of some odd moments with you." Orson had his reasons for inviting Dadda to live with him at a time when he knew he would be under enormous pressure to prove himself worthy of his famous contract. For once, instead of being annoyed by Dadda's effusive praise, Orson actually longed for it. (If Orson did not turn to Skipper just now, it was because the Hills were still urging him to reconcile with Virginia.) Since it was Dadda who had been *first* to proclaim Orson's genius, Orson brought his old mentor to Hollywood to reassure himself of the special status upon which his presence there so entirely depended. If, in the anxiety of those first few weeks in Hollywood, Orson ever secretly doubted that he was a genius, there was Dadda to tell him so.

The studio was also happy to confirm Dadda's image of

Orson: in studio bios and press releases they emphasized his intellectualism. To further the image, Orson kept—and cultivated—the greasy beard he had sprouted for *Five Kings*. Although he protested that he didn't want to shave until *Five Kings* opened on Broadway, it seemed more likely that he wanted to look older and more thoughtful. It was another of his masks. So successful was this persona that, in some hostile Hollywood circles, Orson came to be called the Beard. Perhaps it was *too* successful. One evening, in a nasty incident at the popular Brown Derby restaurant, a massive brute named Big Boy Williams loudly mocked Orson's beard and his manhood as well, and in the ensuing tussle hacked off Orson's necktie with a knife. In a curious way, Big Boy's tirade spoke for all those in Hollywood who resented Orson as an outsider, an intellectual, who hadn't done anything to prove himself.

If his beard was meant to be symbolic, the peculiar outfit of slovenly dungarees and sweat shirt he wore to tour the film studio indicated that he was there to work. The studio assigned a bright young woman named Miriam Geiger to improvise a film textbook for Orson. In it, selected film stills illustrated an assortment of shots and angles. (If Orson's first film, *Citizen Kane*, seemed to use every trick in the book, it may have been because Orson had literally been working out of a book, the dictionary of film language Miriam Geiger had so urgently assembled.) Once he assimilated the techniques named in his handmade textbook, he could begin to label them in the films that were privately screened for him almost daily. With particular interest he examined the German expressionist classic *The Cabinet of Dr. Caligari*, a print of which he had ordered from the Museum of Modern Art in New York. He reviewed John Ford's *Stagecoach* so many times that he lost count. Although *Caligari* and *Stagecoach* would seem to have little in common, Orson discovered in both of them an extreme

stylization of reality. This taste for stylization in film was
a logical development of his taste for theatrical theater,
which Orson had acquired in his formative apprenticeship
at the Dublin Gate, and which he had so brilliantly put into
practice in New York. But Hilton Edwards had taught him
to think that film essentially reproduced reality, while in its
greater artistry theater stylized it. When Orson had first
considered filming Mercury's stage productions, he still
thought of cinema as a mere recording medium. The film
he had in mind would be a transparent rendering of the art
of the stage play. Although he had had an intimation of
film's plastic possibilities as early as his work on the footage
for *Too Much Johnson*, the real revelation came in his first
few weeks in Hollywood as he studied the specifically cinematic techniques a filmmaker could use to stylize reality.
Watching the same film countless times, it was only natural
that he would pay far less attention to its story than to the
way it told that story. He began to think about making a
film that deliberately called attention to its own style. He
wanted the audience to think about the act of seeing as much
as he had in the past few weeks. Fascinated by the way
movies tell stories, he wanted to share that fascination, to
make a movie about it.

From August until September, hungry for knowledge about
every aspect of filmmaking, Orson was scheduled to spend
three hours daily meeting with top studio technicians.
"Everybody was at his beck and call whenever he wanted
to talk to them about film," recalls Miriam Geiger. On his
first tour of the studio Orson had called it "the greatest
electric train set a boy ever had." But if he was as excited
as a kid with a new toy, he could also be childishly impatient.
"I remember screaming, screaming all the time," says Geiger,
at whom, in an infantile rage, Orson once threw an inkwell.
He was in a hurry to learn, and anxious to start shooting
by early October. He feared that he might not be able to

learn what he needed to know in time. Initially he had assigned Houseman to work on a script based on Joseph Conrad's *Heart of Darkness*, a brief radio adaptation of which Mercury had performed on November 6, 1938, the week after the Martian hoax. When Houseman failed at this, Orson proceeded to work on the script himself. His method of adaptation was essentially the same one he had used back at Todd; he marked up the pages of a book, boxing and crossing out the sections to be deleted. Now, however, he used two books, neatly tearing the pages from their bindings and pasting them on white typing paper, on which he scribbled marginal comments.

By August 18, Orson's concept had crystallized into a first memo to RKO management; without going into details, Orson's assistant, Herb Drake, wrote that Welles's *Heart of Darkness* would be "a completely unprecedented experience for the audience since it will see a story told in an entirely new way." Orson's new approach to storytelling was to make the camera consistently represent the point of view of Marlow, who, in Conrad's classic, embarks on an African quest for the enigmatic Kurtz. In the film, Marlow himself would remain always offscreen, his dialogue spoken by Orson (who, in a cinematic twist on the doppelgänger theme, also planned to play Kurtz). Thus, the audience would seem to see precisely what—and only as much as—Marlow does. (A visual pun equated the "eye" of the camera with the spoken "I" of Marlow.) By subjectivizing the camera, by having it consistently represent Marlow's point of view, Orson hoped to compel the audience to identify entirely with Marlow, as well as to call attention to the presence of the camera, thereby suggesting that film isn't merely a passive, objective recording medium. It registers a limited point of view. Fascinated by the way in which the lens frames reality, Orson decided to make the camera into a character. In the theater, Orson had liked to violate the frame, to

transgress its borders, which was precisely what he would
achieve now by keeping Marlow offscreen. The audience
would constantly be thinking about what was going on outside the frame. Orson's playing that offscreen character
ironically alluded to his own career as an unseen presence
on radio. Besides portraying Marlow and Kurtz, Orson also
intended to play himself in a brief opening segment to explain the subjective camera technique (much as he had liked
to frame the stories of *First Person Singular* by introducing
them before metamorphosing into the voice of one of the
characters). In a way, by playing three roles in the picture,
Orson was thumbing his nose at his enemies in Hollywood
who complained that writing, directing, producing, and acting in a film were too much for one man. It was as if, for
Orson Welles, all this still were not enough.

For Kurtz's fiancée, Orson wanted an Austrian actress then
living in France, Dita Parlo, best known for performances
in Vigo's *L'Atalante* and Renoir's *La Grande Illusion*. By
the end of August, Parlo had received a cable from America
offering her $20,000 and first-class transportation to begin
shooting October 1 for three months. But no sooner had the
cable been dispatched than Germany invaded Poland, making Parlo's participation in the project unlikely, since, as an
Austrian national, she was interned in France. The situation
with Dita Parlo betokened a much larger problem for Orson,
and the entire film industry. The outbreak of war in Europe
was certain to diminish drastically the world market for
Hollywood films, a depressing fact that RKO president
George Schaefer tried to explain to Orson in a three-page
wire from New York, dispatched—ironically—on September 15, the very day Orson submitted for studio perusal the
first detailed description of his film's characters. Schaefer
told Orson that, after England and France had declared war on Germany on September 3, business had sub-

stantially fallen off in English and French movie theaters. With people generally wary of assembling in the remaining movie theaters there, it seemed probable that the essential British and French markets could no longer be counted on. The loss of European markets would have a particularly devastating impact on the sort of serious filmmaking Orson had initially been hired to do. Orson found himself called upon to cut costs and stick to the story in his picture, for which, as with other "important" RKO projects, a budget ceiling of $500,000 was imposed. In a return wire to Schaefer, Orson agreed to economize. Grateful as he was for RKO's considering his picture one of its most "important," and eager to prove himself worthy of Schaefer's immense confidence, Orson still did not know whether he would be able to keep this promise since he simply did not know how much making a picture cost. Nor did he have any idea as yet that the studio was not the monolithic organization he innocently imagined it to be, and that Schaefer had his enemies within the organization, who, in turn, were Orson's enemies as well. They would be watching him carefully. Any mistakes he made would be a strike against Schaefer.

In September, the attenuation of the world film market, and its direct impact on his production, were not Orson's only problems. Mercury's weekly radio broadcasts were scheduled to resume on Sunday evening, September 10, and Orson was bound by his Campbell's contract to be back in New York. Nervous that Orson might fail to show up (initially they thought unrealistically that he would have finished his movie by September), Campbell's ad agency had expressed its concern to Arnold Weissberger, even hinting at the possibility of seeking an injunction against RKO. Weissberger replied that he didn't see how they could get one, since the RKO contract in no way conflicted with Orson's radio commitments, as long as he was there reg-

ularly to fulfill them. Orson agreed to fly to New York once
a week for the broadcast; the initial plan was that he would
work three days a week on the West Coast and three days
on the East, with a day between for traveling. The trans-
continental flight took about eighteen hours, with stopovers
in San Francisco and Chicago, during the latter of which it
was Dadda's custom to meet the plane at the airport for a
good talk with his protégé about the Bernsteins' plans for
permanently resettling in Hollywood, where they had spent
the summer. Once, however, at four a.m., so exhausted was
Orson, and so deeply did he slumber, that he didn't even
wake up when his plane landed in Chicago. Nor could
Dadda, or the stewardess he summoned in great alarm, seem
to rouse Orson, however vigorously the doctor shook or
called to him. All of which, of course, occasioned another
anguished letter from Dadda, which was waiting for Orson
on his return to California.

   Although Orson had originally planned to divide his time
equally between the two coasts, his responsibilities in Hollywood were far greater and far more important to him than
those in New York; and so he dispatched Houseman to New
York to supervise the preparation of the radio programs and
see to it that a recorded rehearsal would always be ready
for him the moment he got to town. The morning after the
broadcasts, he liked to catch the nine forty-five a.m. flight
from Newark, New Jersey. One such morning, at nine
o'clock, accompanied by two of his Mercury cohorts, Orson
took a cab from his 57th Street apartment house, but it
stalled on the Pulaski Skyway in New Jersey. The only way
to make the plane was to hitchhike, but when Orson extended the long tapered thumb of his extraordinarily beautiful hand, the only vehicle to stop was a garbage truck,
into which Welles and company promptly crowded. When
asked at the airport what cargo he was carrying, the trucker
barked, "Actors and garbage!" Telling the tale afterward,

Orson quipped that at least they'd gotten top billing. By the end of 1939, Orson would have logged enough miles on TWA to get the airline's annual award for its best customer. In September, on his first trip to broadcast from New York, Orson told Weissberger of his plan to buy a private plane, which would free him from bothersome airline schedules. Weissberger was horrifed at the potential expense. Orson had incorrectly calculated that all a plane would cost him was, at most, $5,000 (for which amount he would have to take a loan anyway—an unwise course since he was already substantially in debt, no money having been advanced as yet from RKO). Outwardly patient but inwardly anxious, Weissberger explained that the plane would cost at least $20,000, and that the upkeep would be extremely costly, at which point, in a rare show of personal economy, Orson voluntarily abandoned the idea.

Orson intended to start shooting *Heart of Darkness* as soon as possible, although in October neither the script nor the budget was ready. Still, by the third week of the month, in the CBS studios at radio station KNX, he was running rehearsals for *Heart of Darkness*, which were recorded on discs for Orson to evaluate afterward, much as he had done preparing radio shows. Meanwhile, composer Bernard Herrmann also studied the proceedings in hopes of creating a score that was perfectly synchronized with the psychological ebb and flow of the action—an important consideration for Orson, who, as a radio man, was inclined to pay special attention to the film's soundtrack. The first draft of Orson's script was ready November 7, but still Orson decided to trim it a bit more, so when, on November 30, he submitted his "revised estimating script," from which RKO would calculate the picture's budget, the text was down to 184 pages. In New York Schaefer heard that *Heart of Darkness* was likely to cost an immense $1,057,761—more than twice the limit he had imposed. Had the war in Europe not cut off a vital market for the sort of serious film Orson was planning to make, Schaefer might have been considerably less alarmed by the big budget. Under the circumstances, however, spending this much just would not do. Orson had reason to fear that, having come to Hollywood with the greatest contract ever, he might soon find himself sent home in disgrace. The preliminary report Schaefer received from his Hollywood office suggested that the budget for *Heart of Darkness* was so high because Orson was simply not conforming to usual studio working procedures.

In fact, Orson was just then seriously considering various options for economizing. He wanted to shoot on location in Latin America, for example, and claims that if he had been allowed to, costs would have been cut substantially. But "I lost my battle to go to the swamps and do it in a real place," Orson recalls. "That was at the height of the period when nobody left the studio. The studio had to have *control*—as it was called—the famous *studio control*. . . . Well, I was more a victim than an authoritative pro like Hawks would have been, because I was the stage actor and director *who didn't know what he was doing*. In other words, there was the theory that the cameraman himself and the unit manager on location couldn't control things as well as in the studio. We had that terrible late-'30s–'40s look in which people kept riding by in front of painted drops. You know that scene in the Westerns with the little gas fire burning away under the twigs when they've drawn the covered wagons around and all? I was shown that and told that nobody could tell the difference. And I said, *I can tell the difference*, and that was regarded as very eccentric. That was a long and bitter fight. It was almost as definitive a reason why we didn't do *Heart of Darkness* as the fact that we couldn't get $50,000 to $75,000 off the budget. I claimed that the extra money came from the fact that we were going to do it in the studio." When Orson gave in to the studio's pressure to forgo location shooting, he wasn't going to settle for a lot of silly backdrops. "I gave in and said, *all right*, it's going to have to be all trick shots. I wanted *my* kind of control. They didn't understand that. There was no quarreling. It was just two different points of view, absolutely opposite each other. Mine was taken to be ignorance, and *I* read their position as, you know, established dumbheadedness." In the absence of authentic locations, Orson proposed the extensive use of miniatures of the jungle, these to be shot *before* the main photography, rather than *after* as Hollywood custom dictated. This approach would cost substantially more, as shooting would be held up until the painstaking work of shooting miniatures was completed. Orson insisted on it so as to match the main photography to the miniatures—a costly reversal of Hollywood routine that enraged the studio bureaucracy, who snidely complained to Schaefer. Back in the WPA, Orson had managed by and large to skirt the bureaucracy and to do pretty much as he wished. He had Houseman to fend for him with the government bureaucrats, and his own cash to pay for things without formally requesting them. At the studio, on the contrary, he always had to go through the proper channels; he had to play strictly according to the rules. Accustomed to thinking for himself, he bristled at these new constraints.

As if the news of Orson's budget were not bad enough, Schaefer learned that only $400,000 in two bank loans had been acquired, so that to make *Heart of Darkness* RKO itself would have to come up with more than $400,000 cash. It was up to Schaefer to decide whether or not to proceed with *Heart of Darkness*. With the production postponed until March, the studio management had already told Orson that the Mercury players he had brought from New York when the radio show had begun to originate from Los Angeles could not be kept on the RKO payroll with nothing for them to do in the interim. The studio's suddenly removing the transplanted actors from the payroll was a big blow to Orson, who needed them for moral support. He began to realize that he was in the middle of an internal struggle between a Hollywood progressive like Schaefer, who, having hired him in the first place, wanted to infuse the studio system with fresh new talent, and those who were quite content to leave things as they were. From the outset, both because of the unusual manner in which Orson had been brought to Hollywood, and because of his independent personality, he represented a threat to studio protocol. It was an image he would never overcome.

Aware that both he and his production were in very serious trouble, Orson turned up in New York that December with a surprise proposal of another film to be made while he completed preparations for *Heart of Darkness*. It was the same strategy he had used to put off *Five Kings* until it was ready. A modest adaptation of Nicholas Blake's thriller *The Smiler with a Knife*, the film would star Carole Lombard—or so Orson told Schaefer, who instantly shared his enthusiasm for the project, which struck him as more commercial than *Heart of Darkness*. But one other problem remained. Under the terms of Orson's contract, his first picture was to have been due by January 1, 1940. Obviously there was no chance of his making his due date, so that RKO would be perfectly within its rights to terminate his contract. Now, in return for RKO's overlooking his tardiness, Orson offered to make not two, but *three* pictures for them for the same compensation. In effect, they would be getting one picture free. At this point *Smiler* was to have been the so-called free picture. RKO would divide the $100,000 they owed him for *Heart of Darkness* between that film and *Smiler*. Although of course Orson would not make either film, he still owed them the free picture that, under duress, he had agreed to make—a fact that would come to haunt him later. In December of 1939, besides buying a very desperate Orson

more time in Hollywood, *Smiler* would presumably get some
of the Mercury players back on the RKO payroll. For Orson
the meeting with Schaefer was a great relief from the negative attitude he had consistently encountered in the West
Coast office. By now Orson's expectations of swiftly making a movie or two and returning to Broadway had disappeared; suddenly he was almost as preoccupied with making
a *big* Hollywood picture as he had been with staging *Five
Kings*. What those who hated him in Hollywood did not
realize was that, instead of discouraging him, the obstacles
in his path only made him more determined to succeed.

All of Orson's business on the trip to New York was not
as pleasant as his visit with Schaefer. Orson had asked
Weissberger to prepare a draft of a separation agreement
with Virginia, who, on October 22, had returned from Europe, where the outbreak of war had temporarily stranded
her. By December, they had agreed formally to part ways.
Virginia was granted three hundred dollars a week, plus
$1,600 a year in child support for Christopher until she
reached the age of ten, when the sum would go up to $2,400
a year until she was twenty-one. Orson promised to maintain
Virginia and Christopher as beneficiaries of his $71,000 life
insurance policy, unless Virginia died or remarried, whereupon it all went to Christopher (a point that would cause
considerable trouble for Orson some years later). Never
having liked Orson in the first place, Virginia's father, Leo
Nicolson, was dismayed by the three-hundred-dollar weekly
support figure. Having read all the publicity about Orson's
famous contract, he presumed that, once Orson got his first
picture under way, he would be making plenty of money
and would easily be able to afford a more generous settlement. Weissberger, on the other hand—knowing Orson's
current circumstances as well as he did—was concerned
that in the event Orson was unsuccessful in Hollywood, he
might not be able to afford the payments to which Leo

Nicolson had objected. The more time passed, the worse his prospects appeared. Thus, after Orson returned to California, it occurred to Weissberger to insert a provision that limited Orson's liability for support of Virginia and Christopher to fifty percent of his income. Any decrease in his income—which Weissberger obviously didn't consider entirely unlikely—would be accompanied by a proportionate cut in his payments to Virginia. Weissberger knew what the public did not: that Orson was massively in the red. If even Orson sometimes seemed genuinely oblivious to the dismal state of his financial affairs, perhaps it was because his agent, Columbia Artists, had not been deducting the very considerable expenses for his radio show, but advancing him the entire amount to live on until production on his film began. Eventually, he would have to repay these funds. Thus the high life Orson appeared to have thought it his *obligation* to lead in Hollywood had been paid for with money he had not actually earned yet.

News of Orson's separation and the impending divorce (the divorce decree was granted in Reno on February 1, 1940) caused no little stir in Hollywood. When he had arrived without his wife six months before, Orson had consistently—and with intimidating firmness—denied any trouble in his marriage. Now all he would say publicly was that since he and Virginia had already been separated for a year, their breakup was not really news. In a way he was right; the news was that he was admitting it.

There was also considerable embarrassing publicity about Orson's having had to postpone *Heart of Darkness*. The mirth with which Orson's professional difficulties were generally greeted is suggested by the press snidely calling *The Smiler with a Knife*, "Mr. Welles's latest forthcoming picture." The script Orson had written was revised by Herman Mankiewicz, then a writer for the Mercury radio show. But the project faltered irretrievably when both Carole Lombard,

whom Orson had originally had in mind for the female lead,
and Rosalind Russell declined. When Orson asked for Lucille Ball, then under contract to RKO, the studio said no.
Even Orson was secretly beginning to question his ability
to work in the studio system when he could not seem to
push through such a relatively routine project as *Smiler*.

It was at about this time that Dadda Bernstein had begun
to pressure Orson to ask Schaefer about appointing him
RKO's studio doctor. Given his problems at RKO, Orson
should probably not have been bothering his sole supporter
about such a thing, but Dadda did not let up. Whenever
Orson looked through his mail there was a new plea signed
"Lovingly and Distractedly Dadda." Hazel called this mainly
one-sided correspondence her husband's "literary work (his
daily dozen to Orson)." Obviously, inviting Dadda to Hollywood for a few weeks had been a big mistake. He had
only stirred him up again. "I am really and truly up a tree
what to do," he wrote Orson, "am very unhappy and am
losing weight and strength from loss of sleep, and worry."
To start afresh in Hollywood where he knew it was important
to look prosperous and "to have a proper address," Dadda
would need a small cash advance from his protégé. Lest
Pookles worry that his Dadda would need too substantial
an amount: "What you spend on one venture I can live on
for life," wrote Dadda. "I am your new Venture, a play
called Dadda." And lest Pookles be concerned that all this
was just a ruse, and that Dadda was really wanting to come
to California to be near him (which was, of course, rather
obvious) he wrote: "Don't think that I want to go to California because of your being there, though that is no draw-
back." Frustrated by Orson's prolonged silence on the subject,
Dadda wrote to Pookles's assistant Herb Drake: "Orson
wired me last Saturday that he wanted to talk to me and as
a result I had very little sleep, bad dreams when I did drop
off, but no phone call. If you should hear of my sudden

death you will know that no one is responsible but Orson. However, I will haunt him in my dreams." Eventually, Orson broke down and sent a telegram to Schaefer about RKO's hiring Dadda. But the bewildered Schaefer saw no reason to import the Chicago doctor, who was, after all, Orson's Dadda, not his.

By now, Orson had far more pressing concerns. Although the studio had expected him to *complete* his first picture by January 1, 1940, by that date he had not yet *started* shooting a film (aside from the abortive plans for *Heart of Darkness* and *Smiler*). As the new year approached, and with it the shame of not having accomplished what he had so confidently come to Hollywood to do, Orson quarreled violently with Houseman, who seemed to him to be serving no useful purpose in his employ. Since he had found himself unable to help with the Conrad adaptation as Orson had asked, there had really been no role for him in Hollywood. Orson calculated that it was best to deal with Schaefer on his own. As Orson saw it, he and Houseman were not really partners anymore. "He was working for me," says Orson. "That's why he hated me so. You know, he was on salary to me in effect."

But Orson was embarrassed by the seeming disloyalty of dismissing Houseman after their four years together. Anxious not to lose face in front of the Mercury players whom he had brought to California, Orson sought to provoke Houseman to terminate their relationship himself. "My job was to get rid of Houseman," Orson explains. The opportunity presented itself shortly before Christmas 1939, at a gathering of the Mercury at Chasen's Restaurant in Beverly Hills. After bickering with Houseman about the company's future, Orson removed a Sterno can from beneath a casserole, threw over the table on which it lay, and hurled the Sterno in his opponent's general direction. Despite this, Orson insists he wasn't really angry at Houseman. "The whole purpose was

to get Houseman to quit and go back to New York," says
Orson. "It was a total piece of theater. I didn't throw the
Sterno within ten feet of him. He'd been sitting at that dinner
table cutting me up for an hour, but I didn't get mad. I
thought, 'I've just got to get him away.' I couldn't say,
'You're not working for me anymore' after all our time
together and all. So that's why I turned over the table. It
was cold-hearted. It wasn't a *big* end of it; it just got him
off salary for a while, which was all I wanted to do." The
beginning of 1940 found Houseman back in New York, just
where Orson had wanted him.

Time was running out. Under pressure to justify his existence in Hollywood, by February Orson finally came up
with the film idea he had been looking for all along. Suddenly he knew that this was it, and that he should abandon
Smiler immediately. This was the project he would be able
to push through and make his name with. The movie he
had in mind was not completely new but drew on key elements of two past projects: his boyhood play *Marching
Song*; and the unrealized *Heart of Darkness* adaptation.
From *Marching Song*, Orson revived the notion of a reporter's quest for "a prophet-warrior-zealot—the most dramatic and incredible figure in American history," about whom
there are various points of view out of which the reporter
(and the audience) compose a picture of the mystery man.
From *Heart of Darkness*, Orson appropriated the idea that
the character who sets out in quest of the mystery man be
a fundamentally shadowy figure himself—the audience's
representative in the film. Thus, it will be recalled that in
Heart of Darkness Marlow was to have remained unseen,
his point of view identical with that of the camera—and,
by implication, of the audience. Similarly, in Orson's new
film idea, the reporter would hardly be present at all. (Pauline Kael pejoratively calls the reporter in *Citizen Kane* 'a

vacuum," as if to criticize the actor—William Alland—
who played him so. But she doesn't comprehend that this
was precisely what Orson had intended: a character who is
nearly as invisible as Marlow was supposed to have been
in *Heart of Darkness*.) Also from the earlier film project,
Orson took the framing device that would prove so decisive
in *Citizen Kane*: the mystery man's story inscribed within,
hence framed by, the vicissitudes of the search for it. Thus
it should be clear to anyone familiar with *Marching Song*
and the *Heart of Darkness* project that from the outset the
new film's matter and manner were both derived from the
two earlier efforts. It was hardly a case of his merely coming
up with a vague subject for a film, then turning to others
to give it substance. In the end, what distinguishes *Citizen
Kane* is less Kane's story than the curious—and, for Orson,
characteristic—way in which that story is told (*characteristic*, because he had told two such stories before).

   Convinced that at last he had concocted a viable first film
project, Orson flew to New York, where, at the 21 Club,
he invited Houseman to return to the West Coast with him.
He had a job for him now. In Hollywood, Orson had enlisted
the services of writer Herman Mankiewicz, who, besides
having recently worked with them in radio, and with Orson
on the abortive *Smiler* script, had a long list of successful
screenplays to his credit. He had the kind of screenwriting
experience Orson needed (precisely as he needed seasoned
Hollywood technicians) to realize his film idea. Under House-
seman's supervision, Mankiewicz was to get a rough draft
of Orson's concept on paper for Orson to cut, embellish,
rearrange, and generally rework. The only problem with
Mankiewicz was his notorious alcoholism. But having kept
Jack Carter from destructive drinking throughout the run of
Doctor Faustus, Orson was confident that, by assigning
Houseman to monitor the writer, he would have equal suc-
cess with Mankiewicz. Orson temporarily exiled Mankie-

wicz to a secluded resort called Victorville in what Orson recalls as "a special departure for drying him out." Perhaps far away from the people and pressures of Hollywood, Mankiewicz would be able to resist some of his more self-destructive impulses.

The plan worked. Rough segments of the script arrived regularly in Hollywood. There Orson pursued his usual extensive rewriting until the new versions were as close as possible to what he had in mind. Nor did the revisions stop there. All his life Orson has been a compulsive rewriter, of his own and other people's texts. Eventually, after Mankiewicz had finished a first rough draft, and with time out for work on another project, back in Hollywood he found himself presented with Orson's new version of the script, which, in turn, he was expected to work over. Even then Orson could not resist fine-tuning the pages Mankiewicz sent back to him. At length, from this prolonged give and take, this rewriting, more rewriting, and still more rewriting of each other's material, Herman J. Mankiewicz and Orson Welles wrote the script for *Citizen Kane* (precisely as the credit onscreen says they did).

Aside from Mankiewicz, Orson had another major collaborator on *Citizen Kane*, cinematographer Gregg Toland, whose credits included an Academy Award for *Wuthering Heights*, as well as a recent stint shooting *The Grapes of Wrath* for John Ford. Despite his extensive experience, Toland, much to everyone's astonishment, applied for work with Orson. Having made a big name for himself, Toland was eager to experiment, to transgress the usual pictorial codes and conventions. Unlike those in Hollywood who feared Orson as an inexperienced outsider, Toland figured that, with his notorious reputation for audacity in theater and radio, the newcomer was likely to have fresh ideas about film too.

Given the previous difficulties Orson had had with the

studio management, he devised a plan to begin shooting surreptitiously, *before* the front office could say anything about it. Chief in Orson's favor was that his enemies in the front office figured he did not know what he was doing. That June of 1940, under the guise of innocently shooting some "tests" for *Kane*, whose script he had not yet finished revising, twenty-five-year-old Orson began actually directing and shooting his first feature. This was a shrewd strategy. Before this, as late as early June, when Orson's plans for *Kane* were approaching their final stages, some of the studio management had been militating to get him to direct a picture called *The Men from Mars*. Evidently they figured that, as long as Schaefer had contracted him to work for RKO, he might as well bring in some easy money by directing a picture that the public would instantly associate with the famous Halloween hoax. Although he was just about to start shooting *Kane* covertly, Orson did not rule out the inane proposal. Instead, through Schaefer, he told them that he simply did not want to be typed "the horror man." He would certainly consider directing *The Men from Mars*—or so he hinted—but only *after* making another sort of film first. For which he wanted to do some tests. By the time they figured out these weren't *really* tests at all, *Kane's* momentum was much too great to stop.

With this new sense of direction, Orson struggled for control, not just of his destiny in the studio, but of himself as well. After a year of profligate spending, Orson had dismissed his butler, maid, and gardener and installed himself in a considerably more modest apartment, the address of which the very agitated Dadda did not manage to get for some time. Orson had also gone on a diet. Planning to portray the film's mystery man himself, he longed to slim down for the scenes that showed Kane as a young man. One of his crazy crash diets of the period had him eating bananas and milk exclusively. But since, in times of stress (which was most of the time), he was wont to cheat with nocturnal steaks, one after another, and so on, in swift succession, Orson took diet pills, whose stimulating side effects were by no means unwelcome. "I was full of energy!" recalls Orson, pointing out that this was long before the harmful effects of diet pills were known. And if crash diets and pills failed to do it, his steel back-brace helped. "Made my stomach look wonderfully flat!" explains Orson. "Nothing will hold in the gut so, like a steel brace!" To which he adds: "*Then* I was told by a whole lot of doctors that I was weakening my back by wearing the steel brace—which is probably true—so I gave it up. But oh, you *do* feel so great in it!" Orson says he also wore arch supports that helped him walk more gracefully than he would have with his perfectly flat feet.

To be certain he was comfortable with his cast, Orson wanted actors he already knew from the East Coast. If he was directing in an unorthodox fashion, the newcomers from New York probably would not know enough about film-making to notice or complain. No one would question his authority. Filling the movie with new faces also had the virtue of making filmgoers think that Orson Welles had personally discovered an entire cast. It was part of his image as the man who does everything. Finally, and perhaps most important, having radio cronies like Joseph Cotten, Everett Sloane, William Alland, Erskine Sanford, and Paul Stewart on the set made Orson feel protected from the often-hostile studio environment. In the two most important male roles besides his own, Orson cast Mercury regulars Everett Sloane (best known for his Sammy Goldberg on radio's *The Goldbergs*) as Bernstein, Kane's indispensable right-hand man, who describes himself as having been with him since "before the beginning"; and Joseph Cotten (fresh from the success of *Philadelphia Story* with Katharine Hepburn on Broadway) as Leland, the drama critic. Both characters were

consciously based on important people from Orson's past.
Bernstein was obviously a fond allusion to Dadda, while
Leland was modeled on the Chicago drama critic and Welles
family friend, Ashton Stevens, who had publicized young
Orson when the boy was still at Todd. But this was not the
only, or even the most important, reason Orson was keen
to allude to the newspaperman. Stevens had regaled young
Orson with the tales of his flamboyant employer, the myth-
ical newspaper magnate William Randolph Hearst, on whom
the character of Kane was in large part based. Thus Leland's
reminiscing about Kane to Thompson is a personal allusion
to Stevens's telling Orson all about Hearst. Since *Citizen
Kane* was Orson's own *re*telling of that story, he must have
thought it fitting to put Stevens into it. For his pair of leading
ladies, Orson cast Dorothy Comingore (whom Chaplin had
discovered) as Kane's mistress and second wife, Susan, and
Ruth Warrick as Kane's patrician first wife. Having met
Warrick on one of his trips to New York, he thought her a
perfect lady. Back at RKO, when he found himself looking
for the right actress to play the genteel and ladylike Emily,
she came immediately to mind.

Although Orson had indeed cast Warrick in the role of Emily for her ladylike qualities, he has considerable difficulty, some forty years later, assessing how properly to assert his own gentlemanliness with regard to her. Orson and I are having lunch together at Ma Maison one day just after he has finished taping a special segment of Good Morning America *to discuss the making of* Citizen Kane. *Ruth Warrick—now far better known as Phoebe Tyler in the soap opera* All My Children—*had been on the show, along with Orson's old friend Paul Stewart (Raymond, the butler). When the taping session was over, Orson tells me, Warrick gave him an autographed copy of her memoirs, which he had promptly gone home and read to discover with horror that she alluded to an amorous encounter she had had with him in what Orson likes to call "the prehistoric past" of his early days in Hollywood. But why would she possibly claim such a thing, Orson vigorously protests over lunch with me, when he certainly never did anything like that with her? At this, I can't resist commenting tongue in cheek that it might not be precisely* gentlemanly *to deny what a lady says. Orson looks genuinely puzzled, apparently realizing that he is in murky water, and drops the subject, but not before he has been unable to suppress a wicked giggle. At the end of lunch I, of course, rush out to buy and read the book.*

A year later, Orson and I are joking one morning about the new woman who "tells all"—the lady star whose graphic memoirs, Orson laughs, have put gentlemen into something of a quandary. Just what sort of chivalric code applies when it is the lady who claims you've shared her favors? Poor Orson, he loves lamenting about the "new woman"—though in truth, he is hardly the male chauvinist he sometimes likes to pretend he is. Not that Orson is seriously upset about the possibility of turning up as a character in his former ladyfriends' memoirs: he mock-solemnly reminds me that "anything a girl wants to tell is a delight to a man—unless she wants to say how terrible he is." Today, however, he is pursuing this subject because the new tell-all mood in some ladies evidently isn't confined to books alone, but can extend to the dinner table. I've just told him about one woman I met the other night at a dinner party in New York. When she learned that I was writing a biography of Orson Welles, she spent the rest of the evening (which was supposed to have been a few hours away from my subject) acclaiming the wonders of Orson's sexual prowess to me in surprisingly graphic detail. The other dinner guests sat in polite silence—some, I suspect, in shock—as this genteel lady of a certain age summoned up from the depths of memory an amazing succession of torrid encounters, meanwhile heartily eating the food and drinking the wine the rest of us barely had the heart to touch. As I joke about it now with Orson, I refuse to tell him her name, and allow only that it was a blond with huge blue eyes. This, however, is not enough for him. If Orson Welles is anything, it is determined. When he wants to know something, he gets what he calls his "mud turtle" mood on and keeps after you. He wants the blond's name—badly. Finally, exasperated by my continued refusal (as if it were he who had been trying to get information out of me all these many months!), Orson announces, in the fashion of Metternich carving up Europe in Vienna, "I'll trade you. And so much for my honor!" He means Ruth Warrick. His mind has been moving in a very Orsonian fashion—measuring where he can give something without giving too much. As long as Ruth Warrick wants to claim him (and has already done so in print), Orson wants to know the blue-eyed blond's name badly enough temporarily to throw over his code of honor. He will "trade" me a Warrick admission for the mysterious blond's name.

"You're so awful," I say, "the day you told me it wasn't true I thought, this is really twisting honor backward."

"Well," retorts Orson, "of course you don't tell on those kind of things."

"Of course you don't tell," I agree, "but if somebody else tells and then you deny it, it's worse!"

A mock-worried Orson queries, "Is that rude?"

"I don't know," I say. "I was trying to think that through after you said it."

"Then it's true," he bursts out, referring to Ruth Warrick.

"Only when told that it was rude to deny that you had a relationship with her were you willing to admit it," I complain.

"Well, I think that's the correct thing," says gentleman Welles. "I don't know what one's supposed to do in those circumstances. I think stout denial—at all times. But I am not going to make any effort to find out who this girl was— I'm just kidding you. But if I were Warren"—he means Warren Beatty—"and you were talking to me, he would have it by a week and he would drop everything to find it. You don't know what he would do. I made a terrible mistake once—because the only way I can hold Warren's attention is to cease to be a gentleman and trade off marks on the gun, you know. It's the only way an old man could keep him interested. He'll listen for hours to anything." This time, the particular story Orson regaled him with concerned

another actress from Orson's "prehistoric past" with whom he had a relationship—but in this case he lost her to Billie Holiday, who swept her away for a lesbian fling in Mexico City. As to how Warren Beatty responded to Orson's tale of lost love: "He was so fascinated with it," says Orson, "that he stopped for a week until he got to know the girl and asked her if it was so."

"He's *that* obsessive?" I wonder aloud.

"He's *that obsessed* by the subject," says Orson. "It struck him as so exotic and unlikely and probably a lie. And he found out it was true. That's *all* he thinks of, day and night. Oh yes, he's a real satyrite."

"But how does he have time?" I want to know. Warren Beatty seems awfully busy to me.

"That's all he does," says Orson. "Yes, he spends an awful lot of time. He spends as much time as we've spent on the phone"—we've been talking at this point for some four hours—"calling different people all morning long to be sure that in the evening there's going to be somebody new. You know, that's the real *Casanova.*"

"I think eventually it must just be sort of boring after a while," I say.

"Of course," agrees Orson. "Of course it is."

"And he's been doing it for an awfully long time."

"Yes, and he's not doing it as much now. He's not leaping out of moving cars in order to introduce himself to a girl he sees on the street, you know."

"That's an improvement."

"Yes, it's an improvement."

"I read the Joan Collins autobiography," I say, thinking of her affair with Warren Beatty.

"She's a cow," Orson rumbles angrily at the mention of her name.

"She said Warren Beatty was insatiable and left her feeling exhausted."

"I wish women would write that kind of thing about me,"
Orson says a bit wistfully.
"Only Ruth Warrick," I remind him.
"Only Ruth Warrick."

CHAPTER 19

The Power
of Ambition

By the end of July, Orson had the go-ahead to start shooting officially. Word went out to the press that Orson's "tests" had been so excellent that, now that he had actually begun *Citizen Kane*, there was no need to reshoot them. This convenient version of the events added to Orson's reputation for genius. Besides, it would have looked bad for Orson, and especially for the front office, if it were known that he had hoped to use the tests all along, and that his real motive had been to get *Kane* started before anyone could stop him.

The first official scene was the breakfast sequence with Welles and Warrick. By showing glimpses of the Kanes at the breakfast table over the course of years, Orson would chart the disintegration of their marriage. He wanted Warrick to play it the same throughout, decorous and ladylike, while he would change drastically, seeming to grow more and more distant from her. Expressly to save money, and thereby presumably to calm the anti-Welles faction in the front office, Orson avoided taking a scene numerous times by rehearsing extensively before he ordered the cameras turned on. No less anxious to have the press on his side (for he seemed to have his enemies among them as well) Orson threw a cocktail party for journalists. Told that they would be able to watch him shoot his first scene, they learned upon arriving that he had already finished it. Since Orson had a reputation in Hollywood as a late starter, telling the press he was far ahead of schedule was strategic. Here he was, driving past in an antique automobile and wearing a top hat. But the most curious aspect of his appearance—at least for those who had known him only in Hollywood—was that he had shaved the beard he had vowed to keep until he directed *Five Kings*.

Orson threw himself into *Kane* with all the energy that he felt had been pent up for more than a year, and that came through now with a rush. "When he was doing *Kane*," recalls editor Robert Wise, "that seemed to be his whole life. He was really, really concentrating on that. Absolutely! Boy, *that* was it—and very little else in his life." The unusual ferocity of *Citizen Kane*, its irresistible exuberance, was, in part, Orson's reaction to the impotence, the inability to express and thereby to assert himself, that had frustrated him thus far in Hollywood, and that had been all the more painful for the immense mastery he'd exerted on Broadway. Orson put in sixteen-, even eighteen-hour days, and began as often as not at four a.m. It took about four hours for the makeup man to age Orson, who, stuffed in a barber chair in his studio bungalow, used the idle time to confer with Toland and the other members of his staff. As usual, Orson was strangely exhilarated by being molded and made up. If thus far he had felt diminished in Hollywood, now he longed to be sculpted into an outsize figure even more imperial than he already was. While altering one's appearance is part of any actor's regimen, with Orson the ritual itself sometimes seemed almost more important than the result.

Besides the rubbery ears and noses and chins the makeup man pasted on Orson to show the passage of half a century, now there were specially coated contact lenses that seemed to age the eyes as well. They also made it difficult for Orson to see clearly. To insert them, a doctor was hired. But no matter how gingerly the doctor worked, the lenses were painful. During the filming of the sequence in which a furious Kane breaks up his second wife's bedroom at Xanadu, suddenly Orson could be heard screaming madly for the doctor. Blood streamed down his hands. His impaired vision had resulted in his cutting open his wrist on the furniture he "angrily" hurled about. An even more serious accident occurred when Orson fell ten feet in the scene where Kane pursues Boss Gettys down a flight of steps. X-rays at Good Samaritan Hospital showed two chips in his ankle. For two weeks thereafter, he directed from a wheelchair. Metal braces on either side of his ankle permitted him to act. One other mishap was a small fire caused by the series of burning sleds Orson needed for the camera to get the name "Rosebud" immersed in flame. When Orson had nearly exhausted his supply of sleds, and still had not managed to get the precise image he wanted, the doors swung open and in flew the fire fighters, summoned, it turned out, because an inadequate flue had caused a fire on the roof. When one of the men asked Paul Stewart who Orson was and Stewart told him, the fire fighter replied, "It figures!"— a sarcastic reference to the Martian hoax.

Accidents were not the only impediments to shooting *Kane*. No matter how swiftly and economically Orson worked, his enemies in the front office persisted in harassing him. Orson felt that the front office had stalled with Toland's contract in hopes that in the meantime the master cinematographer would accept another offer. Losing Toland would have been a big blow for Orson, who needed his technical expertise. Also, much to Orson's dismay, the clause in his contract stipulating that there was to be no interference from management was not always respected. The front office had in fact intercepted all copies of the script at the very moment Orson awaited them to begin shooting; only when Orson appealed were the scripts released, but not until a copy had been covertly dispatched to New York, where the hitherto secret subject of the film was leaked to reporters. Nor did the front office hesitate to call in studio employees to report on Orson's day-to-day activities, or to turn up unannounced on the set, even though his contract stipulated that he was supposed to be left entirely alone. No sooner would these uninvited guests arrive than Orson would cheerily invite cast and crew to a game of softball. Unathletic as he may have been, slowed down by his ankle brace, his back brace, and pounds of makeup, Orson would play ball till the intruders left.

This infighting notwithstanding, Welles had finished shooting by the end of December, having exceeded his preliminary schedule by only twenty-one *shooting* days (as opposed to *idle* days). Orson was elated. He showed his gratitude to cast and crew by hiring an orchestra and a striptease act for a gluttonous beer and spaghetti party. Already he and Toland were dreaming of their next project: the life story of Jesus Christ. In order to film it Orson had applied for, and secured, the endorsement of Bishop Fulton J. Sheen (among other clergymen to whom Orson had written from Hollywood for advice about the role he most wanted to play after Kane).

Did the twenty-five-year-old Orson Welles know what he had wrought in *Citizen Kane*? Did he have any inkling as yet that it might be one of the greatest films ever made, as well as one of our century's greatest works of art? Although his first months in Hollywood had proved disappointing and at times humiliating, he had known very great artistic success before. He had already made theater history. However much maddening frustration he had experienced in Hollywood thus far, however often he had secretly feared having to leave in disgrace, now it seemed only natural to him to conquer the cinema as well. It had merely been a question of outsmarting the studio, getting his picture made without their interference. This was the boundless ambition that

Martin Scorsese cites as having been widely resented in Hollywood. It was expressed not only in Orson's having written, produced, directed, and starred in his picture, but in its emphatic, self-assertive style. As he had in New York, now in Hollywood he created himself as the star-director. The unusually low camera angles, the deep focus, the long takes, the overlapping sound, the often unnerving cuts between scenes, these and other shock effects call as much attention to what is going on behind the camera as in front of it.

"You have to hate the camera and regard it as a detestable machine because it should be doing better than what it can do," says Orson, for whom film has been not just a means of recording reality, but of making his mark on it. "You have to totally dominate the camera and hate it. Like Simon Legree with a slave, you have to whip it through a movie and not approach it on your knees." Hence the mightily self-assertive style that, from *Citizen Kane* to *F for Fake*, has been the essence of his cinematic art: "You could write all the *ideas* of all the movies, mine included, on the head of a pin," says Orson. "It's not a form in which ideas are very fecund, you know. It's a form that may grip you or take you into a world or involve you emotionally—but ideas are not the subject of films. I have this terrible sense that a film is *dead*—that it's a piece of film in a machine that will be run off and shown to people. That is why, I think, my films are *theatrical*, and strongly stated, because I can't believe that anybody won't fall asleep unless they are. There's an awful lot of Bergman and Antonioni that I'd rather be dead than sit through. For myself, unless a film is hallucinatory, unless it becomes that kind of an experience, it doesn't come alive. I know that directors find serious and sensitive audiences for films where people sit around peeling potatoes in peasant houses—but I can't read that kind of novel either. Somebody had to be *knocking at the door*—I figure that is the way Shakespeare thought, so I can't be in bad company!"

While one may remember *Citizen Kane* as a continuous story, in the actual viewing it is, even by today's standards, exceedingly *dis*continuous. This was Orson's way of keeping his audience awake. Since the film tells Kane's fractured story from multiple points of view, the spectator apprehends it in bits and pieces, the jagged fragments of a life: his boyhood inheritance; his being taken as a boy to New York by his detested guardian, Thatcher; his taking over a newspaper, *The Inquirer*, shortly after he turns twenty-five, and his subsequent escapades as its publisher; his first doomed marriage to the genteel niece of an American president; his illicit affair with, then his second unhappy marriage to, a hopelessly untalented singer; his lonely death in the ostentatious mansion he calls Xanadu. All this—Kane's story— is just the movie's raw material. And it is precisely this raw material that stays in the mind afterwards, which is one reason why in retrospect, the film may seem far more continuous than it really is. Although the reporter himself never discovers the meaning of Rosebud (Kane's dying word), the spectator does: as the film draws to a close, in the process of clearing out Xanadu, a workman has thrown Kane's boyhood sled—labeled *Rosebud*—into the flames. One suddenly recalls the boy's having thrown the sled at Thatcher when the detested guardian came to take him to New York. However one wishes to interpret Kane's dying word in this light, the viewer's inevitable mental flashback to the much earlier scene of the boy's resisting Thatcher tends to make one think of Kane's life as a continuous whole—extending fluidly from boyhood to old age—rather than the disjunctive fragments one actually experienced in the course of watching the film. But it isn't Rosebud that makes *Citizen Kane* a great film—if it were, every film in which a mystery is eventually solved would be great.

The special genius of the film is of course not Kane's story—which, in itself, is really little more than a routine melodrama—but the peculiar way in which the film discloses that story. The film could have been made without multiple perspectives, as a straight narrative; but to subtract the conceit of the reporter's quest for Kane and to subtract the successive points of view of those who knew him (Thatcher, his guardian; Bernstein, his manager; Leland, his best friend; Susan, his second wife; Raymond, his butler) is to eliminate the artistic essence of *Citizen Kane*. Still, the structure of multiple narrators isn't in itself what gives Kane its unique fragmented texture. If *Kane* is a curiously disconcerting film, it isn't because the different points of view contradict one another (for they really don't). Nor is it because the story is told entirely out of chronological order (for, after the film's introductory sequence establishes the motif of the reporter's quest, although Kane's story is narrated to Thompson by different people, it is told in a fairly chronological way).

What *is* so curiously disconcerting is the way Welles repeatedly deceives our expectations, as when, for instance, he lulls us into the dark, dreamy opening sequence of Kane's muttering "Rosebud," then, suddenly, blasts us out of our seats with the brassy mock-newsreel of Kane's life story. Then, the very moment that life story is over, there follows another shock. The film within the film stops dead. There's a projector still running, an eerily blank screen, a small shadowy audience of journalists. When the newsreel runs out like this, one feels duped, let down. After the extreme upbeat of its conventional pace and narration, the blank screen is a potent metaphor for death. By contrast with the murky, dreamlike close-up of a pair of monstrous lips issuing an enigmatic word—Rosebud—the newsreel had seemed, well, *real*. It comes as a bit of a shock to be reminded that it was simply a reel of film, and the people it showed were really shadows—which is why the group of spectators

(Thompson among them) who constantly remain in the shadows is an especially nice touch. Now there is an extraordinary shot in which, as he speaks about the film he has (and we have) just seen, one of these shadowy spectators looms in front of the bare, white movie screen: a frame within the frame. Fascinated by frames, by the borders between things, Welles was inclined to give the audience a jolt whenever the movie moves from one scene to another. Hence the shock effect between the Rosebud sequence and the newsreel, between the newsreel and the screening-room sequence. The newsreel's suddenly stopping dead, and the sense of emptiness, of loss, that follows, suggests Welles's idea that, unlike theater, film is "dead," and that the filmmaker has to do something about it.

Consider the shot of Charles Foster Kane as a very young boy saying "Merry Christmas"—this followed by a "reverse" shot of his guardian, Thatcher, saying "And a happy New Year." The single sentence would initially appear to suggest that the two shots are parts of a single space, that Charles is looking at Thatcher, who, looking back at him, completes the familiar phrase. But no: many years have passed—Thatcher goes on to say that Charles is now twenty-five. The familiar phrase (anyone in the audience could have filled in the second part) leads one to expect that the second shot is only a moment later. The resulting shock, the disjunction in both time and space, is Welles's way of making the medium come alive by making it theatrical. In another strongly stated sequence: Kane, Bernstein, and Leland are reflected in the office window of the *Inquirer*'s rival paper, the *Chronicle*. They are covetously looking in at a group photograph of the *Chronicle*'s excellent reporting staff. Slowly the camera moves in on the photograph so that the reflection of Kane and his companions disappears as the image of the Chronicle staff grows larger. Suddenly, it seems, the photograph comes to life. It is several years later. Kane has gradually hired them all away from the *Chronicle* and they are posing for a new group photograph. The old photograph's unexpectedly springing to life, the sudden lapse in time and space, is another example of the kind of disorientation Welles so brilliantly used to theatricalize his first feature film.

Strangely enough, this most stylized of films has sometimes been described by critics as a cardinal example of cinematic realism in which art aspires to conceal art. The source of this interesting error is the film's marked use of the long take whereby, instead of cutting up individual scenes into numerous shots, Welles and Toland tried whenever possible to show the action within the scene as fluidly as they could. They would let the camera roll, cutting only when the scene was done. But the actual effect of this rather startling device was hardly to conceal the film's art, as some critics have suggested. In fact, these majestic long takes, crammed with detail, were so startling that they could not help but dramatically call attention to themselves and to the audacious star-director who was responsible for them. If Orson Welles's self-assertion, his seemingly boundless ambition, provoked hostility when he got to Hollywood, it has also excited—and inspired—subsequent generations of filmmakers of whom Martin Scorsese says: "The one key element we learned from Welles was the power of ambition. In a sense, he is responsible for inspiring more people to be film directors than anyone else in the history of the cinema."

CHAPTER 20
Rosebud

Late that August of 1940 Herman Mankiewicz was enraged when in her popular column Louella Parsons quoted Orson as having said, " . . . so I wrote *Citizen Kane*." But although Mankiewicz may not have realized it himself, the real source of his rage at that particular moment was more complicated than Orson's remark to a gossip columnist. Mankiewicz had just been looking at rushes from *Kane*, and what he saw there had surprised him, for it was certainly not the film he had envisioned. Mankiewicz had had a far more visually conventional film in mind. A glimpse at the rushes, and he knew enough about film to know that Orson was making a very different sort of picture. A memo to Orson from Herb Drake reported Mankiewicz's complaint about "not enough standard movie conventions being observed." Moreover, Mankiewicz was troubled by Orson's puzzling tendency to eschew closeups, and thereby to show the action theatrically. These complaints notwithstanding, Mankiewicz pronounced the footage "magnificent." Emphasizing that while "from an aesthetic point of view" he approved of Orson's approach, still he suspected that the audience might not understand it all.

Here was a curious—and revealing—contradiction in

Mankiewicz's reaction to the footage. Evidently at pains to approve of it in aesthetic terms, he criticized it precisely for its highly unconventional aesthetic approach: the theatricalization of the action—shown whole rather than in close-up or with numerous cuts—that Orson had hoped to achieve. The contradiction is quite understandable: at the same time he realized the film was going to be "magnificent," he realized it was not his. Whatever he had contributed to the film—and this had been a great deal—it had already become something entirely different. No wonder he was upset. And no wonder, shortly thereafter, he was thrown into a fit of agitation when he read Louella Parsons. Having realized that this "magnificent" film was not what he had had in mind, suddenly Mankiewicz now felt compelled to put his claim on it, to make it somehow his when he had just realized it wasn't. But according to the contract he had signed, Mercury might or might not credit him for his work. Since Orson's much-publicized contract with RKO specified he was to act in, direct, produce, and *write* the picture, Weissberger had thought it best to leave it open as to whether Mankiewicz would get a credit onscreen. Mankiewicz agreed. Paid $22,833.35 for his labor, Mankiewicz certainly had not balked at signing his contract.

In fact, correspondence between Welles and his lawyer, Arnold Weissberger, clearly indicates that Orson had never intended to deny Mankiewicz a credit on the finished film. The provision in Mankiewicz's contract had been Weissberger's idea to protect them lest RKO insist Orson be credited as having entirely performed all the roles for which he had contracted. Knowing of the antagonism toward Orson from the front office, Weissberger wanted not to give anyone any excuse to break his contract. Still, Orson had told Weissberger that he definitely wanted Mankiewicz to get a cocredit onscreen. There was certainly nothing strange about Orson having told Louella Parsons that he had written *Kane*. As Mankiewicz knew perfectly well (having had far more experience in Hollywood than Welles had) Orson was not *just* a director or an actor or a writer, but a public persona. And when public personae chat with gossip columnists, their job is to talk about themselves—which was especially true of someone like Orson, whose image was as the guy who does everything. Finally, although he intended all along to give Mankiewicz an onscreen co-credit for the writing he had undeniably—and quite brilliantly—done, Orson was in fact responsible for the concept of both the film's story and structure. Besides which he had extensively revised and rewritten whole chunks himself. But shooting his first film, Orson had discovered that onscreen spoken words inevitably lose something of the weight and substance they have on-stage. Writing a film was far more than getting the words down for the actors to speak. In a lecture titled "The New Actor" that he hired himself out to deliver in the idle days at the end of October and the beginning of November he stated: "The writer has a new thing to write, which isn't words—which is pictures." These were the very pictures that had so upset Mankiewicz when he first saw them. He was upset because he, the word man, hadn't written them. Orson had.

If, in a famous *New Yorker* essay of 1971 titled "Raising Kane," Pauline Kael revived Mankiewicz's charge that Orson is a credit stealer, it was, in large part, because of her unmistakable psychic identification with Mankiewicz. For, like Kael, Mankiewicz had been a staff writer on *The New Yorker*. And as Mankiewicz had done long before her, Kael had aspired to go to Hollywood to work in pictures. (When, eventually, she did, in 1979, her stay there proved abortive, and, shortly thereafter, she returned to work at *The New Yorker*.) That the *writer's* pilgrimage to Hollywood will be a principal theme of her piece is suggested, early on, when Kael establishes a lineage of *New Yorker* staffers who went West. Kael needed to discover Mankiewicz onscreen because, at length, she longed to find herself there too. So anxious is she to unearth the *literary* presence in *Kane* that she flagrantly disregards the most basic principles of literary analysis by not comparing *Kane* with Welles's earlier efforts. Although she briefly mentions *Heart of Darkness*, she appears not to know how much, and how obviously, *Kane* reworks that early effort. And on the subject of *Marching Song*, Kael is entirely silent. The sort of fundamental textual comparison missing in Kael's essay (between *Kane* and *Marching Song*, and *Kane* and *Heart of Darkness*) is precisely the means by which literary scholars routinely establish authorship. But if she had done that—if she had stopped trying to find *her* writer in the picture—she might have come up with the wrong *auteur*.

Kael's argument was an outgrowth of the critical polemic in which she had been engaged since 1963, when she attacked Andrew Sarris's influential argument for a film criticism that focuses on the director as the picture's *auteur*, or author. But besides her prior polemic against the *auteur* theory, and besides her strong personal identification with Mankiewicz, there was still another subtext to Kael's attack on Welles: she used Houseman as a principal source without having spoken to Welles himself. Asked about Kael's essay, Houseman replies, "Obviously, a certain amount of that material she got from me. I lunched with her, gave her stuff. *The New Yorker* kept calling me to doublecheck." In conversation, Houseman goes so far as to argue that Orson did no writing whatsoever on *Kane*. "He claims he wrote a parallel script," says Houseman. "That's all bullshit. He never wrote a word. I can tell you positively, he didn't." This assertion will seem odd to anyone who has examined Houseman's personal papers deposited at UCLA, among which is a telegram from June, 1940, in which Houseman tells Mankiewicz that he has received and mostly liked Orson's new scenes for *Kane*.

Initially, Mankiewicz had threatened to attack Orson's credit stealing in full-page ads in the trade papers, and warned that his friend Ben Hecht would write an exposé of the matter in the *Saturday Evening Post*. But the most perplexing threat was that Mankiewicz would complain formally to the Screen Writers' Guild. Evidently fearing that he was going to be denied any screen credit at all (which, as the correspondence between Welles and Arnold Weissberger makes clear, certainly was not the case) Mankiewicz decided to claim that he had written the *whole* script—and that it was Orson who did not deserve any credit. But since Mankiewicz had signed away the right to any credit, and since he was going to get a co-credit with Orson anyway, the RKO legal department assured Weissberger that, should Mankiewicz complain to the Screen Writers' Guild as he was threatening to do, there was nothing to worry about. Having vacillated for several months about whether to carry out his threat, by January Mankiewicz had decided to register his complaint formally. Fully confident that eventually Mankiewicz would have to agree to a co-credit (which, at length, he did, when at the end of January he asked the Guild to drop the matter), Weissberger was nonetheless greatly dismayed that Mankiewicz had brought action just when Orson found himself amid yet another, and vastly more serious, controversy.

Press tycoon William Randolph Hearst, on whom the fictional character of Kane was unmistakably based, had just then expressed his immense displeasure about the very idea of the film, especially its depicting in an unflattering light his real-life mistress, Marion Davies (whose beloved nephew, screenwriter Charles Lederer, had recently married Virginia Welles after her divorce). Somehow, before making the movie, Orson had found out the secret name that Hearst used to refer to Marion Davies's genitalia: Rosebud. To Hearst, it was bad enough that Rosebud be mentioned throughout the picture, but even worse was the idea that Kane died with Rosebud on his lips. *Kane* was scheduled

to open at Radio City Music Hall in New York on February
14, 1941. At the beginning of January, although Orson had
not finished post-production work on the film—it was still
without its music track—Mercury decided to give the critics
from *Life, Look,* and *Redbook* a secret preview that would
allow them to meet their deadlines for the next month's
issue. Better to risk showing them an unfinished film, Mercury figured, than lose the timely publicity early reviews in
big-circulation magazines could afford. Almost instantly,
however, all Hollywood had heard about the secret screening, on the morning of which, gossip-columnist Hedda Hopper informed Orson's publicist, Herb Drake, that although
uninvited, she planned to attend. Afterward, unlike the other
critics who had much admired what they'd seen, Hopper
made much ado about being appalled by what seemed to
her Orson's "vicious and irresponsible attack on a great
man." Nor did she hesitate to sneer at what she took for
corny writing and old-fashioned photography. Still, her
strictly artistic judgments were far less dangerous to Orson
than her public protest at his film's being about Hearst. But
if Hopper was clearly an enemy of Orson's, columnist Louella
Parsons was a staunch supporter—or so Orson thought. She
was the last person Orson would want to alienate just now,
and it is easy to imagine his upset when he learned that the
forthcoming issue of a magazine was about to quote him as
having wondered why, in her columns, Louella Parsons was
so nice to him: "This is something I cannot understand,"
Orson was supposed to have said. "Wait until the woman
finds out that the picture's about her boss." Claiming never
to have uttered anything like this, Orson confronted the
magazine's editor, who, admitting that his source for the
quote was fallible, offered to run Orson's protest. It was
too late, however, to stop the press, or insert Orson's denial
in the same issue. Lest she bristle at the offending misquo-
tation, Orson sent Parsons an apology for any embarrassment it should cause her as well as his assurance that the

quote was fallacious. On the same day she received Orson's note, she also received word from San Simeon, the palatial Hearst retreat (a fantasy version of which appears as Xanadu in *Kane*). Having learned about *Kane* from Louella's rival Hedda Hopper—who did not even work for him—Hearst expressed his supreme displeasure about the film to Louella Parsons, who *did*. It was imperative that she act quickly lest her employer think Hedda Hopper more loyal to him than she. That it was about to be printed that Orson had made a fool of her enraged her all the more.

At midnight, January 8, all Hearst papers were instructed to refuse RKO advertising. The next day there was a series of furious calls from Parsons to RKO. First she called Drake to inform him that he was to arrange a screening of *Kane* for her the next day. Never did she *ask* to see *Kane*, she *insisted*. Then she called Schaefer, and announced to his startled secretary that her call involved a life and death matter. Told he wasn't there, she demanded his home telephone number, adding that RKO was about to have a massive lawsuit should they release *Kane*. Nor would RKO suffer alone for *Kane*. In yet another call, Parsons warned Schaefer's secretary that Hearst was going to attack the entire movie industry.

As promised, Parsons arrived for her screening on the afternoon of the 10th. She identified her two male escorts as reporters from the *Examiner*, Hearst's Los Angeles paper. In fact they were Hearst's lawyers, there to advise Parsons on just how libelous *Kane* really was. Later, having demanded that Schaefer shelve the picture (which he was clearly not inclined to do), and having warned the Radio City Music Hall management not to show it, Parsons contacted several movie moguls, among them Louis B. Mayer, to whom she is supposed to have said, in a now famous phrase, "Mr. Hearst says, if you boys want private lives, I'll give you private lives." Hearst figured that the best way to stop Hollywood from disclosing the secrets of his sex life was to threaten to expose theirs. Perhaps Parsons could scare the moguls into pressuring Schaefer to pull back. (It is ironic that the movie shows Kane's image being ruined by sensational newspaper stories about *his* sex life, precisely what Hearst threatened to do to the moguls.) Nor was the RKO board of directors safe from threats of their *fictionalized* life stories in the Hearst papers.

Orson, too, found himself suddenly threatened with a well-researched exposé of his furtive nightlife. If at this particular time he was especially vulnerable to this threat, or felt himself to be so, it was because he had something to hide from the scrutiny of the press: his liaison with a married woman substantially older than he, Lolita Dolores Martínez Asunsola López Negrette, better known to her public as Dolores Del Rio. Like Dolores, Orson had still been married at the outset of their relationship. Those close to him had perceived that his powerful attraction to her had completely—and permanently—precluded any lingering chance of his returning to Virginia. Now the beautiful black-haired Mexican actress, who, Orson recalls, "never wore any dress more than once," anticipated a divorce from her second husband, and perhaps even a marriage to Orson. Still, she and Orson persisted in conducting their affair with the utmost discretion. Although he had been having erotic fantasies about her since adolescence, Orson actually met Dolores, he recalls, "at a huge Hollywood party given by Jack Warner. We all moved to Darryl Zanuck's ranch, and there I met her. We went swimming together in the evening. Oh, she swam beautifully!" What Dolores did not know was that Orson had watched her swimming once before in a movie he had seen, and subsequently dreamed about, in youth. "That's when I fell in love with her," he says. "I was about eleven. She was in a picture about the South Seas, a silent, with a lot of underwater scenes. You know, her little feet fluttering! She was as *undressed* as anyone I'd ever seen on the screen, and *maddeningly* beautiful! I had some young lady in the back row with whom I was fumbling. It changed my life!" But it wasn't his young girlfriend who had excited Orson. "It really was the movie," Orson recalls. "I just waited till I could find her. Oh, I was *obsessed* with her for years!"

Now, some years later, here she was in the flesh in exactly the same aquatic poses that had first gotten Orson going. Soon Orson focused on a new aspect of her allure. "You should have seen her underwear!" he exclaims, four decades later. "Unbelievable! It was all handmade, very hard to find, so *erotic* it was indescribable!" From the moment he discovered where she got her flimsy lace-edged slips and gossamer embroidered silk nightgowns, at the swank Juel Parks in Beverly Hills, he became a longstanding and much-valued customer there. (Even after he had broken off with Dolores, he liked the women in his life to wear the kind of lingerie he preferred.) One aspect of ladies' lingerie that Orson grew to abhor was the garter belt. "From my happy time, the first cloud that fell over the horizon was the garter belt," says Orson. "Before that they wore garters, and above the garters nothing. They had their slip, which was delicately connected under the legs—*very delicately*! And garters, you see, on silk stockings. Then came nylon stockings and garter belts. That was bad enough—and then they invented the stockings that go right up. Just making an approach, you had to begin saying, 'Do you want to screw?' There was no other possible approach!" But Dolores's sensuous, if rather impractical, underwear presented no such problems. "You cannot believe what Dolores paid, and what she looked like in those!" he reiterates. "You know, the only thing that can have equaled it was the high fashion of the nineteenth century, which is described in 'The Old Chevalier,' a wonderful story of Dinesen's—a long description of what it was to undress a woman in the days when there was all this to take off. It does convince you that that was foreplay with a vengeance!" Another thing about Dolores that particularly excited Orson

was what he describes as "that sightless beautiful look of
hers, which was a great turn-on, you know." At such moments what seemed to him like her perfectly "black eyes"
would freeze into "this wonderful fixed expression." Because Dolores was still married and hesitated to be seen
with Orson in public, they often brought along Marlene
Dietrich to make it all seem innocent enough. "Marlene was
the 'beard,' you see, for Dolores when she was married,"
says Orson. "I would take out Dolores by taking out Marlene
too. Who would guess with those two girls what I was
up to?"

Unfortunately, Hearst had guessed, or found out, exactly
what Orson and Dolores were up to. But Hearst's greatest
threat against Orson was not gossip. What vexed Orson
most was the possibility of Hearst's permanently, irrevoc-
ably blocking the release of *Kane*. Rumors of what Hearst
and Louella were going to do next flew in every direction,
and Orson seemed to have heard, and endlessly mulled over,
all of them—especially the one that had Louis B. Mayer
offering RKO a lordly sum to buy the film in order to destroy
it. Acutely agitated as he was, Orson could not resist being
just a bit too expansive with the press, as when he declared
of *Kane*: "It is not based on the life of Mr. Hearst nor anyone
else. On the other hand, had Mr. Hearst and similar financial
barons not lived during the period we discuss, *Citizen Kane*
could not have been made." Once before, Weissberger had
sternly advised Orson not to apologize for the chaos of the
Martian scare, lest he seem to admit any guilt for all that
had happened. Now, reading Orson's statement in the papers, his attorney was appalled by Orson's having unnecessarily qualified his denial of the picture's being based on
Hearst. Why had he felt compelled to continue his denial
with: "On the other hand . . ."? In his attempt to deny a
connection, he seemed almost to be admitting it. Thus,
Weissberger sent strict orders that Orson's future denials
were to be absolutely unequivocal. Under no circumstances

was he to succumb to his natural, almost irresistible, impulse to expand on the subject. After having heard that Hearst's lawyers were busily annotating a copy of the *Kane* script in preparation for securing an injunction against the picture and for bringing suit on grounds of libel or invasion of privacy, Orson called Weissberger at four one morning. Rousing himself from sleep, Weissberger ventured the educated guess that, although Hearst might initially succeed in securing a temporary injunction from a lower court, an appeal from Orson would almost certainly be successful. And ironically, Hearst himself would have made the picture's premiere even more of an *event* than it might otherwise have been. Weissberger suspected, too, that, in the long run, Hearst would not actually go through with a suit for fear of having to testify in court about his extramarital relationship with Marion Davies. To be certain of scaring off Hearst, one of Weissberger's colleagues had suggested threatening him with publicly disclosing that, in Mexico, Marion Davies had once covertly given birth to twins, the birth certificates for which could be produced. Hearst's greatest weapon, however, was not a lawsuit, or even the threat of one, but the implicit, and massive, threat of using the power of the press to harass the entire film industry. In particular, Hollywood feared an attack on its widespread employment of aliens at the expense of American labor. Because of the war in Europe, there was a particularly strong foreign presence in Hollywood just now. Hollywood was most content to have the benefit of all this European talent, but feared lest the Hearst press portray the industry as somehow unpatriotic.

In helping Orson to plan his counterstrategy, Weissberger calculated that, since Schaefer had staked so much on Orson, and become so fully associated with him in the eyes of RKO's stockholders, he was most unlikely to abandon him now. Defending Orson and his controversial first film was clearly in Schaefer's best interest. But Weissberger also

figured that, since *he* knew where Schaefer's interest lay,
so probably did RKO's controlling stockholders. Faced with
the threat of exposés of their private lives, as well as with
intense pressure from elsewhere in the industry, they might
decide to ignore Schaefer's recommendations with regard
to *Kane*. According to this possible scenario, whatever the
obvious consequences for Schaefer, they would decide to
save themselves by prohibiting the release of *Kane*. Thus
Weissberger's tactic was to give Schaefer the ammunition
to use against these controlling interests should they show
signs of having turned against Orson. He advised Orson to
intimate to Schaefer that he would bring suit against RKO
in the event of its failing to release *Kane*. Once it was made
public in March, Orson's threat of a lawsuit may have seemed
impetuous or hotheaded. But in fact it had been most carefully calculated to give Schaefer the leverage he needed
against any of RKO's controlling stockholders who opposed
releasing the picture. Finally, meeting with board members
to argue his own case, Orson pointed out that, ironically, it
was none other than Hearst himself who had brought so
much attention to the idea of the film's being about him,
and that no one was doing more to publicize Kane's identification with Hearst and to make the picture a box-office
sensation than his own columnist, Louella Parsons.

While Hearst himself seemed to identify with the film's
central character, as an actor Orson deliberately did not
(especially not with the older Kane). One reason the portrait
is so unsympathetic is because Orson so entirely distanced
himself from Kane that, many years later, he would describe
him in conversation as "a hollow man." Says Orson: "The
secret was there really was no secret." Encrusted with four
hours' worth of makeup, old Kane was almost like one of
Gordon Craig's *übermarionettes*: the giant dummies that
Craig had proposed to replace live actors. Craig had been
one of the spiritual sources of the antinaturalistic theatrical
theory Orson had assimilated at the Gate. As an experienced

puppeteer, Orson was really outside Kane, pulling the strings. Back at Todd, having put his puppet-teachers through some humiliating turns, he now did the same with his puppet-tycoon.

Although Orson had publicly denied that Kane was really Hearst, in private he took a different line. Hearst was undeniably a public figure; and to Orson's mind, the facts of a public figure's life were always readily available for writers to shape and restructure. Weissberger had succinctly articulated the issue in the form of a rhetorical question to Orson: "Will a man be allowed in effect to copyright the story of his life? For both Weissberger and Welles the implicit answer was—resoundingly—no. Only the treatment of that life was subject to copyright: its form, but not its content. As a brilliant pioneer of entertainment law, Weissberger had raised a question that remains controversial today, especially at a time when popular biographers and the makers of TV docudramas have found themselves threatened with legal action because of their attempts to reinvest the facts of a public figure's life into a narrative structure of their own design. However unabashedly frivolous some of these productions may be (especially by contrast with a work of art like *Citizen Kane*), the basic issue is still the same: whether the public figure should be able to prohibit the writer from appropriating the facts of his or her life. Orson thought not. The Welles case was further complicated by the film's explicitly being a work of fiction, so that in the screenplay Hearst's life had been liberally mingled with the careers of two other figures: Robert McCormick (who, like Kane, had promoted a lousy opera singer because he loved her) and Samuel Insull (builder of an ostentatious opera house whose publicity director was Skipper Hill's old friend John Clayton). To distinguish the tycoon character even further from Hearst, after a special screening in New York for film industry mahatmas who wanted to see what the uproar was all about, the editor had removed a few snippets of dialogue that would too readily call Hearst to mind. Weissberger suspected, however, that in the unlikely case that there were flagrantly libelous matter in the film, even the fictional frame might prove an inadequate defense. Thus Weissberger was dubious when an RKO attorney suggested that Orson tack onto his picture a foreword, or an afterword, to claim that in the narrative the central character is seen from the viewpoints of other characters, and that none of these limited views purports to show the man as he really was. Presumably this disclaimer would allow individual characters to say anything at all about Kane without the filmmaker's being responsible for it. The suggestion seemed perfectly reasonable from a literary perspective, but literary and legal answers to a single question need not always be the same and such a disclaimer probably would not stand up in court. Weissberger told Orson: "If you had a character in a picture get up and say, 'Hearst is a thief,' it would not be a defense to a libel action to answer, 'I didn't say that—the character in the picture said it.' "

Orson had plenty of time to mull over all of this when he and Dolores went to New York in February of 1941. At Houseman's invitation, Orson was to stage Richard Wright's *Native Son* on Broadway at the St. James Theatre. "I thought it was a shame that our relationship should have broken off with a whimper," explains Houseman. "I owned *Native Son*, and I asked Orson to come and direct it and produce it with me." Richard Wright's story of a black man's accidental murder of a white woman was precisely the kind of politically controversial material that by now so strongly appealed to Orson. Although Orson had suspected that Houseman had maliciously set Mankiewicz against him, he welcomed this break from Hollywood as an opportunity to get away with Dolores (even though her mother accompanied them) and to plan the movie he hoped to make with her soon in Mexico, his hopes for playing Jesus Christ never having crystallized in a script. Lest anyone get the mistaken idea that, because of the crisis with *Kane* and the abortive Jesus project, he was not planning to return to Hollywood after *Native Son*, he issued a press release to announce the transfer of all operations of Mercury Productions to the West Coast.

When Orson and Dolores had visited New York together once before, it had been strictly in secret. To avoid the press finding out about their rendezvous, she had checked into a hotel under an assumed name. After all, she was still a married woman. This time, however, the divorce proceedings from Dolores's second husband were already under way, so she felt free to go about openly with Orson—much to the dismay of Dadda, who claimed that Dolores was too old for Orson, and that she had probably lied about her age anyway. And even if Orson could steal a look at her birth certificate (which was advisable), Dadda's professional opinion was that Mexican birth certificates were not to be trusted, as it was common for the birth dates of well-to-do Mexican ladies to have been substantially altered. In New York, Orson and Dolores installed themselves in separate suites at the Ambassador Hotel on Park Avenue. Dolores's was filled with her beloved gardenias, but also by her watchful mother, an elderly lady of aristocratic background ("a real royal mama," as set designer James Morcom describes her).

To Orson, Dolores represented everything that was glamorous about Hollywood. Returning East with her now was a sign of his success there. "He was mad about her," explains James Morcom. "He just couldn't believe that probably one of the most beautiful women in the world would give him ten minutes. She wasn't terribly bright at that time. She was terribly sweet, but he could buffalo her, you see. She was so in awe of him and his genius, and he *loved* that, lapped it up. He was goggle-eyed that she would even hang around."

Although one of Orson's principal motives for briefly returning to Broadway had been to make some quick cash (much as he'd gone to Hollywood to do), he once again found himself spending more than he could possibly earn. Nor did he stint on his production of *Native Son*. At rehearsals his adamant refusal to economize caused him to quarrel openly with Houseman, who was as anxious to minimize expenses as Orson was to maximize them. Of course all the other lingering tensions between them formed the subtext of their financial disputes; Orson would bellow that he had paid for something out of his own pocket, to which Houseman would sarcastically reply: "What pocket?" And, too, Orson had been dazzled by the extensive technical resources of Hollywood, in comparison to which Broadway now seemed plodding, inefficient. His impatience caused him to spend, or to want to spend, more than he should have. Perhaps the most meaningful expenditure of all, however, was also an exceedingly modest one: Orson mysteriously ordered a sled to be placed on the stage with the word Rosebud painted on it. Since *Citizen Kane* had not yet opened, the allusion was not obvious. All Orson would say when asked about the sled and the cryptic inscription was that the prop was for good luck.

At first, the sled brought better luck to the play than to the film from which it had been borrowed. When *Native Son* opened on March 24, 1941, *Time* called it "by all odds the strongest drama of the season." And of Orson, Brooks Atkinson wrote in *The New York Times*: "When he applies the theatricalism of his personal nature to a stage problem something exciting comes into existence. The space and the sound of the theater, which are only partly used in ordinary productions, yield a fresh sensation. It is as if the theater had been shaken up and recharged with life." Not everyone was as delighted by Orson. Thus Hearst's *Journal American* hurled the nasty epithet "Communist" at the play as a first step toward discrediting Orson. Wright's leftist sympathies were generally known, so initially it might have seemed reasonable to assume that he, not Orson, was the principal object of the attack. Shortly thereafter, however, Orson found himself the direct object of red-baiting when both the Hearst press and the American Legion attacked as "definitely Communistic" a series of patriotic shows about the Bill of Rights, aired on CBS, and titled *Free Company*. Along with Orson, the show's eminent unpaid participants included Sherwood Anderson, George M. Cohan, Ernest Hemingway, and William Saroyan. But Welles was singled out for attack. Since there was certainly nothing remotely subversive about the program Orson had scripted, which involved liberal quotation from the Bill of Rights, it seemed obvious that labeling Orson a Communist was simply the latest tactic for smearing the man who made *Citizen Kane*.

While at first Orson declined to comment publicly on the charges, he soon felt compelled to respond to them head-on: "The Hearst papers have repeatedly described me as a Communist. I am not a Communist. I am grateful for our constitutional form of government, and I rejoice in our great American tradition of democracy. Needless to say, it is not necessarily unpatriotic to disagree with Mr. Hearst. On the contrary, it is a privilege guaranteed me as an American citizen by the Bill of Rights." Not everyone was convinced, however; back in Hollywood after *Native Son*, Orson received a visit at the studio from a government investigator. The mysterious investigator promptly asked if Welles was a Communist, to which Orson replied that the fellow would have to define what he meant by Communist. Told that by definition a Communist is someone who gives his money to the government, Orson quipped that, indeed, he must be eighty-seven percent Communist, since that was the amount of his income he paid in taxes. The remaining thirteen percent, he assured his visitor, was all capitalist.

All this pressure had begun to take its toll on Orson's health. In Hollywood, he visited a doctor who was terribly alarmed by Orson's bloated, exhausted body; despite all the diet pills, the twenty-five-year-old Orson weighed in at 218 pounds. Besides his chronic back pain, bronchial asthma, and hay fever, Orson now suffered from "knifelike pain in his chest" accompanied by "sensations of smothering." The doctor counseled Orson to leave Hollywood immediately for at least sixty days and to go on a Spartan diet.

Orson had good reason to be suffering from nervous exhaustion. "My nights are sleepless and my days are a torture," he telegrammed Schaefer, whom, in a fit of paranoia, he suspected of having begun to avoid him. At the outset of the trouble with Hearst, Orson and Schaefer had regularly conferred by phone, often twice daily. Suddenly Orson seemed to be having trouble reaching Schaefer at all. Suffering from insomnia, agitated by hate mail, and fearful that Schaefer had turned on him, Orson sat up into the middle of the night repeatedly dialing his number to find out when and if *Kane* was going to be released.

After publicly threatening to sue RKO for withholding his picture, and even grandly offering to buy the picture from them for a million dollars, Orson finally learned that the studio had decided to go ahead with a New York premiere of *Kane* on May 1. Since Radio City Music Hall had stubbornly refused to show *Kane*, the Palace Theater was second choice. But the good news came much too late to calm Orson's overly agitated nerves. In New York for a round of advance publicity, Orson dispatched Arnold Weissberger to Los Angeles to escort Dolores and her friend, actress Fay Wray (whom King Kong had hauled to the peak of the Empire State Building), back to New York to join him for the premiere. As there had already been a spate of laudatory advance reviews, Orson did not have to worry about the picture's critical reception. In *Newsweek*, John O'Hara had hailed Orson as "the best actor in the history of acting" and *Citizen Kane* as probably "the best picture" he had ever seen. Said *Time*: "It has found important new techniques in picture-making and story-telling." And *Life*: "Few movies have ever come from Hollywood with such powerful nar-

rative, such original technique, such exciting photography."
But Orson worried about what the mass audience would
think. How effective had the smear campaign against Orson
been? What would be the result of the powerful Hearst
press's refusal to run ads for *Kane*? Most important, would
the masses *understand Kane*? Would they be irritated or
baffled by its dense structure, its complex framing devices,
its multiple points of view? Orson feared that it would take
weeks, perhaps even months to tell.

The premiere Orson was really anticipating most anxiously, however, was not the big one in New York, but the
Chicago opening, several days later, on May 6, his twenty-
sixth birthday. For there, he and Dolores were to be met by
Skipper and Hortense Hill—to whom, as always, Orson
liked to turn in periods of stress. Nor did Skipper disappoint
him this time. To the tune of "Happy Birthday to You,"
Skipper had composed a sweet ditty about the *Kane* controversy as a special surprise for Orson, and when Orson
and Dolores entered the theater lobby the night of the opening, they saw a cake topped with twenty-six candles—and
a radio crew and commentator to report on Orson's blowing
them all out. After which a quartet of Todd boys, led by
Skipper's fifteen-year-old son, Roger Gettys Hill, sang:

> Happy Birthday to you,
> Felicitations we strew
> On our dear friend in Orson
> From the boys old and new.
> Let the Hearst face turn blue,
> Shouting red bunk at you.
> Those who know you, dear Orson
> Know you're white through and through.
> If he thinks Kane's like him,
> It's his privilege and whim.
> But if Kane's after Abel,
> Why you're able to win.

So we'll sing it once more
Though this tune's apt to bore.
Happy birthday, dear Orson,
Happy birthdays galore.

Much to Orson's humiliation, however, the theater was surprisingly empty. "Nobody came at all," Orson recalls with horror. "It was an awful, awful embarrassment with Dolores, who was used only to glamour." The poor turnout that terrible night in Chicago presaged what was to come.

However successful *Kane* had been with the critics, it failed at the box office. Although it grossed $23,878.99 the first week in New York, by the ninth week, receipts were down to a dismal $7,279.99. After expenses, this meant a loss of $18,057.67 for the nine-week engagement. Except for Seattle, the premiere engagement theaters—in Boston, Chicago, Los Angeles, San Francisco, and Washington— also reported losses. "People were too scared of it to even know what it was," explains Orson. Although Hearst never actually brought suit, the fear that he would persisted, and this kept the picture from being distributed as widely as it might have been: the distributor Spyros Skouras told Weissberger that he did not plan to screen *Kane* in the theaters he controlled, since he suspected that Hearst was waiting to sue until after the picture had been running for a time. Although Skouras said that he personally had liked *Kane* very much, he didn't want to encourage more movies about public figures, because the purpose of film was to entertain people, not to cause trouble.

Ironically, all its publicity had worked against *Kane* by making it seem somehow forbidding. The ad campaign for its popular-price release attempted to make it seem less so by identifying it with a familiar popular genre: the torrid love story. "How much love can you buy for $60,000,000?" asked one ad. Another: "What made this cutie walk out on $60,000,000? A girl who never made more than $15 a week—wed to the world's wealthiest man! But neither she— nor any woman—could endure his kind of love!" In short, *Kane* had become "the love story they said *dared* not be filmed." Still, however hard the ads tried to change the picture's threatening image, the initial damage had been done at the box office.

Having come to Hollywood as a much-resented outsider, Orson was still a pariah, even now that he had mastered the medium and made a picture that was widely recognized as a new breakthrough in the art of film. In an unprecedented sign of scorn for the man who made *Citizen Kane*, there were boos and guffaws when the movie was mentioned at the Academy Awards ceremony in February of 1942. Nominated in nine categories, *Kane* received only a citation for best screenplay—a mocking allusion to the Mankiewicz controversy. Figuring they had to honor *Citizen Kane* for something, the industry picked that part of the film to which Orson's contribution had been seriously—and publicly— called into question. This was another way of humiliating him. It did not really matter that, in the end, Mankiewicz had agreed to the co-credit he deserved. The nasty innuendo about Orson Welles had been made, and like the myth about his being a Communist, it persisted in some people's minds.

CHAPTER 21

Comeuppance

"If there was a downfall, then it was entirely of his own doing," says John Houseman of Orson's Hollywood career after *Kane*. "I mean, nobody stopped him from producing more *Citizen Kane*s." But the facts tell a very different story.

After the great artistic and critical triumph of *Citizen Kane*, Orson knew better than anyone that people would be watching him intently. If he could not repeat his earlier performance, they would gleefully write him off the way they do the brilliant first novelist who cannot match his first effort. Moreover, Orson appreciated that Schaefer had taken a big chance on the *genius*'s being able to make an intelligent first film that also made money. Now, unfortunately, his controversial investment in Orson seemed highly unlikely to pay off at the box office and was almost certainly not going to make the kind of cash Schaefer needed to appease his and Orson's antagonists among major RKO stockholders. Schaefer's position—and, as an immediate consequence, Orson's—was seriously weakened.

Orson was aware that his choice of a second picture project was a crucial decision in terms of his future in Hollywood. By now the Jesus film was definitely out, and so was the passing idea he had had of directing W. C. Fields in Dickens's *The Pickwick Papers*. In February of 1941, Orson had sent a finished script for his so-called *Mexican Melodrama* to Schaefer. Partially based on Arthur Calder-Marshall's novel *The Way to Santiago*, the film was supposed to star Dolores Del Rio. In his enthusiasm, Orson had even briefly scouted locations in Mexico. But the government there was not amused by the film's theme—Nazi spies in Mexico—and refused Orson the permission to shoot. Although Dolores resolved to intercede with the Mexican government on Orson's behalf, negotiations would take time.

So Orson hit upon a new plan. He urged RKO to buy from Alexander Korda the Ben Hecht script for *Cyrano de Bergerac*. Orson had personal reasons for his interest in the property. Although his natural nose is perfectly adequate (if, at certain angles, a trifle small for the rest of his physiognomy), Orson has always thought it his weakest feature. Hence the vast museum of false noses beneath which, on stage and screen, he has generally preferred to conceal his own. Fearful that this upturned button of a nose was not grand enough for serious leading roles, Orson now decided to play a character whose nose was too grand. Unfortunately, however, a Gallup poll regarding potential film projects had indicated minimal public interest in *Cyrano*, and Schaefer and RKO were therefore not especially excited about Orson's latest idea.

When Orson conferred with the story editor Schaefer had dispatched to suggest potential properties to him, *Cyrano* was still his first choice. Much to the editor's astonishment, Orson appeared to have already read and considered any story she mentioned. By the end of their hectic two-hour session in Orson's suite at the Ambassador in New York, they had rapidly discussed no fewer than forty stories, among them works by Maugham, Daudet, O'Neill, Dostoevsky, Dreiser, Twain, and Hemingway. Orson's brain was a crowded archive of plot outlines.

Not all of these plot outlines came from fiction. It had

been in conversation with a French lawyer of his acquaintance—whose partner had defended the infamous Landru, who had married and murdered a series of women—that Orson had thought of making a movie about this modern Bluebeard, starring Charles Chaplin. Orson's imagination had been activated by the fact that the lawyer had witnessed Landru's decapitation. A moment after his client had been properly positioned, face downward, in the guillotine, the lawyer leaned over to inquire what the *real story* of the murders was. Landru blandly replied, "That's my little secret." Then down went the blade. Hearing all this, Orson was determined to unearth the story that supposedly died with Landru—or, better yet, to imagine one. The first step was to accumulate masses of research on the case, the next somehow to assimilate it all, then, finally, to synthesize it into a *story idea*. He took all this to Chaplin, who, reluctant to act under Welles's direction, bought Orson's idea, which would form the basis of *Monsieur Verdoux*. In his memoirs, Chaplin would say that Welles had given him merely the raw idea for a film about the Lándru case, although in fact Orson had suggested specific incidents and scenes that he had planned to use had he directed the film. In 1941, Orson told the press that he had sold Chaplin the material because he thought him the single living actor capable of playing the part. "There is one tableau, and it is the key to the whole picture," Welles said to a reporter. "There is Chaplin, dapper and blithe, clipping the hedges, making his hands and the shears dance like sunlight, while out of the chimney in the background pour vast clouds of dense black smoke."

Chaplin exerted a great fascination for Orson in part, no doubt, because in Chaplin's reputation as the film artist who did everything, Orson recognized a kindred spirit. Orson was fascinated by Chaplin's immersion in his public persona. Chaplin told Orson of an afternoon when, day tripping with a friend in a small rowboat off the coast of France, Chaplin was suddenly stricken with violent diarrhea. Swiftly rowing to shore, Chaplin jumped out of the boat and rushed along the beach toward a rustic outhouse in the distance. But no sooner had the locals spotted Chaplin than they closed ranks around him to ecstatic cries of "Charlot! Charlot!," the name by which the French affectionately called the waddling little tramp of the silent cinema. "W.C.! W.C.!" he moaned in response, desperately trying to shake off his persistent admirers. But the more fiercely he struggled, the more they laughed and danced around him, repeatedly calling his name. Assuming that the famous Charlot was putting on a special show for them, they wanted to demonstrate their utmost appreciation. It never occurred to them he wasn't joking. In fact, by now Chaplin was ready to burst—and probably would have if he hadn't reached the outhouse just in time. Still standing, he pulled the flimsy door shut, positioned himself on the precarious metal footrests, dropped his pants, and, at long last, and with great fanfare, exploded into the pit. "Charlot! Charlot!" he could hear the locals singing and laughing outside. For, as far as they were concerned, the show was still on. They even took his repeatedly breaking wind for an especially excellent series of sound effects.

Welles's admiration of Chaplin was not, however, entirely blinding. Once, when the two of them had gone to take a shower after they had been in the steamroom together, Orson witnessed what he calls "a terrible embarrassment." He inadvertently cast a glance in the direction of Chaplin's genitalia, which reminded him of nothing so much as "a little peanut." (This eyewitness testimony of Orson's is completely contrary to standard Hollywood legend that portrays Chaplin as unusually well endowed.) Chaplin did not flinch from alluding to his organ's small size—at least not with Orson. Thus he told Orson all about his amorous encounter in London with the famous evangelist Aimee Semple McPherson, who used to wear immense white angel's wings onstage. In the audience at one of her melodramatic appearances, Chaplin began to fantasize about having sexual intercourse with her still hooked into the white wings. Later, Chaplin could not resist calling on the aging evangelist backstage to invite her out with him for the evening. After several hours in London's nightclubs, he found himself alone with her in her hotel room, but since, up close, her face seemed to Chaplin "like a quilted bedspread," he wasn't sure he could go any further. Telling himself to concentrate on the wings, he requested that she put them on. After which—as he told Orson—"I managed to *thumb* it in."

While Orson's plan to film Chaplin as Landru never got far, he was considerably more successful in initiating three other picture projects (he eventually directed only two of them, and only completed one). The first was an adaptation of Eric Ambler's *Journey Into Fear*, although from the first he preferred to produce it with someone else directing. While RKO was intrigued by the idea, there was substantial disagreement about who should direct. The second of the projects Orson was discussing with the studio was a mélange of fact and fiction with the ironic title *It's All True*. Having inserted a mock-documentary in *Citizen Kane*, Orson was taken with the idea of subtly mingling documentary and fictive segments (much as he would many years later in what is doubtless his most eccentric film, *F for Fake*: its title an ironic allusion, perhaps, to the abortive *It's All True*). Thus, for instance, on the documentary side, one tentative section of the assemblage Orson initially had in mind for *It's All True* was a short history of jazz, to be scripted in association with Duke Ellington; while on the fiction side, Orson planned to do a little story titled *Bonito the Bull* about Mexican bullfighting that Mercury had acquired from Robert Flaherty.

Fully aware that he needed urgently to put a new film into production, Orson had to admit to himself that *It's All True* was not a viable second project. At this point he absolutely could not afford another false step such as *Heart of Darkness* had been, and he knew that it would be a while before he could fully develop his still-germinal concept. Determined to keep working on *It's All True*, Orson seized upon a far more practical project, one that he could launch into almost immediately. Booth Tarkington's novel *The Magnificent Ambersons* appealed to Orson for several reasons. First, he had already thought through the material when Mercury had performed a radio adaptation back in 1939. But while he considered the book Tarkington's best, his interest in *Ambersons* was not entirely literary; Orson felt a strong personal connection with the novel because he suspected that Tarkington had based the key character of Eugene the inventor on his friend Dick Welles (to be played in the film by Orson's friend Joseph Cotten). The novel also strongly appealed to Orson because of Georgie Minafer's relationship with his beloved ill-fated mother. *George* was in fact Orson's real first name, and he vividly remembered that the last time he saw Beatrice Welles before she died, she had called him "Georgie Porgie." In the scene at Isabel's deathbed (the fictive mother sitting up and stifling her pain much as Beatrice had) the filmmaker would discover, and explore, reserves of feeling about his own mother. To play her, Orson would lure Dolores Costello, who had been married to John Barrymore, out of retirement. (Unfortunately, the harsh studio makeup of years past had badly scarred her cheeks, which appeared almost to have been eaten away, and this posed a daily problem for—ironically—Orson's makeup artists.)

Although he had played Georgie on the radio, and although he was still only twenty-six, Orson knew he looked far too old for the role of a college boy. He might be able to manage it by losing a great deal of weight, but since this was completely out of the question, another actor, film-cowboy Tim Holt, would be cast. The obnoxious Georgie is Orson's dark alter ego, an intensely ironic version of his own compulsive eating and self-obsession. Only an artist

with a great deal of perspective on himself could give us
so merciless and grotesque a self-caricature. "It's like *Dallas*," says Orson, alluding to the obnoxious J. R., "fascinating to see what happens to the spoiled boy!" The theme
of the brat getting his "comeuppance" was especially resonant to Orson just then when at least half of Hollywood
appeared to be waiting for him to suffer the same fate. It
occurred to him that there was no more fitting and ironic
way to begin his second film than by his narrating the story
of Georgie Minafer's comeuppance, as if to indicate that he
knew perfectly well what some people in the audience had
come to see.

Before starting the script, Orson decided to get Schaefer's
approval, so he played him a recording of Mercury's 1939
radio broadcast. Today Orson recalls that, after listening for
five minutes, Schaefer dozed off, awakening just as the old
program was drawing to a close. "*Fine*, do it," he told
Orson. But the conditions under which Orson made *Ambersons* were entirely different from those of *Kane*. *Ambersons* was *not* part of Orson's original contract that had
afforded him total artistic control. *Ambersons* and *Journey
Into Fear* were the results of a completely new and separate
deal Orson struck with RKO. Having agreed to do a free
film to buy extra time in 1939, and not entitled to any profits
from *Kane* until it made back $500,000 (which seemed most
unlikely in the near future), Orson would not be paid again
until he made a third picture under the original contract
terms. So he signed a new, and unfavorable, contract under
which he directed *Ambersons* and produced *Journey Into
Fear*—a contract that no longer required him to appear in,
or even actually to direct, his projects, and in which he lost
the coveted right to final cut (so that RKO was legally within
its rights to recut *The Magnificent Ambersons*—as it eventually did).

The fact that *Ambersons* was made under a new contract
is often overlooked and vital to comprehending precisely

what happened to Welles in Hollywood. Orson himself is quick to point out the absurdity of the oft-repeated charge that Hollywood turned against him because he was "unbridled." "People are always saying I need control," he explains, "and the irony is that *Citizen Kane* was the one film on which there was the *least* control over me." In Welles's new contract he had no choice but to sign away the complete control that had allowed him to make his masterpiece. Although at first this major concession seemed harmless, the studio's right to final cut would make a big difference later on.

For now, however, Orson was anxious to get started on the *Ambersons* script, so he and an assistant repaired to Catalina Island for a week in late July and early August. Orson did much of the actual writing on board his friend King Vidor's yacht. According to Orson, Vidor was one of the cheapest men in Hollywood, the other being Chaplin. Orson recalls that Chaplin and Vidor regularly dined together at Ciro's. Waiting to see which of the misers would finally consent to pick up the check this time, the waiters would put the chairs up on the tables all around them, while Chaplin and Vidor stalled in hopes that the *other* would break down and offer to pay. If by offering him the use of his private yacht King Vidor was exceptionally generous with Orson, it was only because he had been so immensely impressed by *Kane*. After seeing it, Vidor had telegrammed Orson to tell him that he was "the best actor, the best writer, and the best director in the business"—praise indeed coming from one of film history's giants. Best of all, King Vidor had joked that Orson ought to change the spelling of his first name to A-W-E-S-0-M-E.

At the time he was preparing *Ambersons*, Orson also signed on to do a major new weekly radio show for Lady Esther Face Powder and Face Cream. Having resisted his usual compulsion to overcommit himself while making *Kane*, he now decided to resume juggling several projects all at once: in addition to the three films more or less in the works and the radio show, Orson made regular forays into vaudeville and country fairs where, billed as The Ace, he appeared to cut Dolores Del Rio's arm off. Lady Esther paid him $8,000 a week, but out of that he had to pay an eighteen-piece orchestra, script writers, production people, and guest artists. This time there was no live studio audience, so Orson could silently clown at the sponsor's expense. There was a tall, elegant, blond lady who enunciated the flowery Lady Esther commercials, and while she did, off to the side, and with eloquently exaggerated gestures, Orson pretended to inspect the plump red tip of his elbow, fingering it, and holding it up to an imaginary mirror to test if it had what the announcer solemnly called *Lady Esther qualities*.

But Orson wasn't always so amusing. In particular, some of his secretaries failed to find him funny. He could not seem to hang on to secretaries, either because they hated him or he hated them, or because the antipathy was mutual. Orson was almost constantly dictating; a thought might come at any moment in his eighteen-hour days, and he expected his secretaries dutifully to get it down for future reference. Nor was a secretary's day finished when she went home. In the dead of night she might hear her doorbell ringing, which invariably meant that Orson had dispatched his valet, Alfalfa, to bring her back to work. Orson had had a thought and it could not wait. Secretaries often resigned in tears.

The new secretary at the time of *Ambersons* was a tall, slender, dark girl named Shifra Haran. After her interview one of Orson's male assistants drove her home. The bashful new girl really didn't know much about Orson, so the male assistant helpfully filled her in. For more than two hours in the car he detailed how terrible Mr. Welles was. Miss Haran was open-mouthed. Nor initially did Mr. Welles belie this portrait of him; Miss Haran's first few days were spent listening to his wild tirades, all of them conducted in perfectly proper English. It seemed to Miss Haran that he was testing the devotion of his employees. The more devoted employees were, the more he seemed to berate them, although he would have been crushed if they left. Other employees he clearly despised, evidently because he genuinely believed they were persecuting him. So disconcerted was Miss Haran by her peculiar new employer that when she got home most nights she felt like vomiting. Dinner was out of the question. Then one night, at about three a.m., much to the alarm of her mother, the front buzzer rang. It was Alfalfa.

There followed many such late-night calls, even though Miss Haran's day generally did not end until ten p.m. Her mother was appalled, but dutifully Shifra got dressed whenever Alfalfa summoned her in the wee hours. Sometimes Orson would doze off after dictating for hours, but he would expect her to stay awake to type the notes. It was not unheard of for Orson to keep her working for as long as twenty-four hours. Another of Miss Haran's duties was rousing Orson in the morning, no easy task, since when he slept, he was a deep sleeper. As she followed Welles from home to office to the set it was Miss Haran's responsibility to carry an immense accordion folder in which she crammed anything Mr. Welles might need in the course of the day: documents, tea, snacks, articles of clothing, scripts. Expected to anticipate whenever Mr. Welles might be hungry or thirsty, Miss Haran would make sure his tea was ready exactly when he was, or risk Orson's wrath. He only berated her when other people were around to watch, never when they were alone, which suggested the extent to which Orson's temper was a public performance. Perhaps Miss Haran lasted for four years in his employ because she, in turn, liked to perform her anger at him, as when, just before serving his tea, in full view of everyone but Orson and much to the delight of all the other underlings, who knew exactly what her gesture meant, she stirred the tea with her finger.

In Miss Haran, Orson had met his match, for she was

fully as energetic as he. Still he persisted in complaining about her—but most people around him would know enough to disregard entirely those hollow laments. The exception was Dadda Bernstein. By now, Dadda had given up watching the Chicago skies, idly dreaming that one of the planes soaring past might be carrying Orson; he had finally installed himself and Orson's mother's furniture in Beverly Hills, where, between the checkups he administered in his new general practice, he had ample time to check up on Pookles. Even though RKO had spurned him as its studio doctor, he was in frequent attendance there; and he took Orson's tirades about his new secretary most seriously. Because nothing should be done to upset poor Pookles, Dadda secretly launched an extensive national search for her replacement. Dadda's medical office on North Camden Drive became the headquarters of this intensive recruitment campaign. So many resumés arrived that Hazel Bernstein had to pitch in to help sift through them all. At last, after months of discussion and debate, they agreed upon one lucky candidate from Chicago. Thereupon Dadda entered into animated correspondence with her so that he might more carefully scrutinize her letters for grammar, spelling, punctuation, and neatness. Dadda rushed these *perfect* letters in to Pookles, who glanced at them, nodded his approval, and began dictating. Immersed in her steno pad, Miss Haran knew nothing of what Dadda was up to. Satisfied that Miss Chicago was the very *best* there was, Dadda instructed her to quit her job immediately and fly to Hollywood, where "the temporary girl," Miss Haran, would secure a hotel room for her. Miss Haran could not figure out why Dadda and Hazel were suddenly so gleeful. Eventually the mystery lady arrived. Per Dadda's instructions, Miss Haran picked her up at the airport, took care of her abundant luggage, and promptly drove the visitor to the Mercury office, where both Bernsteins warmly greeted her, before Dadda ceremoniously ushered her into Orson's office. Miss Haran was instructed to wait outside. Twenty minutes, half an hour passed. Suddenly the office door flew open. "Get me out of here! I can't stand it!" the visitor was heard to scream. Now she stood sobbing and shaking in the outer office. Appearing from behind, Dadda discreetly instructed Miss Haran to arrange for the hysterical girl to fly back to Chicago as quickly as possible. Perhaps she could get her old job back. "That beast!" she muttered—presumably referring to Orson—as a perplexed Miss Haran packed her into the car.

A far more successful addition to Orson's ménage was Gary Cooper's pudgy ex-manager, Jack Moss, who signed on as Houseman's replacement as the administrative end of Mercury enterprises. Mercury's lack of organization was one of Orson's principal complaints; but no sooner had Moss painstakingly established strict office rules, schedules, and lines of command than Orson began compulsively to undermine them, as if chaos was most conducive to his personal manner of working. Orson seemed more pleased with Mercury's move from RKO on Gower Street to Gloria Swanson's old bungalow at RKO Pathé in Culver City, where Moss installed an intricate buzzer system for Orson. Wherever he was, Orson always had a buzzer within easy reach. His new toy afforded instant gratification, for he had only to press it and all came running. Moss also took it upon himself to watch Orson's weight, an absurd task considering his own substantial girth. Diet pills had been temporarily discontinued, since Orson grew unusually flushed and his eyes seemed to pop out of his head when he took them. Thus Moss had hired a maid to prepare healthy lunches of boiled beef and cooked vegetables to keep Orson within range of his 210-pound goal. Unfortunately, this lunchtime regimen only seemed to work up Orson's appetite; by dinner time he was ready for the three steaks he was used to downing in swift succession.

• • •

Meanwhile, Orson had completed the final version of the *Ambersons* script, on which shooting was scheduled to begin at the end of October. The Screen Actors' Guild issued a stern warning against using any of the "tests" in the finished film, as Orson had so notoriously done in *Citizen Kane*. Although the Guild had overlooked the matter before, they certainly would not do so now. Anxious to avoid union trouble, Moss swiftly denied any such intentions on Orson's part. Orson *did* intend to rehearse his cast extensively and to record those rehearsals on discs to be played back the day of shooting. "We rehearsed for two weeks," Orson recalls, "and I prerecorded the whole show so that the actors would listen to the way they played it in rehearsal. Because the tendency of all actors in front of the camera is to slow up, I wanted them to hear how quickly and brilliantly they played it in rehearsal. This sound would never be heard in a movie theater. It would only be heard by actors about to perform in front of the camera. It was a device to avoid the tendency of all actors to forget the fine points of the rehearsal when they think of their face being recorded as well as their voice." Despite these extensive rehearsals, Orson refrained from discussing the movie as a whole with the actors, choosing instead to focus entirely on their individual performances: "It's very much against my principles to tell a cast of people what I intend a picture or play to be like, because it sometimes turns out to be something else and they shouldn't catch you making a mistake. That's one reason. And the second is, they're all thinking about themselves anyway, so talk about them. Don't talk about the grand canvas. You know, they start chewing gum and looking out the window."

While Orson would not actually appear in the picture ("I was so happy not to be acting in front of the camera. You know, that was the joy of my life. Oh yes, to be the director *only*, that was a wonderful thing!"), he would make his presence felt in the voice-over narration, and even more important, in the picture's self-assertive style. In this he was abetted by cinematographer Stanley Cortez, who sums up working with Welles thus: "When you're doing a picture with Orson Welles, Orson runs the show, and if he doesn't, his voice does." Hired the day before shooting began, Cortez was instantly impressed by Welles's consummate pictorial sense, his instinct for framing things as the camera would. Perhaps the most extraordinary instance of this was the immensely ambitious—and justly celebrated—ballroom sequence, which Orson had envisioned as a single sensuous crane shot through a succession of rooms, the walls of which ascended on invisible chains so that Orson's kinetic camera might seem magically to pass through them.

Besides pacing the onscreen sweep of the camera and the offscreen ascent of the walls, Orson deftly choreographed his cast, all of them guests at the Ambersons' ball, so that, at measured intervals, and in tempo with the camera, they floated into and out of the frame. Shooting the scene took an average of ten hours daily for nine days with about one hundred men operating the crane. This emphatic camera movement was the artist's brush stroke, his sweeping, self-assertive mark on the canvas.

Setting much of the film's action in the evocative twists and turns of the huge house afforded Orson ample opportunity to demonstrate his visual wit and virtuosity. In another key sequence involving emphatic camera movement, Isabel and her brother are viewed in conversation on the first floor: suddenly the camera drifts upward to disclose Georgie's eavesdropping on them. The effect is slightly unsettling. We could not have guessed the extreme height of the ceiling above the spot where Isabel and her brother confer, nor that Georgie would be looming there. And there is a further small shock in store: the very moment we see Georgie, we hear a woman's voice exclaiming, "Well!" The camera drifts still further upward, and there is Georgie's Aunt Fanny (Agnes Moorehead) spying on his mother. This witty second

shock is a particularly good example of Welles's delight in
deceiving our expectations cinematically: it is not simply
the plot that deceives us here, but the space in which it
unfolds.

Perhaps the most arduous shooting occurred in an old ice
house in Los Angeles that Orson had scouted for the film's
snow sequences. The entire building was permeated with
the sickly stench of dead fish, great mountains of which
were pushed to the sides for the filming. Planning to shoot
twelve hours daily, Orson stuffed himself into a leather suit
and a knit cap with a big pompon on top; since he did not
have to appear in front of the camera, Orson suddenly seemed
to have blown up to even more gargantuan proportions. It
was so cold in the ice house that the 10,000-watt bulbs used
to light the set constantly popped during the shooting—
which meant that Orson would wearily have to order another
take, lest the flash be visible onscreen. Cortez recalls that
he and Orson kept warm with a bottle of brandy. The actors
wore red long Johns beneath their period costumes—although the whole idea was for them to feel the cold, to see
their breath when they exhaled. (When they inhaled, they
smelled fish, which slightly spoiled the psychological effect.)

After the day's shooting was over, Orson and Joseph
Cotten would repair to a local steam room to discuss the
screenplay for *Journey Into Fear* on which they had decided
to collaborate. They would continue working on the script
over dinner at Chasen's. Orson, of course, was operating
on several fronts simultaneously; besides *Ambersons* and
the screenplay for *Journey Into Fear*, *It's All True* was still
very much on his mind. Having dispatched his friend, the
erstwhile leading man Norman Foster, to Mexico to do
second-unit work on the *Bonito the Bull* segment, Orson
flew down periodically to monitor his progress. Orson calculated that once he had finished *Ambersons*, the *Bonito*

footage and the *Journey* screenplay would give him a substantial head start on whichever was to be his next project.

By now, Orson's conflicts with the industry had forced
him to formulate a specific position for himself with regard
to Hollywood. He outlined this position late in November
of 1941 to the Sigma Delta Chi fraternity of newsmen. Orson
argued that it was the filmmaker's task to elevate, rather
than to lower, the artistic taste of the general public. It
seemed to Orson that producers vastly underestimated the
artistic maturity of the audience for Hollywood films. Perhaps—Orson snidely suggested—this was because it was
the producers who were immature, and not the public. Although the artist who abased the standards of his art might
be rewarded in the short term, in the long term he, like all
his fellow artists, would suffer from this degeneration. To
speak so audaciously to the press only made his enemies in
the industry all the more anxious that he get his comeuppance—and that he get it soon.

At about this time, Orson also disclosed to the press that
he and Dolores intended to marry as soon as her divorce
was final. It was evident that his sustained relationship with
Dolores had been highly beneficial to his work on *Kane* and
now on *Ambersons*, since it allowed him to concentrate more
fully on his filmmaking than if he had been unattached.
Outside a steady relationship like this, women were likely
to be less understanding of his peculiar work habits and
more demanding of his time and attention. Dolores was
there when he needed her, at whatever odd hours.

Orson's already crowded work schedule was to become
even more hectic when, after the bombing of Pearl Harbor
on December 7, he was summoned by Washington to help
the war effort. The evening after the surprise attack, when
Orson appeared on the air in his regular slot for Lady Esther,
he used the opportunity to address the events that, by now,
all America knew about. "Ladies and gentlemen," he said,

"as we all know, our country has answered a vicious and an unprovoked attack by declaring war on Japan. This is a time for energetic and unashamed patriotism on the part of all of us: I know we all agree to that because I know that none of us will be satisfied with anything but complete victory." If Orson's physical condition made it highly doubtful that he would be drafted for active duty, he would now be called upon to serve his country in another way. Having entered the war against Japan, Germany, and Italy, the U.S. faced a danger from South American nations, which Roosevelt feared might be lured into fighting on the side of the Axis. The Axis powers had embarked on a concerted propaganda effort in South America that included radio broadcasts and free films. South American newspapers received free access to news services, whose *real* aim was to spread the totalitarian word. German and Italian professors were dispatched to key teaching positions in South American universities. To counter antidemocratic propaganda, Roosevelt named Nelson Rockefeller the coordinator of Inter-American Affairs, charging him with building up cultural ties between the U.S. and South America. One of Rockefeller's tactics was to send a number of goodwill ambassadors to South America—and one of these was Orson Welles. In Washington, the man who made *Citizen Kane* was not the pariah he was considered in certain quarters of Hollywood. This unexpected call from Washington revivified Orson's vague desire to get involved in politics. Rockefeller invited Orson to make use of his matchless oratorical skills on behalf of his beleaguered country. The original idea was for Orson to embark on a lecture tour throughout South America. Ultimately, however, the Rockefeller Committee agreed partially to finance a film Orson would make in Brazil, where the government had proposed the topic of the yearly carnival in Rio. The conditions for this partial financing were that the Committee approve the treatment, and that Orson appear in the picture. Besides disseminating goodwill in the form of culture from the U.S. throughout South America, the Rockefeller Committee hoped to interest the people of the U.S. in their neighbors to the south, something Orson's film would presumably help to do.

Orson knew that he would not really be able to say what he would do with the carnival topic, or whether he could do anything at all with it, until he saw it. A treatment was out of the question. He in fact regarded the trip to Rio as an unexpected and fortuitous opportunity to proceed with *It's All True*. Since the government was bankrolling part of the new picture, the studio (in which Rockefeller himself was—conveniently—a major stockholder) figured it had better put up the rest of the cash Orson needed. Orson decided to quicken his already breakneck pace and finish shooting *Ambersons* by the time he left in February. That would be a challenge in itself—but it was not the only goal Orson set. He also decided to get *Journey Into Fear* into production before he left.

On examination, his plan was not as impossible as it sounded. Orson had never really intended to direct *Journey Into Fear*, only to write the screenplay, produce the film, and perhaps act in it. Since his Mercury Theatre days in New York, Orson had had it in mind for *other* directors to work under his auspices. This time Orson chose Norman Foster to direct, mainly on the basis of the superb rushes for *Bonito* that had come back from Mexico. Lest the studio protest Orson's decision, he announced that he and Foster would co-direct, although it was clear from the outset that this was only a pretense. "My influence on *Journey Into Fear* is so exaggerated," says Orson. As proof that he did not secretly direct *Journey*, Orson points out that he was actually gone during most of the shooting; and that Foster once even ejected him from the set when, appearing in one scene with Joseph Cotten, Orson kept cracking up.

Orson knew that he had plenty of serious preparation to do for his goodwill lecture tour (including studying elementary Portuguese for his stay in Rio), so he dispatched Miriam Geiger to gather background information on the South American countries he might find himself visiting. Having succeeded so efficiently in preparing Orson's film textbook when he first came to Hollywood, Geiger had later done various sorts of research to feed into Orson's brain. When Orson was planning *Heart of Darkness*, for example, he sent Geiger off to find photographs of footprints: a curious mission perhaps, but one that is unusually revealing of Orson's hunger for the most specific sorts of information. Now Geiger was charged with assembling the morass of random details about South America that, in turn, Orson would sift through, assimilate, and, finally, recycle into his mellifluous speeches. Orson wanted to know everything: facts and figures about geography, linguistics, politics, economics. He wanted his data in volume, and he wanted it quickly.

Cramming, finishing one film, and starting a new one left Orson little time. Since his rush was linked to Roosevelt's Good Neighbor Policy, the studio agreed to Mercury's patriotic proposal to add steam and rubbing rooms to Orson's Culver City bungalow so he would not have to trek all the way to Beverly Hills. To save time, Orson could hold conferences in the steam room. At times, it began to sound as if allowing Orson to take a steam on the premises was part of the war effort. Having learned of the great luxury of Orson's new facility, a number of RKO biggies longed to take a steam there too from time to time, but Orson wouldn't hear of it. The steam bath was solely for Mercury business. Because Mr. Welles was doing so much serious thinking lately, Miss Haran refrained from speaking to him unless he spoke to her. If she had a question about something, she wrote it out so that her boss could answer simply yes or no. Then she left the question in a special basket. When he was good and ready, he checked either the yes box or the no box by way of answering.

The steam bath, the massages, the respectful silence from Miss Haran, and the instant gratification of his buzzer system were not enough, however, to soothe Orson's nerves. It seemed that anything could set him off, as on the day when, from the new steam room, he could be heard madly ringing the buzzer. Moss, Dadda, and Miss Haran all responded to the danger signal, but it was too late. There stood Orson hastily draped in his jumbo terrycloth robe. He might have looked like the Buddha, except that he dug his teeth into a massive fuming cigar. "My testicles are painted purple and hanging down to my ankles!" rumbled the voice of God. "And all, all because of this woman!" At which both Moss and Dadda shot inquiring glances at a rather perplexed Miss Haran, who—it was subsequently disclosed—had failed to draw Mr. Welles's bath when she perfectly well should have known he would want it. But even Orson must have known that he'd gone too far this time. Later that same day, when he buzzed again for Miss Haran, she broke her rule of never initiating conversation between them by apologizing for having been so stupid as not to . . . but here Orson interrupted her by suddenly retracting all he'd said earlier.

Orson's relations with Dolores were ostensibly less mercurial—but only ostensibly. For while Dolores was anxious that her divorce be completed so that she might instantly marry Orson before he left for Brazil, the prospective bridegroom was having serious second thoughts. He never let on to her, however, that he felt the slightest hesitation about remarrying. And had it not been for a quirk of fate, he probably would have gone through with the wedding. But fortunately for Orson, Dolores's lawyer had forgotten to file an important document and the divorce had been temporarily held up—for just long enough that he might slip away without ever having to explain that he intended it to be for good. This way they would drift apart naturally, without a violent rift. So completely did Orson conceal his feelings that not even Dadda was aware that Pookles was dodging this marriage. Nor could Dolores have known, and she would certainly not have guessed from the intimate gifts Orson selected for her for Christmas in 1941—a splendid robe decorated with white doves; a bed jacket and bedroom slippers; three bottles of perfume; a mirror, a brush, and a comb. Still, on the brink of his South American adventure, Orson was quietly content that his affair with Dolores was drawing to a felicitous close, and that no one—she least of all—suspected.

To his daughter, Christopher, Orson sent four Christmas toys: a horse, a panda, a pink bear, and a doll; and to her mother, now Mrs. Lederer, he sent a huge floral arrangement. Unbeknownst to Orson, the Lederers were visiting Aunt Marion at Hearst's San Simeon, where, on account of *Citizen Kane*, the child was, she recalls, "persona non grata with Hearst." Evidently he felt no resentment toward Virginia, but Hearst identified Christopher with her despised father. She was told to stay out of Hearst's way, which was not especially difficult since the place was so big. Christopher slept in the tower. Mornings, her nanny would tell her that if she did not finish her oatmeal the men inside the suits of armor that lined the dining room would come out and get her. After breakfast, the nanny would take her out for the day, which lessened the chance of running into Hearst.

The other family member whom Orson remembered at Christmastime was his brother, Richard, to whom he had been discreetly sending monthly checks of eighty-five dollars or so, in hopes that Richard would not get it into his head to appear in the press again as the author of "War of the Worlds" or any of Orson's other projects. After the to-do with Mankiewicz, the last thing Orson needed was for Richard to announce that *he* had written *Citizen Kane*. At the moment, however, Richard was too busy with other more pressing activities—shortly after the holidays, Orson received a letter from him that began bluntly: "During the course of the Christmas festivities, I contracted gonorrhea." This was by way of informing his successful kid brother that he and his wife, Mildred (whom he had met in a midnight mission for derelicts), had decided to pay Orson a little visit before he left for Rio. Orson had sent Richard a pair of silver ashtrays and a silver cigarette box (all suitable for hocking) and Mildred a purse and a scarf, so when Mr. and Mrs. Richard Welles turned up as promised at the Mercury office, they came bearing a belated Christmas gift for him: a bottle of pickled watermelon rind, which even Orson managed somehow to resist.

Orson had little time to spend with Richard and his wife, so the task of entertaining them was left mostly to Dadda, Hazel, and Miss Haran. To expedite *Ambersons*, Orson had two units working simultaneously on two sets, with other cameramen brought in to supplement the necessarily slower, more meticulous work of Cortez. It is part of the standard Welles myth that, as a director, Orson lacks discipline; as his crowded work schedule of January of 1942 suggests, nothing could be further from the truth. Says Robert Wise: "The whole latter part of *Ambersons*, he was not only directing in the daytime, he was also many nights shooting all night on *Journey Into Fear*. . . . And sometimes he would come in to run rushes in the morning after a night's work of acting. I don't know how he kept going!" Small wonder he had begun taking Dexedrine.

Orson finished shooting *Ambersons* January 31, 1942, and on February 2 he completed his role in *Journey*. That night, on radio, he bid farewell to his Lady Esther audience: "This is the last time for some while I'll be speaking to you from the United States. Tomorrow night the Mercury Theatre starts for South America. The reason, put more or less officially, is that I've been asked by the office of the coordinator of Inter-American Affairs to do a motion picture especially for Americans in all the Americas, a movie which, in its particular way, might strengthen the good relations now binding the continents of the Western Hemispbere. Put much less officially, the Mercury's going down there to get acquainted. We the people of these United Nations of America now stand together: we're going to have to know each other better than we do. My job—the Mercury's job—is to help with the introductions.... And now it's time for goodbyes. As always, we remain *obediently* yours....

Although Orson had to go to Washington immediately for briefing, he arranged to meet Wise in Miami afterward to consult on editing problems and to complete additional narration. There, for nearly three continuous days and nights in the cutting and dubbing facilities of a local cartoon studio, the director and editor of *Ambersons* worked on the rough cut of the film. At dawn of the fourth day, Wise saw Orson off on the flying boat he had booked to Brazil. It had been agreed that as soon as Wise finished cutting, he would join Orson with the film in Rio to confer on last details. As it turned out, however, they were not to see each other again for years.

Orson and his dog Caesar. "The word *genius* was whispered into my ear the first thing I ever heard while I was still mewling in my crib," laughs Orson, "so it never occurred to me that I wasn't until middle age!" *(Courtesy Orson Welles)*

Orson's mother, Beatrice Ives Welles, maintained a strict policy that "children could be treated as adults as long as they were amusing," Orson recalls. "The moment you became boring, it was off to the nursery."*(Courtesy Orson Welles)*

Dadda Bernstein. Having fallen in love with Beatrice although she was married to Dick Welles, Dr. Maurice Bernstein encouraged Orson to call him *Dadda*, which disturbed Orson's real father. "To him," says Orson, "Dadda Bernstein represented everything that had made his marriage to my mother impossible." *(Courtesy Orson Welles)*

Orson sucks in his cheeks to make himself appear thinner in the Todd School production of *Wings over Europe*. *(Courtesy Orson Welles)*

BELOW, LEFT: Eleven-year-old Orson in *Finesse the Queen* at the Todd School for Boys in Woodstock, Illinois. His deep voice kept him from being cast as a girl. *(Courtesy Orson Welles)*

BELOW, RIGHT: Orson's host in Morocco, Thami el Glaoui, Pasha of Marrakesh, leader of the Glawa tribe of the Western Atlas. "He had killed one of his sons with a bow string," says Orson, "but he also knew how to sit in the Ritz Hotel and chat it up with Claudel." *(Pictorial Parade)*

Orson, Louise Prussing, Hilton Edwards, Constance
Heron, and Micheal MacLiammoir at the Todd
Summer Theatre Festival. "They were away from
home, and they went through Woodstock like a
withering flame," says Orson of MacLiammoir and
Edwards, the directors of the Dublin Gate Theatre.
"*Nobody* was safe, you know. It was a rich harvest
there for both of them, and they knew no shame."
(Courtesy Hascy Tarbox)

Orson and his first wife, Chicago socialite Virginia Nicolson. "We really only got married in order to live together," says Orson. "It wasn't taken very seriously by either of us." *(Courtesy Orson Welles)*

Micheal MacLiammoir camping it up in *Czar Paul*. "What Micheal liked was vigorous nonhomosexual types," says Orson, "good family men, preferably with large black mustaches, and ideally, members of the police force." *(Courtesy Hascy Tarbox)*

"*Suddenly* I was one of the most successful radio actors ever." (CBS)

Orson and Dolores Del Rio dancing at The Stork Club. "I tell you, I was a dude!" (The Stork Club)

LEFT: Orson, Dolores Del Rio, and Charles Chaplin in Hollywood. *(AP/Wide World Photos)* BELOW: Dolores Del Rio at her dressing table. "You should have seen her underwear!" says Orson. "Unbelievable! It was all handmade, very hard to find, so *erotic* it was indescribable!" *(Cinemabilia)*

OPPOSITE: Or... *Citizen Kane.* "The one key
element we lea... ambition," says d... *m* Welles was the power of
he is responsible for ... Scorsese. "In a sense,
directors than anyone e... *rtin* ...ore people to be film
cinema." *(Courtesy RKO P*... Orso...ty of the
Shifra Ha...
six-inch-tall
gentleman, Sho...
Shifra Haran)

The battle with his
weight. *(Courtesy RKO
Pictures, Inc.)*

"Rita had great *natural* dignity," says Orson of his
second wife, Rita Hayworth. *(AP/Wide World Photos)*

Errol and Nora Flynn with Rita and Orson on Flynn's
yacht, the *Zaca*. *(AP/Wide World Photos)*

Before divorcing, Orson and Rita co-starred in *The Lady from Shanghai.* "I had reached the end of my capacity to feel such total failure with her," says Orson. "I had done *everything* I could think of and I didn't seem to be able to bring her anything but agony." *(Courtesy Columbia Pictures)*

Orson, Rita, and Hortense and Skipper Hill. "Until she met Hortense," says Orson, "there was nobody, no woman that she could *believe* . . ." *(Courtesy Orson Welles)*

ABOVE: Seated beside Helen Keller at Madison Square Garden in New York, Orson has just introduced Henry Wallace at a mass rally to reelect Franklin Delano Roosevelt in the 1944 presidential campaign. When Orson and Miss Keller left the rally, crowds shook their limousine and yelled, "Wallace and Welles in the White House in '48!" *(AP/Wide World Photos)*

RIGHT: In 1944, Orson and fellow campaigner Frank Sinatra listen to Franklin Delano Roosevelt's speech at Fenway Park in Boston. *(AP/Wide World Photos)*

Orson and one of the dancers in his ballet "The Lady in the Ice." "I got terribly interested in ballerinas. I didn't consciously go out to collect them, but life just worked out that way," says Orson. "...I had never noticed those calves before!" *(AP/Wide World Photos)*

Orson talking to Hilton Edwards in Paris. Between them is Eartha Kitt, who co-starred with Orson in *Time Runs*. "Orson Welles really introduced me to a marvelous gourmet type of living," says Miss Kitt. "Him and Rubirosa. I tell you, I was absolutely spoiled by the best kind of men!" *(AP/Wide World Photos)*

ABOVE: Orson and his third wife, Paola Mori, the Countess di Girfalco (second from left), with Mr. and Mrs. Joseph Cotten at The Stork Club. *(Pictorial Parade)* BELOW: Orson directs Laurence Olivier in Ionesco's *Rhinoceros*. "He doesn't want anybody else up there," says Orson to explain the discord between them during rehearsals. "He's like Chaplin, you know. He's a real fighting star." *(John Timbers, London)*

Orson and his friend Marlene Dietrich in *Touch of Evil*. "She was the good soldier of all time," he says. *(Universal Pictures, a division of Universal City Studios, Inc. Courtesy MCA Publishing Rights, a division of MCA Inc.)*

Orson and Oja Kodar, star of *F for Fake* and *The Other Side of the Wind*. *(Pictorial Parade)*

Orson, Kiki, and Henry Jaglom. "See, the thing that nobody knows about Orson—the big secret to him—is that he has no false ego at all," says Jaglom. "It's not just that he's important—he's so human, he's so sweet." *(Courtesy Henry Jaglom)*

CHAPTER 22
The Man
in the Red Suit

Orson figured that once he got to Rio the best tactic was to get as much raw newsreel footage of the carnival as possible, then to restage it afterward in a local studio. "The picture was made off the cuff," Orson points out. "It had to be. There was no script. I'd never *been* to a carnival! I had to go and find out what it was like and shoot what was going on, and then go on *re-creating* carnival for a while." At this stage, however, there was really no telling how much would have to be restaged. That would depend on what happened at the carnival and how Orson's imagination responded to it all. Although today Orson claims not to have been particularly fond of carnivals, in Rio he seems brilliantly to have concealed whatever distaste he may have felt for the general orgy by rushing about for seventy-two hours with the slightly demented look of someone who was really enjoying himself. But all this was by way of *research*. While many documentary filmmakers would prefer relative obscurity for themselves, so that the natives might proceed as naturally as possible, Orson made himself highly visible, cruising about in an immense convertible heralded by a pair of motorcycle escorts whose persistently screeching sirens led the revelers to cry, "Orson is coming! Orson is coming!"

It was not long before people instantly associated the sirens with the Yankee filmmaker's impending arrival, so that there was vast disappointment whenever the sirens turned out to be merely the police or an ambulance rushing to an emergency. With 16mm camera in hand, Orson immersed himself in the action, which included the carnival's notorious perfume battles. The atomizers with which the revelers sprayed one another only looked like they held perfume. "It wasn't perfume at all," Orson points out, "it was pure ether. The entire city of Rio got stoned out of its head. Everybody high and low went around with a spray of ether and sprayed it into the face of everybody they saw. So if you didn't want to get high on ether, you were going to anyway. The whole carnival smelled like a cheap hospital." Having gotten in the proper mood, Orson quickly learned to samba. At each new carnival, original sambas were created around the personalities of celebrities, and this time one was fondly called "The Man in the Red Suit" in homage to Orson. He, in turn, had suddenly discovered the theme he had been seeking for his film about the carnival: the story of the samba.

To this theme he wisely decided to add a focused plotline based on a magazine item he had read, about a group of four poor fishermen from Fortaleza, in the remote north of Brazil, who had bravely traveled the turbulent waters to Rio on a precarious raft known as a jangada to plead for assistance for their impoverished people from the Brazilian dictator, President Vargas. As a result, the jangadeiros had become Brazilian national heros. It was Orson's idea to restage segments of the perilous pilgrimage to Rio, then to intercut this footage with the samba material. The two plot strands would be logically connected by the carnival's taking place just as the jangadeiros arrive in Rio. Thus the story of this noble mission would add narrative drive to the carnival scenes that the Brazilian government had invited Orson to shoot in the first place.

But there were two important problems with this scheme.

The first was expense: Schaefer figured that if Orson wanted to shoot the jangadeiros sequences in Fortaleza he'd better do it in black-and-white, even though the carnival footage was in color. However, Orson assumed that because the studio had okayed shooting the carnival in color, it was in poor faith for them to insist now—as they seemed to be doing—that he shift to black-and-white, since he logically saw the jangadeiros sequences as an integral part of his Rio assignment. This was the kind of elementary disagreement that could have been swiftly settled one way or the other had Orson been back in Hollywood. But in wartime Brazil the extreme difficulties of communicating with Hollywood only exacerbated the mutual misunderstandings. Telephone service was abominable—either one didn't get a line or one got cut off almost as soon as one did—and the mail was even worse. Schaefer resorted to a series of cables begging Orson to forgo color film for the disputed segments or to face a confrontation with the hostile board of directors. If gradually Orson began to waver somewhat on the color-film issue, it was not out of loyalty to Schaefer, whom he considered to have been his faithful advocate only because his own reputation was on the line with Orson. But Orson did know that without Schaefer he was unlikely to survive at RKO, even though he had a contract to make another picture for them. Thus Orson decided to adopt a wait-and-see policy on the color controversy. If it looked as if using color for the jangadeiros sequences was going to jeopardize seriously Schaefer's position at RKO, Orson would be willing to go with black-and-white—even though it was aesthetically unsound.

In the meantime, Orson was faced with an immediate problem here in Brazil when the authorities learned with horror that he had been shooting in the *favelas*, the terrible slums in the hills of Rio, and that he had even been poking into the local practice of voodoo. There was instant political pressure on him to let up—as well as less diplomatic pressure by the angry thugs who pummeled Orson and company with bottles, rocks, and bricks. At pains to keep local reporters away from the sealed studio where Mercury was covertly staging scenes of low life in the *favelas*, Orson's press man feared that if the Brazilian papers found out what was really going on inside "they would write Orson out of town."

As it turned out, however, it was not the Brazilians who wrote him out of town—but, rather, the good people of Pomona, California, who, entirely unbeknownst to Orson, had in great numbers attended a sneak preview of *The Magnificent Ambersons* on March 17, before the director had even had a chance to finish the film himself. Although on March 1, Robert Wise had been scheduled to bring the footage on which he'd been working to Brazil, a sudden American government embargo on civilians' flying overseas had precluded his doing so. A rough cut was shipped to Rio on March 11, but that was only six days before the sneak preview, and it would be weeks until Orson would receive it. An RKO contingent, which included Schaefer and Wise, turned up at the Fox Theatre in Pomona to see how the locals liked *Ambersons*; they would have to like it a lot to justify its having gone more than $500,000 over budget. But Schaefer did not have to wait to read the standard comment cards the audience would fill out afterward. Almost from the outset, the surprise screening was a disaster. Large numbers of people walked out, and those who remained guffawed at all the wrong moments. "Boys your [*sic*] slipping," wrote one connoisseur. Others called the film "putrid," "much too long and dragged out," "overdone," and "a very disastrous attempt."

A panicked Schaefer wrote Orson that the Pomona screening of *Ambersons* was the worst experience in all his twenty-eight years in the film industry. Never had he seen an audience react so violently. Listening to them hoot and holler at the screen made him feel as if he were being repeatedly socked in the jaw. When Orson got back, he and Orson were going to have a "heart-to-heart" talk about Orson's shifting to more commercial, down-to-earth pictures. Meanwhile, as Wise recalls, the studio edict was, we've got to get a picture that the audience will sit for, that we can release." There followed a period of massive cutting (about forty-five minutes' worth) and reediting to compensate for the cuts and to give the picture a standard happy ending. Entirely new scenes were shot, which had not been in Orson's script. Meanwhile, in Rio, Orson simply assumed—as he had all along, and as he had every right to—that he would have an opportunity to rework the film himself. Welles never intended for the film to be released before he got his hands on it again. He had planned to work on *Ambersons* in Rio, and the fact that Wise was unable to fly to Rio on March 1 as originally planned was a quirk of fate.

When Orson learned of the disaster at the Pomona preview he cabled thirty-seven pages of revisions to Wise, but still he presumed that he would have an opportunity to work on the picture himself. "I had no idea that they would prevail," says Orson. "I thought that what I would say still carried some weight." In retrospect, Wise remains equivocal about the revisions he and others made without Orson's consent: "Let me say two things. I think undoubtedly, as a work of art, it probably was a better picture in its original-length version: as an *accomplishment*. I don't think there's any doubt about that. But we were faced with the reality of not art, but business, and what to do with something that wouldn't play. But I also think that the fact that it has come down through the years as something of a semiclassic at least means that we didn't *destroy* the picture, did we? I can tell you, everybody strived as hard as they could to retain every bit of the feeling, the quality of what Orson was trying to do."

Wise is right when he suggests that the greatness of the picture is still there. But as to how this final version actually compares with Orson's original, one can only speculate since, despite David O. Selznick's noble suggestion that the original be copied and deposited in the Museum of Modern Art in New York, the studio considered this too costly to do. According to Orson, the loss is immeasurable. However marvelous the famous ballroom sequence may be in the recut version, Orson says that it was far superior as he directed it. "The entire sequence was *one* reel without a single cut," says Orson. "It was shot that way and it was only cut afterward by Wise." Wise asserts that the sequence had to be cut because "there were things in it that didn't work. . . . It became part of what was cut into because of overall problems the picture presented." To which Orson replies: "Of course it worked! It was the greatest tour de force of my career! No way of saying it didn't work. That was just Wise taking over." According to Orson, the shot-reverse shots in which the camera alternates between Cotten and Costello were originally achieved through camera movement from one character to another, then back again— rather than in cuts that diminish the original fluidity. "We got to the reverse shots by camera movement," Orson explains. "They just *seem* to be cuts now. In other words, that's part of the single one-reel shot." Orson bristles at the implication that moments of the ballroom sequence were better deleted: "See, the one thing on which I am totally without self-doubt is the technical side of the theater, radio, and movies," says Orson. "And I never did anything that wouldn't work. I did things people didn't *like*. But any story you hear about something not working: *not true*! I am the only director in the world that I've ever heard of, or anybody that I've ever talked to has heard of, who comes on a set and puts his closed fist in a certain position in the air: *this will be a 40, right here*. Without a viewfinder, without anything—and I know exactly what will work. I am the absolute technical master of the medium. I have no shame in saying it. So if people say something doesn't work, they don't know any better. That's all I can say."

Ambersons also suffered thematically in the recutting. Orson explains that the film as he shot it treated the glory and the fall of the Amberson family as integral parts of the same story. In fact, the fall was for him the crucial component. But what one discovers in the existing version is only the buildup to the fall of a family, whose way of life was destroyed by the changes in society symbolized by the introduction of the automobile. The fall itself wound up on the cutting-room floor as the kind of dark material audiences presumably would despise. *The Magnificent Ambersons* as Orson intended it exists nowhere except in its script and in the dazzling fragments that remain, hacked apart, reedited, and interspersed with the perfectly banal scenes the studio shot while Orson was in Rio. "Nobody stopped him from producing more *Citizen Kane*s," declares Houseman, but as their corruption of the text of *Ambersons* demonstrates, the studio certainly tried.

"Who knows what happened? says Orson of the reworking of Ambersons in his absence. "I was all covered with confetti, trying to pretend I like carnivals, you know. I hate carnivals. . . . The plot of course was really what they took out. Using the argument of not central to the plot, what they took out was the plot. . . . They got it absolutely upside down. I got a letter from Joe Cotten in which he said, You don't realize that you've made a sort of dark movie. It's more Chekhov than Tarkington. I got that in Rio. And of course I did it very clearly and intended it that way. You see, he was distressed for me. It was a very sweet letter all about, You know, we're doing our best to protect you but there was this terrible preview, and you don't understand you've made a movie that, in spite of yourself, turns out to be very dark. Yes, exactly! That's just what I was making! He had become, with the best will in the world, an active collaborator with Wise, and the janitor of RKO, and whoever else was busy screwing it up. They used him. First they convinced him, undermining his confidence by the preview, convinced him of their point of view, and then used him with me. In other words, there's your good friend, you know, the fellow who wrote Journey Into Fear with you, and your old pal and all that. If he feels that, then it isn't just us Hollywood people. *And he was genuinely persuaded by them ... and that was just because they laughed in Pomona.*"

Cotten's *having agreed to appear in the new scenes that Orson had not written was obviously a great blow to Welles.* "It's my theory of Judas, you know," *Orson explains.* "I think that Judas was the most passionately committed of the disciples and that he betrayed Jesus in order to fulfill the prophecies. Well, that's my theory. I don't think that anybody who had lived and been a disciple of Jesus would have sold him for thirty pieces of silver. I think he took the thirty pieces of silver to convince the Romans that it was a genuine sellout. And I think he's the greatest martyred saint of them all—at least I had a whole play written on that basis once. And I think in a way, Joe was that kind of Judas. He was helping to protect me from this disaster, which the movie would have been had it been released in anything resembling my form. That was a heartbreaking thing because it was very hard for me to reply to that. I don't think I even answered it. As I remember, I couldn't think of any way to argue that, except to say that that's what I meant and then have him write me back that* the audience doesn't like it, *and then me to say* screw the audience.*"

Welles *is understandably bitter with regard to the cutting of such dark—but decisive—scenes as one showing George Minafer's long walk through the desolate Amberson mansion, or another showing Eugene (Joseph Cotten) visiting Georgie's Aunt Fanny (Agnes Moorehead), who, after the downfall of the Ambersons, has found herself in a boarding house.* "Of course I expected that there would be an uproar about a picture which, by any ordinary American standards, was much darker than anybody was making pictures. First I* charmed *them, you know, then I* tore *the thing to shreds. Everything, including a six-minute conversation on a talk show in America, or a thirty-second commercial, has a*

happy ending: Now she uses Rinso and her husband makes
it with her five nights a week! *There was just a built-in
dread of the downbeat movie, and I knew I'd have that to
face, but I thought I had a movie so good—I was absolutely
certain of its value, much more than of Kane—that I had
absolutely no doubt that it would win through in spite of
that industry fear of the dark movie. If you see the movie
you'll see that it's like all the preparations for the betrayal
of Falstaff. It's exactly like that, you know. It's a tremendous
preparation for the boardinghouse with Aggie Moorehead
and Joe Cotten, and the terrible walk of George Minafer
when he gets his comeuppance. And without that, there
wasn't any plot. It's all about some rich people fighting in
their house. I'm an enemy of great length in a movie, but
this* had *to have—a kind of awful pompous word—a certain
epic quality. When you do a family and the change of American life because of the automobile, it has to have a kind
of size to it. And there was nobody who even apparently
had an idea what was in my head. And you know, I never
would have gone to South America without a guarantee that
I'd be able to finish the picture there. That I think is a
matter of record. And they absolutely betrayed me and never
gave me a shot at it. You know, all I could do was send
wires, and I knew I was already in an area of compromise
when I was sending wires. But I couldn't walk out on a job
which had diplomatic overtones. I was representing America in Brazil, you see. I was a prisoner of the Good Neighbor
Policy. That's what made it such a nightmare. I couldn't
walk out on Mr. Roosevelt's Good Neighbor Policy with the
biggest single thing that they'd done on the cultural level,
and simply walk away. And I couldn't get my film in my
hands."*

Reminded that, despite his subsequent sense of having
been betrayed, RKO was legally within its rights to reedit
his picture, since by contract he did not have the right to
final cut with Ambersons and Journey as he had in Kane,

*Orson replies: "Yes, but I expected it! But the point is that
my mind didn't even go to 'final cut.' I thought that it went
without saying that, if it had to be previewed, my best rough
cut would be shown and then we would talk over anything
that didn't work. But I was against a preview, as I was with
Kane. See, people don't understand how many people disliked Kane when it came out. People shouted to me in the
street, Hey Ors, what's that Kane about?—you know, as if
I had made The Blood of a Poet. And I expected the same
thing on Ambersons, and a stronger backlash of approval,
because I was certain of the quality of what I was doing.
. . . I'd loved the material! There wasn't a tiny cloud in the
sky in my mind when I left that there would really be trouble
with that picture. And if there ever would be, it would be
after I'd shown what I was doing to lots of people and a
big argument had been held. But all those arguments were
held behind my back—including my best friend, who had
become their ally."*

CHAPTER 23

Bordello de Luxe

As he continued to shoot the Brazilian film, communications between Orson and RKO deteriorated substantially. The months passed, and still there was a work call each morning in the local studio to shoot additional footage of reenacted carnival life; one obviously exasperated company member wrote home that they had already shot enough film to reach from Rio to the United States. Orson's rationale, however, was that since he could not view rushes until he got back to the States, he had better shoot extensively to be certain of having enough usable material to edit later. After three months, Schaefer cabled angrily that RKO had expected him back long before (after all, the carnival itself lasted only three days), and that he had been spending far too much money: $33,000 in March, $10,500 the first week of April, and $15,000 a week for the four weeks after that. If Orson did not wind things up soon, they would order everyone back to the States.

RKO had heard—and been seriously disturbed by—rumors that Orson was planning to spend $25,000 reconstructing Rio's Urca Casino to shoot a sequence in it, and that he had already spent studio money on a national broadcast he did from the casino in honor of the Brazilian dictator's birthday. Neither of these rumors was true. Although Orson did plan to shoot in the casino, whose mirrored walls would have to be covered so that the cameras would not be reflected, he certainly had not planned to rebuild it. And although he had indeed been host at the birthday broadcast for President Getúlio Vargas, the studio had not paid a penny for it. (Orson recalls that he had struck up a friendship with the Brazilian dictator, who insisted that he visit him weekly so that Vargas could recite a list of the girls Orson had cavorted with since his last audience with the president. Orson quips that it is a measure of the efficiency of Vargas's secret police that the lists were unfailingly accurate.)

Word also drifted back—and these charges, alas, were not unfounded—that Orson's relations with his crew had broken down. One of the RKO men in Rio suggested that Orson was prolonging his stay there merely to avoid being drafted back in the States. Anxious to go home to their families, the crew was often irritated by Orson's disappearing for hours on end with the seemingly endless supply of women listed in Vargas's comprehensive weekly reports. While he had been working diligently on the film and successfully delivering goodwill speeches, it is also true that, far away from Dolores, who angrily broke off their engagement when he would not take or return her calls, he celebrated his freedom by relentless womanizing. "He had not just one-night stands," laughs Shifra Haran, "but afternoon stands, before-dinner stands, and after-dinner stands. Quickies by the thousands! Before lunch, after two o'clock tea—but *no one* in residence." Eager as he was for sexual conquest, he was surprised, and often disconcerted, by the unusually aggressive Brazilian women. "It's Portuguese, not Spanish," says Orson to explain the women of Rio, "and the women have all the balls. They decide who they go to bed with. They *tell* you. Believe me, it was very hard for me to cope with that." Orson says that the Brazilian women he encountered were particularly interested in foreign men.

"Look what they have to turn to—Portuguese men," he
says. "If you'd ever been to Brazil, you'd see why. When
men spit, they don't lean forward, they just spit and the
sputum falls directly down in front of them and just misses
their suit, and lands on the floor."

Orson got in trouble for his erotic exploits when what he
suspects was an enraged husband or brother shot at him
through the window as, dressed in a beautiful navy silk
Japanese kimono, he lay reading in his pink satin bed. The
bullets, which narrowly missed him, lodged in the tufted
headboard. "I rolled over to the other side, away from the
window," Orson recalls, "and rolled out onto the balcony,
and went along on my stomach to the next room, and went
in." There he escaped through the back door, and rushed
down several flights to Avenida Atlantica, where he bumped
into a friend from New York who, before Orson could say
that he had just been shot at, announced that he was on his
way to a gathering of leading Brazilian painters. Within
minutes, still dressed only in his kimono, Orson found himself deep in conversation with the artists, to whom he never
got around to mentioning what had just happened. Afterward, reluctant to go home, Orson checked into the Co-
pacabana Palace Hotel, where he telephoned a local
government official of his acquaintance to request special
police protection. The official was not at home, but his sons
were, and they told Orson that, after having been shot at
like that, above all a man needs to relax and they knew
exactly the place. "They said the thing to do is to go to a
bordello *de luxe* to get my nerves in order," says Orson.
They asked him to meet them immediately at a fashionable
address, to which, *still* in the kimono, Orson hurried. "So
for the first time I went to a bordello *de luxe*," Orson laughs.
"I've never been to one before or since. And I must say
that my performance in that bordello was the *greatest* of
my entire life. Nothing like being shot at to improve your
performance!"

Perhaps the high point (or nadir, depending on how one looks at it) of Orson's bachelor life in Rio was the day he and a Mexican diplomat had one convivial drink too many in Orson's large, rather grandly furnished apartment. By the time they decided to take some air on the terrace, they were most pleasantly intoxicated. As they sat talking, they placed their crystal glasses on the ledge; inadvertently, Orson knocked one of them over. In his condition, its crash to the pavement four stories below seemed a lovely sight, so he pushed the other glass over, and it too shattered on the sidewalk. "Have we got anything else we could throw over?" Orson called to Miss Haran, who was inside talking to the cook. At first she brought some lemons and eggs, then the rest of the glasses, all of which the two men hurled over the side, followed by the porch furniture, a chaise longue, a jug, a Chinese vase, then large pieces of furniture from indoors. At which point the other tenants in the building, all of them sedate, well-bred people, began pounding on the door to complain. "It was marvelous!" Miss Haran recalls. "It lasted three or four hours. The street was a shambles. Everything shattered down there that you can think of. I didn't try to stop them. I thought, this is a marvelous experience—they are loving it—and if ever I had the courage, it's what I wanted to do. They didn't really stagger or anything. Mr. Welles, when he's excited, his eyes pop and they're shiny. They almost exude light instead of absorbing light. There's a flush that comes to his face. He gets that even when he's sitting around with writers and flips for an idea. He's so excited, he gets heady on the idea. Well, this time he was heady on the idea, plus whatever they'd been drinking." The bedlam ended with the two men slipping out the back door of the apartment, leaving Miss Haran to tell the angry neighbors that she was sorry but Mr. Welles was not home at the moment.

By May the studio was ready to summon Orson back to Hollywood. They were opposed to Orson's further developing the jangadeiros plotline, but Orson hoped nonetheless to persuade them to let him intercut it, and he proceeded to restage the arrival of the jangadeiros in the Rio harbor. Then, in mid-month, a great tragedy occurred. In the midst of filming the arrival sequence in Rio, the leader of the jangadeiros drowned. Having become a national hero for braving the treacherous waters between Fortaleza and Rio in so flimsy a vessel as a jangada, Jacare had now died, not for the cause for which he had risked his life, but in the making of a movie.

Most of the company left on June 8, but Orson and a handful of the faithful remained behind. The studio had agreed to release an additional $10,000 for Orson to go to remote Fortaleza to finish the saga of the jangadeiros; evidently Jacare's drowning had convinced the studio that the jangadeiros were a delicate international matter, and that Orson should proceed with his filming. Fortaleza was a provincial town on the coast north of Rio. The poor people whose life Orson had come to record lived outside town in huts so precarious they blew away in an especially strong ocean gust. There Orson shot for a month, using dreadfully inadequate equipment, which he suspected one of the RKO men had deliberately given him to sabotage his work in Fortaleza. It was a strange pensive time he spent there, cut off from the rest of the world. He filmed all day, often shirtless, his great white trousers rolled up so he could wade in the water. Because of the defective equipment he had no way of knowing whether all his work that month might be for nothing. At night, after a typical dinner of rice and beans and fish, Orson slipped away to write for hours. Sometimes he could be seen sitting in the darkness silently, calmly thinking. The peace was shattered, however, when one evening at dinner in a local restaurant he was approached by a reporter, who had come all the way from Rio to talk with him. How did Mr. Welles feel, he asked, about having been *terminated* at RKO? It was the first time Orson had heard the word "terminated," but he took the news quietly, as if he already knew.

What had happened was this: Schaefer had been ousted at RKO, and Orson no longer had a protector there. Days after Schaefer was displaced, Mercury had been curtly notified to vacate its office at RKO within twenty-four hours. Not even a hysterical Dadda Bernstein had been able to keep Orson's personal effects intact. In revenge, one Mercury employee had had the presence of mind to unscrew the valve in Orson's steam room, and when, towel in hand, one of the RKO executives later rushed in to take a steam he was foiled in his attempt to do so. (The bungalow was not the only property reclaimed from Mercury: *Journey Into Fear* was also confiscated and recut by the studio without Mercury's participation.) While the new regime at RKO was eager to be rid of Orson—"All's well that ends Welles," one studio mahatma had quipped—they did not interfere with his work in Fortaleza, because they suspected that if *anything* was to be salvaged from all the film Orson had shot in Brazil it would be the jangadeiros material. He could stay there until he used up the $10,000. But they hoped to sell the negative of Orson's film to the office of the coordinator of Inter-American Affairs, or if Nelson Rockefeller did not want to buy it, they might edit the footage themselves without consulting Orson. Nor, if they could avoid it, did RKO intend to go ahead with the third picture Orson was entitled to direct under his contract.

But in Fortaleza all Orson knew was that he had been *terminated*—whatever that meant. Hollywood was worlds away. Here the natives were unabashed in their delight at their big visitor whom they chased along the beach. Orson did a great deal of shooting on the beach, where he would often dig a hole in the sand for the cameras so as to shoot the jangadas from an especially low angle. One such time, barefoot, shirtless, and quite tan, Orson picked a spot on the beach from which he wanted to do a low angle shot.

No sooner had he begun to dig than he realized that he had made a terrible mistake. The natives had not warned him that this was an area of the beach where people routinely defecated, afterwards covering their deposits with sand. By the time Orson realized this, it was too late. For there he found himself, twenty-seven years old, world famous, and standing in shit.

CHAPTER 24
Wild Nights

"Nobody was ever more cowardly in the world than Nelson, you know," says Orson of Nelson Rockefeller, the coordinator of Inter-American Affairs. "He didn't want to be near anything that was under any kind of shadow." By the time Welles got back to the States, Rockefeller was definitely not interested in acquiring the Brazilian footage from RKO, who were trying to unload it. Orson felt that since he had gone to Rio at Rockefeller's request in the first place—he calls his sojourn in Rio "the Nelson caper"—the coordinator might have taken a greater personal interest in his subsequent plight at RKO. Afterwards Orson could not help but look upon the trip itself as a false move in his career—and in his heart, he blamed Rockefeller. "I was unhappy being in South America because I was away from America at a time when I wanted to be there," says Orson. Not until he came home did Orson fully come to terms with the fact that *Ambersons* had been wrested away in his prolonged absence. He would never really know if he had been able to match in his second film the majesty of his first, since, in effect, the *Ambersons* he had made no longer existed as he had intended it. As to why he had stayed in Rio so long, Orson says: "I was in the ridiculous position of having to say, 'Let me stay here to finish it,' when I would have preferred to have somebody else do it."

"It wasn't at all daring," Orson says of the footage that had been shipped back to the United States, never to be edited. "*It's All True* was not going to make any kind of cinematic history, nor was it intended to. It was intended to be a perfectly honorable execution of my job as a goodwill ambassador, bringing entertainment to the Northern Hemisphere that showed them something about the Southern one." Since one of the missions of the so-called Nelson Rockefeller Committee had been to generate interest in Latin America among the citizens of the United States, financing the editing of the Brazilian footage to be shown to them in theaters across the country would have been perfectly in order. But as Orson points out, *It's All True* was by now under a shadow: the controversy and discord that were widely associated with it—and that scared off Rockefeller, who declined RKO's sales pitch. If the subject of the abortive Latin American project is highly charged for Orson, it is because—as he well recognizes—his failure to finish the picture was a shadow that would remain with him for his entire career. "Disaster scares people," says Orson of the effect the history of *It's All True* would have on his later career in film. Orson goes on to say of the other big disasters in his career: "All these kinds of breakdowns are really worse than not having success. That's *really* what hurts me, not the lack of blockbusters. *That's* what scares them, you see. They think that something goes with me, either because of my character or because of my luck—or a combination of both that scares them. *What's going to happen with it?* you know. And it began of course with South America, but it repeated itself enough to look like a character failing of mine. And I keep thinking maybe it is. It's like somebody who every time he goes out gets struck by lightning."

• • •

But when he left Rio on July 29, 1942, Orson did not yet perceive himself as having been struck by lightning. For there was still a chance, however slim, that he could finish his film back in the States. Even RKO was willing at least to hear what Orson proposed. But before he flew to New York, Orson had several stops to make in his role as goodwill ambassador. Among them was a courtesy call on the Bolivian president. Having arrived in Bolivia and checked into his hotel, Orson almost did not make it to the presidential palace, however: "I had been in the Amazon," says Orson, "and my only pair of trousers (because my luggage hadn't come) had gotten covered with the pitch with which the canoe had been held together, so that whenever I sat down I took away the upholstery with me. I sent this suit out to be cleaned, and it came time to go and visit the president and the suit hadn't come back. So I called the presidential palace and asked to speak to his secretary, and a voice said, 'I'm sorry, the secretary isn't here, but I'm the president. What can I do for you?' " When Orson explained the embarrassing situation (without his pants he couldn't exactly pay a call on the presidential palace), the president offered to send over one of his own suits. Orson got his own pants back in time for his next diplomatic mission: a stopover in Mexico City to see Dolores Del Rio for their first confrontation since she had called off the marriage. Whatever ill feelings there might have been between them swiftly dissolved, and after Orson had dispensed a little of the goodwill for which he'd become so famous in Rio, another rendezvous was set, for several months hence, at the Sherry Netherland Hotel in New York.

At their Mexico City rendezvous Orson refrained from telling Dolores what he had told others, that he already had his next wife in mind. Even the representative from the coordinator's office who had arranged the meeting with the Bolivian president had heard all about Orson's sudden passion for an actress he had seen in a magazine after he had left Rio. It sounded like nothing more than a bit of levity when Orson confidently announced that he planned to marry Rita Hayworth as soon as he could arrange to meet her. Orson knew enough not to mention his little fantasy to Dolores while in Mexico. It would certainly have cast gloom over the party that she gave to celebrate their reconciliation at the Hotel Reforma the night before Orson's departure. Dolores had invited the ambassadors from Argentina, Brazil, China, Cuba, Peru, and the United States, as well as the poet Pablo Neruda and the painter Diego Rivera. The party was her gift to Orson, who in turn told everyone that he had intended to bring Dolores a gift of his own, a costly Peruvian necklace, which he had inadvertently left behind in a hotel in Guatemala.

Back in the States, it was not long before Orson was on the radio again with two shows of his own design. Every week on *Hello Americans*, Orson planned to inform his countrymen about their South American neighbors. Orson conceived the Sunday-night sustaining program on CBS as boosting the efforts of the coordinator's office to publicize the importance of South America to the continued strength of the U.S. His other show, on Mondays, also had a political slant. Titled *Ceiling Unlimited*, and sponsored by Lockheed and Vega Aircraft, it dealt with aviation's role in the war effort. Both productions were elaborate affairs, and Orson proved his usual omnipresent self. In part, it was this amazing capacity for doing everything at once that accounted for Orson's image of being "unbridled," an image that he resented fiercely.

A newly appointed advertising-agency account executive who visited a last-minute rehearsal of *Ceiling Unlimited* experienced this resentment first hand. When the agency fellow showed up, two hours before air time, Orson was rushing about the set as always, barking instructions at actors, musicians, and technicians. The visitor edged up to Orson's new business partner, Jackson Leighter (formerly of the coordinator's office), and in a very low voice asked him, "Mr. Leighter, how do you handle this man Welles?" At which remark Orson suddenly stopped dead. A moment before, the set had been a hive of activity, but now no one was moving. "Young man," boomed Orson, who was only twenty-seven years old himself. "You *handle* horses!" Without a word more, he repaired to his office, threw on his hat and coat, and left for the night. So definitive was his exit that Leighter knew he'd better quickly find a replacement.

Orson's image had almost entirely infected his relations with the new studio management at RKO. Although his contract with them entitled him to make—and be paid for— a third picture, they certainly were not inclined to let that happen. Behind closed doors, it was argued that the studio would probably get off much more cheaply by waiting until Orson legally forced them to pay him the agreed $125,000 for a third picture he never *actually* made than to allow him to make it. There was, of course, always the possibility that he would not bring any pressure to bear at all, and would just quietly go elsewhere.

If Orson was still of any interest it was because they suspected he was the only one who might be able to salvage the Brazilian footage, for which the only script was in Orson's brain. "There'd be no way to make a picture unless I made it," says Orson, "unless they just used it as production material for a bad musical." There was also considerable studio interest in his being brought in—although without compensation beyond basic expenses—to put a few finishing touches on *Journey Into Fear*, since they realized that they had pretty much made a mess of it when they wrested it from Foster to rework themselves. Orson agreed to do some recutting in hopes of salvaging *Journey*; to his horror, he discovered that RKO had retained the basically "naive" story on which the film was based, but had hacked away the rich "atmosphere" that he found to be the source of the material's appeal. To the studio's way of thinking this merely impeded the progress of the story. As if they were doing him a favor, the studio allowed him no more than fourteen days to do what recutting he could and to shoot an additional scene with Joseph Cotten, who, like Orson, would not receive any compensation for his efforts.

As for *It's All True*, Orson was told he could submit a script and a schedule for work yet to be done, as well as a reasonably accurate idea of how much that might cost. Whatever Orson's hopes might have been at first, he soon realized that the studio had not been very serious about salvaging the footage, and had been leaning toward abandoning it and taking a tax loss. They had only called him in to see what he would propose, if by chance it gave them a better business deal. "It was a tax write-off, so they lost nothing," Orson explains of their final decision to give up on the film. "See, it's a tremendous temptation to studios and networks in situations of that kind because if they get to a place where they can argue that the thing is unusable or blocked some kind of way, point their finger at somebody, they can write it right off, and they haven't lost a thing. *I'm* the only one who lost, you see. . . . Otherwise, they would have been struggling to get something out of it. However bad, they could have made a bad musical out of just the nightclub footage. They would have got a return on their money. But they didn't want a return on their money. It was better for them to drop it in the sea, which they did. I found out that a lot of it was literally thrown in the sea"— this last assertion a reference to what Orson believes eventually happened to the footage.

If finishing the South American film became something of an obsession for Orson, it was not only because the *It's All True* fiasco had damaged his credibility, but also because it had done him considerable psychic damage. "I had that and *Ambersons* together, you see," Orson explains. "It left its mark." The myth that he had abandoned *Ambersons* (thus forcing the studio to take it over) had already begun to take root, and there was little Orson could do now that the studio had foolishly released it in its corrupt form. But Orson felt (probably correctly) that he could still save the South American footage—and, more important, his reputation. For the fact was that whatever carousing and womanizing Orson had done in South America—and he had done plenty—he had also done plenty of work, and only the finished film would prove it. Without a film he had nothing to show for the period—nothing except the reputation of a director whose films were either taken out of his control (*Ambersons*) or abandoned altogether (*It's All True*).

Having finally persuaded the studio to let him examine some of the footage, Orson decided that he should cut it at his own expense, an idea that was well-nigh unthinkable in Hollywood, where directors do not pay, but get paid, to make movies. And since the studio had not even bothered to have the jangadeiros footage developed, Orson decided to pay for that costly procedure as well. This was how he had operated back in the WPA. Although from the first, Orson had been an outsider in Hollywood, the desperate decision to play by his own rules and pay for the cutting of his picture was the start of an even more exacerbated state of alienation—one that would persist for many decades thereafter. For now, however, Orson still held out hope that the partially assembled South American film would attract a buyer among the other studios. If no buyer materialized, Orson would need somehow to raise the cash to release the picture. But how was Orson possibly going to pay even to begin cutting when he had not been paid for any of his work on the film thus far?

His scheme was to raise cash by hiring himself out as an actor. This was to be the first of many such arrangements in the course of the years: he would pay for his own offbeat film work by acting in a more mainstream picture. In this case, the picture was 20th Century–Fox's *Jane Eyre*. Orson agreed to play Edward Rochester for a considerable price tag of $100,000, the same sum he had been paid to act, direct, produce and write *Kane*. "Part of my deal," says Orson, "was that I was to be given a Moviola and allowed to work on my South American picture. And I did—during lunch periods and all that, with whatever material I'd been able to get, trying to show people a part of it to persuade them that it was worth finishing."

Eager to accept the role of Mr. Rochester when David O. Selznick offered it to him, Orson still had his conditions. This time, he was in a good position to bargain. When the top producer invited him to lunch at Romanoff's, Orson knew about the package that Selznick and British director Robert Stevenson were earnestly putting together to sell to 20th Century–Fox. Selznick sorely wanted Orson to co-star as the darkly romantic and mysterious Rochester opposite Joan Fontaine's Jane Eyre. Back in 1940, Orson had played this very part—and played it well—on radio. After the formidable RKO advertising campaign for *Kane*'s general release, which portrayed Orson as a dashing romantic lead, it had become clear that Orson could be sold in this sort of part to audiences. It would mean rigorous dieting and once again hauling out Kane's corsets, but as Rochester, Orson would reach the high point of his shortlived career as a romantic lead. Before Orson was forty, his ever-escalating weight would make his playing such parts impossible. But now, at twenty-seven, he could still very convincingly will himself into shape for such a role.

But if Selznick was primarily concerned with Orson's image as an actor, Orson himself took a broader view. How would it appear for the great actor-director-producer-writer suddenly to cast off the last three of these roles? What would become of his reputation as the *wunderkind*—especially if in the credits his name would appear *beneath* Joan Fontaine's? Thus Orson adamantly insisted on first billing, his name *above* Fontaine's, and Selznick agreed. Although he eventually grew to be very fond of Stevenson, Orson was

also concerned about someone else directing him. Another
condition for his signing to play Rochester was that he also
be appointed associate producer, which would guarantee his
being allowed basically to shape his own performance without intervention. Eventually Selznick regretted this concession, and persuaded 20th Century–Fox not to list Orson
onscreen as associate producer (even though this role had
been clearly stipulated in the contract). He feared that audiences would perceive the film as secretly being Orson's
when in fact Stevenson was principally responsible for its
conception and execution. This was to be an unmistakable
irony of Orson's career: that coupled with the spurious rumors that somehow he was not *really* the *auteur* of his
masterpiece *Citizen Kane* were other rumors—these last
not always entirely unfounded—that in fact he was the
secret *auteur* of many of the films in which he ostensibly
only acted. Closer to the truth perhaps is that, as in the case
of *Jane Eyre*, Orson often tended to direct his own performance; through the ineluctable force of his personality, he
would momentarily take control of those whose job it was
to control him.

If *Jane Eyre* was sometimes a trying experience for Orson, it was because he was bored to be only acting, and his
imperial instincts frequently began automatically to assert
themselves on the set. Perhaps it was that same ennui that
caused him to play an extended practical joke on an un-
suspecting production assistant who, as Orson likes to tell
the tale, was informed that according to the terms of Mr.
Welles's contract it was part of the assistant's job to waltz
with him. The assistant had heard many rumors about Orson's eccentricities, but this was going too far. Seeing how
shocked and disconcerted the poor fellow was, his inform-
ant—one of Orson's cronies—told him that otherwise Mr.
Welles was really very easy to work with. His only quirk
was that he liked to waltz with a partner. Lest the assistant
fear that this might be a prelude to more intimate embraces,

the crony assured him that he was expected *only* to waltz with Mr. Welles, nothing else. If at first the assistant discounted what he had just heard, he could do so no longer when suddenly waltz music boomed forth from Orson's dressing room. Finding himself sent to fetch Orson, the by now distraught fellow nervously knocked on the dressing-room door, behind which he could hear Orson loudly humming along to the familiar tunes. When, rhythmically swaying to and fro, Orson flung open the door, the assistant meekly refused to enter the dressing room for fear that he would have to perform his dancing duties with the madman. From then on, whenever Orson encountered the assistant about the set he would routinely inquire, "And which Strauss waltz is your favorite?" or "Which Offenbach do you prefer?"

But Orson's mirth disappeared whenever six-year-old actress Margaret O'Brien was around, especially the day she arrived amid much fuss in the adorable white gown she was to wear onscreen in her role as Mr. Rochester's tiny ward. Thrilled by her own outfit, she kept glancing in the mirror, much to the shared delight of the rest of the cast and crew— all except Orson, that is, who snidely muttered to his secretary that the kid was nothing but a "little scene stealer." Of Orson's attitude toward the child actresses in the film— ten-year-old Elizabeth Taylor was another—Shifra Haran says, "Well, he didn't cozy up to them, if you know what I mean." But of little Elizabeth Taylor, Orson has a somewhat different memory. Unlike some other figures in Hollywood, Orson has never found himself attracted to very young girls. "That's something I'm very puritanical about," he says. "I just believe that it's off limits." Only once, he recalls, did he faintly comprehend the impulse, and this was in the presence of little Elizabeth Taylor. "When I read *Lolita*," says Orson, "I undersood what he meant, because of Elizabeth Taylor as a child. I just never saw anything like her. She was unbelievable."

As to Orson's working relationship with the lovely Joan Fontaine, the cast and crew seemed to think that Orson was deliberately holding his on-camera embraces with her a bit longer than necessary. Miss Fontaine was then married to British actor Brian Aherne, whom Orson had never forgiven for having displaced him as Mercutio in Katharine Cornell's *Romeo and Juliet*. Orson decided to play a little joke on his co-star by regaling her with tales of his wild sex life. "I wasn't having a very brilliant love life because I was working hard on the picture," Orson recalls. "And I used to make these terrible jokes—as we'd stand there in the dry ice waiting for the smoke to gather, I'd say, 'There you are going home to have roast beef with Aubrey Smith, who I suppose is your guest tonight, and I on the other hand am going with two Siamese girls.' I made up this tremendous sex life for myself hoping to torment her, this steady tale of wild nights with mixed races." Orson says that a rumor he had heard about the sexual habits of British men had motivated his teasing her in this way. "A girlfriend of mine from London had told me the terrible thing about English men was that when they finished with you they slapped your flank the way they do when they get off a horse. That made a big impression on me." With this image in mind, whenever Orson caught sight of his co-star he remembered that her husband was British: "I kept thinking of that and looking at her down there in the mist—you know, coming, as she did, a little below my navel, and thinking of her going home to dinner with this thigh-slapper. So I thought the only way to get at her was to, in a sort of friendly way, like one actor to another, describe these *incredible* combinations that you would find only in what used to be sold under the counter." Orson's fun was spoiled, however, when his chauffeur took it upon himself to tell her the truth.

His wild tales of debauchery notwithstanding, with time out for an occasional date, Orson's real schedule was mostly crammed with work. Even his daily trips to the 20th Cen-

tury—Fox steam room involved business. He went there to
put in a good word for Stevenson's picture—although not,
as one might expect, with the studio executives. "The steam
room at 20th," says Orson, "was entirely controlled by a
very bad masseur who sweated on you as he worked, and
whose opinion was eagerly sought for the rushes every day
as being *the voice of the people*. I was smart enough to get
in terribly well with the masseur so that the word would
come down from him that everything was well."

After he had finished in the steam room, Orson devoted
most of his spare hours to readying some of the Brazil
footage to show to prospective buyers. For a work space
20th Century—Fox had given him Shirley Temple's former
bungalow, which he shared with a group of white mice that
an admirer had given him as a gift for his magic act. Seeing
no particular use for them, however, Orson in turn gave the
box of mice to Miss Haran, who, figuring that they would
simply run away if she freed them, bravely opened the lid.
Out came the white mice much as she had anticipated, but
instead of fleeing the premises they decided to stay. Visitors
to Orson's bungalow were often startled by the sight of them
scurrying about on Miss Haran's typewriter. More often than
not the mice preferred the solitude of her second desk drawer,
however.

Orson had managed to squeeze a massive bed into the
tiny bungalow, although he preferred to do most of his
napping in the back seats of automobiles while his new
chauffeur, a hunchbacked dwarf named Shorty, drove here
and there. These naps fortified him for his all-night working
sessions, which he held in his temporary living quarters in
the onetime haunt of the New York literary exiles in Hollywood, the Garden of Allah. Located on Sunset Boulevard,
just across from Schwab's Drugstore, the Garden of Allah
was owned by the ailing silent-screen star Alla Nazimova,
who occupied the rooms directly above Orson's. Agitated
by ringing telephones, Miss Haran's typing, and Orson's

booming dictation that routinely persisted through the night, Nazimova periodically roused herself from bed to pound furiously on the floor with her cane. But intent on whipping *It's All True* into shape, Orson would not diminish his pace. (So Nazimova did not regret Orson's eventually abandoning her establishment for a rented house in the Hollywood Hills, on Woodrow Wilson Drive.) Orson had it distinctly in mind to interest the legendary studio head at 20th Century–Fox, Darryl Zanuck, in his Rio footage. Zanuck may have struck terror in the hearts of some of his underlings, but he in turn often seemed rather frightened in Orson's presence. The two became friends, and while an invitation to Zanuck's luxurious private steam room was much coveted in Hollywood, Orson had been told to drop by whenever he liked. Eventually Orson strategically returned the invitation by asking Zanuck to drop by the screening room for a look at what he had been working on.

There was no dialogue or narration as yet, so Orson had to hold Zanuck's attention with the full force of his voice and personality as he explained what was—and what was not yet—on the screen. In the darkened screening room Zanuck sat on the verge of growing as mesmerized as Orson wanted him to be. The world outside had just about evaporated, when the door flew open and in popped Shorty, a sobering stream of light gushing in from behind him. "Boss, I'm goin' home t'wash out a few things! G'bye!" He quickly closed the door but the frail spell had been broken. Even Orson had to accept that there was no point in continuing. Zanuck could not stop laughing at this unexpected glimpse of the mighty Orson's domestic circumstances.

Shorty had a bad habit of butting in when he shouldn't have. "I used to pay Shorty *not* to talk," recalls Orson. His quips and comments on everything and everybody thus painfully bottled up within him, Shorty was given to making vivid Italianate gestures and operatic noises to express himself without forfeiting the extra cash. Fifty-six-inch-tall

George Chirello had been bestowed on Welles by Joseph
Cotten, who had discovered him dispensing towels in the
steam room at the New York Athletic Club. Born into extreme poverty on the Lower East Side of Manhattan, Shorty
had turned to a life of crime, and by the time Cotten met
him, he was a "two-time loser," scrupulously trying to avoid
a return engagement as the warden's much-prized chef at
Sing Sing. Having labored early on with a gang of burglars
who easily pushed him up and into windows so he could
let them in the front door, during Prohibition Shorty had
graduated to smuggling booze from Canada by hiding the
bottles in the secret pockets of a massive fur coat that,
stuffed to capacity, weighed more than one hundred pounds.

Orson prized Shorty's domestic talents and unwavering
personal loyalty as much as the warden at Sing Sing had.
"He was one of the most trustworthy men," says Shifra
Haran of her beloved former co-worker, whose ashes are
now enshrined in her front lawn. "You know, there's nothing
like a reformed crook for honesty." When every now and
again Orson's financial circumstances took a temporary turn
for the worse, Shorty could even be counted on to lend the
Boss money from his personal savings. To drive, Shorty
had to have special wooden blocks attached to the pedals
of the car, so that he could reach them. Besides driving and
cooking, Shorty took over Miss Haran's dreaded task of
rousing the Boss, as well as keeping him in Upmann cigars
and what he called *snotters*, or handkerchiefs.

They made a peculiar pair, the giant and the dwarf, but
as Miss Haran fondly points out, "Of course that was part
of the *greatness* of it!" However drastically different they
were in stature, they shared (and seemed to admire each
other for) an innate, often irresistible, appeal to women.
"Shorty was more sought after by women than any movie
star," says Shifra Haran. "He was another man with enormous appetites, an enormous success with women." But it
was the Boss's amorous exploits about which Shorty liked

to boast, as when, for instance, he told film editor Ernest
Nims about women's reacting to Orson like "bitches in
heat." All the Boss had to do, it seemed, was "walk down
the street and ... women would come from all over!"
Apparently snoozing wasn't the only leisurely activity
Orson undertook in his automobile as Shorty drove him
about: "They were sittin' in the back seat swappin' spit,"
as Shorty was given to describing it in his singular manner
of speaking.

To judge from the mash notes from women with which
Orson was routinely flooded, he had plenty of opportunities
for dalliance: "It's really only been a few days since I saw
you in Lucy's Restaurant and you sent the headwaiter to
ask my name, and whether I was interested in motion-picture
work, but they've been the longest days of my life," begins
one typical example. "You see I've long suffered from a
bad case of wanting to be an actress, severely complicated
by 'hero worship' for you and the kind of acting you've
always represented. Bang! I see you. And Bang! you send
someone to ask me whether I'm interested in moving-picture
work! That's a Big Event in the life of a girl visiting from
Seattle. . . . Will you be able to see me before Thursday,
when my parents are dragging me back to Seattle?"
But these brief encounters did not distract Welles from
his determination to be introduced to Rita Hayworth. "He
made a great point of it," recalls Jackson Leighter. She had
been spending much of her time with muscle-bound actor
Victor Mature, whom she planned to marry, but Mature had
joined the Coast Guard and he had been shipped out by the
time Orson, who had been classified 4-F, finally managed
to arrange a party, where he could meet her as if by accident.
At first she adamantly refused his attentions. "It took me
five weeks to get Rita to answer the phone," Orson recalls,
"but once she did, we were out that night." She was not
quite the glamorous screen star he had been expecting. Cer-

tainly, with her lush mane of red hair and her supple dancer's
body, Rita was every bit as beautiful in life as on the screen.
But her immense vulnerability, her complete lack of affec-
tation, drew Orson out of himself—something few people
had ever managed so effectively to do.

Margarita Carmen Cansino had been born in Brooklyn in
1918. "She's half gypsy, not half Spanish," says Welles of
the standard story that her father, Eduardo Cansino, was a
Spaniard. "The mother was a show girl with Ziegfeld." By
the time Margarita was thirteen she was partner to her father
in a Spanish dance act. Underage as she was, Margarita
wouldn't be allowed to work in American night spots that
served liquor, so the Dancing Cansinos played Tijuana and
Agua Caliente in Mexico, where no one was likely to ask
how old she was. "He was a terrible man," says Orson of
Eduardo. "And she really hated him." Orson confirms that
when she and her father were dancing professionally, Margarita had to pretend that she was his *wife*, not his daughter.
"She couldn't deal with him at all," Orson recalls. Spending
too much time locked up in her dressing room when her
parents were out, Margarita was denied her youth and the
formal education that should have gone with it, and the
latter loss would henceforth prove a source of embarrassment to her. Too early in life, Margarita was encouraged to
be sexually provocative onstage, although she was an intensely shy child offstage. This dichotomy between the
flamboyant Rita and the shy Rita would persist into adult-
hood—and, initially drawn to the former, Orson found himself entirely, unexpectedly captivated by the latter. Eventually
Rita's inability to integrate the two aspects of herself would
prove disastrous. Having been conditioned early on to provoke men sexually, an adult Rita would sometimes seem to
feel appreciated by Orson only when he was explicitly dem-
onstrative in his physical affections. Shifra Haran (who
worked for Rita both when she was with Orson and when
she was with her third husband, Prince Aly Khan) points

out that she was "not sexually shy in a room with a man, but very shy at meeting people. I think she could only believe that people loved her when they were making love." Rita had never outgrown the withdrawn little girl who had been taught to hold her audience, especially the men. "When it came to the man in her life, she had to have *all* his attention," says Elisabeth Rubino, who also did secretarial work for Rita during both her Orson and Aly periods. "*Why* she had to have all that attention is because she was not really grown up. She was immature."

Her father was only the first of the men in her life who exploited her beauty. Next came a small-time wheeler-dealer named Edward Judson, more than two decades her senior, whom she married at eighteen after having come to Hollywood two years previously at the invitation of a studio vice president who had seen her dancing in Mexico. Judson, whom Orson characterizes as "an indescribably awful man," merchandised her somewhat more shrewdly than Eduardo had. Having changed her name to Rita Hayworth, the former car salesman managed to sell her to that virtuoso of vulgarity, Columbia Pictures' Harry Cohn, who, says Orson, "had been lusting for her ever since he signed her, and chasing her around the desk." The mogul was known to poke his letter opener into the mouths of aspiring starlets to pull down their jaws so he could inspect their teeth; and would quickly use the same opener, now moist with saliva, to lift their skirts for a glimpse of their thighs. Cohn, says Orson, "felt a tremendous *proprietary* sense for Rita." While she would not accede to his sexual demands, she really had no choice but to bear the humiliation and verbal abuse he heaped upon her in the course of years. Even after having divorced Judson, Rita found herself subject to Cohn's tyranny. So jealously did Cohn guard his prize actress that he even bugged her dressing room, lest any aspect of her life escape his obsessed attention.

A woman as insecure about her lack of education as Rita

could only be flattered by the attentions of a reputed genius like Orson. He, for his part, was not only a brilliant talker but a brilliant listener. He actually seemed interested in what she had to say—something that she had not much experienced in men. He was neither vulgar nor tyrannical nor exploitative. He did not want to perform with her, to merchandise her, or to own her. He responded to Rita's sweetness with an unexpected sweetness of his own. "Rita had great *natural* dignity," Orson recalls. By contrast with Dolores Del Rio, who always seemed to be impeccably made up and ready to face her adoring public, Rita was a great natural beauty who didn't need to comb her hair or make herself up to look perfectly stunning in the old blue jeans and rumpled shirt she enjoyed wearing in private. In short, Rita combined the image of sophistication Orson had enjoyed in New York and Hollywood and the genuine simplicity of his Midwestern background. The press was still talking about Rita's impending marriage to "Vic" the day Miss Haran was dispatched to pack away anything she could find in Rita's apartment with the monogram "VM" on it. Although Rita continued to maintain her apartment in Beverly Hills, in fact she discreetly moved in with Orson on Woodrow Wilson Drive.

For Orson there remained the matter of the rendezvous with Dolores that they had agreed to when he saw her last in Mexico City. Although she had previously broken off their engagement when she realized that he was declining to take her calls in Rio, their relationship had briefly flared up again in Mexico City. But now that Orson was involved with Rita he needed to make a clean break with Dolores, of whom he remained genuinely fond.

The trip to Rio had saved Orson once from a face-to-face confrontation with Dolores when he was eager to end their relationship, but this time he had no such convenient escape. In a few days' time he was expected promptly at six at Dolores's suite in the Sherry Netherland Hotel overlooking

Central Park. It is a measure of how genuinely fond of Dolores Orson was that he felt compelled to appear at all, and a measure of how apprehensive that he appeared five hours late, after fortifying himself with quite a few drinks. Orson found Dolores in her bedroom, which lay behind a beaded portiere. How could he begin to explain to her that their relationship was definitely finished now? First he would have somehow to excuse his lateness. As she watched from within, he reached up and grasped a handful of colored beads dangling above him. Nervously tugging at them he went into his speech when suddenly the portiere collapsed and he with it. In his anxiety he probably had not realized how hard he had been pulling. Glancing up at her from the floor where he lay all entangled in beads he could see that she had dissolved into laughter at his awkward plight—both in having fallen and in having been so nervous about his confession.

Orson successfully sorted things out with Dolores so that they both could remain good friends; and he returned to Hollywood and Rita. It was at this point that he saw, but was not alarmed by, the first signs of Rita's grave insecurities. He did not realize that these fits of jealousy betokened anything serious. "Later I began to know," he says, "but I didn't at the very beginning, because I was being *super* virtuous and she had *absolutely* no reason to be jealous. I wasn't smart enough to know that it was neurotic. I just thought it was gypsy, and I said, this is that gypsy kick and I've got to cure her of that." Besides, he hardly noticed the occasional jealous scene, when most of the time she was, as he says, "just so sweet and darling." Happily, they embarked on their first show-business project together.

Los Angeles was packed with milling servicemen waiting to be shipped off to battle. Many celebrities, Rita and Orson among them, had donated performances at the local USO. Having been kept out of the service by his poor health, Orson felt a special responsibility at least to entertain the brave young men who would be fighting abroad. This was the impetus for the wild ninety-minute tent show he and Rita began to cook up.

Principal among its attractions would be Orson's hypnotizing a chicken he had painstakingly taught to freeze at "Dr. Welles's" stare. Unfortunately, no sooner had Orson managed to train the bird than it sprouted a tumor on its leg. Picture the general dismay in the crowded waiting room of a fashionable Beverly Hills veterinarian when the mothers and fathers of the most mandarin of dogs and cats found themselves joined by Miss Haran with Mr. Welles's sick chicken cradled in her arms. Since the chicken was about to donate its services to charity, the doctor agreed to remove the tumor free of charge. Back at the Shirley Temple bungalow, Orson ordered a big box filled with straw to be placed on a table, and there the chicken briefly recuperated after surgery. Another of the curious tricks Orson practiced for the *Mercury Wonder Show* was swallowing a packet of needles that he seemed to regurgitate mysteriously threaded. There was also the stunt Orson taught Joseph Cotten: Cotten would climb into a sack and invite some of the GIs onstage to tie it in a trunk, which in turn they would carefully tie again, only to see Cotten entering at the back of the tent where he would proceed down the long aisle to join them onstage. For eleven weeks Orson's *Wonder Show* company—Rita, Cotten, and Agnes Moorehead among them— rehearsed their magic in a little theater Orson had rented in Hollywood. Shorty was Orson's comical onstage assistant, while backstage Miss Haran frantically manned the abundant props and kept an eye on the chicken. *Princess Nephrotite Cut to Ribbons Yet She Lives! Joseph the Great Escapes Alive! Doctor Welles, All Nature Freezes at His Glance!* went the hoopla. Meanwhile, Victor Mature, shivering out at sea somewhere in the North Atlantic, heard that Orson had daily been preparing to saw Rita in half and lamented that it was "a hell of a way to woo a girl."

However, when the *Wonder Show* finally opened in a tent near the USO it was not Rita Hayworth whom Welles "cut to ribbons" as promised, but Marlene Dietrich. Marlene Dietrich had become Orson's friend during the period when he and Dolores Del Rio were still dating secretly. But the Marlene he had come to know and adore was not the un-attainable, androgynous screen goddess whom director Josef von Sternberg had created in movies from *The Blue Angel* on. Every bit as ravishingly beautiful offscreen, Die-trich was in fact the antithesis of the cold, impassive image Sternberg had so brilliantly created for her. Instead she was, says Orson, more like a German *hausfrau*, warm, caring, domestic. Orson noticed that, above all, the man who most successfully brought out these qualities in Marlene was her lover Jean Gabin, the powerful French actor well known for his performances in such films as Renoir's *La Grande Illusion* and Duvivier's *Pépé le Moko*. A cigarette perpet-ually dangled from his lips. Gabin's craggy face was not conventionally handsome, but his air of masculine strength made him tremendously appealing to women. When Dolores had openly split up with her husband, she and Welles fre-quented chic night spots like the Mocambo with Marlene Dietrich and Jean Gabin. So at the last minute, when Rita could not go onstage with the *Wonder Show*, Orson im-mediately thought of Marlene to replace her. "She was the good soldier of all time," says Orson of Dietrich. "The reason that she was in the magic show was because Harry Cohn wouldn't allow Rita to be in it. It's a total legend that I sawed her in half. She rehearsed it, and on opening night was told by Harry Cohn and her lawyers that she would be sued. So she said, 'I'm going anyway.' I said, 'No, you're not.' And I called Marlene, and she says, 'Come teach me the tricks and I do it.' So that's how I got Jean Gabin as a stagehand. He was backstage every night, loading rabbits and everything so he could keep an eye on Marlene." Orson taught Dietrich to do a telepathy act, which she performed in a form-fitting skin-toned gown which was covered with sequins. Says Shifra Haran: "When she came on the stage with that gown—she was really *no* chicken, you know—and with her *knowing* look, she just devastated everybody. The soldiers went insane." Every night one of the GIs in the audience found himself recruited to participate in Dietrich's mind-reading routine. Of how shy they typically were with Dietrich, Shifra Haran recalls: "Those guys practically peed in their pants on the stage."

Of course *The Wonder Show* was only a diversion for Orson. Unable to interest anyone in the Brazilian footage, he realized he would have to concoct a new picture project. Once again he ordered whole carloads of books, which he feverishly marked up and tore apart in quest of film ideas. To Orson a story was only raw material, to be hacked apart and made his own by telling it in a new way. The question Welles had to answer for himself was what kind of project he should develop at this point in his career. For the moment, however cruelly he had been dealt with by the general public in Pomona, whose rejection of *Ambersons* had been absolutely devastating to him, Orson remained convinced that that same public deserved the sort of serious filmmaking he had tried to give them in his first two pictures.

A lecture that Orson delivered to a group of New York University film students shortly after returning from South America indicates his frustration in Hollywood. Orson lamented Hollywood's mercenary refusal to treat film as "the great art form of our century": "It is just too bad that it is not taken more seriously than it is," said Orson, "because it is so very powerful and yet so very meaningless most of the time. When I tell that to people in Hollywood they get mad at me and they say that 'You are just arty.' " The power to which Orson referred was film's ability directly to reach immense numbers of people in a way that, say, the novel or painting simply could not. But it was a power that, he felt, the moguls seemed basically uninterested in exploring.

"It is too bad that there is no money spent in Hollywood for experiment," said Orson. "If you take any other large industry—General Electric, chemistry, automobiles—you spend at least ten percent—maybe twenty percent—of your profits on a laboratory where experimentation is done. There is not one cent spent by anybody in Hollywood for experiment and there is not one cent spent in the world today, except Russia once did experiment, but Russia did not have the equipment to be able to go forward in any particular direction. Hollywood expects you to experiment on a film which must make money and if they don't make money you are to blame because your job is to make money. Movies can only go forward in spite of the motion-picture industry. I don't want you to take an exceptional picture for granted and believe that Hollywood is a place where a good picture is made as a normal course of things, because it is made against more odds than you could possibly guess." The reference to the movies' going forward *in spite of* the industry was a veiled allusion to Orson's resolve to go it alone if he had to. The bitter experience of *Ambersons* had dramatically confirmed his suspicions about the bad faith of an industry with which he had already had his perplexing difficulties over *Kane*. On top of that, the South American experience, in particular the euphoria of public speaking and diplomatic activity, had intensified his fascination with the potential power of mass communications. If the movie industry wasn't interested in exploring and tapping that power, so much the worse for them. Pomona may have rejected him, but Orson persisted in arguing, as he had in the past, that the mass audience would welcome more intellectually stimulating pictures. "Audiences are more intelligent than the individuals who create their entertainment," he echoed his past sentiments. But what about Pomona? Here was Orson's answer: "Naturally, I am concerned about the audience. They vote by buying tickets. We must remember our audience. I can think of nothing that an au-

dience won't understand. The only problem is to interest
them; once they are interested, they understand anything in
the world. That must be the feeling of the moviemaker."

Late one night Orson thought he had found the right story
out of which to make a third film that, unlike its two prede-
cessors, would interest a mass audience. Unable to wait
until the next day, he promptly sent Shorty to fetch Jackson
Leighter, who, like most people at four in the morning, was
asleep. In response to Leighter's dismay at being so brutally
roused from sleep, Shorty announced that Mr. Welles had
told him to say only that Mr. Leighter would not be mad if
he knew *why* he had been summoned thus. Curious, Leighter
hastily threw on a robe and left with the dwarf. He found
his host poised above a set of publisher's galleys. Inviting
Leighter to have a seat, Orson proceeded to read aloud,
from beginning to end and with great passion, Antoine de
St. Exupéry's *The Little Prince*.

"So?" Leighter inquired when, eventually, Orson had
drawn to a close. "Was this why?..."

Yes, Orson explained—for this was to be his next picture.
He had summoned him in the wee hours so that Leighter
could hear *The Little Prince* in its entirety in time to contact
the publishers before anyone else did. Later that morning,
after a series of calls, Leighter did indeed secure the film
rights for Orson. Orson's concept for *The Little Prince* was
to mix live action and animation: "What I wanted to do with
The Little Prince," says Orson, "was a very small amount
of animation. It was only the trick effects of getting from
planet to planet. The *people* that he saw weren't going to
be drawn, they were going to be real comedians—you know,
Joe E. Brown was going to be the drunk and so on. There
weren't going to be *cute* cartoon people on those. They were
all going to be real people. But the special effects, which
are now in a regular way used as scenery by science-fiction
people, were going to be drawn."

From his stint at the coordinator's office, Leighter knew

Walt Disney, who, shortly before Orson, had toured Latin America for Rockefeller on behalf of the Good Neighbor Policy. (By contrast with Orson, Disney *had* gotten a finished film out of the experience: a montage of animation and live action called *Saludos Amigos*.) It was not so much Disney himself as the master animators gathered around him that—Leighter figured—Orson sorely needed now for the animation sequences in *The Little Prince*. Orson was ambivalent about Disney, whose *Saludos Amigos* he had at one point hoped could be shown at Radio City Music Hall with *It's All True*. Orson had gotten this idea when he had heard that the Disney picture, which *also* included material about the Carnival in Rio and the samba, was perhaps a bit short to run as a feature. Having discussed the matter with RKO, and having written about it to Rockefeller, Orson could only have been disappointed when the Disney film instantly became an immense hit on its own, while Orson's lay unfinished. "*That* was to save the oats of the coordinator of Inter-American Affairs as headed by Nelson" says Orson of Disney's successfully having finished and released his film when Orson couldn't. "He was very right-wing," Orson explains about Disney—which in Orson's view seemed to suit Rockefeller's purposes: "Because he [Rockefeller] was worried that he was being thought of as too much of an Eastern liberal and Disney was a welcome sun-belt neo-Fascist. You see, he [Rockefeller] was already running for president. He wouldn't have *bothered* being coordinator of Inter-American Affairs if he hadn't had that in mind. Covering Nelson and making him look good was the whole name of the game in that coordinator of Inter-American Affairs caper." Nor was Orson without his serious reservations about the Disney style: "Disney had such horrible taste and was so ineradicably German that I just couldn't bear it," he says.

Still, a lunch meeting at the Disney studios was arranged, with Orson at one end of the long table, Disney at the other, and Leighter and the animators between them. All heads were turned toward Orson as he brilliantly, seductively discoursed on the topic of his new picture project. But Orson had not been at it for long when Disney was tapped on the shoulder to take a phone call in the adjoining room. Disney was still out when, a moment later, Leighter found himself summoned in a similar manner. Actually, neither of them was wanted on the phone. While everyone else was raptly watching Orson, Disney had discreetly signaled an aide to pretend there was a call, when all he wanted to do was explode at Leighter. Shaking with rage that his own people had ceased paying attention to him the moment Orson had arrived, Disney exploded: "Jack, there is not room on this lot for two geniuses!" (In 1945, Disney would come out with another Latin American film that Orson could only have eyed with regret for *It's All True*: "There's a song right from *our* movie in it!" says Orson of the presence of "Bahia" in the Brazilian segment of Disney's *The Three Caballeros*, in which there is also a Mexican segment with a bullfighting theme. But horrible as Disney's visual taste may often have been—and in the case of *The Three Caballeros* a number of critics appeared to agree with Orson—Disney managed with this picture to appeal directly and powerfully to the sort of vast audience Orson had consistently hoped to reach with more intellectually challenging fare.)

Without Disney's help, the technical problems posed by the mixture of animation and live action proved too formidable for Orson to proceed on his own with *The Little Prince*, so eventually it seemed most judicious to sell the rights to someone else, which he did for a tidy profit. By now, Orson had another picture in mind—*War and Peace*, to be shot in London for Sir Alexander Korda with Orson as Pierre. Having been criticized with regard to *Ambersons* for not having treated a *timely* subject for a country at war, with *War and Peace* Orson would be *timely* with a vengeance. One imagines that Orson would have made a splendid outsize Pierre, slightly awkward, intelligent, and kind. Unfortunately, however, although negotiations to make the picture dragged on interminably, financial and logistical problems would keep it from ever being realized. "It was a completely finished script," laments Orson of its final incarnation. "And I was going to be Pierre. And there was going to be Larry [Olivier] and Vivien [Leigh] and *everybody*! And we were going to go to Russia and do it with the Red Army retreating as Frenchmen through the snow. Alex's *entire* intention in doing it was to get himself an office at Metro. He got his brother, that saintly brother, wonderful man, to draw all these wonderful pictures of how it was going to look on the screen. And I don't think beyond the third week he had the *remotest* intention of producing it."

During this period, as Orson struggled unsuccessfully to get a third picture going, a political group calling itself The Citizens' Committee for the Defense of Mexican American Youth asked Orson to act as its spokesman. Orson's involvement with this organization was momentous because it was in effect his public debut as a serious political activist, a role he would increasingly seek to cultivate. Eventually he would even consider abandoning the movies for politics. The first controversial public issue in which Orson actively involved himself was the notorious Sleepy Lagoon murder case in which seventeen Mexican Americans had been imprisoned in connection with the murder of José Diaz on August 2, 1942. That the famous Sleepy Lagoon where the crime was said to have taken place was really just a mud puddle within a gravel pit affords an idea of the wildly sensational manner in which the case had been treated in the press. In fact, as the defense committee contended, much of the case had actually been constructed by the press in Los Angeles, anxious to invent a Mexican American "crime wave" even before Diaz's body had been found. The Hearst press in particular heralded the "crime wave" among the so-called zoot suiters—Mexican American youths in peg-top pants, bulky coats, and ducktail haircuts. This sensationalism played right into the hands of those among, and sympathizing with, the Axis who longed to undermine Roosevelt's Good Neighbor Policy in Latin America, and to turn Mexico (who had declared war against the Axis) and other Latin American nations against the United States. As for the murder case itself, it was evident that *all* seventeen youths had not killed Diaz, and that, in fact, there was no evidence to prove that any *one* of them had. Indeed, two years after the case, the court of appeals freed them on account of insufficient evidence. The police harassment of the Mexican American community in Los Angeles that followed the discovery of Diaz's body (he had been run over by an automobile) was symptomatic of the intense wartime racism in the United States. The next night, as they left the local dance halls, young Chicanos were confronted by police who tore into their zoot suits with razor-tipped pokers. As many as six hundred of these "zoot suiters" found themselves hauled in by the police for questioning. The grand jury's much-publicized indictment of the members of the 38th Street Gang was followed by an amazing public statement by the Foreign Relations Office of Los Angeles, which shamelessly declared that, in assessing the guilt of the young men, "the biological basis is the main basis to work from." The statement from the sheriff's office went on to speak of the "total disregard for human life . . . throughout the Americas among the Indian population." While all this talk of a "biological basis" for crime sounded strangely like Nazi rhetoric, the Axis did not fail to use the subsequent convictions as the basis for its own anti-American propaganda in South America. The very day the zoot suiters were convicted, January 13, an Axis Spanish-language broadcast beamed all through Latin America announced: "This is justice for you, as practiced by the 'Good Neighbor,' Uncle

Sam, a justice that demands seventeen victims for one crime."

Welles's association with Roosevelt's Good Neighbor Policy, as well as his inherent hatred of racism and of Hearstian yellow journalism, caused him to become intensely interested in the case, and he agreed to pen the foreword to a political pamphlet about the trial and its international implications, which was published in June of 1943 with his name displayed prominently on the cover. Inside, he told the story of a Mexican American named Pete Vasquez, whom he had met at the military induction center while waiting for the standard physical. (Earlier that year Orson had requested the much-publicized Army physical to put to rest any speculation about why a young man as apparently robust as he was not fighting in the war.) As Orson reconstructed it, Pete spoke out against the discrimination he and his fellows experienced, and said, " 'If the cops catch you on the street after eight o'clock, usually they run you in— or rough you up, anyway. If you look like a Mexican you just better stay off the street, that's all. And where can you go? It's real bad. I'm going into the Army, and it's all right with me. I'm glad to be going. Things'll be better in the Army, and I'm glad of the chance to fight. It makes it hard, tough, for a lot of our fellas to see things that way. They want to fight for their country, all right—but they want to feel like it's their country.' " Although Welles put the passage in quotation marks, it was most probably a paraphrase that he infused with dramatic life. Pete became the persona through which Welles made his point; and this acute dramatic instinct would be a key characteristic of his best political performances.

At this point, however, politics was still just a tantalizing possibility. Although he continued to think of himself as a filmmaker, Orson had begun seriously to question his continued presence in Hollywood. It was not only a question of his inability to sell the Rio footage or to launch a third

picture project. More than that, he sometimes secretly wondered whether there had been any point in continuing after
making instant film history with *Citizen Kane*. Whatever
annoying difficulties he may have been experiencing in Hollywood, he knew that with his first film he had unquestionably established himself as one of its great artists. Perhaps
it was best to assert himself in some other area. His satisfying involvement with the Sleepy Lagoon murder case
confirmed what he had dimly suspected as early as his visits
to Washington in the WPA period—that politics might be
a field in which to test his ambition. Was it too much to
dream, as he had begun to do, that in a period of charismatic
political leaders like Roosevelt and Churchill, the equally
dynamic Orson Welles might someday make a successful
politician?

But Orson did not emerge as a truly political being until
he encountered the last of his mentors, a gangly Lincolnian
figure even taller than he, who went by the name of Louis
Dolivet. Dolivet was an emigré and a figure of some mystery: as far as anyone knew, he was a Frenchman and former
Partisan who had fled from occupied France. He was penniless when he arrived, but his charm and fierce intelligence
soon won him acceptance in the inner circles of American
and exile wartime politics. His rise was helped by his subsequent marriage to actress Beatrice Straight, who was also
a Whitney heiress; through the Whitney alliance, Dolivet
had easy access to the ranks of the American plutocrats.
Before long, he had begun to put together an organization
he called "Free World"—whose purpose was to further world
cooperation and put an end to isolationism in the interests
of winning the war and establishing the foundations for a
truly lasting peace. Originally based in New York, Dolivet
decided to expand his operations to the West Coast.

Arriving in Hollywood to gather support for the International Free World Association, Dolivet was referred to
Jackson Leighter by a mutual friend, and through him made

contact with a host of Hollywood celebrities, among them
Charles Boyer (who allowed the association to operate out
of his palatial home) and Orson Welles. There was a mutual
intellectual attraction for the two men. "You can talk to him
for hours and he's a *significant* mind," says Orson. "I was
fascinated by him, and *very* fond of him." For his part,
Dolivet perceived Orson as weary of Hollywood filmmaking
and keen for political engagement. Although Dolivet found
Orson relatively unsophisticated in the complexities of world
affairs, he saw that the showman possessed what he took
for the "right instincts" with regard to political issues. To
Dolivet, these instincts appeared to come from what he calls
Orson's "natural humanism" as an artist. If Dolivet was
generously willing to spend the time and energy to undertake
Orson's political education, it was because he suspected that
the eloquent young man had a most promising future in
public life. "Oh, he had great plans!" says Orson. "He was
going to organize it so that in fifteen years I was going to
get the Nobel Prize." As curious as that idea may seem, it
is well to recall that since Dadda Bernstein had proclaimed
him a genius when he was still only a baby, Orson was
perfectly accustomed to his mentors' having the very *greatest* expectations for him—and, quite often, to his actually
fulfilling them. It was Dolivet's theory that artists have a
responsibility to contribute to society through political ac-
tivism. Once when Orson told Dolivet that movie stars are
our "crown princes," Dolivet soberly replied that power,
money, and especially glory can be corrupting forces.

Early on in their friendship, Orson appeared to Dolivet
not fully to see the profound difference between making
political moves and making movies. This was never so clear
as on a trip to Washington that Dolivet and Orson took
together not long after they met. Dolivet was scheduled to
give a talk on internationalism in Washington to a group of
top Roosevelt aides, and as he and Orson traveled cross-
country by train, Dolivet had been outlining his speech.

Unexpectedly he suggested that Orson should give the talk in his place. This would be a test of Orson's ability to grasp the nuances of all Dolivet told him; and Dolivet trusted that whatever Orson may have lacked in knowledge he would probably make up for with oratory. As Dolivet had predicted, Orson was perfectly marvelous at delivering the speech in Washington. The trouble came afterward when, in casual conversation with one of the aides, Orson grew arrogant—prompting the aide to fire off a battery of questions that Orson could not answer. Dolivet tried to answer the questions himself, but the aide protested that since Orson had given the speech it was entirely up to him to field the questions that followed. It was a harrowing experience for Orson, who was so shaken that he burst into tears back in his hotel room. Dolivet told him that this would have to serve as a lesson in humility. Perhaps he could bluff with film people, but not with politicians. If he didn't know exactly what he was doing, they would destroy him.

CHAPTER 25
Great Days

The morning of September 7, 1943, Rita was shooting *Cover Girl*, at Columbia. Then, without entirely removing her heavy makeup, she discreetly changed into a tan fitted suit with stylishly padded shoulders and a matching wide-brimmed hat with a tiny veil. Wearing a dark chalk-striped suit and a bow tie, Orson accompanied her to pick up a marriage license; so anxious were they that when the city clerk gave them a blank application to fill out, they assumed it was the license itself and started to leave. Fortunately, the clerk noticed them on their way out and told them they had better complete the application and wait for their license before repairing to the Santa Monica courthouse. There Dadda and Hazel Bernstein, Jackson Leighter and his wife, and best man Joseph Cotten and his wife were waiting. No one else in town was supposed to know that twenty-four-year-old Rita and twenty-eight-year-old Orson were to be married that day—especially not Harry Cohn, who would have stopped at nothing to avert Orson's winning the mogul's prize beauty. Somehow, however, word had leaked out to the press, who crowded into the courthouse in hopes of catching a glimpse of the couple. Before Judge Orlando

H. Rhodes of Santa Monica Superior Court, Orson fumbled getting the wedding ring out of its box, then could not seem to get it onto Rita's finger. The judge helpfully suggested that Orson hold her ring finger with his other hand; no sooner had Orson managed to slip on the ring than Rita burst into tears. Afterwards, the newlyweds stopped off at a hotel in Beverly Hills so Orson could get some money from Miss Haran before driving Rita back to Columbia to resume shooting *Cover Girl*. Cohn surely would have heard by then, but it was too late.

That weekend Orson was scheduled to speak at the Mass Rally to Win the Peace at Chicago Stadium. The trip there afforded an ideal opportunity for Orson to introduce his bride to Skipper and Hortense Hill. Rita found them absolutely charming. They obviously had the kind of model marriage she dreamed of establishing with Orson. In particular, she felt herself powerfully drawn to Hortense Hill. "Until she met Hortense," says Orson of Rita, "there was nobody, no woman that she could *believe*, you know." In Hortense, Rita discovered the friend and confidante she had longed for. Rita's desperate insecurities led her to take great comfort in the warmth and motherliness Hortense had cultivated in her role as headmaster's wife, and to respond to her much like a schoolgirl might. As glamorous as she may have seemed onscreen, Rita longed for the homespun simplicity and honesty the Hills embodied for her. In turn, Hortense had a taste for the Hollywood high life that she had indulged with vacations with Virginia at Marion Davies's beach house in Santa Monica, and that found new satisfaction in her friendship with a glamorous star like Rita. The frantic week of his marriage, Orson had had little time to prepare a speech for the Chicago rally beyond scratching some rough notes on the back of an envelope. So when he got to Chicago, while Rita and Hortense got to know each other better, Orson more fully worked out his speech in his hotel room, while the ever-helpful Skipper typed it up for him.

At the outset Rita was wonderfully supportive of—and receptive to—Orson's political inclinations. Dolivet tutored Orson, and Orson in turn did the same for Rita, whose inherent altruism made her especially receptive to his views on racial injustice. But whatever the issue, as Shifra Haran points out, "if he believed in it, she believed in it." Never having been taken especially seriously before, Rita was delighted by Orson's patiently explaining world affairs to her. One of the things that had intrigued Orson about Rita from the first was her basic indifference to the Hollywood milieu. However much a Hollywood star she was, Rita would not be disinclined to give it all up should Orson decide once and for all to make the transition to a life in politics.

The amused press dubbed Rita and Orson Beauty and the Brain. Hollywood was awhirr with snide talk about how stupid Rita was and how utterly inappropriate she was for a genius like Orson. But Orson did not see it that way. Moody and given to prolonged ruminations, he valued Rita's respectful silences, her constant willingness to listen attentively. What Orson did not like were some of Rita's plebian girlfriends from the film studio: beer-drinking, foulmouthed functionaries from the hairdressing and wardrobe departments who had latched onto Rita—who felt strangely more comfortable with them than with her ostensible peers. The last thing Orson needed was a houseful of tough girls cursing, guzzling beer, and filling Rita's head with studio gossip. Appalled by what he perceived as their commonness and vulgarity, Orson swiftly put a stop to Rita's bringing them home. Still, they persisted in hanging around Rita when she was working, and she welcomed what she perhaps misconstrued as their friendship. Eventually they would find a way of exacting revenge against the big snob who had banned them from his and Rita's home. For now they had nothing on Orson. They would later use whatever gossip they could gather, and there was plenty of it to be had, to encourage Rita's already acute insecurities about her husband. Orson had probably made a mistake in so overtly antagonizing them.

This lack of hospitality also extended to Eduardo Cansino, whose visits to his daughter Orson was anxious to discourage. According to Orson, Rita was equally dismayed by her father's appearances. In Orson she seemed to have found a protector against the sort of exploitative men in her life of whom her father had been only the first. But however much Rita may have "hated" her father (as Orson says she did), appearances between them were kept up. (A glance at the Welleses' Christmas list the first year of their marriage suggests a subtext of hostility toward Rita's parents—for next to the presents an assistant had proposed for them, the usually generous Orson has written "Too much.")

Rita's pathological shyness, coupled with Orson's workaholic habits, kept them from the regular round of Hollywood parties to which they were invited. Impulsively they decided to buy and renovate a grand and tumbledown house overlooking the wild surf at Big Sur in an effort to seclude themselves from public pressures. Having split the purchase price between them, they enthusiastically dispatched Miss Haran to Big Sur to take measurements amid the countless spiders and mounds of dust in the abandoned old house (in which, as fate had it, they were never to live).

In October of 1943, having acceded to Dolivet's urging that he familiarize himself with world issues so that he might stand on equal footing with the serious political figures with whom he increasingly found himself mingling, Orson was one of the five main speakers at the Third Free World Dinner held at the Hotel Pennsylvania in New York. Besides Orson, the other main speakers were Harold Butler, the British

Minister to the U.S. and former Director of the International Labor Office; Wei Tao Ming, the Chinese Ambassador to the U.S.; J. Alvarez Del Vayo, the Minister of Foreign Affairs of the Spanish Republic; and Col. Evans Carlson, of the U.S. Marine Corps—heady company indeed for a young movie actor and director with no political experience to speak of. Orson, identified in the official program as representing the Hollywood Free World Committee, was the only speaker who came from outside the political realm. Ironically, having functioned as a stranger in Hollywood, Orson was perceived as a stranger from Hollywood in his new milieu. The dinner was a prelude to a three-day Free World Congress on the destruction of Fascism and the quest for a lasting peace and a democratic world order. At the closing session, Orson delivered an address to the international colloquium on behalf of the American Free World Association. In the first weeks of November in New York, he delivered two more political speeches on behalf of the movement, one to the Overseas Press Club, the other to the Soviet-American Congress. Having put the painful humiliation he had experienced in the Washington incident behind him, Orson began very seriously to consider the possibility of seeking public office, perhaps as a senator. At an age (twenty-eight) when most men are getting their first career started, Orson—having already made history in theater, radio, and film—was boldly embarking on his fourth.

That October, Orson had made his first appearance in the political journal *Free World*. "A magazine devoted to democracy and world affairs," it had been founded two years before by Louis Dolivet. *Free World* explored the possibilities for international cooperation, a position that adumbrated the formation of the United Nations after the war. Beginning with the October 1943 issue, Orson began to work out some of his political ideas in print, usually not as successfully as he delivered them publicly; he was by in-

stinct an orator, not a writer. In his articles Orson attempted
to discover an authentic voice with which he could seem
politically credible to an audience that he knew thought of
him primarily as a showman. It was only natural that one
of Orson's key social concerns in this period was the internationalism espoused by the Free Worlders in opposition
to the isolationism that still infected much of America. "The
war per se has given the individual his naturalization papers
as a world citizen," Orson would argue. "He will henceforth
increasingly assume the responsibilities of his office and
participate accordingly." While isolationists hoped to cut off
the U.S. from Europe and the rest of the world once the
war was won, internationalism held that there could be no
lasting peace unless all nations found a way to work co-
operatively. During the war years, however, it was not unusual for isolationists to label internationalism a Communist
conspiracy and to call those who actively advocated international cooperation Red secret agents. Having been labeled
a Communist at the time of the Hearst controversy, Orson
was once again subject to intimations and epithets. According to Louis Dolivet, there was even a rumor in circulation that Orson was actually a Russian—its strange
source being that Dadda Bernstein had in fact been born in
Russia. The fact that Dadda was not really Orson's *father*,
but only his legal guardian, had been overlooked.

Orson parried the charge that he was a Communist in the
first of his essays for *Free World*—a revised version of
"Moral Indebtedness," the speech he had delivered to the
Mass Rally to Win the Peace in Chicago. "The scaly dinosaurs of reaction," wrote Orson, "will say in their newspapers that I am a Communist. Communists know otherwise.
I am an overpaid movie producer with pleasant reasons to
rejoice—and I do—in the wholesome practicability of the
profit system. I'm all for making money if it means earning
it. Lest you should imagine that I'm being publicly modest,

I'll only admit that everybody deserves at least as many good things as money buys for me. Surely my right to having more than enough is canceled if I don't use that more to help those who have less. This sense of humanity's interdependence antedates Karl Marx. . . . I believe I owe the very profit I make to the people I make it from. If this is radicalism, it comes automatically to most of us in show business, it being generally agreed that any public man owes his position to the public."

The inherent wisdom of the people had been a theme of Orson's since he and Skipper had planned *Everybody's Shakespeare*, and the troubled relationship between the privileged artist/intellectual (such as he clearly was) and the general public was to become an important subtext of Orson's politics. In his case, it was a relationship that had been seriously put in question at the *Ambersons* screening at Pomona, which, for Orson, had epitomized the mass audience's unexpected rejection of what he had hoped to communicate to them. Politics now afforded Orson another chance. After Roosevelt's reelection in 1944, Orson's political involvement would give him the sense of oneness with the public at large that he had not been able to achieve as a filmmaker. "The intellectual has often found a kind of comfort in the avowal of a minority opinion," he would write. "But now there is no more of that queer comfort for American liberals. The election [of 1944] forces on all of us the duties and the responsibilities of participation in the cause of the majority. We can none of us proclaim again that the masses are unprepared for what we have to say to them. If we make such queer claims we are only admitting that we haven't yet managed to interest the people. The first liberal in our land has held their attention for twelve years. They have listened to him and it is a matter of record and a fact in history that he has listened to them."

It is not too much to suppose that here Orson was trying

to work out what must have been his confused feelings about
the masses' not having been ready for films like *Ambersons*
or—more abstractly—*It's All True*, when that very same
populace flocked to kitsch like Disney's *Saludos Amigos*.
He was afraid that as a filmmaker he had failed on the one
count that mattered: "The only problem is to interest them,"
Orson once said of the mass audience. "Once they are interested they understand anything in the world. That must
be the feeling of the moviemaker." It was also, clearly, the
feeling of the politician; and Orson's political participation
allowed him the sense of having communicated—of having
communed—with the masses, the majority. His confidence
in the inherent wisdom of the people had been renewed.

Not long after his debut in *Free World* Orson's name
began to appear on the journal's masthead as an editorial
writer. Over the next year and a half he commented on
political issues: in "The Good Neighbor Policy Reconsidered," Orson warned of the danger of Fascism in Latin
America, especially Argentina: " . . . our hemisphere is host
nowadays to at least one wholeheartedly Fascist government," wrote Orson. "Indeed, Fascist domination of Latin
America seems more than a threat. . . . With the democratic
man it is a certainty that freedom can expect no sanctuary
anywhere until its enemies are found out in their last ambush
and laid low." And in "Race Hate Must Be Outlawed,"
Orson harped on what was for him by now a familiar theme:
"This is a time for action. We know that for some ears even
the word 'action' has a revolutionary twang, and it won't
surprise us if we're accused in some quarters of inciting to
riot. *Free World* is very interested in riots. *Free World* is
interested in avoiding them. We call for action against the
cause of riots. Law is the best action, the most decisive.
. . . This is our proposition: that the sin of race hate be
solemnly declared a crime." His final editorial in September
1945 titled "Now or Never" dealt with the atom bomb and
how the vast destruction that had been a mere fantasy at the

time of his "War of the Worlds" broadcast was now a reality—
hence, by implication, the need more than ever for a democratic world order.

In 1943 the series of speeches he had delivered for the
Free World movement in New York that October and November spurred Orson to think of moving East again, where
he and Rita seemed to be spending more and more of their
time. Although he had devoted five days that fall to filming
a condensed version of the *Wonder Show* for a picture titled
Follow the Boys (in which both Marlene and Shorty appeared with him, and for which he earned $30,000), his
interest in film centered at the moment on its potential as
a social and cultural force among the masses it was capable
of reaching. Orson was seriously enough considering abandoning Hollywood to give up the rented house on Woodrow
Wilson Drive and to wistfully relegate to storage some finery
he thought might be unsuitable to his new political persona:
a blue Chinese gown with gold trim; a red wool three-piece
suit; a white coat with satin lapels; a red and white striped
magic robe. But in New York ill health distracted Orson
from his work on behalf of the Free World Association. His
old back trouble flared up, this time so seriously that the
New York doctors he consulted unanimously recommended
surgery. To make matters worse, he was suddenly stricken
with jaundice. Obviously this combination of ailments precluded much in the way of speech making or general pol-
iticking. Concerned friends advised that Orson repair to
Florida, where the sunshine might afford some relief to his
precarious health. So the new year of 1944 saw Orson and
Rita ensconced in the Roney Plaza in Miami Beach, where
the sun did seem to Orson to work wonders with his jaundice. His back, however, persisted in tormenting him, so
that by January 7 he had decided to return to Hollywood,
where he knew that Dadda would tend to his condition in
a way that no other doctor could.

At the end of a five-and-a-half-day train trip west that in

his frail state of health Orson found "pretty rough," the Welleses checked into the Beverly Hills Hotel, where Leighter had secured a suite for them until a rented house on Fordyce Road was ready. During the war, even so plush an establishment as the Beverly Hills Hotel was subject to meat rationing, a hardship to which Dadda was determined that the ailing Pookles not be subjected. Thus in his capacity as Mr. Welles's physician Dr. Bernstein crisply informed the hotel management that his patient was "under a strict diet necessitating large quantities of proteins. This means meats!" Lest the management hesitate to serve Mr. Welles as much meat as he required, Dr. Bernstein assured them that he would promptly secure an order from the Food Rationing Board.

Dadda's alarm was not unfounded. Orson's strength did appear to have been sapped in what must have been the physical breakdown about which doctors had been warning him for some time. Having relentlessly driven himself both physically and spiritually throughout his twenties, Orson had little choice now but to submit himself to sunshine, a high-protein diet, and—above all—rest. The unbearable stress Orson had been feeling after the debacle of *Ambersons* and Rio and during the difficult passage between careers that followed could only have contributed massively to his diminished health.

Despite his ailments, Orson felt compelled to keep working, however: he was negotiating a new theatrical project with top Broadway producer Billy Rose. Orson had declined a previous invitation to work with Rose, but now he was definitely receptive to a fresh proposal to stage Donald Ogden Stewart's *Emily Brady*, first in San Francisco, then in New York, where, after a recuperative hiatus of several months, he would resume active political involvement. While Orson still had not been able to secure the financial backing he needed to complete *It's All True*, here was "all the money in the world" to put on a modest play—something he could do with relative ease and predictable success. Although it was not exactly what he wanted to be doing, the play seemed like a perfect therapeutic interim project. Still Orson could not have been terribly disappointed when, at length, irremediable casting problems caused him to abandon the show.

Nor was *Emily Brady* the only project Orson undertook while convalescing. Shortly after returning to California he commenced a variety radio show for Mobil Oil titled *Orson Welles' Almanac*, the principal ingredients of which were comedy and jazz (the latter considerably more successful than the former), and a pilot for which he had prepared in New York before falling ill. Briefly—and successfully— guest-hosting Jack Benny's radio show the year before had inspired Orson to try comedy, a genre that had not much occupied him in the past. Benny's crack team of writers had built a hilarious series of shows around Orson's personality, including a secretary-character based on Shifra Haran, except that instead of constantly getting bawled out as Miss Haran did, the comic secretary was given to taking her employer to task for everything he did wrong. Now, unfortunately, because *Orson Welles' Almanac* lacked the generally ingenious writing of the Benny show, its comedy often fell flat. Before going on the air Orson would do a warm- up act for the studio audience in which he mixed mind reading and magic tricks—and gleefully threatened that if they did not laugh during the show, an ice pick would shoot up out of their seats. Even this seemingly simple production was not exempt from behind-the-scenes tensions; in hopes of appeasing bigoted listeners, a production person casually suggested to Orson that when Duke Ellington appeared on the program, he be identified in the script not as Orson's *friend*, but as his servant. Orson adamantly refused: told that this was just a "minor change," Orson snapped that it certainly was not minor to call his friend his servant.

However energetically Orson worked on his theatrical plans and on his radio program, by early April of 1944 he had not recovered sufficiently to travel to New York, and so asked his friend Elsa Maxwell to deliver a political speech for him there. Afterward she wrote to tell him that she had had to resort to "a great deal of what you call 'mass hypnotism,'" considering that the audience had been expecting a handsome leading man and not a fat little lady like her. By the end of April, however, Orson felt well enough to deliver a speech at the Council for Civic Unity at the Philharmonic Auditorium in Los Angeles. This was to be only a prelude to the absolute frenzy of activity into which he plunged when Secretary of the Treasury Henry Morgenthau asked him to produce a live radio broadcast in Texarkana, Texas, on June 12 to launch four weeks of the sixteen-million-dollar Fifth War Loan Drive, the purpose of which was to finance what was hoped would be the conclusion of the war. The efficacy of celebrity broadcasts was proven; the year before, in a single radio marathon, Kate Smith had brought in almost forty million dollars for the war effort. In his capacity as a consultant to the Treasury Department, Orson would be paid one dollar a year. Early in May, shortly after Orson had agreed to assemble the show, word came down from the office of General George C. Marshall that the script ought to be based on the impending—or, perhaps, current—invasion of France. As it turned out, D-Day—the Allied invasion across the English Channel into Normandy—took place on June 6, six days before Orson's broadcast.

Orson was preparing for the Texarkana broadcast when he heard General Dwight D. Eisenhower's recorded announcement about D-Day on the radio; on June 7, Orson scrapped the comedy routine that had been planned for that night's regular *Orson Welles' Almanac* in favor of a moving dramatization of a letter to a little boy from his mother about what had just happened in Normandy, read by Agnes Moorehead. The Allied invasion was also to form the background for the Texarkana broadcast. Scheduled to meet with Secretary Morgenthau before the big broadcast, Orson and Miss Haran flew to Hot Springs, Arkansas, where they found themselves placed under the official protection of treasury agents who dutifully trailed about after Orson and stood guard at his hotel-room door. Orson of course managed to give them the slip one night, and he and Miss Haran took a drive in the back of a horse-drawn landau, which was hit from the rear by a car. The carriage driver dropped his reins and the horses broke loose, charging blindly into a shop window. After the crash Miss Haran realized with horror that Orson had lurched forward, and his eyeglasses had cracked on impact. Sitting up silently to compose himself, Orson had a stunned look on his face. The secretary dashed to the nearest open shop, a grocery, where a handful of locals listened impassively as she blurted out what had happened. No one budged. Further agitated by the stony lack of response, Miss Haran rushed back to the landau, where the driver was tending to the injured horses. Orson, however, was precisely as she had left him. It appeared not to have occurred to him to get out of the carriage to see if anything could be fixed. All he wanted to do was go back to the hotel room to resume work on the radio show as if nothing had happened.

After Texas, Orson repeated the War Loan show in Los Angeles, then in Chicago. Because of the large cast and crew required for the live broadcasts, producing the gala program had been an exhausting undertaking, especially for someone so recently ill. On the way back to California from Chicago, Leighter thought it best to stop for the night in Kansas City. During the show the two of them had been drinking quite a lot of aquavit and beer to keep themselves going, and now this probably contributed to Orson's over-

whelming fatigue. Unfortunately, the stopover afforded little
in the way of comfort. The moment Orson entered the hotel
lobby, a man rushed up and began to pound him mercilessly
with his fists. "I'm going to kill you! I'm going to kill you!"
shouted the assailant. "I *promised* I'd kill you if I saw you!"
So unexpected was this sudden violence that, for a long
moment, the people in the lobby watched incredulously. As
for Orson, he was already in far too much of a stupor to
fend off the repeated blows. It was Leighter who finally
pulled the madman off, while others in the lobby shoved
the drowsy victim into an elevator. By the time the madman
was subdued, Leighter's nose was bleeding. This had been
no case of mistaken identity. Unable to continue his rampage
the assailant blurted out that Orson was responsible for the
suicide of his wife on the night of the famous Martian
broadcast. Ever since, he had vowed he would murder Orson. Whether or not the fellow was telling the truth was
anyone's guess, but on hearing this, Leighter had him set
free without filing any charges against him.

An unanticipated outcome of the War Loan show had
been to launch Orson's endeavors as a political speech writer.
Orson had written an appropriate text for Morgenthau, who
was so impressed that he asked Orson to do additional speech
writing afterward. In speech writing Orson applied the reworking and revising skills he had spent years developing
in theater and film: the *bricoleur*'s knack for producing
something wonderfully new out of the material that is given
him.

There followed the halcyon days of Orson's marriage to
Rita. In March, during Orson's recuperation, she had become pregnant. She had one last bit of film work to do
before retiring until she gave birth to her first child: a role
in *Tonight and Every Night*. Having determined that the
house on Fordyce Road was too cramped for a family, the
Welleses rented a far grander place on Carmelina Drive in

Brentwood, which boasted a swimming pool with a center island from which palm trees sprouted. Rita's preference for nude sunbathing gave Orson the idea to build a roofless solarium, so that only Peeping Toms in low-flying airplanes posed a threat to her privacy. In the living room of the new house was a fish tank built into a wall so that one could watch the goldfish from both sides.

To show off their new place, and to celebrate their impending parenthood, Rita and Orson did what they rarely had the time or inclination for: they gave a huge party. Orson drew up the invitations—"Please come to our house. This Saturday. Any time after 10 p.m. Rita and Orson Welles"—that included a scribbled map, lest anyone not know the way to Carmelina Drive. Most of the invited guests did manage to find their way, although at the evening's end, opinion was definitely divided as to whether the highlight of the party was Rita's appearing in a stunning long white evening gown, or zany actor Hans Conried's falling into the pool.

The only cloud on Orson's horizon in this period was a lawsuit against him that his first wife, Virginia, had filed on behalf of their now six-year-old daughter, Christopher, whose interest in Orson's estate she sought to protect before the arrival of the new baby. According to Virginia, Orson had not properly provided for Christopher in his will and life-insurance policy as he had agreed to do at the time of the divorce. The lawsuit caused Orson much embarrassment and personal anguish: although he wanted to treat his daughter fairly, he blamed her stepfather for having stirred up the dispute, and the fact that Lederer was genuinely fond of little Christopher did not diminish his resentment. To make matters worse, while Lederer was off in the armed services, Virginia and the child were ensconced on the Santa Monica estate of Marion Davies: hardly a comfortable place for the creator of *Citizen Kane* to visit as he had to when he went to pick up his daughter for a visit to Carmelina Drive. For the most part he would send Miss Haran to fetch Christopher and her nurse. On such days Orson's tendency to show up only for half an hour or so suggests that, as Miss Haran puts it, fatherhood "wasn't his thing." At length Orson had little choice but to accede to most of Virginia's financial demands, among them a substantial hike in his child-support payments.

The pain that the lawsuit caused him could be partly forgotten in the pleasure he and Rita took in an extended visit from Orson's "family," the Hills. But when Orson, Skipper, and Hortense played word games in the enormous living room, Rita preferred to watch and listen from the sofa; she feared that she was not intelligent enough to participate, and that if she tried she would only embarrass herself. Orson never talked down to her, but always seemed to assume that she understood everything he said. In her desperation, she sought to educate herself, when she thought no one could see her, by studying the books that Orson had been reading. And she loved to listen to every word of Orson's intellectual conversations with Skipper—both of them seemed almost to metamorphose into schoolboys when they were together.

Nor was Skipper the only figure from the past capable of turning Orson back into a boy. Rita was incredulous at the effect Skipper's father, autocratic old Noble Hill, had on Orson. It was one time when she seemed far more mature than her husband. One weekend the Hills and the Welleses set out on a long drive, taking advantage of the extra gas coupons Todd's headmaster was entitled to. They found themselves near the retirement home of the man they had called *the King* back at Todd. At Hortense's suggestion that they stop for a surprise visit, Orson protested, explaining to Rita that he was frightened of the King. After the visit, Rita said that she did not see why Orson was afraid of such a nice old man, to which a still-tense Orson replied that while Noble Hill may have seemed like just a nice old man to her, to him he remained the King—and he was scared to death of him.

Hortense spent a good deal of time with Rita during the ensuing fall of 1944, while Orson was off campaigning for Roosevelt's reelection. Besides Hortense, Rita's other companion was an adorable white and gold spotted cocker spaniel named Pookles, which had been a gift from Dadda, one of whose dogs had recently had a litter. With Orson's departure that September, the halcyon days of the marriage drew to a close. While campaigning, Orson operated out of a suite in the Waldorf Towers in New York, where he mapped out his far-flung speaking tour on Roosevelt's behalf. Traveling mostly by train (since both he and Miss Haran were unusually tall they felt cramped and uncomfortable on the tiny planes of the day), Orson was constantly dictating speeches, which he would rewrite endlessly as was his custom. It was not simply the content of his speeches he labored to get absolutely right, but their spoken rhythms as well. For whether in person or on the air he would typically hold his audience with the sheer spell of his voice and verbal manner. In each new town, Orson and Miss Haran were met by local Democratic leaders, who provided Orson with local anecdotes and references with which to pepper his speech. Orson maintained a dizzying schedule of speech making and radio broadcasts, which often kept him going for as long as twenty-four hours at a stretch.

Roosevelt was running for his fourth term as president against Governor Thomas E. Dewey of New York, who was not above insinuating that the incumbent had accepted Communist support, or that his poor health would preclude his serving out his term. Roosevelt had strategically dropped his former vice president, Henry Wallace, whose social radicalism made him a liability on the ticket at a moment when, despite Roosevelt's evident popularity as wartime commander, there was considerable national unrest about his progressive domestic policies. As a concession to the conservative drift in public opinion, he had replaced the outspoken Wallace with Harry Truman. Still, Wallace nobly agreed to campaign actively for Roosevelt, and it was Orson who introduced Wallace on September 21, 1944, at a mass rally at Madison Square Garden in New York. Other speakers included Sinclair Lewis and Helen Keller, the latter of whom Orson led through the great mass of onlookers with what she later called "knightly gallantry."

Miss Keller described the dramatic evening as "tense with a historicity that I do not suppose mortals feel twice in a lifetime." Orson's appearance before the great mass oddly recalled his impersonation of Kane delivering a similarly resounding election speech in the film, except that these were not hollow words—they were spoken from the very heart that Orson's *übermarionette* of a Kane had lacked. *The New York Times* later reported that "Mr. Welles was received with great enthusiasm." If, as Miss Keller told him, she had read Polly Thomson's Braille translation of his speech "over and over," it was because of the "thunder of a waking social conscience" it so effectively imparted. In particular, Orson's incantatory repetition of key words and phrases—the word "they" chanted incessantly to conjure up the Republican opposition; the mighty opening line, "These are great days," spoken thrice to punctuate the text at strategic moments—infused the speech with extraordinary rhetorical force. Orson complemented the text with an unusually impassioned performance that caused some people in the audience to think that he had had too much to drink. "I came down from the platform with my eyes dazed from the lights," Orson recalls, "and two or three people afterward told me how amazing it was that I spoke so well when it was obvious I was drunk." At the close of the

Madison Square Garden rally, Orson and Helen Keller made
their way outside to a rented limousine. The excited crowds
leaving the rally swarmed around the automobile, shaking
it, and yelling, "Wallace and Welles in the White House in
'48!" (Many of them were upset that Roosevelt had dropped
Wallace from the ticket.) For Orson, that enthusiasm made
his wildest dreams of political power seem possible.

Having spoken out in his Madison Square Garden address
against what he called "the partisans of privilege—the
champions of monopoly—the old opponents of liberty—
the determined adversaries of the small business and the
small farm" (among whom he specifically mentioned his
old adversary William Randolph Hearst), Orson was not
winning very many friends in America's upper class. Never
was the animosity that he elicited from them clearer than
on October 18, when he filled in for Roosevelt to speak
opposite Dewey at the *Herald Tribune Forum*, broadcast
nationwide from the Waldorf Astoria in New York. So incensed by Welles were the ordinarily genteel Republican
dowagers in the audience that many of them stood up to
scream and shake their programs at him. The effect of their
wrath was magnified even further by Orson's address having
been cut off midway on the air: although rumor had it that
Orson's speech had been censored, the fact was that it had
merely exceeded the allotted time and that the next scheduled live radio show was ready to begin.

Orson's personal service to Roosevelt was not limited to
filling in for him at the *Herald Tribune Forum*. "He liked
to be directed," Orson recalls of Roosevelt's often asking
him for advice about his speeches. "He was a pure actor.
You couldn't direct Churchill, but you could him." One
speech with which Orson helped Roosevelt was in his defense against the charge that, having forgotten his dog Fala
on an Aleutian island, Roosevelt had squandered taxpayers'
money by sending a destroyer to fetch him. It was Orson's

idea that Roosevelt turn the charges into a joke by claiming that the Republicans had libeled his poor Scottie, who, after having heard the allegations, had "not been the same dog since." Orson ad-libbed the basic joke for a delighted Roosevelt, who had a final version written up by one of his staff. After Roosevelt delivered the famous Fala speech, he wanted to hear Orson's opinion of his delivery. "He loved it," Orson recalls, "and he asked me afterwards, 'How did I do? Was my timing right?' Just like an actor!" Later Roosevelt quipped to Orson that they were "the two best actors in the world." Orson had not said a word about his own political ambitions to Roosevelt, so he was delighted when the President suggested that he seek public office. Roosevelt counseled Orson that if he ever wanted to make a bid for the White House, he should start by running for the Senate. But if Franklin Roosevelt had high hopes for Orson, Eleanor Roosevelt clearly did not. "Mrs. Roosevelt didn't like me because Mr. Roosevelt did," Orson explains. "There were very few people who were in good with both of them. She disapproved of me very strongly. It was only just before she died, the last few years, that she was convinced that I was not an irresponsible drunkard and Hollywood bum." Mrs. Roosevelt had taken offense at things she had heard about Orson Welles. "Missy [FDR's secretary] used to complain that I'd get him to drink another cocktail at night," says Orson. Nor was the First Lady amused by Orson's disparaging remarks about White House hospitality. "I made fun of the food at the White House," Orson admits. "The worst that has ever been known was under the Roosevelts." Even his tireless and quite effective efforts on behalf of Roosevelt's reelection did not change Eleanor Roosevelt's mind about Orson. "She thought I was just a sort of pubescent back-room boy," he laughs.

Late in October of 1944, Orson fell ill with a 104° fever and a throat infection. Evidently the ceaseless campaigning about the nation had worn away his resistance. Roosevelt wired Orson his best wishes for a speedy recovery, Helen Keller wrote to say that she prayed his health would improve, since he simply couldn't be spared at "this crucial time" in the campaign, and an obese Southern Democrat of his acquaintance arrived at the Waldorf with a small gift: a pack of pornographic playing cards, each of which showed a group of naked people cavorting that was equivalent to the numerical value of the card (2, 3, 4, 5, 6, etc.). Just a glance at them and, utterly repelled, Orson hurled the whole deck across the room from where he lay. No sooner had the fever broken than Orson dictated a letter to Roosevelt: "This illness was the blackest of misfortunes for me because it stole away so many days from the campaign. I cannot think I have accomplished a great deal but I well know that this is the most important work I could ever engage in." Two days after he promised Roosevelt that he would be back on the road by the following week, Orson broadcast a ten-minute campaign speech on CBS. As if willing his health to improve, Orson went on the road again, against the advice of his doctors. On November 4, he accompanied Roosevelt, who was winding up the campaign at Fenway Park in Boston, where they were joined by another show-business campaigner, Frank Sinatra. "We were coming into the ball park in an open car under the great arc lights," Orson recalls his arrival with Roosevelt. "There was a Secret Service man on our running board. I was sitting next to Roosevelt. I was riding with him because he didn't want to ride with a local ward heeler, so he wanted the place taken up by somebody. When we got to the entrance the Secret Service man had forgotten whether they were to turn right or left, and I said, 'Mr. President, you've never gone wrong when you've turned left!' So he roared with laughter, and he turned left." But Orson's most important contribution to the last days of the campaign came when on election eve, over four networks, at Roosevelt's personal request, he broadcast a speech for the Democratic National Committee.

Two days after Roosevelt's reelection, Orson and Miss Haran left for California. When their twenty-one-passenger plane stopped in Wichita, Kansas, there was an announcement that a military wife whose husband was about to be shipped overseas from Los Angeles desperately needed a seat, all of which were occupied. Orson instantly piped up that of course his secretary would be delighted to give up her seat. Unexpectedly stranded in Wichita, a somewhat startled Miss Haran found herself being interviewed about Orson by the local press, to whom she confidently announced that "he will really and truly be one of the great men of our time, and he is only twenty-nine."

"Shifra?" Orson Welles stammers in disbelief at the mention of her name. "You found Shifra Haran? Now there's someone who knows everything about—where is she? I have to see her!" But exceedingly fond as she is of him, Orson's former secretary isn't certain she is brave enough to see him: 'Just the thought of his seeing me makes me tremble!" she says, all of her young girl's shyness sweeping over her again, several decades after she left his employ. But still she has a message for him: "Well," says Miss Haran, "if he asks, tell him that Shorty's in my front yard." For when the dwarf chauffeur died after retiring to Hawaii, his ashes were shipped to his devoted friend Miss Haran—who installed them in an urn in her front yard. Her pet mallard duck, Esther Williams, tramps around it. "That's wonderful!" says Orson, apprised of Shorty's whereabouts. "That's perfect for him!"

When it rains, Miss Haran, who is tall and slim, with a deep, throaty laugh, digs up snails to feed Esther Williams. "Now there was a man who knew an awful lot about Orson Welles," she says, recalling Shorty's revelations about Welles's amorous encounters. "Shorty used to tell me some things I can't even repeat! Now in those days Shorty was

*his cook, chauffeur, valet, everything. When he had com-
pany, he used to bring out the finger bowls, and Shorty
would go out—he was a little hunchback with this beautiful
face—pick geranium petals and float them in concentric
circles in different colors in the finger bowls."*

Nor was Shorty alone in discreetly observing the Boss's
amorous encounters: *"No one woman in the time that I
knew him could satisfy him,"* says Miss Haran of Orson's
affairs. *"I don't know whether he lusted after them or was
trying to prove something to himself or them."* Like Louis
Dolivet, who saw Orson's womanizing as motivated by a
more general desire for power, Miss Haran speculates: *"I
always felt that he was trying to prove his virility."* With
Rita, Miss Haran did her best to cover up Orson's transgres-
sions. Says Miss Haran about Rita: *"The books don't begin
to tell the truth about her, what she was really like. Sweet,
beautiful, charming, nice—she was another one who could
never believe anybody loved her unless they were in bed
with her. That was the only thing she could equate with
love."* And of Rita's final breakup with Orson: *"Maybe if
I had hung around, it wouldn't have happened. I was able
to cover up a lot of things that he did that she didn't have
to know about. She trusted me, which was good because
she didn't trust anybody anymore. You know at that time
they were both in the eye of the storm, and there were all
kinds of people who wanted to penetrate that and bring them
down and do them dirt. People are rotten lots of times."*

"Oh, she was great!" says Orson of his long-lost secretary. *"There was nothing too daring that she wasn't ready
to do."* In retrospect, however, Orson admits that in what
he describes as *"my youthful arrogance,"* he perhaps asked
Miss Haran to do rather too much for him. If Miss Haran
somehow survived, it was partly out of curiosity: *"You never
acted surprised around Mr. Welles. You never knew what
you were going to come across"*; and partly out of esteem:
"In ways that people don't realize, Mr. Welles was just a

demon for work. I've worked for other people and no one worked as hard as he did. Just drove himself relentlessly, and apparently reveled in it." So much in a hurry did he always seem that once as she drove him up into the perilous, winding roads of Bel Air, she felt his big foot pressing on hers to make the car go faster.

In one of the new scenes that were inserted in The Magnificent Ambersons while Orson was in Rio, a sign in the corridor of the hospital where Georgie is confined reads: "Miss Haran, Head Nurse." Orson's cronies, Jack Moss in particular, had placed it there as a secret homage to the one person who did indeed seem capable of tending to Orson's multitudinous personal and psychological needs.

"One of the greatest girls in the world," says Orson today. "She was miraculous. She was absolutely miraculous!"

CHAPTER 26
Olé! Olé!

When Orson returned to Los Angeles from the campaign trail, Rita was eight months pregnant, and thrilled to have her vagabond of a husband back. Rebecca Welles (Rita had found the name in *Ivanhoe*) was born by cesarean section on December 17, 1944. She bore a vivid resemblance to her father. Still, Miss Haran recalls that Orson was "not really all that interested" in Becky: "I don't really think Mr. Welles ever paid any attention to her—just not in the cards. Now on the contrary, Prince Aly [Rita's next husband] played with her, talked to her. He was *crazy* about her. Mr. Welles never did that."

If Orson seemed distracted at the moment, it was because, having concluded his campaign activities, he had wasted no time in making new professional commitments, principal among them a daily column in the *New York Post*, to begin in January after the presidential inauguration. For five columns weekly, Orson was guaranteed a minimum of three hundred dollars salary plus fifty percent of syndication sales, which, owing to Orson's celebrity, the *Post* predicted would be substantial both in the U.S. and possibly abroad. He saw it as a way of establishing himself as a popular political commentator.

"I don't take myself seriously, but I take my job as a columnist seriously," Orson told the press, about his latest undertaking. "No ghost will write my stuff, for I'm going to say what I want to say in my own way. Certainly, I love the stage and screen. But things are happening in the world today that are more important than the theater. Everybody with sense knows that this is the supreme crisis of civilization and if we don't come through it, then what does it matter? I don't have the answers to the world's problems and I'm not founding a new religious cult. But I do believe that if I can stir the people to debate and think about our problems, we'll find a way out." Among the researchers Orson hired to feed him raw material about Washington for use in the new column was Geneva Cranston, the first wife of the future California senator and presidential hopeful Alan Cranston, who was also one of Orson's secret sources. "The column is so important," Orson told reporters, "that I plan to devote almost all my time to it as soon as I can. I've given up all my Hollywood work except to act in one picture each year." This was an allusion to the latest picture he had signed to appear in: *Tomorrow Is Forever*. Shooting was set to begin in March of 1945, and his salary would be $100,000.

Starring opposite Claudette Colbert, Orson played a husband, disfigured in the war, who returns home incognito years later to find his wife has remarried. Since the picture was little more than what he recalls as a "weepy," Orson viewed it mainly as a way of making money. His contribution limited to acting the banal role of the man whom nobody recognizes, Orson was noticeably bored not to be directing or producing as well—a fact that may explain the outrageous practical joke to which he resorted in hopes of passing the time. In anticipation of the scene in which Miss Colbert had to keep her head on his lap, Orson had the prop man rig up what he describes as a "very impressive" fake penis, which, when Orson pulled a hidden string, would expand to gargantuan proportions in his trousers. But much to Orson's disappointment, as his artificial member swelled wildly beneath her, the actress showed no sign whatsoever of anything being wrong, nor did she mention the incident afterward. Orson speculates today: "She probably didn't know what to do. She didn't know whether to jump up and slap my face, to be complimented, or to ask me for a date!" Finally: "It could have worked wonders for my reputation!" quips Orson, who actually liked Miss Colbert a great deal but was simply trying to diminish his unbearable boredom.

Although Orson claimed to be basically winding up his affairs in Hollywood (except for acting in one lucrative picture a year), he persisted in his obsession with the Brazilian footage. "Too much effort and real love went into the entire project for it to fail and come to nothing in the end," Orson had written to one of the jangadeiros he had known in Fortaleza (and who served as guardian of the late Jacare's family). "I have a degree of faith in it which amounts to fanaticism, and you can believe that if *It's All True* goes down into limbo I'll go with it." And in a sense Orson kept his word. For he struggled desperately to save *It's All True* at what would be great personal cost. When Leighter and Orson sought to buy the film from RKO, the studio suggested that, as part of the deal, Orson sign away his right to a percentage of *Citizen Kane*. But Leighter wisely would not hear of it. As far as he was concerned, buying *It's All True* had nothing whatsoever to do with the profits that Orson might eventually realize from *Kane*. Afterward, over lunch at the Brown Derby, Orson and Leighter discussed RKO's offer. Then Orson left suddenly on the pretext of having a date with a girl—which Leighter found highly unlikely because at that point Orson was still faithful to Rita. Leighter's suspicions proved correct. The next morning a messenger from RKO arrived to ask Leighter for a $20,000 check. Aghast, Leighter inquired what this was all about. It seemed that the day before, Orson had gone straight from the Brown Derby back to RKO, where he foolishly signed away any claim to *Kane*, and freed RKO from any further obligation to him with regard to a third picture. In exchange for a promissory note for a lordly sum, plus the $20,000 in advance, the negative of *It's All True* would be released to Orson. The irony was that that negative would ultimately have to be returned to RKO when Orson could not pay the $197,500 he had promised. Meanwhile he had relinquished his claim to profits from his first film, which—when it was widely released after Hearst's death—would have been immense.

Another of the projects that Orson had undertaken after returning from the Roosevelt campaign was to prepare a regular fifteen-minute radio program for Eversharp pens and pencils. But while the Eversharp people envisioned a show that was strictly entertainment, Orson longed to do political commentary, what he called a "radio column" based on the column he was about to begin in the *Post*. Anticipating their resistance to the proposal, Orson assured Eversharp that there was "real showmanship—and the best kind of show-manship—in the idea of Orson Welles doing a big national column." A number of things are interesting in this remark, chief among them Orson's referring to himself in the third person, as an image: an alienated sense of himself that he would increasingly come to have. But Orson's having anticipated Eversharp's objections suggests another more immediate kind of alienation—the evolving conflict between himself as an artist and as a politician. Which was he? Insisting that his political commentary would be a kind of showmanship may have been a shrewd way of conning the sponsor. But it also suggests the possibility that Orson was still unsure as to which role he was playing, or that—as Dolivet had thought—he did not entirely distinguish between them. The sponsor wanted an Orson Welles who acted

and directed fictions, who told stories, and, above all, who
entertained. But that was not the Orson he was willing to
sell them.

In the meantime, he continued his speaking engagements
on political topics, and in January attended the Inauguration
in Washington as an "Honored Guest." Despite Mrs. Roosevelt's having invited the Welleses to luncheon at the White
House the day before the Inauguration, Rita finally decided
against what would be perhaps too strenuous a trip for her
so soon after giving birth. The Inauguration proved a disappointing experience for Orson, who was shocked by both
Roosevelt's all-too-obvious ill health and what suddenly
struck him as Truman's ordinariness (especially by contrast
with Roosevelt's undeniable star quality). Greatly disheart-
ened, Orson skipped the reception that followed at the White
House and returned to his hotel full of snide remarks about
the blandness of Truman's inaugural speech.

Before the end of January, Orson was in New York to
deliver a speech about Fascism titled "The Nature of the
Enemy" as part of a lecture tour that would continue on to
Baltimore and Washington, D.C. While Orson was traveling
the lecture circuit, Rita, still recovering from Becky's birth,
received the news that her mother had died. Although she
had explicitly told Orson by phone that he need not cut short
his speaking engagement to return for the funeral, it later
seemed to Orson that that was exactly what she had expected
him to do—and the conflict created considerable tension
between them. Orson returned to Los Angeles, and the
Welleses, the Hills, and Miss Haran set off on a vacation
trip to Mexico, which patched things up somewhat. Becky
was left behind with her nurse, but Orson—under pressure
to churn out five columns weekly—brought with him a
thick stack of up-to-the-minute notes on the Washington
scene his researchers had industriously provided. Since it
was wartime he did not want the Mexican customs inspectors
to see the material, which might be politically sensitive.

Miss Haran was enlisted to roll up the pages as tightly and compactly as possible and jam them in the sleeve of her fur coat, the cuff of which she fastened with a rubber band to keep the notes from slipping out. The plan was that, as she prepared to pass through customs, she would leave her coat behind in the waiting room. Inspection completed, she would seem suddenly to remember her coat and hurry back to get it. As it turned out, however, at the very moment the inspection had begun, a helpful customs girl rushed up to Miss Haran with the coat she had ostensibly forgotten. Orson and Miss Haran exchanged bug-eyed glances. But against all odds, and much to the relief of a very pale Miss Haran, the stuffed sleeve escaped notice.

This was not the least of Miss Haran's tribulations on the trip. The night before they were scheduled to return home, Orson instructed his intrepid secretary to wake him and Rita at six sharp. Embarrassed to enter the hotel room where they slept together, Miss Haran nonetheless did as she'd been told. Neither would budge. Ten minutes later she tried again, without success. In three hours she tried to rouse them no fewer than thirty times, meanwhile packing their luggage so that, should they finally awaken, they might still somehow catch the plane. As it turned out this was precisely what happened: the Welleses drowsily threw on some clothes and caught the plane just before it was about to take off. That was the day Miss Haran decided to quit Orson's employ. Much as she adored him and Rita, she had had enough. So she placed her letter of resignation in the basket in which she routinely put her requests for Orson. For weeks and weeks the note lay untouched. Only when she heard him mention her leaving to someone else did she know for certain that he had read it. Still she stayed on for several months more: Orson was so very busy it seemed impossible for her to leave him.

As usual, he was preoccupied with several projects at once. One of these was teaching Rita to bullfight. Orson

had discussed the project over lunch with an incredulous
Jackson Leighter. When Leighter protested that he did not
see how Rita was possibly going to learn bullfighting in Los
Angeles, Orson replied that he just wanted to get his business partner's approval for something to take place in the
future. Afterward, Leighter returned to his office shaking
his head at the nonsense Orson had spent the entire lunch
discussing. At three o'clock that morning Leighter was
awakened by his telephone. It was Miss Haran to say that
Mr. Welles's bullfighter had just arrived at the airport and
needed some money. Unable to reach Mr. Welles, Miss
Haran sought Mr. Leighter's approval to advance the Mexican the cash. "Well, by all means!" said Leighter, hanging
up and returning to sleep. The next morning, still trying to
make some sense of all this, Leighter was idly thumbing
through a weekly magazine to which he subscribed when
he came across a strange picture labeled "Orson Welles's
Bull." The photo showed a wheelbarrow to which a great
bull's head was attached for Rita Hayworth to learn bullfighting. A few days after reading this, when Leighter drove
up to Welles's home to discuss some urgent business, he
heard cries of *Olé! Olé!* issuing from the living room. There
he found Rita, dressed as a bullfighter, waving her big red
cape at a bull-headed wheelbarrow manned by her father,
Eduardo Cansino, as Orson and a number of other guests
cheered them on.

   The cancellation of the proposed Eversharp radio column
had eroded Orson's recent resistance to doing the kind of
radio drama with which he had been widely associated in
New York. So in March of 1945 he began a new program
titled *This Is My Best* for Cresta Blanca Wines (". . . a wine
to serve proudly saying, *This is my best, this is Cresta
Blanca*") in which he enacted literary favorites like *Heart
of Darkness* and *The Master of Ballantrae*. The show was
prematurely canceled after little more than a month. As with

his perfunctory performance in *Tomorrow Is Forever*, his heart was not in it.

But when Orson was involved in something he really cared about, his authentic emotion infused every word. When in April of 1945, having returned from the Yalta Conference, President Roosevelt died of a cerebral hemorrhage in Warm Springs, Georgia, Orson took no more than an hour to prepare a text for a eulogy that, as it turned out, was broadcast in almost every corner of the nation. "It was absolutely stupendous," says Leighter. "Orson could write better for Orson than he could write for anything else. He never was a great writer in pieces, but when Orson was writing for Orson, he approached greatness." In the Roosevelt eulogy, as in the superb speech he gave to introduce Henry Wallace, *Orson was writing for Orson*: that is, expressing what *he* really thought in the cadences of his own unique voice— something he found himself basically unable to do in the pieces he was writing daily for the *Post*. Pressed to come up with five columns a week, Orson often found himself spewing forth raw chunks of unassimilated data his researchers had provided. Nor did this failure go unnoticed by the newspaper publishers across the country who, expecting great things from Orson, had so keenly bought the column from the *Post* and who dropped it months after it had begun.

But Louis Dolivet had far grander aspirations for Orson than his serving as a newspaper columnist. Less than two weeks after Roosevelt's death, fifty nations dispatched delegates to San Francisco for the United Nations Conference on International Organization (UNCIO), whose mission was to draft the United Nations Charter. Roosevelt had been especially anxious for the charter to be drawn up before the war was over lest any of the nations have second thoughts about international organization. It was while the delegates were meeting in San Francisco, on May 7, 1945, that Germany surrendered. (The Japanese surrender would not come until September 2.) At the time of the San Francisco meeting, Dolivet's singular plan was to put forth as a candidate for the Secretary General of the United Nations the name of Orson Welles. His reasoning, as he explains it today, was that the United Nations should be a world organization not of governments, but of people. This being so, the best candidate for Secretary General would be a figure not explicitly identified with any particular government. Known around the world as a symbol of the boldness of youth, Orson was Dolivet's idea of a perfect candidate for the job. Asked about just how conscious he was of Dolivet's plan when he and Miss Haran took off for San Francisco, Orson says, "I knew about it, I did. And I never took it very seriously. But I knew that the talk was serious. . . . I was terribly flattered that people were talking about it." In any event, Orson's relative lack of political or diplomatic experience had doomed his mentor's wildly ambitious plan from the outset. Nor was Orson particularly enthusiastic— or so he asserts today: "I wasn't very keen about it," Orson recalls. "I was in on the founding of the thing, and at the founding it was apparent to me that all the limitations we know now were inherent in it, and that we were eventually going to be imprisoned by what is now called the Third World. So I had a dim view of its future." Despite Dolivet's efforts to plunge him into the very center of activity, Orson's role as a journalist afforded him a certain aesthetic distance from the proceedings. Besides his column, there was his lively new weekly radio show titled *The Free World Forum* on which Orson's guests were eminent conference participants, with whom, consummate master of the radio medium that he was, Orson seemed always to hold his own. In the euphoria of the international conclave, Orson caroused with the foreign representatives by night, drinking, dining, and generally carrying on. In one case, the next day he didn't feel up to attending a meeting at which he was scheduled to speak, so he dispatched his secretary to secure a pair of crutches, on which he hobbled out when the organizers came to pick him up.

By now Orson had begun to resort to deception at home as well. Although he had initially been faithful to Rita, she had often angrily accused him of cheating. "Every night I would come home, and I would find her in tears," Orson recalls sadly. "She said, 'I know what goes on in the studio!' Oh, it was terrible! It was just so awful." Rita's experience of having been used by men all her life was responsible for her ingrained lack of trust. Seeing how genuinely tormented Rita was, Orson understood that she could not control her jealousy. It seemed to him that there was no rational way of convincing her that he had been faithful and that he loved her. In time, although he continued to love her very much, her accusations and tantrums began to drive him away, and, ironically, he embarked on the extramarital affairs she imagined he had been conducting all along. These included a brief illicit relationship with Judy Garland, who, after their affair ended, became a good friend of his. (In later years she would call on him twice when she was contemplating suicide, once in Los Angeles, once in London.) During their love affair, Orson frequently brought Judy great loads of flowers. One night, however, returning home from a visit with her, he suddenly noticed that his car was still full of flowers, which he had forgotten to give to the proper party. Instinctively, Miss Haran rushed out quickly to conceal the card to Judy before Rita, who assumed the flowers were for her, noticed it. When he spotted Miss Haran hauling the flowers inside Orson went dead silent. But he soon realized that Miss Haran had discreetly disposed of the incriminating card.

Did Rita know about Judy Garland and the others? If Miss Haran had tried to keep it from her, there were those who did not—including her former friends from the studio whom Orson had expelled from the house and who were eager for revenge. Unfortunately, it was Rita who was hurt by their insinuations. Her feeling unwanted could result in terrible scenes, as in New York when Orson had been working frantically with a group of writers and his New York secretary, Elisabeth Rubino, in the living room of his hotel suite, and suddenly Rita's weeping could be heard issuing from the bedroom. This was no ploy. She was genuinely upset that Orson was neglecting her. Anxious to get back to the marathon of work, Orson dispatched one of his men to escort her to the hairdresser. But hours later when they returned, Orson and the writers were still hard at it. Hoping that Orson would comment favorably on her new hairdo, Rita stared at him for a long while without his so much as saying a word to her. This threw her into an even worse fit of agitation than before. Only then did Orson seem to notice her hair, and when she rushed off into the bedroom, he followed her. When Orson closed the bedroom door behind him, the writers packed up to leave. They knew from experience that when Orson closeted himself with Rita at such tense moments in their relationship, it would be a long time before he emerged again.

In addition to the trouble in his marriage, Orson also began to experience serious professional problems when his newspaper column failed. For all his success in the Free World movement and the Roosevelt campaign, Orson had not managed to sell himself as an all-around political commentator to the general public. By May the *Post* felt compelled to ask Orson voluntarily to take a cut in his weekly guarantee. As far as the paper was concerned, the problem was that the public automatically expected news of the entertainment world rather than of politics from Orson Welles. The *Post*'s general manager referred specifically to "the public consciousness" in which Orson was associated with "Hollywood, the theater, radio and arts generally." To save the column Orson was advised to change its emphasis to an area on which he was indisputably "an authority"—namely show business. Orson's swift refusal was framed in terms of an issue that had preoccupied him in the past: the question of whether there is a "serious public" out there and how to reach it. If previously the Hollywood audience had rejected him because they found him too serious, now in turn serious readers were doing the same because they associated him with Hollywood. Orson argued that he needed time to teach them to take him seriously. To Orson's mind, shifting to writing mostly about the entertainment world as the paper evidently wanted him to do could only keep him from finally reaching the serious public for whom he'd been longing. "Why would I want to write *another* kind of column?" Orson asks today, still bristling at the very idea of it.

Once again, intense psychological pressure had seriously diminished Orson's health. Alarmed by his physical condition, Dadda Bernstein sternly ordered him to suspend the column or find himself in the hospital. Orson woefully complied. In the meantime, a letter from Orson's editor at the *Post* cogently outlined a reason for the aesthetic failure of Orson's column. He wisely counseled Orson to permanently dismiss his researchers: for "the material which pours from you instantly, apparently almost instinctively, will be likely to be truer, warmer, and more convincing than anything gathered in your behalf by others, no matter how competent or how concerned." A second attempt to write the column failed as before, and if by November he decided to stop writing altogether, Orson did not stop trying to discover an authentic voice for himself as a political commentator. He would have to do what his editor had advised: to trust his instincts and speak from the heart. This at length he would finally manage to do on radio.

CHAPTER 27

On Schedule
and Under Budget

Marlene Dietrich was an important source of comfort to Orson in this difficult period. "He was crazy about her," says Shifra Haran. Fresh from entertaining the troops ("She was broke," Orson recalls), Marlene was the Welleses' houseguest in the big house on Carmelina Drive, and she asked Orson to introduce her to Greta Garbo. When Dietrich began to be popular in Germany in the '20s, the press often compared her with Garbo. Orson recalls that Marlene absolutely "worshiped" Garbo but had never found herself in a room with her. So he arranged for the actor Clifton Webb (who always entertained with his mother) to give a party to which they would invite Garbo, and to which Marlene would come with Orson so that the pair could meet "inadvertently." Knowing Garbo and Dietrich as he did, Orson suspected that their meeting might not be a happy one. Says Orson of Garbo: "She was essentially very dumb, you see. And Marlene was very bright." To illustrate, Orson tells of a certain evening he spent with Garbo: "This was during the war," he explains. "I was having dinner with her and we came out of the restaurant and there was a soldier in uniform without a leg, standing on his crutches with an autograph book and she refused it. That is how dumb she was! She refused him, yes, in front of my eyes! And of course Marlene was a very different kind of cat."

Orson and Marlene were already at Clifton Webb's party when Garbo arrived. It was only natural that Orson would take Marlene over to meet her. But when Dietrich complimented her peer by comparing her to a goddess, Garbo uttered nothing more than a polite thank you. "She turned into the dumb Swede that she really was," says Orson of the silent Garbo. Initially undaunted, Marlene kept praising Garbo, who persisted in saying thank you, over and over. That was the extent of their meeting, which ended finally when Marlene gave up earnestly trying to engage Garbo in conversation. On the way back to Carmelina Drive afterward, Marlene did not say a word until suddenly she turned to Orson to pronounce: "*Her* feet aren't as big as they say!" Back home, a few drinks seemed appropriate, and Marlene got going on her subject. "They say, no makeup!" Orson remembers her having exclaimed. "She has beaded eyelashes! Do you know how long it takes to have your eyelashes beaded?"

But Orson had more important things on his mind at this time than one screen goddess snubbing another. He had finally sold the radio show on politics that Eversharp pens and pencils had rejected. The buyer was Lear Radios, who agreed to sponsor a fifteen-minute weekly broadcast on Orson's choice of topics. The first program was scheduled for September 16, 1945, at ten-fifteen a.m. Naturally, Orson saw this as an opportunity to try to work out some of the problems of presentation that he found himself unable to solve in his newspaper column.

But a weekly fifteen-minute radio show was not going to pay the rent. Although Orson did not completely give up on the *Post* column until November of 1945, by the end of the previous summer it had become evident that perhaps he should reconsider his well-publicized decision to limit his Hollywood work to acting in one picture a year. The public still thought of him, after all, as an entertainer. In September of 1945, then, when International Pictures expressed serious interest in his directing a film for them, Orson was so delighted he accepted an entirely unadvantageous contract. He had acted in *Tomorrow Is Forever* with Claudette Colbert for International, whose co-founder, William Goetz, had been with 20th Century–Fox when Orson appeared in *Jane Eyre*. Goetz had seen Orson act in two movies and he wanted to give him the chance to direct again. But what Orson calls the "disaster" of *It's All True* had given him an unjust reputation as a director who does not finish films. So that September of 1945 when he signed the contract to direct his next picture, he was required to submit to the humiliation of agreeing to indemnify the moneymen should he fail to finish the picture. He and Rita signed a guarantee that, should he default in his duties, he would owe International as compensation any money he earned, from any source, beyond $50,000 a year. Also Orson agreed that in the event of an artistic dispute with the studio, he would submit to their wishes. This was the exact opposite of his original Hollywood contract: complete control. Having once been granted complete artistic control by RKO without giving the slightest proof that he could direct a movie, now that he had indeed made two of the greatest films in the history of the cinema, suddenly Orson was required to prove himself.

The film that resulted from this curious new contract was supposed to eliminate Orson's reputation as unwilling to take orders (an image that had issued in large part from the widely resented total artistic freedom afforded by Orson's first contract). The genius had to show himself willing to submit to the system. This new picture would be Orson's penance. For it he would be paid $2,000 a week plus

$100,000—*if* he successfully finished the film. As a way of checking Orson's natural inclination to take charge, someone else—Sam Spiegel (S. P. Eagle)—would produce. There would always be someone watching over Orson lest he be tempted to indulge in secret excesses. But precisely what were these mysterious excesses from which Orson was supposed to abstain? Although there was much talk of the exorbitant expense of *Kane* and *Ambersons* (which in fact had not been terribly extravagant at all), the real issue seemed to be his artistic excesses, his unabashedly self-assertive style, in an industry that valued neater, more efficient films than a free spirit like Orson Welles was inclined to make. In short, what Orson was expected to prove here was that he was as capable of grinding out a bland and artistically undistinguished picture as the next guy.

The Stranger, the movie that Orson made under the terms of this new contract, is surely his least interesting—as, in a sense, it was supposed to be. This lack of artistic interest is also the source of its immense critical interest. *The Stranger* shows us exactly the sort of artist Welles was not. More important, it shows that Orson's submitting himself to strict external control—as he undeniably did in *The Stranger*— did not result in better filmmaking. On the contrary, *The Stranger* is as nothing beside *Kane* or even the mutilated *Ambersons*. Jorge Luis Borges once wrote that *Citizen Kane* is a "labyrinth without a center"—a phrase that quite captures the vertigo, the curious indeterminacy of meaning that one discovers in all of Welles's films—all except *The Stranger*.

The Stranger is linear, straightforward, continuous in a way that Welles's other films simply aren't. It proceeds at a far brisker pace than one discovers elsewhere in his cinema, where atmosphere and texture play a principal role largely denied them in *The Stranger* in the interest of telling its tale as simply and swiftly as possible. Not that simplicity and directness may not be artistic virtues—they are simply antithetical to Welles's fundamentally baroque sensibility.

Welles had a second motive for making so uncharacteristically linear a movie. Thematically *The Stranger* dealt with one of his key political concerns of the period: the persistence of Fascism after the defeat of the Axis. Based on a story by Victor Travis, the script for *The Stranger* was written by Anthony Veiller with uncredited assistance from John Huston and Orson Welles. Its protagonist was a handsome former Nazi officer who after the war lives incognito as a boys' schoolmaster in an American small town, where he secretly prepares for the resurgence of Fascism. Clearly, Orson conceived of *The Stranger* as a film with a political message (the postwar danger of Fascism) and he hoped that an unobtrusive style might allow the story to speak for itself. Viewed in this light, *The Stranger* was Orson's confrontation with the problem of political cinema: whether the filmmaker with a message is wisest to make his audience think (as mosaics like *Citizen Kane* or the best Soviet avant-garde films of the '20s do) or to tell his audience what to think (as smoothly linear narratives like *The Stranger* and Soviet socialist realist films of the '30s do).

But for Orson, experimentation in political filmmaking was of secondary importance to improving his Hollywood reputation. At least it was the latter that he talked about when to his co-workers he stressed the importance of finishing the picture on schedule and under budget. After *Ambersons*, Hollywood thought Orson made movies that were too long and too slow. Thus *The Stranger* was *pre*edited. That is, editor Ernest Nims cut what he considered to be extraneous elements from the script *before* Orson started shooting. Orson knew that accepting these cuts early on meant saving money. Nims recalls Orson's having basically agreed to most of the suggested cuts in the interest of showing that he could work quickly and efficiently. But Orson tells quite another story. Says Orson of Nims: "He was the great supercutter, who believed that nothing should be in a movie that did not advance the story. And since most of the good stuff in my movies doesn't advance the story *at all*, you can imagine what a nemesis he was to me." Even with the preediting, there were further cuts afterward, and these Orson says he vehemently protested. "I fought him tooth and nail all through it and won in the case of *The Stranger*, except that he took out everything which is interesting in the great long sequence in Latin America before we even get to that village, which was very strange." These lost scenes would have shown Orson's fleeing Nazi in Latin America prior to going into hiding in the small town in the United States where most of the film is set. "You don't know what it was like on the screen!" says Orson. "And I have to this day a deep wound in my leg where I stepped on a baby's coffin in one of the scenes—the wood cut into my leg—and it always reminds me of what was lost from that movie. At least they kept the story—" which was more than RKO did, Orson thinks, with *Ambersons*.

How then is one to reconcile these two apparently contradictory views of Orson's attitude toward the editing of *The Stranger*? Orson was probably far more malleable on this particular project than he realizes. He was making the picture to make himself marketable, and at the time it appeared that Nims's suggestions would help do just that. As it turned out, however, *The Stranger* did not particularly enhance Orson's reputation in Hollywood—and its failure to do so could only have made him resent its artistic failure all the more. Nor on some subliminal level could Orson fail to blame himself for having largely submitted to all the external constraints that were imposed on him. These resentments focused on Nims—the "supersurgeon," as he calls him—who for Orson came to embody what he perceived as Hollywood's inclination to hack apart his films.

Nor, one suspects, are Orson's retrospective comments on the editing of *The Stranger* uninflected by his subsequent encounter with Nims, more than a decade later, on *Touch of Evil*, when the film was taken away from the director's control and given to the editor to cut as he wished.

Any resentment that Orson may have felt while making *The Stranger* he seems mostly to have repressed or concealed at the time. Says production manager Jim Pratt: "I'd say that during *The Stranger* he was about as well balanced as he ever was in his career in the business. . . . There have been a few authentic geniuses in our business—not many—but he's one of them, that's for sure, if you could have harnessed him so as to avoid the excesses. In other words, there has to be an editorial function. There has to be someone who finally says no, that's as far as we're going to go, and so on. Whether they're right or they're wrong, there has to be this kind of a situation." But Orson did not allow himself to be "harnessed" in all things. Although a doctor arrived two or three times a week to give him shots to help him lose weight, he typically devoured double portions of his meals at the studio commissary. Orson spent most nights in a suite of rooms he had taken over at the Goldwyn studios, where he was shooting *The Stranger*. There was little time to go home when, besides quickly making a movie, he was writing a daily column, doing a weekly radio show, and—a new addition—actively working on the concept for a projected stage production of Jules Verne's *Around the World in 80 Days*. Another advantage of the suite was, of course, that Orson could discreetly meet girls there. Just before shooting had started, Rita had thrown Orson out of their house on Carmelina Drive after an argument over his extramarital affairs. "When I was thrown out of the house by Rita the first time," Orson recalls, "I went and lived with Sam Spiegel." Shortly thereafter Rita allowed him to come home, but because of the continued tension between them he felt much more comfortable living at the studio. Rita would visit there when she could, mostly in the evening, although she too was busy, having just begun work in September on *Gilda*, in which she starred opposite Glenn Ford.

In this period, Orson was torn between needing to pursue the other women who were so easily available, and not wanting Rita to be hurt by what he was doing. His constant fear of publicly embarrassing her made him susceptible to a blackmailer who threatened to accuse him of attempted rape. The incident was supposed to have taken place in a car Orson was driving. In September, Orson had acquired his first driver's license even though, as he says: "I don't drive well. I pay no attention, but I love to drive fast, very fast. It's the only thing that keeps me from being bored." The night in question he had gone to pick up a script from a Hollywood nabob, who in turn asked Orson to drive his typist home. "'Certainly,' said I," Orson recalls. "And she got into my car. And they'd been drinking a bit, and she slumped to the side of the car, and I started across town. In Beverly Hills, you know, they have those big bumps to stop you from going fast. And I hit one and the car door opened and she fell out. . . . And so I stopped the car and tried to find her. And she hadn't been hurt, but she could be heard running through the underbrush of the Hollywood villas, you know, calling for help, as though she'd been raped. *Very* ugly girl—." After searching all about for her in vain, finally Orson gave up and drove back to tell the nabob what had happened. When he got there, there she was. "So I said, 'I suppose you don't want to drive with me anymore,' " Orson says. " 'I apologize. I didn't close the door strongly enough.' Anyway, that was the end of that and I went home. The next morning I went to my office . . . and they said, 'There's a lawyer out there who wants to see you.' And I said, 'Oh.' And in came the lawyer, who said, 'Mr. Welles, I wonder how much your wife, Miss Hayworth, would like to read in the newspaper that you attempted to rape my client and that she had to throw herself out of a moving car.' And I said, 'I wouldn't like that at all.' And he said, 'Well, that'll be $20,000.' And I paid him and never drove again. . . .'' As far as having given up driving was concerned, Orson had no regrets: "I was a very bad driver and I needed the first excuse to tell myself, like knocking off liquor because you don't know how to drink, you know. . . . So then I never drove another inch. . . . I never minded at all. I was delighted to give up driving. I only drove because I was made to by public opinion.'' And what of the blackmailer? Did he regret having paid her off? "I couldn't bear to let Rita read that,'' says Orson. "And no use saying how *ugly* the girl is!''

By contrast with his messy and confused relationship with Rita, production on *The Stranger* went without a serious hitch. In the end, as Pratt happily points out, "It was *on* schedule and *under* budget.'' Pratt routinely interceded with the actors to get them to work overtime without complaint, so that Orson could keep to his schedule. But Orson sometimes had to make concessions to keep the cast happy. Thus when Edward G. Robinson (who played the investigator searching for Orson's Nazi) protested that Orson was persistently shooting his bad side, Pratt convinced Orson that it would be wise to photograph what the actor was absolutely convinced was his *good* side. There was also a curious concession to Loretta Young (who played the innocent young American who marries the Nazi). In a scene that did not find its way into the finished film, she was to meet the handsome mystery man for the first time as she prepared to enter church one Sunday, and to walk off with him into the woods instead of attending Mass. But as a devout Catholic, Miss Young was greatly dismayed at the idea of being shown onscreen cutting church, so Orson changed their meeting to another day of the week when she was simply out walking her dog. Loretta Young also objected to members of the cast and crew swearing on the set. Because nothing much could be done about people's natural tendency to utter an offending word or two now and then, she set up a "swear box" to which anyone who did had to contribute a quarter for charity.

Since the principal point of *The Stranger* was to show that Orson could keep himself in check, no wonder it is his least personal film. Perhaps things had gone *too* smoothly. Missing was the disjunctive cinematic style that Orson had made his signature in *Kane*. Orson tried to compensate for his new picture's essential impersonality by imbuing it with private allusions that no one but his intimates could possibly get. In fact he had originally hoped to shoot *The Stranger* on location at Todd, and to use one of the current Todd Troupers as Loretta Young's little brother. At length, neither idea worked out. But the boys' school where the Nazi teaches history is clearly modeled on Todd, down to the name of one of its beloved staff members, Coach Roskie, appearing on a sign in the gymnasium. And in his jaunty schoolmaster's outfit—his tweed jacket and V-neck—Orson even looks a bit like Skipper, as, one suspects, he was supposed to. But gratuitous personal touches like these could not make *The Stranger* a personal film. Often in his career after *Kane* other men have tried to repress Welles's films by cutting and reworking them, but still they are *his*, unmistakably so. The difference in the case of *The Stranger* is that this time he had *agreed* to repress himself.

"I was ready never to act again," says Orson of the difficult period after the unsatisfying experience of making *The Stranger*. Having scrupulously kept his self-assertive instincts in check (except in his philandering), he felt restless, unfulfilled. He kept thinking of Roosevelt's suggestion that he run for senator. "Imagine the great orator he would have

been in the Senate!" says Louis Dolivet. But if he were
going to pursue this path, it seemed to Orson that he probably should have started a bit earlier and run for office in
1944. "If I had run at the last Roosevelt campaign," he says,
"even at my age I had a very good chance." On January
14, 1946, *Time* magazine reported: "In California, where
anything can happen, Orson Welles—who has impersonated
William Randolph Hearst, campaigned with Franklin Delano Roosevelt and sawed his wife in half—thought of
running for the U.S. Senate." Today, Orson explains that
the main reason he finally decided against running on the
West Coast was Alan Cranston, who discouraged him. "He
was a power in California politics," says Orson of Cranston.
"He knew everybody and everything, and was the smartest
fellow behind the scenes in Sacramento." But when Orson
went to see him he was instantly disappointed. "He told me
I couldn't win. I know why he didn't want me to win:
because *he* wanted to be senator, that's why. He said that I
would carry northern California, but I could never carry
Los Angeles because of the strong Communist objections
to me. There was an element of truth in it. None of the left
wing in Beverly Hills or Bel Air would have voted for me.
There were a lot of card-carrying fellows—never forget
that—and I was very much not of their group. They were
older and jealous of a younger and at that time extremely
visible American celebrity. Just plain old Hollywood envy!"

Convinced that because of this important opposition he
could never carry southern California, Orson briefly thought
of establishing residency in New York, then settled on the
idea of possibly running in Wisconsin, the state of his birth.
But the problem that faced him there was Joseph McCarthy.
"Joe McCarthy had the dairy people behind him and there
was no way to beat him," says Orson. Some of Orson's
political cronies advised him to go up against McCarthy
nonetheless. "I didn't," Orson says wistfully. "And that's

how come there was a McCarthy. It's a terrible thing to have on your conscience. I was convinced that I wouldn't beat him." He feared that if he lost his first race, he would be finished in American politics forever. "It isn't like England, where you can go and contest two or three seats and make your name and then finally go to one that you can win," says Orson. "It doesn't work like that, you see."

It also seemed to Orson that his faltering marriage to Rita was a serious impediment to realizing his great dream of running for president some day. "Like a thousand other people I thought it might be a possible future," he says. "But I had this lingering conviction that having been divorced and having been an actor was perhaps an insurmountable objection to ever getting into the Oval Office"; he now laughs uproariously in light of Ronald Reagan's having succeeded in surmounting both these obstacles to win the presidency. Although Orson did not expect his marriage to break up in the very near future, he sensed that Rita would eventually leave him. "Rita was very unhappy, and I didn't believe that she was going to stay with me," he says. "I didn't see it coming soon, but I thought that she was somebody who would finally break down in one way or another. Then my substitute, you see, for public office was education. That's when I went to all the big foundations and said that I would give up all acting and so on and use my skills for popular education to try to rejuvenate the idea of a civilized generation of students, and nobody was remotely interested. But Rita was absolutely willing to give up everything for it. And I thought she'd be happier in education than she would in Washington. She didn't like to be left alone and I knew that a junior senator or congressman doesn't have much home life." Finally, of his unrealized political ambitions Orson sighs: "It was just a big missed boat." As to why, after failing to sell his educational program, he did not resume his quest for public office, Orson says: "I didn't run away from it. There was just nowhere to go—that was really it." At the time, returning to the New York stage, where he had known tremendous success in the past, seemed the most prudent course to follow. It was time to assert himself again.

In the months of the 1984 presidential campaign, Orson keeps receiving letters signed "Nancy" and invitations to one Republican shindig or another——but nothing from the Democrats, who appear to have forgotten how vigorously, and effectively, Orson campaigned for Roosevelt.

"Roosevelt used to put me on prime time, and I wasn't running for anything," says Orson.

"Why did Roosevelt think it would be effective to have somebody who was a non-candidate do it?"

"All the more so, he thought. It's a concerned citizen and a popular artist who is going to say it better than anybody in the political world. He was responsible for the kind of space and time that they gave me. Now, even though Jack Nicholson and Warren Beatty are sitting at Gary Hart's side, they're not heard from."

"Why not?" I ask. (At this point, Gary Hart is still a serious contender for the Democratic nomination.)

"Have you noticed that they're not heard from?" says Orson.

"Yes, I read in one story that they were working on the cutting of a Hart commercial."

"Well," says Orson, "they're doing that kind of thing,
but they also both want to be president."

"Both of them?" I gasp—Beatty doesn't amaze me, but
the idea of Nicholson does.

"Oh sure," says Orson "and so does Robert Redford,
and so does the chunky fellow who's the head of the Screen
Actors' Guild."

"Asner?"

"Asner," says Orson. "He seriously wants to be president."

But apparently with Warren Beatty it is more than just a
case of his simply wanting to be president: "Warren deeply
and profoundly believes that he will be president," says
Orson.

"He really believes it?" I ask.

"Yes," says Orson, "he told me that."

"Do you think he ever could be?"

"No," says Orson. "Not a chance."

Our conversation returns now to why Hart hasn't made
much use of his movie-star supporters like Beatty and Nicholson.

"They would like to be used," says Orson, "but there
has grown up this tight little group of experts on cam-
paigns—and they won't give Warren or Jack five minutes
on the six o'clock news, ever, because he's getting in the
way of their man."

"Every second of that five minutes," I begin.

"Has to be their man," Orson finishes my thought. "And
they aren't doing his man any good, because what they need
is their man. They don't want him to look like another
Hollywood"—by which Orson means that since the Republicans already have a former movie star in office, the Democrats must somehow maintain their distance from
Hollywood.

"The strength that they have," he says of the Democrats,
"is that they are not from Hollywood. In other words, these

two poor movie stars" —he means Beatty and Nicholson—
"are down there hoping somehow to get a foot into the door
of the American political process, and they should be told
that the scene is hopeless. The last thing you want is a
candidate who is chummy with the superstars and Hollywood. "

Does this mean that Ronald Reagan has eliminated the
possibility of another actor's being elected president in the
near future?

"I think it's almost impossible for another actor to be
president, certainly for fifteen years," says Orson. "That's
what I've carefully told Warren, Jack, and the Chunky
Man."

"A lot of people take Warren Beatty seriously," I say,
"but I can't imagine Jack Nicholson."

"No, no, never," says Orson. "I think he sees himself as
Harry Hopkins. "

"To Warren's president?" I ask.

"Warren or whoever gets it," says Orson. "And you see
they've all missed it, because there's only going to be one
actor to be president, and the right one—as I kept telling
him, he would never listen to me—was Gregory Peck. Bad
actor, but he'd be a hell of a president, you know."

"Great for the role," I agree.

"Sure," says Orson, "and his heart is politically in all
the right places, you see. I kept nagging at him but he
wouldn't do it."

"So Ronald Reagan got it," I say.

"That undoes it all," Orson groans. "It had to be a
second-rate actor."

CHAPTER 28

Citizen
of America

Rita's announcement came as a great shock to Orson. He had flown to New York to talk to Cole Porter, who was going to do the music and lyrics for the adaptation of Jules Verne's *Around the World in 80 Days*, which Orson saw as his triumphant return to Broadway. But Orson's excitement was greatly diminished when he heard the startling news that Rita had told the press that she and her husband were separating. Rita found herself left alone too much of the time, and with Miss Haran gone, there was no one to keep reassuring her of Orson's devotion, peculiar as it may have been. For all Orson's talk of finding a way to avoid their being apart so often, he was indefinitely off on his own again. Having made her unhappiness public, Rita was waiting until she finished *Gilda* before repairing to Palm Springs for a recuperative vacation.

Orson decided that it was probably best not to contact Rita, whom he still loved very much. He had to admit that at this point she had good reason to be dissatisfied with their relationship. He was brokenhearted, but also strangely relieved that the difficult marriage was over at last. "I could have patched it up in a day," he says, "but I had reached the end of my capacity to feel such total failure with her. I

had done *everything* I could think of and I didn't seem to
be able to bring her anything but agony." He suspected that
it would always be the same between them, and that as
much as he loved Rita he would never be able to make her
happy. "I really thought that maybe somebody else could
make her happy, because I could see that there was no way
I could, except to give her some *moments* of joy during the
week. I was going to come home every night for the rest
of my life to a woman in tears. I felt so *guilty*—and I adored
her! Oh, it was awful!"

Back in Hollywood to put some finishing touches on *The
Stranger*, he refrained from calling Rita as he longed to do.
With Christmas approaching he was terribly lonely and depressed, but at the same time he could not bear to see his
friends, or to spoil their holiday with his dark mood. "I
went to Mexico to be not in the Christmas world," he says
of his sudden departure from Los Angeles. "I checked into
this hotel, which had been built when the hemp industry
was enormous, and each room had its separate swimming
pool." But however much he craved solitude, Orson was
not destined to spend the holiday alone. "In the hotel, a
marvelously distinguished old gentleman, as you find only
in magazine stories, came up to me and said, 'You are alone,
Señor Welles. We recognized you. May we invite you to
come to the country for our Christmas?' And I said yes.
We got on a little tiny train with the narrowest gauge you've
ever seen in your life, exactly like something in Turgenev.
Here were all these aunts and uncles and little cousins and
all that, and we went through the jungle in this tiny train.
When we got off, we all got on donkeys and went on through
the jungle till we came to the great hacienda of this fellow."
In the preparations for the Christmas feast, Orson was called
upon to help. "I was given a matador's sword, and I killed
the bull," he recalls. "They made a great stew of that, and
after drinking all through the night, next morning we had
this marvelous meal." Sensing that Orson wanted to be alone

for a while, the Mexicans gave him a horse and directions to the Mayan ruins about five miles away. "I climbed to the top of the biggest pyramid, and sat there on Christmas day, all alone in the ruins of the Mayans. I've never been so happy in my life."

In January, after stops in Havana and Miami, Orson went on to New York, where he learned that, although he had not expected her to move so quickly, Rita had instructed her lawyer to proceed with the divorce. In anticipation of a settlement between them, the lawyer had requested Orson's financial statement, but Orson wanted to stall the proceedings however he could. In particular there was the touchy matter of the $30,000 that Rita had loaned Orson in the course of their marriage, and that she wanted back now. She asked that at the very least he agree to a schedule of payments, but he was about to launch an expensive new show, and was reluctant to part with *any* cash at all.

Finally Rita's lawyer threatened that if some amicable settlement could not be reached soon, she would bring suit. By and by it was decided that since Orson and Rita had contributed equally to the purchase price of the house in Carmel, the proceeds from its sale could be used to pay off Orson's debt. Although Rita was not seeking alimony or a substantial settlement, she did want some financial provision to be made for her and Rebecca in the event that she stopped working. Rita also felt that she had a community interest in Orson's profits from *The Stranger*, as well as in the potential profits that might accrue from the stories to which Orson had purchased rights in the course of their marriage. Negotiations resulted in Rita's agreeing to relinquish her claim to any profits from *The Stranger* in exchange for half of Orson's interest in *Around the World in 80 Days*. As it turned out, had the papers ever been finalized, this would have been a terrible deal for Rita. After all the haggling back and forth, Rita seemed to hesitate, and Orson did nothing to encourage her to bring matters to a conclu-

sion. Meanwhile, she had moved out of the big house on
Carmelina to a smaller one, which she rented in anticipation
of buying and decorating a home of her own.

Orson moved out of his costly quarters at the Waldorf
Towers to a much less expensive apartment on East End
Avenue to which Rita had shipped a trunkful of his clothing
and magic equipment. The prospect of financial commitments to two ex-wives made Orson at least temporarily eager
to economize. But still he felt like a veritable spendthrift
beside one of his New York cronies of the period, drama
critic George Jean Nathan, whom Orson fondly recalls as
"next to Chaplin, the tightest man who ever lived." At that
time, Orson tended to run into Nathan at "21," where both
of them were regulars. To illustrate how cheap Nathan really
was, Orson likes to tell the following wicked and outrageous
joke about him: Nathan resided across the street from the
famed Algonquin at the Hotel Royalton because it was
cheaper. After years of not being tipped, a disgruntled room-
service waiter would "piss a bit in Nathan's tea each morning." Day by day—Orson says—the waiter increased the
amount till finally he was serving Nathan *all* piss. Once,
when Nathan was dining at "21"—Orson recalls—the critic
exploded over the tea he was served, "Why can't anybody
else make tea like they do at the Royalton?"—at which
everyone else dissolved into laughter, because Nathan was
perhaps the only person left in New York who hadn't heard
about the waiter's revenge.

Money was much in Orson's thoughts now as he tried to
put together a rather costly production of *Around the World
in 80 Days*. That January, Mike Todd, a successful Broadway producer since 1936, had agreed to back Orson's writing and directing the show (in which he did not initially
plan to appear). The contract gave "full, complete and un-
restricted authority" to Orson, who was expected nonetheless to consult with Todd on expenses. Orson conceived
Around the World as a zany extravaganza on the order of

his early *Horse Eats Hat*—but on a much grander scale.
Beginning in London in 1872, where Phileas Fogg bets that
he can go around the world in eighty days, the show would
follow his fantastic journey from one colorful locale to another until he reached England again. There is every reason
to suppose that the vast proportions of the production were
an antidote to Orson's having kept himself so strictly in
check with *The Stranger*. Paid $2,000 weekly as an advance
against royalties that would accrue to him after the show
opened, Orson was well into rehearsals and about to begin
out-of-town tryouts when suddenly, unexpectedly, Mike Todd
withdrew, saying he had run out of cash. Orson's flamboyant
idea of rigging up a gushing oil well onstage was said to
have been the deciding factor for Todd. Orson was aghast.
He had been counting on his spectacular return to the New
York stage to be the massive success that had been stubbornly eluding him lately. Now he was faced with yet another disappointment; he feared that his reputation, let alone
his spirits, might not be able to stand this setback. Not for
one moment had it occurred to him that Todd was considering pulling out. At this point, Orson would probably have
been wisest to abandon the idea of opening in New York
in the spring of 1946. Had he postponed it until the fall, as
Cole Porter advised him to, he almost certainly would have
been able to replace Todd with another backer. But Orson
felt compelled to assemble the cash himself immediately.
And although they certainly may have appeared so, his
motives were not entirely irrational.

For in the meantime, Orson had struck a deal (or thought
he had) to direct Charles Laughton in the premiere of the
English version of Bertolt Brecht's *Galileo*, for which rehearsals were set to begin August 1. Orson had thrilled to
the idea of working closely with Brecht, whose radical theories of acting and staging came as a revelation to him in
his preparation for the production. Although Brecht had
been a name he had heard from both Hilton Edwards and

Marc Blitzstein, Orson had never paid much attention to his essays. But when he studied them now, he was intrigued by Brecht's notion of an alienated style of acting whereby, instead of identifying with the character he is playing, the actor views his role critically, from a distance (much as Orson may be said to have done in *Kane*). Along the same lines, in the sort of theatrical performance Brecht envisioned, instead of becoming emotionally involved in the dramatic action, the spectator would maintain his own critical distance, all the better to form his own judgments. Having gone so entirely against the grain in making a naturalistic film like *The Stranger*, Orson was especially eager now to put Brecht's antinaturalist theories into practice. Although eventually he would not get to work with Brecht as he had anticipated doing, Orson's study of Brecht's theatrical theory in this period would bear a decisive—and entirely unexpected—influence on the next film he would make in Hollywood, and on much of his work in film thereafter.

The dropping of the atomic bomb on Hiroshima on August 6, 1945, had caused Brecht to re-think substantially the character of the scientist in *Galileo*, the first version of which he had written in German in 1938 and which, in collaboration with Laughton, he had been slowly translating into English since December of 1944. For Brecht, the "atomic age" had been initiated the day Hiroshima was hit. It seemed inevitable to Brecht that since Galileo was "the founder of modern physics" the fact of Hiroshima should somehow be worked into the play, and this he and Laughton did in their translation. Putting off *Around the World* until the fall might mean forfeiting the opportunity to work with Brecht, something Orson was determined to avoid at all cost—although he could not then have even remotely suspected just what that cost would be.

To open the ill-fated show that spring, Orson acquired cash by all possible means. In exchange for Orson's promise to make a picture for him that summer, Harry Cohn lent Orson $25,000. And in hopes of getting a film or perhaps a London production out of it, Alexander Korda invested $125,000. Once, to meet a payroll, Orson even had to borrow $4,000 from Shorty. To make matters worse, the immense sums of money Orson regularly put into the play were ultimately disallowed by the Internal Revenue Service as business expenses; instead Orson was forced to take them as a personal loss. Without these anticipated deductions, Orson suddenly found himself owing a tax debt that would take years to escape—and which, at length, would be the major inducement for Orson to remain in exile from his own country for as long as he did.

The money from Harry Cohn had arrived at a moment when, at the Opera House in Boston for the first tryout, what Orson called "this damn costly behemoth of a spectacle" seemed on the verge of collapsing altogether. Even with Cohn's help, opening night in Boston was a grand disaster. *Nothing*—lights, props, scenery—was as it should have been. "Is this London?" one actress proclaimed as the stagehands fumbled with a succession of backdrops, none of them London. "Yes, this is London, all right," answered an actor, standing incongruously before a vast image of the Rocky Mountains—a surrealistic mixture typical of the evening's sustained incompetence. Fearful that there was not enough cash to pay the actors, Orson fled during the abortive performance, feeling, as he said later, "like a man wanted by the police." When he woke up the next morning he realized that he had not bothered to undress. At the second performance, Orson turned up onstage when his Phileas Fogg, Arthur Margetson, fell ill with a heart ailment. The budget had not provided for understudies. No sooner had Margetson returned that week than Orson had to fill in as Passepartout, whose lines he seemed to know even more imperfectly than he had Phileas Fogg's. When Margetson ribbed him onstage by exclaiming, "Passepartout, you don't know what you're talking about!" a frazzled Orson responded, "You've never said a truer word!" Later Orson called his precarious performance that night "among the most remarkable audacities ever perpetrated in the American theater."

Stops in New Haven and Philadelphia followed, during which Orson managed finally to tame the "behemoth" before taking it to the Adelphi Theatre in New York in May of 1946. Along the way, the production had gained a new cast member, Orson himself, who had decided to play Fogg's pursuer, Dick Fix — and for which he accepted the minimum Equity wage of sixty dollars weekly (a mere formality since he was consistently putting many times as much of his own money into the show). But although all thirty-four scenes ran fluidly one into the other, and although this time Passepartout *did* know what he was talking about and London *was* really London, and although the preview and first-night audiences seemed perfectly, pleasantly dazzled by it all, the critical reception was, with a few exceptions, rather poor. Wrote Robert Garland in the *Journal American*: "With countless interludes, and twice that many characters, with magic, movies and music thrown in for no good reason, it is a show shown by a show-off, full of sets and costumes, signifying nothing in particular." In the *New York Post* Vernon Rice wrote: "Seldom has Welles been accused of understatement, but this time he can be charged with making one when he calls his work an 'extravaganza.' There is hardly a word descriptive enough to fit this musical fare. It is mammoth, it is gigantic, it is lavish. It is also dull."

Orson, in defense, used his weekly spot on the air for Lear Radios to blast the critics, whom he claimed had been "outvoted by the paying customers." He railed against the unreasonable power of a handful of critics swiftly to close a show: "Displease more than three of these powerful personages," said Orson, "and no matter what the paying audience thought of your show, it's a lifeless corpse by the second edition." Reminding the critics of what had happened in 1936 to Percy Hammond after he panned the Harlem *Macbeth*, Orson pointed out that "my voodoo friends are still in New York. I can always get them together for a special event like this one . . . I'm not threatening you, I just thought I'd mention it." Having suffered when he had not pleased the general public, Orson felt it unjust that this time the critics weren't giving him credit for doing just that. "It's entertaining, and it gives the audience a lot of fun," Orson told the press, referring to the unmistakably enthusiastic response of the first few evenings' audiences. "But what did the critics do? They handled it as though it was an Ibsen play." Orson felt as if somehow he were eternally being criticized for having been too serious or else, as now, not serious enough.

But Orson was very serious about keeping the show running. It was inordinately expensive, however, and although it had its cultists who, as they had with *Horse Eats Hat*, bought tickets night after night, *Around The World* needed packed houses to continue. To raise additional money, Orson had added another radio commitment to the Lear broadcasts, *The Mercury Summer Theatre*. But finally nothing could save the show, which closed early in August. "Tragic news," Cole Porter called it, adding that Orson had "made more than human efforts to keep our poor little show running so long."

The money he had had to pour into *Around the World* when Mike Todd walked out had made it impossible for Orson to pay the first installment of the $197,500 for *It's All True*, for which he had given RKO a promissory note. Thus RKO successfully moved to foreclose on the chattel mortgage they held on the Brazilian footage, which had been put into storage in a Salt Lake City vault. Orson would never have another chance to retrieve and edit it. As if all this were not enough, there came a third misfortune when, suddenly, Brecht and Laughton announced that they had appointed, of all people, Mike Todd to produce *Galileo*. For Orson it was the bitterest stroke of all. In correspondence with Orson, Laughton accused him of "inevitable procrastination," a particularly unjust charge considering the immense personal and financial risks Orson had taken in order to be free to do *Galileo* in the fall as scheduled. And now Brecht had secured the services of the man whom Orson held responsible for having brought him to the edge of economic ruination.

It was only natural that Orson would angrily resist Laughton's suggestion that he direct the play with Mike Todd producing. Still Laughton said he hoped that Todd and Orson could work out their differences. Never having "spoken ill" of Orson, or so Laughton claimed, Todd had said only that he was rather "afraid" of him. But Orson was adamant. There was no question of his working with Todd, who had contributed to Orson's losing—as he put it with great bitterness—"more money than I'll be able to make for some time." Besides which, never would Orson have undertaken so immense a financial burden had he not been absolutely determined to do the Brecht play, which he had planned to begin rehearsing in Los Angeles that August. But now this would be impossible. Orson would have even more cause for bitterness when, shortly thereafter, on the basis of Todd's inept ideas for the play, Brecht decided against his doing *Galileo*—so that Orson's angrily pulling out had not been necessary after all. Nor could Orson fail to resent that, a decade later, Todd went on to make a great fortune from producing the film version of *Around the World in 80 Days*— the very property that, because of ensuing complications with the tax authorities, had financially done Orson in for some years to come.

Galileo, Around the World, the South American footage, and the *Post* column—all these had ended in disappointment. Orson's sense of loss in this period was compounded by still another: Lear Radios' decision in July of 1946 not

to take up their option on Orson's fifteen-minute weekly
broadcast, principally because they objected to what they
perceived as his stubborn insistence on political themes. It
was the same old litany. Although the sponsor had fled,
ABC agreed to continue the show on a sustaining basis until
a new sponsor was found (which never happened). Instead
of the $1,700 weekly salary Orson received from Lear Ra-
dios, however, he now grossed a pathetic fifty dollars per
show. Orson was advised that if he wanted to continue as
a political commentator he needed somehow to convince
listeners of his credibility, indeed of the special interest of
what he had to say. This obviously he had not yet done. An
analysis of his previous shows, in which he talked about
current politics with occasional digressions to his personal
experiences, suggested that he had actually alienated the
mass audience by intermittently describing a glamorous life
they could never hope to lead, in honeyed words they could
never hope to speak. The consultant who was brought in to
scrutinize Orson's show argued that Orson had to persuade
listeners of his moral courage, of his willingness to say what
others dared not say—and to say it plainly, so not to intimidate them with his verbal virtuosity. Quite simply, Orson
scared people—and in ways more subtle than his Martian
broadcast had done.

Then, at long last, and with a topic no one else dared
discuss on the air, Orson discovered his natural voice as a
political commentator. He found a way of effectively communicating, of powerfully dramatizing, his beliefs. Knowing Orson's sustained commitment to racial justice, and
hoping for some publicity, the NAACP had sent him an
affidavit signed by a black veteran, Isaac Woodard Jr., who
had served for fifteen months in the South Pacific and earned
one battle star. Just after his discharge, Woodard had been
the victim of an unprovoked police beating in South Carolina
on February 12 that had left him blind. Only after several
hours had passed did he receive medical treatment—but it

was too late. On Sunday July 28, 1946, two days after
Orson had first laid eyes on Woodard's testimony, listeners
to his Sunday radio show heard him begin, "I'd like to read
you an affidavit." Orson brilliantly dramatized the case by
inserting himself into it as a character who directly addressed
the unidentified police officer responsible for blinding the
black veteran: "Wash your hands, Officer X," Orson bellowed. "Wash them well. Scrub and scour." Orson turned
the case into a public mystery, which in turn he promised
to solve. "We will blast out your name. We'll give the world
your given name, Officer X. Yes, and your so-called Christian name." It was a stunning use of the potential of radio:
the audience could not but have been titillated by the knowledge that the faceless Officer X was listening to all this at
the very same moment as they. Most important—Orson used
the opportunity dramatically to create himself as the voice
of moral authority—all the more awe-inspiring for being
perfectly disembodied: "Officer X—after I have found you
out, I'll never lose you. If they try you, I'm going to watch
the trial. If they jail you, I'm going to wait for your first
day of freedom. You won't be free of me. . . . You can't get
rid of me. . . . Who am I? A masked avenger from the comic
books? No, sir. Merely an inquisitive citizen of America."

From week to week the drama persisted as Orson reported
new developments in the case, which, as a result of the
attention he had given it, had aroused nationwide concern.
To those who asked what business it was of Orson's to speak
openly of America's racial tensions, let alone to rout out
Officer X, he replied: "God judge me if it isn't the most
pressing business I have. The blind soldier fought for me
in this war. The least I can do now is fight for him. I have
eyes. He hasn't. I have a voice on the radio. He hasn't. I
was born a white man and until a colored man is a full
citizen like me I haven't the leisure to enjoy the freedom
that colored man risked his life to maintain for me. I don't
own what I have until he owns an equal share of it. Until

somebody beats me, and blinds me, I am in his debt. And so I come to this microphone not as a radio dramatist (although it pays better), not as a commentator (although it's safer to be simply that). I come, in that boy's name, and in the name of all who in this land of ours have no voice of their own. I come with a call to action."

Orson's passion brought forth equally strong reactions from his listeners. There was a spate of hate mail directed at him: "Please don't come to Georgia," wrote one listener, "we don't think it would be very healthy for you down this way." From Chicago: "I called up the Radio Station and they tel [sic] you are a Jew, which doubtless accounts for quite a bit in your broadcast." But the drama also aroused an ongoing search for the man responsible for blinding Woodard. The investigation was a dramatic device that Orson had used most effectively in the past—in particular, with *Kane*. Now Orson liked to include up-to-the-minute bulletins from the NAACP investigators—greatly to the consternation of the ABC censors, who repeatedly had trouble getting a finished script to vet even two hours before air time. Orson, however, was exhilarated by the sheer theatricality of improvising, of reworking at the very last minute.

His efforts finally paid off when, that September, the Department of Justice brought charges against the officer who had admitted beating Woodard. The NAACP wired Orson to tell him that, as a result of his broadcasts, he more than anyone else was responsible for the Justice Department's having moved in the case. But there was another way in which this had been a triumph for Orson. More than ever before he had spoken directly to the mass audience from whom he had felt himself cut off, and whom he had been longing to reach. Although he claimed not to be speaking as a "radio dramatist," it was precisely because of the drama with which he infused his broadcasts that they were so extraordinarily eloquent. This being so, the Woodard broadcasts constitute an important and little-known instance

of the art of Orson Welles. They also mark the virtual conclusion of Orson's career as a political commentator on
radio. For that September, Orson received word that ABC
could no longer continue his show on a sustaining basis.
His final broadcast was scheduled for October 6, 1946.
Assured and reassured that his getting kicked off the air had
nothing to do with the national race controversy he had
created, Orson suspected otherwise, especially in light of
the country's general swing to the right after Roosevelt's
death.

One quite positive result of the *Around the World* calamity
(although Orson did not regard it as especially fortunate at
that time) was his owing a picture to Harry Cohn, who had
lent him $25,000 for the show. The film that resulted, *The
Lady from Shanghai*, is an extraordinary artistic achievement that, unfortunately, has not found its proper place in
film history. With Cohn's approval, Orson had secured the
rights to Sherwood King's novel *If I Die Before I Wake* in
hopes of turning it into a suitable screenplay. Thus began
what would be Orson's fourth finished picture: *The Lady
from Shanghai*. Orson would pay back his loan out of the
money he earned for the picture: $2,000 weekly (for a total
of $24,000) plus an additional $100,000 if, and *only* if, it
made enough money at the box office to cover Columbia's
expenses. Finally, he was entitled to fifteen percent of the
picture's ultimate profits. It was not a very good deal for
debt-ridden Orson, since his only up-front money was the
weekly salary. At the time of the loan, Orson had agreed
to make a movie for Cohn that summer, but his appearance
in *Around the World*—which he had planned solely to direct—meant that shooting on Cohn's picture could not actually start until October of 1946. If Orson seemed especially
eager to finish the film as quickly and as cheaply as possible,
it was because, in the meantime, he had had what he considered to be an attractive offer to make three pictures for
Alexander Korda in England, for each of which he would

receive $75,000 plus a percentage of the gross. Orson was particularly inclined to accept the offer because of the sunny opportunity it afforded to work abroad, where, after the series of dismal disappointments with which he had met recently in the States, he hoped he might fare somewhat better. That September he contracted to start shooting for Korda January 1—"He was an absolutely superb man!" says Orson—so there was little time to lose on the picture he owed the less-appealing Harry Cohn.

The schedule called for Orson to have finished shooting the film for Cohn on December 23. From the first, however, there was substantial disagreement, as Cohn balked at Orson's idea to shoot on location in New York. A number of meetings at Columbia resulted in Orson's scouting locations in Mexico and San Francisco. Nor was Cohn receptive to Orson's plan to cast a young French girl he'd met and been intrigued by as the female lead. So intrigued had Orson been that, in time, he personally put her under contract (not to the studio, but to *him*) *and* paid for English lessons. Cohn left the girl's private tutoring to Orson. It was Rita whom the mogul already had firmly in mind to star opposite Orson in *The Lady from Shanghai*. There was a certain irony in Cohn's seeking to reunite the couple now, when in the past he had sought to keep them apart. But their appearing together would be splendid publicity for the film—which on account of Rita's participation would have to be far grander in scale than Orson had initially envisioned. Cohn was sure things were really finished between them, and so they seemed to be. Although Orson and Rita were still married, when Orson went out to California to discuss *The Lady from Shanghai*, there had been no question of his staying with her. Rita was just then settling into a lovely new home on Rockingham Road in Brentwood that had been smartly appointed by Wilbur Menefee. A Columbia set director, Menefee's services had been provided as a bonus from Harry

Cohn, who could only have been delighted by Rita's setting up her own establishment.

On arrival in Los Angeles, Orson had checked into the Bel Air Hotel, where he fully expected, and Cohn expected him, to remain. But Rita had other ideas. After Orson had accepted her starring in *The Lady from Shanghai*, she suddenly called Menefee to say that Orson would be staying with her presently. Nor did Orson find himself relegated to a guest room. Rita explained to Menefee that while the bed he had made for her was absolutely perfect for *one* person, something much larger would be necessary for the two of them (especially considering Orson's bad back).

Orson had never stopped loving her. Remembering vividly the many nights he had found her in tears when he came home (even before their marriage had begun to go awry), Orson was filled with sadness and guilt when she suddenly told him now, "You know, the only happiness I've ever had in my life has been with you." It seemed to him to be a terrible commentary on Rita's experience: "If that was happiness," he says, "imagine what the rest of her life had been." He felt himself again wanting to protect her, to give her whatever small measure of happiness he could. Although at first he had been apprehensive about Rita's starring in his picture, he saw now that it meant a great deal to her. She hoped Orson's directing her might cause people to take her acting seriously, to treat her as more than just a love goddess. The cynics who speculated that the Welleses' reunion was a mere publicity stunt were wrong. Unintentionally, Harry Cohn had played Cupid. Hundreds of Orson's books arrived at Rockingham Road, where a room was quickly converted into his private study. Although, as Orson says, Rita wanted the part in *The Lady from Shanghai* as a chance to do some serious acting, another of her motives must have been the possibility of reconciling with Orson.

After all, as if anxious not to make a *final* break, she had persistently hesitated to complete the property settlement her lawyers had taken such trouble to draw up.

When they went to shoot on location in Acapulco, Orson gave Rita a lavish birthday dinner—complete with an orchestra and two singers—at the Hotel de las Americas. One of the guests there was Errol Flynn, on whose famous yacht, the *Zaca*, the film was being shot. Orson recalls that it was with Flynn on the *Zaca* that he first tried cocaine. The experience thrilled him beyond his expectations. Orson muses that if he had had another life to live he might have given himself over to cocaine. But knowing that *this* was his only life, he figured that he had better abstain, which from then on he did. The trip to Acapulco was not entirely pleasant; one by one, the members of the company were stricken with dysentery. Worst of all, one of the technicians had died of a heart attack shortly after arriving—an event that cast a general gloom over the days that followed. Nor could Orson devote himself entirely to Rita, for seven-year-old Christopher Welles was there too. Since he had not spent much time with her for a while, Orson had sent for his first daughter, who arrived in Acapulco with her nanny. Christopher was not always well behaved. Once while Orson was shooting, she threw a tantrum, stamping her feet and crying that she wanted to be in the movie too. Finally Orson had had enough. Indeed, she could be in the movie, he promised. She was to play a little American girl, a *brat* eating an ice-cream cone. Then, handing her a cone, he instructed her to begin eating it. "Okay! Ready! Action! Camera!" he shouted, as the cameraman pretended to film her.

Shortly after the shooting in Acapulco was over, Orson and Rita took a week's break in Mexico with Skipper and Hortense Hill. It was like old times. Skipper had brought with him a tiny plane in which he and Orson flew above the coast, while the women waited below. Orson had taken to wearing the Navy pea jacket and T-shirt that were part of his costume as the handsome Irish rogue he played in the film. He had not looked so fit in a long time, for he had spent many hours in the steam and massage rooms at the Biltmore Baths in New York in hopes of retrieving the proper figure for a dashing romantic lead. Perhaps he looked the part a bit too much. Passing through customs at Tijuana, Orson was harassed by an MP who apparently mistook him for the sailor he was dressed as. And because Orson had gone through a wrong door, he found himself hit in the stomach with a nightstick, then further manhandled by three additional MPs who had heeded the whistled summons of the first. The MPs never found out who the victim of their bullying was, for Orson refrained from complaining to the authorities lest he encourage rumors that he had been drunk.

It was a pity that the short vacation had ended with so stressful an incident. Orson had enough on his mind already. Even as he filmed *The Lady from Shanghai*, he was planning the pictures he was to make for Korda. First he would do Stevenson's *The Master of Ballantrae*, he told himself, then *Carmen* with Paulette Goddard. But early that fall, Korda had excitedly wired him that he had secured the rights to Oscar Wilde's *Salome*. Since there was a problem with prior registration of the Stevenson book, why not start with Wilde? Orson agreed at once, but sorely wanted Olivier to play Herod. According to Korda, however, the role Olivier really longed to do was not Herod, but Cyrano. This news of course triggered Orson's memories of his own abortive *Cyrano* project: it was this that he wanted to do as his second picture, although Korda tried to coax him back to the idea of *Carmen*. But what really was the point of their haggling over Orson's second picture when his first had yet to be made? To this end, Korda had dispatched a scenarist to accompany Orson on the Mexican shoot. It is difficult to say where Orson possibly found the time to work with Korda's man, but before long there was a script, to which eventually Orson hoped to append a version of Wilde's *The*

Happy Prince. Although Orson had initially hoped to cast Vivien Leigh as Salome, he was unable to, and his thoughts strayed to the young French actress still under contract to him at $350 weekly. Korda, however, had his own obscure young actress in mind; but on seeing her photograph, Orson protested that she lacked the "quality of [the] perverse little girl, which Salome must have." This heated transatlantic exchange seemed pointless when it became obvious that Orson would not be finished with *The Lady from Shanghai* in time to start *Salome* on January 1, so the project was postponed until at least the spring of 1947.

A strike at Columbia had inevitably held things up, as had Rita's state of exhaustion, which culminated in her collapsing on the set in December. Lovely as she may have appeared in the publicity photos showing Orson clipping her trademark long red tresses in preparation for the film (in which she wore her famous hair short and tinted blonde), behind the scenes her poor health kept her from working to capacity, much to the detriment of the picture's shooting schedule. Both Orson and Rita were ill that Christmas of 1946. Indeed it was necessarily a lean holiday for debt-ridden Orson, who had to repress his lavish generosity. Instead friends received only a program for the defunct *Around the World* and the message: "This is a souvenir of the expensive reason why the (otherwise deliriously happy) O. Welles family cannot this year wish you Merry Christmas with flowers or anything except this." Orson had not allowed his abysmal finances to keep him from giving Rita, among other things, four sheer nightgowns from Saks, a sheer half-nightie and a negligee-nightgown from Juel Parks, a sterling-silver milk jug for her bedside, and an ounce of a very expensive Egyptian perfume, however.

If Orson had given Rita exactly what she wanted that Christmas, he did not do the same for Harry Cohn, who had expected a finished film. Nor was Cohn satisfied when he *did* get the picture, rather belatedly, in March of 1947.

By then *The Lady from Shanghai* was $416,421.92 over budget. Even worse, as Orson suspected, Cohn could not understand the movie, which, as if in reaction to *The Stranger*, was probably Orson's most disorienting to date. Gravely disappointed at not having been able to work with Brecht, Orson had, by way of compensation, made a film that very subtly embodied key principles of Brechtian theatrical theory: most notably the actor's distance from his role, which also prohibits the spectator's identification with the action. Orson's having recently read and assimilated Brecht in preparation for their collaboration explains the peculiar presence of the otherwise incongruous (and hitherto mysterious) Chinese theater sequence toward the end of *The Lady from Shanghai*. In that sequence, Orson's sailor boy, Michael, while fleeing from the police, slips into the auditorium of a Chinese theater, where a performance is under way onstage. If at first Michael seems distinctly out of place among the entirely Oriental audience, the other members of the audience seem surprisingly unfazed by his presence — even when he is joined by the femme fatale Elsa (Rita Hayworth). In a celebrated essay on Chinese acting (published in English translation in 1936) Brecht had argued persuasively that the Chinese theater epitomized his theory of "the alienation effect." Because of the alienated style of acting employed in Chinese theater, "the audience can no longer have the illusion of being the unseen spectator at the event." But, most ironically, this is exactly what Michael has come to this particular Chinese theater to be: an *unseen spectator*. In light of Brecht, the auditorium of a Chinese theater is the last place the fugitive should have picked in which to hide.

Brecht's essay also explains why, when Michael and Elsa talk rather loudly and conspicuously to each other, no one turns around to hush them, for according to Brecht, since it prohibits passive identification with the action onstage, the alienated acting of the Chinese theater is perfectly tol-

erant of interruptions and disturbances. Whereas in a typical
Western theater the spectators would undoubtedly be furious
if the illusion onstage were violated by fellow members of
the audience, according to Brecht this would not be so in
the Chinese theater, where neither the actor nor the spectator
is in a trance. Perhaps the most extraordinary moment in
the sequence occurs when police storm the theater. Brecht
writes that the Chinese actor occasionally looks directly at
the audience, even as he continues his performance—and
so it is in this sequence when the police arrive. The Chinese
actor onstage casts them a curious glance but continues
acting. In a desperate attempt to remain an *unseen spectator*,
the fugitive puts on a performance of his own, as he and
his companion lock in a lovers' embrace intended to conceal
them from the police. In the heat of its pretend passion, it
is quite a different sort of performance from the coolly
distanced one that continues onstage. Brecht argues that the
Chinese actor's performance is never "heated"—as this mock-
lovers' parody of onscreen romance surely is. In fact, *The
Lady from Shanghai* generally maintains so rigorous a distance from the emotions it depicts that an amorous embrace
like this can perhaps *only* be parodic.

In a sense the Chinese theater sequence illuminates the
distinctly odd—almost chilly—acting style that permeates
the film as a whole. Under Orson's careful direction, so
strangely distanced are the performances in general that, in
what has often been taken as a major artistic defect of the
film, it is rather difficult for audiences to identify with them.
"The artist's object is to appear strange and even surprising
to the audience," writes Brecht of the Chinese actor—a
notion that might equally apply to the singularly strange
performances one discovers in *The Lady from Shanghai*.
The Chinese theater sequence is then Orson's distinctly ironic
indication that this *strangeness* is hardly ineptitude (as many
spectators, critics among them, have mistakenly presumed)
but fully intentional: an exploration of the artistic possibil-

ities of the sort of alienated acting that is so clearly anti-thetical to the naturalistic style that Hollywood held to be the norm, and that Orson had used rather uncritically in *The Stranger*. If *The Lady from Shanghai* has been generally underrated in film history, it is in part because its expressly Brechtian aspirations have been consistently overlooked. An awareness of the filmmaker's subtle application of Brechtian theory makes it possible historically to assimilate this major film as it has not been in the past.

Harry Cohn was surely no connoisseur of film style, so that Orson ascribes much of the mogul's agitation to his utter incomprehension of the picture's "shock effects": "The shock effects were unknown movie devices at that period," says Orson. "They'd had them earlier and they had them later to some extent, but *that* was the period when movies were at their most homogenized. And of course that would have had to do with it." In a memo to Cohn, Orson suggested that he had hoped for "something off-center, queer, strange"; to give the entire film a "bad dream aspect." "Our story escapes the 'cliché,'" he warned, "only if the performances and the production are *original*, or at least, somewhat *oblique*." To keep the film "from being just another who-dunit," Orson argued, would require the "quality of *freshness* and *strangeness*" with which he had tried to imbue it. Queer? Oblique? Strange? To Harry Cohn these were pe-jorative words. But influenced as he was by Brecht's way of thinking, Orson saw strangeness as a criterion of artistic value precisely as Brecht did. Orson's repeated reference to strangeness in the memo to Cohn is further evidence of how much Brecht's theories were on his mind at this time. (Not that he expected Cohn to recognize the allusion!)

Brecht is generally thought to have acquired this privi-leged term in his theoretical vocabulary from the Russian formalist critic Viktor Shklovsky's key concept of estrange-ment (*ostraneniye*) in art, whereby the artist views things from a new, and therefore especially revealing, angle. But so *entirely* new is this angle that the spectator may take some time to adjust himself to its utter strangeness. (Much as the spectator of the famous hall-of-mirrors sequence in *The Lady from Shanghai* finds himself initially unable to gauge just where the characters are—or, more important, who has shot whom. Showing the climactic chase to the death in the multiple and fragmented images of a "crazy house" hall of mirrors in an amusement park was Orson's *original*—and, quite literally, *oblique*—way of imbuing the cinematic convention of the chase sequence with what is here its eloquent *strangeness*.) For Shklovsky, and in turn for Brecht, the process of estrangement applies *both* to form and to content: that is, it is not simply reality (content) that is viewed afresh in the successful work of art, but art (form) itself. The artist must do away with artistic clichés, stale modes of perception, by inventing forms capable of viewing the world in original, oblique, perhaps somewhat startling ways. These ideas, which Orson had assimilated through Brecht, are clearly echoed in what had been his hopes for *The Lady from Shanghai* as he expressed them in the memo to Cohn.

For all the impossibility of communicating his ideas to Cohn, Orson says, "I had a curious respect for him." Notwithstanding Cohn's ensuing efforts to ruin his picture, Orson found himself terribly amused by something Cohn said of their unhappy business relationship: "'Well, it's taught me one lesson,'" Orson recalls Cohn's having said. "'Never have a leading man who's the director, 'cause you can't fire the director!'" "I kind of liked him for it," says Orson of Cohn's quip. "I always had a soft spot for him at his worst. He always struck me as funnier than he was frightening. You know Billy Wilder's great joke—the greatest Hollywood one-liner ever made. Cohn had this *huge* funeral. Nobody ever had such a big turnout as for Harry Cohn. Billy Wilder says, 'Well, give the people what they want!'"

The basically negative reaction of the preview spectators confirmed Cohn's dismay with *Lady from Shanghai*. It was Pomona all over again. Says Orson: "All the changes that were really made were made after the preview with this terrible woman that he brought in. . . . I sat with him and said yes to everything she said. And then when I was alone with her I fought like a tiger and lost most of the battles." Orson attributes her apparent compulsion to alter the footage, even when he was clearly able to show her that something was best as it was, to her sense of herself as having been hired for the film "to show that she'd made it different." Although the preview spectators had indicated that they liked the music Orson had temporarily affixed to the film, the studio somewhat perversely concocted an entirely new score that, according to Orson, has "nothing to do with what's going on. It's as though you were playing a radio while you were sitting and watching the movie, playing Muzak or something." Although Orson had hoped to have some input in the selection of the music, this the studio flatly denied him: "See, I wasn't even there when they scored it!" Given Orson's antipathy to what he considered to be Disney's kitsch tendencies, it is not surprising that when he complained to Cohn about the new score he explicitly evoked Disney. Thus, of the music that now accompanies a shot of Rita Hayworth diving, Orson lamented that it might be more suitable for "a pratfall by Pluto the Pup, or a wild jump into space by Donald Duck"—but not for *The Lady from Shanghai*. In retrospect, Orson points out that all in all the studio's approach to the film he had turned in was to "pay no attention to what the director says, which of course has been the rallying cry of this town since the beginning of celluloid, you know. The director is the big boss until the picture is over and then see what you can do to screw him up!" Fortunately, the mutilation of *Lady from Shanghai* was far less extensive than that of *Ambersons* had been. "He took about twenty percent off the picture," Orson says of Harry Cohn's handiwork. "It's about twenty percent less than it would have been, maybe a little more—"

Orson suspects that, in addition to wanting to eliminate some of the film's more blatant *shock effects*, Cohn may have had another reason for cutting up his film. "This was a *Rita Hayworth* picture," says Orson, "and Harry Cohn felt a tremendous proprietary sense for Rita. And I think part of all that was to try to make it something that wasn't my picture. No matter what. I think that's part of the explanation." If Orson's having lost artistic control of yet another film left him understandably disappointed, Rita was in even gloomier spirits when she realized that the public had not taken her appearance in the film as seriously as she had hoped: "I thought she was great in it," says Orson, "and she was proud to be in it and all that. And then everybody treated her as though she'd been slumming, you know, and so they didn't give her *that* satisfaction!"

One bit of secret satisfaction that Orson had from his film was artistically settling a score with a powerful political enemy of his: "*He* always called everybody 'fella,' " says Orson of Nelson Rockefeller, "and I used that for Glenn Anders in *Lady from Shanghai*. In fact Glenn Anders was doing kind of a parody of Nelson Rockefeller and Glen looked a little like him, so it was perfect!" The character Anders plays in the film is a duplicitous villain—a lawyer, actually—who bullies Orson's naive Irishman (whom he persistently calls *fella*) into a scheme that will presumably benefit the sailor boy, but that, at length, nearly destroys him, exactly as Orson perceived Rockefeller to have done to him: "I thought he was the one who really let me down. Because the movie companies you *expect* to, but I really didn't expect to be scuttled by him." Nor does the sailor boy in *Lady from Shanghai* expect to be scuttled by the Rockefeller look-alike to whom he plays the "fall guy." There is even an explicit reference to Fortaleza in *The Lady from Shanghai*, when Michael describes having been fishing there and the sharks' devouring each other precisely as the lawyer and his equally grotesque partner (as played by Everett Sloane) do. Rockefeller, Fortaleza, sharks—these allusions suggest that *The Lady from Shanghai* contained within it Orson's ironic meditation on what he rightly considered the most terrible episode in his career. Hence the film's underlying theme of guilt and innocence: as *The Lady from Shanghai* ends, the sailor boy, having been proved innocent of a crime he did not commit, contemplates his still somehow being considered guilty. This was Orson's present plight as he saw it: widely thought to be wasteful and rebellious, it seemed to him that he had vindicated himself with the footage he had brought back from Rio and, more important, with his concession to Hollywood, *The Stranger*.

CHAPTER 29
Desperate Adventure

"In his best vein he can make Ernest Hemingway seem like a Vassar girl in a daisy chain," asserted Orson in trying to persuade Harry Cohn to bankroll a picture that he wanted to direct based on Prosper Merimée's *Carmen*. Since Merimée's name was sure to mean nothing to Harry Cohn, who would have automatically associated the title *Carmen* with its opera, Orson described the French writer as "the James Cain–Raymond Chandler of his time." It was not what he called "the operatic dilution" that Orson wanted to do on-screen, but what he saw as "the original melodrama of blood, violence, and passion." The rhetoric of his sales pitch to Cohn suggests that for once Orson really knew his audience. By now he had figured out that the money men liked their narratives quick and simple—hence his strategic description of Carmen as a last-moving story, hard-boiled and modern." And figuring that Cohn was always alert to new uses for Rita, Orson pointed out that *Carmen* was "a great star vehicle"—there was no need to name the star he had in mind. But when in 1948 Rita did indeed appear in a Columbia picture called *The Loves of Carmen*, Orson would not be the director. Harry Cohn's dissatisfaction with

The Lady from Shanghai put an end to his willingness to invest in Orson, who was forced to look for cash elsewhere.

By the time *Lady from Shanghai* was finished Orson also had to look for someplace else to live, since his and Rita's attempted reconciliation had gone awry. Not that they had not earnestly tried to repair their marriage. As late as January of 1947, they had both applied for passports in anticipation of Orson's working for Korda in England that spring. Planning to accompany her husband for a month or longer, Rita had scheduled meetings with several British producers to explore the possibilities of working in films there. Orson had also requested passports for Christopher and her governess so that they might join him in London for a holiday.

But none of this was to be. The old problems with Rita began almost the moment they had finished working together on *Lady from Shanghai*. As her director, Orson had been focused on her in the single-minded way she liked—but when that attention ceased, so did their marital happiness. Rita accused Orson of seeing other women, and Orson felt as helpless and guilty as he had in the past. Once again, his bewildered response to her seemingly uncontrollable jealousy was to do exactly what she accused him of: to turn to other women. When she decided to go through with the divorce once and for all, he did nothing to stop her. He could not bear to have caused so much pain to a woman he had loved so much.

In March, Korda wired him that it would not be possible to begin *Salome* April 1 as they had planned. A somewhat startled Orson learned that, at the very earliest, he might be able to start shooting at the end of July. Once again, just when everything had seemed so promising, the ground had fallen out from under him. The studio had taken over—and torn apart—his brilliant new film. Korda had told him not to bother coming to London for a time. And he had lost Rita.

After Rita threw him out, Orson installed himself in a

beach house next door to the palatial Marion Davies estate,
where his first wife, Virginia, and her husband, Charles
Lederer, were living. In the past, earnestly trying to protect
the best interests of Virginia and, particularly, of Christopher, Lederer had had angry run-ins with Orson, whom he
accused of not living up to the divorce settlement. Now, in
the unlikeliest of turnarounds, Orson and the witty, intelligent Lederer became great chums. Lederer even jokingly
admitted to Orson that some of his original animosity toward
him had been resentment of Virginia's famous first husband:
the abstract villain who had so shamed his Aunt Marion. "I
liked them together," says Orson of the Lederers, with whom
he entered into a friendly relationship that he describes as
a "strange design for living at the beach." There was an
occasional awkwardness, however, particularly when Aunt
Marion came to call. "You see, he'd have Marion Davies
for dinner," Orson recalls. "Virginia would say, 'Now you
stay away. Don't be seen.' And so I'd come up to the window
where their dinner table was, with my coat collar up as
though it were snowing outside, and just stare in at them
eating."

Korda's postponement of *Salome* made Orson think of
two other offers he had had recently but not considered
seriously. One was a proposal from the British producer
Sidney Bernstein to direct a film of *King Lear* (a play Orson
had vainly hoped to do one night a week with his *Around
the World* cast); the other was an inquiry from the American
National Theatre and Academy (ANTA) in New York about
Orson's directing something at the Utah Centennial Festival
in Salt Lake City. ANTA wanted him in May, however, and
by then of course he had planned to be abroad doing *Salome*.
Luckily, Utah was persistent, and suggested that he stage
Lear as one of the festival's four productions. This fortuitous
pair of offers suggested distinct possibilities to Orson, especially now that he would not in fact be starting *Salome*
in April as he had anticipated. As a film director it had been

Orson's custom to rehearse his cast extensively before shooting. Now it occurred to him to adumbrate the movie he
might make of *Lear* with a stage production in Salt Lake
City. The concept posed both practical and aesthetic problems: it would be exceedingly difficult and expensive to
haul Orson's production across the ocean. And Orson would
have to decide which, if either, of the two productions
should take precedence. Obviously he was not about to
inform Utah that its production was basically a dress rehearsal for a film; or London, that its was to be a bit of
canned theater. Saying that the two productions fed into
each other would not be entirely honest. Before he knew
much about film, it had seemed perfectly acceptable to
Orson to film a theatrical performance (and to claim it was
a *film*)—but not so now. Initially it might have seemed that
Orson was disposed to regard the theatrical production as
the more important of the two, since he decided to focus
his energies on the Utah festival, although he accepted their
offer with the stipulation that it was *Macbeth* that he do,
not *Lear*. This particular play had worked so well in his
New York directorial debut that it seemed lucky to him, and
luck was what he needed to execute his rather complicated
and ambitious plans for this new production. For if one had
thought that Orson was abandoning the idea of doing a
Shakespeare film, one would have been wrong. The coincidence of the two offers had given him an interesting idea.
He would rehearse and run his play in Salt Lake City and
film it, shortly thereafter, not in London, but in Hollywood.
Having worked out his concept onstage, he would be able
to work with unusual economy in Hollywood. Hence the
raison d'être of Orson's fifth finished picture: to show once
and for all that Hollywood could actually earn a profit on
serious film fare.

Orson's pitch to Harry Cohn about the "strong commercial
aspects" of *Carmen* epitomized his determination to sell
Hollywood on the potential profitability of quality pictures.

Even if at first there was only a small serious audience for this *Macbeth*, the film would have been made cheaply enough to make money nonetheless. This was to be precisely the sort of cinematic experiment Orson had protested the money men were not willing to back. Perhaps if they saw that an experiment like this could be profitable, they would change their minds. In addition, Orson would be able to free himself from his reputation for profligacy and wastefulness—for just now Harry Cohn was making much ado of Orson's having gone wildly over budget on *The Lady from Shanghai*. Not that Orson planned to repress his own artistic inclinations as he had in *The Stranger*. Within the very strict limitations of time and budget he imposed upon himself, he would make a *Macbeth* absolutely as expressive—and eccentric—as he wished.

Orson did not, however, delude himself into thinking that his *Macbeth* would be a work of art of the magnitude of *Kane*. This time, his aspiration was more modest, more practical, than anything he would have conceived of doing when he had first come to Hollywood. Now, having lost his innocence, Orson had accepted the necessity of the Hollywood director's paying as much attention to economics as to self-expression. Hollywood had not been willing to invest in a Shakespeare picture since the disaster of Reinhardt's *Midsummer Night's Dream* in 1935. But the healthy box office for Olivier's *Henry V* in 1944 made it quite feasible for Orson to seek money for his *Macbeth*. Olivier had shown that the movie audience would come out for the Bard. Otherwise Orson probably would not have dared to hope for Hollywood backing, which, at length, he found in perhaps the least likely of places: Republic Pictures, known mainly for horse operas starring the likes of Roy Rogers, Gene Autry, and Johnny Mack Brown. "I went there because I figured it would be cheaper," says Orson. "Everybody would be used to working faster." For their part, Republic was not especially interested in Orson's rather high-toned project of somehow raising Hollywood's cultural level; but if he could indeed make *Macbeth* as cheaply as he genuinely seemed to want to, and if perhaps he could reach a hitherto untapped film audience in the process, he might succeed in finding a new way for Hollywood to make money—and that seemed appealing. And although there was abundant laughter in Hollywood at the very idea of Orson's having wound up at a plebeian studio like Republic, Orson thought it ideal for his experiment.

Thus, he was in the very best of spirits as he embarked upon his pair of *Macbeth*s, the leads of which would appear in both, while the rest of the cast would be different in Salt Lake City and Hollywood. He had to move quickly now. The Utah production was set for May, and Orson's proposed twenty-one days of filming would start that June. Orson cast himself as Macbeth—after all, he had played it in black-face when, in Indianapolis, Jack Carter's replacement had taken ill—and, when neither Geraldine Fitzgerald nor Tallulah Bankhead was available for Lady Macbeth, he settled upon Jeanette Nolan, with whom he had first worked on radio's *March of Time*. Orson explained that the entire production would be delivered in a Scottish burr, a challenge he knew would particularly delight the versatile Miss Nolan, who loved to mimic dialects. Two of his more curious casting decisions were made for the small parts of the film version: Shorty was Macbeth's "personal attendant," Seyton—a role that he could play from life; and Christopher was Macduff's son. Little Christopher had harped on his giving her a role during the film's preparations until finally Orson relented, but since there were no parts for little girls, he explained, she would have to play a boy. That was all right with Christopher, who received one hundred and fifteen dollars weekly.

Having rehearsed his principal actors in Los Angeles, Orson took them to Salt Lake City, where they were joined for further rehearsals by the locals from the university, who

rounded out the cast. But for Orson the Utah festival production was itself only a foreshadowing of the movie. However warm its reception, Orson could not help but regard it
critically in terms of the screen images it would yield. Thus,
for instance, Orson decided to change entirely the costume
Dan O'Herlihy had worn in Utah as Macduff, which made
his "pot belly" much too prominent. Something of an expert
on this particular problem, Orson recommended a heavy
corset and padding in O'Herlihy's upper chest and shoulders
to compensate for what Orson complained of in a memo as
"no muscles whatsoever." Furthermore, Orson lamented of
O'Herlihy that "after one step he starts to crack at the
seams"—a problem Orson hoped to solve with a costume
specially designed "so that he can't bulge or sag." And as
for Roddy McDowall as Malcolm, Orson noted that his
costume "should suggest the young prince rather than the
third page boy from the left. That's what he looked like in
Salt Lake City."

When Orson began shooting late in June of 1947, the talk
at certain Hollywood dinner parties often strayed to whether
he would stick to his $884,367 budget and his twenty-one-
day schedule. The precedent of *The Stranger* notwithstanding, the odds were against him. Orson worked relentlessly
to finish *Macbeth* on time and, as it turned out, substantially
under budget. He only seemed to let up for the revivifying
massages of a powerful chap named Abdullah. For Christopher, these were hardly the idyllic hours with Daddy she
had hoped for. Orson was much too preoccupied to keep
her from becoming frightfully bored on a hot indoor set that
reeked of urine from the picture's horses. Fortunately, there
was a little boy actor with whom she could steal away to
watch the B Western being shot on the next set. At which
miraculous vision Christopher mused about why her father
couldn't be making an interesting movie like that.

"I had Duke Wayne on the set all the time, all through
Macbeth, watching!" says Orson, who was not unaware of,

or unamused by, the incongruity of his own presence at Republic. "I had only one day with a big extra call," he begins a joke he likes to tell about his experience at Republic. "So I did two things. I had two cameramen dressed up as extras, with cameras, moving around among them. And then, when they had to charge the castle, which they were loathe to do because it required a little energy and moving, I shouted, 'Lunch!' And what you see when everybody charges the castle is everybody running off to eat lunch. They were special Republic extras who hadn't been asked to do anything, you know, in forty years. 'Lunch!' "

The president of Republic Pictures Corporation, Herbert J. Yates, could not fail to be impressed by Orson's achievement in *Macbeth*, and wrote to tell him so, once shooting was done. Indeed never in his thirty-four years in show business had he been *so* impressed as by Orson. The entire film industry had been watching Orson's experiment, Yates told him, and he had proved an "inspiration" to them all. Yates congratulated Orson on having "demonstrated beyond a doubt" that a "superior product," as Yates called it, could be made economically and profitably. And in case Orson did not already know it, *Macbeth* was, Yates assured him, "the greatest individual job of acting, directing, adapting and producing that to my knowledge Hollywood has ever seen."

All that remained was the post-production work. But surely there would be no problem given the impeccable manner in which Orson had handled himself thus far. And surely after working under such intense pressure to finish filming Orson deserved the therapeutic trip to Europe that he planned to take during the preparation of the rough cut. That trip was not all pleasure though; one stop on his itinerary was London, where he would see Sir Alexander Korda to discuss the pictures that they still anticipated making together, although by now it was *Cyrano* they particularly wanted to do first. In London, Korda told Orson that Laurence Olivier

and Ralph Richardson would be thrilled to have Orson Welles
join them on the London stage. "They would just love it!"
Orson recalls Korda's having told him. "It would be like
the three musketeers!" Today Orson is dubious that he would
have received as warm a welcome from Olivier and Richardson as Korda imagined: "You know," says Orson, "Korda
in his innocence—and he had a big slice of it because he
was so in love with actors and impressed by them in a way
that only Middle Europeans are—kept saying to me, 'You
must come to work with Larry and Ralph, who will be
delighted to give you the great roles! They're doing too
many things anyway. They will want you here!' *Want me!*
I've listened to the stories from them—how they were fighting *each other* for the next play, but he really believed they
would just say, 'Oh, how marvelous! Now we have Orson!'
I would have been tripped up with piano wires by Larry the
first night!"

Eager to work with Korda, Orson was not very encour-
aging to the representatives of director Gregory Ratoff, who
approached him to star in a movie titled *Cagliostro* (*Black
Magic*) to be filmed in Italy. Even if *Cyrano* or any of the
other projects he discussed with Korda did not materialize,
surely Orson's having been an "inspiration" to the rest of
Hollywood would get him other directing jobs, and directing
was what he mainly wanted to do. It looked as if, with
Macbeth, Orson had finally changed his image—or would,
once the post-production work was finished, and he planned
to take care of that the moment he returned from Europe.

But Orson had not been back in the States for long when
Republic began to suspect that something was amiss. The
editing seemed to drag on in a sluggish manner, and Orson
appeared not to be spending as much time at the studio as
the management felt he should have. To make matters worse,
it seemed that Orson was leaving for Europe again. His
dismal finances, and Korda's further postponement of *Cyrano*, had led him to change his mind about *Cagliostro* after

all, in preparation for which flamboyant role he swiftly
undertook a regimen of fencing lessons. But instead of all
this parrying and thrusting they heard about, Republic wanted
him to finish cutting his film. Before he left for Italy, Orson
did have time for a brief affair with twenty-one-year-old
Marilyn Monroe, who was still an obscure Hollywood star-
let. One night at a crowded Hollywood party, Orson had
repaired to an upstairs bedroom with Marilyn, to whom he
was making love when a jealous husband, mistakenly thinking that his wife was inside with Orson Welles, banged open
the door. The raving brute threw a solid punch to the side
of Orson's head before discovering that he had made a
terrible mistake.

When, having wrapped up his fencing lessons and his
affair with Marilyn, Orson departed for Rome, he left his
latest partner, Richard Wilson, behind in Hollywood to supervise post-production on *Macbeth*. Republic was thrown
into a fit of agitation. It was almost as if, in some subliminal
way, Orson had felt compelled to repeat the grave mistake
he had made in leaving *Ambersons* unfinished in the hands
of Jack Moss. If Orson had proceeded blindly in taking off
for Rio when he had not completed *Ambersons*, and if he
had lived to regret his error in doing so, this time he certainly
should have known better. Having worked so feverishly to
come in on schedule and under budget, both of which he
had unquestionably succeeded in doing, why possibly would
he want to blow it all now? The fact was that, as far as
Orson was concerned, *Macbeth was* in a sense finished—
not as a film, of course, but as an experiment. In *Macbeth*
Orson had never intended to make a great film; just to prove
a point, to show what could be shot quickly and cheaply.
Having come in on schedule and under budget, he had fully
worked out the artistic problem he had set for himself, and
that was that. Since his experiment had involved the efficient
shooting of a quality picture, he really saw no reason why
the post-production work he had planned could not be left

to other hands in his absence. It was only natural that Republic should see things differently. The studio took no
comfort in Orson's intention to put the finishing touches on
Macbeth in Italy once the basic post-production work was
finished; they wanted him to finish it now.

In Rome where he installed himself in grand style at the
Excelsior, Orson seemed far more worried about the supply
of false noses he had inadvertently left in Hollywood than
about his unfinished picture. Until he received a package
of noses from home he would somehow have to conserve
the ones he had. Without Shorty there to attend to him,
Orson was somewhat at loose ends, and frantically wired
home that he could not find his Proloid diet pills or his
Dexedrine, both of which Shorty was supposed to have
packed for him. By return wire Dadda explained how Orson
could get the pills in Rome until he received the supply that
had been mailed to him. Orson was in control again by the
time he began work on Ratoff's *Cagliostro*. Evidently he
was rather more in control than he was supposed to be. A
visitor to the set one day was surprised to see Orson on top
of a coach directing a grand mob scene populated by numerous extras in costumes. "Where is Grisha?" inquired the
visitor of the whereabouts of the Russian-born director.
"*There* he is," called Orson, pointing to the mob of extras,
a fully costumed Gregory Ratoff among them. An easygoing
director who adored Orson, Ratoff seemed perfectly content
to let his friend Orson take charge now and then.

Orson's particularly expansive mood in this period is indicated by a strange scene that occurred one afternoon in
the lobby of the Excelsior, where Jackson Leighter heard
him authoritatively lecturing a trio of stunned red-robed
cardinals on, of all topics, Catholicism. When finally Orson
had bid them farewell Leighter heard one of the cardinals
mutter that somehow Orson knew more about Catholicism
than they did! What these princes of the church could not

have known was that back in the States, Catholicism had been one of the subjects on which Orson had paid his researchers to feed him raw data. Although no project had come of the information he had assimilated, his interlude with the cardinals had afforded him an excellent opportunity to invent himself in the unlikely guise of an ecclesiastical expert.

But, according to Orson, the cardinals were far from his most significant encounter with the Church while he was in Rome, for in his capacity as a famous actor and director he was granted an audience with Pope Pius XII. "Pope Pius XII had hands like lizards," Orson laughs. "They were as dry and hot as lizards. They gave off almost a palpable vibration—he had such a strong papal personality!" But what did Orson and Pope Pius talk about? "I had forty-five minutes alone with him," says Orson. "He held my hand and never let it go. There we sat alone, and he said, 'Is it true that Irene Dunne is contemplating divorce? What do you think of Ty Power's marriage coming up?' All the *hot stuff* from Hollywood is what we discussed."

Not all of Orson's Rome encounters were of a spiritual nature. "I was chased all over Italy by Charles Luciano—known as 'Lucky' by ignorant newspaper readers," says Orson. But why would the famous gangland figure want to talk to Orson Welles? "In order to persuade me to make the true story of his life," says Orson. "He thought I should do it. I should write it and direct it and act it. I could elevate him to the proper position historically." But the sort of crime with which Orson was preoccupied at the moment was very different from Luciano's variety. In Rome, Orson had a gypsy girlfriend from the circus who was trying to break into movies. In exchange for his help, she taught him one of her best gypsy tricks. "She taught me how to steal a chicken and walk away with dignity," Orson recalls, "The only thing: you had to have a dress on. A live chicken with the feathers—you keep it between your legs, and learn to walk in a dignified manner. It was one of the first things she'd been taught as a child, and she thought I should know it." Orson, however, refused ever to put on the dress she kept offering him, so his education in petty crime was incomplete: "I never tried it with a dress," he admits. "But I know all the moves."

As a foreign film celebrity Orson received many invitations during the making of *Cagliostro*, one of them to a dinner party given by a very wealthy young man, whom Orson describes as "the prince of evil in Rome." Orson points out that his decadent twenty-one-year-old host "used to shoot up through his gold lamé trousers." "I accepted what I thought was an ordinary engagement," says Orson of having excused himself from his chicken-stealing lessons to have dinner with the prince of evil and his aristocratic guests. And so it seemed—at least until they finished eating. "After dinner, it was put to us, what exhibitions would we enjoy *pour commencer*?" Exhibitions? *Pour commencer?* Orson wondered what was possibly coming next. "Somebody said, 'Oh, it had better be *pédé* because it's so much more visual!' " Orson recalls. Whereupon he discovered that besides giving his guests dinner, the young Italian aristocrat regularly entertained them with demonstrations of their most elaborate sexual fantasies.

Meanwhile, back in Hollywood, the Republic management was absolutely enraged that he had been working on another director's picture when he should have been finishing his own. Orson simply did not realize the damage he was doing to himself by remaining abroad. Even if he had left part of the post-production work to the technicians but stayed in Hollywood, things would have gone more smoothly. But as it was, the studio even threatened to bill Orson for what they perceived as the costly delays his absence had caused. When Orson decided it was time to inspect the post-production work that had been done on the picture thus far, the studio initially hesitated to comply with his wishes. But Orson had his way, and on November 25, 1947, Republic dispatched to Rome the unfinished footage and the cutter who had been diligently working on it. Not until March 6, 1948, did the cutter return from what was to have been a short stay in Italy. To make matters worse, Republic heard that, having gone to Rome expressly to finish the film with Orson, the cutter had spent part of his time there working on *Cagliostro*! No news could have infuriated the studio more than this. It seemed to Republic as if anyone who came even remotely within Orson's orbit lost all purpose and direction. Nor did it help that the film the cutter brought back with him still was unfinished. The work print reflected the changes Orson had supervised in Rome. But he had also sent notes for further changes to be made in Hollywood. The score for the picture presented another complication; Orson had originally had Bernard Herrmann in mind, but that deal fell through, and in Italy he had negotiated with composer Jacques Ibert to do the music as soon as he received a contract from the studio. On their part, Republic did not want to send him anything in writing until they received the music. The triumph Orson had scored in shooting *Macbeth* on schedule and under budget had degenerated into a failure to finish the picture, which in effect, finished him in Hollywood for years to come.

With the recent loss of his wife, and of his political career, there was nothing to keep Orson in the United States. During *Cagliostro* he—like others in the Hollywood film industry—became tantalized by the distinct possibilities for shooting cheaply in postwar Italy. An Italian producer whom Orson had met when he was acting in *Cagliostro* had suggested directing *Othello* in Venice next. And since at first the producer seemed genuinely interested in bankrolling the picture, Orson saw it as an excellent backup in the event of Korda's putting him off again. "I had no intention of doing a movie of *Othello* until he began saying I should do it," recalls Orson. "I thought if this great producer wants to put up the money for *Othello*, I'll do *Othello*."

But it finally appeared as if Orson would indeed make *Cyrano* for Korda now. In Paris Orson had mapped out the production with the celebrated art director Alexander Trauner. Says Orson: "We were going to do all the sets where I was shot with big doors and high door knobs, and so on— so I'd look very, very short, because I always thought that Cyrano should look up at everybody." As for the magnitude of the false nose he would wear in the part, it seemed he would need several different sizes: "I discovered a wonderful thing about Coquelin, who created the part, that nobody knows," recalls Orson, "which is that in every act his nose got shorter. Isn't that brilliant? Absolute genius! And so of course I was going to do that." But Orson's film of *Cyrano* was never to be. "We were within weeks of starting," he recalls. "We had sets built. We were finally going to shoot in Italy . . . I was ready with everything, and then Alex came to me and said, 'My dear fellow, I have not a sou of hard currency.' " Korda told Orson that he wanted to sell the property for the Hollywood version of *Cyrano* to star José Ferrer. "He owned the rights, you see," says Orson of Korda. "A butcher in Chicago sued Rostand, claiming that he had sent him the plot and that Rostand had stolen it from him. So that the rights to *Cyrano*, in America, belonged to the heirs of this butcher. And Alex had obtained these rights"— which made the proposed American film of *Cyrano* entirely dependent on Korda's selling them. "So I said, 'Of course that's all right, Alex!' " Orson sighs. "But my whole time with Alex was things like that. I kept doing projects for him, which *I* did not abandon but which *he* did. I didn't abandon one single project—in each case he said he didn't have the money or it wasn't the right time and why not do something else?—but I didn't care, I loved him so!" Korda was the sort of magnificent dreamer Orson adored.

"He cost me years of my life and I can't hold a minute against him," says Orson, "because every time he would start on a dream he not only sold me, but I knew he'd sold himself."

In addition to *Cyrano* and *Othello*, Orson thought of directing The *Shadow* and *Moby Dick* in Italy, but none of these projects had seemed a particularly good bet to the attorney back in the States to whom Orson had turned for financial counsel. To his dismay, Orson found himself advised to give up at least temporarily the idea of directing, at which labor he was unlikely to make as much sure money as he could acting in other men's movies. As an actor Orson could command about $100,000 a picture, which, even if the film flopped at the box office, subjected him to no financial jeopardy. As a director, however, he had to cope with deferred payments and precarious percentages. As a case in point, to date for *Macbeth* he had received only $50,000 for his work, whereas the remaining $100,000 for which he had contracted was deferred until the requisite profit percentage was reached (which of course might never occur). But Orson simply could not accept this practical advice. All that mattered to him now was to direct.

With Korda's *Cyrano* out of the picture, Orson turned to his backup project, *Othello*, but he could not depend entirely on the Italian producer who had suggested the film to him and whose investment in lire would have to be supplemented by American dollars. The American producer of *Cagliostro* had briefly shown some interest in *Othello*, but decided against backing any more pictures in Italy, where the political situation worried him. To judge from what he said, it also looked like *Othello* could be a difficult project to sell to American backers, who might think the black central character to be a box-office liability. It was no help either that Orson wanted to do another Shakespeare picture when there had been such widely conflicting reports about the job he had done on *Macbeth*. But it was precisely because of the

very, very modest *Macbeth* he had been compelled to make
in America that he wanted to do Shakespeare a little more
grandly now, and the less-costly production conditions of
postwar Italy encouraged him to try. Still, *Macbeth* loomed
unfinished; so in April, a year after Republic had first excitedly announced his bold experiment, Orson returned to
Hollywood to wrap up the post-production work, which had
dragged on so interminably that, its strict twenty-one-day
shooting schedule notwithstanding, the picture no longer
proved what Orson had meant it to. On the contrary, *Macbeth* only seemed to confirm the deadly rumors of Orson's
unreliability.

Orson had planned to return to Europe the moment he
finished fine-tuning *Macbeth*, but he contracted chicken pox
from his daughter and was not well enough to leave until
June. "I had a lot of fun with the chicken pox," says Orson,
who recuperated in New York at the Waldorf, in the convivial company of Charlie Lederer, whose script for *The
Shadow* Orson had hoped to direct. Orson recalls with glee
that he and Lederer kept two producers "imprisoned in the
Waldorf Astoria for three days by what we said was the Port
Authority on the grounds that I was in quarantine." Nor was
this the last of his pranks. As soon as he got to London
from New York, Orson was scheduled to meet with Korda,
who knew nothing of the children's disease that had befallen
him. Orson says that when he was no longer contagious he
"touched up all the sores and then arrived in London and
kissed Alex on the lips." When, much to his horror, Korda
noticed the strange speckles all over Orson's face, he nervously inquired about them—to which Orson replied that
"I didn't know what it was that I was suffering from."

Orson arrived in Europe intent on starting production for
his film of *Othello* immediately, although without any American money behind him this seemed improbable. Never was
he more determined to begin, however, than when he heard
that another *Othello* film was already in the works in Italy.

Although he had not wanted to take acting work simply to shore up his finances, this suddenly seemed like the best way to get the cash he needed for *Othello*. He'd done it before: putting his own acting money into *It's All True* when no one else would help. The modest sum Orson felt he needed to get started on *Othello* was $150,000—and he could easily make that much by appearing in a single picture. But Orson did not anticipate the horrors that lay ahead as he embarked upon financing his own film. The Italian backers were soon to back out. And his own money would disappear all too quickly into the production.

That summer, he asked Skipper Hill to send him some film stock with which to begin. There was something boyish and impulsive about the entire precarious project so that, for Orson, it was only natural to think of, and to appeal to, the Todd School when no one else was about to help. Todd, and Skipper Hill, were cherished symbols of security and rootedness to Orson—he had even enrolled his daughter Christopher there, as the only girl in an all-boys' school, where she boarded with Skipper and Hortense.

When Orson went to Cap d'Antibes on the French Riviera to talk to Darryl Zanuck about the acting work he needed to help finance his new film, he learned that Rita, whose divorce from him was not yet final, was vacationing there too. She had brought along Orson's former secretary, Shifra Haran, whom she had hired especially for the trip. The two of them were staying in a hotel on the hill above Zanuck's cabana—where Orson was filled in on the details of Rita's ménage by professional gossip Elsa Maxwell. (Miss Maxwell's claiming to be on the most intimate of terms with virtually everyone had moved Orson and Cole Porter to play a devilish prank on her. "Cole Porter and I trapped her," Orson recalls. "We were both terribly fond of her. If you mentioned *any* name in the world, any famous name, she'd say, 'He's one of my most intimate friends.' And we said, 'We're going to get her on one that is so impossible even

she is going to stop and gasp.' We set it up, a whole long
conversation, and mentioned Mihailović, the Partisan leader.
She said, 'One of my most intimate friends,' and turned
white, realizing that she'd gone too far.") It seemed that
Rita had left their daughter, Becky, at home in the care of
an elderly aunt and the Filipino houseman. Pookles, the
cocker spaniel that Dadda Bernstein had given to Orson and
Rita, was also left behind. On the trip one of Miss Haran's
duties was to carry in her purse $10,000 in cash for Rita;
another duty, which she shared with Rita's maid, Angel,
was to try to lift Rita's spirits. For although Rita had had a
great professional triumph with the film *Gilda*, she was prey
to persistent depression: "Whenever she'd act kind of funny,"
says Miss Haran, "Angel and I would put on an act and
we'd get her to smile and pull herself together." But it was
not easy. As they left for New York by train, Rita's new
picture, *The Loves of Carmen*, was about to be reviewed;
when the train stopped in Kansas City, Miss Haran dashed
out for the papers. Rita was used to the critics' making snide
remarks about her acting, but this time, for a change, the
reviews were quite kind to her. "You know, I always thought
that if I ever got good reviews, I'd be happy," she told Miss
Haran in a small, sad voice. "It's so empty. It's never what
I wanted, ever. All I wanted was just what everybody else
wants, you know—to be loved."

Her troubled state of mind manifested itself on the ocean
liner from New York when everyone seemed to turn and
look at her the moment she and Miss Haran entered the
dining room. Rita found this kind of intense public scrutiny
unbearable. This was her holiday, and it seemed not to have
occurred to her that, on the ship, she would be instantly
recognized. The captain's courteous invitation for Rita and
Miss Haran to join him at his special table—elevated slightly
above the rest—was an acute agony for Rita, whose new
position in the dining room made her all the more vulnerable. But the first night she really had no choice but to

accept. Not so afterward. "We never went back to the dining room because she couldn't stand being looked at," Miss Haran recalls. "We ate in the room. And then we would go walking when it was darkest, when there weren't too many people around. She was virtually a prisoner in her room."

In Cap d'Antibes, Rita was the object of quite another sort of attention—and this she did not find displeasing. In much the same way as Orson had seen and fallen for Rita in a magazine photograph, Prince Aly Khan had been obsessed with *Gilda*. Orson recalls that he had known the Muslim prince long before Rita did, since the two of them had played together as young boys on the Riviera. Just as Orson had had a party arranged where he and Rita might seem inadvertently to meet, now Aly Khan asked Elsa Maxwell to arrange a gathering at Cap d'Antibes for which he secretly paid. Contrary then to the story that Elsa Maxwell had spontaneously played matchmaker between them, it was Aly Khan who had deliberately engineered the meeting— although Miss Maxwell was only too willing to take credit. On this trip Rita was generally disinclined to accept any invitations to parties, for she was much too retiring to walk into crowded rooms where she knew no one. Still, since Elsa Maxwell was an old friend through Orson, Rita accepted this one invitation. She could not have suspected how much it would change her life. However richly he deserved his reputation as an international playboy, the darkly handsome thirty-eight-year-old eldest son of the Aga Khan was in his own way as sensitive and insecure as Rita. Because of his considerable fortune and position, Aly constantly perceived others as fawning on him in hopes of some reward. Distrustful of the motives of those around him, he despaired of finding anyone to talk to in a more than superficial way. Despite their material generosity with him, his father and stepmother appeared to withhold the personal warmth and affection that he longed for. Behind the public persona of the relentless womanizer there was a loneliness

and a genuine need for love that Rita found immensely
appealing. Not long after they met, she and Aly repaired to
his French villa, the magnificent Château de l'Horizon, then
set off for Spain together. "It should have been a summer
romance that ended at the end of the summer," says Shifra
Haran, who observed behind the scenes what the press
could—and did—only speculate about. Rita herself wondered whether it had in fact ended when as fall approached
she set sail for New York on her way back to Hollywood,
where she was expected to resume work at Columbia. But
any doubts she may have had about her romance with Aly
were instantly dispelled when he turned up in Hollywood
in pursuit of her.

For Rita, Cap d'Antibes had been the start of a new
romance, but although one evening Orson and Rita did
indeed dine together, the Riviera had been strictly business
for Orson. "I had no time to swim," says Orson. "I was
moving around looking for money." Of *Life* magazine's
having photographed him shirtless, however, Orson laughs:
"It was to enter into *the spirit of the thing*! It looked better
than Swifty Lazar, who once came tiptoeing out to see me
when I *was* in a bathing suit on the sands in San Sebastián.
And there was Swifty and he had patent-leather shoes on!
Now if you've never seen patent-leather shoes on the beach,
your life isn't complete until you do!" But at Cap d'Antibes,
Orson's entering into "the spirit of the thing" (as he puts it)
paid off, for Zanuck helped him get the movie roles he
needed to pay for *Othello*. That August in Rome, Orson
appeared as Cesare Borgia in *Prince of Foxes*, a new Tyrone
Power picture for Zanuck's 20th Century–Fox, for which
he earned $100,000. From then on, Orson would appear in
many of what were to him routine roles like this in which,
generally, he invested very little of himself. In hopes of
directing movies worthy of the name Orson Welles, he rented
out that name and the familiar face and voice that went with
it. Eventually this strategy would result in Orson's becoming

distanced not only from some of his characters but from himself as well, since he spent so much time working on projects with which he did not identify, and that gave him so little satisfaction.

Satisfaction was what he hoped to derive from the pictures he directed. Hence his perplexity when, that September, *Macbeth* was poorly received at the Venice Film Festival. He had, in fact, suspected that there might be a problem, and had withdrawn *Macbeth* from the official competition in which it had initially been entered: for Laurence Olivier's far costlier—and more conventional—*Hamlet* was also to be screened at Venice, and alongside this film Welles's eccentric *Macbeth*, with its queer costumes and unabashedly makeshift settings, might look shoddy by contrast. But *Macbeth* was not supposed to look like Olivier's *Hamlet*. Orson had eschewed the polished, classical approach to Shakespearean production epitomized by Olivier's *Hamlet* in favor of the strangeness that had been his aim in *Lady from Shanghai*. The controversial barbarism of this *Macbeth* reflected both the severely limited means at his disposal and the determination to view the classic play from a new angle. Perhaps it was too new and startling for most viewers—but Orson had never intended the film for a mass audience anyway (the limited potential audience had been a principal reason for making it so cheaply). Wrote Jean Cocteau: "Orson Welles's *Macbeth* leaves the spectator deaf and blind and I can well believe that the people who like it (and I am proud to be one) are few and far between." By way of rationalizing the humiliating reviews, Orson told others, and perhaps himself, that there was much prior animosity against him among the Italian press corps, who resented Gregory Ratoff's having ejected reporters from the set of *Cagliostro*, and having steadfastly kept them from talking to Orson. To his friend Ratoff, Orson lamented that he was hated in Italy—a state of affairs that seemed all the more painful since he had fled to Italy in hopes of starting anew.

The sound track—the Scottish burr in which the dialogue was spoken, and which Orson had chosen precisely for its marvelous strangeness—became a subject of immense controversy for English-speaking reviewers who complained that they could not understand it. In response to the controversy about the sound track, Republic studios decided to redub the picture to get rid of the Scottish burr—they hoped, misguidedly, that doing so would make the picture suddenly accessible to a mass audience. But criticism of the notorious Scottish burr had merely indicated a more general feeling among the film's detractors that nothing in Welles's *Macbeth* quite made sense: for those who despised the film's eccentricities, the sound track was probably just the most obvious thing to complain about. Since Orson was hardly about to return to the U.S. to dilute his own picture at the very moment he was trying to get started on a new one, it fell upon Wilson to supervise the arduous reworking of approximately sixty percent of *Macbeth's* sound track. Later, Orson himself would fiddle with the track in London. This prolonged additional work on *Macbeth* further—and fully— obliterated any hope of the picture's serving as a model of efficient production. Who in Hollywood would possibly take a chance on Orson again after this?

But if he was a bit less hysterical than he might have been about the great disaster of *Macbeth*, it was because Orson's thoughts were just then on a homely Italian actress, with whom he had fallen madly in love. "She had a face like a spoon," Orson recalls, "but when she was young, in spite of her looks, she had a tremendous allure for men. I wasn't the only idiot. They really were falling all over themselves for her—inexplicably, but they were." Like his many rivals, Orson was unfazed by her physical unattractiveness. "I was blinded, unable to see," he recalls. "It was real low comedy and I knew it. I knew perfectly well that I was acting like an idiot. I couldn't help it! The reason is so egotistical and

unspeakable. You see, I have been blessed by some kind
of interior sexual mechanism, where if a girl is not ever
going to say yes, something clicks, and I don't want it. This
had given me the impression that no woman in the world
would refuse me if I tried hard enough. You must understand, at this point I hadn't made it with her. It was the
total novelty: I had everything to offer her and she wouldn't
have anything to do with me. I couldn't cure myself. Charlie
Lederer [to whom Orson had written letters about his unrequited love] told me that I should visualize her sitting on
the toilet picking her nose. And I wrote him back and said,
'It's the most enchanting vision I've ever thought of!' "

For the first time in his life Orson took perverse pleasure
in a woman's mistreating him. "She treated me like dirt,"
he explains, "and I had *never* had that experience. I think
I turned, briefly, as one might turn into any sort of pervert,
into some kind of masochist. I did all the jealous bits! I
knew that she was humping away with other men, and there
I was out in the garden looking at the window! And don't
forget that I was in Hollywood during the war, when there
was no competition! You know, there's *nobody* I missed.
That's all I can tell you. I was the only man in Hollywood.
So I didn't know what it was not to have a garland of beauties
fighting for my attention. And here was this pockmarked
little beast! So anybody who was talking to me during this
period was talking to a madman.

"I took her to Venice, and we went to all the grand balls
and the dinners, and all she did was snarl at everybody.
Everybody hated her—except me. I probably hated her, but
I didn't know what I felt except that I was going to get her
into that bedroom or else. All this happened at a point when
I was really reaching young middle-age or elderly youth—
I had my comic men's menopause ten years too early, like
everything else!"

At the beginning, their relationship had been further complicated by neither one's being able to speak the other's

language. "When I didn't know what she was shouting at
me it was just marvelous Italian theater," says Orson. "She
made scenes all over Italy. She didn't leave out a single
province. The point is that my interest in her—which is a
mild word—began when I didn't speak a word of Italian,
and she didn't speak a word of English. But through the
months, she learned English, and I learned Italian, and we
discovered that we detested each other." What Orson did
not know was that, even as he was madly pursuing her, she
was regularly sleeping with a member of the film crew he
had assembled for *Othello*. Ironically, this was the only other
man besides Lederer to whom Orson had confessed his
passion. He was also the first person to hear when at last
Orson succeeded in getting her to bed. "I had *one* night
with her," Orson says. "*One* night. In Venice. And it was
not a night to remember—but I *did it*! I'd finally climbed
up to that balcony, you see. And the first thing I did was
to run and tell him that I'd had victory, not knowing that
he was the man. And he complimented me! What happened
was that I slowly realized that she was going to bed with
him all the time, and had been from the beginning. It slowly
dawned on me that I was the biggest cuckold in Italy. And
he was the man I used to confide in my difficulties with
her. He'd hold my hand and encourage me." By the time
Orson found out about his rival, however, he had fallen out
of love. "I wasn't in love anymore," he recalls, "but I was
stupefied by my own stupidity!" But having finally gotten
what he'd wanted all along, a night with the woman whose
face was like a spoon, did Orson have any regrets? "I had
a role to play, and I was going to *get in there*, and I did,"
he says philosophically, "but it wasn't worth it, believe me."

When Orson was still pursuing the elusive actress, and
shooting a bit of (eventually discarded) footage for *Othello*
in Venice, Alex Korda sent word that at last he had a project
for him—not to direct but to act in: *The Third Man*, to be
directed by Carol Reed, and to co-star Joseph Cotten. David

Selznick, who had the American rights to the picture, wanted Reed and Korda to use Noel Coward in the role of the enigmatic Harry Lime, but Reed held out for Orson Welles. Although the part was absolutely central to the film, it was quite small and would not require Orson to spend much time away from Italy. Orson was reluctant to break off his preliminary work on *Othello*, however, and as much as he adored him, he resented Korda's offering him acting work when all their previous deals for Orson to direct had fallen through. Still Orson badly needed the money to get on with *Othello*. Having decided that he had little choice but to take the acting job, Orson figured that, before he accepted, he would play hard to get. "I knew I was going to do it," laughs Orson, "but I was going to make Alex pay for all those movies I hadn't done." So when Korda sent his brother Vincent to track down Welles and bring him back to London to sign the contract, Orson deliberately kept giving him the slip all over Italy. "I thought if they really want me for this," says Orson, "they're going to have to chase me, and I'm going to make it just as unpleasant as possible." When at last Vincent Korda caught up with Orson, he loaded him into a private plane for London. Orson shared the back seat with Vincent's young son, Michael, and a magnificent basket of fruit that Vincent had prepared for his brother, and that Orson proceeded to wreck by taking one bite out of each fruit. "It was going to be offered as a great present," says Orson of his wicked little joke. "He'd gone and carefully picked each piece of fruit. It was too good to be true! I knew Alex wouldn't touch any of it if it had been bitten into!" When he finally signed Korda's contract in London, Orson's need for immediate cash to make *Othello* caused him to make a very bad deal. "I was given a choice between $100,000 or something like twenty percent of the picture," Orson recalls, "and I took the $100,000. Picture grossed, you know, something unbelievable. Because in America it was only a success, but in the rest of the world it was an

absolute bombshell—it was *The Sound of Music*, you know.
There never was such a hit in twenty-five years as there
was in Europe. I could have *retired* on that!"

As it happened, the night before Orson went to Vienna
to appear as scheduled in *The Third Man* was also the night
he finally got to sleep with the spoon-faced Italian actress
he had been pursuing. He arrived in Vienna "still numb"
from the experience, so that when he met the beautiful
female star of *The Third Man*, Alida Valli, he barely seemed
to notice her. "I'd lost my mind in some way," Orson admits.
"I didn't *see* Alida Valli, the sexiest thing you ever saw in
your life. It didn't even register with me that she was female.
We had long conversations about Austria and all that—
instead of me leaping into action! Crazy! Completely mad!
And I see her now and she excites me beyond words. I was
right there—next door to her in the hotel. Just a little knock
on the door and, you know, borrow some salt. I see *The
Third Man* every two or three years—it's the only movie
of mine I ever watch on television because I like it so
much—and I look at Alida Valli, and I say, 'What was in
your mind when you were ten days in Vienna and you didn't
make a move?' She drives me mad with lust when I see her
in it!"

Orson did not wish to leave his pock-marked ladylove
unguarded while he was in Vienna. She was about to go
abroad to make a film of her own, and since there was no
question of his accompanying her, Orson instinctively did
what he always had in such circumstances: he wired Hortense Hill to come to Europe at his expense. It seemed to
Orson that Hortense could always be counted on to watch
over his women in his absences. The series of wires that
Orson dispatched to Woodstock struck Skipper as "frantic."
Hortense had only recently undergone an operation, which
had left the Hills short of funds. But Orson sounded so
genuinely "desperate" to Skipper that he borrowed the cash
to get his wife over to Europe. Once she got there, however,

Hortense disliked the spoon-faced actress as much as most other people did. Nor did she succeed in doing what Orson says he secretly hoped she would: "To try to persuade her what a *wonderful* fellow I was."

That November Rita's divorce from Orson became final. Having pursued Rita to America Aly Khan had installed himself in a house across from hers; openly moving in with Rita and little Becky was certain to stir up even more of a scandal in the press than the couple already had. In 1948, the fact that Aly Khan was still officially married to someone else made his affair with Rita seem especially titillating. Reporters hounded them wherever they went, which was a source of immense agitation to Rita, so that Miss Haran was generally the one to show the prince around Hollywood and Beverly Hills. Rita was also unhappy with her part in *Lona Hanson*, which Harry Cohn insisted she do next. Hoping to get away at least temporarily from both the press and Harry Cohn, Rita fled, with Aly and Miss Haran, to Mexico City. Much to Rita's horror, the desk clerk at the hotel at which they had reservations had sold the information about their secret arrival to the local papers, and the party had to slip away to another hotel. Only Rita and Miss Haran signed the guest register, so that if the reporters found them it would seem that the prince was not there. Several of Miss Haran's relatives, among them a rabbinical circumciser, aptly named David Klip, lived in Mexico City, but she had no time to contact them as she busied herself with supervising the hauling of a large bed into the room reserved for the lovers. Hours later, after midnight, in the tiny room where she had gone to bed herself, Miss Haran was abruptly awakened by the arrival of her local family members. When she inquired how they possibly knew she was there, they waved before her the front page of a newpaper proclaiming that Rita Hayworth and Prince Aly Khan (whose real name was Shifra Haran) were in town. It certainly had not taken long for the press to find Rita and Aly at the hotel. An elevator operator and a maid were reporters in disguise, who thought they had uncovered the secret name of the man all the world knew as Aly Khan, but who, they disclosed, was *really* Shifra Haran. With so much pressure on the relationship, it is not surprising that Rita's grave insecurities surfaced in an explosion of jealous rage when Aly spent ninety minutes at the manicurist. That he calmly told her where he'd been, and that Miss Haran had been with him all along, didn't placate Rita; as with Orson, she couldn't seem to bear their being apart, even for so short a time. The prince chose to disregard this bad omen.

On their return to Hollywood, Rita learned that Columbia Pictures had suspended her for not having shown up to make *Lona Hanson*, and so Rita and Aly moved on, staying in Hollywood only as long as was necessary to pick up Becky before they set sail for Europe on the *Brittanic*. On the day of departure, they arrived at the ship separately in hopes of throwing off the reporters and photographers; Rita wore a dark mink coat and looked terrified by the flashing cameras and persistent questions as she scurried up the gangplank clutching Becky's hand. She found some refuge from the press at the prince's great house in Ireland, where the weary travelers rested after the crossing, but her mercurial behavior perplexed the prince. He confided his anxieties to Miss Haran, who, since she had known Rita longer than he, might help him to make some sense of Rita's moods. In private this notorious international playboy revealed himself to Miss Haran as "shy, bashful, misunderstood"—and quite unable to understand the woman he loved; but he took a warm and special interest in Orson's daughter. "The prince was wonderful to Rebecca, just wonderful!" says Miss Haran. "She needed someone."

Soon thereafter Becky and her father had a strained reunion in Paris at Orson's hotel, where Miss Haran (who accompanied Becky for the occasion) was startled by Orson's shabby, soiled, "down-at-the-heels" appearance. How different he seemed from the Hollywood days when she or Shorty had followed him about with spare shirts in case he wanted to change, which he sometimes did several times a day. She remembered him as impeccable, immaculate—so unlike the rumpled bohemian who ushered her into his suite. If at the moment he was not spending his money on new clothes, it was to put every last penny into *Othello*. But he had spent a good deal of money on presents for Becky, which filled the room. She took little interest in them, however, and she bawled uncontrollably while Miss Haran unbundled her from her rain clothes. Orson seemed unsure of what to say to her; for her part, Aly Khan had already supplied her with more toys than she needed, so the gifts from Orson went unnoticed. At the end of this exceedingly awkward visit, as Becky started to bawl again the moment Miss Haran began to dress her, Orson threw the child a long glance and muttered, "Same as me—no discipline! That's my trouble: I never had any either!"

What he did have at this moment was an obsession: to assemble and complete *Othello*. The footage he had shot earlier had to be discarded now that his Iago, Everett Sloane, bailed out of the picture. Tormented by what he perceived as his own physical unattractiveness, Sloane maintained an ambivalent relationship with Orson, who had directed him in his greatest roles—Bernstein in *Citizen Kane* and Bannister, the crippled attorney, in *Lady from Shanghai*. Sloane bitterly resented his inability to be cast as the handsome leading man Orson typically portrayed, and this resentment of Orson would have made Sloane a natural Iago to his Othello. But as it turned out, Sloane was disinclined to tolerate the sporadic manner in which Orson was apparently going to have to shoot *Othello*. To replace him, Orson asked Carol Reed's help in getting James Mason, who, years before, had followed Orson at the Dublin Gate. But Reed told Orson that Mason was entirely wrong for the part. Instead, he suggested that Micheal MacLiammoir might be the perfect Iago for Orson. Orson was not so sure. He had not seen MacLiammoir and Hilton Edwards since the Todd Summer Festival in 1934, and he had not forgotten his resentment at how shabbily they had treated him in Dublin and in Woodstock. Although they had been out of his life for a decade and a half, they were distinctly present in his thoughts, particularly because of *All for Hecuba*, the graceful memoir MacLiammoir had since written, and which Orson had hurled across the room when he got to its portrait of him.

Micheal dreaded seeing Orson too; all his worst fears of Orson's one day becoming his better had more than come true. Never had Micheal been more aware of his jealousy of Orson than when the film of *Jane Eyre* opened in Dublin at the same time he was appearing onstage there as Rochester. Two *Jane Eyres* and two Rochesters were more than Dublin needed. The competition from Orson had come as a devastating blow to Micheal, who, as a passionate devotee of the Brontës, had been waiting all his life to play Rochester, which he did now in the manner of Sarah Bernhardt. Wherever he went in Dublin, Micheal was confronted with people who insisted on comparing his and Orson's performances. "You know," says Orson, "Micheal told me he'd go into the restaurant and they'd say, 'Ah, you're not as good as Mr. Well-es. He's the man for the part, sir!' 'Oh well, he's a star of the fil-ums, sir. Ya can't go up against that!' "

Micheal had another reason as well for hesitating to accept Orson's invitation to Paris. Having recently suffered a nervous breakdown, and having put on a bit of weight, Micheal had for the most part lost his looks, and he shuddered to think of the screen test that Orson proposed. As it turned out, Micheal went to Paris, and Orson never did subject him to the ordeal of the screen test. Years before, when Orson had invited the Dubliners to Todd, it had been Micheal

who talked a dubious Hilton into going. This time it had
been Hilton who had gently persuaded him.

Although Welles and MacLiammoir had increased in girth
since their last encounter in America, the subliminal tensions
between them, and their efforts to mask those tensions behind a show of affection that, deep down, neither of them
really felt, were quite the same as they had been before.
"He was always *on*—ferociously *on*—" says Orson of
MacLiammoir, "not to show his jealousy about Hilton, you
see. Because Hilton loved me—I think Hilton genuinely
did—at the moments when he was not under Micheal's
influence." As in their youth, Orson was anxious to impress
the Dubliners, and so—despite his struggle to raise money
for *Othello*—he spent vast sums in the costliest of restaurants, where time and again, Micheal, and indeed the rest
of Orson's entourage, were his guests and his audience.
"One did rather have to grit one's teeth as one came into a
restaurant with him," says Orson of MacLiammoir, at whom
people inevitably stared. Did Micheal intentionally make
up his face to look a bright orange? Did he know that his
toupee kept slipping off his head, or that his mascara was
almost always running? "I told him he looked like an unemployed gypsy fiddler," Orson recalls, "and that he ought
to try and pull himself together." As for the huge restaurant
bills, Orson figured that in restaurants where they knew him
he could always run up a tab, and that, at length, he could
always earn enough quick cash by acting to pay off at least
his most urgent debts. When he had spent money he did
not really have on Hilton and Micheal in New York it had
been to create in them, and perhaps in himself, the proper
spirit; now, with *Othello*, he did not want his cast and crew
to think that this was only a low-budget picture. The grand
style in which they were treated set the tone for the com-
parable generosity of spirit with which it was hoped they
would work.

Only Desdemona remained to be cast. By March when rehearsals began Orson had settled on a young French actress named Cécile Aubry, whom Henri-Georges Clouzot had been talking up. But after only three days of work on *Othello*, she announced that she was leaving to do another film. As Orson had as yet no contract with Miss Aubry, she was quite without obligation to him. Orson decided that even without a Desdemona (later he cast the Canadian actress Suzanne Cloutier) he could start filming those scenes in which she did not appear. But discovering that he was without funds again, he went to London and hired himself out to the very same movie for which Cécile Aubry had decamped. In Henry Hathaway's *The Black Rose*, much to Orson's delight, he would have to be thickly and laboriously made up to play a Mongol chieftain. As in *Prince of Foxes*, his co-star was Tyrone Power.

Before he had run out of money, Orson had already hired a crew to go with him to North Africa to begin *Othello*. Although he had postponed beginning his own film to act in *The Black Rose* in Morocco, some of the *Othello* crew showed up there anyway to be certain they got paid. "So there was a whole crew for a movie that wasn't being shot!" laughs Orson. He put up his *Othello* cast at his own expense in a villa outside Rome until he returned.

Initially Hathaway was delighted at the opportunity to direct Orson: "I wanted Welles—who wouldn't want Welles in a picture?" says Hathaway. "He's a great actor and everything—but he's only trouble." This *trouble* was perhaps the result of Orson's shifting back and forth between being the head of his own company and a member of Hathaway's, a transition he didn't always negotiate smoothly. "He doesn't like direction," says Hathaway, who was certainly not the sort of director to encourage Orson's taking over. Even at the dinner table Orson asserted himself in a manner that irritated Hathaway. "Welles would take over every time," complains Hathaway, who finally decided to set up a small table in a tiny room off the kitchen, where he and his wife, and Tyrone Power and his, could dine quietly. But it was not long before Orson figured out where they were and, leaving his own entourage in the dining room, went back to Hathaway's table to inquire if they were being served what he called "special food" there. "No," said Hathaway, "we don't want *special food*. We want quiet!" But this seemed to escape Orson, who was sure they were indeed eating better in the back room and not telling him, so the next night, when Hathaway arrived there, he saw that Orson had ordered two tables set up, one of them for him to hold court. Content to allow Orson to get all the "special food" he wanted, the Hathaways and the Powers returned to the main dining room.

On the set Hathaway bristled at what he perceived as Orson's resisting his directorial authority. Thus, Hathaway describes a scene in which he had trouble getting Orson to do what he asked. "We did it, and we did it, and we did it," recalls Hathaway of the many takes. "And finally he said to me in front of the company, 'Mr. Hathaway, I've played this scene every conceivable way that I know how to play it. I've played it fast. I've played it slow. I've played it loud, and I've played it soft.' And I said, 'Mr. Welles, you're a genius, but you've played it every single way *but* the way I've asked you to play it.' And he looked me straight in the eye and we went and did the scene and I printed it." All of which suggested that Orson knew exactly what the director had wanted all along, and exactly how to do it. "He's such a conniving bastard," says Hathaway. Orson's consolation for having had to postpone *Othello* to act in *The Back Rose* was the affair he conducted with the "great, tall, dark, tattooed creature," as he describes her, who had been provided by the production company to translate for him with the locals. After dinner, Orson and his six-foot Berber girlfriend could often be seen riding off into the mountains on burros.

• • •

To work out last-minute details on *Othello*, Orson had gone
to Rome, where, much to his surprise, he received word
from Rita that she needed to see him. "She sent for me and
asked me to take her back," says Orson. "She sent me a
telegram in Rome. I couldn't get any plane, so I went, stood
up, in a cargo plane, to Antibes." There, he says, he went
straight to her hotel, where Rita was waiting. "There were
candles and champagne ready—and Rita in a marvelous
negligee," says Orson. "And the door closed, and she said,
'Here I am.' " Did Orson know that Rita was about to get
married? "She didn't tell me she was going to marry him,"
says Orson. "She said, 'Marry me.' I didn't even know it
was anything but a romance, one of those in-the-newspaper
things." The next day Orson sadly returned to Italy. Having
seen her like that, he realized that he still loved her, but
that he could not bear to make her unhappy again.

Shortly thereafter word came that Rita had married Aly
in the village of Vallauris, near Cannes. At Château de
l'Horizon, where the reception was held, white flowers
floating in the pool formed the intertwined initials M and
A for Margarita and Aly. Although the couple would have
preferred it otherwise, their wedding was copiously docu-
mented in the international press, who could not seem to
take enough pictures. Wearing a blue Jacques Fath dress
and a delicately floppy picture hat, Rita looked lovely as
she cut the many-tiered wedding cake with a great saber.
And there in the pictures of the happy event that flashed
around the world was little Rebecca Welles, wearing a dotted
organdy dress—and looking distinctly like Orson.

A month later, in June of 1949, Orson and his *Othello*
company finally landed in Mogador on the northern coast
of Morocco, where Orson had tramped about in his youth.
To pay for costumes and sets Orson had been counting on
the lire from the Italian backers. But Orson says: "When I
arrived in Mogador I got a telegram that they'd gone bank-

rupt. And we didn't even have return tickets. Sixty people! No costumes, no money, no return tickets, nothing!" Looking around at the actors he'd brought with him to North Africa, Orson decided that "if I had them, I might as well shoot a movie. I had a wonderful cast. I couldn't just send them away." If he had, he points out, "I never would have forgiven myself."

Not without cause, Welles describes the films of his European period—of which *Othello* was the first—as a "desperate adventure." The first scene shot was to have been the killing of Roderigo. But the costumes did not turn up as expected, and Orson was forced to improvise by setting the action not in the street, where the actors would have to be costumed, but in a steam bath, where towels alone would do. Perhaps it was the unanticipated bankruptcy of the Italian backers, perhaps the need constantly to improvise, to make something out of nothing, that plunged Orson into the oddest of moods: "There was no hotel there," he recalls, "and we had to go to the public baths, and walk in our nightgowns through the streets, and it was heavenly! I was convinced I was going to die. The wind blew all the time, which seemed to me associated with my death. And things were so terrible, there didn't seem to be any way out of it. And I was absolutely, serenely prepared never to leave Mogador. I was sure they were going to carry me out dead." These dark premonitions notwithstanding, Orson describes his work in Mogador as "one of the happiest times I've ever known, despite all the struggle."

It was also a happy time for Micheal, who, although Hilton had joined him in Morocco—"to keep him company and out of trouble," says Orson—discovered among the local population a great many masculine forty-five- and fifty-year-old men to his liking. Micheal's nocturnal activities did not escape the amused attention of Mogador's governor. "The governor of Mogador, an enormously sophisticated character, insisted on giving me every day the report of everybody's behavior in Mogador the night before," says Orson. "At first I pretended I didn't want to see it. But when I told Micheal that I knew what he'd done the night before, and saw what delight it gave him, then I read it like a newspaper! Here he was, you know, with some type with a great long mustache and five children!" Because Micheal had a superb ear for languages, it was not long before he could chatter away with the locals: "He picked up from the policemen that he took home with him at night a great deal of useful Arabic," says Orson.

But Orson had other things to worry about besides the Moroccan policemen with whom Micheal spent the night. Whenever the production was cut off for lack of funds, he had to go out into the great world to find cash where he could. One of these forays took him to Antibes again, where the phone rang in Darryl Zanuck's hotel suite to say Mr. Welles was waiting in the lobby. Zanuck was about to go out to dinner with Henry Hathaway and his wife, who had come to call for him, and he was in no mood to be bothered. But when he told the desk to send Orson away, they called him back seconds later to say that Mr. Welles refused to leave until Zanuck saw him. So the three of them went down to the lobby, where Orson instantly threw himself on his knees before Zanuck. "*You're* the only one in the world who can save me!" "Get up! Get up!" said Zanuck, mortified at Orson's making a scene like this in a busy hotel lobby. "I'm destitute!" Orson went on. Anxious to put an end to this embarrassment Zanuck agreed to give Orson $85,000 in lire. Thereupon Zanuck called the head of Fox in Rome to order the release of the money. Orson's putting up his company in expensive hotels even when production was suspended did nothing to help the *Othello* budget. Each excursion to raise money cost him vast sums for the company he had left behind. "I was beleaguered in that movie," says Orson. "It was an *unbelievable* strain to try to keep those people happy. I didn't send them home and wait for money. Everybody was kept on salary." To the subsequent rumors that he irresponsibly abandoned his actors in these intervals he responds: "You know one place where I left them? The Colombe d'Or—that's one place I left them! I left them in the Gritti Hotel, on full pension! It was a pretty rough life they had!"

Although Orson was utterly exhausted when he and his *Othello* company landed in Venice, he felt a new surge of energy on seeing for the first time in more than a decade the first of the beautiful ballerinas with whom he had carried on in his New York theater days. "Still looking great," says Orson, "not me, but she was! She had aged absolutely marvelously—not a wrinkle you would take away. I had a marvelous time with her—again!" Micheal MacLiammoir, on the other hand, was a good deal less fortunate in his Venetian romances. Micheal's social life had serious repercussions for Orson's production company. "One night in his amorous behavior with a gondolier," says Orson, "Micheal managed to knock the gondolier into the Grand Canal!" The accident threatened to cause a great scandal in Venice, and it cost Orson a good deal to hush it up. "You can imagine what we had to pay!" says Orson. "The gondoliers cost you lawyers' fees just to row across the canal anyway. If you knock them into the canal making forbidden love to them—!"

Back in the States, Richard Wilson was running what was in effect a shadow organization. He could hardly make commitments for Orson if he was not even sure where Orson was at a given moment. But in his role as the American end of Mercury Enterprises he persisted in trying somehow to operate on Orson's behalf. All claims against Orson—not just Republic's, but also Skipper's for the film stock and Hortense's plane ticket, and Shorty's for the storage of some of Orson's effects in his home—were filtered through Wilson, who tried to maintain Mercury Enterprises. Frustrated by the absence of detailed information on what was going on with Orson's *Othello*, Wilson lamented the lack of organizational procedures in the Mercury's operations in Europe and North Africa. Indeed if any kind of organization had ever existed, it had by now disappeared entirely.

Each time Orson returned from one of his fund-raising forays, shooting resumed. At intervals there had been shooting sessions in Mogador, Venice, Rome, and other farflung locales, and the sporadic manner in which Orson filmed *Othello* is reflected in its fractured texture. If the actors needed in a scene were not all there when Orson turned up, he had to split the scene into various short takes that could be filmed at different times and reassembled later (as shots and countershots). For what seemed to him a very long time, Orson despaired of ever finishing the shooting, not to mention the post-production work, on his beloved film.

Even as he struggled to film *Othello*, his thoughts were filled with two other projects he was anxious to embark on. To Skipper Hill, Orson wrote about his desire to do a film based on Homer's *The Odyssey*, which, should Skipper agree to join him, Orson proposed to begin in December of 1949 in Cairo. In addition to assisting Orson in shooting the picture, Skipper would help supervise the sailing sequences. Skipper and Todd were especially on Orson's mind just now because Christopher and Virginia had been to visit him in Rome during *Othello*, and the three of them had jointly sent "a brief declaration of love," as they called it, to Hortense, each of them scrawling part of the message. Virginia's marriage to Lederer had ended and she had married now for the third time. Her new husband was about to take the family to South Africa, so for the moment this would be farewell between Orson and his elder daughter. This sad leave-taking was counterbalanced by the revival of an almost-forgotten dream: all over Woodstock that June posters were plastered, announcing the belated world premiere of *Marching Song*, directed by none other than Todd's other genius, Hascy Tarbox. "The forty-five characters and ten scenes required in this play make it so expensive to stage that, as yet, it has had no New York production," announced the poster (obviously this was still a sore point with Skipper). "But here in Woodstock, Hascy Tarbox, scene designer extraordianry [*sic*] has stunningly staged this tremendous pageant with the most breath-taking sets and lighting ever presented in the Opera House." No wonder that, to this day, Orson still refers to "this boy, Hascy Tarbox," as if, having remained behind at Todd, Hascy seemed to Orson never to have grown up, to have remained always the brilliant Todd boy. Orson was in Paris with Micheal and Hilton when he received the poster for Hascy's production from Hortense, accompanied by a scribbled request that Orson meet briefly with a group of traveling Todd boys in Europe. Skipper, however, would not be joining him to work on *The Odyssey*.

But *Marching Song* was not the only play of Orson's about to be staged now. For in Paris, he had proposed to Hilton and Micheal that they collaborate with him on the production of two of his more recent literary efforts: one of them an adaptation of Marlowe's *Dr. Faustus (Time Runs)*, the other an original play about Hollywood (*The Unthinking Lobster*). Orson's plan was to open the double bill at a little theater in Paris, then, if all went well, to take the show on a European tour. Devoting himself to a small-scale theatrical production like this was not exactly the shrewdest professional move Orson could make now. But he didn't intend it to be shrewd. Approaching thirty-five as he was, Orson had had several very formidable professional careers by now. The double bill was to be a departure from the grand scale on which he had typically been operating. Eventually when word of what Orson was up to drifted back to New York and Hollywood, people there pronounced him mad to be wasting his time like this. But not only did Orson figure that he *deserved* the simple theatrical pleasures of the tour, he *needed* them. Having completed most of the principal photography for *Othello* during five weeks in Mogador,

Safi, and Mazagan, this time in the happy company of the
cameraman who had been with him in Fortaleza, Orson's
thoughts strayed from the additional shooting and post-
production work that remained to *Time Runs* and *The Unthinking Lobster*, for which he booked the Théâtre Edouard
VII in Paris for June of 1950. Orson had asked Duke Ellington, then in Europe, to write the music for his updated
version of *Faustus*. Of course Orson planned to portray
Faustus; for his Mephistophilis he cast Hilton Edwards (although later Micheal replaced Hilton on the road); and for
Helen, he took a chance on an obscure black beauty named
Eartha Kitt.

CHAPTER 30
The Best Kind of Men

"Eartha Kitt was obviously a star," says Orson, "You could tell that." He first saw her dancing with Katherine Dunham, and, later, performing in a Parisian nightclub that Eartha Kitt describes as "a highly sophisticated supper club run by a lesbian. Her name was Fred—one of the most beautiful women you ever want to see in your life, *always* dressed as a man. All of her women dressed like this. Fred was like the queen of this little beehive. And they used to tell me that Orson Welles was in there all the time sitting at the bar, but I never saw him." More than three decades later, Eartha Kitt still has the tiny, lithe dancer's body and the exotic beauty of an expensive Persian cat that, along with her matchless voice, instantly appealed to Welles. When she heard that Orson wanted to see her, she did not believe it: "One of the ballet dancers of Dunham called me up and said, 'Orson Welles has been looking for you.' I thought it was a joke. And he said, 'To prove it to you, I will take you to the Théâtre Edouard VII for the audition for Helen of Troy.' Well, as a joke I went to the theater with him. And I was thrown out of the theater by the stage manager because the part was already cast. Orson had given the part to Suzanne Cloutier. When I left the theater after being thrown out, I passed by this car. I was walking down the alleyway—because there was an alley that goes from the front of the theater to another street—I was walking down this little alleyway and it turned out to be Hilton Edwards who had been sitting in the car. I saw him out of the corner of my eye. But because of my embarrassment and losing face by being thrown out of the theater, I didn't want anybody to see me. So this man jumped out of the car, I was scared to death. He had a derby hat on and a cane, and said, 'Hey miss, hey miss, hey miss, I know you've just gone in there for an audition for Helen of Troy. The part is already cast, but you have an interesting look about you. I think Mr. Welles would like very much to meet you. So will you come back tonight at midnight? He will be there.' So I went back and saw Orson and they gave me the script. And he said, 'Read this.' I was supposed to come by the next day, which was Tuesday. I went back and Orson took me into this room, way at the top of the theater, and he turned his back. I was sitting in the middle of the room, and Orson was listening to me with his back. When it was over, he said, 'I don't know what I'm going to do. I have given the part to Suzanne Cloutier. But I love the sound of your voice! You have the part—and I will talk to Suzanne Cloutier.' Now that's how I got in to play Helen of Troy with Orson."

Her immense excitement about having gotten the part was all the greater for Orson's being the director with whom she would be working: "I'd seen *Citizen Kane* five times because Orson Welles was one of the people I had worshiped as a kid!" As it happened, Orson hammered together his production days before it was set to open. "We started rehearsing that Tuesday and we opened the same week," says Miss Kitt. "In twenty-four hours I learned my whole part. We built the scenery and we painted the scenery. We did *everything*! We practically made our own costumes, except for mine, because Orson just bought me a sweater and a pair of slacks." After rehearsing and painting scenery all night: "We would walk from the Théâtre Edouard VII, in the wee hours of the morning, up the Champs-Elysées. I was staying at the Plaza Athénée. He would walk me to the hotel and he would leave me there and go on about his business after the concierge opened these big doors. He would push me in front of those huge French doors and he would leave. It was fascinating for me to be walking the Champs-Elysées with the sun coming up. We would look at the sights, window-shop, and he would recite Shakespeare to me, and all sorts of fantastic authors. To me it was a marvelous experience. I'd never had such a wonderful time in my life!" Another thing that especially delighted Miss Kitt was Orson's hosting wonderful lunches for selected members of his company. "He used to take us to Calvados in Paris," she recalls. "When we got there the table was already laid upstairs. He had ordered everything for us from soup to nuts, and everything he had ordered for us naturally he wanted part of. I think this is what Orson's life had always been about. He gave me the impression that he wanted a bit of everything. He wanted something of everything that he thought was going to help him create his character. So he was sopping up everything he could from us, he was draining us—even those of us like myself who were more or less silent in his company. I had nothing to say because I was busy absorbing Orson, sopping up Orson's energy." As to how Orson paid for all these wonderful meals, Miss Kitt has her suspicions: "I mean it must have cost a fortune, but I don't think Orson ever paid for anything. He *never* paid the bill!"

Part of Orson's fascination was his unpredictability. "I never knew what the hell he was going to do," says Miss Kitt. To illustrate, she describes the strange scene on opening night of his *Faustus* adaptation. Miss Kitt played a young student who, seeing a statue of Faust in a museum, falls in love with him. The action that unfolds is the daydream she

has about the statue's coming alive. As the spotlight falls
on Orson he begins suddenly to move. "And he stretches
his arm out," Miss Kitt recalls. "The girl gets up on the
other side of the stage. As she gets to Orson he takes her
in his arms and he says, 'Helen, make me immortal with a
kiss.' He's talking to the *audience*, and as he says, 'Helen,
make me immortal with a kiss,' he pulls me up to him, he
kisses me, but he *bites me* at the same time. I mean that he
bites me to such an extent that it was very painful." Miss
Kitt suspected it was the conspicuous presence in the front
row of an older gentleman friend of hers from the States
that triggered Orson's jealous outburst: "I asked him later
and he said that he was jealous. He said he got excited."
As Orson's teeth dug into Miss Kitt's lip, she tried not to
let on to the audience what was happening."I couldn't get
away from him because he was too strong," she explains.
"Because the curtain is up, you don't let the audience know
what's going on. You keep acting." Shortly thereafter, when
the curtain dropped, but only for a moment, the student was
supposed to metamorphose into Helen. Says Miss Kitt: "It's
only down for like five seconds—just gives her enough
time to run to the side of the stage and get an apron, a white
apron, and she comes back and she puts this half-apron
around her. But as I came back onstage, I wiped my mouth
because it felt as though moisture was around my mouth.
Blood had been dripping down and it was turning cold. I
wiped my mouth and I saw all of this blood on the apron
so I kept hiding the apron so that the audience would not
see that there was blood on it. The show went on, and as
I was singing a little song that Duke Ellington had written
my face was getting bigger and bigger and bigger." When
at last the final curtain dropped, she rushed downstairs to
the basement, where the dressing rooms were, and where,
at length, she angrily confronted Orson: "I was hitting him
against the chest and saying, 'Why did you bite me?' He
sort of pushed me aside and said, 'I got excited.' "

No sooner had the show opened than it became obvious that the dazzling Eartha Kitt was its principal attraction, a situation Orson dealt with simply. Says Miss Kitt, "I was five feet two, and I must not have weighed more than one hundred seven pounds. And when the audience accepted me in the manner in which they did, Orson would walk in front of me, and everything that I was saying as Helen of Troy looked as though it was coming out of Orson Welles!" But as far as Miss Kitt was concerned, working with Orson had its distinct compensations: "There was a marvelous hotel just outside of Paris, and he would call me and say, 'Meet me out there.' And he would send a car for me. I would go out. We'd have lunch together. We'd sit and talk. We'd walk around the gardens. He would recite fantastic soliloquies from God knows what. We had *fantastic* meals. I was eating marvelous gourmet food, drinking champagne. I mean, Orson Welles really introduced me to a marvelous gourmet type of living. Him and Rubirosa. I tell you, I was absolutely spoiled by the best kind of men!"

Although the French audience had more difficulty than Orson had anticipated they would in trying to follow the show in English, the production was a great hit, and it made Eartha Kitt famous in Paris. Her acclaim spread when Orson took the show on the road; although he had planned to open in London, he changed his mind and went to Germany with a revamped show titled *An Evening with Orson Welles* that included his *Faustus* (with Micheal replacing Hilton as Mephistophilis), a condensation of Wilde's *The Importance of Being Earnest*, in which Hilton had directed Orson and Micheal, a few songs by Eartha Kitt, Orson's magic act, and assorted Shakespearean soliloquies thrown in as well. "The first part was the *Faustus*," says Miss Kitt. "Then Orson had to go dress, put heavy makeup on with a hunchback, and he had to do a soliloquy. And it took him a little longer than fifteen minutes to put his makeup on. So he threw me out on the stage to sing what they called the Peanut

Concert. I had to sing three songs—one I had written in English, one was in Spanish, and somebody had written me a little German song, so I sang that one. I remember the dress I had on—it was a gold lamé striped dress, very, very sensuous, split up on one side." Orson was supposed to follow her onstage immediately thereafter, but the wild applause that filled the auditorium told him otherwise: "So I go back through the curtain, and Orson is supposedly ready," she recalls, "but the audience did not stop applauding. So as he's standing there in his makeup and his hunchback and his lantern in his hand, he said, 'Get back on the stage, dammit! Don't you see they want you?' And so I had to go back out and invent another song. I think I ad-libbed the whole thing because I was scared to death. Now the papers came out and they said, 'Orson may think it's an evening with Orson Welles, but it's really an evening with Eartha Kitt.' Orson became very jealous. He didn't talk to me for a month. We were living in the same hotel, right across from one another, and I would walk out of my room at the time he did, and he would pretend I didn't even exist!"

Not that the German audiences failed wildly to appreciate Orson. "They used to applaud forever," Orson says of the Germans. "And in Hamburg, I literally got so fed up with taking a bow and thought it was so undeserved after what seemed to me like an hour and twenty minutes of bow-taking, that I went to my dressing room and got dressed, and started to go out of the theater. And the stage manager came and said, 'They're still out there applauding.' I was ready to leave for the hotel. Of course I had to quickly take off my overcoat and *try* to look like I was just milking the applause or something. That didn't make me unhappy, but my reaction wasn't the typical actor's one: I *become* a director—my psyche moves out to the box office and the fifth row where the director sits. I don't stand up there surrounded by the applause. It *alienates* me in some funny way. That's why movies are a much happier place for me."

In Hamburg, Orson was the object of considerable attention outside the theater as well. "I was writing a series of articles while I was touring in Germany: on postwar Germany as it was then," Orson remembers. "And I wrote one piece which was entirely made up of quotation marks—cab drivers and bartenders and intellectuals and poets and actors and everybody: what they thought of Germany today. And they said, *We are the criminals of the world, we should be trampled under*, all this. And I printed all that and it got translated into German as though it was my opinion! So when I got to Hamburg—which is a city I adore—on the front of the marvelous hotel, literally on the front of it, the whole length of the hotel, was an enormous sign saying, 'Out of bounds for Orson Welles.' " The German antipathy toward Orson had no effect in the theater, but it *did* at the movies, where *Prince of Foxes* had flopped badly as a result of Orson's being quoted in the press as saying he doubted that there were many genuine anti-Nazis among the German people. So alarmed was the studio by the dismal fate in Germany of *Prince of Foxes* that they decided not to release *The Black Rose* there because of Orson's starring role. Not all the frenzied reaction to Orson in Germany was political—frequently he found himself pursued by young women who had fallen in love with him from his portrayal of Harry Lime. "*Der Dritte Mann! Der Dritte Mann!*" they called when they saw him. But Orson was not flattered. It would always be a source of aggravation to him that people seemed to identify him far more with his performance in Carol Reed's film than in any he had directed himself.

Micheal MacLiammoir was thrilled to be in Occupied Germany with its great abundance of uniformed soldiers. "Oh, he'd never had it so much in his life as when he was in Germany," says Orson. Hilton Edwards had had to return to Dublin to look after the Gate, which left Micheal particularly free to seduce soldiers. But Hilton had a dark secret of his own that only Orson knew about, and that Hilton had pleaded with him not to disclose to Micheal. "When we were playing in Paris he fell madly in love with one of the *girls* in the cast, and got the clap from her!" says Orson. As far as Orson could determine, it was the first time Hilton had had sexual intercourse with a woman in years. "He said to me, 'For God's sake, don't tell Micheal it was a *girl!*' " Orson recalls.

Before Orson's company left Germany, he had an unexpected visitor from America, a beautiful, well-to-do young woman who announced that she had come to Europe expressly to give herself to him, and to live with him forever. Orson had never met or heard of her before. "I sent her back," he says, with a tinge of regret. "Of course she was a total nut, but she was terribly attractive. The temptation to exploit her was enormous, but I didn't." This was neither the first nor the last time in his life that Orson was aware of his appeal to all sorts of strange people. "If I'm at a large dinner party—which very seldom happens nowadays, thank God—and there's *one* pair of wild eyes, I know that they're going to end up being fixed on me," says Orson. "I do have some appeal for those who belong in quiet rooms."

From Germany Orson hauled his little extravaganza to Brussels, then to Italy, where, having installed Eartha Kitt and the others in an elegant hotel near Lake Como, he found himself out of funds. The company waited at leisure, some happily rowing on the lake, as he struggled to scrape together the cash to open. But he was unable to do so, and *An Evening with Orson Welles* came to an end. The modest tour had afforded Orson a measure of contentment that he had not known for some time (and that almost distracted him from his intermittent fits of anxiety about finishing *Othello*). It would be hard for him to accept the fact that the tour had substantially damaged his already tarnished reputation; the executive secretary of ANTA, who had been interested in Orson's doing another production for them, complained to Wilson that Orson's vagabond tour had convinced people that he was a "lost cause" and—even worse—that he needed a "keeper." By returning to the States, it was suggested, perhaps Orson could "get a firm footing." But ANTA despaired of reaching Orson, let alone getting a clear commitment from him. As when he had been in Brazil, inaccessibility was a great part of Orson's problem now. ANTA lamented that everyone had grown "afraid" of Orson—and one suspects that much of this fear issued from a simple lack of information and the attendant misconceptions about his activities. There was barely any awareness of the *Othello* project in America (and even those few who knew about it figured he would never finish it anyway), so besides what sounded like nothing more than a traveling vaudeville show, Orson's only apparent activities for the past three lost years had been to turn up now and then in ludicrous roles in equally ludicrous movies, and to be photographed shirtless by *Life* magazine at Darryl Zanuck's cabana in Cap d'Antibes. That the movie roles and the posing at Eden Roc were both attempts to raise money to make *Othello* seems never to have occurred to those back home who proclaimed that Orson was wasting his time abroad.

The most stinging attack was to come from critic Walter Kerr, who described Orson in print as an "international joke, and possibly the youngest living has-been." Wrote Kerr: "Welles has let himself turn into a buffoon, and buffoonery is a quality hard to erase from the public mind. In fact, the imprint of the clown is by now so firm that the talents Welles once displayed as a serious, or at least respectable, director, producer, and scenarist have been all but obliterated." From afar Orson was much too easy a target. From afar it did indeed sound as if Orson had abandoned his sense of himself as a serious artist. But about Orson's struggle to film, and now to finish, *Othello*, Kerr was of course silent. It would have spoiled his argument. Far from having abandoned artistic seriousness, Orson was so entirely motivated by it that he insisted on making movies his own way—at whatever personal cost. Rambling about with *An Evening with Orson Welles* had given him renewed vigor to complete *Othello*. Contrary to those who have argued that Orson never likes to complete anything, he has in fact consistently labored against all odds to finish troubled films like *It's All True*, *Othello*, and—some years later—*The Other Side of the Wind*. That he has not always been successful in doing so in no way suggests that he has not tried.

Having dispersed his traveling company, Orson did not cease to travel himself. Now he alighted in Italy, where he was a regular house guest at the palatial villa of a tycoon from whom he raised some cash to finish cutting *Othello*, and on whom he eventually based the character of Mr. Arkadin. In England, he launched a popular radio show for the BBC titled *The Adventures of Harry Lime*, in which he re-created his famous character from *The Third Man*. He figured that as long as people seemed inevitably to associate him with Harry Lime, he—and *Othello*—might as well benefit from the fact. Not only was the show a great hit, but Orson impressed the radio people with the uncanny speed with which he was capable of knocking together an entire show. 'He was a powerhouse," says actor Robert Arden, who appeared regularly in the Harry Lime series. "To those of us more used to working with the BBC in radio shows his technique was a revelation. At the BBC they would take three days to record a half-hour show. Orson had it all together and recorded inside one morning." Orson would also host a popular radio show titled *The Black Museum*, which rehashed famous Scotland Yard murder cases for the BBC, and act in an adaptation of *Sherlock Holmes*, in which he portrayed Moriarty with John Gielgud as Holmes and Ralph Richardson as Watson.

Nor were his artistic activities in London confined to radio. Having derived the movie of *Macbeth* from the stage production he had done in Utah, in the fall of 1951 Orson reversed the process by doing a stage version of *Othello* derived from his still-unfinished film. He discussed the production, and especially his interpretation of the title role, with Laurence Olivier first, and Olivier "implored me to commit suicide by bringing out a small curved knife and cutting myself from ear to ear," says Orson. "I thought it was a very bad idea—and he went ahead and did it years later." Welles had his own advice for Olivier: he says he suggested to Olivier that he would make a great Iago, to which Olivier instantly replied, "Why not Othello?" "Because to play Othello you need a bass voice," said Orson. At this Olivier's eyes lowered, and the discussion ended. According to Orson, Olivier then went to a voice coach, who, by the time Olivier appeared in *Othello* in 1964, had made him sound rather like James Earl Jones. If Olivier had to change his voice to play Othello, Orson had to regain his, for in the midst of assembling the show he found himself suddenly hoarse. Fortunately, by opening night his voice was as mighty as ever—and as beautiful. Several decades later when Orson revisited London there were still people there who garlanded him with praise for his *Othello*. "*That* made me so happy," says Orson, "because a stage thing is written on sand, and when people start telling you how they loved you in St. James's Theatre, you'd rather hear that than anything, because it's gone forever." In retrospect Orson thinks his performance of the role onstage—with Peter Finch as his Iago—superior to what he had already done onscreen. "I'd play it better again the third time," claims Orson. "I think I played the last scene as well as I know how to play it. In general, I was better because I had less to think about. I was beleaguered in that movie."

Renowned for his eccentric staging, Orson this time wanted

to fit into what he saw as the mainstream of contemporary British theater by mounting a production that was, as he describes it, "essentially conservative, but self-effacing, in order to reveal the acting." In short: "I wanted to play a great classical part in London, and I simply wanted a production that would support it." When Welles's *Othello* opened, Kenneth Tynan wrote a devastating review that particularly upset Orson because of the great esteem in which he held this brilliant critic. "No doubt about it," wrote Tynan, "Orson Welles has the courage of his restrictions." He described Orson's acting as simply "a huge shrug": "Welles's Othello is the lordly and mannered performance we saw in *Citizen Kane*," said Tynan, "slightly adapted to read 'Citizen Coon.'" It seemed to Orson that Tynan had attacked him for not doing what, on the basis of the legendary productions of Project 891 and the Mercury, the critic had expected from an Orson Welles production. "He went waiting to see the English theater turned upside down by a new way to do *Othello*," says Orson, who had simply never intended to do that in this production. "I wanted to do as much of an English *Othello* as I could," says Orson, "and Ken went to see the Mercury." Orson's friend, writer Wolf Mankowitz, suggests that, besides this, Tynan may have had other reasons for being agitated by Welles's performance: "Tynan was a very quirky fellow," says Mankowitz. "And I think, you see, if Tynan had been the actor he would have liked to have been, he would have been Orson. And I think that Tynan was really rather jealous of Orson's bravura and his character, personality qualities, and command of the situation, and so on. I think Tynan was an actor manqué. I mean an actor with a stutter as bad as that doesn't stand too good a chance anyway, but even if he hadn't had the stutter, he didn't have the talent." While this stage *Othello* had been otherwise quite well received, Tynan's eloquent sarcasm would linger in Orson's thoughts forever after.

There were worse disappointments in store. Shortly after *Othello* closed, Orson went to Dublin to see Hilton and Micheal, who, in the meantime, had proposed transplanting one of the Gate's new productions for a London run. But if he had expected his return to the Dublin Gate to be marked by a good deal of fanfare, Orson did not anticipate the unfelicitous form it would take. "This was a very strange event," says Orson, "because I went to see a play and there were people out there demonstrating against the fact that I was going to sit in the audience. 'Go back to Moscow, Stalin's star!' they said." Outside the Dublin Gate more than a hundred angry protesters from the Catholic Cinema and Theater Patrons' Association declared Orson a Communist whom they warned to "Stay out of Ireland!" Picket signs charged that Orson's "spiritual home" was Moscow. Press reports at the time indicated that the demonstrators hurled bottles at the police, who tried unsuccessfully to disperse them, but who did manage to keep them from storming the theater. Hoping to avoid Orson's having to confront the demonstrators out front, Hilton arranged for him to be sneaked in through the adjoining maternity hospital. "They got me in through the maternity hospital," Orson recalls, "so I wouldn't see the crowd, and up through the back where I'd been as the Ghost in *Hamlet*, and into the audience." Nor when the curtain went up did the chanting outside diminish. Afterward : "I was then asked up on the stage at the end of the play, and had to address the audience to calm them," says Orson, "because all during the play we'd heard the roars of this group, which was led by some insane priest. And I had to make a political speech on the stage of the old Gate." This was by no means the peaceful, happy vacation Orson had fondly anticipated. Even when he called on Hilton and Micheal at home he was confronted with agitation, unrest. The two were embroiled in a terrible spat, which Orson observed through the open door. "I came to pick them up for lunch, and Micheal had hold of the bed, and Hilton had hold of Micheal, and he pulled the bed and Micheal to the door of the apartment," Orson recalls. "And he was trying to continue to pull, but the bed was too big! They were screeching at each other like macaws." Thinking it best to leave them to their rituals, Orson quietly left, and returned to London.

Although it was rumored in New York theatrical circles that Orson would soon be returning to do his London *Othello*, and although he had done nothing to discourage these rumors, he was still entirely preoccupied with finishing the film that he had been working on sporadically for four years now and that, thanks to the money he made on radio, was very nearly ready. Besides, if he returned to the States he would have to contend with the Internal Revenue Service, who wanted money from him that he preferred to spend on *Othello*. There were those in the film world who laughed at Orson's having paid for the picture himself; those who said that he'd never finish it; and those who thought he had been foolishly squandering his time and money How very wrong they were was evident at the Cannes Film Festival of 1952, at which, finished at last, Orson's *Othello* was screened, acclaimed, and awarded the grand prize (which it shared with another picture).

But it would be equally wrong to think that the great artistic success of *Othello* would considerably improve Orson's reputation. In the States, the unusual way in which he had made his new movie seemed like further proof of the eccentricity, the queerness, that Hollywood had ascribed to him all along. The fact that he had taken four years to complete *Othello* only because he lacked the cash to do it more quickly was overlooked; his perseverance, his self-reliance—ironically these were widely interpreted as character flaws! From Hollywood's point of view he had merely been obstinate, and this being so, *Othello* wasn't the personal triumph for Orson that, on the basis of Cannes, one might have expected it to be. But it was a very great film, and within the bounds of the woefully limited financial and technical resources available to him, Orson had made it entirely on his own terms. For the first time since *Kane* he could feel that he had made quite the movie he set out to.

CHAPTER 31

The Glorious Gypsy

When King Farouk offered to back a modern-dress film of *Julius Caesar*, Orson wrote a script for the picture, which, he says, was to be "shot like a newsreel," but word of a Hollywood *Julius Caesar*, directed by Joseph Mankiewicz (Herman's brother) and produced by John Houseman, soon killed the project. "My Egyptians immediately ran for cover!" laughs Orson of King Farouk's response to news of the rival picture.

In between acting jobs Orson threw himself into writing the libretto for a ballet, "The Lady in the Ice," which was performed by Roland Petit's Ballet de Paris in London, as well as two slender novels—*Une grosse légume* and *Mr. Arkadin*, the latter of which he would eventually adapt for a film of his own. It is not surprising that Orson wrote to Hortense Hill from Rome about *Arkadin*, for the nabob who had inspired him to write this book about a wealthy man of mystery lived there. Actually, Orson had two millionaire models for Arkadin: "One of them loved to buy out all the whores from some nightclub in Rome and bring them up to his villa," Orson says of the Latvian Jew who was his host in Rome, "and the other, a Hungarian, had the biggest expensively bound pornography collection in Europe."

The search for identity, the quest for an enigmatic self, this was a theme that had engaged Orson as early as *Marching Song* and as recently as *Citizen Kane*. But if Orson had consciously based his fat mystery man on others, it is not too much to suppose that, perhaps less consciously, he also drew substantially on his personal experience of self-invention and celebrity. Thus the book begins with what could have been a description of Orson as he perceived himself: "Yes, everybody had heard of him, but nobody knew much about him. Who was he? What sort of man was he? The stories told about him were endless and legion; were they not produced by the fertile brains of those gossip columnists who must daily dish up a ration of rumors, jokes, slanders, insinuations, sly digs for the anonymous multitude concerning whom nobody ever bothers to write anything?" In a sense, this was how Orson thought of himself: as misunderstood as he was famous. It seemed to Orson that, in America, although *everybody had heard of him, nobody knew much about him*. They did not know what sort of man he really was. Ironically, the "anonymous multitude" who read about him so avidly in the American popular press were the very people with whom he perceived himself as having tried, and basically failed, to communicate.

A speech that he had been asked to deliver at the Edinburgh Festival in 1953, in conjunction with the summer film school of the British Film Institute, afforded Orson the opportunity to work out his feelings about the "anonymous multitude" that, for better or worse, constitutes the principal audience for film. It was a topic that Orson had been stalking for years — but the experiences of *Macbeth* and *Othello*, and of living in exile at a great physical and spiritual distance from Hollywood, allowed him to articulate the problem in a new light. Orson pointed out that unlike most other artists, the filmmaker was *expected* to create something that would speak to sixty million people. "If I were to play King John at the Edinburgh Festival I would know the shape of my public, but a film is manufactured and shipped out to a series of halls throughout the world into which a huge and amorphous public pours. Nobody really knows anything about it. It is made up of everybody, of kings and queens and cleaners and clerks. The best thing commercially, which is the worst artistically, by and large, is the most successful; and that being the fact, how can we be surprised if the level of film goes down and down?" Thus Orson called for an international conference to scrutinize the nature of the mysterious public on whom the economics of the film industry depend. He had by now largely abandoned his initial faith in the innate wisdom of the public, but this skepticism did not mean that he was about to start making avant-garde films for a tiny audience. Hence his conviction that the serious filmmaker had to discover some middle ground between the avant-garde film and "the big commercial film": Orson argued that instead of aiming at the select few, on the one hand, or the mass audience, on the other, the filmmaker might address, and build, the potential third audience that lay somewhere between them. "The biggest mistake we have made is to consider that films are primarily a form of entertainment; they are only incidentally a form of entertainment. The film is the greatest medium since the invention of movable type for exchanging ideas and information, and it is no more at its best in light entertainment than literature is at its best in the light novel." But as he knew only too well from having made *Othello* mainly out of his own funds, the filmmaker, unlike the writer or painter, who could create in relative poverty, needed immense sums of money to put anything onscreen. Hence the importance of an experiment such as Orson's *Macbeth* had been to make films quickly and cheaply for this third audience: ". . . we have to find a way of making films—and here television may help us—by which, if two or three million people see them, we have a return for our money. . . ."

Orson's curiosity about the aesthetic possibilities of television made him particularly receptive to Peter Brook's offer to star in his American television production of *King Lear* to be aired from New York in December of 1953. In his Edinburgh address Orson had said that unlike film, television was an actor's rather than a director's medium, so that he was thrilled to have been offered the role of Lear. Far from regarding this as just another acting job, Orson saw it as an opportunity to look into the matter of American television. Because of Orson's substantial tax debt, a deal had to be worked out in advance with Uncle Sam. Recalls Virgil Thomson, who did the music for *Lear*: "It was arranged that he could come in, work, live in a good hotel, but he could spend no money beyond his actual expenses." The rest went to pay off a tiny bit of what he owed the government. "He didn't have money to buy cigarettes or anything like that," says Thomson, "so that he would borrow from friends and pay them back in France." One of these friends was Micheal MacLiammoir, who had joined Orson in New York to play the role of Edgar.

New York seemed to expect the worst from Orson, who behaved himself impeccably. Anxious to alter his frivolous image in the public mind, Orson earnestly explained to the press that he was not the dilettante people thought him. He told them about the books he had been writing, and the new film he had been planning. He made himself seem industrious, especially in *King Lear*, by which most critics were enthralled. Hailed *Cue*: "Like a confidently patient boxer who lets his opponent flail away for eight or nine rounds and then calmly steps in to finish the fight with one blow, Orson Welles burst into television (after several years of watchful waiting) and knocked everything for a loop. The performance he gave as King Lear established a new high for the medium in terms of power, heart and sheer artistry." Indeed, it was widely hoped in New York that Orson would turn up again very soon on American television. But this Orson was not especially anxious to do; his top priority was

to rush back to the Continent to get started on the movie of
Mr. Arkadin, for which his old political mentor Dolivet had
successfully arranged the initial financing.

In London Robert Arden was appearing in *Guys and Dolls*
at the Coliseum, where one evening the stage-door keeper
told him, "Some madman has been telephoning you from
somewhere and will call back during the intermission." The
only other information the puzzled Arden could pry out of
the fellow was that the crazy call had been "foreign." He
would have to wait until intermission, when, as promised,
he was summoned to the phone, where a Spanish operator
told him to hold, and then suddenly he heard an absolutely
unmistakable voice that he had not heard for some time
now: "How soon can you be in Madrid?" asked Orson.
When they had worked together in the Harry Lime and Black
Museum radio shows, Orson had told Arden that he would
like to make a movie with him someday, and now that day
had come. Orson told him nothing whatsoever about the
part, just that they were waiting for him in Spain. When
Arden protested that he was in the middle of a show, Orson
told him not to worry—his "London representative" would
promptly extricate the actor from all contractual obligations.
Arden had to return to the show following the intermission,
however, since Orson's "agent" would not be calling him
until the next morning. No less amazing than Orson's call
was the one that Arden received at eight a.m., when Orson's
London representative turned out to be none other than Sir
Carol Reed, who summoned Arden for breakfast at his home
to explain that Orson wanted him for the male lead in his
new picture. Within four days Sir Carol had bought Arden
out of *Guys and Dolls*, Orson had cabled instructions about
the clothing he should bring, the script had arrived, and
Arden had left for Madrid.

No sooner had Arden checked in to the Palace Hotel than
he received a message that he was to come to dinner in
Orson's suite at the Castillana Hilton. There actor Akim

Tamiroff opened the door, to reveal Orson, Dolivet, and Orson's newest love, the exquisite Italian Countess di Girfalco, Paola Mori, whom he had cast for the female lead. "Orson welcomed me into the suite as though we had last seen each other the day before," Arden recalls. Never one to waste a moment, Orson decided to start rehearsing after dinner. Orson played old Arkadin, the countess his beloved daughter from whom he wishes to conceal his sordid past, and Arden the investigator he hires to ferret out anyone who knows too much about that past. When they broke at two-thirty a.m. the young actor learned that shooting was to begin the very next day at two p.m. "Talk about being thrown in at the deep end," he says.

The next day when Arden and Tamiroff reported for work, Orson told them he had been up all night rewriting the script to tell the story in flashback, so there were entirely new pages to shoot. Further problems would be resolved later by dubbing. Arden ascribes Orson's tendency to rewrite to the director's old problem of losing interest in what he had already worked out in his thoughts. Says Arden: "Part of the problem with *Arkadin* was—in my opinion—that once Orson had written the script of the film and got it done in his head and on paper, he then lost interest in the actual filming . . . and then, to maintain his flagging interest he would keep changing things, always saying that any discrepancies could be fixed up in the dubbing. Hence the occasions when the lips aren't saying what the sound track is saying." Orson's conviction that the sound could be taken care of afterward caused him to lash out at a sound engineer who got in his way the second day of shooting. As Arden recounts it: "The sound engineer asked, just before a take, if some carpet could be put down to cover the camera track noise he was picking up. Orson exploded! But I mean really exploded! For the next five minutes, and with his magnificent voice getting louder and louder, he proceeded to tear into the unfortunate sound man. Everybody else around seemed to wish that he were some other place. The gist of it all was to the effect that sound was the servant of the film and not the master. Eventually it was over and we got on with the work. . . . Later, driving back to the city from the studio, I said to Orson, 'Man, you really go when you go!' He laughed as though I had said the funniest thing. Then he said, 'One good tantrum at the beginning of the shooting solves all future problems. Then they know there is only one boss.' 'So are you performing?' I asked him. He gave his Harry Lime grin and said, 'If you think so.' "

But it was no performance the time Orson exploded at Arden, who, with a number of other actors, had spent several hours waiting for the director on location at Barajas Airport. When at last Welles appeared, Arden casually greeted him. "I said, 'Hi.' No more than that," Arden recalls. "He turned to me. 'Hi?' he said. Then he let loose. 'You don't say hi to the director.' . . . He proceeded to tell me that he had picked me up from nowhere and could drop me right back there. . . . This and about four million other things were pouring out at an alarming rate—his voice booming away as only that incredible instrument can." Furious at being treated so, Arden stormed off to another part of the airport, where, shortly thereafter, Dolivet pursued him to try to patch things up. But Arden insisted that he just wanted to escape this "madhouse" and to get away from "that goddam maniac." "Dolivet asked me to calm down," Arden explains, "and I remember saying to him that he had better give that advice to Welles. Two minutes later, and my own fury was abating, when a huge hand descended on my shoulder. It was Orson. He asked me to forgive him for an unpardonable outburst. He had been feeling unwell—hence his late arrival—was looking for an argument with somebody—anybody—and I was the first person to give him any opportunity. I told him to forget it, and then, with tears on his face, he said, 'We mustn't fight, you and I—I don't want to forget it, I want you to forgive me.' There was something so forlorn about this huge man (not only huge in stature) that my anger vanished and I said, 'Okay, let's get back to work.' He put his arm around my shoulder, walked me back to the crew and other artistes, and we got on with the filming. Not another word was said by either of us, about this incident, and I think that Orson had probably forgotten the whole thing minutes later." Arden eloquently characterizes Orson as "the most gifted fourteen-year-old I've ever known. He is perpetually fourteen. With the enthusiasm, energy, and confidence that only extreme youth seems to be able to produce in totality. He is gifted beyond human requirement with charm. He can, literally, charm the birds off the trees—and to me he will always remain the complete Renaissance man. His conversation, his interest in so many different facets of life, and his ability to make you feel that you are important to him—if only momentarily—are gifts indeed. More than any one human being should have."

But there was one person whom Orson did not manage to charm during this prolonged period of shooting in Spain, France, and Germany—and that person was Dolivet. Before agreeing to produce the film, Dolivet had predicted that there would be trouble between them, since he planned to take an active role in the making of the picture. But in the end, the acute tensions between the two old friends were caused mainly by the production's requiring substantially more time and money than expected. If Dolivet was frequently absent it was because he had taken off for Switzerland in quest of more cash, some of it earmarked to appease Orson's flock of continental creditors. Every now and again even Orson was called upon to dress up in what he liked to call his "Go to See the Banker" suit to do the same. Dolivet was furious about what he perceived as Orson's intolerable slowness in cutting the picture, and he finally took Orson aside to tell him that he would have to learn something about efficiency. In turn, Orson ascribed Dolivet's criticism to the producer's inexperience in making movies. "Louis had never been near an editing table!" says Orson. "And I'd made quite a lot of pictures by then, and I knew exactly how long it takes to edit a picture!" Orson argues that it was the pressure of the Swiss investors' clamoring for a finished film that turned Dolivet against him: "It was *my* fault because he didn't have a finished movie and he had told them that for that money he would. I had told him all along that we didn't have a budget, that we were flying blind, and that we'd have to go on selling territories until we saw what we could bring it in for. Louis would go off to Switzerland and sell another piece of the picture and come limping back again, groaning with pain. And he turned on me because I take three days cutting to one day shooting. That's my ratio. And he wanted the picture about three weeks after it was finished."

Orson could never have anticipated what disaster was to follow. In Hollywood he had several times lost control of the movies he was making, but he did not expect that that would happen to him working independently in Europe. "They took it away from me!" says Orson of *Arkadin*. "And they completely destroyed the movie! More completely than any other picture of mine has been hurt by anybody, *Arkadin* was destroyed because they completely changed the entire form of it: the whole order of it, the whole point of it . . . *Ambersons* is *nothing* compared to *Arkadin*!" According to Orson, the recut film was more linear than anything he intended: "It was told in a very complicated and strange way," he says of his original version, "which is what made it, I think, more palatable and interesting. They tore that apart, threw out scenes." Nor was this humiliation all. Afterward Dolivet brought suit against Orson for his purported misbehavior during the making of *Arkadin*, which included excessive drinking in nightclubs and on the set, and which resulted in lost time. Orson hotly denies these charges. The beautiful Italian Countess di Girfalco was another point of contention in the lawsuit; Dolivet charged that Orson had hired her for personal reasons and to the detriment of the film. Under the professional name of Paola Mori, the countess, whose parents were highly regarded members of the Italian colonial diplomatic service in Africa, had been acting in an Italian picture with his friend Errol Flynn when Orson met and embarked on a passionate love affair with her. In preparation for *Mr. Arkadin*, he had sent her to Dublin to work on her English for six weeks under the tutelage of Micheal MacLiammoir and Hilton Edwards. Although the suit against Orson was eventually dropped, the recutting of the film and the implications about Paola's acting ability created too much ill-will for Orson and Dolivet to resume their once-intense friendship. Ironically, when *Arkadin* was released, *The New York Times* proclaimed it "from start to finish, the work of a man with an unmistakable genius for the film medium." But Orson took a darker view, convinced that the version released to the theaters "made a mess out of what was the *best* movie story I'd ever thought up."

After *Arkadin* Orson and the countess settled into a large apartment in Paris, and although his funds had dwindled to almost nothing, he persisted in living (which, in large part, meant eating) very well indeed. "His way of life wasn't really seriously affected ever by his financial difficulties," says Wolf Mankowitz. "All he requires is another couple of thousand dollars and he can get through till whenever it is it spins out. He lives from hand to mouth—I think he always has. He's a great genius—but he's also an artist and a bohemian, and this is reflected in his attitude toward money. I sympathize, I have a similar attitude myself. Now did it affect his state of mind or his way of living? I think you could say substantially no. I mean, he always ate too much and his state of mind was always very evanescent. Any project that caught his eye, that tempted his imagination, he would spend a few hours with, and if it mate-

rialized from there, okay, if not, something else would turn
up." One such project was Mankowitz's idea of selling
Orson's *Arkadin* manuscript as a way of paying for his and
the countess's ticket to London, where, at Mankowitz's
suggestion, he would return to the stage. But when, as
promised, Mankowitz did indeed make the sale in Paris,
Orson suddenly seemed to have other ideas about what to
do with the cash. "I sold *Arkadin* as a serial to a Paris
newspaper," says Mankowitz, "and got a certain amount of
money for him up front—I think quite a lot at the time,
relative to having nothing anyway. Actually, when he got
the money he spent quite a lot of it taking me and my wife
out with Paola and him to the most expensive restaurant in
Paris, the Grand Vefour. And then after that he wanted to
go to a nightclub, a fiddle joint, because he likes fiddles—
and he tipped very heavily and we drank too much stuff,
and I don't know how much was left of that money! Orson's
attitude towards money is never very realistic, never was."

Orson's cronies were thrilled to see him so utterly content
with Paola Mori. "She obviously worshiped him," says Robert Arden, "and he seemed to feel the same way about her."
From the outset the countess took over the formidable task
of looking after Orson's every need. "She was a tower of
strength, really," says Wolf Mankowitz, "a very pragmatic,
practical Italian lady, very beautiful, and very nice indeed.
She really looked after him awfully well. . . . I mean, it takes
a very extraordinary person to be able to live with Orson
anyway." As to the secret of their relationship Mankowitz
speculates: "There was a kind of division of labor: he made
the mess, and she cleared it up!" In particular, his friends
marveled at the countess's unrelenting loyalty to Orson,
from whom it was obvious that she could expect little in
the way of domestic stability. "If *I* was a woman," fancies
Wolf Mankowitz, "not at present of course, but in the past,
I would have preferred to have a sort of wild affair with
Orson in some exotic and ridiculous place rather than get

lumbered with the whole ongoing production. I mean, Orson is a traveling bohemian actor—man of the theater—and, you know, you don't bring people like that home to your mother."

Eager to work with Orson in England, Mankowitz made a deal with the BBC for a series of television shows titled *The Orson Welles Sketchbook* that would pay enough to keep Orson going until they put together something for the London stage. Mankowitz had created the television show to fit what he saw as Orson's innate restlessness: "The problem with Orson," says Mankowitz, "was to get him to stay in the same place in front of the camera for very long. So as he draws quite amusingly well, I had the notion that we could have him with his sketchbook, and that we would simply cut to the drawings when we wanted to get off him. You see, we simply needed a device to intercut so that we could lay his voice over and then when we had him back in the eye of the camera, pick it up from there." The BBC programs turned out to be a big hit, and Orson was eventually offered a second series, titled *Around the World with Orson Welles*.

But Orson and Mankowitz saw *Sketchbook* as little more than an expediency. Once again, Orson was possessed by the dream of founding a repertory theater, as he and Houseman had done. He would stage his own dramatic versions of Melville's *Moby Dick* and Hemingway's *The Sun Also Rises* (with Marlene Dietrich in the latter), as well as an adaptation of a Mankowitz novella.

In the end, however, only *Moby Dick* found its way into production with the financial backing of two New Yorkers, Henry Margolis and Martin Gabel, who hoped to bring the show to New York next. The wealthy Margolis had heard from his and Orson's mutual friend, columnist Leonard Lyons, that Orson's *Moby Dick* script was in the spirit of his wonderful New York productions that had used, as Margolis puts it, "imagination more than money"—exactly what

an investor wants to hear. It had been this remarkable ingenuity that had so greatly impressed Martin Gabel when
he worked with Orson on *Danton* in the Mercury days. And
indeed the *Moby Dick* script on which Orson had been
laboring intermittently and, in various forms, for years (at
one point he had even envisioned it as a cantata with a score
by Honegger) had strong affinities to his work in the New
York theater, most obvious among them the preoccupation
with breaking down the frame of the dramatic work of art.
This time his strategy was to insert a play within a play.
Orson's Melville adaptation concerned itself with an American theatrical company of the 1890s that is rehearsing its
own Melville adaptation by day while doing *King Lear* by
night. Hence Margolis's delight at Orson's using "imagination more than money"—for the conceit of the rehearsal
permitted Orson to do without costly stage properties. Har-
poons? Oars? Telescopes? According to the script, these
would be "indicated in gesture and mime." Captain Ahab's
peg leg? For the moment a simple walking stick would
suffice. In the kind of subtle theatrical irony Orson loved,
the *bare* stage on which the mock-rehearsal takes place is
not in fact bare at all: "It would not be true to say that there
is no scenery," writes Orson. "The stage is not bare; it is
interestingly and even romantically dressed with all the lum-
ber of an old-fashioned theater."

Orson's *Moby Dick* opens with an actor's pronouncing
the famous phrase "Call me Ishmael"—but after several
lines of blank verse, this reality dissolves into another: that
of the theatrical company's getting ready to begin the rehearsal that the actor had merely gotten a head start on
moments before. The effect of this abrupt transition between
the *play* and the ostensible reality of the theatrical company
is rather like the shock one experiences watching *Citizen
Kane* when the newsreel about the tycoon's death spins out,
and there suddenly is the screening room in which a small
audience has been watching. The preparations for the re-

hearsal, the incidental discussions among the ragbag of actors and the pungent actor-manager (Orson) who will take the role of Ahab, these constitute a shrewd device for distancing the wildly extravagant tone of the dramatic action that follows.

But Orson did not *frame* the action of Melville's novel merely to allow himself (as Ahab) to get away with otherwise laughable histrionics, as some of the critics suggested at the time. In general, Welles criticism has consistently overlooked the important Brechtian strain in his temperament as an actor: his tendency to distance himself from a character as if to watch himself acting. In his play of *Moby Dick* Orson had contrived a dramatic means for stepping into and out of the role of Ahab—for both performing onstage and watching himself from the fifth row. More than that, the master stroke of the play was to portray the action of Melville's novel in an out-of-date, hence legible, style of acting that allowed Orson to represent the character of Ahab without *embodying* him and without the audience's identifying with him.

But the imminent opening of *Moby Dick* was by no means the most important event in Orson's life just now. Two days after his fortieth birthday he married the twenty-four-year-old Countess di Girfalco in a civil ceremony at the Caxton Hall registry in London. Paola wore an elegant suit and white gloves, in which she clutched a sprig of lilies of the valley, and Orson put in a rare appearance in a business suit and tie. But with the production about to open, there was certainly no time for an extended honeymoon. They had taken rooms in St. James's Chambers, where one morning Mankowitz glimpsed somewhat more of Orson's flesh than he was probably accustomed to seeing: "The picture of Orson being rolled over in order to get his jabs for the day, arguing with Paola meanwhile, is an unforgettable image!" Mankowitz exclaims. "He looked like a huge white whale that had gotten beached in St. James's!" As if the combined pressure of getting married again and mounting a new show were not enough, Orson was hotly pursued by his creditors, whose flunkies waited outside his home to serve him with a writ the moment he issued from the front door. Once, Mankowitz found himself enlisted to impersonate Orson, whose coat and hat he put on for the brisk trip out the front door and down the street. A fellow with a writ dashed after him, while, in the meantime, Orson discreetly escaped through the back door.

His creditors were not the only ones to be paying close attention to Orson now that he had set up in London, where there was much amused speculation in theatrical circles about how he was going to do Melville's mighty novel onstage. Wrote the London *Times*: "It is difficult to imagine how he will get on the stage a classic of the sea in which a mad whaling captain, Captain Ahab, pursues an albino whale, Moby Dick, into the Antarctic and there seals the doom of himself and his crew." The fact that John Huston had been working on a still-unfinished film version of *Moby Dick* (in which, ironically, Orson himself had played the cameo role of Father Mapple), made people wonder too if Orson had any hope of making a decent showing beside so expensive a superproduction.

Although Orson played the actor-manager Ahab, he preferred not to rehearse onstage with the other actors. Instead, during rehearsals he positioned himself behind a microphone in the darkness of the stalls, from which he spoke his lines and barked instructions to the others—"like Big Brother!" thought Gordon Jackson, who played Ishmael. Orson had had the sound man hook up the loudspeaker system and kept it at full volume, because he feared straining his voice as he had before the opening of *Othello*. Only when the rehearsal period had nearly ended and the play was about to open, did Orson emerge from the shadows to do his lines onstage. "He *hated* actors who mumbled or played 'under,'" recalls Gordon Jackson. "He called that 'kicking the shit under the bed' style acting! I was inclined to get over-emotional at times, and developed a throb in my voice. He *hated* that too! 'SELF-PITY! SELF-PITY!' he used to scream at me, through his loudspeaker, from the stalls. And he whispered that to me a lot during the actual performances in the run! He never stopped directing on the stage *during* the performance. Quite distracting sometimes! If you were wallowing in a soliloquy, he'd come up behind you and hiss, 'Hurry up!'"

For all his bluster during rehearsals, Orson was certainly not too haughty to ask the considered advice of his company. When an actor burst out laughing at one of the complicated visual effects Orson had devised, the director stopped the rehearsal to solicit the opinions of the crew. "When the *Pequod* took to sea," says Gordon Jackson, "a great curtain of ropes descended from the flies—and these ropes swayed from side to side, giving the impression of a ship at sea. During one of Orson's big Ahab soliloquies, we all had to stagger from side to side to give the impression of a storm at sea. This was very tricky, and had to be meticulously orchestrated, so that we all staggered on the *same* syllables—and in the *same* direction!" It was all this staggering, and an intimation of how ridiculous it might look opening night, that caused one of the cast members to snicker. But overall the crew liked the effect, which Orson retained, and which ultimately proved to be a real crowd pleaser.

The complex lighting on which much of the production's visual impact depended was executed by Hilton Edwards, whom Orson had summoned from Dublin. If at the Todd Summer Festival Edwards had refused to help young Orson with the lighting for *Trilby*, now, says Wolf Mankowitz, "Hilton *deferred* to Orson." Still Orson counted on Hilton's impeccable taste and matchless technical know-how—which seemed especially fitting since in the end the production so

successfully put into practice what had been Edwards's principal artistic legacy to young Orson many years before: the
exquisite dream of a *theatre theatrical*.

Although in retrospect Orson says that "*Moby Dick*, I
think, is the best thing I ever did in *any* form—and I seriously think if I ever did anything really good, that was
it," shortly before it opened he seemed somewhat less certain
of what he had wrought. This insecurity was to be expected,
however: "I don't think Orson's ever been satisfied with
any production he's done," says Wolf Mankowitz. "I think
if he could tinker along with them for years he would do
so—and then probably throw the whole lot in the garbage
can and get on with something else." But when at last *Moby
Dick* opened that June of 1955 at the Duke of York's Theatre,
with few exceptions the press and public were enchanted
by what they saw. Even Kenneth Tynan, whose response
Orson particularly valued and who had clobbered *Othello*,
raved: "Mr. Welles has fashioned a piece of pure theatrical
megalomania," Tynan wrote, "a sustained assault on the
senses which dwarfs anything London has ever seen since,
perhaps, the Great Fire. It was exactly fifty years ago last
Wednesday evening that Irving made his last appearance in
London. I doubt if anyone since then has left his mark more
indelibly on every second of a London production than Mr.
Welles has on this of 'Moby Dick.'" Tynan went on to say
that if spectators "wish to exert themselves, to have their
minds set whirling and their eyes dazzling at sheer theatrical
virtuosity, 'Moby Dick' is their opportunity. With it, the
theatre becomes once more a house of magic."

On his part, Orson was no less enamored of the London
theatergoers, who impressed him with their consummate
seriousness: "I enjoyed it much more than I did in New
York," says Orson of working in the London theater. "I
don't think there is any New York theater anymore. I don't
think I could have *happened* if I'd started three years later.
I think it's just sheer luck I got to New York just when I

did because it closed in and became impossible, you know. By the end of the war, Broadway had ceased to be an attractive place for a legitimate play. They all say, 'Why is everything great in London?' Everything's great in London because they take plays and actors seriously. It's as simple as that."

In keeping with his sense of *theatricality* as anything being able to happen onstage, Orson constantly varied his performance of Ahab: "I ad-libbed every night a great deal," Orson recalls, "and tried to take the mickey out of all the actors. They were all young and solemn." Instead of being put out by his nightly ad-libbing as they very well might have been, the others were exhilarated by it. Says Gordon Jackson: "He's a *big* man who *thinks* big! His idea of 'ham' acting is to do the same thing every night. According to Orson, you must search for something different, in interpretation, or effect. Some nights—because of this attitude—he'd go all out, and find himself at the end of a limb, with egg dripping down his face. Other nights, he absolutely soared, and was *magnificent*! That's what I consider great acting." Doing it a little differently every time was also a way of warding off the inevitable boredom of repeating the same role nightly: and Orson was especially prone to ennui: "He won't do more than a limited season in the theater," says Wolf Mankowitz. "He can't stand the strain of the regularity. He's no good at that. He needs a fluid kind of situation. Films suit him better because it's different every day. He gets bored, he gets bored. Being an actor in the theater requires the capacity not to be bored with what *is* essentially boring—going on and doing the same thing for the same type of audience, again and again." One variation that Orson did not intend, but that certainly enlivened his performance the night it happened, was the gradual loss of his false nose in the course of one of Ahab's soliloquies. "Tell Orson his nose is falling off!" one of the actors whispered in panic. But Orson knew it already. He could feel it slipping off, then dangling from the end of his own nose, till it dropped off entirely; as if nothing untoward had happened, he discreetly kicked it into the audience.

Orson's happiness in London was marred slightly by an unpleasant meeting with John Houseman and his wife at the Caprice restaurant. That the meeting would be highly charged for both men was only natural, since *Moby Dick* was Orson's most important theatrical production since the Mercury, whose spirit it was generally thought to have revived. As Houseman depicts it in *Front and Center* Orson exploded when he said that he did not know which night he would be coming to see *Moby Dick* since he was waiting for a much-coveted ticket to Olivier's *Mácbeth*. But Orson tells a different story: "Houseman started in on me again, in exactly the same way he'd done at Chasen's. . . . I never said a word. There was *no* scene. There was Houseman quietly cutting me down, and me taking it all because I didn't want to embarrass him. I wasn't going to start to argue with him. I was just sitting there taking it because so many years had gone by. That was Jack going on. I wasn't even bothered by it, but his wife was, and gave him this terrible dressing down. Isn't that funny that it should be turned into a tantrum on *my* part!"

Orson had hoped to make a television movie of his hit play, which he began to shoot at the Hackney Empire in London, but, shortly thereafter, he abandoned the idea. "Orson's attitude is a very pragmatic one," says Wolf Mankowitz. "He thinks until you get on the set with the actors and the lights and the rest of it, you don't know whether it's going to work or not. And he simply reserves the right as an artist to sort of drop it if it doesn't work. This is always very upsetting to the financiers, who think that they're dealing with a finite and static creature when they're dealing with a creative concept." Persistent rumors over the years have hinted that there is a finished film of Welles's *Moby Dick* stashed away somewhere, but Orson had barely started the film when he gave it up. "We shot for three days," he recalls, "and it was obvious it wasn't going to be any good, so we stopped. There was no film made at all. We only did one and a half scenes. I said, let's not go on and waste our money, because it's not going to be any good." Leaving the Hackney Empire after a day's shooting Orson got into a cab and barked, "Take me home!" to which the driver replied, "Where's that, sir?" "I don't know!" gasped Orson, realizing he couldn't recall the name. Rolling down the window he called to the actors who had just issued from the stage door, "Will someone please tell me where I live?" To complicate Orson's having forgotten his address, there was indeed a sense in which Orson lived nowhere in particular, and in which nowhere was home. As Gordon Jackson puts it, "In a strange way, Orson is a glorious gypsy!"

While preparing *Moby Dick* in London, Orson discovered for the third time in his life that he was going to be a father. By the time the run of *Moby Dick* was over, Paola was visibly pregnant, and they repaired to the island of Torcello in the Gulf of Venice, where Orson quietly worked on *Around the World with Orson Welles* and planned his assault on New York. Margolis anticipated his staging *Moby Dick*, for which the London run had presumably been only a preparation. Although by now Orson felt supremely confident about the play and the production, he was less sure about his own performance as Ahab: "I have a feeling that I didn't play it very well, and I think I should have. I tried very hard to play it very well, but I was *enormously* impressed by the actor who was playing Starbuck [Patrick McGoohan], and I kept thinking how good he'd be in the part of Ahab." Still, it was not insecurity that caused Orson to decide against bringing *Moby Dick* to New York. Apprised of the Equity rules that would not let him work with his actors round the clock as he had in the past, Orson decided that *Moby Dick* was much too complicated a production to rehearse properly

in the three weeks allotted him. "On those terms I could
never do anything like my London *Moby Dick*," says Orson.
"It would be an exercise in futility. That's why I gave it
up." By contrast, in London his actors had kept working
on rehearsals for as many hours as he thought necessary.
We had four weeks of nobody sleeping in order to get *Moby
Dick* on," says Orson of the London production, "and I
knew I wasn't going to get that in New York. We used to
do that in the old days in New York, but now Equity had
tightened its rules. So I said, 'It's just impossible: there's
too much choreographed material for anybody to learn in
that time.' " Since his performance in the television *King
Lear* had been so successful, he decided now to do *Lear*
onstage in New York, possibly alternating it with *Volpone*.
For both productions he would bring over a number of
British actors in hopes of establishing his own repertory
theater on or off Broadway. But to attract the funds to do
that, his first show would have to be a smash hit.

In October of 1955, Orson and Paola crossed the Atlantic
on the *Andrea Doria*. Since Paola was going to give birth
the following month, an airplane was out of the question.
In New York Margolis gave his apartment at the Hotel
Volney to the Welleses; he also kept Orson in meals, cigars,
and three books daily. Despite Orson's squeamishness about
the idea, Paola was determined to have the baby at home,
as one often did in Italy—even if for now home was a
borrowed hotel suite. "She was the one who thought she
could tame the beast," Margolis says of Paola. "She was
determined to restrict him to some kind of home life." Elisabeth Rubino, an Italian-speaking former secretary of Orson's, was summoned to assist the countess. "The Volney
Hotel is no place to have a baby with *Orson Welles* in the
same apartment," says Miss Rubino, so at last Paola resigned herself to the idea of the hospital, where, that November of 1955, Orson's third daughter was born. Miss
Rubino was at home when Orson telephoned and asked that

she come to the hospital immediately. When she got there she assumed from his manner that something dreadful had happened. But all Orson would say was that the baby had arrived and that he *had* to get out of there. Moments later, when she found Paola, the secretary discovered why he had been so anxious to escape. "She was fighting with the attendants, and he couldn't stand it," says Miss Rubino. "He can't stand fighting! She was fighting with them because she wanted the baby to stay in the room with her." On one topic Paola was substantially more acquiescent. Orson says that she instantly accepted his idea to call the baby Beatrice, in memory of his mother, because "Beatrice is a good Italian name." It is oddly fitting that Beatrice should be born just as he was preparing *Lear*; in a sense she would be his Cordelia, the beloved youngest of three daughters. Quips Margolis: "He had just married and had a new baby—that accounts for the fact that he *only* worked eighteen hours a day!"

Much to Orson's disappointment, however, instead of being booked for Broadway, *Lear* was set to open in the cavernous City Center on West 55th Street: "Terrible theater!" Orson rumbles. "The worst theater I've *ever* been in! It's built to destroy a play! It's a big *shelf* up there!" Obviously the place has bad associations for him—and with good reason, for from the first all was not well with this production of *Lear*, on which his dream of starting up a repertory company so clearly depended. Having abandoned the idea of doing *Volpone* with Jackie Gleason in the title role, Orson was having a bit of trouble with the company he managed to assemble for *Lear*. Equity did not allow him to import the mainly English cast he had assembled: "I had a whole English cast which were refused entry, and I had to hurry and find people to take their place," he recalls. "I had a Cordelia who had *her coach* out there during rehearsals— the Method was in full swing with the actors. And they all read the small print in the Equity book and quit in the middle

of a sentence when the day's work was done! All this was
so new to me!" Accustomed to rehearsing all night, Orson
was disconcerted by actors who flatly insisted on regular
hours. "If you're going to stop because it's exactly five
o'clock, I don't know what to say," Orson explains of the
terrible shock he felt on returning to the New York stage.
"I wasn't angry—I was really frightened about not having
enough time to *get it on*, you see. I was running scared!"
It seemed to Orson that most of the cast under his direction
were unwilling to make the sort of total emotional "family"
commitment to the production that he expected: "I felt that
they were all in there to do their job with their little books
ready—that didn't go for all of them, some of them were
wonderful—but there were enough of them to give me a
feeling of being in a foreign land—which I hadn't felt being
in foreign lands. Nobody brought out little books in Amsterdam, you know, only in New York. And how much
Shakespeare had they had in the last twenty years? Why
wasn't this a great experience for them? And I felt that it
wasn't for anybody. I couldn't get that feeling from most
of the people that we were all engaged in a great adventure!"

As if this disharmony with his cast were not misfortune
enough, shortly before the opening Orson tripped during a
rehearsal and broke his ankle. Still, accustomed since youth
to humoring his unreliable ankles, Orson appeared as scheduled on opening night: "I think I may have been very bad
opening night," Orson recalls. "I was hurt, but the thing
that *really* did it to me was the applause when I appeared.
It was so enormous and so long and so sustained that it
completely disoriented me. I ceased to be *Lear*. I just thought,
*these people think they've got a great actor come back, and
oh Christ, what can I do*? I hate to be applauded except at
the end, you know. When they do all that and I look down
and see people I know clapping their hands and smiling
with happy anticipation, the energy runs right out between
my toes. And I think that happened to me to some extent

on *Lear*. . . . I think I gave my *worst* performance opening night. Suddenly I felt a very strong sense of not belonging to that audience or to that town, even though they gave me that reception. It's very curious." But why is Orson invariably disoriented by the kind of warm reception that would thrill most other artists? "Because it means that they *like* me," Orson says of the audience, "and I'm afraid I'll disappoint them. That applause is what really *destroyed King Lear* in New York. Because I came on as King Lear and there were three minutes of applause. I stood there and suddenly all my concentration went out to all the apartments in all New York where I had ever been with friends. I spread right out over the whole city! And I almost wept because I hadn't expected anything like that, I'd been away so long. And it was so wholehearted, and it was such an incredible greeting, that I knew I couldn't possibly do justice to that."

That night, after the final curtain dropped, Orson tripped again and injured his other ankle. By then Orson could not believe his ill fate, so when he scanned the generally negative reviews that followed, it was with an air of resignation. Wrote Brooks Atkinson in the *Times*, in what was one of the better notices: "To judge by the 'King Lear' that opened at the City Center last evening, Orson Welles has more genius than talent." It was the sort of remark that was likely to pain Orson even more than his unsteady ankles. Orson's *bête noire*, Walter Kerr, did him no favors in the *Herald Tribune*: "His heart seems to have nothing to say. . . . There is nowhere an emotional line. . . . He sounds a bass-note at regular intervals, pauses metronomically, varies from blast to whimper on a prearranged schedule. The result is an intelligent automaton at center stage."

Unable to walk, the "automaton" wondered how he was going to get onstage the second night of the run, which he recalls with a shudder as "the worst night I ever had in my life": "I now had two broken ankles—not sprained, broken—and had to be carried in a stretcher into the theater."

That afternoon, as he lay on the stretcher on his way into the City Center, Orson's reveries carried him back to his earliest childhood memory. He had never known that he could remember this far back: to being pushed along in his perambulator. "I suddenly remembered that I remembered the view from the perambulator," says Orson of being carried on the stretcher. "And I saw *exactly* the pictures that I saw in the perambulator: the sky and the buildings and everything."

"That's why bee-ographers are born!" Orson teases me. He has sensed my acute embarrassment at asking him a sort of amateur-psychoanalyst's question. I couldn't help asking, even if I was setting myself up as an easy target for the "rough-kidding" in which he specializes. A month or so ago, he had mentioned his suddenly returning to his earliest childhood memory while being carried into the City Center to do his ill-fated Lear. When he had finished describing the memory of being pushed in a carriage and seeing the sky and buildings above, I tried to prod him for more. "Nothing else comes?" "No," he said, "that's it." And then his tantalizing afterthought: "No mommy leaning over and saying, 'How are you?' Nothing. Just this trip, you see."

That afterthought nagged at me for weeks. Why had he brought up the fact that, in his memory, his mother wasn't there? Was there some hidden connection between his mother and the Lear production in New York? Or was I making a big deal out of nothing? I knew that Orson was still the same fellow who had related bogus dreams to the psychologists who examined him in boyhood. So I held my breath

*now when I asked him, several weeks after we had first
discussed it, whether his feelings about the* Lear *production
in any way reminded him of how he'd felt when his mother
died. A farfetched, even a ridiculous question, perhaps—
but I had a hunch.*

"I knew when I told you the story," Orson says sarcastically, "I could feel the beginnings of a great ferment."

"I don't usually ask that sort of question," I say in my
own defense.

*But Orson really has me now, and has no intention of
letting me off the hook. I try to explain that the reason I
made the connection between the two seemingly disparate
phenomena—the* Lear *production and his mother's death—
was his having said spontaneously, "No mommy." Why had
he brought up his mother's absence?*

"The trouble with it is that my mother never pushed me
in a pram in her life!" *Orson laughs.* "In that age people
of our class—excuse the expression—never pushed their
children in a pram."

*Although we have both been laughing until now, I feel
myself growing exasperated with Orson's sparring. It occurs
to me that if he's going to treat me like a pop psychologist,
I may as well act like one.*

"Were you angry when your mother died?" *I ask bluntly.*

"Not a bit," *says Orson, no longer even slightly sarcastic.*

*My asking a terribly indelicate question in so abrupt a
manner isn't the way we usually talk to each other. Sensitive
to my having bristled this once at his teasing, Orson grows
profoundly serious. With the greatest of candor he describes
for me his feelings about his mother. I am very moved. This
is the other side of Orson: his gentleness, his sensitivity.
Even though he does not particularly want to, he earnestly
tries to examine something he knows is important to me:*
"The thing about 'no mommy there' may be Freudian. I
wouldn't argue about it because I don't understand it. I*

told you what my real feelings were, because my basic feeling was one of shame."

Shame? Suddenly he isn't talking about his mother's death anymore—but about how he felt doing the ill-fated Lear. The two phenomena—his mother and the production—have crossed circuits in his thoughts.

"I don't know how my mother came into it," he thinks aloud, "except the basic of not coming up to her expectations, which is what I felt about both my parents. I always felt I was letting them down."

Why as he was carried on a stretcher into the City Center to do Lear did he flash back to his earliest memory? The common feeling was one of shame, of not living up to his parents' expectations in childhood, and not living up to his audience's expectations as an adult. When he botched Lear in New York, he felt that he was letting people down, a fear he had harbored in one way or another all his life.

Farfetched? A connection invented by Orson because he knew it was what the pop psychologist in me wanted to hear? I don't think so. Although it is impossible to prove that something like this is or is not true, I think I know Orson well enough by now to sense when he is being candid, authentic. In such cases, truth is a hunch.

At the beginning of nearly two years of interviews for his biography, it was Orson who directed the course of our conversations. He knew what he did and didn't want to tell "this biographer-woman." But gradually he let his guard down. He let things slip that I suspected he later regretted having said to someone who was, after all, a journalist. He had an almost grotesque sense, as I did, of somehow turning his life over to me, piece by piece, every time we talked. It was unsettling, disturbing. He knew that I was mixing what he told me with what others told me and with what I found in documents, so that we began to joke gruesomely about there being my Orson and his Orson: two versions of a

*single life. But which of them was true? I was surprised—
and, I must say, impressed—when he didn't seem annoyed
by my Orson's not being identical with his. "A biography
is more reliable if it's like a portrait," he told me. "It is
admittedly the viewpoint of one person, and therefore it has
a kind of authority, no matter how wrong it is. It has the
authority of being somebody's picture of somebody."*

*I did not entirely accept that, however. Although I knew
it was not quite possible, I wanted my Orson to be the true
Orson. I wanted to tell what really happened, not just what
I thought happened, based on what the people I interviewed,
Orson among them, thought happened.*

*How exactly is one to know the truth about Orson Welles
or any biographical subject? Sometimes, I discover, regarding the truth about himself even Orson is not quite
certain, as when he tells me the following curious story:*

*"I got a letter the other day from a woman," he says,
"written very charmingly, giving a picture of her—she looked
quite nice—and saying, 'We agreed when I was pregnant
that you would not take any responsibility for my child,
but I would like you to see what a fine boy he's grown up
to be.' And there's a picture of a grown-up boy on the
beach." Which is all well enough, except, says Orson, "I
don't remember having met her."*

"Do you think it's true?" I asked.

*"I can't decide," says Orson. "I don't believe it's true
because I don't think I have that poor a memory. But anything is possible! I don't see myself ever saying that I wouldn't
be responsible for a child—unless she made that condition
herself." I sense that Orson is quite genuinely puzzled as
to whether he may once have slept with and impregnated
the lady.*

*"Quite well written," he says of the letter, trying to assess
its intent. "In other words, it's not a nut's letter, you see."*

"Does the child look like you?" I ask the obvious.

"A little," says Orson, "a little. In other words, she could sustain an illusion, or it could be so. But I don't remember the name, the woman, the circumstances. The period of time she says it was seems unlikely because I was then making a damn fool of myself over somebody else." He pauses to think a moment, then: "Isn't that strange?" he asks, as much of himself as of me. He is unsure as to whether, or how, to answer this letter, which in fact asks for no reply.

"I don't know how to answer her," he says. "You know, saying, how nice of you to write, and I hope whatever-his-name-is is happy."

"Don't write back," I warn him, "in case it's not true."

"Or true!" Orson laughs.

In such cases, I want to tell him, truth is a hunch.

CHAPTER 32

Bring Up
the Lights

"I was put in a wheelchair and pushed out onto an empty stage," says Orson of the second night of *Lear* at City Center, "and the idea was to try to tell the audience not to go to the box office and ask for their money back." There sat Orson, his legs propped up before him. Beside the wheelchair was a table with a glass and a pitcher of water. Instead of his Lear costume, he wore a suit and tie. Having expected Lear, some members of the audience quickly expressed their displeasure. "A lot of them began right away to stand up and go," says Orson, who, if he wasn't already uncomfortable enough, was even more so when, looking out into the audience, he instantly recognized a familiar face looking right back at him. It was the last face in the world he wanted to see just then. "When I talk to an audience I always bring up the house lights, which was my great mistake that night," says Orson, "because under the brightest part of the chandelier sat John Houseman in the third row! *Me* in a wheelchair trying to tell interesting stories of the theater and recite from other well-known plays, just to try to give people a feeling of their money's worth. *His* head tilted up in that disappointed tortoise expression. I don't know how I got through it."

By the third evening, however, Orson was back in the role of Lear; delivered nightly to the City Center by ambulance, he performed in full costume in a wheelchair until the end of the limited run. Although he carried on as nobly as he could, Orson's hopes that the production would lead to backing for a permanent repertory company had been dashed by the bad reviews. "*Lear* broke me badly," he says of his terrible disappointment in New York.

After *Lear*, when no one would back his dream of a new repertory theater in New York, Orson took Paola, Beatrice, and the family dog to the Riviera Hotel in Las Vegas, where, in March of 1956, he hired himself out to do magic tricks, and Shakespearean recitations from *Julius Ceasar* and *The Merchant of Venice*. It was obviously a great letdown for Orson but he dispatched himself gracefully with an eminently successful, twenty-five-minute act, the most popular feature of which was the Shakespeare. (He had wanted to saw Paola in half, as he had Dolores and Rita, but at the last minute she backed out.) Who would have anticipated that a high-toned, and rather incongruous, act like this would be a big hit on the Vegas strip? Orson wished he had been so successful in New York.

Having picked up some much-needed cash with the Vegas nightclub act, the Welleses left the desert for Hollywood, where Orson had signed to act opposite Betty Grable in a television version of the Ben Hecht–Charles MacArthur play *Twentieth Century*. As long as he was not going to be able to launch his repertory company in New York, he figured he might as well capitalize on the phenomenal success he had had acting in Peter Brook's *Lear* on television. Orson remained puzzled by the immense disparity between the reviews his acting had garnered in Brook's *Lear* and in his own. But the fact remained that he could make money on television that he simply could not in the theater, and with a wife and baby to support, that was an important consideration. A deal with Lucille Ball and Desi Arnaz's

Desilu Productions to put together a television series of adaptations of classic stories followed. The pilot that Orson shot, however, an adaptation of John Collier's "Fountain of Youth," was not picked up for a series. Ironically, in 1958, long after Orson had despaired of selling the series, the pilot was shown on national television as part of the Colgate Theatre and won the coveted Peabody Award for Excellence. At that time, Harriet Van Horne wrote in the *World Telegram*: "Should an eager chap from one of those opinion surveys corner you and ask, 'What, in your judgment, does television need right now?' look him straight in his avid eye and say, 'Orson Welles.' . . . Now, why can't we see Mr. Welles every week?" But Orson had already learned the networks' answer to that question in 1956 when he made, and failed to sell, the subsequently critically acclaimed pilot. The networks had thought it possibly too sophisticated for "the average viewer"; and furthermore they had been reluctant to take on any of Orson's directorial projects, in which—they felt—he might be inclined to experiment as he had liked to do on radio. However excellent the series pilot was, it was to be only a one-shot deal. The networks doubted that from week to week, month to month, they could depend on "a glorious gypsy."

Orson then made an abortive attempt at putting together a deal to direct Charlie Lederer's script titled *Tip on a Dead Jockey* for MGM. But almost as soon as the deal was announced it fell through. Still, the disappointing experience had suggested to Orson that his hopes of getting a directing assignment in Hollywood might not be in vain; in the meantime, Orson accepted one of the many acting roles that were readily available to him, this one as a "heavy" in a picture titled *Man in the Shadow (Pay the Devil)*.

If Orson wanted to show Hollywood that he was a changed man, he seemed to give no evidence of it his first day on the set when, having made a grand and noisy entrance, and having effusively greeted both cast and crew, he suddenly produced a sheaf of pages and announced to all concerned, "You'll be interested to see the changes for today!" The producer was promptly summoned, and the consensus was that Orson's unanticipated revisions were a distinct improvement over the original, so that, the relevant actors having learned their new lines, shooting began several hours late.

Before long Orson received an offer from the producer of *Man in the Shadow*, Albert Zugsmith, to act in another picture, *Badge of Evil* (later changed to *Touch of Evil*), which was about to be shot at Universal, and for which Zugsmith also sought to hire Charlton Heston. Shortly after Charlton Heston was offered a part in the picture, he not only accepted, largely so as to work with Welles, but as an ardent admirer of Orson's films, he forcefully proposed him for director. Heston realized that being directed by Orson could enhance his own development as an artist. (He was right to think so; his performance as Vargas in *Touch of Evil* was a great triumph.) Heston's was the best kind of recommendation Orson could have had: "I was by that time in a position to exert certain leverage," Heston recalls. "Let's put it this way: I was at a point where my views on who was going to direct the picture had to be taken into account."

"He has gargantuan vitalities of all kinds," says Charlton Heston of Orson, a quarter of a century after they worked together on Touch of Evil. *"This is part of his charm. He is an overwhelming person. It's difficult to withstand him. This is part of why he is a good director—he is a leader, a captain." Heston points out that when he first met Orson back then he was "a very young actor dealing with a man who was already perceived as one of the cinematic giants." But today Heston is himself a Hollywood giant who observes his old friend with the perspective the intervening years have afforded. Unlike some people who have worked with Welles, Heston clearly has no personal stake in advancing a particular view of a man whom he praises and criticizes with equal sympathy.*

As to why, at the time of Touch of Evil, *Orson hadn't worked in Hollywood since* Macbeth, *Heston says: "One of the reasons that he couldn't get a directing assignment was that he was considered a profligate and wasteful director. The tragedy of Orson's life is that he was not beginning to make films five years ago, ten years ago—this is the age of the independent filmmaker. The studios don't want to make movies, the studios are afraid to make movies!" And*

Orson, argues Heston, was someone who simply could not operate successfully in the studio system: "He was just unable to function that way. It's accepted wisdom that Orson deserved better of the film industry than he got; it is also true that the film industry deserved better of Orson than it got. There's some kind of perverse, suicidal refusal to deal with the people—I mean, he can charm actors and stage-hands and drivers and makeup people: why can't he take a little time and charm the men who are going to give him the money to make the movies? I think he disdains them, and I think he is contemptuous of their intelligence, and outraged that they nevertheless control what he does. See, film is the only art form whose raw materials are so expensive that the artist cannot afford to buy them for himself. Orson wouldn't have had this problem if he'd been a painter or a writer. But he has to grovel to some studio head for whose intelligence he has little respect and who he recognizes has no talent at all. That's not what he does. He thinks, why must I be nice to this man? That's my theory."

But if Heston is critical of what he views as Orson's "inability" to charm the Hollywood money men, he is quick to point out that their image of him as being wasteful is entirely wrong: "The fact that he is an extravagant director is a big canard. It is simply not true. I mean, Warren Beatty can spend sixty million dollars making Reds half an hour too long and it crosses nobody's lips that that's too much money to spend. But there's no reason to say it about Welles. You can say other things about him, but not that."

Among these other things, Heston is particularly critical of Orson's acting: "He's a very careless performer. He is not highly disciplined. Mind you, I am speaking from a small sample, but in my experience he is careless about learning his lines and about details of his responsibilities as an actor." Heston shakes his head about Orson's appearing in so many films in the course of years: "I guess almost invariably he has been willing to commit to act in

*almost anything. He maintains that he doesn't like acting:
I don't believe that. I think he disdains acting as an insuf-
ficiently weighty undertaking—and indeed in film it doesn't
compare to directing in importance."*

*As a director Orson seemed to Heston to work especially
well with actors—the secret of which success Heston explains quite simply: "He makes it enormous fun. He per-
suades you that every shot you're doing happens to be the
most important shot in the whole picture, and the key to
your role, and he then proceeds to get you to agree to that
by cajolery and imagination."*

Throughout Touch of Evil *Heston was conscious of Orson's doing more than just making a movie, of his feeling
that he had to prove something besides: "He can work fast,"
Heston says. "I think that perhaps on* Touch of Evil *he was
in part trying to demonstrate that, and he did it. You can't
make a picture that good that fast unless you know how to
do it!"*

CHAPTER 33
Sisyphus

Heston's recommendation that Welles direct *Touch of Evil* fell on receptive ears at Universal, where post-production head Ernest Nims had (from his point of view) worked happily with Welles on *The Stranger* and had already suggested several times the possibility of bringing him to direct something at Universal. But whereas Nims was clearly delighted by the one Hollywood picture Orson had done strictly according to the rules, he mistakenly assumed that Orson wanted to make another movie just like it. In retrospect Orson felt that *The Stranger* had been an artistic mistake, and that he shouldn't have allowed himself to go against the grain in making it. It was, however, the atypical precedent of *The Stranger* that influenced the studio to give Orson another shot at making a movie in Hollywood. Another veteran of *The Stranger* who liked the idea of Orson's directing again was Jim Pratt, who was now second in charge of production at the studio, and luckily it was to him that his boss, production head Ed Muhl, turned for advice about Charlton Heston's proposal. Pratt assuaged the considerable nervousness the studio predictably felt about giving Orson another chance.

On the basis of Pratt's reassurance, the studio offered

Orson the job to act, direct, and—if he liked—to rewrite
the script, all for the same $125,000 (but this time with no
percentage) that he had been offered years before by RKO.
The sum suggested that the money men looked upon Orson
as having to start all over, to prove himself again. It was a
grotesque fact of Orson's filmmaking career that so much
of it had been spent proving himself—like Sisyphus, who
eternally rolled a big rock all the way to the top of the hill,
then watched it roll back down again, and then started over.
So it didn't seem strange to him to have to do so again.
But his idea of proving himself in this case was to make
the film as efficiently as possible, to satisfy the studio brass
that he was not the slobbering wild man they seemed to
fear. One major element of *The Stranger* he *never* intended
to emulate, however, and that was its linearity, its conventional form. Hence the inevitability of the terrible conflict
that would eventually ensue between Orson and the studio.
They had hired him to make a movie very different in style
and structure from what he intended to do. At first this
disparity was evident to neither of them. On everyone's
mind (including Orson's) was the importance of getting the
shooting done quickly. When Orson went to Tijuana to scout
locations, the studio balked at the idea, since they would
not be able to monitor him there—and everybody in Hollywood knew what had happened when Orson went to Rio!
The studio's having adamantly forbidden his shooting in
Mexico suggested two things to Orson: that they would be
watching him very carefully; and that, in order to keep them
from watching too carefully, he would have to devise a
strategy to soothe the front office on the first day of shooting.

But before shooting began he felt compelled exhaustively
to rework the script. In the film Orson would play the
dissipated police chief of a sleazy American town on the
Mexican border who is in conflict with the principled Mexican narcotics inspector played by Heston. Says Heston:
"He took what was a very routine police story, the kind they

do on television, on *Hill Street Blues* or something, and rewrote the whole thing in a couple of weeks, and gave it what distinction it had. That was entirely his." To play the Mexican's new bride Orson had cast lovely Janet Leigh, whose most famous role, in Alfred Hitchcock's *Psycho*, would be foreshadowed here. Even before her agent had told her anything about Orson's offer, a puzzled Miss Leigh had received a telegram from the director to say how delighted he was that they would be working together. Correctly calculating that she would be as pleased by the idea of being directed by him as Charlton Heston was, Orson had figured that the telegram would get her at a lower price than if he had to negotiate with her agent first. Unfortunately, Miss Leigh broke her arm shortly before shooting began. But instead of deterring Orson, the thought of her playing the young newlywed with a cast on her arm held a certain perverse appeal for him. Before long, however, he abandoned the idea, and managed to conceal the arm in a variety of ingenious ways of shooting Miss Leigh—except in the famous motel-room scenes, for which she had her cast sawed off, then put back on afterward.

As he planned every detail of his production, which, at Pratt's suggestion, was to be shot by Orson's equally gargantuan pal Russ Metty (who went back with Orson as far as RKO, when he had been an assistant, and who had been chief cameraman on *The Stranger*), Orson was particularly careful about setting up the crucial first two days of shooting, on which he knew the worried front office would be keeping close tabs. Years before when John Ford had visited the set of *Citizen Kane*, he had pointed out to young Orson the studio spy who had been assigned to report the fledgling director's every move to the front office. Since then Orson had entirely lost his innocence about being spied upon. Not only did he expect that there would be a spy or two, but now he knew enough to put on an edifying little show expressly for their benefit. (Ford turned up on the set of

Touch of Evil as well, but this time it was to offer Orson the acting role that eventually went to Spencer Tracy in *The Last Hurrah*. Orson says that he admired Ford so much that he would have done the part on any terms Ford was willing to offer, but Welles's representative, unaware of this, asked too high a fee—and without another word to Orson, Ford turned to Spencer Tracy. It was a lost chance Orson regretted forever after.)

That February of 1957 when Orson appeared on Stage 19 to begin directing his first Hollywood picture in a decade, what he did *behind* the camera was every bit as much a performance as the dramatic action in front of it. He knew, and quite perfectly executed, the role his hidden audience wanted him to play. He knew the studio honchos were anxiously huddled in the Universal production offices, where they waited for the phones to ring with news of what Orson Welles was up to. He knew exactly what they would be thrilled to hear, and he made sure it happened. Having started the show promptly at 9 a.m., Orson had made his first shot by 9:15 a.m. when, much as he imagined it would, the phone rang in the front office, where there was much elated back-slapping and self-congratulation at finally having tamed Orson Welles. As if getting a first shot in a mere fifteen minutes was not impressive enough, at 9:25 the phone rang again, to report that, wonder of wonders, Orson had gotten his second shot! That both these shots were exceedingly simple close-ups never seemed to occur to the front office, nor did it occur to them that Orson was deliberately trying to impress them. Nor when, much to their horror, the camera did not roll again until 6:25 that evening, did they suspect that the perpetrator of *The War of the Worlds* was merely building up unbearable suspense, and that, at 7:40, when the camera stopped, he would have shot eleven pages of script in a single remarkable take. At the end of the first day Orson would be two days ahead of schedule.

The second day was another carefully calculated performance; Orson shot another thirteen and a half pages of script, at the exuberant end of which he was heard to say, "Okay, now that we've taken care of the front office, we'll go ahead and make our picture!"

Besides this, Orson's major strategy for maintaining control of the shooting of his picture was to move it out of the studio to quaint Venice, outside Hollywood, where initially he said he planned to work for only a couple of days. Secretly, he intended from the first to remain there until he finished most of the shooting. To make it even more unlikely that the studio brass would turn up in Venice to see what was going on, Orson shot at night. "They really didn't know what was happening," Janet Leigh says of the studio whom Orson had so successfully eluded. Orson's quest for total creative freedom also took the form of his constantly rewriting the script; when everyone else was asleep, Orson seemed almost always to be working on the script. Says assistant director Phil Bowles: "The sun would be coming up and he'd go home and rewrite. He'd come in the next afternoon and he'd pass out the pages to the actors. I don't know *when* he slept!" This daily rewriting made Orson the only person there who always knew just where they were headed on a given night. Thus according to the film's other assistant director, Terry Nelson: "He assumed absolute creative control by rewriting constantly so that nobody really had a firm fix on all the requirements except Welles." Orson's extreme flexibility, his willingness to let actors create their own performances, differentiated him from a director like Hitchcock, of whom Janet Leigh (who would work with both masters) says: "With Mr. Hitchcock the picture is over for him before he even starts shooting." Not so for Welles, who, as Miss Leigh points out, afforded actors a degree of freedom to improvise that Hitchcock, having worked it all out for himself in advance, would not have brooked. Orson did not worry that new turns in the script might contradict the dialogue in scenes he had already shot, since he could always loop in entirely new dialogue later.

One of the most curious characters in the film, a neurotic motel clerk, played by Dennis Weaver (best known then as Chester of the *Gunsmoke* television series), was largely built up out of the actor's inspired improvisation. Orson gently encouraged him to depart from the script as much as he needed to evolve the unexpectedly complex minor character, who so clearly anticipates the hysterical kook that Anthony Perkins portrays in *Psycho*. In *Touch of Evil*, a Mexican narcotics inspector and his bride are on their honeymoon in a border town. When he takes time out to compete with a dissolute American police chief to crack a case, the Mexican inspector's wife checks into a motel to wait for him. There she encounters the spindly voyeuristic clerk, whom Hitchcock would subsequently rework for his own film, in which Janet Leigh would again encounter an equally odd motel keeper. Says Weaver: "We went into his whole background—about his mother and how he was a mamma's boy. He had this terrible guilt about sex and *yet* he had a large sex drive. There were no words to indicate such a thing in the script at all—but it gave him an interesting behavior pattern when we put it all together. The main thing was his attraction to women and his fear of them at the same time. *That* was the thing that was basic to his character." And, one might add, to the character of Norman Bates in *Psycho*, except that in the later film the repressed wierdo acts out his goriest fantasies about the beautiful blond. In *Touch of Evil* a gang of hoodlums who invade the motel sadistically abuse the wife in a way that seems simultaneously to appall and excite the wimp of a clerk. (The presence of the same art director, Bob Clatworthy, on both films may be a clue to some of the vivid visual similarities between them.)

Another marvelous minor character was Marlene Dietrich's Tanya, a part that she played entirely as a favor to

Orson, and that, once she got to Venice, they expanded considerably when Orson saw how crisp was her interpretation of the steamy prostitute who, when he asks her to read his fortune in a deck of cards, sadly—and accurately—warns that his future's *all used up*. "Oh she's marvelous!" says Orson of her performance. "It's her last great role. She was such a wonderful soldier about it. I called her literally the night before. I got this brainstorm. I said, 'You've got to come to work tomorrow in this movie.' There was no talk about reading the script or what the part was at all. She said, 'What should I look like?' I said, 'You should be *dark*'"—which gave Marlene the idea of putting together a costume of exotic odds and ends she had worn in previous pictures. "She looked superb!" says Orson. Orson had not told the studio about Marlene, who worked only one night in Venice. Later on, when they inspected the footage, they were flabbergasted to see the superstar there. "They were subjected to a lot of shocks during *Touch of Evil*," laughs Orson.

But if most of the cast found Orson to be exceedingly receptive to the nuances of costume and behavior they wished to bring to their characters, they found he could also be suddenly inflexible. He demanded that Akim Tamiroff (cast as the petty gangster who despises the Mexican inspector for having nailed his brother on a narcotics charge) overcome his revulsion at sticking the butt of a lamb's tongue in his mouth for a pungent death scene in which, as Orson had initially envisioned it, the crook's tongue was to appear to pop out of his head. Until moments before the scene was shot Tamiroff knew nothing of Orson's special plans for him. Recalls Terry Nelson: "When we got ready to make the shot, Welles had the prop man bring out a large tray with a dish towel. Off comes the dish towel, and it's an assortment of lambs' tongues, four or five inches long." When he saw how Tamiroff instantly recoiled at the nauseating sight, Orson firmly instructed him to hurry up and

bite down on the butt of one of the tongues so shooting
could get started. If, after much cajoling, Tamiroff relented
and stuffed the ghastly pink object in his mouth, probably
it was because having worked with Welles before he was
used to acceding to his most peculiar demands. Says Wolf
Mankowitz of Tamiroff: "He expressed the kind of despair
in relation to being asked to do things by Orson one might
adopt towards an irresistible destiny." As it turned out, however, the shot with the lamb's tongue proved much too
disgusting to show onscreen, so that, fated as he may have
been to experience it, Tamiroff's ordeal had been for naught.

Apparently, working on *Touch of Evil* proved something
of a physical ordeal for Orson, who, shortly after the move
to Venice, had tumbled into one of the canals that weave
through the little seaside community. His weighing nearly
300 pounds by now had probably exacerbated his injuries,
which included a sprained wrist, ankle, and knee, a swollen
foot, and a badly bruised face—all these copiously detailed
at a mini-press conference that Dadda Bernstein held in
Venice immediately after Orson's nocturnal mishap. But ill-
timed injuries were nothing new to Orson, who kept going
night and day, despite the sling and splint he wore on his
arm when not in front of the camera; the bad leg in fact fit
in nicely with the gimpy physical wreck of a character he
was playing. And since he had to wear great gobs of makeup
to weather his own baby-fat face, his bruises would not be
evident. On *Touch of Evil* Maurice Seiderman, the same
virtuoso makeup man who had once turned twenty-five-
year-old Orson into the monstrous *übermarionette* Kane,
took two hours daily to make forty-one-year-old Orson into
the cantankerous Quinlan. He pasted plastic bags under his
eyes, replanted his hairline, stuck on an ugly nose they had
chosen from seventeen equally ugly possibilities, and stuffed
his suit with mounds of padding to make the fat man even
fatter.

If onscreen Orson absented himself by disappearing en-

tirely into the grotesque body of the character he was playing, he was himself most vividly present elsewhere, in the
Wellesian self-assertive style that the big money and unmatched technical capacity of Hollywood facilitated. Working in Hollywood again after a decade of self-imposed exile,
Orson had to come to terms with the fact that, as an artist,
he could be most himself in the very town where they
seemed most intent on repressing him. He thus brilliantly
asserted himself in the film's bravura long takes, the most
celebrated of which is the opening scene, in which Welles
shows us the planting of a bomb in an automobile near the
Mexican-American border, and the havoc that ensues—all
of it situated in the rich visual context of the abundant
passersby, Vargas and his bride among them, who cram the
frame. Every move had to be timed precisely so that, finally,
just as the newlyweds kiss, the bomb detonates offscreen.
There is a strange sensuality to the long, seemingly effortless
sweep of the camera that imbues the street scene with an
electric excitement it would clearly lack if broken into conventional shots. Much as Hitchcock's famous shower-mur-
der sequence in *Psycho* depends for its potent impact on its
myriad of shots, the opening of *Touch of Evil* would be
immeasurably diminished without its *single* majestic boom
shot—whose apparent (and hallucinatory) effortlessness issued from long hours of diligent labor that stretched through
the course of an entire bitterly cold night. "It took all night
to set up," recalls Janet Leigh. "We would do it, and then
something would go wrong. Obviously he'd stop it *before*
the explosion. We did it quite a few times, then finally when
everything was right in the scene, and we realized it was
really going to happen, there was *pink* in the sky!" For all
his shrewd calculations, one instance of Orson's mastery
amazed even him. About to resume shooting a scene begun
the night before, he realized that now the wind was blowing
in the *opposite* direction. Ordinarily this would not have
made much difference, except that in the scene he had

already started, he had deliberately shown the flight of debris in the strong gust. The wind was just as strong tonight, but if he picked up where they had left off, it would be obvious to the audience that the debris was blowing the wrong way. "You've got it going the wrong way!" Orson declaimed at the sky in his mightiest voice—and to everyone's amused astonishment, including Orson's, the wind suddenly turned around.

When he had finished shooting *Touch of Evil* in April of 1957, it looked like Orson had finally turned his fortunes around. From the first, and for a change, his handling of the front office had been impeccable. The rushes they periodically inspected had pleased them enormously. The stylistic "strangeness" which he had sought to achieve in *The Lady from Shanghai* and which had so terribly infuriated Harry Cohn was evident in *Touch of Evil*, but far from balking, as Orson initially feared they might, the studio was consistently emphatic in their approval. Its murky low-key lighting, its tortuous long takes, its eccentric camera angles and pictorial compositions—these posed no problems to the boys in the front office, who were seriously talking about signing Orson to do another five pictures for Universal. As had been the case with *Macbeth*, all that remained was for Orson to put the picture together, and he would have vindicated himself in Hollywood. Back in 1947, when Orson had decamped for Europe at that crucial moment when he should have been editing *Macbeth*, it had been because he had conceived of this modest film as no more than an experiment in swift and efficient shooting whose postproduction work was really secondary to what he had set out to show. Not so with *Touch of Evil*, whose editing Orson deemed absolutely decisive, and into which he threw himself with all the gusto of the great artistic success that was *almost* his.

Even before principal photography had been completed,

Orson and the first cutter who had been assigned to him
hadn't hit it off. Now, post-production head Nims sent in
editor Virgil Vogel, with whom, almost instantly, Orson got
along just fine. "I could immediately see the kind of *startling*
film he was shooting for—it was very apparent—and that
it needed *that* kind of editing," says Vogel. Not only were
the images themselves to be startling, but so too the relationships between them—and that of course was where the
editing, the meticulous juxtaposition of shots, came in. Orson Welles has sometimes been drastically misread as a
filmmaker who cares less about the reciprocities between
shots than about their individual contents, but from *Kane*
on, this simply has not been the case. His taste—and talent—for cramming an abundance of dramatic action into a
single amazing shot no doubt accounts for this misinterpre-
tation. But in Welles's cinema, the bravura long take is a
shock effect of no greater (or lesser) importance than the
sort of assertive editing that made, and still makes, *Kane*
so startling an experience. Hence, night after night, he joined
Vogel in the editing and proved unusually willing completely
to reinvent dialogue as long as the duration of, and relations
between, shots were precisely as he wanted them. In fact,
directing one sequence in Venice, Orson had not had the
actor speak any real lines at all. Instead he told him just to
keep his mouth moving, to recite the Declaration of Independence if he could, and that the dialogue would be written
and put in after the material had been edited for visual effect.
Later, when Vogel inquired what the actor was supposed to
be saying in the context of the story, Orson replied that it
was none of Vogel's business what the words were supposed
to be. As editor, all he was to concern himself with was
"pictorial value." It was the *rhythm* of the cuts that concerned Orson far more than their advancing the story line.
Only after Vogel put the images together without any prior
consideration of sound did Orson repair to a typewriter to
bang out dialogue to fit the edited sequence. This was hardly

the common practice of repeating scripted dialogue in the
course of looping; it was also a laborious and time-
consuming enterprise, which the front office was unlikely
to comprehend. As the editing dragged on, Orson mystified
what he and Vogel were doing by adamantly refusing the
front office even a peek at the work in progress.

When the editing was nearly completed, Orson flew to
New York to do a Steve Allen show, and much as he had
predicted to Vogel, the moment Orson was gone, Nims
called on behalf of production head Ed Muhl to set up a
screening. But Orson had happened to call Vogel from Chicago en route to New York, and upon hearing what had
happened, he angrily blurted out, "You tell them if they run
it, I'll fly back there, and I won't use an airplane!" In
deference to Orson, Nims called off the screening, but in
the meantime, Vogel had decided he had done all he could
on the picture, and that perhaps another cutter ought to put
the final touches on it. After returning to Hollywood, Orson
was apprised that a new cutter had been assigned to the
picture. This time perhaps it would be better, or so Orson
was told, if he stayed out of the cutting room and let the
new fellow, Aaron Stell, work alone. Orson agreed not to
bother Stell (although he had hardly been bothering Vogel,
who had greatly appreciated, and learned from, his immense
contribution to the editing), but first he wanted to run through
the whole picture with him. During the screening, Stell was
rather uncomfortable when Orson scrutinized the cutter and
not the film, presumably to measure his reaction to the
footage. Meanwhile, Orson planned to do a few brief re-
takes, but after completing one of them in less than two
hours, he was suddenly refused studio permission to proceed
with several inserts he thought he needed for narrative clar-
ity. Nims had decided that since Orson would probably have
to do a few more inserts anyway once the picture had been
cut, it would be cheaper to wait and do them all at the same
time. Orson was absolutely furious at what he took for a

personal insult, and this unfortunate incident set the tone for the major dissension that was about to occur when, over Orson's strenuous objections, Nims and Muhl decided that it was time to inspect the picture.

Whereupon Orson left for Mexico; while it seemed to Nims that he had stormed off in anger, actually he had planned to go even before this to work on a sort of "home movie" of *Don Quixote* he had been intermittently fiddling with since 1955 in Paris, and which he hoped to work on while wrapping up *Touch of Evil*. Although he had not rashly departed in a moment's ire, he certainly should have reconsidered his plans to leave just then, for, knowing that Nims and Muhl were about to screen his work-in-progress, he should have been there to present, explain, and, if need be, defend it to them despite his resentment. But Orson miscalculated that since the front office had had nothing but effusive praise for the rushes they had seen, they would be just as enthusiastic about the shape he'd given his material. Besides, it had been the studio who had suggested that he remove himself from the editing room, where he had been working like mad to finish his film, so it seemed to him perfectly reasonable briefly to take off for Mexico. But the experience of having lost control of the equally magnificent footage for *Ambersons* when he went to Rio to work on another picture should have taught him how important it was to stick around until a picture was finished to his satisfaction, or as close to it as possible (even though, this time, the studio wasn't letting him do very much to finish it). He must have decided that in his absence nothing much could happen to his film—but he of all people should have known better. Not being there for the screening of *Touch of Evil* and its immediate aftermath was a drastic mistake— one of the worst mistakes of Orson's career.

The Muhl screening did not go well. What seemed to the bigwigs like faults of continuity made portions of the picture hard to follow. "Here was a great picture," Nims recalls, "but he had really messed up the first five reels. He was ahead of his time. In those days, you must remember that smoothness of continuity was very important in pictures," and Orson's picture unmistakably lacked this conventional smoothness. Clearly what posed serious problems for the studio was Orson's taste for fragmentation and discontinuity, his habit of splitting a story asunder, which, Nims argues, would be far more acceptable to today's popular audience than those in the '50s, who would have expected Orson to tell his story in a more linear way than he cared to. "He was ahead of his time," Nims repeats. "He was making those *quick* cuts — in the middle of a scene you cut to another scene and then come back and finish the scene and then cut to the last half of the other scene"—that is, simultaneously developing two *different* lines of the story. Nims offered to supervise the tentative recutting of the offending reels to try to give them the smoothness and continuity that, following the innermost impulses of his artistic sensibility, Orson had deliberately eschewed. There is no question that Nims proceeded with the best of intentions. He appears to have honestly thought that he was somehow doing Orson a favor, straightening out the promising footage Orson had "messed up." Where Orson had been editing for pictorial and rhythmical subtleties, Nims set about telling a straightforward story. From the studio point of view, the complications to which Orson had subjected his narrative were needlessly vexing—as were the auditory shock effects he had devised for the sound track. A month passed, during which, in Orson's absence, Nims had made, and reedited, a duplicate print of the initial reels so that when Orson got back presumably he would be able to *compare* the two versions— or so Nims told him in a letter in response to Orson's telegrams about when he could come back to work. (For, having been prohibited to shoot inserts, and having agreed to let the editor work on his own, Orson perceived himself in effect to have been shut out, and to need permission to return.)

When indeed Orson returned to Universal that August, Nims's new version of the first five reels was a fait accompli, and ready to be screened. Orson could not believe that this had happened to him again. He tried to be diplomatic, but he was aghast at what he saw as Nims's having undone all his painstaking labor in the editing room. Suddenly he felt powerless again. However much he might protest, and he was invited to do so, the massive fact of the new version (and the antithetical approach to moviemaking it indicated) remained, and there seemed to him to be nothing he could do about it. Having heard that Orson had taken off for Louisiana to appear in Martin Ritt's film *The Long Hot Summer*, the studio did not receive his critique of Nims's revisions until November (which of course was another major tactical error on his part). Although Orson would assert that he had dispatched the critique earlier but that apparently it had been lost in the mail, Universal was not amused by what they perceived as Orson's stalling, whereas despair and confusion would have been more accurate. While at length the studio would agree to correct certain small errors Orson had pointed out, they refused to make the more drastic changes in the editing that he had called for. They also moved to lock him out entirely, which meant sending in another director (much as had happened on *Ambersons*) to do inserts, which Charlton Heston describes as "really just geographical shots" (although the thought that another director would add even a shot to his film was absolutely devastating to Orson). Says Heston of the studio's motives: "The film is less linear than they made then—now it wouldn't be considered so, but it was then—and they felt they wanted some shots which straightened you out as to where the hell you were." Out of loyalty to Orson, both Heston and Janet Leigh recoiled at appearing in the film's new shots: "We both resented changing it and bastardizing it," says Miss Leigh, "because what we did made it almost normal"—the very opposite of the *strangeness* for which Orson had characteristically aimed. The inserts posed a moral dilemma for Heston, which caused him nobly to assume the financial responsibility for canceling a call at the last minute when he still could not decide whether to go ahead with it. Finally, he discovered that, having signed a contract, he was legally obliged to do as the studio asked, and he agreed to appear in the controversial shots. By then Orson had relented and wanted desperately at least to be allowed to direct the inserts himself (even though he objected to them aesthetically), but the studio would not hear of it. Says Heston: "In the end he said he would do them for nothing, and do them the way *they* wanted them done, but they were sore at him by then"— *sore at him*, it appears, for his resistance to having yet another film wrested away from his artistic control.

By now, Orson thought of the picture as no longer really his. This alienation from his own artistic labor was precisely what he had hoped to avoid this time in Hollywood. He had meant to restore his reputation there, to show that he was not fated always to exist in discord with the studios, whose financial and technical resources were so important to him as a filmmaker. But having failed again, having lost control of yet another picture, it seemed perhaps that he had failed for good. Who in Hollywood would back him now? When the Welleses sailed for Genoa, Italy, shortly after Christmas of 1957, it seemed as if the dark prophecy hurled at him by Marlene Dietrich in *Touch of Evil* was all too real, all too true: "Your future is all used up."

CHAPTER 34

Crazy Welles

When I was beginning to outline the chapters of Orson's biography that deal with his work as a director in Hollywood, I happened to mention the intense admiration his films have always made me feel for him (and that first made me want to write about him). At which offhand remark Orson groaned, "It will turn to *hate* by the time you get me to Genoa." There was an air of resignation, of inevitability about his prediction, but at the time it seemed much too intentionally cryptic for me to ask what he meant—and there were more pressing matters about which I had to ask him. Still I did not forget what he had said, and as I continued to follow the narrative line, the itinerary of Orson's life, without consciously articulating it for myself I was all the while on the lookout for Genoa. Just what was it that would have happened when he—and I—got there? And how would I react to it? Would Orson's prophecy come true? Would I hate him by then, and if so *why*?

Early in 1958, amid a flurry of charges and counter-charges between Orson and Universal, the Welleses disembarked at the port of Genoa. The *Exorchorda* of the American Export Line had been their second choice for the crossing, the first having been the French liner *Liberté*;

which, at the last moment, had denied them permission to take their long-haired miniature dachshund, Columbina. This had been more than just an ordinary crossing. In effect it seemed to mark the end of Orson's career as a Hollywood director. "I really was never going to come back," says Orson. If anyone in Hollywood had doubted that Orson was as unbridled as legend had it, *Touch of Evil* seemed conclusive evidence. Once again it appeared that he had not finished a film as promised, that he had brought upon himself the intervention of the studio, who had to finish it for him. Once again he was known to have been working on some other film when it was his own project that needed completing.

Around Orson Welles an undeserved reputation for deliberately not finishing his films would accrue, which, at length, writer Charles Higham would elaborate on—and disseminate—in a destructive book titled *The Films of Orson Welles*, which argued that "all his blame of others for wrecking his work is an unconscious alibi," whereas in truth, he never really wanted to finish in the first place. Thus he had run off to Rio instead of finishing *Ambersons*—and had been running off ever since. Higham's speculation that "his unconscious drive was to avoid the agony of editing and scoring and finishing *Ambersons* in 1942" is widely accepted as the definitive explanation for Orson's Latin American sojourn. That the U.S. government had asked the filmmaker to depart for Rio in time for the carnival, which the Brazilian government wanted him to film, that the studio had fully encouraged him to comply with Washington's request that he leave just then, and that he fully expected to be able to finish *Ambersons* either in Rio or upon his return—these facts Higham does not allow to get in the way of his thesis, although they so obviously provide a perfectly rational explanation for Orson's departure, which Higham prefers to ascribe to darker motives. In a sense, Higham merely gave critical credence to what was already the public perception of Orson Welles as somehow irrational: hence the wide-spread acceptance today of the fear-of-completion thesis, even by people who have neither read nor heard of Higham's book. If indeed Orson feared completion, why would he have tried to finish *It's All True* at his own expense? Why would he have subsidized his films with his own acting money? And how does one explain the struggle to finish *Othello* at such great personal cost? The fear-of-completion thesis simply does not fit the facts. For Higham to say of Orson's involvement in *Touch of Evil* that "characteristically, he left before final cutting" is to overlook available facts that clearly contradict his thesis: in particular, that Orson had been working like mad to finish the picture's final cut, and that eventually the studio had discouraged Orson's persistent presence in the editing room. And it is terribly misleading to say, as Higham does, that "Welles never saw a finished cut or even a rough cut; he obviously could not bear to do so. The one partial cut that Stell ran for him he did not look at; he looked at Stell, to study his reactions, instead." This last incident occurred at the outset of Stell's tenure as editor; it was considerably after that that Orson viewed the drastically revised version Nims had prepared, and to which the director submitted a detailed critical response. That the disagreement between Orson and the studio was mainly on *aesthetic* grounds, that the studio essentially took the picture from him once they saw how strange, how *un*conventional a narrative Orson was painstakingly preparing—this information is of less interest to Higham, it seems, than the same silly business of Orson's purportedly not wanting to complete his cut. For someone who supposedly did not want to finish the picture, Orson certainly spent a lot of time and effort in the editing room trying to do so.

None of which is to say that Orson was entirely blameless for some of the ill fortune that had plagued him in Hollywood. Although he could not have known it then, going to

Rio was a strategical error that in time he would come sorely
to regret. A more serious professional blunder came somewhat later when, although he considered his experiment in
Macbeth to involve showing how efficiently he could shoot
it, his departure for Rome to act in Ratoff's *Cagliostro* had
merely confirmed his reputed unreliability. Nor on *Touch of
Evil* had he acted shrewdly in leaving town as planned when
the studio bigwigs finally insisted upon a screening of what
he had been up to with the editing. Nor should he have let
so much time elapse before registering his formal protest
about the footage the studio reedited in his absence. Still,
these were by and large tactical errors, miscalculations that
hardly add up to the pathology that Higham and others have
ascribed to Orson. Unfortunately, however, that fabled pathology, the myth of his madness, would blight Orson's
filmmaking career, making it difficult for him to attract
backing for pictures that the money men feared he did not
really want to finish. "He gets bored with his pictures is
one of people's favorite stories," laments Orson of the public
perception of him. "Oh, it's just the opposite! I go on fighting for them at the expense of something else." To illustrate,
Orson points to *Othello*, which he steadfastly refused to
abandon until at long last he finished it. But even Orson's
perseverance in this regard was used as evidence against
him. "Because it took me so long to get all the money
together, I had to keep stopping," says Orson, "and friends
of mine, people who before and after had been very loyal
to me, like Darryl Zanuck, said, 'We don't know what's
wrong with Orson. He keeps making a picture and stopping
because he gets bored with it and goes away.' *I had no
money!*"—this last a perfectly rational explanation for why
Orson had to make *Othello* in the intermittent way he did.
Years after *Othello*, when a lawyer of Orson's approached
Zanuck to back a picture Orson had in mind, Zanuck said
that although he was fond of Orson and thought him a
genius, his having taken four years to finish *Othello* sug-

gested that backing him would be an unsound investment. To Orson's horror, Zanuck seemed to have forgotten the terrible financial difficulties that had beset Orson during *Othello*—difficulties that he certainly should have recalled, since he had been among the people Orson had hit for cash! "I even got money from him for *Othello*," says Orson, "and he'd forgotten that, and had swallowed the story that somehow *Othello* took four years to make because *Crazy Welles* took four years to make it."

Crazy Welles—it is an image of himself that Orson thinks especially unjust because, as he argues, rather than growing bored with his films, he grows obsessed with them, with finishing them against all odds. "Once I get into it," says Orson, "I'm like a mud turtle, I don't move. The legend is so detached from the facts that it's absurd. I've never been bored. I have a sense of obligation to anything I start." As to the source of Orson's notorious reputation for being unbridled, this in part he ascribes to what had been his public persona in the early theatrical days in New York: "I took over the mantle of John Barrymore and von Stroheim. That's a sort of ready character and the public *wants* somebody like that." From the outset this *Crazy Welles* with whom Orson sincerely finds himself unable to identify had attracted a vast amount of publicity to his stage productions. "I didn't like the publicity," Orson claims (although one suspects that this is something he feels more in retrospect than he did at the time). "But there was nothing I could do about it, because Houseman and people like that were on their way up the ladder by showing that *they* were able to control me. I had to be wild in order for their function to be important. I had to be irresponsible, capricious, unreliable, and so on for wise old heads like that to have their value. It was greatly to the advantage of anybody who became a producer or associate of mine to be the steadying influence to this brilliant but out-of-control force. People don't understand that you can't really put on a play if you're out of control, or

direct a picture or finish it unless you're *more* in control
than anybody."

And indeed by the time he got to Genoa early in 1958,
he had to his credit an amazing number of major plays and
pictures: a record of artistic achievement that clearly belies
the now-popular idea that Orson tended to grow weary of,
and wantonly abandon, projects before bringing them to
consummation. Quite simply, what other figure in America
could lay claim to a long list of the greatest accomplishments
in film, theater, and radio? Still, for Orson, that illustrious
career had been tinged with sadness. Besides feeling alienated from the public perception of him, he also could not
always recognize himself even in his own films because too
often they were mutilated, reedited, or rescored in the end
by others. In both his style and sensibility Orson was plainly
an artist of self-assertion, so that it was all the more painful
for him when it was not always his own self that his films
asserted. Still, they were all films by *Orson Welles* in which,
to varying degrees, he recognized an imperfect version of
what he had wanted to do. By the end of his stay in Hollywood, he believed that *Touch of Evil* was somehow no
longer his picture, but he took a different line when at the
1958 Brussels World's Fair, much to the surprise of the
studio, which had shown little interest in seeking the proper
distribution or publicity for it in America, the film won top
prize in the international competition, and Orson cheerfully
accepted. The award was particularly gratifying to Orson
in light of the film's having virtually disappeared in the
States. But however much he seemed in public to have
changed his tune about precisely whose picture it was, still
his gratitude for the award was mingled with a secret sense
of loss, of alienation from a work of art that both was and
wasn't his.

"It will turn to *hate* by the time you get me to Genoa,"
Orson had predicted of my feelings about him, as I worked
my way through his life. Although he would flit in and out

of Hollywood in the ensuing years, and although eventually he would even unofficially resettle there (while maintaining his official residence in Las Vegas), there was also a sense in which, after Genoa, there was really no turning back. As far as Hollywood was concerned, Orson had proved the validity of, had entirely *become* for all time, the image of him that they had had all along. "Sometimes *he's* just out there and I don't know who he is," says Orson of that image—as if it were one of the many often-ridiculous roles he has played in other men's movies, as if—Brechtian to the bitter end—he has resisted *identifying* with the part he has generally been assigned to play in his own life story.

From Genoa the Welleses headed south toward Rome. Orson had no clear idea of where—or *if*—he wanted to settle down. They talked of making a home either in Sicily or Tuscany, but nothing was certain. Orson remained terribly confused about all that had just happened in Hollywood. The partial vindication of the Brussels World's Fair was still several months away, so he was filled with anxiety about the fate of his new picture. For Orson, Italy meant exile, rootlessness, but for Paola it was home. She said that although Orson wanted her to act with him again, she preferred the role of wife. The scornful response to her performance in *Arkadin*, the intimations that Orson had cast her only because she had been his girlfriend, these could not have been easy for her. But if Paola chose now to throw herself into the role of wife, it was also because some semblance of home, of an establishment, however precarious, was what Orson needed now that he took up a life of ceaseless peregrination, as often as not with his little family in tow. His first daughter, Christopher, compares Orson and Paola's marriage to Skipper and Hortense Hill's, which in some small part was probably its model. Hortense had allowed Skipper entirely to immerse himself in his projects, to stay out all night if he had to get things done. Now, on a far grander scale than Skipper had, Orson would steal away for days, weeks, at a time, usually to make a well-paid cameo appearance in another man's movie. But always he would return home, which, eventually, meant Fregene, outside Rome, where besides the addition of Orson's mother-in-law, the Welles ménage included a bevy of cats, who, like Orson, periodically came and went. "We had about two hundred cats, it seemed to me—I suppose it was twenty," says Orson. "But there was one absolutely *wonderful* cat that I'd found and brought back, who was uncatlike in that when we would drive up he would run to meet the car and do uncatlike things. He depended *so much* on us." But Orson's delight in this creature was to end in terrible sadness. "When we had to leave," Orson recalls, "he had gone away on one of his three- or four-day binges, and I said to my mother-in-law, 'You drive out there and wait till he comes back and pick him up and take care of him and bring him back to Rome.' And she *never* did, and I'll *never* feel the same about her, that's all! So he came back and there was nobody there, and he just died of hunger and a broken heart. That's just too awful to think of!"

Orson sustained a more serious loss while living in Italy, when he heard of the death of Dadda Bernstein, who had fallen off a ladder in his yard. Once before, Dadda had had a similar accident but survived it. "He got up early in the morning and went to his office to fix the wiring," says Orson, "and went down in the cellar and climbed a ladder and fell down. That was the accident he lived from. Then he was told by everybody never to get up on a ladder again." Apparently, however, Dadda failed to heed these warnings, so that, not long afterward, he suffered the fall that killed him. Recalls Orson: "On this day he leaned a ladder against a tree and went up to prune it and fell down and killed himself. Poor Hazel found him dead." When he heard the news, Orson had mixed feelings about this first of his mentors. Mingled with his profound regret, with his memories of their early days together, was something else. Indeed, much as he genuinely loved Dadda, Orson also resented him for having kept much of the money Dick Welles had left Orson in his will (a fact of which Skipper did not hesitate to remind Orson). Says Orson: "There is a moment when you wonder how he can *possibly* have justified keeping all that money. He bought a big house in Los Angeles out of *my* money, and decorated it entirely with furniture which had belonged to my mother." Not that Dadda ever consciously thought of himself as having *stolen* from Orson. "I do not think that Dadda Bernstein had any *notion* that he was actually stealing from me," says Orson. "It was all for my own good. I don't think he could have had a moment of conscience. It was all justified in his mind." Probably Dadda honestly believed that the money was best spent maintaining the home for Pookles that had been lost when Beatrice died (whether that new home was in Ravinia or Los Angeles!). To illustrate how Dadda was able to rationalize a somewhat smaller theft from his Pookles, Orson tells the story of a visit Dadda and Ashton Stevens paid to his dressing room in Philadelphia during *Five Kings*. "I had a box of very expensive Havana cigars on my dressing-room table," Orson recalls, "and when I came back after the show to get my makeup off, I saw that three-quarters of the cigars were gone. It turned out that Dadda Bernstein had taken them all, and his justification was that the stagehands could walk in and steal them from me. Now he kept these cigars, but he had *protected* me from the theft of them by the stagehands." The news of Dadda's death made Orson dream of the possibility of retrieving some of his mother's possessions, especially her piano, to haul about with him in Europe. "The house was entirely decorated with things I had seen as a child in my mother's house," says Orson of Dadda's Beverly Hills home. "And there was a famous prayer rug—of museum quality—which my father tried to get out of Dadda Bernstein, and I remember their quarrels about it

as a child. The famous prayer rug! *There* it was in Los
Angeles! It was the only thing my father really thought he
wanted. He'd bought it, you see, himself. It was the kind
of thing he'd like. He used to travel with it. When he would
be on a Pullman car, he liked to have it to put his feet on
when he'd get out. 'Where's my goddam prayer rug?' "
Orson recalls his father's habitually lamenting, when Dadda
had taken it after Beatrice's death. But neither the prayer
rug nor the piano nor any other of his mother's things found
their way into Orson's possession, for Hazel dispersed them
among Dadda's Hollywood friends before she repaired to a
retirement home. "I would have liked to have had my mother's piano!" Orson grumbles, still obviously miffed by its
having gone to perfect strangers who weren't about to return
it to him. "He always painted me as hopelessly ungrateful,"
says Orson of how Dadda talked about him to friends late
in life. "They all looked steely-eyed at me and regarded
him as a kind of saint. And *all* he talked about, day and
night, was me to them. 'When have you seen him last?'
'Oh, not in years!' "

But even if Orson had managed to get his hands on the
prayer rug, or any of the other family heirlooms he coveted,
still he would be left with the practical problem of earning
a living, of supporting his mobile ménage, and perhaps even
of scraping together the cash to resume work on *Don Quixote*. Orson had not been back in Europe for long when, in
quest of cash, he found himself briefly in the States again,
to narrate a Cinerama picture, and to talk up a possible deal
(of which nothing ever came) with some TV panjandrums
in New York. Then it was back to Italy, and off to Africa,
where, in the 125° heat of the Cameroons, he was to act
opposite Errol Flynn and Trevor Howard in another of Zanuck's pictures, *The Roots of Heaven*, directed by John Huston. As if the unbearable and unrelenting heat was not enough
to drive everyone batty, Errol Flynn's desperate need for
fixes of heroin, which the shocked hospital nuns refused to

provide, threatened to impede the production, until Zanuck shrewdly offered the grateful Mother Superior a new wing for her hospital in exchange for her providing Flynn all the dope he wanted. Flynn had deteriorated substantially since Orson had taken cocaine with him on the *Zaca* during the making of *Lady from Shanghai*. (Orson knew in detail about Flynn's drug habits from Dadda Bernstein, who, for a time, had served as Flynn's doctor in Hollywood. But although Dadda was perfectly willing to prescribe speed for Orson, he balked at supplying the hard drugs Flynn routinely asked for, and subsequently lost him as a patient.) In Africa, Flynn was also drinking heavily, as was Trevor Howard, with whom one night on the set he became far too groggy to continue shooting. Next morning, when they returned to the same set, neither seemed to remember having been there the night before. "Errol, have I seen this set before?" asked Howard. "No, no, absolutely not!" insisted Flynn—and he wasn't kidding. However awful was his health, Flynn managed to impress Orson with the beautiful young lady he had in tow. Not that Orson had been particularly impressed by Flynn's taste in women in the past: "He had, in my opinion, spent his entire life, this man over whom girls swooned, picking *dogs*. I went on a cruise with him and when we would come into the port all the crew, including myself, would get dibs on the good-looking girls in the port, and the *dog* that was left would go to Errol." But in Africa Orson changed his tune: "He turned up with a fifteen-year-old girl who would have made a Polanski of *anybody*! She was sensational! It made a very strong impression on everybody that *he* was sustaining the interest of this healthy young child since he was coked to the gills, and on the big H, and drunk. He was still managing to get around, looking pretty awful."

When the production moved on to Paris, Orson was installed at the Ritz, which struck him as a far more congenial setting than the bush. Having recovered sufficiently from the heat to talk of his imminent plans to the French press he announced that, besides *Don Quixote*, he hoped soon to direct a TV special he envisioned with Gina Lollobrigida. In between shooting, he squeezed in stops at Cannes for the film festival, and at Brussels, where he saw, and was hailed for, *Touch of Evil*. Notwithstanding the acclaim with which *Touch of Evil* was garlanded at Brussels, and elsewhere in Europe, where almost instantly it became a cult classic, it was mostly overlooked in America. So when Orson accepted an acting job from Zanuck, which meant his returning to the States for the major role of defense lawyer Clarence Darrow in *Compulsion*, to be produced by Zanuck's son Richard, and directed by Richard Fleischer, it was not without a certain amount of bitterness that he had not been asked to direct. "He was jealous of my directing the picture," says Fleischer with understanding of why this would be so, "because why shouldn't he be directing *Compulsion*?" From the first, Fleischer was acutely sensitive to the awkwardness of the situation. "We were all worried," he says about the anxious anticipation on the set before Orson came over from Europe. "Orson Welles had always been a great idol of mine, and I was in awe of him for my whole life. *Citizen Kane*— I believed then as I do now—is the best picture ever made, and the idea of working with Orson Welles was quite overwhelming. I was very nervous about it!" To make matters worse, Orson's contract required him to work on the picture for exactly ten days, after which he had booked passage on a freighter to the Orient, where he was scheduled to arrive in time to act in a film in Hong Kong. Fleischer knew that if he did not get everything he needed from Orson in that time his picture could be ruined, and this added to his agitation, which did not abate in the slightest when at long last Orson arrived.

"You don't know how to grab on to him," says Fleischer of his first physical impression of Orson. "You don't know how to handle him. You don't know which way he's going to jump. He's got this overpowering voice and presence. You really have to feel your way for a while to see whether you can direct him or whether he's going to direct you. He knows so damn much. He knows what you're doing before you think of it yourself." Fleischer sensed that Orson's first impression of him would be crucial in determining the success or failure of their ten days together. "You have to be very careful directing Orson," Fleischer says. "You have to gain his confidence. If he has no confidence in you, he will steamroller you, flatten you right out. So he has to get to feel that he can trust you. He watches the director to see how the director has prepared and how he handles the crew and the other actors—he's *very* mindful of that." Fleischer mentions one incident in particular to illustrate the subtle struggle for power between them. Orson was to make an exit at the end of a corridor, on the left side. Never imagining that this could pose a problem, the director told the actor what he wanted him to do: "Orson, you go down to the end of there and turn left and go out the door." "I'd rather go out the right side," Orson replied. "You can't go out the right side," said Fleischer. "Why not?" "There is no set on the right side. If you turn right and we pan with you, there's no set. You'd see the stage wall. Nothing there." Orson seemed to think deeply about it for a minute. Then: "You know what *I'd* do if I were directing this picture?" he asked. "No," Fleischer replied. "I don't know. What would you do?" "I would wait until they built the set for me." "Orson," said Fleischer, "this is the reason why I am directing this picture and you are not." "You are absolutely right," said Orson. "I will exit through the door." And he did.

Whatever tension there may have been between them, the work they did together on the film was extraordinary. "I don't think Orson *feels* any great emotion when he's acting," says Fleischer, "but he is very intellectual and very technical. I don't care how an actor gets a performance. I don't care whether he feels it or he doesn't feel it, as long

as it's what you're looking for. I don't think Orson works
internally, but his *technique* is a master's." A good example
of this distanced technique is the lengthy and dramatic speech
that Clarence Darrow delivers at the end of the movie's
murder trial. Fleischer's likeliest approach would have been
to film the speech in sequence. But considering the numerous changes in camera setup and lighting that would
have been required, doing the speech in sequence would
have taken much too long, and Orson was available for only
ten days. Thus Fleischer decided to shoot the courtroom
speech out of sequence so that all segments of the speech
to be covered by a particular camera angle would be shot
together, thereby cutting out much of the time it would
otherwise take to shift the cameras and lights. But as Fleischer
points out, this time-saving device "required great concentration on Orson's part because we might do one part of the
speech where he's speaking very quietly, and then the next
section, which might have been two or three pages down,
where he was back in relatively the same angle, and he
might have had to come in in the middle of a sentence, very
emotional and very excited." From the outset of his moviemaking career in *Citizen Kane*, Orson had viewed film as
an assemblage of parts, the myriad relations among which
he kept constantly in mind while working. Because of this,
and because his distanced approach to acting typically kept
him from inhabiting, from feeling, the role, he was able
painlessly to shift gears while performing out of sequence
different parts of the speech. Says Fleischer: "I don't think
I could have done it with anybody other than Orson."

Sometimes Orson's ability to put his *technique* into practice was not without its peculiar requirements, such as asking
that other actors not look him in the eye when he was in
the middle of a speech. "Orson has a great deal of trouble
looking people in the eye," said Fleischer. In one scene,
for instance, when Orson was supposed to address E. G.
Marshall, whose back would be turned to the camera, he

asked Marshall to keep his eyes closed so that he would not flub his lines. Since no one would see him doing so, Marshall complied. Equally unbearable to Orson was to have an actor watch him from off-camera. "When he has to do a scene where he is talking to someone off-camera," Fleischer explains, "he does not want that other person there." Fleischer points out that most actors prefer talking to someone whom they can see, and who actually delivers the appropriate dialogue in response to what they have just said—but not Orson: "Orson doesn't want *anybody* there," Fleischer continues. "He doesn't want the actor *on the set*! And he doesn't want anything in his eye line right to the stage wall. You have to clear that side of the camera where that other actor would have been, and *then* he will do the scene perfectly, with the proper pause for the other actor's dialogue and with the overlap in the right place. He'll react to something the other actor is saying. He'll laugh or he'll get angry or whatever. He'll play the whole scene without the other actor's being there or the dialogue being read, and it'll be perfect!" Never was it clearer that Orson was intensely conscious of every move off-camera than when, in the middle of rehearsing a scene in which he interrogated a witness, Orson spotted the publicity man, who, much to Orson's ensuing embarrassment, had not followed his instructions to cancel an appointment with an important journalist. Breaking off in the middle of a line of dialogue, Orson suddenly lashed out at the publicity man, whose eyes actually welled with tears at the humiliation to which Orson's mighty barrage subjected him. No sooner had he violently broken out of character than Orson was Darrow again, shrewdly interrogating the witness on the stand. By then the moment's evanescent rage seemed more like acting, like artifice, than the measured legal patter that had so suddenly replaced it. Was the explosion merely a performance for the benefit of cast and crew—or did Orson really feel the fury that he had just enacted? Precisely as Orson intended, it was impossible to tell—although shifting gears like that had indeed made his little tirade all the more effective. The intentional ambiguity of his actions contributed substantially to the "Crazy Welles" image that has persistently done him so much harm. People couldn't always read him—nor did he want them to. "He is mercurial," says Fleischer of Orson. "You think you know him, you think you've got a hold on him, you don't. Maybe he doesn't want you to. I just don't think that you can ever understand him."

The publicity man's inefficiency was not the only source of Orson's irritation. It was on this trip to the States that he discovered that, much as he had feared, there was no chance of retrieving his mother's piano or the other property that Hazel had freely dispensed before settling into a retirement home. Orson was so annoyed that after the first visit with Hazel he did not want to go back to see her again, but Paola insisted that it was his duty. (Orson points out that in the end his pretend-devotion paid off when Hazel left him some money in her will. Says Orson: "Since all of it was stolen from me I was glad to have it!") Besides working on *Compulsion* and visiting Hazel, Orson also found the time for a swift foray into Mexico to shoot additional footage for *Don Quixote*. Like *Kane*, *Don Quixote* was to be as much about the *telling* of the tale as the tale itself, whose frame was Orson's narrating the adventures of the Don to a little girl played by Patty McCormack, the brilliant child-star of *The Bad Seed*. She appears to have seen a side of Orson Welles that eluded many others. "The impression I had of him through others was someone to be feared," Miss McCormack recalls. But to the youngster there was nothing fearful about him—on the contrary, his manner with her was extraordinarily gentle. Where others saw the public persona that Orson calls "Crazy Welles," she saw only the "twinkle in his eye" that gave it all away as an act. She knew he was playing.

But he wasn't *always* playing; there were moments when

his rages were spontaneous, deeply felt—and more often than not caused by economic pressures. At the end of Orson's work on *Compulsion*, he hoped to collect his check and sail for China the next day. All that remained was for him to look at the dailies and do the looping. But first, Fleischer had assembled a little farewell party for Orson, who was holding court with some members of the company across the room when Fleischer spotted Richard Zanuck arrive. The producer looked stricken. The Internal Revenue Service, to whom Orson still owed an immense sum in back taxes, had stepped in at the last minute to garnishee his salary. If Orson had blown up at a publicity man for a relatively minor offense, what would he possibly do when he did not get his money? Zanuck feared telling him, lest Orson balk at doing the looping. But Fleischer figured that they had to, since Orson might want to call a lawyer, and because they might be legally liable if they withheld the news. But whatever trepidation they had about telling him appeared to have been unnecessary. Fleischer held his breath as Zanuck crossed the room toward Orson, who kept laughing and talking even after the producer had obviously disclosed the bad news. They even had a convivial drink together after which Zanuck went back to Fleischer to say that Orson seemed somehow to have expected the tax people's action against him, and had thanked Zanuck for telling him about it. Fleischer, however, said that he was still going to hold his breath, and as things turned out he had good reason to do so. In what must have been a delayed reaction to the bad news, while screening the dailies Orson exploded at what he claimed was the utter incompetence of the footage. Each of them in turn, Fleischer, Zanuck, and the cameraman, fell victim to his eloquent tongue-lashing. But if Fleischer and Zanuck refrained from fighting back because they knew the real source of Orson's agitation, the cameraman grew enraged at the furious spate of abuse, and was ready to smack Orson when Fleischer grabbed his arm and told him to be quiet. By then Orson had blustered outside, where he sped away in a jeep. Having sworn off driving the momentous night the woman fell out of his car and accused him of trying to rape her, Orson was again behind the wheel, disappearing in a cloud of smoke. What was Fleischer to do without Orson's looping in the necessary dialogue? The sound work scheduled for that evening was absolutely essential. After a drink to calm their agitated nerves, Fleischer and Zanuck went to the looping room to dismiss the crew. There, however, they discovered Orson, who, in a great huff, had started work without them. The session was an unmitigated disaster. Orson's bitterness about not having been asked to direct the picture had been compounded by this final humiliation of not even getting paid for his acting. He covered—or thought he was covering—the pain he felt with a great show of asperity. In a boiling rage, he sped through his lines, refusing to backtrack when the soundman complained that he was all out of sync. One particularly difficult speech that Orson had already done to perfection was unusable because of the camera noise. Now he really boiled over when asked to try it again. The camera noise hadn't been *his* fault. "I refuse to loop this scene!" he fumed. "Orson, listen to it," said Fleischer, trying to reason with him. "It's not acceptable." "I refuse to loop it! This is now a matter between you and the Screen Actors' Guild. Good night!" Orson wasn't kidding. He barreled off, never to return. Within hours he was on his way to Hong Kong, and Fleischer was left with a small but indispensable part of his sound track badly marred by camera noise. Since the scene could not be cut, the editor reconstructed it out of words, even syllables, culled one by one from Orson's dialogue elsewhere in the film, in an arduous process that Fleischer compares to "hand-knitting." "We screwed Orson!" exults Fleischer of their having salvaged the scene. But Orson's nasty exit notwithstanding, Fleischer did not bear a grudge. Says Fleischer: "I got a letter from Orson from the ship really apologizing for his behavior the last day of the picture, and saying what a wonderful experience it was, and how patient we all were with him, and how much he appreciated it." Having cooled off a bit at sea, Orson must have suspected the artistic importance of the performance he had just turned in, and which, along with *The Third Man*, would generally come to be thought of as the apex of his acting in pictures other than his own. Indeed, with his two co-stars in *Compulsion*, Bradford Dillman and Dean Stockwell, Orson would share the prize for best actor at Cannes in 1959. Much of his other acting work, however, was far less creatively rewarding. But as he liked to say, he had to "pay the rent."

Next, while filming in Hong Kong, Orson had a happy reunion with Christopher that compensated somewhat for acting in a picture that held little artistic interest for him. On the ferry to Macao with Orson, Christopher met an old schoolmate from Europe, a Portuguese girl whose family lived there, and to whose home Christopher and her famous father were invited. Although the large Portuguese family was clearly quite nervous about entertaining *Orson Welles*, he quickly—and skillfully—put everyone at ease by showing them the sunny side of his personality. The more food they brought for him to eat, the more he sweetly sang their praises. Missing was the haughtiness, the air of superiority, one might have expected, and in its place, a warmth and genuine lack of pretension he rarely exhibited in public but which was, in its way, every bit as much a part of his personality. This was the private Orson, who could be as sweet and self-effacing as the public Orson was often quite the opposite.

Orson was neither sweet nor self-effacing the day in Paris when, a few pictures later, he reported to work for Fleischer again. "You're going to have a much more difficult time with me!" Orson announced at the outset of the new picture, *Crack in the Mirror*. "Why?" Fleischer asked. "Because my interest span on a picture is very short," Orson explained. "The ten days we had on *Compulsion* was just about right, but this is a much longer thing. I'm going to get very impatient and short-tempered because I don't like being on a picture this long." In the interval since *Compulsion*, his resentment about it had been festering, so much so in fact that, one Friday night during *Crack in the Mirror*, after he and Fleischer had had several drinks, Orson blurted out his conviction that it had been he, not Fleischer, who was responsible for the success of *Compulsion*. Fleischer of course hotly denied it, and, thinking better of what he had said, Orson apologized after a long painful pause. But Orson had *needed* to say it, perhaps not so much because he believed he had somehow directed *Compulsion*, but because, more than ever, he believed he should have directed it. Fleischer tried to ease some of the tension by saying how much he admired him: "I think I really won him over when I told him in all sincerity that he'd made the greatest movie ever made and that was good enough." But it was not good enough. Perhaps it might be for *history*, but not for forty-four-year-old Orson, who was not about to start thinking of himself in the past tense. His restlessness, his discontent manifested itself in the way he seemed to sabotage the other cast members by telling them elaborate stories just before a take, so that when the cameras went on, the actors were so immersed in what Orson had been saying that they flubbed their lines. "He was devilish that way," says Fleischer. "He did that over and over again and made them look very foolish. I felt he was doing this on purpose. It's playful— he's so accomplished an actor that he can outmaneuver other actors if they're not really on top of things." To Orson this was just a little game to amuse himself. It was not really a question of sabotaging the others, however, as much as it was of demonstrating how easily he could shift gears from telling a wild tale to acting his part in the picture. If the others stumbled while he soared, so much the better.

But Orson did not always soar, and one time on the picture he stumbled badly. In one scene the character he played was supposed to fall into an excavation. At the bottom of the fifteen-foot drop were mattresses resting on cardboard crates. At first there had been no question of Orson's actually taking the fall, which would be done by a stunt man, but Orson insisted that he wanted to do it himself so that the camera could move in close for the accident. "Orson, you can get hurt!" the director protested. "You know you have very weak ankles and you're not the lightest-weight person in the world." "It's perfectly safe," Orson shot back. "I *insist* on doing it!" Fleischer relented. When it was time to get the shot, Orson approached the edge of the excavation, which crumbled on cue so that he disappeared into the big hole. "Okay, Orson!" Fleischer called after he cut—but much to his alarm, there was no reply. Panicked, everyone rushed to the edge of the hole. At the bottom they saw that Orson was wedged in the very narrow space between one of the mattresses and the wall. The possibility of his falling just there, let alone his getting stuck in so small a space, had never occurred to anyone, least of all to Orson, who looked mortified at his plight. "We couldn't get him out for a while," Fleischer recalls. "It was his own damned fault. It was so funny seeing him wedged in there!" Apparently, only Orson was un-amused by the delicate operation of dislodging him.

If Fleischer and company rescued Orson from the hole into which he had thrown himself, it was up to his erstwhile mentor Hilton Edwards to bail Orson out of his more general and far more painful plight. When Edwards visited Paris during the making of *Crack in the Mirror*, Fleischer glimpsed an aspect of Orson he had not so far observed: "He has a facade that he puts up, he has an image—but not with Hilton. With Hilton he was just a little boy." Once again, then, Orson played the little boy to Edwards's mentor type. That this was as much a mask as any other, and always had

been, Fleischer could not have suspected. Once again, Orson needed a stage from which to launch himself, and once
again Edwards provided it. In partnership they would patch
together a new version of the Shakespearean crazy quilt
Orson had attempted in the botched *Five Kings*. "It's the
essential idea I had for *Five Kings*," says Orson of this
ambitious new production, which he called *Chimes at Midnight*, "except that *Five Kings* made the dramatic mistake,
I think, of going and doing *Henry V* in the same evening,
which it shouldn't have done. The basic idea to do the two
*Henry*s as a single play and take the main theme and stay
with it is what I was trying for." That main theme, as Orson
isolated it in stitching together bits and pieces of the history
plays, was the complex relationship between young Prince
Hal and his mentor, Falstaff. Under the auspices of the
Dublin Gate, Orson would play Falstaff to Keith Baxter's
Hal in Belfast and Dublin—and then, if all went well (which
it would not), in London. Finally, if all went exceedingly
well, and a backer materialized, Orson hoped to translate
the stage production of *Chimes* into a film, to be shot in
Yugoslavia, which had begun to rival Italy as a cheap place
to make movies.

On February 13, 1960, *Chimes* had its world premiere at
the Grand Opera House in Belfast. A week later, it moved
on to the Gaiety Theatre in Dublin, where, in a typical
critical reaction, the correspondent for *Variety* hailed it as
"an evening of considerable entertainment" in which Orson
gave "a standout performance" as Falstaff. But still, Orson
recalls the production as having been "a terrible flop in
Ireland," where the theatergoing public gave it a chilly reception after a massive public-relations blunder. Hoping to
economize on the living arrangements for his family, Orson
decided not to stay in a hotel in Dublin. Instead he secured
an old house, which had come highly recommended to him
by several prominent Dubliners. Unfortunately, he had not
actually inspected the house before renting it, so that when

he and Paola arrived in Dublin on the eve of rehearsals, they were dismayed to find that it was "thick with dust" and that none of the lights inside worked. Far worse, when they repaired to the bedroom, they discovered that the chamber pots beneath the bed had not been cleaned. There was no question of Orson's subjecting his wife to even a night of such unbearable filth, and the Welleses promptly left in disgust. Having checked into a hotel for the duration, Paola made the fatal mistake of passing a snide remark or two in public about the memorable chamber pots. "In this case it was really the fault of my beloved wife," says Orson. "She was the one who in that uninhibited Italian way allowed herself to tell the world exactly how dirty this house was. *I* would have crept quietly to the Shelbourne and shut up." She should have been more discreet. The eminent Dubliners who had heartily recommended the house to them in the first place took great offense at their being offended. And so, as these things happen, word quickly spread about Dublin that Orson Welles thought the Irish dirty—a rumor that Orson blames for the ensuing box-office failure of his production. In addition to the dismal box-office receipts, none of Orson's former friends came backstage to congratulate him, which suggested the intense ill-will with which Dublin seemed to regard Orson as a result of the chamber-pot incident. To make amends with the Irish, he tried declaiming a national classic by J. M. Synge from the stage of the Gaiety. "By the second week," Orson recalls, "I was reduced to reading *Riders to the Sea* in order to keep the theater *open*." But even that did not seem to help much. The only locals who did not seem suddenly to hate him were those who confused Orson with James Mason, who, years before, had appeared as Brutus on the Dublin stage. "I had an occasional good word in a pub," laughs Orson. "Somebody would say, 'We'll never forget your Brutus, sir!' And of course *James Mason* is the one who played Brutus. We looked a lot like each other back in those days! Yes, he was very bitter about it. *He* has a square face, and *I* have a round one, and he doesn't have *much* nose. When we were young, people mistook him for me—to his *great* irritation. He looked like I tried to look in stills when I sucked my cheeks in." By 1960, however, even if Orson sucked in his cheeks there was little hope of his looking much like James Mason. Following two entirely unsuccessful stays at the fashionable Italian spa Montecatini—"Everybody walks around carrying glasses of that stinking water," he had complained to the press—Orson seemed to have despaired of ever slimming down.

Orson's weight—this is the inescapable issue. People want to talk about it far more than they do about who wrote Citizen Kane *or why Orson Welles could not work in Hollywood or what happened to* The Other Side of the Wind. *"How did you get so fucking fat?" commercial director Harry Hamburg once asked, to which Orson glibly replied that, having created works of art when he was a young man, he'd finally decided to make himself into a work of art. If in a curious way Orson's weight provokes anger in some people, I suspect it's because they resent a once exceedingly handsome man's having let himself turn into what strikes them as grotesque. "There is no reason to be that gross for Orson Welles, who was such a beautiful man!" director Henry Hathaway says indignantly. "He's like a heap of Jello!" comments actor-producer Martin Gabel. "I don't understand all that. As a kid he used to be fat and thin within a month—literally thin to very fat. But nothing like this. This is grotesque!" "It's like an addiction," says screenwriter and novelist Wolf Mankowitz of Orson's eating. "It's like a drug addict who hasn't reached rock-bottom and can't face the fact that he's an addict. He has an addiction to food."*

Orson and I are having dinner at Pat's Fish House, another of his pet names for Ma Maison, based on the first name of its owner, Patrick Terrail. As a regular, Orson depends on the chef's recommendations for the day. Today it is a fish St. Pierre with a lobster sauce. Orson accepts, but specifies that for him, not me, the sauce is to be "on the side." The days of the legendary Lucullan feasts are over. Orson eats well but—as far as I can see—sparingly. Not only does his fish arrive plain but, also by request, it is unsalted. Even the vegetable (which is spinach) has come "au naturel." The chef can't resist sending Orson a little silver boat of a "special" sauce in addition to his lobster sauce, but Orson is not tempted. He barely tastes either. I have learned to dread the moment of dessert when dining with Orson; he will insist on something profoundly caloric and sinful for me, and fruit for himself. Tonight it is sliced kiwis. "Toujours simple," he laughs when ordering. As usual, there is a bottle of champagne for me, but he drinks only glass after glass of Perrier. The people who see him regularly in Los Angeles observe the same thing I have: at least in public, Orson eats relatively little and drinks nothing remotely alcoholic.

I dare not ask him about his weight, however—certainly not in the first stages of our friendship. I would be much too embarrassed even to mention it. Sometimes, surprisingly, he brings it up himself as he does tonight in Ma Maison, when he jokes about what he describes as "the thousands of pounds" he has lost and gained back in his life. He is a bit less mirthful about the diet pills that were routinely prescribed for him in the early Hollywood years, when no one, he reminds me, seemed to have the faintest idea that they were harmful.

People who have never met Orson Welles often presume that his size is almost all one can think about in his presence. But my experience is very different from that. In fact, I have considerable trouble identifying the man I am talking to with the outsize creature he has become. It is as if he is buried somewhere inside himself. I am repeatedly startled by how intact is the beauty that others lament has entirely disappeared. Although he is a veritable Gargantua, at least twice the bulk of many men, if you watch him from the right angle, you find yourself glimpsing the old sex-symbol Welles of decades back—the dashing star of Citizen Kane *or* The Third Man. *At such unsettling moments, one face suddenly emerges from within the other, then slips back inside again. Just as when telling stories at the dinner table Orson is capable of pefectly impersonating, of becoming, Greta Garbo or Charlie Chaplin, is this merely one Orson Welles impersonating* another?

The more Orson and I talk over many months, the more I realize how much anguish his fat causes him—anguish at being laughed at because of his size. "Fat jokes" is what he bitterly calls the mockery to which he is subjected—even by a friend like Burt Reynolds, of whom he was an early supporter in Hollywood. Appearing with Reynolds on a television show, Orson made a joke about the actor's having named a theater after himself in Florida. "It was meant as what the Spanish call rough kidding, which in life *he likes," says Orson, who is silent for a moment as if suddenly remembering another part of the story, which he had originally repressed. His voice alters noticeably, there is a catch in his throat as he tells me, "He immediately did a fat joke— just as a knee-jerk. Quick—did a fat joke and then went on." Orson can take plenty of rough kidding himself but clearly, I realize suddenly from the brooding tone of his voice, fat jokes don't fall into that category. Until the '70s, when Orson's weight shot up beyond a point of no return, he had still been quite capable of joking in public about his size. It was clear back then that he felt more joy in eating than he did pain in the fat jokes. All that is very different*

*today—which is why, even when we finally know each other
well enough for me to feel comfortable asking him just about
anything, his size is one subject I steer clear of.*

*One day, however, I find myself talking to him openly,
and in a fairly lighthearted manner, about his feelings about
being fat. It starts by our discussing, of all things, the many
people in Hollywood who have had cosmetic surgery, much
of it very bad.*

*"I think the worst plastic surgeons in the world come to
Hollywood because they seem to be in a sort of conspiracy
to make everyone look worse," Orson laughs. "There are
some good ones somewhere, because every once in a while
I meet some girl that I've known in the prehistoric period
who looks absolutely divine, as though the years haven't
passed at all. So somewhere, in some towns, there must be
good ones."*

*I know the particular girl he's thinking of, an actress
with whom he had a fling some forty years ago. Just the
other day she came up to his table at lunch and looked
much as she had decades before. From the way he told me
about this, I sensed that, even as he marveled at how very
much the same she appeared, he trembled to think of how
entirely different he must look to her.*

*"There's one who's supposed to be the greatest in Lon-
don," he continues on the subject of plastic surgeons. "He
doesn't like to do it because he's an old war hero. He's the
best man at putting a face back on a man who has no face,
and he spends all his time doing that. He does one or two
cosmetic operations a week, and you have to book two years
ahead of time or something. He looks at you with contempt
because you have a face to begin with." I'm beginning to
wonder how Orson knows all this when he says, "I went to
see him because I wanted to know if I could get my fat cut
off."*

*"You were just going to have it cut off?" I say, as startled
by his talking about it so candidly as by the idea itself.*

"Yes," says Orson, "they can really do it. But he said it was a very major operation, and that nobody should have a major operation unless it were life and death. They do it all the time very cheerfully. People have slabs of lard cut off daily, you know."

By now we are both giggling—I, a bit nervously—but still I know he is absolutely serious about having wanted to get his fat cut away.

"It's a terrific idea," I laugh.

"Yes," he laughs back. When I suggest that it would of necessity be only a temporary measure, because new fat would soon take its place, Orson says philosophically, "That's true of anything to do with fat. That's automatic." And what about the physical pain of the operation? "It isn't that so much," he says to explain why he didn't try it, "as just that the shock of the surgery is considerable."

As long as we are on the subject, I mention a television talk show I watched the other morning about a doctor who suctions away fat in his office. "Yes, that's the new one, and I've thought of doing it," he says. "I was very pleased with that, and I went hurrying, hurrying for advice." He can't resist another gale of laughter here. "And they said the same thing: Big Shock."

"That really looks ugly and unpleasant," I say of what I saw on television.

"It was very ugly, that awful vacuum cleaner," Orson agrees. "But it seemed to me an awfully nice idea, theoretically—just turn on the Hoover, and away goes the fat, you know."

I wonder aloud now how the doctor possibly suctions off the same amount of fat from the different parts of the body.

"Oh, you're going to be oddly shaped," Orson explains authoritatively, as if I were the prospective patient. "The point is that you'll be thinly oddly shaped."

CHAPTER 35

So Shall
the World Perceive

The financing failure of *Chimes at Midnight* in Dublin precluded Hilton Edwards's taking the production to London. But having finally solved the aesthetic problem of focus that had stumped him in *Five Kings*, Orson did not abandon the dream of eventually raising money for a film version of the Fallstaff-Hal relationship that had come to preoccupy him. In the meantime, however, if *Chimes* was not going on to London, Orson was—for he had just received a timely invitation to put on the London premiere of Eugène Ionesco's *Rhinoceros*, which Wolf Mankowitz was producing, an invitation that pleased Orson all the more for the long-awaited opportunity it afforded to direct Laurence Olivier, who was set to play Bérenger. Playing the role of Daisy was Joan Plowright, whom Orson had directed in the London production of *Moby Dick* in 1955, and with whom Olivier, still married to Vivien Leigh, had fallen in love when they appeared together in *The Entertainer*. It was during the run of Orson's *Rhinoceros* that their affair would erupt into the open when Vivien Leigh shocked the press and public by disclosing that her husband wanted a divorce. But all this was still in the future when Orson happily embarked on rehearsals late in March. As it turned out, *Rhi-*

noceros was a dreadful disappointment for Orson, who had initially intended to outdo Jean-Louis Barrault's hit production then running at the Odéon in Paris. But the more he labored on the production—directing, designing sets, and even reworking some of the action, transposing the setting to England—the less sympathy he seemed to feel for Ionesco's play, in which he had taken no onstage role for himself. "It's a terrible play," says Orson. "I *hate* it. But I wanted to do it because of Larry." Although, in London, there was much keen anticipation of the production, when it opened in April of 1960, it was quite surprisingly overshadowed by what had been the far less trumpeted premiere of Harold Pinter's *The Caretaker*. "Nothing could have been more fatal," says Orson of the effect of the other production on his. As for the golden opportunity to direct Olivier, this was the worst disappointment of all. "He behaved terribly during the show," says Orson of Olivier. "He's always very sinister and does strange things. The way he *got* me in this was to take all of my directions like a perfect soldier, never argue with them, and always do them—I gave him some wonderful things to do, I must say—and he took every actor aside and told them that I was misdirecting them." Orson explains Olivier's strategy thus: "Instead of making it hard for me to direct *him*, he made it almost impossible for me to direct the *cast*. He got them off in little groups and had little quiet rehearsals having nothing to do with me." For all his notoriety as an actor who was not averse to taking over another man's production and directing it himself, Orson did not like it one bit when someone else did the same to him. Orson says that eventually Olivier sent him away from his own production, and that for some inscrutable reason he heeded the actor's command. "Then he did something which he had done to John Gielgud before, when he was playing *Twelfth Night* with Vivien," says Orson. "He told John Gielgud four days before the opening that he shouldn't come for any more rehearsals,

he was upsetting them. And he *didn't* come! Then he [Oli-
vier] did the same thing to me. He told me to stay home,
and I *did*! I was so humiliated and sick about it that you
can't imagine. I *had* to come for the dress rehearsal because
I'd designed the sets, and I had to supervise that, and light
it, and so on." Afterwards, however, Orson couldn't bear
to return to the play, which he felt had been wrested away
from him in rehearsal. "I never went back to the play," he
recalls. "They changed the cast, and they had Maggie Smith
in, and they had Alan Bates, and they moved to another
theater. But I didn't go to rehearsals. All those actors think
very badly of me because they think that I simply wasn't
interested—I was so humiliated, I didn't *know how* to come
back! All those actors thought that I was just unthinkably
cavalier, but I didn't have the *guts*! *He's* the leader of the
English stage, *he's* playing the leading role, and directing
it all the time! What was *I* going to do? Yes, it was a black
moment." As to why Olivier would do any of this, Orson
has his theory. "He *had* to destroy me in some way," says
Orson. "He did it to John G., and he took it perfectly
cheerfully!" But why possibly would Olivier want to destroy
Orson? "Well," says Orson, "he doesn't want anybody else
up there. He's like Chaplin, you know. He's a real fighting
star."

   "Being in show business today is like being a cherry
picker," Orson told the press that May as he prepared to
leave London. "We go where the crops are." Given the lack
of money to film *Chimes* as, more and more, he longed to
do, Orson had no choice but to hire himself out for the
usual round of acting chores. "It's like the cherry crop," he
added. "Whatever's going, we take. Except that I'm choos-
ier about what I direct than what I act in." Surely he was
not being choosy when, for instance, he pursued the crop
to Zagreb, Yugoslavia, where he appeared with Victor Mature in *The Tartars*. Not that Orson and his long-ago rival

for Rita Hayworth's affections would actually appear together very much. The artful use of doubles could make it seem that *both* of them were onscreen when only *one* was really there. The few times they did work together, however, did not quite work out. The production schedule called for Orson to shoot his entire part first, then for Mature to arrive to do his. Whatever work they had to shoot together, they did shortly before Orson left. Their first big scene began with Orson seated on a raised throne toward which Mature marched down a long aisle lined with palace guards, at the end of which Orson would dramatically descend the steps from his throne to meet him. It was simple enough direction, but not for these two, who appeared to be worried about which of them would seem the larger when they stood side by side. "Orson was a really big man, and so was Mature," says the production manager, Prince Alessandro Tasca di Cuto, "but Mature wasn't satisfied. He had to be even bigger. So we started the scene, and I saw Mature come in *wobbling*—he had heels several inches high so that he'd be much taller than Orson and dominate him! Orson saw this. He came down—but not *all* the way down. He stayed on the last step, so that he was one step above, and played the scene, all throughout, *one step above* Victor Mature!" Even after Orson departed from Zagreb, Mature seemed determined not to let himself be overshadowed by him. Told that there was a crisis on the set, Tasca rushed there to find Mature engaged in a furious dispute with director Richard Thorpe. "You son of a bitch!" Mature was heard to address the gentlemanly director. "What's wrong, *Mr*. Mature?" interjected the prince, who deliberately refrained from ever calling him Victor. "You're a son of a bitch too!" he replied. "Well, *Mr*. Mature," Tasca said calmly, "maybe I am a son of a bitch, but what is this all about?" "In this scene you shot two close-ups of Orson Welles, and the son of a bitch wants to do only one close-up of me!" said Mature. "I want *three* close-ups!" With which request Tasca loudly advised the director to comply, while more quietly instructing the cameraman only to *pretend* to film the extra shots.

"It was a *terrible* picture!" the prince wryly admits of *The Tartars*. Unsatisfying work like acting in *The Tartars* made Orson more resentful of his temporary inability to direct, to make the movies he wanted to, while kitsch like this seemed to have no such trouble attracting funds. Back in Italy after his stint on *The Tartars*, Orson was perhaps more anxious than ever to get behind the camera again. But with no one as yet in sight to put up the cash for *Chimes*, he had little choice but to unpack six years' worth of disparate footage for his "home movie" of *Don Quixote* and start tinkering. The more pieces there were, the more Orson liked experimenting with new combinations, new permutations. His interminable approach to telling the tale of *Don Quixote* was an apt (if ultimately impractical) response to the Cervantes masterpiece, which is itself the most vertiginous of narrative structures: a series of stories within stories, frames within frames, that threatens never to end, to keep multiplying, to keep reworking itself from within— and in a curious way, this is exactly what happened in Orson's ill-fated version. Now, however, determined as he was to finish it, to come up with the right combination of images, Orson kept creating new images that he hoped would make the parts of the puzzle fit together. With this in mind he enlisted the services of Prince Tasca, who, having completed his labors as production manager on *The Tartars*, happily joined Orson on *Don Quixote*. In order to shoot more footage Orson even accepted an offer from Italian television to do some documentary work in Spain that would enable him to work on his "home movie" on the side.

Then something unexpected happened. Having employed Orson as an actor in the past, the father-and-son producing team of Michel and Alexander Salkind proposed to back him in a picture of his own. Presented with a list of literary classics that were in the public domain, Orson was asked to choose one quickly. "The only thing that was *conceivable* for me was *The Trial*," says Orson of his choice. "I *never* would have picked it out." Despite what he describes as his own "lack of profound sympathy for Kafka," he agreed to do *The Trial* in Yugoslavia with Anthony Perkins as Joseph K. But even now he was harried by money problems; not long after he started shooting exteriors in Zagreb, the Salkinds ran out of cash. Worst of all, the moment they suspected that the production was in financial trouble, the Yugoslav authorities, who had agreed to put some money into Orson's picture, balked at constructing the elaborate sets he had designed. With the exteriors already shot, the production was at a virtual standstill. Another director might have panicked, but not Orson, who had great experience with financial calamities. But it did seem to him that fate must have had something to do with his being out of funds again, even when he had begun the picture with what looked like perfectly stable backing and the best will in the world from his backers, who hadn't foreseen the sudden crisis.

Orson's state of mind in the midst of this crisis may have been helped by his having recently met a young woman in Zagreb who instantly struck him as among the loveliest and most intelligent he had ever encountered. A gifted sculptor, Oja Kodar had also tried her hand at script writing, and Orson was genuinely impressed by the original scenario of hers that he read. He was also impressed by what he recognized as her unusual independence of spirit. From the first she came to him as an equal—and so he accepted her. "He's very impressed that she doesn't need him to exist," says producer Dominique Antoine, who has known them both for more than a decade. "He worships her, he really worships her, because it's the first intelligent woman he has had in his life." Having discovered such a woman, he was determined not to lose her. In time he would make her his companion, his artistic collaborator, his confidante. But for

now they had only just met. Besides, Orson had serious
decisions to make immediately about *The Trial*, the production of which old Michel Salkind had sadly suggested
he close down.

But Orson had other ideas. He explained to Salkind that
if they could get the company to Paris, he could finish up
for next to nothing. Orson proposed they all skip town on
a train that left in half an hour. "You pay the hotel bill, and
we won't pay anything else," Orson recalls his having told
Salkind. "We'll just go home and find a way to shoot it."
In Paris, Orson improvised brilliantly by seizing upon the
derelict Gare d'Orsay to shoot interiors. Because of the dire
shortage of funds, Orson sometimes found himself paying
actors out of his own pocket lest they refuse to continue.
He edited the film that summer of 1962, commuting between
the cutting room in Paris and Malaga, where he had rented
a retreat for Paola and Beatrice, and where he could attend
the bullfights in August. Originally set to premiere at the
Venice Film Festival in the early fall (the festival management threatened to sue him when, at the last moment, he
disappointed them), *The Trial* was not ready until winter.
When it opened in Paris, Orson was widely criticized for
having badly miscast Anthony Perkins as K. "I think everybody has an idea of K. as some kind of little *Woody Allen*.
That's who they think K. is," speculates Orson. "But it's
very clearly stated in the book that he is a young executive
on his way up." It was K.'s "aggressiveness," as Orson calls
it, that he specifically had in mind in casting Perkins, and
against which he is convinced people reacted.

Soon Orson had a new project; he longed to make a movie
of Joseph Heller's *Catch 22*. "It's the movie of the century,"
a hopeful Orson told the press in Paris, but his vigorous
efforts to secure the film rights proved unsuccessful. (He is
still wistful when he speaks of having missed out on *Catch
22*, which he argues could have been "a groundbreaking
movie—exactly the sort of movie Mike Nichols did not

succeed in making when, several years later, he, not Orson, directed it. "You can't watch it," complains Orson of the Nichols version, in which, ironically, he played a small role. "It's really dreadful!") For a while, it looked like instead of doing *Catch 22*, Orson would direct the Jacob segment of Dino De Laurentiis's superproduction of *The Bible*. But that too failed to happen, although Orson had thrown himself into writing the segment, and his uncredited script material would eventually find its way into the finished film. The closest he came to directing anything from the Bible was *portraying* a Hollywood director of a biblical epic in a movie titled *RoGoPaG*. But he seems to have played the part too well, for upon viewing the satirical sequence in which he appeared, the Italian authorities took umbrage at what they deemed a travesty of the crucifixion and ordered the arrest of the real director, Pier Paolo Pasolini.

To direct another picture of his own, Orson would have to wait until he had moved his family from Italy to Spain, where, in 1964, he and Tasca finally managed to lure backers for *Chimes at Midnight*. "Spain was the only country that didn't know that black-and-white wasn't commercial!" jokes Orson about why he made *Chimes* there, although in truth he was glad to have the chance to do it anywhere. "This was the picture he had in his heart," says the prince to explain why they forged ahead with the production, although they feared from the outset that the financing was to be a precarious affair in which Orson would never really see all the cash that he had been promised by the Spanish money men. The idea was to make the movie for whatever small sums they could extract, and at length Orson did it for a measly $800,000, when he had expected, and any other director would certainly have needed, at least several times that. Having made *Othello* as he had, Orson was perfectly accustomed to cutting corners without looking as if he had done so. Two of the film's stars, Jeanne Moreau as Doll Tearsheet, and John Gielgud as Henry IV, were

available to him for only five and ten days respectively, so
that, as he had on *Othello*, Orson made very extensive use
of doubles. "Whenever it's not her face, it's a double," says
Tasca of Jeanne Moreau. "*Even* in the love scene. Every
reverse shot is a double." Orson reports that Gielgud achieved
his splendid portrayal of the king in spite of the constant
carping of an apparently malicious Hungarian friend "with
a bright orange complexion coming from some medicine he
was taking to make himself look sunburned," says Orson.
"All this terrible Hungarian kept saying to him was"—here
Orson slips into a mock-Hungarian accent—" 'John, you
are terrible old fashion! Old hat, old hat! Nobody wants
you.' *All day long!* And Gielgud was saying"—here the
exact voice of Gielgud—" 'I know, I know, it's perfectly
true, perfectly true, every word of it is true!' "

Orson's own experience as an actor who typically alighted
on a given movie set for only a few days at a time did not
hurt when it came to his using actors with maximum efficiency. He knew exactly where he needed their faces, and
where he could get away with a double. To keep costs down,
Orson released actors the moment he could. Whether in
Barcelona, Madrid, or elsewhere on location, there were
always locals willing to rent their backs to him if he needed
to double the real actors later. He also used them to simulate
vast numbers of people by means of clever cutting. Perhaps
the most dazzling example of Orson's ingenuity was the
crowded canvas of the vivid battle sequence. "We never had
more than one hundred and eighty people on the battlefield,"
says Orson, although at a glance it *seems* like many, many
more. "And that took *a lot* of doing!" Still, he could not
entirely compensate for the ineptness of certain of his local
technicians, whom he did not have the funds to replace.
One particularly irritating incident occurred when a tearful
Margaret Rutherford as Mistress Quickly brilliantly declaimed her sad little speech upon the death of Falstaff.
There was a spontaneity, a tender beauty to her performance

that Orson was instantly afraid might be marred by the persistent hum of the generator. But the technician profusely assured him that there was no problem since the mike wouldn't pick up the offending noise. "Either this man is a genius or he is an idiot," Orson told Tasca, both of them strongly suspecting the latter. Unfortunately, their worst suspicions were confirmed when, long after Miss Rutherford had gone, they discovered that the generator was indeed audible. Later, meeting with the prince in Paris, she tried desperately to lip-sync the speech, but she couldn't do it. Somehow she couldn't recapture the passion, the authenticity, of the original, which, at length, Orson decided to use despite its flaws, which he obscured wherever he possibly could. If you listen to Miss Rutherford's speech in the finished film you can indeed hear the hum of the generator in the background, but the eloquence of her performance is such that you barely notice it. A technical blunder that particularly nettles Orson, and understandably so, is that the entire first reel had come back from the lab slightly out of sync. The sound was off only slightly, but this made all the difference in the world. Nor were there funds available to redo the reel, which would be shown in America in its imperfect form. This technical ineptness, and the lack of funds to rectify the ensuing errors, were a source of immense agitation to Orson, who, in the editing, had been relentlessly *self*-critical. It vexed him enormously to have to accept defects in the fabric of his film. Although they would hardly be as noticeable to audiences as they were to him, Orson saw these spot defects as an indication of his sorry fate as a filmmaker, whereas the grace, the grandeur, of the film as a whole indicates for us how mightily he had transcended that fate.

But there is another kind of transcendence here as well. That *Chimes at Midnight* was for Orson an intensely personal film is widely accepted. But precisely *why* it is so personal a statement cannot be ascertained without a knowledge of Orson's past, of his personal mythology. During the making of the film Orson described its focus as "the triangle between the king, his son, and Falstaff (who is a sort of foster father)." This focus he had finally hit upon while preparing the Irish stage production. Concentrating on the triangle solved the aesthetic problem that had stymied Orson in years past when both his Todd and Mercury productions of the history plays seemed somehow to lack an organizing principle. But the triangle was more than just a formal solution. With it Orson managed to bring into the foreground a dramatic story that had personally obsessed him all along: the story of the father, the mentor, and the young man's quandary about which of them to reject for the other. For this is the story Orson tells in *Chimes at Midnight*: Hal's renunciation of drunken Falstaff in favor of the father, the king. In a curious way this was also the story that as a youth he had lived out when he rejected drunken Dick Welles in favor of Skipper Hill. In Shakespeare it is the mentor whom the young man throws over, and who dies as a direct result, while in life it was his father whom Orson rejected, and for whose ensuing death he would always feel responsible. Both men elicited a mixture of love and embarrassment. It was the Hills who had encouraged Orson not to see Dick Welles on account of his chronic alcoholism (the same "excess of wine" for which Hal spurns Falstaff), and when Dick suffered a lonely death Orson ultimately felt guilty of having killed his father. So it is not too much to suppose that the reversal of his actual situation that Orson discovered in Shakespeare—the young man's rejecting the mentor, the foster father, rather than the real father—unconsciously appealed to him as a way of artistically denying the guilt that nagged at him. Significantly, Orson's Falstaff mingles traits of both Dick *and* Skipper. Like Orson's father, he drinks and frequents whores (where Hal, like Orson, observes him); also like Dick he misleads youth and takes young Hal carousing. He depends on the young man to bail him out. Like

Skipper, Falstaff is the beloved mentor, the desired foster father (following Dick's death, Orson had asked Skipper to be his legal guardian), the exuberant director of travesties in which the protégé performs. Like Skipper, he sometimes seems younger than his protégé. Not by accident, in May of 1964, shortly before he began shooting *Chimes at Midnight*, Orson wrote to Skipper, whose sixty-ninth birthday came days after Orson's forty-ninth: "I am so disastrously old that the mind boggles at the thought of what the age must be that you are celebrating—if 'celebrate' is the word I'm looking for. But then (in the best sense) you will always be younger than I was when I first checked into Clover Hall." The betrayal of Falstaff in *Chimes* is not only a restaging of what Orson considered to have been the betrayal of Dick Welles; by making Falstaff a peculiar amalgam of Dick and Skipper, he allowed himself to repeat the scene of rejection while changing the outcome, so that, in the film, the father is not spurned. The drunkard is spurned, yes, but *not* the father.

In Hal's dramatic renunciation of Falstaff, Orson heard an echo of his own. "I think it's one of the greatest scenes ever written," says Orson, "so the movie is really a preparation for it. *Everything* prepares for it." Having learned that his boy is the new king, Falstaff rushes to observe him from the crowd, much as when a drunken Dick Welles alighted on Woodstock between his far-flung journeys— "stained with travel" is how Falstaff describes himself—he had slipped into the theater at Todd to watch Orson from the back of the auditorium. But Hal is his boy no longer: "Presume not that I am the thing I was; / For God doth know, so shall the world perceive, / that I have turn'd away my former self; / So will I those that kept me company." Betrayed by the one who was his boy, sternly warned to reform himself, Falstaff hopes that this was all just a public display, that Hal will send for him in private. But this was not to be—just as Orson, having betrayed Dick in hopes that he would reform himself, never again saw him alive. Turning away from one's former self, as Hal announces that he has, was a theme of special interest to Orson, who would perceive himself as doing so more than once in life—not only with Dick Welles, but with Skipper and Dadda as well. While writing to Skipper and Hortense from Europe that first season after Todd, Orson would consciously think of himself as having changed, as merely acting the part of the boy they'd known before. And with Dadda there was the same explicit sense of having abandoned a former childish self named Pookles. As he had not with his father, with his two boyhood mentors Orson would oscillate between his old and new selves. He would watch himself enact what he once was—much as he does in the film when, as Falstaff, he watches Keith Baxter's Hal make the same mistake he had in youth. Watching himself like that was the kind of built-in distancing device that inherently appealed to an actor like Orson, who had so often resisted losing himself in the dramatic parts he played, all the better to maintain a critical distance from them. In *Chimes* Orson achieves perhaps the most mordant irony of all by costuming his daughter Beatrice as a boy and making her Falstaff's page, who as the film draws to a close is principal mourner at his master's death. That she vividly resembles the boy Orson once was— quite literally his "former self'—will be evident to anyone who has seen his early childhood photographs. Thus one version of young Orson, Hal, is responsible for the drunkard's death (as Orson thought he was), while another version, the page boy, mourns it (as in fact Orson did). At the end of the film it is said that Hal has "killed his heart"— which, in a realized metaphor, Orson remorsefully shows himself to have done by playing the part of the one who is killed. As Prince Tasca says, *Chimes at Midnight* was the film Orson "had in his heart"—words that take on new meaning in light of the autobiographical allusions that underpin this magisterial work. Unfortunately, the aftermath of *Chimes at Midnight* was less satisfying to Orson than the making had been. Bad press, as well as inadequate distribution, kept it from reaching the wide audience he had hoped for—and deserved. "Almost nobody has seen it in America, and that drives me nuts," says Orson of the picture in which through a battery of self-distancing devices he manages to explore, and to involve us in, his most personal preoccupations as intensely perhaps as an artist can. In this delicate balance between critical distance and painful intimacy lies the source of the film's resounding greatness.

CHAPTER 36

Fact and Fiction

After his experience making *Chimes at Midnight* with relatively little cash at his disposal, it seemed odd to Orson,
not long afterward, to act in a lavish production like Charles
Feldman's James Bond spoof, *Casino Royale*, in which
expense was clearly no object. Everything about the mis-
guided production was so utterly absurd—"a frightful mess"
is how scenarist Wolf Mankowitz describes it—that it left
Orson little time to brood about the absurdity of his personal
situation. "What criteria do you use for selecting acting roles
offered to you?" the press had asked Orson at the Cannes
premiere of *Chimes at Midnight*. "Money," he replied. For
Casino Royale, Feldman, who had produced *Macbeth*, hired
a bunch of script writers, Orson and Wolf Mankowitz among
them, but tried to keep them from learning of one another's
existence. "We were not supposed to know the other one
was working on the picture!" says Orson. But it was not
difficult to find out, since the scenarists had been installed
on different floors of the same hotel, and could not help
but bump into one another in the elevator. Feldman's scheme
had been to keep them from discussing the script because
he was convinced that they would only dilute one another's
best ideas. This way he figured he was getting the most for

his money. Without telling Feldman, the scenarists lunched together daily, where, quite naturally, they discussed the picture, which, says Orson, was supposed to be "the Bond that out-Bonded Bond. But it was the *worst* one. It didn't even have *Bond* in it!" Feldman never found out about the little lunches he had hoped to prevent. Recalls Orson: "We would arrive at various hours at Charlie's house with our secret scripts, which he would take and put in the safe on the theory that our ideas were so brilliant that people would try to steal them." Orson thought this highly unlikely since the popular television show *The Avengers* was, week after week, clearly superior to anything they were doing in terms of spoofing Bond.

In addition to the writers Feldman had hired, actor Peter Sellers hired several writers of his own to work only on his scenes. When Sellers refused to work with Orson, their scenes together had to be shot separately. On-camera Sellers spoke to a double's back, while Orson spoke his lines at another time. Orson was used to working this way for convenience, not because the other actor hated him. A further peculiarity of this awkward situation was that Sellers's having hired his own writers sometimes created curious disjunctions when he and Orson seemed to be talking about two diferent things. "When he asked me a question my answer didn't make any sense at all," says Orson, who was working from another script. "Now this gave a marvelous surreal quality to the whole thing because there had been no coordination whatsoever between us. Since we weren't on the set together, there was very little we could talk over." Mankowitz thought that Sellers refused to play with Orson because he was intimidated by him. "He was a treacherous lunatic," says Mankowitz of Sellers, with whom he had had a business partnership that had ended unpleasantly shortly before *Casino Royale*, "and he became more so after *The Millionairess*, which is the film we did together with Sophia Loren. He fell in love with Loren and it drove him right

over the top. He went completely barmy. My advice to
Charles Feldman was not in any circumstances to get involved with Sellers. But Sellers was at his peak at that time.
I told Charlie that Sellers would fuck everything up: he
wanted different directors, he wanted to piss around with
the script. He knew nothing about anything except going
on and doing funny faces and funny voices, and he wasn't
really a great actor. He was *terrified* of playing with Orson
and converted this into an aversion for Orson before he even
met Orson." He made his aversion perfectly clear when he
and Orson encountered each other in the elevator of the
Dorchester; Sellers was descending from his penthouse suite
when the elevator stopped, and Orson and Mankowitz got
in. Sellers took one look at Orson's outsize proportions and
wondered aloud whether the elevator might not drop from
the weight. "Sellers had got very thin and thought he looked
like Casanova," says Mankowitz by way of explanation.
Orson may have been the greater actor by far, but from the
first he was an easy target for Sellers on account of his
considerable heft.

On his part, however, Orson was not especially impressed
by Sellers, whom he found pretentious. "He wasn't terribly
bright, but he came on as *a great actor*," says Orson, who
had had several run-ins with him before Sellers had ruled
out their being filmed together. The first incident occurred
when Sellers arrived on the set and heard one of the beautiful
girls remark of Orson, "Isn't he sexy?" This remark enraged
Sellers, who was, since his weight loss, unbearably narcis-
sistic. Then there was a session in Sellers's hotel suite during
which he tried unsuccessfully to make Orson laugh. He was
not only defensive about acting with Orson, but he also
feared that Orson did not find him funny. What finally came
between them, however, was Princess Margaret, with whom,
unbeknownst to Sellers, Orson had become quite friendly
when he directed *Othello* in London. "The fact that she was

stopping by every day at my house was unknown to him," laughs Orson. Never suspecting that Orson could be acquainted with her, Sellers darted about to tell everyone he could find that he had invited Princess Margaret to lunch and that she would be there presently. "Then Princess Margaret *came*," recalls Orson, "and walked on the set and passed him by and said, 'Hello, Orson, I haven't seen you for days!' *That* was the real end. *That's* when we couldn't speak lines across to each other. 'Orson, I haven't seen you for days!' absolutely killed him. He went white as a sheet because *he* was going to get to present *me*."

For a director like Orson who had worked for four years on a single picture it was strange to see directors come and go on this production: "A director would say, 'Excuse me just a minute' and he'd go off and a door would open, and in would come another director!" is how he describes it. "Then at the end of it," Orson continues, "having fired several directors—they used to be *led* off the set—Charlie hired John Huston, and John *immediately* moved everybody to Ireland because he wanted to do fox hunting." People thought Feldman had lost his senses to keep putting immense sums of money into a film like this. But they were proved wrong when *Casino Royale* was a smashing success at the box office. It must have given Orson pause—why did he have the madman image when a picture could get made in this perfectly irrational manner and no one complained? What accounted for a "frightful mess" like *Casino Royale*'s becoming a big hit with the public? "I think it was the poster," says Orson, *half*-kidding. "It was a great naked girl entirely covered with tattoos. *Very* sexy, superb poster! That's the *only* explanation. There were so many of us on it that they had to put us down in tiny letters, so people had no idea that there wasn't any Sean Connery." Of his not very strenuous acting role in the picture, Orson sums up, "For two months I sat in a white dinner jacket, for a very high salary, on alternate days. It was all very cheerful except for Peter, because he was whirling and giving off little clouds of smoke."

The Welleses were living in an eighteen-room stucco villa named Mi Gusto that Orson had bought in Aravaca, outside Madrid. For Orson, the high life, the endless rounds of bullfights and fashionable *boîtes*, to which he tirelessly devoted himself in Spain was a way of forgetting, of temporarily escaping, what he saw as his professional plight. In Spain he was thought of as just another frivolous American émigré. "That's why I lived happily in Spain in a bullfighting and aristocratic ambience, which is not stimulating in any way," says Orson, "but it *is* a complete world in which I was accepted without questions. Nobody asked me what I was doing, and I wasn't doing *anything*. I didn't have any movie or anything, but nobody asked me. . . . My *whole* conversation was just about bulls."

Before long, however, he had a new project: a modest adaptation of Isak Dinesen's *The Immortal Story* for French television. Once before, Orson had hoped to put Dinesen onscreen, and had thought he had proper backing from a Hungarian émigré in London who claimed to have arranged for him to film an anthology of Dinesen stories in Budapest. Orson and his cronies spent several weeks there, living it up in preparation to start shooting. But when Orson realized that the self-styled émigré producer was actually quite penniless, and that, shock of shocks, the tab at the hotel was entirely in the name of Mr. Welles, he had little choice but to slip away quietly at four o'clock in the morning. In addition to *The Immortal Story*, which he filmed from September through November, and which, despite its being intended for television, would eventually also find its way into theatrical distribution, Orson was immersed in plans for a full-length film based on Charles Williams's suspense novel *Dead Calm* that, if all else failed, he planned to finance out of his own pocket. He sent the script to Skipper, who, having sold Todd, had retired with Hortense to Florida, where they ran a charter-boat service. Orson asked Skipper to check for technical accuracy those portions of the script that pertained to yachting. After a string of acting jobs, the proceeds from which Orson had hoped to use in part at least to begin filming *Dead Calm*, he quite unexpectedly received an offer from Dean Martin to appear on his television shov back in the States. Delighted as he was, Orson could not figure out why Dean Martin wanted to pay his passage all the way to America just to do a television spot. He gathered that someone named Greg Garrison had been responsible for the invitation, but Orson knew no such person.

In September of 1967 Orson made the first of what would be many guest appearances on *The Dean Martin Show*. It was his second opportunity to become a television personality. The first had come in the '50s when a quiz-show producer invited Orson to his suite at the Hampshire House in New York, where he guaranteed that Orson would win immense sums of money if he would appear as a contestant. Orson's reputation as a *genius* would be perfect for the program. When Orson expressed doubt that he would be able to answer the kind of questions they'd probably throw at him, the producer told him not to worry since he would know the questions and answers in advance. Orson wisely passed up the generous offer, and he was glad he had when several years later he read about the chap from Hampshire House when the big quiz-show scandal broke in the press. As for the mysterious producer Greg Garrison, who had sought out Orson in Europe to go on television with Dean Martin, Orson seemed to recognize him now, but could not place where they had met. Whereupon Garrison told the story of their initial encounter many years before when, as a young college student, he had taken a job as a stagehand on the ill-fated *Around the World* when it played Philadelphia. His first day on the job he saw Orson throw a tantrum about one of the innumerable things that were going wrong with the production. So enraged was Orson that he hurled his walking stick in no particular direction. It hit Garrison, who in turn took the stick, marched up to Orson with it, and whacked him back. "Out! Get him out!" Orson bellowed, at which Garrison practically found himself thrown out on his ear. Very late that night, Garrison was asleep in the boardinghouse where he lived, when a knock at the door to his room awakened him. It was the landlady to say he had a visitor. A moment after he had sent her away saying he was not expecting anybody at that hour, there was another knock. "Who is it?" asked Garrison. "It's Orson Welles," came the unmistakable voice. "May I come in?" Orson was there to apologize. "I'm sorry, I didn't realize the cane hit you. I was wondering if you would come back to work tomorrow." That was in 1946. Now, in 1967, Garrison was a top television producer and able to return the kindness by inviting Orson to come to work for him. "That brought me to Hollywood twice a year when I was *Europe-bound*," says Orson of his association with *The Dean Martin Show* that led to his working with Garrison on other TV projects later on, among them a talk-show pilot for which there were, alas, no buyers.

In Europe after this first stint for Garrison, Orson repaired to Yugoslavia, where, between acting roles in pictures by local directors who were overjoyed to have him, he worked on *Dead Calm*, or *The Deep*—work that was ultimately never to be completed, Orson says, because of the death of leading man Laurence Harvey in 1973, after the production had dragged on and on because of the usual financial calamities. The unorthodox manner in which he patched together the ill-fated film is suggested by his enlisting Skipper to shoot some footage in the Bahamas, where Orson arranged briefly to appear with Oja Kodar, and a collection of costumes, in tow. Although he remained married—and quite devoted—to Paola, and although to all intents and purposes he continued to live with her, his presenting Oja to Skipper was a significant gesture. For Orson it bestowed a private legitimacy on a relationship that had flourished since *The Trial*. But this was not the principal reason for the trip. Before he rushed back to Zagreb to appear as Winston Churchill in a World War II movie about battling Yugoslav Partisans and the Nazis, he filmed a scene in which he toppled off the ketch Skipper had secured. That was to be followed with a bloody underwater knife fight between Orson and an adversary—except with Orson gone, it was Skipper's job to find a jumbo double for the underwater action. Finding someone big enough for Orson's enormous trousers would be hard enough, but the chubby would also have to know his way around underwater. It was a tough set of requirements. When at last Skipper found someone who was fat and could dive well he also turned out to be blond. Skipper talked him into dying his hair. Unfortunately when Skipper filmed the sequence the fake blood went green underwater.

Before long the press had spotted Oja. Orson's openly traveling about with a woman of such exceptional beauty could not go unnoticed. But Oja's presence did not mean that his marriage to Paola was finished as some observers mistakenly presumed. Orson needed both relationships. Paola and Beatrice continued to mean *home*. He might wander far afield, but he always came back. Even when he was with Oja, his home address was wherever Paola and Beatrice were. For many years Orson would divide his time between the two women in his life, so that, in its own way, his relationship with Oja was every bit as stable as that with Paola. In collaboration with Oja, Orson successfully reworked a film script of his titled *The Sacred Beasts*. In its original form it concerned an old Hollywood filmmaker who, much as Orson perceived himself to have done, had given himself over to bullfights and café society in Spain.

Now Orson and Oja wrote a new version of the script titled *The Other Side of the Wind*, the making of which was to be one of the most personally vexing—and widely misunderstood—episodes of his career.

In *The Other Side of the Wind* the action of *The Sacred Beasts* is transposed to Hollywood, where the old director is trying to launch a comeback. At the suggestion that he might have modeled the character of Jake Hannaford on himself, Orson insists otherwise: "He's based really more than anybody on Rex Ingram," he says. "He was considered a great filmmaker at one time—and he *wasn't*. He made terrible movies. They're awful! He was a great *fascinator* like John [Huston], in the high style of a great adventurer, a super-Satanic intelligence, and so on. He was a great director *as a figure*, in the way that John is. That's why John is so perfect for it." But even before he had cast the film Orson was convinced that, perhaps more than *The Deep*, *The Other Side of the Wind* was capable of restoring his reputation in Hollywood. With its possibilities for satire and parody, it seemed suddenly the more audacious idea. Also there was an *openly* erotic element in the script of the sort that had been mostly absent from his earlier work. Dominique Antoine says that this was Oja's influence: "This is a new thing in Orson's oeuvre, that it's erotic. He never touched all that before. He couldn't touch it, and she opened all that in him." Confident that this was the right project for the moment, Orson was ready once again to invest his own money. But this time it looked like there would be a source of funds besides his acting jobs, for CBS had invited Orson to direct several specials during the next few years. When he arrived in Hollywood he tried to lure backers to put up some of the money for *The Other Side of the Wind*; there were no offers, but Orson was undeterred. The television money would keep him going. Shooting intermittently, Orson and Oja together sank what he says was about $750,000 of their own funds into the picture.

Then his old tax trouble from *Around the World* came back to haunt him. For his European films he had used a production company based in Switzerland to which he had asked that the television producer at CBS send the money owed him for one of the specials. Says Orson to explain the Swiss address: "If you're shooting in different European countries you have to have a banking place of origin. It was not at all a company to siphon off money so I could go off on my yacht." But the tax people did not agree, and much to Orson's amazement, they seized the money, saying that what he claimed was a production company in Switzerland was really a holding company. "That was a real nightmare," says Orson of finding himself embroiled in the tax troubles that had kept him in Europe for so long. While he haggled with the Internal Revenue Service, trying somehow to work off, and perhaps to renegotiate, his vast debt, he had little choice but to seek investors again—but to seek them with a desperate need that may have made him ripe for falling victim to a swindle. In hopes of diminishing his monstrous tax bill, in Paris he hit upon a plan to assemble a new television special from footage François Reichenbach had shot of an art forger in Ibiza named Elmyr de Hory, about whom Clifford Irving had written *Fake*. As a filmmaker Orson was adept at taking shots that meant one thing by themselves, and making them mean something quite different by cutting them up and juxtaposing them. But while in the past he had worked with film footage for which *he* had been responsible, this time he used *found* footage. Affording shape and meaning to someone else's footage appealed to the *bricoleur* in Orson.

Reichenbach provided Orson with an editing room in Paris, where, driven by the desire somehow to get back to *The Other Side of the Wind*, he worked at the feverish pace that had astonished people in the early days in New York and Hollywood. When he was not locked up in the editing room he was busy sniffing out potential investors among

film people in Paris. Meanwhile his wife and daughter lived
in London, where the Welleses had moved after renting the
Spanish villa. Orson was nearly finished putting together
the television documentary about de Hory when news broke
in the press about Clifford Irving's spurious claims to have
had Howard Hughes's cooperation for a new book about
the recluse's mystery life. "My God, we're absolutely in
the middle of this!" said Orson, since the Reichenbach footage included a brief interview with Irving. "Let's forget
about TV, and do a long feature about Clifford!" It was a
bold move. Not only had Reichenbach initially shot the
footage expressly for French television, but there was not
very much of it, and certainly not enough about Irving, for
a full-length feature film. Until now the art forger de Hory
had been the center of attention. Irving's role had been
limited to commenting on de Hory. Orson quickly decided
to shift the balance of the material to give equal weight to
Irving and de Hory. The new picture would be about *both*
fakers, and since there still was not enough here to make a
feature film, by shooting additional footage he would add
a *third* faker to the cast of characters: himself.

As long ago as his radio program *First Person Singular*,
Orson had enjoyed turning up on both sides of the frame
by oscillating between the roles of narrator and character,
thereby calling into question the line between fact and fiction—which was precisely the vertiginous effect now in *F
for Fake* when he and Oja appeared *both* as themselves and
as actors in a purely fictive scenario about Oja's bogus
encounter with Picasso that Orson had shrewdly improvised
to fill out the film. When toward the end of *F for Fake* they
jointly tell the tale of Oja's purported involvement in the
dissemination of Picasso forgeries, the spectator assumes it
actually happened. For, in the first moments of the picture,
Orson announced that everything he was about to recount
in the next hour would be *true*. That hour is a frame. By
the time Orson and Oja recount the Picasso affair, although

we probably have not noticed, that hour is *over*, having been filled with diverting accounts of hoaxes: Elmyr's, Irving's, and, as it turns out, Orson's (the Martian scare that makes of Orson as much a faker as the other two). As the film draws to a close, having just laughed at the victims of a triptych of famous frauds, we fall victim ourselves to a fiction that we take for truth. Orson, who has just gleefully confessed to being a charlatan, still deftly puts one over on us. It is his old theatrical trick (a favorite device from the early days in New York) of making us forget the frame.

Throughout *F for Fake* Orson wears away a whole series of frames by intercutting footage from a variety of sources so that for instance he, Elmyr, and Irving appear to converse when they were very obviously filmed at different times and different places. Here the unabashed artifice of the technique bears ironically on Orson's experience as a film actor who had often only seemed to converse, to occupy a single space, with the other actor in the scene; and as a director who out of necessity had often assembled his films from quite disparate footage so that, for instance, when his actors weren't really there he had had to fool us into thinking that they were. In *F for Fake*, however, Orson took immense pleasure in baring the device, in making it work and exposing it at the same time—much as he had as early as *Citizen Kane* when, for instance, still a little boy, Charles says "Merry Christmas," and in the "reverse" shot (actually many years later) Thatcher adds "And a happy New Year!" But if, like *Kane*, *F for Fake* delights in its own artifice, it does so in a way that is at times even richer than its very venerable predecessor. The shock effects in *Kane* bespeak the wonderment, the excitement of a new toy. Young Orson wanted to try everything—and he did so with the fluency, the sophistication of a master's touch. In *F for Fake*, by contrast, the acknowledged master examines his medium in retrospect; he shows how, through cutting, a filmmaker can make something out of next to nothing. But for all Orson's

supreme virtuosity there is an endearing roughness to it all,
more than ever a fearless sense of improvisation, of experimentation, of not only showing but of seeing for himself
what he can do. It is the film of a collagist, a composer of
sounds and images, an artist who had waged a relentless
battle for the final cut because for him perhaps therein lay
the art of cinema.

CHAPTER 37

Again!

The news of the Hughes case had been opportune for Orson, who was understandably proud of himself for having seized the moment. He began to get the feeling that perhaps he had finally reversed his long run of bad luck when, on the verge of finishing *F for Fake*, he seemed to have found the investors he had been seeking for *The Other Side of the Wind*. Suddenly it looked like he would be finishing not one, but two pictures in swift succession. This was a particularly comforting thought, for he had been badly stung by the 1970 publication of Charles Higham's book, with its assertion that he actually feared completing pictures. Then, in 1971, Pauline Kael's disparaging essay had brought him to tears in a conversation with his lawyer, who advised him against a lawsuit, which would only attract more attention to the piece. The travesty of the Hollywood milieu in *The Other Side of the Wind* included wicked caricatures of both Higham and Kael. But Orson knew that he was best vindicated in having two big new films to his credit. "Bad luck is unforgivable," says Orson of how the public regarded his adversities. He had to show them that, once and for all, he had shaken the bad luck that had hounded him—and with *F for Fake* almost finished, and two major new sources of money for *The Other Side of the Wind* in the offing, he seemed about to do just that.

The first of the backers Orson managed to find in Paris was a Spanish acquaintance of his from the international film community who enthusiastically agreed to kick in $350,000, a little less than half of what Orson and Oja had already invested. Shortly thereafter an equivalent sum was pledged by a French-based Iranian group headed by Medhi Bouscheri, the brother-in-law of the Shah. Part of the Shah's program for modernizing his country was to cultivate the arts, film among them. In addition to beefing up local film production, the Iranians hoped to enter into prestigious co-productions with eminent Western directors. Hence they were on the lookout for a filmmaker of Orson's stature. Dominique Antoine, a Frenchwoman, made the deal with Orson on behalf of the Iranians, for whom she was setting up a film production company in Paris, and for whom she also bought *F for Fake*, which they subsequently distributed under the Iranian imprint of Les Films de l'Astrophore. In the negotiations for *The Other Side of the Wind*, Orson explained that he had already shot about an hour and a half of film, and that once the Iranian deal was clinched, he and Oja would repair to Spain to shoot some more. The Iranians having signed on made it a three-way co-production. After he put the finishing touches on *F for Fake*, Orson left France with the understanding that the Spanish partner would act as his intermediary with the Iranians in Paris. As the money was ready, the Iranians would give it to him, and he would bring it to Orson.

But no sooner were Orson and Oja in Spain than trouble started. "We were perfectly all right as long as I was using Oja's money and mine," says Orson, "but the moment we got associates!" The Iranians appeared not to be living up to their end of the deal. Orson heard from the Spaniard, who had flown in from Paris, that the Iranians had not given him the money they had promised. There were heavy rains and flooding in Spain, so Orson and Oja were basically cooped up in their hotel, where they worked on a new script together. The Spaniard returned to Paris to try again. "In a minute they're going to have it," he told Orson later. "It looks all right." In lieu of the Iranian funds, he gave them very small sums of money, which he said were part of the investment he had agreed to make. Not until afterward did Orson discover that the Iranians had indeed been giving the Spaniard the promised money, which had come from Iran in *cash*, and that, instead of bringing it to Spain, the sly fellow was pocketing it. Says Orson: "We just sat, month after month, while he went to Paris, received the money, and came back and told us that they wouldn't give him any money. He was very convincing to us, and very convincing with them in Paris. He kept flying back and forth extracting money from them. We didn't know *them*, you see. We knew *him*." The small sums of money he had been giving Orson as if from his own pocket actually came out of the Iranian funds. His constant reassurance to Orson that the Iranians were about to come through was calculated to keep Orson in Spain out of contact with them. On his part, Orson did not want to interfere in what he presumed were his emissary's delicate negotiations with them. It simply never occurred to him that the fellow was lying—and had never had any money of his own to invest in the first place.

Meanwhile, on account of the foul weather, Orson had decided to abandon Spain for Arizona, where John Huston and a host of other faithfuls joined him and crack cameraman Gary Graver to shoot in the desert. Resigned to his lot, Orson had begun to put his own money into the production again, but by now his personal funds had just about run out. "Orson found himself completely lost in Arizona," says Dominique Antoine of his wearily forging ahead without backing. The swindler continued his game of collecting cash from the Iranians, who, having heard only from him, still did not know that anything was wrong. When they received

a telex purportedly from John Huston's agent to ask for a
$60,000 advance, Dominique Antoine did ask for further
verification. But this did not deter the swindler, who sent
her a Screen Actors' Guild form with a bogus Social Security
number and signature from the States. The Iranians dispatched the $60,000, which was pocketed by the Spaniard
rather than by Huston, who, out of friendship for Orson,
was actually working for much less. After having sent the
money, Dominique Antoine had second thoughts about it.
Until now she had deliberately left Orson alone because she
sensed he preferred it that way. But now something told her
that there was a problem. "I think I have to go there," she
told Bouscheri, "even if Orson isn't pleased." Since Orson
had yet to receive a penny from the Iranians, their French
representative was the last person he expected to see in the
Arizona desert. He could not have been happy to see her.
When almost instantly he asked her where the money was,
and she nervously told him that she had been making regular
payments to the intermediary, who obviously hadn't passed
them on to him, he broke down. *"Again!"* Orson muttered
to no one in particular. *"It's happening again!"* He felt like
such a terrible fool. Over and over he tried to make sense
of what had happened, and, even more, of why irrational
disaster was repeating itself in his life. He oscillated between
incredulity and anger. Orson grew especially furious when,
after all the swindler had done, he brazenly resisted being
written out of the partnership. Back in Paris, however, a
new agreement was drawn up between l'Astrophore and a
company formed in Oja's name. (Orson's Swiss company
remained a matter of dispute with the tax people.)

Although when he left Arizona he was nearly broke,
Orson *had* managed to shoot a substantial portion of the
footage he wanted, and was ready to start editing. The
Iranians stipulated that he work in Paris, but Orson went to
Rome to labor on the footage in peace. He had good reason.
The American Film Institute had notified him that he was

to be the next recipient of the coveted Life Achievement Award, and while at first he was struck by the immense irony of the film industry's rewarding him for artistic achievements that, in the course of years, it had not exactly helped him to bring about, he was also struck by the possibility of this being the perfect opportunity to sell *The Other Side of the Wind* to the Hollywood money men. Perhaps in the end the making of *The Other Side of the Wind* would not have been such a disaster after all. When the Iranians moaned about his having violated their agreement by secluding himself in Rome, Orson patiently explained that if all went well both he and they could instantly recoup their investment. Nor were the substantial fringe benefits of Hollywood-style publicity and distribution to be sneered at. It could be everything they had hoped for. Led by the Shah's brother-in-law, a party of Iranians excitedly prepared to accompany Orson to Hollywood, where they would charge all of their considerable travel expenses to the picture. As his departure for Los Angeles approached, Orson redoubled his efforts to assemble enough of the footage to give the moguls a good idea of what he was selling. So deftly had he edited that to anyone else the picture might have appeared nearly finished. At least that was how it looked to the Iranians. But for the perfectionist in Orson all this was only a preliminary step. It seemed as if *The Other Side of the Wind* might conceivably be the turning point for him and he didn't want to bungle it with anything less than the major work of art for which he had been striving. Orson likes to say that when he was a young man in New York and Hollywood he was in competition with all the other jerks, but that when he grew older, it was the young Orson Welles who was judging him. On some level Orson saw *The Other Side of the Wind* as his contest with the man who made *Citizen Kane*—it was a contest he *had* to win. But he needed more footage to work with, or so he had decided. The Iranians agreed to put up the money for him to film in Los Angeles, but that meant l'Astrophore would have to get a bigger percentage of the profits later. He agreed that each time he took an advance from them he forfeited part of his percentage, which had begun at fifty percent. Eventually, the Iranians would end up owning more than eighty percent of the film.

In February of 1975, led by the Shah's brother-in-law, Bouscheri, the Iranian contingent gleefully arrived at the Los Angeles Room of the Century Plaza Hotel, where the American Film Institute was about to give Orson its trophy. Film clips of the first two winners, director John Ford and actor James Cagney, flashed on a giant screen, as the announcer said, "Tonight, we honor *the third man*." Nelson Riddle and his orchestra struck up the theme from Welles's most famous acting role, *The Third Man*. Spotlights focused on the paneled door, as the announcer continued: "The American Film Institute spotlights a director, an actor, a writer, a producer—and here *they* are—Orson Welles."

Into the glare slid the massive, gray-bearded Orson. For all his bulk, he rolled quickly and forcefully ahead, his great flat feet as close to the ground as the treads of an armored tank. His hair slicked back, he wore a jumbo tuxedo and flowing silk tie nearly the size of a pillowcase, and carried a script under his arm. He took his place at the red-draped dais facing a stage plastered with blowups of his many eminent film roles: the young shirt-sleeved maverick in *Citizen Kane*; the white-haired hulk of a Falstaff in *Chimes at Midnight*; the handsome Irish rogue in *The Lady from Shanghai*; the obscenely fat, dissipated slob in *Touch of Evil*.

To his right sat the darkly beautiful Paola and to his left his towering blond look-alike daughter Beatrice. Oja Kodar may have been his partner in all this, but Paola was still

Mrs. Welles, and the place of honor was hers. Pecking wife and daughter on the cheek, Orson turned to acknowledge the electric applause of the banquet hall, whose round pink tables were filled with Hollywood elite like Charlton Heston, Jack Lemmon, Johnny Carson, Natalie Wood, Rosalind Russell, and Groucho Marx, as well as assorted moguls and money men who had come to toast his filmmaking as having "stood the test of time."

Frank Sinatra sang "The Gentleman Is a Champ," which Sammy Cahn had set to "The Lady Is a Tramp"—an unfortunate irony in light of Orson's having tramped about Europe for years. America's greatest living filmmaker had not been able to make a movie in Hollywood since *Touch of Evil* in 1957; and before that he had spent another down-at-the-heels decade making marvelous low-budget pictures in Europe whenever he could scrape together the cash. Excerpts from Orson's now-classic pictures were screened, including the one from *Touch of Evil* in which Marlene Dietrich predicts he has no future—a line that turned the crowd's applause to embarrassed silence.

Said Ingrid Bergman in testimonial: "I think that it must have been a great burden for him to have made a masterpiece when he was twenty-four years old. And it must have been very hard to live up to it all those years. . . . I've been working in Europe when Orson Welles was working in Europe, and we had hardships—both of us. . . . I knew how he was working, and we saw pictures produced by Orson, directed by Orson, written by Orson, arranged by Orson, acted by Orson, clothes by—he had done everything. Still, he had his troubles. And the joke started in Europe saying that Orson Welles is running out of countries."

There was much laughter at this, indicating how aware all Hollywood was of Orson's plight; and no one howled more than he, his pudgy eyes crinkling with delight. For Orson grasped the evening's irony better than anyone, and

was prepared now to milk the occasion for all it was worth.
He was here for the honor, of course, but for something
else as well.

"Now he has come back to his own country," Bergman
continued, "and in great style. I'm so happy that the American Film Institute has asked me to come so I also can pay
my tribute to you and thank you that you have shown the
world what real *courage* is and *tenacity* and, of course, your
dazzling talent. So therefore I say, Bravo Orson, and hit us
again with your talent."

But to do that—everyone knew—Orson needed money.
This being an industry affair, money was on everybody's
mind—why a supreme film artist like Orson hadn't made
money, and why nobody in Hollywood was willing to back
him now.

"Too often we measure a film only by its bank account,"
said then AFI head George Stevens, Jr., broaching the indelicate subject in his introductory address. "Remembering
the stormy seas that Orson Welles has weathered in his long
career, hear what the writer John Ruskin said, a hundred
years ago, in noting that many of the most enduring works
in art and literature are never paid for. 'How much,' he
asked, 'do you think Homer got for his *Iliad* or Dante for
his *Paradiso*. Only bitter bread and salt and walking up and
down other people's stairs.'"

So tonight all Hollywood gathered to offer Orson something more than bitter bread and salt—a big meal, plenty
of booze, and a "handsome" trophy.

"He reminds us," said Stevens, "that it is better to live
one day as a lion than a hundred years as a sheep."

Now, clasping Orson's hand, Sinatra led him to the transparent Plexiglas rostrum, where he pressed the trophy to
his great stomach.

"My father once told me," gentleman-Orson began, "that
the art of receiving a compliment is of all things the sign

of a civilized man. And he died soon afterward, leaving my
education in this important matter sadly incomplete."

If the crowd tittered somewhat nervously, it was because
they were not sure whether this was supposed to be a joke—
a joke about someone's father *dying*?—a typically Wellesian
effect calculated to throw people off.

Still—and this is also typically Wellesian—Orson was
the perfect gentleman, *at least* during this first part of his
speech.

"My heart is full," he cooed, "with a full heart—with
all of it—I thank you."

He seemed to have finished now, but no sooner had everyone applauded than he picked up again.

"There are a few of us left in this conglomerated world
of ours," he said, "who still trudge stubbornly along the
lonely, rocky road and this is, in fact, our contrariety. We
don't move nearly as fast as our cousins on the freeway.
We don't even get as much accomplished, just as the family-
sized farm can't possibly raise as many crops or get as much
profit as the agricultural factory of today. What we do come
up with has no special right to call itself better. It's just
different. No, if there's any excuse for us at all, it's that
we're simply following the old American tradition of the
maverick. And we are a vanishing breed. This honor I can
only accept in the name of all the mavericks. And also as
a tribute to the generosity of all the rest of you—to the
givers—to the ones with fixed addresses."

Fixed addresses.

On these words Orson paused, raised his eyebrows, and
stared intently at his evening's benefactors, who were not
unaware that he was playfully indicting them, using the
occasion to remind them that they had shut him out, that
they had been cozily ensconced in Hollywood while he—
the genius, the *dazzling talent*—had kicked around the world.

Generosity.

What generosity had they shown, denying him the money to make films all these years?

"A maverick may go his own way," Orson continued, "but he doesn't think that it's the only way or ever claim that it's the best one—except maybe for himself. And don't imagine that *this* raggle-taggle gypsy is claiming to be free. It's just that some of the necessities to which *I* am a slave are different from yours. As a director, for instance, I pay myself out of my acting jobs. I use my own work to subsidize my work. In other words, I'm crazy. But not crazy enough to pretend to be free. But it's a fact that many of the films you've seen tonight could never have been made otherwise. Or if otherwise—well, they might have been better. But certainly, they wouldn't have been mine."

Finally, "just by way of saying goodnight," he introduced a clip from his unfinished movie, *The Other Side of the Wind*—about a legendary director named Jake Hannaford and his desperate struggle to raise funds.

This was what he had really come for. Suddenly intense, he was a salesman making a pitch, which he hoped the evening's embarrassment would help put over.

"The scene that you're going to see," explained Orson, clasping his hands, and glancing about him, "takes place in a projection room, and waiting there is the capital 'B' Big Studio Boss."

The director, Orson went on, "has a stooge, and the stooge is trying to sell the unfinished movie that Jake is making, which needs *end money*—"

End money.

This was what Orson really wanted from them—and deserved—not the trophy with the silver star on top. But whether, after the applause and the tributes and the toasts, he would get the Hollywood cash he had come for remained to be seen. Would one among them heed his unorthodox appeal?

Not long after, the offer Orson had been dreaming of did

indeed come from one of the moguls, who, on the basis of what he had seen and heard at the AFI banquet, wanted to buy *The Other Side of the Wind*. It was, says Orson, a "wonderful offer," but l'Astrophore turned it down on the assumption that an even better offer would come. "I am really sorry," says Dominique Antoine of the calamitous decision, "because I think the picture would have been finished now and released"—that is, if they had accepted promptly. Says Orson: "The whole story would have been over!" Instead Antoine settled in to wait for a better offer, which did not come. "And *of course* the phone never rang!" Orson groans.

In the meantime, unbeknownst to Orson, the mood at l'Astrophore in Paris had changed drastically, and by no means in his favor, when a new administrator arrived from Iran. His job was mainly to represent the film-production company that had been newly formed in Iran to complement at home the international co-production activities based in Paris. Events in Iran put Bouscheri at a disadvantage against the officious newcomer. In an attempt to cast himself in a more favorable political light, the Shah had ceased uniformly to protect the hitherto unassailable interests of family members, which meant that brother-in-law Bouscheri could expect no support in the ensuing internal power struggle with the new administrator at l'Astrophore. No sooner had the new man inspected the books in Paris than he began to raise a great fuss about, of all people, Orson Welles and why he had not yet finished *The Other Side of the Wind*. He singled out Orson as a prime example of the inefficiency that had blighted l'Astrophore until now, and that he was determined at all costs to expel. Little did he care that the Spaniard had swindled Orson, or that the Iranians had just blundered by turning down the deal that they had all presumably been waiting for. Although Orson did not know it, the newcomer at l'Astrophore was about to launch a holy war against him as part of a power play against Bouscheri.

In Paris at Christmastime, Orson met with Dominique Antoine in his suite at the Plaza Athénée, where, entirely unaware of the trouble he was in with the Iranians, he talked of his anxieties about his and Oja's rapidly diminishing percentage of the film, which was down to less than twenty percent. For all their tireless labors, neither he nor Oja (who appeared in the picture, as Orson had declined to do lest people say Hannaford was a self-portrait) had made any money whatsoever. It seemed terribly unfair to him to be forced to sign away bit by bit their half of the picture. Immensely sympathetic to his plight, Antoine was inclined to agree. But she also knew that given the climate at l'Astrophore, it was imperative that he swiftly edit *The Other Side of the Wind* and be done with it. So she offered him a deal whereby she would propose to the Iranians that the fifty-fifty percentage split be restored, as long as he agreed to supply her with a post-production budget, and to finish cutting by a stipulated date. The date could be anywhere up to a year away, but for every month he was overdue he would lose ten percent. Accordingly, Orson agreed to finish by May of 1976. It remained only for Antoine to solicit the approval of the Iranians and to meet Orson with the new contract in Los Angeles, where, contemplating an end to his years of self-exile, he planned to edit.

But not only was the new administrator at l'Astrophore unwilling to renegotiate the percentages, he wanted to take the picture from Orson and finish it himself. In a fit of anger, Antoine blurted out that before he did that he would have to walk on her frozen corpse. But the Iranian persisted. He had a lawyer in Los Angeles draw up a contract whereby Orson would indeed be allowed to edit a version of the footage, which he could screen privately for friends three times only. Afterward, however, the footage was the Iranians' to reedit as they pleased. In the peculiar detail of Orson's being permitted just three private screenings of his cut before the man from Teheran forever undid his labors there was a note of perverse condescension. Antoine warned that if the Iranians dared to insult Orson with such a contract, they would probably never hear from him again, nor indeed *should* they. Her adamant objections notwithstanding, the Iranians went ahead with the ugly proposal, and as she had predicted, Orson retreated into silence. Eventually, a contingent from l'Astrophore met with Oja Kodar in Los Angeles, but nothing was settled. For Orson, losing final cut when he had given so much of himself to *The Other Side of the Wind* was unthinkable. After l'Astrophore botched the Hollywood deal, Orson's spirits had picked up again when he had agreed to finish the film by May with his proper percentage restored. But this new letdown was too much for him to bear.

His ensuing attempts to buy out l'Astrophore's share of the picture were unsuccessful. Orson did manage to interest a Canadian backer in making a deal with the Iranians, but because of the precarious political situation in Teheran, where the Shah might fall at any moment, Bouscheri wanted to be paid entirely in cash before he would give up the negative and l'Astrophore's percentage of the picture. Any hope of a deal was extinguished, however, when the Shah fled, after which title to Iranian foreign assets was put in jeopardy by Khomeini's taking power. Watching helplessly from afar Orson knew that these assets included l'Astrophore—which meant that the negative of *The Other Side of the Wind* might end up as the property of the Iranian people. In that event he would be unlikely ever to get his hands on it again. There was nothing Orson could do but wait until Khomeini's representatives inspected Bouscheri's files to determine which of l'Astrophore's properties they wanted. Only then would Orson have any idea of who had possession of the film that, in better days, was to have been his Hollywood comeback.

"There was no way of explaining it to anybody!" says Orson of his frustration when the press and public kept asking why he had not finished *The Other Side of the Wind*.

Ironically Orson had hoped that this picture would put Higham's thesis to rest. Instead, by not finishing *The Other Side
of the Wind*, Orson seemed only to prove his detractor correct. "You know, I had these long years of trying to justify
myself in Latin America," says Orson, "and here it was
again. It was a nightmare to end all nightmares!" How could
he communicate that *The Other Side of the Wind* was in
limbo through no fault of his own, that it had meant everything to him to finish it properly, and that he had spent
virtually his last penny trying to do so? How could he begin
to tell anyone about the Spanish swindler, the rain in Spain,
the botched Hollywood offer, the new man from Teheran,
the fall of the Shah, and now the long wait for Khomeini's
representatives? Says Orson: "It's too *particular* to make a
story that anybody could write in a newspaper article, or
absorb as an alibi." Hence the fate of *The Other Side of the
Wind* was widely—and unjustly—viewed as yet another
manifestation of his reputedly unreliable and self-destructive
character. "Even when the legend starts to die," Orson broods,
"some other damned thing crops up!"

CHAPTER 38

The Marionette

Reading a book at a pebbled-glass table on a sunlit patio, there was Orson in a king-sized flame-red sport shirt. "Margaret Mitchell began writing *Gone with the Wind* in 1926 and she finished it ten years later," he said, as if realizing we'd just joined him. "The writing of a great book, or"— Orson paused now for what aestheticians call a *pregnant moment*, to gaze fondly at the bottle on the table, his studied silence implicitly linking *great book* and *great wine* before he'd even said it—"the making of a fine wine, takes time," arching his eyebrows as if he had just disclosed something important.

"What was true nearly a century ago is true today," he *enunciated*. "Paul Masson will sell no wine"—again, the pause; the eyebrows: all to convey meaning to the meaningless—"before its time."

For someone who supposedly could not make a commercial movie, Orson certainly seemed comfortable selling products on television, which, more and more, he began to do as a way of earning what he calls "grocery money." Top commercial director Harry Hamburg, who worked with him on ten or so spots, contrasts him with some of the other stars he has directed who find commercial work "a little unnatural."

"Not Welles," says Hamburg. "He goes into commercials like he's thought of the idea. He understands the dynamics of advertising. He respects the craft he's doing. He wants to do the best possible job. He reviews how much the product is selling from the marketing people. I mean, he really goes into this shit."

In 1978, when Paul Masson hired Orson as spokesman, it was to reassure people that Paul Masson wines were the right choice. "People have this incredible feeling and insecurity that they're going to serve wine to their friends, and then they're going to start laughing at them," says John Buckingham, the winery's account executive at Doyle Dane Bernbach. "Or they're going to order a wine in a restaurant and the maître d' is going to laugh at their choice." Orson, says Buckingham, "obviously has the image of a person who likes food, and so people find it very believable and find him very credible when he talks about wine."

Orson would arrive on the set with his makeup already done—by himself. Acutely conscious of his appearance in commercials, he has very specific ideas about how he should be lit and photographed. "I know what makes me look the best," he told Doyle Dane Bernbach. Before his first day of shooting on the Masson campaign he dispatched written instructions to the cameraman. Hamburg reports that Orson favors the brooding look he gets when the camera is positioned above his eyes so that he has to look up slightly. Also, he likes the hard light, three-quarters on the left side. Hamburg says he would set up everything to Orson's specifications, so that Orson would not balk the minute he showed up on the set: then, once Orson was satisfied, the director quietly altered the lighting and camera angle to his own liking. Hamburg insists Orson never noticed—although, given Orson's expertise in film lighting, he probably did notice and just decided not to say anything and get on with it.

Orson is agreeable to doing extra takes during shootings, but he insists upon each one's being justified.

"Why do you want it different?" Orson asked Hamburg, who had just ordered another take. "If you say it faster, you can't use it, and if you say it slower, you can't fit it."

"We're getting a hum from a refrigerator," said the director, who did not want to tell Orson the client wanted him to speak louder. "If you talk a little louder, you'll talk above it, and we can drown it out."

When Orson did the take, Hamburg decided upon yet another.

"Orson, you sound like you're really selling," said Hamburg.

"Well, Jesus," Orson replied. "I don't want *that*."

Another day, when Orson took sixty seconds to do a thirty-second bit, Hamburg protested.

"It's too long," he told Orson.

Orson disagreed. "It can't be said any shorter," he said.

"Well, we can't cut any copy," said the worried director. "That's what we need."

"I'll give it a try," said Orson, "but it's not going to work."

Orson launched into action, taking forty-five seconds to say the lines. He tried again, and took forty seconds. Again, and he had reduced them to thirty. The astonishing thing was that each time he sounded exactly the same, seeming to speak as slowly and with the identical phrasing.

To maintain his credibility, Orson has been known to balk at saying things that would be entirely out of character for him. Presented with the lines "Stradivarius took three years to make one of his violins; Paul Masson took..." Orson was dismayed.

"Come on, gentlemen, now really!" he admonished. "You have a nice, pleasant little cheap wine here. You haven't

got the presumption to compare it to a Stradivarius violin.
It's odious."

Another time, while shooting a champagne commercial,
Orson found himself posed in a living room with a particularly plastic collection of extras, all of whom were overjoyed to be working with the great man. Welles looked
disconcerted by their presence.

"Who the hell are these people?" he asked Hamburg.

"They're at a party, Orson," Hamburg explained.

"A party at *my* house?" Orson said.

"Yeah."

"*I* wouldn't have these people at a party," he said. "I
mean, this is really lousy. I wouldn't have these people at
a party at my house. These people look like a party that
Robert Young would have."

When he is making a commercial Orson does not like
anyone besides the director to talk directly to him. Even the
clients have to communicate with him through the director,
or through the cameraman, who refers their comments to
the director.

Once when he was working on another commercial in
England, a production assistant made the mistake of violating that cardinal rule. Orson and the director were dis-
agreeing over the timing of a voice-over.

"Peas grow there," Orson had said, monitoring the commercial for which he was doing a voice-over.

"I'd start half a second later," interrupted the British director.

"Don't you think you really want to say 'July' over the
snow?" Orson asked. "I think it's so nice that you see a snow-
covered field and say, 'Every July peas grow there.'"

Without transition Orson launched into the commercial
copy as if it were a Shakespearean soliloquy: "We know a
remote farm in Lincolnshire where Mrs. Buckley lives. Every
July peas grow there." Breaking again, Orson addressed his

director, "We aren't even in the fields, you see. We're talking about 'em growing and she's picked 'em."

Orson cleared his throat.

Then: "Can you emphasize a bit *in—in* July?" asked the unknowing production person.

"Why?" snapped Orson. "That doesn't make any sense! Sorry, there's no *known* way of saying an English sentence in which you begin a sentence with 'in' and emphasize it! Get me a jury and show me how you can say '*in* July' and *I'll go down on you!* That's just idiotic! If you'll forgive me my saying so. That's just stupid! *In* July'! I'd love to know how you emphasize 'in' in 'in July'! *Impossible! Meaningless!"*

Anxious about having lost control, the director sputtered, "I think all they are thinking about was that they didn't want to—"

"He isn't thinking!" Orson said.

"Orson," the director pleaded, "can we just do one last—"

"Yes," Orson agreed, shifting gears.

"It was *my* fault," assured the director. "I said, 'in July.' If you can leave 'every July'—"

"You didn't say it!" Orson exclaimed. *"He* said it—your *friend—"* making friend sound like a dirty word. " 'Every July.' No, you don't really mean 'every July.' But that's bad copy! *There's too much directing around here!"*

Even with a director like Hamburg, with whom he has worked often and well, Orson can have a bad day. Making a Paul Masson commercial in Los Angeles, Orson was sitting on the edge of his chair as is his custom, so that Hamburg had to get down on hands and knees to instruct him— a position Hamburg compares to taking communion.

"I want to feel piqued in this thing," said Orson. "You know, 'As old Paul Masson said many years ago—' "

"What do you mean, *piqued*?" Hamburg asked.

"Piqued," Orson replied, speaking down. "You know what I mean. Now, you're the director, I'm the talent. You create this emotion. Now do something. Do some directing with me. Get me in the mood."

Hamburg looked up at the bearded Buddha for a moment, then asked, "Orson, what are you doing?"

Orson wasn't smiling. "This is your job," he said. "You get me in the mood now. This is your art, and I want to feel it. You tell me now how I can feel this thing."

By now, all the crew and clients were crowding around them for the showdown.

"Why are you doing this?" Hamburg asked.

"Because this is *your* art," Orson replied, "and this is *my* art, and we're going to combine our arts now. Come on, do it. Do it. Tell me—"

"Well, you're a fat slob," Hamburg said.

"No," Orson shot back, "that doesn't do it. You're just going to make me laugh."

"You're a has-been," Hamburg continued.

"Nah, nah," Orson complained, "that doesn't do it either. You have some pretty weak acid you're throwing in my face."

Really furious now, Hamburg did not care if he ever worked with Orson again.

Orson kept going: "Say something to me that will make me piqued," he urged.

"Well," said Hamburg, "how come you screwed Mankiewicz out of the credit on *Citizen Kane* when he actually wrote it?"

Orson went blood red.

"Obviously," he said, "you can't differentiate between making someone angry and making them piqued. Forget it. I'll do it myself!"

Finally, like all good things, Orson's association with Paul Masson came to an end. After three years, he was replaced by John Gielgud. As for the reason Orson got the boot, the introduction of Paul Masson's *light* wines is among the factors mentioned. "Obviously," says account executive Buckingham, "that would not be appropriate." More pointedly, one insider mentions a Welles appearance on a TV talk show whose host inquired about Orson's recent weight loss, to which Orson replied that he had stopped snacking and drinking wine.

A tape recording of the making of the British peas commercial in which Orson explodes at the director subsequently found its way into circulation among advertising executives in New York, who relished it for the candid glimpse of Orson Welles it afforded. Preparing one kind of performance—a commercial—he had inadvertently given another, and that behind-the-scenes Orson was what the tape recorder had captured. But exactly how inadvertent was it? How candid? This was the role he calls "Crazy Welles" or "Imperial Welles," and on and off he has been doing it for so many years now that we automatically assume that this really *is* Orson Welles: that there is no difference between the man and the mask. As an actor, Orson has frequently been accused of not getting inside his characters enough to convince us: a criticism that, ironically, has never been leveled against his rendition of "Crazy Welles," because he does it so perfectly we forget he's doing it at all. To the rest of us it seems natural—but not to Orson. Since childhood, he has been trying to live up to—to *live*—an image that others, Dadda, his parents, Skipper, had of him: the genius. "I used to play Orson Welles all the time on *Jack Benny,*" he says of the extraordinary radio skits of the '40s in which he parodied himself as brusque, snobbish, insolent. "That's the Orson Welles everybody still thinks I am," he continues. "The secretary used to atomize the microphone before I would speak into it! You know, a lot of people believed it. In other words, the comedy figure rubbed off on me." But it would be inaccurate to say that his public

persona is *just* a role. Surely Orson's early comic version
of himself on the *Jack Benny Show* was based on something
tangible in his character. Otherwise, it would not have worked
effectively as parody.

"I regard it as an enormous and articulated marionette,
which is standing in the hallway waiting for me when I am
called to do a job," says Orson of his image. "You know,
it's *completely* foreign to me—and the part of it that *is* like
me, I don't recognize even though it's there. You see, of
course there must be a lot there, but *I* don't think there is,
because it's an inexpressibly exasperating personage." Having played *Kane* as a kind of *übermarionette*, now this was
how he had begun to regard himself—or that aspect of
himself that the public sees. But whereas onstage and in
films the distance he maintained from his characters had
been entirely deliberate, not so the distance he increasingly
felt from himself. Alienation may have been a device in his
art for mastering emotion, but the alienation he felt from
his mutilated films, from his more banal acting roles, from
his public persona, from the fleshy colossus in which he
was buried, and in which, at intervals, *he* was still visible—
these instances of alienation from his work and from himself
resulted not in mastery but in pain. Since childhood he had
consciously perceived himself as "playing parts to keep
people interested," as he describes it. Now, however, he
realized that, more and more, the part he was playing, the
"marionette" he activated when he went out into the world,
was scaring people away, costing him work. The private
Orson is the antithesis of his haughty public persona. His
friends know him as warm, caring, strangely shy. *He* is the
man who regards "Crazy Welles" with horror.

Orson is especially fond of London, where he has happily lived and performed, so I am surprised to hear him say one afternoon that he does not know if he can possibly accept a cameo role in a film because it is being shot there. The problem, it turns out, is Kiki, Orson's inseparable companion.

"You know," says Orson, "they want me to go to England for this cameo thing and I can't go because of my Kiki."

"That's right," I say. "You can't take her with you."

"No," says Orson sadly, "and she would die *without me, you know. No matter where I walk she's there next to me, you know. It's a terrible burden."*

Orson is not talking about a beautiful woman, but rather his pint-sized black poodle, Kiki. Usually left, as he prefers her, with her fluffy mass of curls unclipped, Kiki can look deceptively innocent. His vigorous protests notwithstanding, I think Orson is more than a little amused by Kiki's terrible mean streak—since it is never directed at him. With Kiki, Orson is the picture of pure indulgence. As far as he is concerned, she can do absolutely no wrong. "With dogs I am like with daughters," he admits, "they can have anything they want."

"I noticed, " I say.

"You never saw me command a dog'" Orson laughs. *"I hate people who* do *go, 'Down, sir' and all that."*

"Somehow or other you get them to mind though," I offer.

"No," Orson says *"they get* me *to mind and it gives the impression of obedience on their part."*

For Orson, mean little Kiki is a source of immense comfort: "I can't sleep at night without some animal in the room with me," he points out. *"Doesn't have to be a dog, but there* has *to be a beast in the room with me."*

Among the other animals who share Orson's life are his budgies, for whom he has built an unusually large cage at home. "I'm insane about all kinds of birds," says Orson. *"Birds are* magic *for me. Their energy is so extraordinary because their temperature is about two points higher than ours and their heart rate is very fast, so you're in the presence of some extraordinary explosive energy. "*

Filled with awe for his budgies, he treats them accordingly: "I can't bear them in a cage where they can't fly," says Orson, who has made sure that his birds have all the room they need. These are not the first birds to whom Orson has been emotionally attached: *"I had a marvelous macaw in Spain,"* he says. *"We were passionately in love. And he'd sit on my lap, lie in my lap. He loved the cat, and they would roll around together playing, he and the cat. Most wonderful bird you ever knew!"* But when the Welleses left Spain, they could not take the macaw with them. *"I had to leave him with a cook who adored him and always took good care of him. But she left the door open and the draft killed him."* Orson is obviously upset by the sad memory. *"About five years before,"* he continues in the same wistful mood, *"he'd had hepatitis and I'd been months feeding him with a dropper and getting him well again. I* loved *him!"*

The haughty, imperious Orson Welles of legend is hardly someone who would take the time patiently to nurse a bird to health with an eye dropper. But the Orson I've observed at dinner in Ma Maison lovingly holding a tiny butter crock of water for Kiki to drink would do nothing less.

"I have a theory that it's a question of honor," he says of his devotion to his pets. "There's a contract we have with animals—especially dogs, who made a pact with us about 10,000 years ago not to be wild and to give us everything they can. We're honor bound to give them more than we can give ourselves, it seems to me, because of that pact that exists between us."

Even as he worries about what to do with Kiki should he go to London, Orson is anxiously trying to arrange an immediate flight to Paris for his ailing Newfoundland puppy, who apparently needs to have steel balls put in its hip sockets. The plane fare alone will be $1,000.

"What are you sending it by, Concorde?" I ask. "In its own seat?"

"That's what it costs in cargo," Orson groans. "He doesn't travel as a passenger. This poor dog has a terrible bone condition, and there's only one doctor in all the world— it's like a bad movie—who can do the operation, and he is in Paris." Although the French doctor has trained a few American veterinarians to do the operation, Orson feels more confident sending his puppy to the man who invented the complicated procedure. "It's breaking my heart, you know," he says of the pain his dog is going through. "He's in the kind of condition that the English would put him down instantly, you know. He's a wonderful, wonderful creature!" Each leg will cost another $1,000, but Orson thinks it is well worth it if the puppy returns in good health. "The alternative is to—awful word—put him down, and I'm not going to do that. They're hostage to fortune," he says of pets, "like children."

Thinking of my own pampered pet beagle, I suggest to Orson that some dogs have awfully nice lives.

"I don't know. I don't know," he says softly. "I think if you love them, they give you more than they get. I always *feel that they've made a contract with us, and most of them suffer as a result of it, you know. It's only a few lucky ones."*

Much to his regret, Orson's gypsy life has caused him to leave behind more than one beloved pet, among them a sheep dog in 1975, when he returned to the United States: *"He'd been great friends with a fellow in a little town outside of Paris, and I gave the dog to him because I thought he'd be better off out in the country. It was a very sad and difficult parting. The years went by, and a few weeks ago the dog was lying on the ground and onto the television in the next room came* Jane Eyre. *The dog woke up and went insane! You would have thought my performance as Mr. Rochester all those years ago wouldn't bear any relationship to what the dog had heard. The dog went crazy!* Why can't I see him? I hear him? *and all that.* Oh, I felt so terrible. Where is he? He's in the next room! He won't even come and see me! *you know, and all that. Isn't that awful? Years had gone by since the dog had seen me. And here's that ancient movie, you know,* and *that voice.* Heartbreaking story!"

But Orson's dogs are more often a source of pleasure and amusement than of sadness. He obviously enjoys having Kiki around as much as she enjoys being with him. Nor is he unaware of the incongruity of their sizes. Before knowing Orson, when I'd first heard about Kiki's existence I'd thought people were making up the image of the giant Welles going everywhere with a tiny ball of black fluff cradled in his arms. I still always get a chuckle out of watching Orson matter-of-factly tuck her under his massive arm whenever he stands up—a marvelous sight that is every bit as sweet as it is funny. But it no longer even strikes me as odd that Kiki often accompanies Orson to dinner at Ma Maison. Like her master, Kiki is an accomplished performer, easily slipping into the role she is expected to play. At Ma Maison, she mostly drops the aggressive watchdog pose to become "Mademoiselle Kiki"—as the staff there calls her—who sits silently and demurely all through the evening on her

own chair immediately to Orson's left. You might not even
notice her unless she poked up her head to take a sip of
water. But when she isn't behaving, Kiki is anything but
unobtrusive. Even at Ma Maison, if she doesn't like somebody, she occasionally bares her teeth, and even Orson's
likes and dislikes in people don't necessarily influence her
feelings toward them.

For instance, Orson loves no one more than he does
Skipper Hill. Apparently, however, Kiki does not feel the
same way toward Orson's old mentor. Nor is Skipper particularly fond of her. Finally, after having known Orson for
more than half a century, there is something about his beloved boy Skipper cannot comprehend. "I don't understand
his attachment to this little dog," Skipper complains to me
when we are alone. "Orson's always been attached to dogs,
but how could he care about that little monster?" I am not
surprised that Skipper feels this way. Several hours ago,
Orson and I were chatting on the telephone in Los Angeles
when, from Kiki's suddenly incessant barking in the background, I gathered that Orson's houseguest, Skipper Hill,
had come into the room. "Roger," said Orson, confirming
my suspicion, "sit down or you'll be eaten by the dog."

CHAPTER 39
In Life

The Welleses moved back to the States when, after the AFI banquet, Orson's lawyer worked out a deal with the tax people to reduce the considerable debt that remained from *Around the World*. After a spell in Arizona, where they had initially planned to settle, they bought a modest house in Las Vegas because of the tax advantage. Mrs. Welles would say that she preferred not to live in Los Angeles. But it was there that Orson would spend much of his time, in the company of intimates like producer Prince Alessandro Tasca di Cuto, director Henry Jaglom, and, of course, Oja Kodar.

On the day in 1979 when Henry Jaglom ran into him again in Los Angeles, Orson was dining with Warren Beatty. Back in 1970, when he was twenty-nine, Jaglom had directed Orson in *A Safe Place*; later, Orson directed him in *The Other Side of the Wind*.

"How are you?" Jaglom asked Orson, whom he hadn't seen in a while.

"I've lost my girlish enthusiasm," Orson replied.

"Why, what happened?" said Jaglom—at which Orson launched into the tale of woe surrounding *The Other Side of the Wind*.

Hearing of Orson's plight, Jaglom decided to take it upon himself to pitch a Welles script directly to the Hollywood baby-moguls, who—like Jaglom—had long revered the man who made *Citizen Kane*. Now in their thirties and forties, these men were Jaglom's contemporaries—and he figured that if only they knew *Orson Welles* was available and willing to work for them, they would jump at the chance. Here, Jaglom demonstrated both courage and common sense—as well as a certain naïveté. Wouldn't anyone who knew anything about the movies want to back Hollywood's most brilliant director?

Orson gave Jaglom a script he had written based on Isak Dinesen's Danish Gothic tale *The Dreamers*, and Jaglom thought the adaptation a "masterwork." But when Jaglom went to his powerful friends they were resistant to the very idea of Welles. Jaglom would remind them of how much Welles had once meant to them, to which they would respond with phrases about separating youthful feelings from business pragmatism. Welles, they claimed, simply was not commercial. His movies never made money—not even *Kane*—so how could they justify bankrolling him now?

Even when Jaglom was able to appeal to their honor and persuade them to look at Orson's script, he met with little success. There was no audience for *The Dreamers*, they told Jaglom—it was too poetic, too fanciful, not pragmatic.

Jaglom remained adamant. He wanted to see Orson Welles direct a Hollywood picture now, and asked his friends how precisely to bring this about. Pressed to the wall, the executives said the only way was for Welles to come up with a more conventional, less poetic script—something mass audiences would respond to. Also, the project would need a big star. These were the ground rules for Welles to work in Hollywood again. Jaglom understood.

Lunching with Orson, Jaglom explained the uniform response to the *Dreamers* script. Then, eyeing his monumental

friend, Jaglom said, "Orson, I want you to write an original
movie."

"I, I can't do that anymore," said Orson. "I don't. : ..
Really, I have this one I want to do—"

Jaglom cut off his protests, saying, "Please, I want you
to write an original movie."

"What about?" Orson asked.

"I don't know," Jaglom said. "Tell me some stories—
just tell me."

Several lunches—and many stories—later, Orson reeled
off something about a presidential candidate and his adviser.
Jaglom asked for more, and Welles kept going—*this* was
it.

"Would you give me just four or five pages?" Jaglom
asked.

Next morning Orson called Jaglom to say he had been
up all night and had twelve pages for him, although he was
not sure they were any good. Jaglom, however, found them
"just spectacularly wonderful" and asked for eight more—
and so on, until, eight months later, Welles finished an
original script entitled *The Big Brass Ring*.

With *The Big Brass Ring*, the idea was for Orson to direct
and act, the kind of setup he has always favored. The story
concerns a young senator, a Vietnam veteran on the brink
of attaining the presidency, and the former Roosevelt aide
whom he discovers in Africa advising a despot. Played by
Orson, the old-timer becomes the senator's mentor, and falls
in love with the younger man without telling him. Instead,
he writes letters about it to a former lover in Florida—so
that the story unfolds as a mystery à la *Kane*.

Day after day, month after month, Jaglom set Orson up
for lunches with an endless array of producers, all of whom
were most anxious to see and be seen with a living legend.
Some of the moguls dined with him for months, but in the
end nobody in Hollywood would touch *The Big Brass Ring*.

One money man was willing to talk business, but wanted to reserve for himself the right to final cut. This, of course, Orson found unacceptable.

With Jaglom and Tasca, Orson had been trying to mount a film version of *King Lear* when in July of 1983, eighty-eight-year-old Roger "Skipper" Hill visited him in Hollywood. In 1978 Skipper had put in a charming appearance at the American Film Institute's *Working with Welles* series, but since then, in 1982, his wife of sixty-six years, Hortense, had died. Afterward, Orson had kept after his old mentor to join him in Hollywood for a real reunion, but Skipper had given himself over to assembling the Todd archives. Still Orson had persisted. When Skipper said, "I've got all this work I've got to do," Orson replied, "I do too. While I'm working you'll be working." Even when Skipper seemed to have agreed, his archival work kept getting in the way, until Orson said, "Come on, I'm going to be dead soon, you'd better hurry." It was a joke, of course, but the fact remained that both the mentor and his protégé were old men now. "You won't recognize me," Skipper said. "I look like a mummy." "What do you *expect* to look like at your age?" Orson replied.

His mentor's impending arrival was not the only event Orson was keenly anticipating. After several years of finding himself unable to sell a film project, it looked as if at last he had indeed managed to attract backing for *King Lear*. At the Cannes Film Festival in May of 1983, there had seemed to be a sudden swell of interest in the project. Confident that the cash he needed was forthcoming, an elated Orson returned to the States in June to plan every aspect of his production. But just as Skipper was about to arrive, the money Orson thought that he had raised in Cannes seemed suddenly not to be coming through. As he ruefully described it then: "At exactly the moment when I've got what I thought were brass balls being juggled in the air, they are turning to soap bubbles before my eyes!"

By the time Skipper got to Los Angeles, Orson's anxieties about *Lear* had plunged him into the blackest of moods, which was made all the worse by a chipped tooth that had become infected. "I feel like Camille in the last act," said Orson, who, on account of the pain from his tooth, and the no-less-excruciating anxiety over *Lear*, took Valium to nap. Otherwise, so wrought up was he that he would just "leap about on the bed." Although one of Skipper's reasons for coming to Los Angeles was to get a second opinion on a serious medical problem of his own, no sooner had he arrived than he grew exceedingly alarmed by Orson's overall condition. When he advised Orson to get a secretary at least to handle the phone for him, Orson replied that he could not bear to have anyone around besides his favorite chauffeur, Freddie. It both touched and amused Orson that, having just scolded his protégé for exerting himself too much, Skipper proceeded to talk on and on about old times for hours, long after Orson had finally said that he was tired and wanted to go to sleep.

Orson knew that his trouble with the financing for *Lear* would not mean much to Skipper, who only recently had counseled him to give up filmmaking, in which he had already indelibly made his mark anyway, and try his hand at political commentary again.

Not that the idea of abandoning the movie business did not sometimes occur to Orson, who, in addition to his troubles with *Lear*, was at this very moment feeling particularly vexed by a Hollywood director who was negotiating to get him to act in an eight-million-dollar thriller (when Orson was having a hard time getting less than two million dollars for *Lear*). He dined with him to discuss the part, but there was trouble from the first. "I don't know how really to relate with you because I call you *Mr. Welles*," the director told

Orson, who, although not exactly keen on "relating with" him, wanted to put the poor fellow at ease. "Well, then, call me Orson," he said. "Oh, that's fine, Orson!" said the director, who added that Orson should call him by his first name as well. "Sure!" said Orson. "Fine!" Having settled this important matter of "relating with" each other, the director was ready to talk business. "Now listen, Mr. Welles," he picked up where he had left off, evidently not noticing Orson's ill-concealed amazement. Now that everyone was *relating* properly, Orson consciously played the role he calls "Pagliacci" or "Laugh, clown, laugh!" as he half-listened to the director announce, "I have my *vision* of the film." Orson groaned inwardly. "You see, when *they* talk to you like that," Orson explains, "you can't say anything. You just say *oh!* and *all right!*" As the Hollywood visionary disclosed his latest vision to the man who made *Citizen Kane*, Orson's thoughts were elsewhere: on Skipper, on *Lear*, on his broken tooth. He knew that it was pointless to interject with more than an occasional "oh!" or "all right!" because the director obviously didn't want to hear anything Orson Welles might have to say. "In any given conversation he has one loop, which you can never penetrate," says Orson of his would-be director. "Sometimes he's quiet enough, so you say something, but then on goes the loop again, and he says exactly the same thing. You *cannot* listen, yet you *have* to."

But there was one thing Orson couldn't resist commenting on, and that was the other male lead, for which the director had in mind a distinguished actor of Orson's generation. On impulse, Orson suggested that a younger, hotter actor like Sylvester Stallone would probably be a much better draw at the box office—at which point the director recoiled, less at the suggestion really than at what he obviously perceived as Orson's trying to take over the picture from him. Ironically this notoriously *non*commercial director found himself

trying to point out the strictly practical implications of casting decisions while the hack with eight million dollars persisted in talking about his *vision*.

"You see," laughs Orson, "he's a poor frightened, blink-
ered man with a strong sense of the *spiritual* and *interre-
lationships* and all that that he, as a director, is going to
provide, and then all the *rest* of it will be provided by the
wise all-knowing studio system within which he's working."
As to why they had ceased to *relate* the moment he made
a suggestion, Orson says: "The director only talks in terms
of *textbooks* that you're sent on the cinema, and I'm only
talking to them about who will go to see this movie, and
how much weight has to be attached to the leading man,
and how it has to operate on the lowest *show-business* terms.
They don't like to talk that way, you know." By *they* Orson
means the younger generation of Hollywood moviemakers,
many of them film-school graduates. "I think everybody
under thirty-five has gone to film school," laughs Orson,
"and they've learned this terrible lingo. They don't think,
just repeat these terrible little slogans." Interestingly, Orson
disapproves far less of the European film schools: "Didn't
seem to hurt them as much! It seemed to help them. I think
they taught them more technique and less horseshit." Also
the European film-school students seem consistently literate,
something Orson misses among the new breed in America:
"They haven't *read*, you see. In Europe, they've read something. Here, they have only seen movies!" In fact Orson
had a personal reason for wanting to play against a vibrant
young actor like Stallone. He secretly feared that if the
casting lacked the proper electricity, and the film flopped,
the way things had been going lately everybody would blame
the failure on him. "What do you expect when you have
Welles in a picture?" echoed in his thoughts as what people,
the director included, would say. But the director also had
personal reasons for not wanting Stallone: "Stallone has

been a director," he told Orson. "Then I would have *two* directors that I would have to deal with."

After playing Pagliacci for several evenings, Orson received a call from the director, in the midst of which Orson's phone went dead. Waiting for his phone service to be restored, Orson failed to consider that the outraged director assumed that Crazy Welles had hung up on him. When he learned from an intermediary that the director was fuming at the imagined insult, Orson could not quite believe that besides entertaining Skipper, salvaging *Lear*, and nursing his tooth, suddenly there was a new complication in his life that week. "Well, you've dropped in at a moment which will give you a rough idea of what my life has been like for the last thirty-five years!" Orson said to me. "It's like a French farce! It's a kind of spiritual Feydeau with doors slamming everywhere!" A few days later, a very worried Orson had to put Skipper into the hospital for tests. Having told Orson that Skipper could check in any time until four-thirty, the doctor who had promised to be there to admit him personally had gone home at four, so that they had to wait on a bench for an hour and forty-five minutes while a nurse endlessly grilled Skipper for details like his grandmother's maiden name. At home the next morning Orson was on the telephone with London when a call came through on the other line. It was one of Skipper's daughters; because of his toothache and all the other confusion, he was not sure which. When Orson told her that her father was in the hospital—"Not for surgery, just for a checkup"—she naturally asked for the name and number. Orson said he would have to look in his address book in another room. Since London was on hold, would she call back in about ten minutes? "You don't sound like yourself—I don't think this *is* Orson," he recalls her saying, before she appeared to him to "get very angry and slam the phone down"—which Orson ascribes to what he perceives as the Hill children's all hating him. ("Oh my God, they hate me!") By now, cut-off phone conversations, and the anxieties that followed, were becoming something of a motif in Orson's week. That very afternoon in fact he was scheduled to have lunch at Ma Maison expressly "to make peace" with the director from the thriller. "I'd rather have four infected teeth than to have this lunch," Orson said before going. "I'd not only put the lunch off, but I'd tell the people to stick their movie up." Orson was convinced that since he had dared to suggest Stallone, and even more, since the famous telephone incident, the director did not really want him in the film anymore. "He hates me, he really hates me," said Orson. "I think what he would like *now* is to have Richard Burton in the part. The director is *convinced* that I want to take over his movie, as most third-rate directors are always convinced of that."

Still Orson went to the much-dreaded lunch determined to conceal his low opinion of the director as "unendurably plodding and limited, and both frightened and stubborn— a combination which I always find maddening." "Being social *costs* me so much," he said in anxious anticipation. "I have good friends who tell me that I use myself up on social occasions. I always think that *I'm* responsible for keeping the ball rolling." But even Orson had a hard time keeping the ball rolling when almost instantly the director confided, "I want to bring out the serious and tragic elements of the story." "You know," said Orson, before the visionary could go any further, "there's all kinds of good theater and movies that shouldn't delve too deeply or they'll be destroyed. Don't you think we should just make this a good thriller?" "*Oh, no,*" said the director, utterly appalled at Orson's attitude. "There's a *resonance* in my vision of the film!" And so went Orson's seemingly interminable three hours at Ma Maison that afternoon, which he describes as "a *typical* Hollywood lunch." Orson would calmly point out the inefficiency of the director's ideas, and the director would reply, *"Oh, no!"* Apparently Orson's fear that the director did not really want him was unfounded, since the fellow made one last clumsy pitch to get Orson to agree. "Here you are," he said dramatically, looking Orson in the eye, "and you're hungry for a commercial success." "Let me correct you," said Orson, gathering up his dignity, "I would be very grateful and happy to have a commercial success—but *hungry* is not the word." Afterward Orson was not sorry he had turned down the lucrative role, only that he had been stuck with the check. "I have to listen to this bullshit and then pay for his lunch!" lamented Orson.

One film role he did accept, although he surely did not want to, was a cameo in a picture titled *Where Is Parsifal?* of which, having read the script, he sneered: "It's like a rerun of a TV movie from ten years ago!" He accepted the tiny part, because he thought it might enhance the possibilities of getting its backer, Alexander Salkind, to put some money into *Lear*. Salkind, who with his father had once produced *The Trial*, seemed to want Orson for the cameo badly enough to help out with *Lear*, into which Orson was even willing to recycle his salary for *Where Is Parsifal?* as part of Salkind's investment. He did not want to agree to anything, however, until he spoke with Salkind, who seemed to him to be "hiding out, jumping from foreign country to foreign country." Trying to get a commitment from Salkind at this of all moments was, groaned Orson, "terrible timing" because the producer's grave disappointment over the box-office receipts for *Superman III* wasn't likely to "put him in the mood" for backing *Lear*.

When he was not phoning all around the world to find the elusive producer, Orson repaired to his editing room with Skipper, who, having been released from the hospital, had broached another of the reasons he'd come to California: he wanted Orson to reedit the conclusion of an old peace film that the Todd boys had made at the end of World War

II under the direction of Skipper and Hascy Tarbox. Skipper was convinced that if it was possible to pep up the ending of *Rip Van Winkle Renascent*, Orson Welles was the man for the job. "Anyone who's been his friend for a lifetime's lucky," said Orson of his mentor, for whom he would do just about anything, even work on Hascy Tarbox's film. But on the subject of Todd's *other genius*, sixty-eight-year-old Orson seemed as genuinely resentful as ever: "Roger loves him and talks about him all the time!" he complained, a note of boyish jealousy in his voice. Now, however, working side by side with his friend and mentor of more than half a century, Orson was suffused with a sense of well-being, of contentment.

Not long after Skipper went home, Orson and Prince Tasca left for Paris to drop off Kiki before Orson turned up in London to do his lines in Salkind's picture. Then it was back to Paris, where, besides trying to raise money for *Lear*, Orson hoped at long last to retrieve the negative for *The Other Side of the Wind*, which Khomeini's representatives had finally declared worthless. For once, Orson was not insulted by people's turning up their noses at his film. Their decision left Orson to fight with the Shah's brother-in-law, Bouscheri, who managed to hang onto the picture as among his post-revolutionary assets until a French court ruled that technically it was Orson's property. But there was a catch to the ruling. Otherwise, Orson could have just sent for the negative and edited the picture in Los Angeles as he'd wanted to do all along. The catch was that, despite Orson's having been declared the owner, Bouscheri still had a financial interest in the film, and wanted Orson to live up to his original agreement with l'Astrophore that he would edit *The Other Side of the Wind* in France. Having invested approximately $750,000 in the picture that he had begun more than thirteen years before, and having received not a penny from it in return, not even a salary for his directing or screenwriting chores (as neither writer-actress Oja Kodar or cameraman Gary Graver had been paid for their labors), Orson simply could not afford to spend the many months in France it would take to finish the film, meanwhile largely cutting himself off from earning a living by doing commercials and voice-overs in Los Angeles. Orson and the prince seriously feared that the Shah's brother-in-law was using the issue of Orson's editing the picture in France as a way of stalling until Orson's death, at which moment the footage could be cheaply slapped together and billed as "Orson Welles's final film"—all of which would, ironically, mean a substantially fatter profit than if Orson had done the job.

But there was an even stranger twist. Having declared the negative Orson's property, the French appeared to have their own peculiar reasons for preventing him from taking it out of the country. Orson realized he was going to pay a price for being loved and revered in France as he simply had not been in his own country. The nation that, in 1982, had awarded Orson the Order of Commander of the Legion of Honor was about to claim him as one of its own by making *The Other Side of the Wind* a French film—or so it seemed to Orson, who suddenly found himself being used as a pawn in the French attack on American cultural values. Having widely and astutely hailed the greatness of *F for Fake* while Orson's countrymen had virtually overlooked the film, the French were about to show that they, not the stupid Americans, knew the true value of Orson Welles. And it was only fitting that the new picture was a mordant satire on Hollywood vulgarity. The French courts put the sticky matter of whether or not Orson could remove the film from France in the hands of a very venerable arbitrator.

When Orson met the arbitrator in court after arriving in Paris from London, the first thing that struck him about the famous fellow was how tiny he was. "He's about two feet

high and ought to be in the Cirque Medrano," Orson quipped
afterwards. "He sits on a platform and studies everybody
with one finger on his cheek, like authors on the dust jackets
of books. You know, that awful pose." Although his lawyer,
whom Orson describes as "a fearless advocate right out of
Daumier," seemed to be rather frightened of this elf with
"an enormous Roman head," Orson could not help but instantly think of what John Wayne once told him about short
men. "He said, 'Always be careful to be sitting down with
them,' " recalls Orson, who, in hopes of winning his case,
tried scrupulously to follow Duke's advice now. From the
first, Orson should have had plenty going for him with the
arbitrator, who could not have failed to notice the Legion
of Honor decoration he strategically wore on his lapel. During his stay in Paris for the arbitration proceedings, Orson
was made a member of the Académie des Beaux Arts, after
which, the arbitrator, who had a news clipping of the event
in front of him, called Orson "Cher Maître." But ironically
it was this very esteem that worked against Orson, who had
come to Paris with news of an excellent deal set up by
Henry Jaglom, who had raised all the money his friend
needed to cut the picture in Los Angeles. But that would
make Jaglom, *an American*, the producer, whereas the courts
seemed intent on its being the French who would enable
their friend Orson to finish *The Other Side of the Wind*.
Although Orson protested that *The Other Side of the Wind*
was not a French film, and that the negative's being in Paris
was strictly an accident, the French thought otherwise.
Meanwhile, the filmmaker Constantin Costa-Gavras was
heard to have commented on the shame of Orson Welles's
not having the money to finish his film; by the time his
perfectly innocent comment was reported to the court, however, it had been twisted into his having volunteered to raise
money for Orson in France, which he certainly had not done.
Whereupon Orson had to find Costa-Gavras, who, he says,

"was really trying to be nice," to ask him to explain what he had actually said, so that the arbitrator would not have an excuse for putting off a decision about the Jaglom deal, the backing for which could easily fall through if too much time elapsed. It was some time before the Costa-Gavras mixup was settled, and the arbitrator then told Orson that he would have to summon Mr. Jaglom to Paris. When Orson said that the busy Jaglom probably could not come, the arbitrator responded with what Orson describes as "a kind of ooh-la-la expression to indicate there's nobody in the world who doesn't want to come to Paris."

If at first glance the zany story of Orson's court case sounds like material for a screenplay, Orson thinks otherwise. "All great comedy, no matter how insane it seems to be, must be based on something which is credible," he says, "and yet there's no connection between *this* and anything an audience would recognize as real life!" Throughout the arbitration proceedings, Orson was in constant physical pain from a pinched nerve that, when he was not in court, confined him to his hotel suite, where he spent his time, as he says, "making Kabuki faces to myself" on account of his aching hand. Instead of walking Kiki at night, he let her out on the shallow balcony that, "by the blessing of God!" he exclaims, his suite possessed. At the end of three months his hotel bill came to $32,000—but after the mess Kiki had made on the balcony Orson feared ever to set foot in the hotel lobby again. Still, the arbitrator had yet to make a decision one way or another. As Orson prepared to leave Paris, his sense of humor was still somehow intact. He joked about "all the psychiatrists among the *cinéastes* explaining my *latest* maneuver to keep from having to finish the picture." But there was heartache as well. Back in the States, reflecting on the many terrible things that had happened to him in connection with *The Other Side of the Wind*, Orson spoke seriously of "a very strong temptation through the last years of all this to just forget about movies. It just was one too many, you know."

Instead of his forgetting about movies, however, Orson persisted in his tireless attempts to raise money for *Lear*, even when, having dutifully appeared in *Where Is Parsifal?*, he found himself unable to strike a deal with Salkind. Although he returned to Hollywood feeling depleted after the fruitless trip abroad, his spirits improved slightly when French television offered to attempt to raise the money he needed for *Lear*. While France's having tried to stake a claim on Orson had worked against him regarding *The Other Side of the Wind*, perhaps now it would prove eminently useful by allowing him to direct *Lear*. But by this point in his life, Orson was not about to whip himself up with too much hope. "When it gets this close," he sagely remarked, "until it happens, I remember how often it doesn't work, and I deliberately keep myself from rejoicing because otherwise it's unendurable if there's disappointment. I have a lot of experience in this field, and I don't allow myself to rejoice over *promises*." While he waited to see what the French could do, he took up what he describes as a "gloomy and hermit-like life" in Los Angeles. In the very midst of Hollywood he often seemed to be living quite apart from it. He did not mind, in fact he rather liked, dining alone, because, as he says, "if you really want to understand what the food is *about*, you sit all by yourself and only think about what you're eating." When he dined with others, not infrequently he preferred the company of magicians to that of movie people, expressly because he could not bear to be asked what he was doing. "Their silence sounds like a judgment, and it's all very painful," says Orson of how movie people inevitably respond when, only because they asked, he explains that, no, he isn't making a movie *just now*.

Orson was filled with dread when in April of 1984 he grimly anticipated Irving "Swifty" Lazar's annual Oscars celebration. "Every year Swifty gives the party of the year," said Orson, bracing himself to put in a rare appearance. "A very select group of rather elderly noncontestants gather for the first part of it at six o'clock. We are given hors d'oeuvres, then we are seated at various tables, and we watch on giant screens all three hours of this. Then afterward, those lucky ones who won, and those unlucky ones who didn't and are willing to face everybody, arrive—and, you know, the *kiss-kiss* never ends. I can't tell you how horrified I am at the thought of doing this!" Most years Orson tended to seclude himself on this particular evening. Wisely he would try to avoid looking at the Awards on television—"I watch old Doris Day movies rather than that!"—lest they provoke too much reflection, too much resentment. Even in 1970, when he was given the Honorary Award by the Academy, he steered clear of the ceremony by pretending to be abroad. "I didn't go because I feel like a damn fool at those things. I feel foolish, really foolish. I didn't go, not because I didn't have respect for it—after all, all the people in the industry vote you something, you should show your appreciation. So I did—I made a piece of film and said that I was in Spain, and I thanked them. John [Huston] introduced me and said at the end, *Good night Orson, wherever you are.* I was in Laurel Canyon!" Orson was weary of being garlanded with useless awards when it was cash he needed to make movies. "Now I'm an old Christmas tree," he told himself, "the roots of which have died. *They* just come along, and while the little needles fall off me, replace them with medallions." He could not bear the hypocrisy of pretending to be terribly grateful: "To come out in the middle of all that, with all the lights shining, and try to get a little glisten in the eye and so on—I just thought I'd be crooked to do it!"

This year, however, having accepted Swifty's invitation—"I have run out of alibis!" admitted Orson—*Mr. Swami* could see it all in advance: "At six o'clock, because of the difference of time, there we are in our dinner jackets in the sunlight. We come in, and we get some kind of drink and sit down. Then there's three hours of nifty entertainment with those *terrible* couples that come out to take the place of Bob Hope with their cute little asides—all of that, Oooooh my God!—and the little buildups of suspense, and then that thing which America loves most, which is the shot that shows all five contestants at once on the screen, and then your eye goes right down to the ones who didn't get it to watch *that smile*, how well they're holding up. I wish somebody would get up and curse, or burst into tears. My feelings about Hollywood are at their lowest around Academy Awards time—probably from sour grapes, but there it is. I suddenly think, 'Where am I living? Why am I in this business?'"

But he knows why—exactly why—when he is working on
a film idea: It is then that Orson is most himself.

    I witness this firsthand as I come to the end of writing
his biography. Orson is still trying to put together the deal
to do Lear, *when an independent producer suggests the*
possibility of his directing a movie about the WPA produc-
tion of The Cradle Will Rock. *Someone has already writ-*
ten the script that the producer has called Orson about. "I
have turned it down cold," Orson tells me the first time he
mentions it in passing, and I don't give it a second thought,
until two days later when he mentions it again. "There's
no way I could do it," he says adamantly, although his
having brought it up a second time suggests he has been
turning it over in his thoughts. Besides, when Orson talks
about there being no *way of his doing something, I have*
learned to suspect that he is secretly wondering if there
really isn't, and how soon he can get started if by some
slim chance there is. Curious, I ask him why he couldn't
do it. "I really don't know this fellow," he says thoughtfully,
not of the producer, however, but of the young Orson who
directed The Cradle Will Rock. *So I was right—he is slightly*

intrigued by the possibility of playing what now he calls "the director of the director."

"I really don't know him. You know him more than I do," he snickers, referring ironically to my role as his biographer who has spent the last few years collecting testimony and documents about him. "I have only memories," he continues. "I know things that fellow was impressed by at various moments. But I really don't know what I was up to." Although he tells me that the young Orson is a "total stranger," it is inconceivable to him at first that anyone else would play Orson Welles onscreen. Thinking it over, he jokes about the actors in the picture having constantly to say, "Orson will be coming at any minute!" "Who's on the phone?" "Orson!" "Tell him we'll call back!"—so that Orson himself could remain safely offscreen.

But what really gets Orson going now is his recollection that once before he did indeed play the director of The Cradle Will Rock—*in a dramatic reenactment on radio of the tumultuous opening night at the Venice Theatre. "I played myself on* The March of Time *afterward," he says. "I played* this *movie on* The March of Time *in a fifteen-minute spot afterward, and it was my sensation of having made it. It was bigger than having seen my name in lights or anything—to have been on* The March of Time *as myself, which nobody had ever been." Having played himself on the air (Orson Welles the radio actor as Orson Welles the Broadway director), suddenly Orson sees in the film a curious new twist: being part of "a story so interesting it's worth a movie," and then getting to* direct *a young actor in the Orson role. As I listen to him describe it this way, I know that, more and more, he is becoming hooked on the tantalizing possibilities of the project.*

A week after he first rather disdainfully mentioned it to me, I pick up the phone to hear, "I have to ask you as the world authority on the subject, how old was I when I did this?" This? *I ask myself. When the phone rang I had been writing about Orson's anxieties in anticipation of Swifty Lazar's Oscars party. This is what is on my mind right now, but it cannot possibly be what Orson is asking about. As has often happened in the course of my writing, Orson has called to talk about a period, a moment, of his life other than the one I am immersed in.* This? *To keep up with him, my thoughts race back to what suddenly I know he is referring to.*

"It was 1937," I say. "And it was June 16 that The Cradle Will Rock *opened. You were just twenty-two.*" "Right!" says Orson, for apparently this is even better than he had hoped. "They want an actor around thirty-five—and I tell them they're crazy!" It is not mere vanity that causes Orson to protest against using an actor in his thirties. "The point is that I was much younger than anybody in the theater," he says, "and baby-faced, looking even younger." "Absolutely," I confirm. "I've got pictures of you from that period. You look like a child." "Like a baby!" he chimes in. "You're still very gangly," I say, idly imagining the photos in my file cabinet. "I'm gangly because I'd dieted myself blind!" "You look like a teenager." "That was the idea," he confirms. "I wanted to be skinny. That was my high-skinny form!" How, he wonders, can he get the producers to see him as he was? "When I was young I was physically so different," says Orson. "I was feline. It's something that's hard for people to imagine, but it's true— and that's the sort of fellow it should be."

I know that by letting himself picture how it should be, Orson has begun in earnest working on the film, even before he has struck a deal with the producer. Having talked mostly about the character of young Orson—still, however, as if it were a "total stranger"—he goes on to recount in copious detail scenes in the script the producer gave him. But the more he talks, the more he begins to shift the scenes around, to rework them, and—tentatively at first, then with increasing, soon absolute *authority—to add scenes entirely of his own imagining.*

"I suddenly see this picture," he says—and with that, he is speaking about this "total stranger," a character called Orson Welles, in the first person singular: "I say . . ." he recounts, or "I am standing . . ."

Orson speeds on, his words pouring out so quickly and so fluently that, before I know it, he has broken loose from reality (the truthful account that I, a mere biographer, have been trying somehow to relate): "The way I want to do it is much more interesting than I was!" he says, as if challenging me to protest.

The laughter between us dissolves, and I am silent, as, image by dazzling image, the sorcerer-seducer effortlessly unreels for himself, and for me, a movie that does not yet, may never, exist.

When, at the end, his great voice dies down, I know that I should say something. But what?

"You're really making it into a movie," I think aloud, as if for a moment I'd forgotten that this is Orson Welles I've been talking to. "You really are."

"I can't help making things into movies," he roars with laughter, "they just don't let me make them!"

Notes and Sources

Previous books on Welles's life and work include: André Bazin, *Orson Welles;* Maurice Bessy, *Orson Welles;* Peter Cowie, *The Cinema of Orson Welles;* Roy A. Fowler, *Orson Welles;* Richard France, *The Theatre of Orson Welles;* Ronald Gottesman, ed., *Focus on Orson Welles;* Charles Higham, *The Films of Orson Welles;* Joseph McBride, *Orson Welles* and *Orson Welles: Actor and Director;* James Naremore, *The Magic World of Orson Welles;* Peter Noble, *The Fabulous Orson Welles.* For general background, I have also read numerous newspaper and magazine articles about Welles.

Page 1 *"I've just walked..."*: Orson Welles to Barbara Leaming, interview, April 8, 1983 (hereafter cited as OW to BL). **1** *"Everybody calls me..."*: OW to BL, interview, June 19, 1983. **1** *"Kiki's terrible..."*: OW to BL, interview, July 25, 1983. **2** *"I only remember..."*: OW to BL, interview, June 19, 1983. **2** *"His memory is...."*: OW to BL, interview, February 9, 1983. **2** *"great age."*: OW to BL, interview, February 1, 1983. **3** *"I think there is a movie..."*: OW to BL, interview, April 8, 1983. **3** *"Has it occurred..."*: OW to BL, interview, July 11, 1983.

CHAPTER 1

My many interviews with Orson Welles were the main source of information about his childhood. Other background material came from interviews with Shifra Haran, Roger Hill, Wolf

Mankowitz, Hascy Tarbox, and Augusta Weissberger Schenker; and correspondence of Herb Drake, Dr. Maurice Bernstein, and Hazel Moore Bernstein.

5 *"My mother and father..."*: OW to BL, interview, July 23, 1983. **5** *Born in Missouri:* death certificate, Richard Head Welles. **5** *"He was lost..."*: OW to BL, interview, May 9, 1984. **6** *"A very rich banker..."*: Ibid. **6** *"aristocratic philistines":* Ibid. **7** *"She had a life..."*: OW to BL, interview, July 23, 1983. **9** *anomalies of the spine:* report of medical examination, June 25, 1941. **10** *"irresistible to women"*: OW to BL, interview, May 9, 1984. **10** *"He had this way..."*: OW to BL, interview, June 5, 1983. **11** *"crazy romantic Russian":* OW to BL, interview, June 22, 1984. **11** *"satisfied with the balcony":* OW to BL, interview, May 9, 1984. **11** *"The word* genius*..."*: OW to BL, interview, June 22, 1984. **11** *"I always felt..."*: OW to BL, interview, June 8, 1984. **12** *"The opposite to Dadda..."*: Ibid. **12** *"I was* taught*..."*: Ibid. **13** *"He left Kenosha..."*: OW to BL, interview, May 9, 1984. **13** *"a paradise that..."*: Ibid. **13** *"My mother used..."*: Ibid. **14** *"a pianist of exquisite..."*: Beatrice Welles obituary by Catherine Pannhill Mead. **14** *"To him, Dadda..."*: OW to BL, interview, May 9, 1984. **14** *"When they separated..."*: OW to BL, interview, June 8, 1984. **15** *"twice the love":* OW to BL, interview, June 5, 1983. **15** *"My father hated..."*: Ibid. **15** *"That's good..."*: Ibid. **15** *"children could be treated..."*: Ibid. **16** *"Everybody thought I was..."*: OW to BL, interview, June 19, 1983. **16** *"Look at the real..."*: Ibid. **16** *"If you tell..."*: Ibid. **16** *"You see, the Italians..."*: OW to BL, interview, June 22, 1984. **16** *"A strange sense of..."*: Ibid. **16** childhood diseases: report of medical examination, June 25, 1941. **17** *"determination to escape..."*: OW to BL, interview, June 5, 1983. **17** *acute yellow atrophy of the liver:* death certificate, Beatrice Ives Welles. **17** *"anguished loss":* OW to BL, interview, June 8, 1984. **18** *"The children, who had..."*: OW to BL, interview, June 30, 1984. **18** *"I was my mother..."*:

OW to BL, interview, June 22, 1984. **18** *"It wasn't that..."*: Ibid. **19** art lecture: "How to Raise a Child" by Alva Johnston and Fred Smith, *The Saturday Evening Post*, January 20, 1940. **20** *"earlier passions..."*: OW to BL, interview, June 22, 1984. **20** *"I had all this experience..."*: OW to BL, interview, August 3, 1983.

CHAPTER 2

Background on Todd came from interviews with Orson Welles, Roger Hill, Bette Hill, Hascy Tarbox, and Joanne Tarbox; and from Roger Hill's privately printed *One Man's Time and Chance: A Memoir of Eighty Years 1895/1975* and the Todd catalogue.

23 *"straighten up and behave"*: OW to BL, interview, February 9, 1983. **23** *"island of lost boys"*: Hascy Tarbox to BL, interview, March 1983. **23** *"knew about Todd..."*: OW to BL, interview, February 9, 1983. **23** *"with a lot of..."*: Ibid. **23** *"She had a group..."*: OW to BL, interview, June 30,1984. **24** *"You know about this..."*: Ibid. **24** *"I was convinced..."*: Ibid. **24** *"I was sent..."*: OW to BL, interview, May 9, 1984. **24** *"left in the spirit..."*: OW to BL, interview, February 9, 1983. **24** *"I hear we've got..."*: Roger Hill to BL, interview, February 19, 1983. **24** *"a beard down..."*: OW to BL, interview, February 9, 1983. **25** *"the snow untrodden..."*: OW to BL, interview, August 3, 1983. **25** *"I feel constrained..."*: Ibid. **25** *"puckish"*: Christopher Welles Feder to BL, interview, June 13, 1983. **25** *"but with much more energy..."*: OW to BL, interview, February 28, 1983. **25** *"sailor's swagger"*: Ibid. **26** *"secretive puffs..."*: OW to BL, interview, August 3, 1983. **26** *"fell in love..."*: OW to BL, interview, February 9, 1983. **26** *"He's always been galloping..."*: Ibid. **27** *"I'm the boy..."*: quoted by Myron Meisel, *Reader*, November 24, 1978. **29** *"It's that Christian..."*: OW to BL, interview, June 19, 1983. **29** *"this gosling in..."*: OW to BL, interview, August 3, 1983.

29 IQ test: Kirk Bates, *The Journal,* February 6, 1940. **29** *"Orson had no friends ..."*: Hascy Tarbox to BL, April 19, 1983. **30** *"During his stay ..."*: Ibid. **30** *"In some ways ..."*: Roger Hill to BL, interview, February 19, 1983. **30** *"He was never ..."*: Hascy Tarbox to BL, interview, March 1983. **30** *"chubby eleven-year-old ..."*: *Time and Chance.* **31** *"Because I wanted ..."*: OW to BL, interview, February 9, 1983. **31** *"the late J.C."*: Hascy Tarbox to BL, interview, March 1983. **31** *"You'd better keep ..."*: Roger Hill to BL, interview, February 19, 1983. **31** *"He loved me ..."*: OW to BL, interview, June 5, 1983. **31** *"a sad drunk."*: Roger Hill to BL, interview, February 19, 1983. **32** *"He didn't want ..."*: OW to BL, interview, June 30, 1984.

CHAPTER 3

33 *"almost the greatest ..."* Hascy Tarbox to BL, interview, March 1983. **34** *"He was as lascivious ..."*: Ibid. **34** *"a dissipated choirboy ..."*: OW to BL, interview, June 16, 1984. **34** *"I had no idea ..."*: OW to BL, interview, June 30, 1984. **34** *"I was, however, not a* wunderkind *..."*: Ibid. **35** *"How they* hired *him ..."*: OW to BL, interview, June 22, 1984. **35** *"We don't have ..."*: Ibid. **35** *"in crocodiles"*: OW to BL, interview, August 3, 1983. **36** *"What I* did *..."*: OW to BL, interview, May 13, 1984. **36** *"Orson would have ..."*: Hascy Tarbox to BL, interview, March 1983. **37** *"I think he felt ..."*: OW to BL, interview, June 8, 1984. **37** *"I knew he'd come ..."*: Ibid. **38** *"lonely and unhappy."*: Ibid. **38** *"he wouldn't be buried ..."*: OW to BL, interview, June 19, 1983. **38** *"On the ferry ..."*: Ibid. **38** *"Your father was ..."*: Ibid. **39** *"That was the last ..."*: Ibid. **39** father's death: death certificate, Richard Head Welles. **39** *"drank himself to death."*: OW to BL, interview, June 19, 1983. **39** *"I've always ..."*: Ibid. **40** *"I didn't think ..."*: Ibid. **40** *"I wasn't prepared ..."*: Ibid. **40** *"I didn't* *discuss . . ."*: Ibid. **40** *"I was supposed . . ."*: Ibid. **40** *"I felt that they . . ."*: Ibid. **41** *"I couldn't stop . . ."*: Ibid. **41** *"She was a witch . . ."*: OW to BL, interview, June 5, 1983. **42** *"I wasn't allowed . . ."*: OW to BL, interview, April 3, 1984. **42** *"I have a headache . . ."*: OW to BL, interview, June 22, 1984. **42** *"Orson, you haven't . . ."*: OW to BL, interview, May 9, 1984. **44** *"casts of thousands"*: Hascy Tarbox to BL, interview, March 1983. **44** *"It was one . . ."*: Ibid. **44** *"I think maybe . . ."*: OW to BL, interview, August 3, 1983.

CHAPTER 4

Background on Welles's trip to Ireland came from interviews with Orson Welles and Roger Hill; correspondence and diaries of Orson Welles; Roger Hill's *Time and Chance;* Micheal MacLiammoir's *All for Hecuba; The Gate Theatre Dublin,* ed. *Bulmer Hobson.*

49 *"it doesn't matter . . ."*: The Gate Theatre Dublin. **50** *"I knew that . . ."*: OW to BL, interview, May 21, 1984. **50** *"He knew that . . ."*: All for Hecuba. **50** *"He was so jealous . . ."*: OW to BL, interview, May 21, 1984. **51** *"His story is . . ."*: OW to BL, interview, April 3, 1984. **52** *"Micheal was kind of . . ."*: Ibid. **52** *"lived a life . . ."*: OW to BL, interview, June 22, 1984. **52** *"In those days . . ."*: OW to BL, interview, April 3, 1984. **43** *"What Micheal liked . . ."*: Ibid. **53** *"Hilton Edwards was a perfectly . . ."*: Ibid. **53** *"Hilton was a born . . ."*: Ibid. **54** *"an attempt to . . ."*: Hilton Edwards quoted in The Gate Theatre Dublin. **54** *"An attempt to . . ."*: Ibid. **54** *"When the theatre . . ."*: Ibid. **55** *"She was the sexiest . . ."*: OW to BL, interview, May 21, 1984. **55–56** *"It was thunderous . . ."*: OW to BL, interview, February 21, 1984. **56** *"That was the night . . ."*: Ibid. **56** *"I got more . . ."*: Ibid. **57** *"From then on . . ."*: OW to BL, interview, May 21, 1984. **57** *"At that point . . ."*: OW to BL, interview, June 5, 1983. **57** *"I had an* *entire . . ."*: OW to BL, interview, May 21, 1984. **57** *"Never trust us . . ."*: Ibid. **58** *"Malice!"*: OW to BL, interview, July 11, 1983. **59** *"Mac, there are no . . ."*: OW to BL, interview, April 3, 1984.

CHAPTER 5

Sources included interviews with Orson Welles and Roger Hill; correspondence of Orson Welles and Dr. Maurice Bernstein; *Time and Chance; Marching Song;* and *Everybody's Shakespeare*.

64 *"I wanted to get . . ."*: Roger Hill to BL, interview, February 19, 1983. **67** *"a play of the stirring . . ."*: *Marching Song,* privately printed. **72** Background on Thami el Glaoui came from interviews with Orson Welles; and from *Arabs and Berbers,* ed. Ernest Gellner and Charles Micaud; and *The Kasbars of Southern Morocco* by Rom Landau. **72** *"He had killed . . ."*: OW to BL, interview, July 16, 1984. **72** *"He lived on a level . . ."*: Ibid. **72** *"An unforgettable moment . . ."*: Ibid. **73** *"Into our tent . . ."*: Ibid. **73** *"He reacted exactly . . ."*: Ibid. **73** *"I've always admired . . ."*: Ibid. **74** *"Here's another queen! . . ."*: OW to BL, interview, June 22, 1984. **75** Background on the Katharine Cornell tour came from interviews with Orson Welles, Shifra Haran, and Roger Hill; correspondence of Orson Welles; and from *Leading Lady* by Gertrude Macy, *Me and Kit* by Guthrie McClintic, and *The Portable Woollcott.* **78** *"Yes, information about . . ."*: OW to BL, interview, April 21, 1984. **79** *"I do tend to . . ."*: OW to BL, interview, June 19, 1983. **80** *"If you're in town . . ."*: Charlton Heston to BL, interview, June 12, 1982. **80** *"You thought he was . . ."*: OW to BL, interview, February 4, 1983. **81** *"I won't, I can't . . ."*: Richard Wilson to BL, interview, July 8, 1982. **84** *"I thought it was . . ."*: OW to BL, interview, August 5, 1984.

CHAPTER 6

86 *"I found myself..."*: The Portable Woollcott. **86** *"the corniest name..."*: OW to BL, interview, February 1, 1983. **87** *"You are suddenly..."*: Ibid. **87** *"They'd have the matinee..."*: OW to BL, interview, April 9, 1984. **88** Background on the Todd Summer Theatre Festival came from interviews with Orson Welles, Roger Hill, and Hascy Tarbox; correspondence of Orson Welles; and *All for Hecuba* and *Time and Chance*. **89** *"Oh, it was wild..."*: OW to BL, interview, August 3, 1983. **89** *"roaring pansies"*: Roger Hill to BL, interview, February 19, 1983. **89** *"probably the only..."*: Hascy Tarbox to BL, interview, March 1983. **89** *"beautiful sixteen-year-old..."*: Roger Hill to BL, interview, February 19, 1983. **89** *"Both of these..."*: Hascy Tarbox to BL, interview, April 19, 1983. **90** *"Hilton and Micheal..."*: Ibid. **90** *"It all started..."*: Ibid. **90** *"inherited"*: OW to BL, interview, August 3, 1983. **90** *"I'll get that..."*: OW to BL, interview, June 22, 1984. **91** *"nubile virgins"*: Roger Hill to BL, interview, February 19, 1983. **92** *"the school was..."*: Ibid. **92** *"laughably referred to..."*: Hascy Tarbox to BL, interview, March 1983. **93** *"I was in..."*: OW to BL, interview, August 3, 1983. **93** *"They were really..."*: Roger Hill to BL, interview, February 19, 1983. **93** *"No matter how..."*: Hascy Tarbox to BL, interview, March 1983. **94** *"disappointingly vague..."*: All for Hecuba. **94** *"his fake chain-mail..."*: Hascy Tarbox to BL, interview, March 1983. **94** *"Pretty dangerous around..."*: Ibid. **95** *"Couldn't you order..."*: OW to BL, interview, June 8, 1984. **96** *"I had to order..."*: Ibid. **96** *"She really did..."*: OW to BL, interview, July 16, 1984. **97** *"She was the essence..."*: Ibid. **98** *"We really only..."*: OW to BL, interview, June 16, 1984.

CHAPTER 7

Background on Welles's relationship with Houseman came from interviews with Orson Welles, Abe Feder, Roger Hill, John Houseman, and Virgil Thompson; correspondence of Orson Welles; and John Houseman's *Run-Through*.

100 *"Houseman started out . . ."*: OW to BL, interview, July 11, 1983. **105** *Bright Lucifer*, privately printed. **109** *"I thought they . . ."*: OW to BL, interview, June 16, 1984.

CHAPTER 8

111 *"Roger, I thought . . ."*: Roger Hill to BL, interview, February 19, 1983. **114** "Suddenly *I was . . .*": OW to BL, interview, June 19, 1983. **93** *"never less than . . ."*: Ibid. **115** *"Just as the . . ."*: OW to BL, interview, December 23, 1983. **117** *"Considering what I . . ."*: OW to BL, interview, August 20, 1984. **117** *"They all hate . . ."*: OW to BL, interview, February 9, 1983. **118** *"There's* this boy . . .": OW to BL, interview, August 3, 1983. **119** *"I got terribly . . ."*: Hascy Tarbox to BL, interview, March 1983.

CHAPTER 9

Background on Welles's New York theatrical career came from interviews with Orson Welles, Walter Ash, Bil Baird, Irma Bauman, Blanche Collins, Millia Davenport, Leonard De Paur, Abe Feder, Martin Gabel, Roger Hill, John Houseman, Paula Laurence, Sam Leve, James Morcom, Augusta Weissberger Schenker, Paul Stewart, Virgil Thomson, Leo Van Witsen, Richard Wilson. Also consulted were interviews conducted by the Federal Theatre Project at George Mason University with

Bil Baird, Philip Barber, David Clarke, Joseph Cotten, Howard
DaSilva, Leonard De Paur, Edward Dudley Jr., Lehman Engel,
Will Geer, Paul Green, John Houseman, Howard Koch, Paula
Laurence, Sam Leve, Norman Lloyd, James Morcom, Carlton
Moss, Wendell Phillips, Augusta Weissberger Schenker, Hiram
Sherman, John Silvera, Virgil Thomson, Arnold Weissberger.
Other sources included videotapes of *Salute to the Mercury
Theatre* at Florida State University (John Houseman, Richard
Barr, Richard Wilson, Hortense Hill, Roger Hill, Paul Stewart,
Sam Leve, Millia Davenport, and others); panel discussion of
the WPA Negro Theatre Project at the New York Public Library;
papers in the Welles Collection, Lilly Library, Indiana Uni-
versity; Lincoln Center Library Theatre Collection; Hallie Flan-
agan Collection at Lincoln Center; Museum of the City of New
York Theatre Collection; John Houseman Collection at UCLA;
Arena by Hallie Flanagan; *The Federal Theatre* by Jane Mat-
thews; *Free, Adult, Uncensored,* ed. John O'Connor and Lorraine Brown; *Run-Through* by John Houseman; *Theater in
America* by Jack Poggi; *Uncle Sam Presents* by Tony Buttita.

123 *"He was beautiful..."*: OW To BL, interview, June 30,
1984. **123** *"He served time..."*: Ibid. **124** *"black Barrymore"*:
Ibid. **124** *"Our conversation was..."*: OW to BL, interview,
June 19, 1983. **124** *"I seduce actors..."*: OW to BL, inter-
view, February 1, 1983. **124–125** *"Jack Carter was..."*: John
Houseman to BL, interview, November 7, 1982. **125** *"Lady
Macbeth* ought..."*: OW to BL, interview, June 19, 1983. **125**
"He would never...": Leonard De Paur to BL, interview, May
6, 1983. **125** *"They really threw..."*: OW to BL, interview,
June 19, 1983. **126** *"They thought he..."*: Abe Feder to BL,
interview, September 11, 1982. **126** *"In those days..."*: OW
to BL, interview, June 19, 1983. **127** *"When I shouted..."*:
OW to BL, interview, July 28, 1983. **127** *"When you're
young..."*: Leonard De Paur to BL, interview, May 6, 1983.
127 *"You're coming with..."*: Abe Feder to BL, interview,
September 11, 1982. **128** *"The atmosphere during..."*: OW

to BL, interview, June 30, 1984. **128** *"The fellow had..."*: OW to BL, interview, June 19, 1983. **128** *"We were pick-eted..."*: Ibid. **128** *"I was caught..."*: Ibid. **129** *"What was so..."*: OW to BL, interview, July 26, 1984. **129** *"Houseman never came..."*: OW to BL, interview, May 9, 1984.

CHAPTER 10

131 *"Suddenly, for no..."*: OW to BL, interview, June 30, 1984. **131** *"Nothing like it..."*: OW to BL, interview, June 19, 1983. **132** *"Who wears a..."*: Leonard De Paur to BL, interview, May 6, 1983. **133** *"He's bad man..."*: Abe Feder to BL, interview, September 11, 1982. **134** *"the only time..."*: OW to BL, interview, June 19, 1983. **135** *"I had con-quered..."*: OW to BL, interview, June 30, 1984.

CHAPTER 11

137 *"magic box"*: OW to BL, interview, June 16, 1984. **137** *"beaten by life..."*: OW to BL, interview, June 16, 1984. **138** *"I think she..."*: Ibid. **138** *"She threw herself..."*: Ibid. **138** *"The backbone of..."*: OW to BL, interview, June 19, 1983. **138** *"Ah, relief-orchids..."*: Ibid. **138** *"By bringing in..."*: OW to BL, interview, June 16, 1984. **140** *"Orson would have..."*: Bil Baird to BL, interview, September 17, 1982. **140** *"He loses his..."*: Ibid. **141** *"The whole time..."*: OW to BL, interview, June 8, 1984. **142** *"He didn't like..."*: Martin Gabel to BL, interview, September 21, 1982. **143** government censorship of *Horse Eats Hat:* interdepartmental memorandum, October 26, 1936, U.S. Works Progress Administration for the City of New York.

CHAPTER 12

145 *"We kept him in..."*: OW to BL, interview, June 19, 1983. **145** *"household money"*: Paula Laurence to BL, interview, October 6, 1982. **146** *"Orson Welles's residence..."*: OW to BL, interview, June 5, 1983. **146** *"Okay, Francis, give..."*: Ibid. **147** *"The world was..."*: OW to BL, interview, July 13, 1984. **147** *"They'd open the..."*: OW to BL, interview, June 19, 1983. **147–148** *"There's no law..."*: Ibid. **148** *"never shaved himself..."*: OW to BL, interview, July 26, 1984. **149** *"I hadn't time..."*: OW to BL, interview, June 16, 1984. **149** *"wild camp"*: OW to BL, interview, June 30, 1984. **149** *"Well, I see myself..."*: Ibid. **149** *"I looked just exactly..."*: Ibid. **149** *"You'd swear he..."*: OW to BL, interview, May 21, 1984. **150** *"This was my..."*: OW to BL, interview, May 9, 1984. **150** *"which I found..."*: Ibid. **150** *"first adulterous weekend"*: OW to BL, interview, December 23, 1983. **150** *"Imagine what it..."*: Ibid. **151** *"the impotence lasted..."*: Ibid. **151** *"He was always..."*: OW to BL, interview, May 9, 1984. **152** *"The one thing..."*: OW to BL, interview, July 13, 1984. **152** *"Charles MacArthur and..."*: OW to BL, interview, June 1, 1984. **154** *"It was lovely..."*: Ibid. **155–156** *"When I don't..."*: OW to BL, interview, June 19, 1983. **156** *"You know I..."*: OW to BL, interview, July 28, 1983.

CHAPTER 13

158 *"He was almost..."*: OW to BL, interview, June 30, 1984. **158** *"He wasn't a..."*: Ibid. **158** *"He was an engine..."*: Ibid. **159** *"He had been converted..."*: Ibid. **159** *"a big Broadway..."*: OW to BL, interview, July 16, 1984. **160** *"I was only..."*: Ibid. **160** *"tempt"*: Ibid. **160** *"saint of the bar-*

ricades" : Ibid. **160** *"You think you'll . . ."* : Ibid. **161** *"He and Virgil . . ."* : OW to BL, interview, June 30, 1984. **161** *"magical production"* : OW to BL, interview, June 16, 1984. **161** *"full of metal . . ."* : Ibid. **161** *"hot ticket"* : Ibid. **161** *"It really belonged . . ."* : OW to BL, interview, July 4, 1984. **161** *"I really did . . ."* : OW to BL, interview, June 12, 1984. **163** *"She didn't become . . ."* : OW to BL, interview, July 16, 1984. **164** *"I was very . . ."* : OW to BL, interview, July 4, 1984. **165** *"My feeling, I . . ."* : Ibid. **166** *"the most beautiful . . ."* : Virgil Thomson to BL, interview, October 8, 1982.

CHAPTER 14

168 *"What do you . . ."* : OW to BL, interview, June 5, 1983. **168** *"the least emotional . . ."* : OW to BL, interview, July 11, 1983. **169** *"a great star"* : Ibid. **169** *"I am totally . . ."* : Ibid. **169** *"He didn't have . . ."* : Ibid. **171** *"His great thing . . ."* : Martin Gabel to BL, interview, September 21, 1982. **171** *"He started out . . ."* : Walter Ash to BL, interview, October 11, 1982. **173** scalpers: Joseph Cotten interview, Federal Theatre Project, February 22, 1978.

CHAPTER 15

175 *"Now look, dears . . ."* : Millia Davenport to BL, interview, October 14, 1982. **177** *"we saw, from . . ."* : OW to BL, interview, June 8, 1984. **179** *"We didn't have . . ."* : OW to BL, interview, July 11, 1983. **179** *"I had a company . . ."* : Ibid. **180** *"What I heard . . ."* : Ibid. **181** telegram: Christopher Welles Feder to BL, interview, June 13, 1983. **181** *"I learned it . . ."* : OW to BL, interview, May 9, 1984. **181** *"The nurse kept . . ."* : Ibid.

CHAPTER 16

184 *"He was used..."*: Ibid. **184** *"I went to..."*: Ibid. **184** *"At that time..."*: Ibid. **184** *"It's her trying..."*: Ibid. **185** *"passionate courtship on..."*: Ibid. **185** *"Mama wouldn't have..."*: Ibid. **185** *"Viennese malice"*: Ibid. **188** *"He was working..."*: OW to BL, interview, June 8, 1984. **189** *"was a real..."*: James Morcom to BL, interview, September 23, 1982. **189** *"a home movie"*: OW to BL, interview, December 31, 1983. **189** *"he got the..."*: James Morcom to BL, interview, September 23, 1982. **189** rehearsals: Joseph Cotten interview, Federal Theatre Project, February 22, 1978. **190** *"I was going..."*: OW to BL, interview, July 13, 1984.

CHAPTER 17

191 *"Danton's Death is..."*: Martin Gabel to BL, interview, September 21, 1982. **192** *"When Reinhardt did..."*: Ibid. **190** *"He did something..."*: Ibid. **192** *"When it became..."*: Walter Ash to BL, interview, October 11, 1982. **198** *"He got fired..."*: OW to BL, interview, June 5, 1983. **199** *"Richard's reaction to..."*: Ibid. **200** *"It was done..."*: Walter Ash to BL, interview, October 11, 1982.

CHAPTER 18

Background on Welles's early period in Hollywood came from interviews with Orson Welles, Walter Ash, Stanley Cortez, Martin Gabel, Miriam Geiger, Milton Goldman, Shifra Haran, Roger Hill, John Houseman, James Morcom, Elisabeth Rubino, Augusta Weissberger Schenker, Martin Scorsese, Richard Wilson, Robert Wise; the Welles Collection at Lilly Library,

Indiana University; RKO files; Lincoln Center Theater Collection; Joseph Cotten's papers at USC; John Houseman's papers and Richard Wilson's papers at UCLA.

202 *"He was so..."*: OW to BL, interview, May 21, 1984. **203** *"They were there..."*: OW to BL, interview, June 19, 1983. **203** *"He preferred to..."*: Ibid. **203** *"He was so..."*: OW to BL, interview, May 21, 1984. **204** *"Nobody had ever..."*: OW to BL, interview, June 19, 1983. **206** two-film contract: memos from Ross R. Hastings to Mr. Koerner, March 23, 1942, and July 11, 1942. **206** *"I would have..."*: OW to BL, interview, July 25, 1983. **206** *"frightened"*: Martin Scorsese to BL, interview, November 28, 1983. **206** *"I think that..."*: Ibid. **206** *"I had all..."*: OW to BL, interview, July 11, 1983. **207** *"Hollywood means big..."*: Martin Gabel to BL, interview, September 21, 1982. **208** Orson's finances: letters from Arnold Weissberger to Richard Baer, November 27, 1939, and December 18, 1939. **210** correspondence of Dr. Maurice and Hazel Bernstein, Lilly Library, Indiana University. **212** *"Everybody was at..."*: Miriam Geiger to BL, interview, January 31, 1983. **213** first memo: Herb Drake, August 18, 1939. **214** Dita Parlo: Mercury memo, August 29, 1939. **215** Schaefer wire to Welles, September 15, 1939. **215** Welles wire to Schaefer, September 18, 1939. **215–216** radio dispute: Arnold Weissberger letter to Welles, July 31, 1939. **217** private plane: Arnold Weissberger letter to Richard Baer, December 18, 1939. **218** *"I lost my..."*: OW to BL, interview, January 19, 1984. **219** *"I gave in..."*: Ibid. **219** complaint about Welles: internal memo to Schaefer, December 7, 1939. **220** actors' compensation: internal Mercury memos. **220** free picture: letters from Arnold Weissberger to Welles, December 20, 1939, December 21, 1939, December 28, 1939; memos from Ross R. Hastings to Mr. Koerner, March 23, 1942, and July 11, 1942. **221** divorce: Arnold Weissberger correspondence 1939–1940. **224** *"He was working..."*: OW to BL, interview, July 29, 1983. **224** *"My job was..."*: Ibid. **224–225** *"The whole pur-*

pose...": Ibid. **225–226** *"a vacuum":* Pauline Kael, "Raising Kane" in *The Citizen Kane Book.* **227** *"a special departure...":* OW to BL, interview, July 29, 1983. **186** shooting of *Kane:* RKO daily production reports. **228** *The Men from Mars:* memo from Schaefer, June 5, 1940. **229** *"I was full...":* OW to BL, interview, February 4, 1983. **229** *"Made my stomach...":* OW to BL, interview, June 19, 1983. **232** *"anything a girl...":* OW to BL, interview, May 9, 1984.

<h2 align="center">CHAPTER 19</h2>

237 *"When he was...":* Robert Wise to BL, interview, June 24, 1982. **238** Toland's contract: "Notes to Schaefer," Mercury Memo, n.d. **238–239** leak to press: Ibid. **240** *"You have to...":* OW to BL, interview, July 11, 1983. **240** *"You could write...":* Ibid. **244** *"The one key...":* Martin Scorsese to BL, interview, November 28, 1983.

<h2 align="center">CHAPTER 20</h2>

245 Mankiewicz's rage: memo #1 from Herbert Drake to Welles, August 26, 1940. **245** *"not enough standard...":* memo #2 from Herbert Drake to Welles, August 26, 1940. **245** *"magnificent":* Ibid. **245** *"from an aesthetic...":* Ibid. **246** Mankiewicz's contract: letters from Arnold Weissberger to Welles, September 6, September 23, October 1, and October 16, 1940, and January 21, 1941; from Weissberger to Richard Baer, September 9, 1940. **246** Welles's intentions: letters from Weissberger to Welles, September 23, October 1, October 16, 1940. **246** Weissberger's idea: letter from Weissberger to Welles, January 22, 1941. **248** *"Obviously, a certain...":* John Houseman to BL, interview, November 7, 1982. **248** *"He claims he...":* Ibid. **249** Houseman telegram to Mankiewicz, June 16, 1940.

248–249 Mankiewicz's initial threat: memo #1 from Herbert Drake to Welles, August 26, 1940. **249** threatened complaint to Screen Writers Guild: letter from Weissberger to Welles, September 6, 1940. **249** Mankiewicz's claim to whole script: letter from Weissberger to Baer, September 9, 1940. **249** legal department assurance: letter from Weissberger to Welles, October 16, 1940. **249** Hearst controversy: letter from Herbert Drake to William Schneider, January 15, 1941. **251** Parsons's calls: secretary's notes, January 9, 1941. **252** *"never wore any..."*: OW to BL, interview, June 22, 1984. **252** *"at a huge..."*: OW to BL, interview, July 26, 1984. **253** *"You should have..."*: OW to BL, interview, June 22, 1984. **253** *"From my happy..."*: Ibid. **253** *"that sightless beautiful..."*: Ibid. **254** *"black eyes"*: Ibid. **254** *"Marlene was the..."*: OW to BL, interview, June 30, 1984. **254–255** Weissberger's orders: letter from Weissberger to Drake, January 14, 1941. **255** four a.m. call: Ibid. **255** Marion Davies's twins: letter from Weissberger to Welles, January 17, 1941. **255–256** Weissberger on Schaefer: Ibid. **256** threatened lawsuit: letter from Weissberger to Welles, January 20, 1941. **256** *"hollow man"*: OW to BL, interview, July 13, 1983. **256** *"The secret was..."*: Ibid. **257** public figures' lives: letters from Weissberger to Welles, January 20, 1941, and January 23, 1941. **258** inadequate defense: letter from Weissberger to Welles, January 23, 1941. **258** *"I thought it..."*: John Houseman to BL, interview, November 7, 1982. **259** *"a real royal..."*: James Morcom to BL, interview, September 23, 1982. **259** *"He was mad..."*: Ibid. **261–262** medical report: June 25, 1941. **262** Welles telegram to Shaefer, March 7, 1941. **264** *"Nobody came at..."*: OW to BL, interview, June 22, 1984. **264** *"People were too..."*: OW to BL, interview, July 11, 1983. **264** Skouras: letter from Weissberger to Welles, October 23, 1941.

CHAPTER 21

266 *"If there was..."*: John Houseman to BL, interview, November 7, 1982. **268** *"That's my little..."*: OW to BL, interview, July 26, 1983. **268** *"There is one..."*: OW quoted in *Baltimore Evening Sun,* October 13, 1941. **269** *"a terrible embarrassment"*: OW to BL, interview, July 25, 1983. **269** *"a little peanut"*: Ibid. **270** *"like a quilted..."*: OW to BL, interview, July 26, 1983. **270** *"I managed to..."*: Ibid. **272** *"It's like* Dallas *..."*: OW to BL, interview, January 19, 1984. **272** *"Fine, do it."*: OW to BL, interview, February 1, 1983. **273** *"People are always..."*: OW to BL, interview, February 4, 1983. **277** *"Get me out..."*: Shifra Haran to BL, interview, November 13, 1982. **278** Screen Actors Guild warning: memo from Ross R. Hastings to Welles, October 4, 1941. **278** *"We rehearsed for..."*: OW to BL, interview, January 19, 1984. **278** *"It's very much..."*: Ibid. **278** *"I was so..."*: Ibid. **279** *"When you're doing..."*: Stanley Cortez to BL, interview, June 23, 1982. **279–281** shooting of *Ambersons:* RKO daily production reports. **281–282** Background on the Nelson Rockefeller Committee came from *The Latin American Policy of the United States* by Samuel Flagg Bemis. **283** *"My influence on..."*: OW to BL, interview, January 19, 1984. **285** *"My testicles are..."*: Shifra Haran to BL, interview, November 13, 1982. **286** Orson Welles's 1941 Christmas list. **286** *"persona non grata..."*: Christopher Welles Feder to BL, interview, June 13, 1983. **286–287** *"During the course..."*: Shifra Haran to BL, interview, November 13, 1982. **287** *"The whole latter..."*: Robert Wise to BL, interview, June 24, 1982.

CHAPTER 22

289 *"The picture was..."*: OW to BL, interview, January 19, 1984. **290** background on Welles's daily activities in Rio: production reports and memos from Tom Pettey to Herbert Drake. **290** *"It wasn't perfume..."*: OW to BL, interview, February 21, 1984. **291** color film controversy: telegrams between Welles and RKO, and Welles and Jack Moss. **291–292** *favelas:* internal Mercury memo, April 14, 1942; memo from Pettey to Drake, May 5, 1942. **292** preview reactions: summary of comment card reactions, March 19, 1942; letter from Robert Wise to Welles, March 31, 1942. **293** Schaefer letter to Welles, March 21, 1942. **293** *"the studio edict..."*: Robert Wise to BL, interview, June 24, 1982. **293** *"I had no..."*: OW to BL, interview, January 19, 1984. **293** *"Let me say..."*: Robert Wise to BL, interview, June 24, 1982. **293** *"The entire sequence..."*: OW to BL, interview, January 19, 1984. **294** *"there were things..."*: Robert Wise to BL, interview, June 24, 1982. **294** *"Of course it..."*: OW to BL, interview, January 19, 1984. **294** *"We got to..."*: Ibid. **294** *"See, the one..."*: Ibid. **296** *"Who knows what..."*: Ibid. **297** *"It's my theory..."*: Ibid. **297** *"Of course I..."*: Ibid. **299** *"Yes, but I..."*: Ibid.

CHAPTER 23

300 Schaefer telegram to Welles, April 16, 1942. **300–301** Urca casino: telegrams between Welles and Schaefer; internal Mercury memos. **301** Welles's goodwill speeches: letter from Welles to Nelson Rockefeller, February 25, 1942; memo from the Brazilian Division of the Coordinator's Office to John Hay Whitney, April 27, 1942; internal Mercury memo, April 23, 1942; memo from Richard Wilson to the Coordinator's Office, May 30, 1942. **301** *"He had not..."*: Shifra Haran to BL, interview, December 18, 1982. **301** *"It's Portuguese, not..."*: OW to BL, interview, May 9, 1984. **302** *"Look what they..."*: Ibid. **302** *"I rolled over..."*: OW to BL, interview, August 29, 1984. **302** *"They said the..."*: Ibid. **302** *"So for the..."*:

Ibid. **303** *"Have we got..."*: Shifra Haran to BL, interview, December 18, 1982. **303** *"It was marvelous..."*: Ibid. **304** death of Jacare: Affidavit of Antonio Rego Passos, May 19, 1942. **304** *inadequate equipment:* letter from George Fanto to Richard Wilson, July 29, 1942; letter from Richard Wilson to Phil Reisman, August 11, 1942. **305** RKO's plans: memo from Ross R. Hastings to Mr. Koerner, July 11, 1942.

CHAPTER 24

Background for 1942–1947 came from interviews with Orson Welles, Louis Dolivet, Greg Garrison, Shifra Haran, Roger Hill, Jackson Leighter, Wilbur Menefee, Ernest Nims, James Pratt, Elisabeth Rubino, John Stransky Jr., Richard Wilson, and Michael Woulfe; correspondence with Jeanette Nolan; Welles's papers in Lilly Library, Indiana University; the Lincoln Center Theatre Collection; USC Library Special Collections; and Richard Wilson's papers at UCLA.

307 *"Nobody was ever..."*: OW to BL, interview, January 19, 1984. **307** *"the Nelson caper"*: Ibid. **307** *"I was unhappy..."*: Ibid. **308** *"I was..."*: Ibid. **308** *"It wasn't at..."*: Ibid. **308** *"Disaster scares people..."*: Ibid. **309** willingness to hear: memos from Peter Rathvon to Charles Koerner, October 22, 1942; and from Koerner to Rathvon, October 26, 1942. **309** *"I had been..."*: OW to BL, interview, February 21, 1984. **311** *"Mr. Leighter, how..."*: Jackson Leighter to BL, interview, December 10, 1983. **311** third picture: memo from Ross R. Hastings to Mr. Koerner, July 11, 1942. **311** *"There'd be no..."*: OW to BL, interview, January 19, 1984. **311** recutting *Journey:* letters from Peter Rathvon to Welles, October 19, 1942, and October 20, 1942. **312** script and schedule: letter from Peter Rathvon to Welles, November 12, 1942. **312** *"It was a..."*: OW to BL, interview, January 19, 1984.

312 *"I had that..."*: Ibid. **314** *"Part of my..."*: Ibid. **314–315** Welles's billing: letter from Loyd Wright to Jack Moss, December 24, 1942. **315** Selznick's regret: letter from David O. Selznick to William Goetz, April 17, 1943. **315** contract: Twentieth Century Fox Film Corporation, December 7, 1942. **316** *"And which Strauss..."*: OW to BL, interview, July 26, 1983. **316** *"Well, he didn't..."*: Shifra Haran to BL, interview, January 1, 1983. **316** *"That's something I'm..."*: OW to BL, interview, February 1, 1983. **316** *"When I read..."*: Ibid. **317** *"I wasn't having..."*: OW to BL, interview, June 22, 1984. **317** *"A girlfriend of..."*: Ibid. **317** *"I kept thinking..."*: Ibid. **318** *"The steam room at..."*: Ibid. **319** *I used to..."*: OW to BL, interview, February 1, 1983. **320** *"He was one..."*: Shifra Haran to BL, interview, November 20, 1982. **320** *"Of course that..."*: Shifra Haran to BL, interview, December 18, 1982. **320** *"Shorty was more..."*: Ibid. **321** *"bitches in heat"*: Ernest Nims to BL, interview, June 26, 1982. **321** *"They were sittin'..."*: Shifra Haran to BL, interview, December 18, 1982. **321** *"He made a..."*: Jackson Leighter to BL, interview, December 8, 1983. **321** *"It took me..."*: OW to BL, interview, July 16, 1984. **322** *"She's half gypsy..."*: OW to BL, interview, July 23, 1983. **322** *"He was a..."*: Ibid. **322** *"She couldn't deal..."*: Ibid. **323** *"not sexually shy..."*: Shifra Haran to BL, interview, November 13, 1982. **323** *"When it came..."*: Elisabeth Rubino to BL, interview, September 12, 1982. **323** *"an indescribably awful..."*: OW to BL, interview, July 23, 1983. **323** *"felt a tremendous..."*: Ibid. **324** *"Rita had great..."*: Ibid. **325** *"Later I began..."*: OW to BL, interview, July 16, 1984. **327** *"She was the..."*: OW to BL, interview, July 23, 1983. **328** *"When she came..."*: Shifra Haran to BL, interview, January 1, 1983. **328** *"Those guys practically..."*: Ibid. **330** *"What I wanted..."*: OW to BL, interview, February 21, 1984. **331** Radio City Music Hall: letter from Welles to Nelson Rockefeller, October 20, 1942. **331** *"That was to..."*: OW to BL, interview, February 21, 1984.

332 *Jack, there is not...": Jackson Leighter to BL, interview, December 9, 1983. **332** *"There's a song..."*: OW to BL, interview, February 21, 1984. **333** *"It was a..."*: OW to BL, interview, December 31, 1983. **333** Background on the Sleepy Lagoon case came from *The Sleepy Lagoon Case* (Citizens' Committee for the Defense of Mexican American Youth) and *La Raza: The Mexican Americans* by Stan Steiner. **337** *"You can talk..."*: OW to BL, interview, February 19, 1984. **337** *"right instincts"*: Louis Dolivet to BL, interview, December 14, 1983. **337** *"natural humanism"*: Ibid. **337** *"Oh, he had..."*: OW to BL, interview, February 19, 1984. **337** *"crown princes"*: Louis Dolivet to BL, interview, December 14, 1983.

CHAPTER 25

340 *"Until she met..."*: OW to BL, interview, July 23, 1983. **341** *"if he believed..."*: Shifra Haran to BL, interview, January 8, 1983. **344** *"The war per..."*: "World Citizenship and Economic Problems" in *Free World*, July 1945. **344** *"The scaly dinosaurs..."*: "Moral Indebtedness" in *Free World*, October 1943. **345** *"The intellectual has..."*: "Liberalism—Election's Victor" in *Free World*, December 1944. **346** *"our hemisphere is..."*: "The Good Neighbor Policy Reconsidered" in *Free World*, March 1944. **346** *"This is a..."*: "Race Hate Must Be Outlawed" in *Free World*, July 1944. **348** *"pretty rough"*: letter from Welles to Leonard Lyons, January 29, 1944. **348** *"under a strict..."*: letter from Dr. Maurice Bernstein to Manager, Beverly Hills Hotel, January 22, 1944. **348–349** *"all the money"*: letter from Welles to Walter Huston, April 27, 1944. **349** casting problems: letter from Welles to Donald Ogden Stewart, May 17, 1944. **349** Duke Ellington incident: Elisabeth Rubino to BL, interview, September 12, 1982. **350** *"a great deal..."*: letter from Elsa Maxwell to Welles, April 11, 1944. **350** General Marshall: telegram from Fred Smith to Welles,

May 9, 1944. **352** *"I'm going to . . ."*: Jackson Leighter to BL, interview, December 8, 1983. **354** lawsuit: affidavit, June 10, 1944; letter from Welles to Loyd Wright, January 28, 1944; letter from Max M. Gilford to Welles, March 13, 1944; correspondence between Jackson Leighter and law offices of Wright and Millikan, March 24, 1944, January 22, 1945, February 14, 1945, and March 30, 1945. **354** *"wasn't his thing"*: Shifra Haran to BL, interview, November 13, 1982. **356** *"knightly gallantry"*: letter from Helen Keller to Welles, October 26, 1944. **356** *"I came down . . ."*: OW to BL, interview, June 8, 1984. **357** *"He liked to . . ."*: Ibid. **358** *"He loved it . . ."*: OW to BL, interview, June 16, 1984. **358** *"Mrs. Roosevelt didn't . . ."*: OW to BL, interview, May 9, 1984. **358** *"Missy used to . . ."*: Ibid. **358** *"I made fun . . ."*: Ibid. **358** *"She thought I . . ."*: OW to BL, interview, June 16, 1984. **359** *"This illness was . . ."*: letter from Welles to Franklin Delano Roosevelt, October 25, 1944. **359** *"We were coming . . ."*: OW to BL, interview, June 8, 1984. **360** *"he will really . . ."*: Shifra Haran quoted in *The Wichita Eagle*, November 10, 1944. **361** *"Shifra?"*: OW to BL, interview, June 5, 1983. **361** *"Just the thought . . ."*: Shifra Haran to BL, interview, February 4, 1983. **361** *"That's wonderful!"*: OW to BL, interview, June 5, 1983. **361** *"Now there was . . ."*: Shifra Haran to BL, interview, December 18, 1982. **362** *"No one woman . . ."*: Ibid. **362** *"The books don't . . ."*: Shifra Haran to BL, interview, January 1, 1983. **362** *"Maybe if I . . ."*: Ibid. **362** *"Oh, she was . . ."*: OW to BL, interview, June 5, 1983. **362** *"my youthful arrogance"*: Ibid. **362** *"You never acted . . ."*: Shifra Haran to BL, interview, December 4, 1982. **362–363** *"In ways that . . ."*: Ibid. **363** *"One of the . . ."*: OW to BL, interview, June 5, 1983.

CHAPTER 26

364 *"not really all . . ."*: Shifra Haran to BL, interview, January 1, 1983. **364** *"I don't really . . ."*: Ibid. **365** *"weepy"*: OW to BL, interview, July 26, 1983. **365** *"very impressive"*: Ibid **366** *"She probably didn't . . ."*: Ibid. **366** *"Too much effort . . ."*: letter from Welles to Fernando Pinto, February 26, 1943. **366** percentage of *Kane*: Jackson Leighter to BL, interview, December 10, 1983; and letter from RKO Radio Pictures to Richard Wilson, November 18, 1948. **367** $197,500: court records, District Court of Salt Lake County, State of Utah. **367** *"real showmanship . . ."*: transcript of tape from Welles to Martin Strauss, November 16, 1944. **370** *"Well, by all . . ."*: Jackson Leighter to BL, interview, December 13, 1983. **371** *"It was absolutely . . ."*: Jackson Leighter to BL, interview, December 11, 1983. **372** *"I knew about . . ."*: OW to BL, interview, December 31, 1983. **373** *"Every night I . . ."*: OW to BL, interview, July 16, 1984. **374** *Post* column: correspondence between *NY Post* and Mercury Productions, November 15, 1944, December 21, 1944, March 23, 1945, May 19, 1945, June 26, 1945, July 4, 1945, July 5, 1945.

CHAPTER 27

376 *"He was crazy . . ."*: Shifra Haran to BL, interview, November 20, 1982. **376** *"She was broke"*: OW to BL, interview, July 26, 1983. **308** *"worshiped"*: Ibid. **376** *"She was essentially . . ."*: OW to BL, interview, July 23, 1983. **376** *"This was during . . ."*: Ibid. **377** *"She turned into . . ."*: OW to BL, interview, July 26, 1983. **377** "Her *feet aren't . . .*": Ibid. **377** *"They say, no . . ."*: Ibid. **378** guarantee to the Haig Corporation and International Pictures, signed by Welles and Rita Hayworth, September 20, 1945. **380** Nims's recollection: Ernest

Nims to BL, interview, June 26, 1982. **381** *"He was the..."*: OW to BL, interview, July 23, 1983. **381** *"I fought him..."*: Ibid. **381** *"You don't know..."*: Ibid. **381** *"supersurgeon"*: Ibid. **382** *"I'd say that..."*: Jim Pratt to BL, interview, July 1, 1982. **382** *"When I was..."*: OW to BL, interview, July 13, 1984. **383** *"I don't drive..."*: OW to BL, interview, July 28, 1983. **384** *"It was on..."*: Jim Pratt to BL, interview, July 1, 1982. **385** *"I was ready..."*: OW to BL, interview, December 31, 1983. **385–386** *"Imagine the great..."*: Louis Dolivet to BL, interview, December 14, 1983. **386** *"If I had..."*: Ibid. **386** *"He was a..."*: OW to BL, interview, May 9, 1984. **386** *"Joe McCarthy had..."*: Ibid. **386** *"I didn't..."*: Ibid. **387** *"It isn't like..."*: OW to BL, interview, December 31, 1983. **387** *"Like a thousand..."*: Ibid. **387** *"Rita was very..."*: Ibid. **387** *"It was just..."*: Ibid. **388** *"I didn't run..."*: OW to BL, interview, May 9, 1984. **389** *"Roosevelt used to..."*: Ibid.

CHAPTER 28

392 *"I could have..."*: OW to BL, interview, July 16, 1984. **393** *"I really thought..."*: Ibid. **393** *"I went to..."*: OW to BL, interview, August 3, 1984. **394–395** divorce negotiations: correspondence between Welles and Loyd Wright, January 14, 1946, and April 8, 1946; wire from I. H. Prinzmetal to Welles, April 17, 1946; letter from Elisabeth Rubino to Welles, January 15, 1946; letter from Frank Belcher to Loyd Wright, April 5, 1946; wire from Loyd Wright to Richard Wilson, April 17, 1946; wire from Mercury Enterprises to Rita Hayworth, April 18, 1946. **395** *"next to Chaplin..."*: OW to BL, interview, February 4, 1983. **323** *"piss a bit..."*: Ibid. **395** contract: letter of agreement from Mike Todd to Welles, January 1946. **397** Background on *Galileo* came from interviews with Orson Welles; letter from Charles Laughton to Welles, July 25, 1946;

letter from Welles to Laughton, July 27, 1946. **398** Background
on *Around the World* previews came from Arthur Margetson's
notes and Welles's Lear Radio broadcasts. **400** *"Tragic news . . ."*:
wire from Cole Porter to Welles, July 29, 1946. **402** NAACP
wire from Walter White and Oliver W. Harrington to Welles,
September 27, 1946. **405–406** Korda deal: letter from Alexander Korda to Welles, September 1, 1946. **406** *"He was an . . ."*:
OW to BL, interview, December 31, 1983. **407** *"You know
the . . ."*: OW to BL, interview, July 16, 1984. **408** shooting
of *Lady from Shanghai*: daily production reports. **408** cocaine:
OW to BL, interview, July 25, 1983. **408** Christopher: Christopher Welles Feder to BL, interview, June 13, 1983. **409**
correspondence between Welles and Korda, September 10,
September 11, September 27, September 28, October 1, October 7, October 10, October 14, 1946. **410** Hayworth's health:
memo from Richard Wilson to Welles, 1947. **410** Welles's
Christmas list, 1946. **411** Brecht: "Alienation Effects in Chinese
Acting" in *Brecht on Theatre*, trans. John Willet. **413** *"The
shock effects . . ."*: OW to BL, interview, July 23, 1983. **413**
memo to Mr. Cohn from Mr. Welles, 1947. **414** *"I had a . . ."*:
OW to BL, interview, July 23, 1983. **415** *"All the changes . . ."*:
Ibid. **415** *"nothing to do . . ."*: Ibid. **415** *"See, I wasn't . . ."*:
Ibid. **415** *"a prat-fall by . . ."*: memo to Cohn. **415** *"pay no
attention . . ."*: OW to BL, interview, July 23, 1983. **416** *"He
took about . . ."*: Ibid. **416** *"This was a . . ."*: Ibid. **416** *"I
thought she . . ."*: Ibid. **416** *"He always called . . ."*: OW to
BL, interview, February 21, 1984. **416** *"I thought he . . ."*:
Ibid.

CHAPTER 29

418 *"In his best . . ."*: memo from Welles to Cohn. **419** wire
from Korda to Welles, March 3, 1947. **420** *"I liked them . . ."*:
OW to BL, interview, June 16, 1984. **420** *"strange design . . ."*:
Ibid. **420** *"You see, he'd . . ."*: Ibid. **422** *"I went there . . ."*:

OW to BL, interview, December 31, 1983. **424** Welles's notes on *Macbeth* costumes. **424–425** shooting of *Macbeth:* daily production reports. **424** *"I had Duke..."*: OW to BL, interview, December 31, 1983. **425** *"I had only..."*: Ibid. **425** Yates's congratulations: letter from Herbert J. Yates to Welles, July 18, 1947. **426** *"They would just..."*: OW to BL, interview, May 13, 1984. **426** *"You know, Korda..."*: Ibid. **428** Background on 1948—present came from interviews with Orson Welles, Larry Aldenhoevel, Dominique Antoine, Robert Arden, Philip Bowles, John Buckingham, Robert Clatworthy, Jean Dalrymple, Joey DiMaio, Louis Dolivet, Richard Fleischer, Martin Gabel, Greg Garrison, Milton Goldman, Harry Hamburg, Henry Hathaway, Charlton Heston, Roger Hill, Gordon Jackson, Henry Jaglom, Eartha Kitt, Diane Latore, Janet Leigh, Henry Mancini, Wolf Mankowitz, Henry Margolis, Patricia McCormack, Terry Nelson, Ernest Nims, James Pratt, Martin Ritt, Elisabeth Rubino, Augusta Weissberger Schenker, Aaron Stell, Paul Stewart, Alessandro Tasca di Cuto, Virgil Thomson, Virgil Vogel, Dennis Weaver, Richard Wilson, Bud Yorkin; also from Welles Collection, Lilly Library, Indiana University; USC Special Collections; Lincoln Center Theatre Collection; Micheal MacLiammoir's *Put Money in Thy Purse* and *Each Actor on his Ass*. **428** *"Where is Grisha?"*: Jackson Leighter to BL, interview, December 9, 1983. **429** *"Pope Pius XII..."*: OW to BL, interview, May 29, 1984. **429** *"I was chased..."*: OW to BL, interview, May 15, 1984. **429** *"She taught me..."*: OW to BL, interview, June 22, 1984. **430** *"the prince of evil"*: OW to BL, interview, May 13, 1984. **430** *"used to shoot up..."*: Ibid. **430** threat to bill Welles: letter from Richard Wilson to Welles, November 20, 1947. **431–432** *"I had no..."*: OW to BL, interview, December 31, 1983. **432** *"We were going..."*: Ibid. **432** *"I discovered a..."*: Ibid. **432** *"We were within weeks..."*: Ibid. **433** *"He cost me..."*: OW to BL, interview, May 13, 1984. **434** *"I had a..."*: OW to BL, interview, December 31, 1983. **434** *"touched up all..."*: Ibid.

435 *"Cole Porter and..."*: OW to BL, interview, April 3, 1984. **436** *"Whenever she'd act..."*: Shifra Haran to BL, interview, January 29, 1983. **436** *"You know, I..."*: Shifra Haran to BL, interview, November 5, 1983. **437** *"We never went..."*: Shifra Haran to BL, interview, December 18, 1982. **438** *"It should have..."*: Shifra Haran to BL, interview, December 4, 1982. **438** *"I had no..."*: OW to BL, interview, April 3, 1984. **439** *hated in Italy:* letter from Gregory Ratoff to Richard Wilson, October 27, 1948. **440** *"She had a..."*: OW to BL, interview, July 16, 1984. **440** *"I was blinded..."*: Ibid. **441** *"She treated me..."*: Ibid. **442** *"When I didn't..."*: Ibid. **442** *"I had one..."*: Ibid. **442** *"I wasn't in..."*: Ibid. **442** *"I had a..."*: Ibid. **443** *"I knew I..."*: OW to BL, interview, May 13, 1984. **443** *"I thought if..."*: Ibid. **443** *"It was going..."*: OW to BL, interview, December 31, 1983. **443** *"I was given..."*: Ibid. **444** *"still numb"*: OW to BL, interview, July 16, 1984. **444** *"I'd lost my..."*: Ibid. **444** *frantic wires:* letter from Roger Hill to Richard Wilson, December 6, 1948. **445** *"To try to..."*: OW to BL, interview, July 16, 1984. **446** *"shy, bashful, misunderstood"*: Shifra Haran to BL, interview, December 18, 1982. **446** *"The Prince was..."*: Shifra Haran to BL, interview, November 13, 1982. **447** *"down-at-the-heels"*: Shifra Haran to BL, interview, December 4, 1982. **447** *"Same as me..."*: Ibid. **448** *"You know, Micheal..."*: OW to BL, interview, June 22, 1984. **449** *"He was always..."*: Ibid. **449** *"One did rather..."*: Ibid. **449** *"I told him..."*: Ibid. **450** *"So there was..."*: OW to BL, interview, May 21, 1984. **450** *"I wanted Welles..."*: Henry Hathaway to BL, interview, June 16, 1982. **450** *"He doesn't like..."*: Ibid. **450** *"Welles would take..."*: Ibid. **451** *"special food"*: Ibid. **451** *"We did it ..."*: Ibid. **451** *"He's such a..."*: Ibid. **451** *"great, tall, dark..."*: OW to BL, interview, May 21, 1984. **452** *"She sent for..."*: OW to BL, interview, July 16, 1984. **452** *"When I arrived..."*: OW to BL, interview, December 31, 1983. **453** *"There was no..."*: Ibid. **453** *"to keep* *him...":* OW to BL, interview, July 26, 1984. **453** *"The governor of...":* Ibid. **454** *"He picked up...":* Ibid. **454** *"You're the only...":* Henry Hathaway to BL, interview, June 16, 1982. **454** *"I was beleaguered...":* OW to BL, interview, December 31, 1983. **455** *"You know one...":* Ibid. **455** *"Still looking great...":* OW to BL, interview, May 9, 1984. **455** *"One night in...":* OW to BL, interview, June 22, 1984. **455** *"You can imagine...":* Ibid. **455** organizational procedures: letter from Richard Wilson to Charles Moses, May 10, 1949. **456** proposal to Hill: letter from Welles to Roger Hill, October 8, 1949.

CHAPTER 30

458 *"Eartha Kitt was...":* OW to BL, interview, July 21, 1983. **458** *"a highly sophisticated...":* Eartha Kitt to BL, interview, January 31, 1984. **458** *"One of the...":* Ibid. **460** *"I'd seen* Citizen Kane...": Ibid. **460** *"We started rehearsing...":* Ibid. **461** *"He used to...":* Ibid. **461** *"I never knew...":* Ibid. **462** *"And he stretches...":* Ibid. **462** *"I asked him...":* Ibid. **462** *"It's only...":* Ibid. **462** *"I was hitting...":* Ibid. **463** *"I was five feet two...":* Ibid. **463** *"There was a...":* Ibid. **463** *"The first part...":* Ibid. **464** *"So I go...":* Ibid. **464** *"They used to...":* OW to BL, interview, February 21, 1984. **465** *"I was writing...":* Ibid. **465** *"Oh, he'd never...":* OW to BL, interview, June 22, 1984. **466** *"I sent her...":* OW to BL, interview, May 9, 1984. **466** ANTA: letter from Robert Breen to Richard Wilson, November 30, 1950. **468** *"He was a...":* Robert Arden to BL, interview, February 25, 1984. **469** *"implored me to...":* OW to BL, interview, December 31, 1983. **469** *"Why not Othello?":* OW to BL, interview, July 26, 1983. **469** *"That made me...":* OW to BL, interview, December 31, 1983. **469** *"I'd play it...":* Ibid. **470** *"essentially conservative...":* OW to BL, interview, May 13,

1984. **470** *"I wanted to . . ."*: Ibid. **470** *"He went waiting . . ."*:
Ibid. **470** *"Tynan was a . . ."*: Wolf Mankowitz to BL, interview, March 12, 1984. **471** *"This was a . . ."*: OW to BL,
interview, December 31, 1983. **471** *"They got me . . ."*: Ibid.
471 *I was then . . ."*: Ibid. **471** *"I came to . . ."*: OW to BL,
interview July 26, 1984.

CHAPTER 31

474 *"shot like a . . ."*: OW to BL, interview, July 26, 1984.
474 *"My Egyptians immediately . . ."*: Ibid. **474** *"One of
them . . ."*: OW to BL, interview, June 8, 1984. **471** *"It was
arranged . . ."*: Virgil Thomson to BL, interview, October 8,
1982. **478** *"Some madman has . . ."*: Robert Arden to
BL, interview, February 25, 1984. **479** *"Orson welcomed
me . . ."*: Ibid. **479** *"Talk about being . . ."*: Ibid. **479** *"Part of
the . . ."*: Ibid. **479** *"The sound engineer . . ."*: Ibid. **480** *"I said
'Hi' . . ."*: Ibid. **480** *"Dolivet asked me . . ."*: Ibid. **481** *"the
most gifted . . ."*: Ibid. **482** *"Louis had never . . ."*: OW to BL,
interview, February 19, 1984. **482** *"It was my . . ."*: Ibid. **482**
"They took it . . .": Ibid. **482** *"It was told . . ."*: OW to BL,
interview, May 9, 1984. **483** *"made a mess . . ."*: OW to BL,
interview, February 19, 1984. **483** *"His way of . . ."*: Wolf
Mankowitz to BL, interview, March 12, 1984. **484** *"I sold
Arkadin . . ."*: Ibid. **484** *"She obviously worshiped . . ."*: Robert
Arden to BL, interview, February 25, 1984. **484** *"She was
a . . ."*: Wolf Mankowitz to BL, interview, March 12, 1984.
484 *"There was a . . ."*: Ibid. **484** *"If I was . . ."*: Ibid. **485**
"The problem with . . .": Ibid. **485** *"imagination more than
money"*: Henry Margolis to BL, interview, November 12, 1982.
487 *"The picture of . . ."*: Wolf Mankowitz to BL, interview,
March 12, 1984. **488** *"like Big Brother!"*: Gordon Jackson to
BL, interview, February 24, 1984. **488** *"He hated actors . . ."*:
Ibid. **489** *"When the Pequod . . ."*: Ibid. **489** *"Hilton deferred*

to...": Wolf Mankowitz to BL, interview, March 12, 1984.
490 "Moby Dick, *I...":* OW to BL, interview, July 29, 1983.
490 *"I don't think...":* Wolf Mankowitz to BL, interview,
March 12, 1984. **490** *"I enjoyed it...":* OW to BL, interview,
December 31, 1983. **491** *"I ad-libbed every...":* OW to BL,
interview, July 29, 1983. **491** *"He's a* big...": Gordon Jackson
to BL, interview, February 24, 1984. **491** *"He won't do...":*
Wolf Mankowitz to BL, interview, March 12, 1984. **492** *"Houseman started in...":* OW to BL, interview, July 29, 1983.
492 *"Orson's attitude is...":* Wolf Mankowitz to BL, interview, March 12, 1984. **493** *"We shot for...":* OW to BL,
interview, December 31, 1983. **493** *"Take me home!"* Gordon
Jackson to BL, interview, February 24, 1984. **493** *"In a
strange...":* Ibid. **493** *"I have a...":* OW to BL, interview,
December 31, 1983. **494** *"On those terms...":* OW to BL,
interview, July 4, 1984. **494** *"We had four...":* Ibid. **494** *"She
was the...":* Henry Margolis to BL, interview, November 12,
1982. **494** *"The Volney Hotel...":* Elisabeth Rubino to BL,
interview, September 12, 1982. **495** *"She was fighting...":*
Ibid. **495** *"Beatrice is a...":* OW to BL, interview, June 5,
1983. **495** *"He had just...":* Henry Margolis to BL, interview,
November 12, 1982. **495** *"Terrible theater!"*: OW to BL, interview, December 31, 1983. **495** *"I had a...":* Ibid. **496** *"If
you're going...":* Ibid. **496** *"I felt that...":* Ibid. **496** *"I think
I...":* Ibid. **497** *"Because it means...":* Ibid. **497** *"I now
had...":* Ibid. **498** *"I suddenly remembered...":* OW to BL,
interview, May 9, 1984. **499** *"That's why...":* OW to
BL, interview, June 8, 1984. **499** *"No, that's it...":* OW to
BL, interview, May 9, 1984. **500** *"I* knew *when...":* OW to
BL, interview, June 8, 1984. **501–502** *"A biography is...":*
OW to BL, interview, May 9, 1984. **502** *"I got a...":* Ibid.

CHAPTER 32

504 *"I was put . . ."*: OW to BL, interview, December 31, 1983. **504** *"A lot of . . ."*: Ibid. **504** *"When I talk . . ."*: Ibid. **505** "Lear *broke me . . ."*: OW to BL, interview, July 4, 1984. **507** *"You'll be interested . . ."*: Terry Nelson to BL, interview, June 25, 1982. **507** *"I was by . . ."*: Charlton Heston to BL, interview, June 12, 1982. **508** *"He has gargantuan . . ."*: Ibid. **508** *"a very young . . ."*: Ibid. **508** *"One of the . . ."*: Ibid. **509** *"He was just . . ."*: Ibid. **509** *"The fact that . . ."*: Ibid. **509** *"He's a very . . ."*: Ibid. **509–510** *"I guess almost . . ."*: Ibid. **510** *"He makes it . . ."*: Ibid. **510** *"He can work . . ."*: Ibid.

CHAPTER 33

511 shooting of *Touch of Evil*: daily production reports. **512–513** *"He took what was . . ."*: Charlton Heston to BL, interview, June 12, 1982. **515** *"Okay, now that . . ."*: Phil Bowles to BL, interview, June 14, 1982. **515** *"They really didn't . . ."*: Janet Leigh to BL, interview, June 15, 1982. **515** *"The sun would . . ."*: Phil Bowles to BL, interview, June 14, 1982. **515** *"He assumed absolute . . ."*: Terry Nelson to BL, interview, June 25, 1982. **515** *"With Mr. Hitchcock . . ."*: Janet Leigh to BL, interview, June 15, 1982. **516** *"We went into . . ."*: Dennis Weaver to BL, interview, June 14, 1982. **517** *"Oh she's marvelous . . ."*: OW to BL, interview, July 23, 1983. **517** *"She looked super!"*: Ibid. **517** *"When we got . . ."*: Terry Nelson to BL, interview, June 25, 1982. **518** *"He expressed the . . ."*: Wolf Mankowitz to BL, interview, March 12, 1984. **519** *"It took all . . ."*: Janet Leigh to BL, interview, June 15, 1982. **520** *"You've got it . . ."*: Terry Nelson to BL, interview, June 25, 1982. **521** *"I could immediately . . ."*: Virgil Vogel to BL, interview, June 18, 1982. **521** *"pictorial value"*: Ibid. **522** *"You tell them . . ."*: Ibid. **523**

"home movie": OW to BL, interview, April 21, 1984. **523** *"Here was a..."*: Ernest Nims to BL, interview, June 26, 1982. **524** *"He was ahead..."*: Ibid. **525** *"really just geographical..."*: Charlton Heston to BL, interview, June 12, 1982. **525** *"The film is..."*: Ibid. **525–526** *"We both resented..."*: Janet Leigh to BL, interview, June 15, 1982. **526** *"In the end..."*: Charlton Heston to BL, interview, June 12, 1982.

CHAPTER 34

527 *"It will turn..."*: OW to BL, interview, July 23, 1983. **528** *"I really was..."*: OW to BL, interview, December 31, 1983. **530** *"He gets bored..."*: OW to BL, interview, April 21, 1984. **530** *"Because it took..."*: Ibid. **531** *"I even got..."*: Ibid. **531** *"Once I get..."*: Ibid. **531** *"I took over..."*: OW to BL, interview, January 19, 1984. **531** *"I didn't like..."*: Ibid. **533** *"Sometimes he's just..."*: OW to BL, interview, February 1, 1983. **534** *"We had about..."*: OW to BL, interview, July 11, 1983. **534** *"When we had..."*: Ibid. **534** *"He got up..."*: OW to BL, interview, May 19, 1984. **534** *"On this day..."*: Ibid. **535** *"There is a moment..."*: OW to BL, interview, April 3, 1984. **535** *"I do not..."*: Ibid. **535** *"I had a..."*: Ibid. **535** *"The house was..."*: Ibid. **536** *"I would have..."*: Ibid. **537** *"Errol, have I..."*: OW to BL, interview, July 26, 1983. **537** *"He had, in..."*: OW to BL, interview, May 21, 1984. **537** *"He turned up..."*: Ibid. **538** *"He was jealous..."*: Richard Fleischer to BL, interview, June 17, 1982. **538** *"We were all..."*: Ibid. **538** *"You don't know..."*: Ibid. **539** *"You have to..."*: Ibid. **539** *"Orson, you go..."*: Ibid. **539** *"I don't think..."*: Ibid. **540** *"required great concentration..."*: Ibid. **540** *"I don't think..."*: Ibid. **540** *"Orson has a..."*: Ibid. **541** *"When he has..."*: Ibid. **541** *"Orson doesn't want..."*: Ibid. **542** *"He is mercurial..."*: Ibid. **542**

"Since all of...": OW to BL, interview, April 3, 1984. **542** "The impression I...": Patricia McCormack to BL, interview, June 25, 1982. **542** "twinkle in his eye": Ibid. **544** "I refuse to...": Richard Fleischer to BL, interview, June 17, 1982. **544** "hand-knitting": Ibid. **544** "We screwed Orson!" Ibid. **544–545** "I got a...": Ibid. **545** "You're going to...": Ibid. **546** "I think I...": Ibid. **546** "He was devilish...": Ibid. **547** "Orson you can...": Ibid. **547** "We couldn't get...": Ibid. **547** "He has a...": Ibid. **548** "It's the essential...": OW to BL, interview, May 9, 1984. **549** "thick with dust...": Ibid. **549** "In this case...": OW to BL, interview, May 21, 1984. **549** "By the second...": OW to BL, interview, May 9, 1984. **549** "I had an...": Ibid. **551** "How did you...": Harry Hamburg to BL, interview, December 29, 1982. **551** "There is no...": Henry Hathaway to BL, interview, June 16, 1982. **557** "He's like a...": Martin Gabel to BL, interview, September 21, 1982. **552** "It's like an...": Wolf Mankowitz to BL, interview, March 12, 1984. **553** "It was meant...": OW to BL, interview, July 23, 1983. **554** "I think the...": OW to BL, interview, June 1, 1984.

CHAPTER 35

557 "It's a terrible...": OW to BL, interview, May 21, 1984. **557** "Nothing could have...": Ibid. **557** "He behaved terribly...": Ibid. **557** "Instead of making ...": Ibid. **557** "Then he did...": Ibid. **558** "I never went...": Ibid. **558** "He had to...": Ibid. **558** "Well, he doesn't...": Ibid. **559** "Orson was a...": Prince Alessandro Tasca di Cuto to BL, interview, February 4, 1983. **559** "You son of...": Ibid. **560** "It was a...": Ibid. **561** "The only thing...": OW to BL, interview, May 21, 1984. **561** "He's very impressed...": Dominique Antoine to BL, interview, March 16, 1983. **562** "You pay the...": OW to BL, interview, May 21, 1984. **562** "I think *everybody...": Ibid. **562** "aggressiveness": Ibid. **562** "a ground-breaking": OW to BL, interview, July 28, 1983. **563** "You can't watch...": Ibid. **563** "Spain was the...": OW to BL, interview, June 5, 1983. **563** "This was the...": Prince Alessandro Tasca di Cuto to BL, interview, February 4, 1983. **564** "Whenever it's not...": Ibid. **564** "with a bright orange...": OW to BL, interview, April 8, 1983. **564** "We never had...": Ibid. **565** "Either this man...": Prince Alessandro Tasca di Cuto to BL, interview, February 4, 1983. **567** "I think it's...": OW to BL, interview, April 8, 1983. **569** "Almost nobody has...": Ibid.

CHAPTER 36

570 "a frightful mess": Wolf Mankowitz to BL, interview, March 12, 1984. **570** "We were not...": OW to BL, interview, May 15, 1984. **571** "the Bond that...": Ibid. **571** "We would arrive...": Ibid. **571** "When he asked...": Ibid. **571** "He was a...": Wolf Mankowitz to BL, interview, March 12, 1984. **572** "Sellers had got...": Ibid. **572** "He wasn't terribly...": OW to BL, interview, May 15, 1984. **572–573** "The fact that...": Ibid. **573** "Then Princess Margaret...": Ibid. **573** "A director would...": Ibid. **573** "I think it...": Ibid. **573** "For two months...": Ibid. **574** "That's why I...": OW to BL, interview, June 1, 1984. **576** "Out! Get him...": Greg Garrison to BL, interview, July 28, 1983. **576** "That brought me...": OW to BL, interview, July 27, 1983. **578** "He's based really...": OW to BL, interview, July 23, 1983. **578** "This is a...": Dominique Antoine to BL, interview, March 16, 1983. **579** "If you're shooting...": OW to BL, interview, January 19, 1984. **579** "That was a...": Ibid. **580** "My God, we're...": Dominique Antoine to BL, interview, March 16, 1983.

CHAPTER 37

584 *"We were perfectly..."*: OW to BL, interview, April 21, 1984. **585** *"In a minute..."*: Ibid. **585** *"We just sat..."*: Ibid. **585** *"Orson found himself..."*: Dominique Antoine to BL, interview, March 15, 1983. **586** *"I think I..."*: Ibid. **586** *"Again!"*: Ibid. **593** *"wonderful offer"*: OW to BL, interview, April 21, 1984. **593** *"I am really..."*: Dominique Antoine to BL, interview, March 16, 1983. **593** *"The whole story..."*: OW to BL, interview, April 21, 1984. **593** *"And of course..."*: Ibid. **595** *"There was no..."*: Ibid. **596** *"You know, I..."*: Ibid. **596** *"It's too particular..."*: Ibid. **596** *"Even when the..."*: Ibid.

CHAPTER 38

598 *"a little unnatural"*: Harry Hamburg to BL, interview, December 29, 1982. **598** *"Not Welles..."*: Ibid. **598** *"People have this..."*: John Buckingham to BL, interview, December 16, 1982. **599** *"Why do you..."*: Harry Hamburg to BL, interview, December 29, 1982. **601** *"I want to..."*: Ibid. **603** *"Obviously, that would..."*: John Buckingham to BL, interview, December 16, 1982. **603** *"I used to..."*: OW to BL, interview, February 21, 1984. **604** *"I regard it..."*: OW to BL, interview, February 21, 1984. **605** *"You know, they..."*: OW to BL, interview, July 11, 1983. **605** *"With dogs I..."*: OW to BL, interview, June 19, 1983. **605** *"I can't sleep..."*: OW to BL, interview, July 11, 1983. **606** *"I'm insane about..."*: OW to BL, interview, May 13, 1984. **607** *"I have a..."*: OW to BL, interview, July 11, 1983. **607** *"That's what it..."*: Ibid. **608** *"He'd been great..."*: OW to BL, interview, June 19, 1983.

CHAPTER 39

610 *"How are you?"* : Henry Jaglom to BL, interview, December 27, 1982. **611** *"masterwork"* : Ibid. **612** *"Orson, I want ..."* : Ibid. **612** *"just spectacularly wonderful"* : Ibid. **613** *"At exactly the ..."* : OW to BL, interview, July 28, 1983. **614** *"I feel like ..."* : OW to BL, interview, July 30, 1983. **614** *"leap about on the bed"* : OW to BL, interview, July 28, 1983. **614** *"I don't know ..."* : Ibid. **615** *"Pagliacci"* : Ibid. **615** *"In any given ..."* : Ibid. **616** *"You see, he's ..."* : Ibid. **616** *"The director only ..."* : Ibid. **616** *"I think everybody ..."* : Ibid. **616** *"Didn't seem to ..."* : Ibid. **616** *"They haven't read ..."* : Ibid. **616–617** *"Stallone has been ..."* : Ibid. **617** *"Well, you've dropped ..."* : Ibid. **617** *"Not for surgery ..."* : OW to BL, interview, August 2, 1983. **617** *"You don't sound ..."* : Ibid. **618** *"to make peace ..."* : Ibid. **618** *"I'd rather have ..."* : Ibid. **618** *"He hates me ..."* : Ibid. **618** *"Being social costs ..."* : Ibid. **618** *"I want to ..."* : OW to BL, interview, August 3, 1983. **619** *"I have to ..."* : Ibid. **619** *"It's like a ..."* : OW to BL, interview, July 28, 1983. **619** *"hiding out, jumping ..."* : Ibid. **619** *"terrible timing ..."* : Ibid. **619** *"put him in the mood"* : Ibid. **620** *"Anyone who's been ..."* : Ibid. **620** *"Roger loves him ..."* : Ibid. **621–622** *"He's about two ..."* : OW to BL, interview, December 23, 1983. **622** *"a fearless advocate ..."* : OW to BL, interview, November 3, 1983. **622** *"an enormous Roman ..."* : Ibid. **622** *"He said, 'Always ...'"* : Ibid. **623** *"was really trying ..."* : Ibid. **623** *"a kind of ..."* : Ibid. **623** *"All great comedy ..."* : Ibid. **623** *"making Kabuki faces ..."* : Ibid. **623** *"all the psychiatrists ..."* : Ibid. **623** *"a very strong ..."* : OW to BL, interview, April 9, 1984. **624** *"When it gets ..."* : Ibid. **624** *"gloomy and hermit-like ..."* : Ibid. **624** *"if you really ..."* : Ibid. **624** *"Their silence sounds ..."* : Ibid. **625** *"Every year Swifty ..."* : Ibid. **627** *"I have turned ..."* : OW to BL, interview, June 8, 1984. **627** *"There's no way ..."* : OW to BL, interview, June 10, 1984. **628** *"I have to ..."* : OW to BL, interview, June 16, 1984.

Index